MW01415454

Saint Thomas Aquinas Meditations

For Every Day

Adapted from the Latin of
REV. P. D. MEZARD, O.P.

By
FATHER E. C. McENIRY, O.P.
Professor at Aquinas High School and
Chaplain of Mount Carmel Hospital
Columbus, Ohio

Author of—
A BOOK FOR BOYS
A NEW LIFE OF ST. DOMINIC
A LIFE OF FATHER ALBERT O'BRIEN, O.P.
—HERO PRIEST OF OHIO PENITENTIARY FIRE

New and Revised Edition
1940

Price $3 per copy. Order from Fr. McEniry, Mt. Carmel Hospital, Columbus, Ohio.

First Edition October, 1938, 1000 Copies
Second Edition, February, 1940, 1000 Copies

Nihil Obstat:
>   Fr. H. J. McManus, O.P., S.T.Lr.
>   Fr. J. S. Considine, O.P., S.T.Lr.

Imprimi Potest:
>   Fr. T. S. McDermott, O.P., S. T.Lr.
>   LL.D., Provincial.

Imprimatur:

COPYRIGHT
Father E. C. McEniry, O.P.
1938, 1940

To

MY MOTHER THE LATE MRS. MARY MCENIRY WHO DIED IN IRELAND, MAY 11TH, 1934, AGED 86 YEARS—THE MOTHER OF TEN CHILDREN; THESE MEDITATIONS ARE GRATEFULLY AND AFFECTIONATELY DEDICATED.

MEDITATIONS OF
ST. THOMAS AQUINAS, O.P.

PREFACE

SECOND EDITION

It is with an earnest desire of bringing the eternal and fundamental thoughts of Saint Thomas Aquinas to those who know not God as well as to those who know much about God that I undertook the translation from the Latin of the collection of "meditations" so judiciously selected by Father Mezard, O.P., from the works of this great Doctor of the Church.

To the writings of Aquinas have gone, through a period of seven hundred years, theologians, philosophers, scientists and literary geniuses from every land and clime. There they have acquired depth of wisdom, clarity of thought and expression, sound logic and clear ideas on topics essential to human happiness and welfare.

In our own day the late Holy Father Pius XI, of glorious memory, has once again proclaimed to the world the influence of this "Guide of Youth" in his glowing encyclical "Studiorum Ducem" in which we are told: "We must hold fast to the teachings of Aquinas more religiously and insistently than heretofore, for Thomas has altogether overthrown the modernists".

And further, in these teachings we find established by him the validity of the human mind in proving the existence of God through philosophy; in matters of faith and theology belief based upon unchangeable truth; the genuine notion of Divine inspiration in Scripture and in social science the principles of social and legal justice in their relation to charity. "Against that freedom of thought, independent of God, of which men commonly boast, he affirms the claims of the First Truth and God's supreme authority over us. It is not surprising that the modernists fear no Doctor of the Church more than they do Thomas Aquinas."

These meditations may truly be called a compendium of the "Summa" since they are culled mostly therefrom to the number of some four hundred and arranged, with references to the original, for daily use throughout the year. In this volume the following distribution is made for the ecclesiastical year.

During Advent will be found excerpts from Saint Thomas on the Incarnation. These are succeeded by sections on the Birth of Our Lord, His Infancy and Public Life. The time of Lent is taken up with reflections on Our Lord's Sufferings and Death on the Cross. Afterwards with the Risen Christ the new life of regeneration through grace, through glorification and inspiration of the Holy Ghost, and through the Eucharist are successively treated, ending with the Feast of the Sacred Heart.

In the second part, extending through July to Advent, will be found five sections dealing successively with God and His Attributes, the purgative, illuminative and unitive ways of spiritual advancement and finally Saint Thomas' treatment of the four last things. Succeeding the meditations proper will be found seventeen topics for spiritual retreats from the Angelic Doctor, with Thomistic prayers, the entire work standing forth as a real synopsis of religion and of the spiritual life.

It is hoped then that these meditations taken verbatim from Aquinas will be to theologians, philosophers, clergy, religious and laymen of all ranks a source of unfailing inspiration and a firm defense of Holy Faith, now made accessible in English dress. Father Mezard, the original compiler of the Latin edition of this work, published in 1905 with the approval of the Very Reverend Edward Hugon, O.P., M.G., says in his preface:

"With regard to the publication of this work the editor makes a double claim. First, that he has taken from all the writings of this great Dominican teacher, whatever is delightful and holy, suitable to inspire the mind and edify the soul. Secondly, that he has arranged the subject matter through all the days of the ecclesiastical year, so that the sweetest sap of this wonderful Cedar of Libanus, in the Summa of Saint Thomas and his other writings, might be collected into one place and daily, during spiritual reading or meditation, what is sweetest and most delightful might be digested and enjoyed for the benefit of heart and mind.

"Frequently indeed, meditations are published for the use of the faithful which appeal neither to the intellect nor to the heart. But you will find in this work not only ideas which inspire the mind but ideas brief, lofty, clear, convincing, replete with true piety and an abundance of the love of God. Some, wearied by a superfluity of words, long for the bread of life and for inspiration set forth in brief style and few words.

"Let us then go to the Angelic Doctor who has not only furnished us with an abundance of material for meditation but also matter most suitable for the reformation of conduct that is capable of nourishing in us the holiest love for Our Saviour."

It only remains for me to express my thanks and appreciation to all those who have contributed to the furtherance of this work, even in the least degree. Grateful acknowledgment is due to the Very Reverend Provincial T. S. McDermott, O.P., S.T. Lr., LL.D., for his continued kindness and encouragement. I am also greatly indebted to those who worked on the manuscript and to Rev. A. B. Coté, O.P., M.A., Ph.D., who kindly assisted me in preparing for the press this second edition.

E. C. McENIRY, O.P.

Mount Carmel Hospital,
Columbus, Ohio.

Feb. 1st, 1940.

CONTENTS

First Part

During the Time of Advent

The Greatness of Divine Love	3
The Suitableness of the Incarnation	4
The Necessity of the Incarnation in Regard to Good	5
The Necessity of the Incarnation in Regard to Evil	6
The Feast of Saint Andrew	7
Annunciation of the Blessed Virgin	8
Mary, Help of Christians	9
The Necessity of the Incarnation to Satisfy Sufficiently for Sin	11
The Incarnation of Our Lord Was a Most Suitable Remedy	12
Saint John the Baptist	13
The Manner of Repairing Human Nature	15
The Wonderful Incarnation of the Son of God	16
If Man Had Not Sinned Would God Have Become Man?	18
Should God Have Become Incarnate at the Beginning of the World?	19
The Feast of the Immaculate Conception	20
The Departing Night	22
The Translation of the House of Our Lady of Loretto	23
The Desire for Our Lord's Incarnation	25
It Was Fitting for the Son of God to Assume Human Nature from the Stock of Adam	26
It Was More Fitting That the Person of the Son Rather Than Any Other Divine Person Should Assume Human Nature	27
No Merits Preceded the Union of the Incarnation	28
The Gift of the Son of God in the Incarnation	29
The Work of the Incarnation Proper to The Holy Spirit	31
The Feast of the Expectation of the Blessed Virgin	32
Penance	33
Fruit Worthy of Penance	34
The Voice of One Crying in the Desert	36
The Heavenly Dew	37
Four Advantages of the Incarnation	38
The Incarnation is a Help for Man Striving for Happiness	39

During the Time of Our Saviour's Birth

The Goodness and Usefulness of Christ's Birth	41
Christ Was Born Subject to Suffering and Death	43
Saint John the Evangelist	44
Concerning Four Blessings of Christ's Birth	45
The Repentant Soul	46
The Circumstances of Christ's Birth	47
The Divine Sonship	49
Christ's Circumcision	50

Suitableness of the Holy Name...	51
The Usefulness of the Name of Jesus	52
The Virginity of Mary.	54
The Fruit of the Womb of the Blessed Virgin	55
The Epiphany of Christ...	56
The Order of Christ's Manifestation	58
The Diligence of the Magi.	59
Gifts of the Magi....	61
Searching for God...	62
Where Jesus Dwelleth	63
Spiritual Marriages	65
Mary Interceding with Jesus	66
Good Wine	67
The Holy Name of God	68
The Threefold Wine..	69
Christ's Conversation and Associations	70
It Was Becoming That Christ Should Have Led an Austere Life	71
The Active Life of Christ	72
Christ's Poverty	73
Christ Conformed His Conduct to the Law	75
Christ's Humility and Obedience	76
The Espousals of the Blessed Virgin Mary	77
The Infinite Grace of Christ	79
The Conversion of Saint Paul—the Apostle	80
The Priesthood of Christ	82
A Compendium of Christ's Preaching	83
The Delightful Well	85
How We Should Be Disposed Towards the Word of God..	86
Keeping the Word of God.	87
The Usefulness of Meditating on the Mysteries of Christ.	88
Jesus at the Door	90
The Purification of the Blessed Virgin	91
The Presentation of Christ in the Temple	92
How to Offer Ourselves to God	93
The Temple of God	94
Following the Lord..	95
The Yoke of Christ	96
The Imitation of Christ	98
The Vine and the Branches	99
The Study of Wisdom—Especially Incarnate Wisdom...	100
The Feast of the Apparition of the Blessed Virgin	102
The State of Sinners	104
Our Conversion Must Not Be Put Off	105
We Must Cling to Christ	106
Christ's Love for His Disciples.	107
Abiding in Christ....	109
Life in Christ	110
Peace and Victory Through Jesus	112
The Narrow Gate	114
The Renunciation of Worldly Things	115

During Septuagesima

We Must Labour in the Lord's Vineyard	117
Good Works	119
Our Reward	120
The Necessity of Carefulness...	122
Interior Reformation	123
Do Good Always	125
Our Lord's Prayer in the Garden	127
The Seed	128
The Goodness of God	130
The Commemoration of Our Lord's Passion	131
The Necessity of Vigilance..	133
Watch Always	134
On Serving God	136
How We Must Worship God..	138
How We Should Serve God on Sundays	139
Sanctity	141
The Scourging of Christ	142

During Lent

Death 143
Fasting 144
The Crown of Thorns. 145
The Grain of Wheat 146
Was It Becoming That Christ Should Be Tempted?. 148
Should Christ Have Been Tempted "in the Desert"? 149
Christ Endured All Sufferings . 150
The Pain of Christ's Passion Was Greater Than All Other Pains 151
Was It Fitting for Christ to Be Crucified with Thieves? 152
In the Feast of the Lance and Nails of Our Lord 154
The Charity of God in the Passion of Christ 155
Did God the Father Deliver Up Christ to the Passion?...... 156
It Was Fitting for Christ to Suffer at the Hands of the Gentiles 157
Christ's Passion Brought About Our Salvation by Way of Merit 158
Christ's Passion Brought About Our Salvation by Way of Atonement 159
Christ's Passion Operated by Way of Sacrifice 161
The Feast of the Holy Cloth.... 162
Christ's Passion Brought About Our Salvation by Way of Redemption 163
We Were Delivered from Sin Through Christ's Passion.. . 165
We Were Delivered from the Devil's Power Through Christ's Passion 166
Christ, Our True Redeemer. ... 167
The Price of Our Redemption... 168
The Samaritan Woman Preaching Christ 169
We Were Freed from the Punishment of Sin Through Christ's Passion 171
We Were Reconciled to God Through Christ's Passion.... 172
Christ Opened the Gate of Heaven to Us by His Passion 173
By His Passion, Christ Merited to Be Exalted 174
The Example of Christ Crucified 176
The Divine Friend........... 177
Lazarus' Death 178
The Most Precious Blood of Our Lord 180
The Liberation of Man Through the Passion 181
The Passion of Christ 182
The Passion of Christ—a Remedy Against Sin 184
The Burial of Christ. ... 186
Spiritual Burial 187
The Greatest Proof of Christ's Love for Us..... 188
The Compassion of the Blessed Virgin 190
How We Should Wash One Another's Feet 191
The Usefulness of Christ's Passion 192
The Need of Perfect Cleanliness of Soul 194
The Washing of the Apostles' Feet by the Saviour 195
Three Things Which Must Be Understood Mystically in Christ Washing the Disciples' Feet 196
The Lord's Supper ... 198
The Death of Christ .. Good Friday 199
The Advantages of Christ's Descent Into Hell 201

During the Paschal Season

The Necessity of Christ's Resurrection 203
The Advantages of Christ's Resurrection 204
The Wounds on the Body of the Risen Christ , ... 205

Christ — the Resurrection and the Life 206
The Three Persons Restored to Life by Christ 207
The New Life..................... 209
The Proof of Our Spiritual Resurrection 210
The Apparition of Christ on the Octave of Easter 211
The Peace of Christ 213
Heavenly Things Must Be Sought 214
The Beginning of the New Life, or Grace 216
Thirsting for the Living Water.. 217
Our Divine Adoption............. 219
The Indwelling of the Divine Persons in the Soul........... 220
Spiritual Regeneration Through Baptism 222
The Penalties of the Present Life 223
The Sacrament of Confirmation. 225
Why the Sacrament of Confirmation is Conferred on the Forehead 226
The Sacrament of the Eucharist.. 227
The Attraction of God, and the Cooperation of Man with God. 228
Should a Man Know That He Is in the Grace of God?........ 230
Gifts of the Holy Ghost......... 232
The Gift of Piety............... 234
The Number of the Beatitudes.. 235
The Rewards of the Beatitudes . 237
The Fruits of the Spirit........ 239
The Number of the Fruits of the Holy Spirit 240
The Merit of Eternal Life 242
We Merit Chiefly Through Charity 243
The Merit of the First Man..... 244
We Can Merit an Increase of Grace 245
Prayer 246
The Advantages of Prayer...... 247
The Lord's Prayer............... 249
Why Our Prayers Are Not Sometimes Answered 250

During Ascension Time

The Ascension of Christ 252
The Advantages of Christ's Ascension 253
The Ascension of Christ Is the Cause of Our Salvation..... 255
Conversation in Heaven......... 256
The Heavenly Father 257
Confidence in Our Heavenly Father 259
The Source of All Consolation... 260
Preparation for the Reception of the Holy Spirit. 262
The Holy Ghost Is Not Given to the World (or to the Worldly) 263
The Workings of the Holy Spirit 265
The Gift of the Most High God. 266
How We Are Moved by the Holy Ghost to do Good............ 268
The Properties and Power of the Holy Ghost 269
The Manifold Fruit of the Holy Spirit 270
The Apparition of the Holy Spirit In the Form of a Dove....... 272
The Spirit Descending and Remaining 273
The Coming of the Trinity Into the Mind 274
The Image of God Is Found in Every Man 276
The Greatest Love and the Highest Worship Belong to God.... 277
The Sin Against the Father, and the Son, and the Holy Ghost.. 278
The Eucharist Confers Grace . 280
How Grace Is Conferred by the Eucharist 281
An Effect of the Eucharist Is the Possession of Glory 282
The Effects of the Eucharist Is Hindered by Venial Sins...... 283

Christ's Love 284
Through the Eucharist, Man Is
  Preserved from Sins.......... 286
Through the Eucharist, Punish-
  ment Due to Sin, Is Forgiven 287
Venial Sins Are Forgiven Through
  the Eucharist 288
The Use of the Eucharist....... 289
The Most Sacred Heart of Jesus 290
The Pure Heart of Mary....... 291

INDEX OF MEDITATIONS

Second Part

On God

The Excellence of the Divine
  Nature 297
The Visitation of the Blessed
  Virgin 298
The Fruit of the Knowledge of
  God 299
The Presence of God Everywhere 300
The Immutability of God 301
Advantages of Reflecting on God
  as Creator 303
The Governor of All Things.... 304
God Our Father.... 305
The Love of God 306
The Threefold Banquet 308
The Vocation of Mankind 309

On the Purgative Life

Darkness and the Shadow of
  Death 310
The Wounds of Nature Conse-
  quent on Sin.. 312
The Infirmities of Sin 313
The Stain of Sin............... 314
Can Sin Be the Punishment of
  Sin? 316
Sin Calls for Punishment 317
Venial Sin and Mortal Sin...... 318
Mortal Sin Incurs Eternal Pun-
  ishment 319
Spiritual Sins 320

To Sin Through Malice Is More
  Grievous Than to Sin Through
  Passion 321
The Excellence or Condition of
  the Person Sinned Against,
  Aggravates the Sin........... 322
The Excellence of the Person
  Sinning Aggravates the Sin.... 323
The Happiness Which Must Not
  Be Sought in This Life...... 324
The Sacrament of Penance 326
The Remains of Sin 327
Contrition 328
The Duration of Contrition 329
Concerning Solicitude and the
  Solicitous 331
The Remarkable Favour of Aris-
  ing from Sin................. 332
The Necessity of Keeping Your
  Heart in God................. 333
The Defect of Hope........... 334
The Love of Oneself........... 336
Folly 337
Sloth 338
Imprudence 339
The Transfiguration of Christ... 340
Precipitation 342
Negligence 343
Intemperance 344
The Daughters of Lust......... 345
The Way to Conquer Lust...... 346

Pride 347	The New Commandment of Love 395
The Wickedness of Pride. . . 348	The Perfect Love of Our Neighbor 396
Pride Is the Beginning of Every Sin 349	Why Love Our Enemies? . 397
The Assumption of the Blessed Virgin 351	Is Mercy the Greatest Virtue? . 399
The Way to Avoid Pride 352	The Fourfold Good of the Law of Love . 400
Vain Glory 353	Other Advantages of the Law of Love 402
Vain Glory Is a Capital Vice 354	The Love of God. 403

The Illuminative Life

	Four Things Necessary for the Love of God 404
The Garments of Virtue . .. 356	The Possibility of Perfect Charity ..,. 406
Virtue, True and Great . . 357	
The Advantages and Need of Faith 359	An Increase of Charity... 407
	Three Degrees of Charity . 409
The Effects of Faith 361	Things Necessary to Acquire and Increase Charity 410
Hope 362	
The Excellence of Charity . 363	The Love of the Highest Good 411
The Fear of the Lord . .. 365	The Causes of Love 413
The Cardinal Virtues.. .. 366	Advancement in Love.. . 414
Prudence 367	The Rosary Feast 415
Justice 368	The Feast of the Maternity of the Blessed Virgin 417
Fortitude .. . 370	
Temperance 372	The Feast of the Purity of the Blessed Virgin 418
The Virtue of Religion... .. 373	
The Interior Acts of Religion .. 375	The Dedication of a Church.. .. 420
The Cause and Effect of Devotion 376	The Effects of Love 421
The Manner of Praying.. . 378	The Guardian Angels . 422
Praying Always 379	The Sign of True Love . 424
Sacrifices Should Be Offered to God 381	

The Unitive Life

The Need of Humility . 382	The Friendship Between God and Man 425
Man Should Subject Himself in All Things 384	
Our Mother's Birthday.. . . . 385	Clinging to God Through Love . 427
Our Lord's Humility Commands Us to Be Humble . 386	The Wonderful Privilege of Love 428
	The Divine Manifestation to One Loving God 429
Patience . . 388	
Advantages of Sorrow and Tribulations 389	The Way to Find Jesus . .. 431
	The Internal Illumination of the Mind 433
The Precepts of Charity 390	
The Precept on the Love of Neighbor 392	Spiritual Joy . 435
	The Peace of God 436
The Death of the Cross 393	Preparation for the Contemplative Life 438
Mutual Love 394	

The Excellence of the Contemplative Life	439
The Happiness Obtained in a Life with God	440
The Merit of the Contemplative Life	442
Things Seen in Meditation	443
The Hidden Manna	444
Spiritual Recovery	446
The Sweet Experience of Divine Love	448
The Coming of Divine Consolation	449
Obstacles to Contemplation	451
Divine Familiarity	452
A Method of Learning Divine Secrets	453
The Effects of Contemplation	454
How to Recover Divine Sweetness	456
The Perfection of the Christian Life	457
The Perfection Which Is Necessary for Us	458
The Perfection Which Comes Under Counsel	459
Perfection Consists in the Precepts	461
The Gospel Counsels	462
Perseverance	464

The Last Things

The Happiness of the Saints	466
Purgatory	467
The Punishments of Purgatory	468
Praying to the Saints	469
The Saints Pray for Us to God	471
Faith in the Resurrection of the Dead	472
The Need of a Final Judgment	473
The Cause in the Final Judgment	474
Fear of the Judgment	476
The Power of the Highest Judge	478
The Time of the Last Judgment	479
Eternal Death	481
The Pains of the Damned	482
The Knowledge of the Damned	483
The Will of the Damned	485
The Eternal Punishment of the Damned	486
We Must Believe in Life Everlasting	488
Seeing God Face to Face	489
Eternal Life	491
The Various Degrees of the Divine Vision	492
The Blessed Virgin's Holy Life	494
Happiness	495
Degrees of Happiness	496
The Endlessness of Perfect Happiness	498
The Fourfold Vision of the Lord	499
Eternal Joy	501

Spiritual Topics for Retreats

Spiritual Topics for Retreats	503
The Voice of God Calling Us	503
Our First Charity Must Be Regained	504
Second Death	506
The State of Perfection	508
The Usefulness of the Vows	509
The Good Use of Time	510
Is Poverty Required for the Perfection of Religion?	511
Obedience Belongs to Religious Perfection	512
The Necessity of the Three Vows	513
The Perfection of Religion Consists in the Three Vows	514
The Vow of Obedience Is the Chief of the Three Vows	515
The Sin of Religious and of Priests	516
The Works of the Active Life	517
How a Religious Who Sins Slightly May Rise Quickly	518

The Study of the Letters (or
    Sciences) 519
The Works of a Religious...... 521
Faithfulness 522

St. Thomas Aquinas, O.P.

Prayers of St. Thomas Aquinas,
    O.P, Before Holy Communion 527
Lauda Sion 527
Verbum Supernum 528
Pange Lingua 529
A Brief Prayer Which St. Thomas
    said daily 529

**Prayers of St. Thomas Aquinas,
O.P., After Holy Communion**

"I Give Thee Thanks, O Holy
    Lord .. Almighty Father"... 529
Adoro Te 530
A Prayer of St. Thomas to Ob-
    tain the Virtues 530
A Frequent Prayer of St. Thomas 531
A Prayer of St. Thomas for the
    Proper Choice of a State of
    Life 531
A Prayer of St. Thomas to the
    Blessed Virgin 532

SAINT THOMAS AQUINAS, O.P.
Patron of All Catholic Schools

Saint Thomas Aquinas, O.P., the most illustrious member of the Dominican Order, officially known as the Order of Preachers, was born in the kingdom of Naples about 1225 and belonged to the noble family of Aquino, which was related to the royal houses of Aragon, Sicily and France.

Our saint lived, therefore, in the thirteenth century, the greatest of centuries. His father was count of Aquino, Belcastro, and Roccasecca. His mother, Theodora, desiring that her son Thomas should not become a priest, threw every obstacle in the way of his entering the Order of Preachers, which had been instituted by the great Saint Dominic. She carried her opposition so far as to imprison Thomas in the ancestral castle for a period of two years; until finally he escaped and in 1243 joined the Order of Saint Dominic. His mother afterwards repented of her misguided love.

He spent his life in teaching, writing and praying, obtaining more inspiration and help from the crucifix than from books. He is known as "the most learned among the saints and the saintliest among the learned."

His fame as a teacher rapidly spread throughout Europe, and in obedience to the commands of his superiors, he taught successively, at Rome, Bologna, Viterbo, Perugia, and Naples.

At Cologne, Thomas had for his teacher Saint Albert, the Great O.P., who foretold the future greatness of his pupil in these words which have been truly fulfilled: "You call Thomas the Dumb Ox (dumb because of his respectful silence and modesty), but I tell you that one day his voice will be heard throughout the entire world." Thus spoke Albert the Great in praise of his student Thomas, who later surpassed Albert in intellectual greatness.

In his lectures as well as in his writings, Saint Thomas is always the revered champion of truth and the builder of a system of philosophy and theology which has been the inspiration of the greatest minds for seven centuries.

His *Summa Theologica*, which is his greatest work and which took about seven years to write, contains some three thousand articles and ten thousand objections—a solution to all the great problems of speculative and practical philosophy; a work or masterpiece so vast that because of its greatness, Thomas has been called the Universal Teacher.

He is also called, because of his sanctity and learning, "The Angelic Doctor," "Prince of Theologians," "The Eucharistic Doctor," and patron of all Catholic schools as well as the patron of youth and of purity.

Pope Benedict XV said of the Angelic Doctor: "The manifold honors paid by the Holy See to St. Thomas Aquinas exclude forever any doubt from the minds of Catholics with regard to his being raised up by God as the Master of Doctrine to be followed by the Church through all ages."

Our saint died on March 7, 1274, when only 49 years of age, and was canonized in 1323. His body is enshrined in the church of St. Sernin at Toulouse. On March 7, the Church in every land and for all ages will sing the praises of Saint Thomas Aquinas, and if we wish to follow his example, let us say daily and devoutly—

"O Blessed Thomas, Patron of Schools, obtain for us from God an invincible faith, burning charity, a chaste life and true knowledge, through Christ Our Lord. Amen."

FIRST PART

From Advent To The Feast Of The Sacred Heart Of Jesus

NOVEMBER 27

The Greatness of Divine Love

"God so loved the world, as to give His only begotten Son; that whosoever believeth in Him, may have everlasting life." (John III, 16.)

The cause of all good things is the Lord and Divine love. For to wish good to anyone belongs to love. Since therefore, the will of God is the cause of things, from this very fact, good comes to us because God loves us. The love of God is also the cause of the good in nature. Likewise, it is the cause of the good resulting from grace. "I have loved you with an everlasting love, therefore, I have drawn thee," namely, through the grace of God.

That God is the Giver of the good resulting from grace also proceeds from His immense charity and hence, it will be shown here, that this charity of God is the greatest charity and this because of four reasons:

1. Because of the Person loving, for it is God Who loves and loves exceedingly. Therefore He says, "God so loved."

2. God's love is the greatest because of the condition of the person loved, for it is man who is the object of God's love, the worldly man living in sin. "God commendeth His charity towards us, because when as yet we were His enemies, we were reconciled to God, by the death of His Son." (Rom. V. 10) Hence it is written, "God so loved the world."

3. God's love is the greatest because of the greatness of His gifts, for love is shown by a gift, as Gregory says, "The proof of love is in the manifestation of action." But God gave us the greatest gift for He gave us His only begotten Son, His own Son, Son by nature, consubstantial, not adopted, but only begotten Son God gave Him to us to prove the immensity of His love.

4. God's love is the greatest because of the magnitude of its effects, because through it we receive eternal life. Wherefore it is written, "Whosoever believeth in Him may not perish, but have life everlasting"; which He has obtained for us through His death on the Cross.

Something is said to perish when it is prevented from obtaining the end for which it was created. But man is created and ordained for eternal life and as long as he sins he is turned away from that destined end. Still, while he lives, he does not perish entirely for he can yet be saved through God's grace and mercy; but if he dies in sin then he perishes completely.

The immensity of Divine Love is referred to by our Lord when He says "that whosoever believeth in Him, may not perish, but may have life everlasting." For God in giving eternal life gave Himself to us, because eternal life is nothing other than to enjoy God forever. Moreover, to give oneself to God is a sign of great love. (In John III.)

NOVEMBER 28

The Suitableness of the Incarnation

1. It would seem most fitting that by visible things the invisible things of God should be known; for to this end was the world made, as is clear from the word of the Apostle (Rom. I, 20), "For the invisible things of Him ... are clearly seen, being understood by the things which are made." But, as Damascene says, by the mystery of the Incarnation are made known at once—"the goodness, the wisdom, the justice, the power, or the might of God"—the goodness, for He did not despise the weakness of His own handiwork; the justice, since on man's defeat, He caused the tyrant to be overcome by none other than man and yet He did not snatch men forcibly from death; the wisdom, for He found a most suitable discharge for a most heavy debt; the power, or infinite might, for there is nothing greater than for God to become Incarnate.

2. To each thing is befitting that which belongs to it because of its nature; thus, to think befits man, since this belongs to him for he has a rational nature. But the very nature of God is goodness. Hence, what belongs to the essence of goodness befits God. But it belongs to the essence of goodness to communicate itself to others. Therefore it belongs to the essence of the highest good to communicate itself in the highest manner to the creature and this is done chiefly by His so uniting created nature to Himself that one Person is made up of these three—the Word, a soul and flesh, as Augustine says. Hence it is manifest that it was fitting that God should become Incarnate.

To be united to God in unity of person was not fitting to

human flesh, according to its natural endowments, since it was above its dignity; nevertheless it was fitting that God by reason of His Infinite goodness, should unite it to Himself for man's salvation.

Augustine says: "God is great not in mass, but in power. Hence the greatness of His might feels no straits in narrow surroundings. If the passing word of a man is heard at once by many, and wholly by each, is it incredible then that the abiding Word of God should be everywhere at once?" Hence nothing unfitting arises from God becoming Incarnate. (3a, q. 1. a. 1.)

NOVEMBER 29

The Necessity of the Incarnation

A thing is said to be necessary for a certain end in two ways. First, when the end cannot be obtained without it, as food is necessary for the preservation of human life. Secondly, when the end is attained better and more conveniently, as a horse is necessary for a journey. In the first way it was not necessary that God should become incarnate for the restoration of human nature. For God of His omnipotent power could have restored human nature in many other ways. But in the second way it was necessary that God should become incarnate for the restoration of human nature. Hence Augustine says, "We shall also show that other ways were not wanting to God, to Whose power all things are equally subject; but that there was not a more suitable way of healing our misery." Now this may be considered in regard to our advancement in good.

First, with regard to faith, which is made more certain by believing God Himself Who speaks; hence Augustine says, "In order that man might journey more trustfully towards the Truth itself, the Son of God, having assumed human nature, established and founded faith."

Secondly, with regard to hope, which is thereby greatly strengthened; hence Augustine says, "Nothing was so necessary for raising our hope as to show us how deeply God loved us... And what could afford us a stronger proof of this than that the Son of God should become a partner with us of human nature."

Thirdly, with regard to charity, which is greatly enkindled by this; hence Augustine says, "What greater cause is there of the Lord's coming than to show God's love for us?" And he afterwards adds, "If we have been slow to love, at least let us hasten to love in return."

Fourthly, with regard to well-doing, in which Christ set us an example; hence Augustine says: "Man who might be seen was not to be followed; but God was to be followed, Who could not be seen. And hence God was made man, that He Who might be seen by man, and Whom man might follow, might be shown to man."

Fifthly, with regard to—the full participation of the Divinity—which is the true bliss of man and the end of human life; and this is bestowed upon us by the humanity of Christ; for Augustine says: "God was made man, that man might be made Godlike." (3a, q. 1. a. 2.)

NOVEMBER 30

The Necessity of the Incarnation

It was not only necessary that God should become Incarnate for our good, but also for our removal from evil.

First, man is taught by it not to prefer the devil to himself, nor to honor him who is the author of sin; hence Augustine says: "Since human nature is so united to God as to become one person, let not those proud spirits dare to prefer themselves to man, because they have no bodies."

Secondly, because we are thereby taught how great is man's dignity, lest we should sully it with sin; hence Augustine says: "God has proved to us how high a place human nature holds amongst us, in as much as He appeared to men as a true man." And Pope Leo declares: "Learn, O Christian, thy worth; and being made a partner of the Divine nature, refuse to return by evil deeds to your former worthlessness."

Thirdly, because, to do away with man's presumption, the grace of God is commended in Jesus Christ, though no merits of ours went before, as Augustine says.

Fourthly, because man's pride which is the greatest stumbling-block to our clinging to God, can be convinced and cured by humility so great, as Augustine says.

Fifthly, in order to free man from the slavery of sin;

which as Augustine says: "ought to be done in such a way that the devil should be overcome by the justice of the man Jesus Christ, and this was done by Christ satisfying for us." Now a mere man could not have satisfied for the whole human race, and God was not obliged to satisfy; hence it behooved Jesus Christ to be both God and man. Hence Pope Leo says: "Weakness is assumed by strength, lowliness by majesty, mortality by eternity, in order that One and the same Mediator of God and men might die in one and rise in the other—for this was our fitting remedy. Unless He was God, He would not have brought a remedy, and unless He was man, He could not have set an example."

And there are many other advantages which resulted above man's apprehension, according to Eccle. III, 25: "Many things are shown to thee above the understanding of men." (Summa 3a, q. 1. a. 2)

NOVEMBER 30

The Feast of Saint Andrew

"Andrew, the brother of Simon Peter, . . . findeth first his brother Simon, and said to him: We have found the Messias, . . . and he brought him to Jesus." (John I, 40.)

1. A clear sign of the perfect conversion of anyone is, when the converted, in as much as he was wrapped up in himself, in his own pride and selfishness, is now on being converted to Christ all the more satisfied. And therefore Andrew, being perfectly converted, did not keep for himself the Treasure he had found, but hastens, yea runs quickly, to his brother to give to him the good things which he himself received. "He findeth first his brother Simon," whom he was seeking. As Simon was his brother by blood, so was Andrew as anxious to make him a brother by faith. "He that heareth let him say, Come." (Apoc. XXII, 17.)

2. Andrew said, "We have found the Messias." Jesus had instructed Andrew in as much as he had acknowledged Jesus to be Christ and hence he said, "We have found." By that statement, Andrew hints that for a long time he sought Jesus with a great desire. "Blessed is the man that findeth wisdom and is rich in prudence." (Prov. III., 13).

3. The fruit of Andrew's labour is evident, "for he brought Peter to Jesus." And here the obedience of Peter is

commended, for he did not delay but ran immediately to Jesus.

Also consider the devotion of Andrew, because "he brought Peter to Jesus." He did not attract Peter to Himself for Andrew realized that he himself was weak and that Christ was strong. All-mighty, All-holy.

And therefore, Andrew led Peter to Christ so that Christ might instruct him, so instructing him that he should become a zealous preacher of the word of God, so that the fruit of his preaching and his zeal might not redound to his own glory but that they might lead other souls in great numbers to Christ, and thus would his preaching and zeal contribute to God's honor and glory. "For we preach not ourselves, but Jesus Christ our Lord." (2 Cor. IV., 5). (John I)

Annunciation of the Blessed Virgin

1 ... It was suitable that it should be made known to the Blessed Virgin that she would conceive Christ.

First of all that a becoming order of the the union of the Son of God with the Virgin might be maintained. Thus Augustine says: "Mary is more blessed in receiving the faith of Christ than in conceiving the flesh of Christ. Her nearness as a mother would have been of no profit to Mary had she not borne Christ in her heart after a more blessed manner than in her flesh."

Secondly, that she might be a more certain witness of this mystery being instructed therein by God.

Thirdly, that she might offer to God the free gift of her obedience which she proved herself ready to do saying: "Behold the handmaid of the Lord."

Fourthly, to show that there is a certain spiritual wedlock between the Son of God and human nature. Wherefore, in the Annunciation the Virgin's consent was asked in place of all human nature. Moreover, the Blessed Virgin did believe explicitly in the future Incarnation, but being humble she did not think such high things of herself. Hence the Angel announced to the Virgin: "Behold, thou shalt conceive in thy womb and shall bring forth a Son; and thou shalt call His name Jesus." (Luke I, 31).

2 ... The Annunciation was perfected by the Angel in a suitable order. For the Angel intended three things concerning the Virgin.

First, to render her mind attentive to the consideration of so great an event. This the Angel accomplished by saluting her in a new and unusual salutation. For to a humble mind nothing is more wonderful than the hearing of its own excellence but admiration especially arouses the attention of the mind and therefore the Angel desiring to render the mind of the Virgin attentive to the announcement of so great a mystery began with her praises: "Hail full of grace." In which salutation he announced her worthiness to conceive from the fact that she was full of grace and he proclaimed the conception when he said: "The Lord is with thee" and he foretold her consequent honor when he said, "Blessed art thou among women."

Secondly, the Angel intended to instruct her concerning the mystery of the Incarnation which was to be fulfilled in her. He did this by announcing that she would conceive and bring forth a Son saying, "Thou shalt conceive in Thy womb and bring forth a Son," and the Angel revealed the dignity of the conceived offspring when he said, "he shall be great and shall be called the Son of the most High," and likewise the Angel revealed the mode of the conception, when he said, "The Holy Ghost shall come upon thee and the power of the Most High shall overshadow thee."

Thirdly, the Angel intended to induce her mind to consent, which indeed he did through the example of Elizabeth and by reason aided with Divine power. (3 a. q. 30, a I and IV.)

Mary Help of Christians

It is related in scripture, how a man—the betrayer, by means of a false suggestion to king Assuerus, caused the sentence of condemnation and death to be passed on all Jewish people living in the provinces of the king. The sentence of death was already published by the king's messengers and sealed with the king's ring and even the day was already set aside for the execution of this cruel decree and nothing now remained to be done but to put the people to death. But through queen Esther's power, the sentence was not executed.

The truth corresponding to this figure is this, namely, through the sin of our first parents, perpetrated by the false suggestion of Satan the betrayer, the sentence of damnation had been passed by Almighty God on the whole human race. The sentence was already passed, already sealed in sacred scripture, already proclaimed abroad by the King's messengers, namely, by the prophets, yea the day of damnation was already assigned. For on the day of our death, we were to descend immediately into hell.

But through queen Esther, that is, through the Blessed Virgin the sentence of damnation passed against us was revoked; namely, through her intercession, through the extension of the King's golden sceptre to Mary and through her kiss on the top of that sceptre we are saved from hell and damnation.

Concerning this Esther, we read in the Book of Esther V, 3: "That queen Esther pleased the eyes of the king, and he held out toward her the golden sceptre, and she drew near and kissed the top of the sceptre. And the king said to her: What wilt thou queen Esther? What is thy request? If thou shalt ask even one half of the kingdom, it shall be given to thee. Then she answered: If I have found favour in thy sight, O King, and if it please thee, give me my life for which I ask and for my people which I request. For we are given to be destroyed, to be slain and to perish;"—through original sin contracted and through our actual sins in addition.

But queen Esther, that is the Blessed Virgin, pleased the eyes of the King in helping to redeem the human race and she found favor in His Presence, not only for herself, but for all mankind.

The King of Kings extended to Mary the golden sceptre and God the Father, our Lord, held out this golden sceptre to us, when from the greatest charity He had for us, He sacrificed His Son in the Passion for our salvation. The Blessed Virgin touched the top of the sceptre, when she conceived in her womb, and later gave birth to the Son of God.

And thus she obtained one half of the kingdom of God, whose Son is the King of Justice. She has therefore revoked the sentence of our damnation and this revocation of sentence has been preached by the Apostles, the messengers of Christ the King; Who sent them especially for this purpose (to preach salvation through our Lord Jesus Christ and His Blessed Mother.)

"Come to her with all thy mind, and keep her ways with all thy power, and on the last day thou shalt find rest with her, and she shall be turned to thy joy. Then shall her fetters be a strong defense for thee, and her chain (The Rosary) a robe of glory." (Eccles. VI, 29.)

DECEMBER 1

The Necessity of the Incarnation to Satisfy Sufficiently for Sin

1. Satisfaction may be said to be sufficient in two ways —first, perfectly, inasmuch as it is condign, being adequate to make good the fault committed, and in this way the satisfaction of a mere man cannot be sufficient for sin, both because the whole of human nature has been corrupted by sin, whereas the goodness of any person or persons could not make up adequately for the injury done to the whole of human nature, and also because a sin committed against God has a kind of infinity from the infinity of the Divine majesty, because the greater the person we offend, the more grievous the offense. Hence for condign satisfaction, it was necessary that the act of the one satisfying should have an infinite efficacy, as being of God and man.

Secondly, man's satisfaction may be called sufficient imperfectly, that is, in the acceptation of him who is content with it, even though it is not condign and in this way the satisfaction of a mere man is sufficient. And inasmuch as everything imperfect presupposes some perfect thing by which it is sustained, hence it is that the satisfaction of every mere man has its efficiency from the satisfaction of Christ.

2. The Incarnation gives us confidence in regard to the forgiveness of our sins.

Just as virtue prepares man for heaven, so sin debars him therefrom. Now sin, which is opposed to virtue, debars man from heaven not only because it brings disorder into the soul by leading it away from its proper end, but also because it offends God, to Whom, as the Director of human actions, man looks for his heavenly reward. Moreover, when a man is conscious of sin he loses hope, which he needs in order to reach heaven. Therefore, as sin abounds in the human race man needs a remedy for it.

But no one can provide this remedy except God alone, Who is able not only to move man's will to good, so as to bring him back to the right order, but also to forgive the offence committed against Himself; since an offence is not forgiven except by the person offended.

But in order that man's conscience may be eased of his past sin he must be made certain of God's forgiveness. But he cannot be certain of this except by God Himself. Hence it was fitting to the human race and expedient for the possession of heavenly bliss, that God should become man, so that man would both receive from God the forgiveness of his sins and be made certain of that forgiveness by God made man. Hence our Lord said (Matth. IX, 6): "That you may know that the Son of man hath power on earth to forgive sins"; and the Apostle says (Heb. IX, 14): "that the blood of Christ . . . shall cleanse our conscience from dead works, to serve the living God." (Contra Gentiles IV, 54.)

DECEMBER 2

The Incarnation of Our Lord Was a Most Suitable Remedy

That sacred union of the Divine nature with the human nature was most suitably ordained for man's salvation, for even though another way was possible for God, still nothing was so fitting as the Incarnation. For it was suitable to the Repairer, to the repaired and to the reparation.
1. It was suitable to Christ, the Repairer of our fallen nature, to Whom it was becoming to manifest His wisdom, His power and His goodness. For what was or could be more powerful than to unite extremes in the highest manner. For great was the power manifested in the union of unequal elements, greater in the union of those elements to the created spirit and greatest in the union with the Increated Spirit, where exists the greatest difference. Truly what could be more wise, as to the completion of the whole universe, than the union of the First and the Last, that is, the Word of God, Which is the beginning of all things and the union of human nature, which among the works of six days, was the final work of created things? For what could be more gracious than that the Creator of all things should will to communicate Himself to created things? And this kindness was great in the union of Himself with all things by His Presence; greater became His kindness when He communicated Himself to good things by His grace and His kindness became the greatest, because He communicated Himself to the Man-Christ and consequently, by unity of person to the family of nations.
2. This way of redemption was most fitting also to the person or people redeemed, because man through sin had fallen into infirmity, ignorance and wickedness by which he had become unfitted to imitate or acquire Divine virtue or know truth or love goodness. Therefore, God became man, so that

He might give Himself to man to be imitated, to be known and to be loved.

3. This way was most suitable in regard also to our reparation, because the Son of God became incarnate, so that in the form of a slave, He might procure the salvation of the slave. Indeed, this suitableness extends to the things proper to the Son and to those virtues appropriate to Him.

First, because the Son is the Word, the Image of the Father and the Son. Moreover, man through sin, had lost three things, namely, a knowledge of wisdom, the likeness of grace and possession of glory. Therefore, the Word, the Image and the Son were sent into the world.

Secondly, this suitableness of the Incarnation appears more and more from the part of the virtues of the Son of God, because in the work of creation, His power especially shines forth; in the work of restoration, His wisdom is seen; while in the work of retribution, His kindness is apparent to all men. (Humanity of Christ)

DECEMBER 3

Saint John the Baptist

"John was a burning and shining light." (John V, 35.)

John was the accepted witness for Christ, and this is proved by three things which were accomplished by John. The first thing pertains to the condition of nature, namely, "John was a light." The second pertains to the perfection of his love, because John was "a burning light." The third refers to the perfection of his intellect, for "John was a shining light."

1. John was perfect in nature for he was a light, that is, he was illuminated by grace, and illuminated by the light of God's Word. The light (in John) differed from ordinary light, for ordinary light is that which shines by its own power; but this light in John was a participation of the Divine Light. For according to John I, 9, "Christ is the true Light. That was the true Light, which enlighteneth every man that cometh into the world." John, however, was not "the Light," but a light, for he was enlightened "to give testimony of the Light, that all men might believe through him," (John I, 8) and

be led to Christ. It is written of the light which shone in John: "I have prepared a lamp for Christ, my anointed (One)." (Ps. CXXXI, 17.)

2. Likewise the love that was in John "was burning and shining." For there are some lights that shine only in regard to duty but are extinct in regard to love (of God). For just as light or a lamp cannot shine unless it is first enkindled and inflamed by the fire of charity. And hence the flame of love shines forth to enlighten because through the burning flame of charity the knowledge of truth is communicated. "I have called you friends, because all things whatsoever I have heard of My Father, I have made known to you." (John XV, 15.) And again: "They that fear God will prepare their hearts and in His sight will sanctify their souls." (Eccl'us II, 20.) Fire has two qualities, namely, it burns and shines. But the heat from fire represents love by reason of three things:

First of all because among all things material fire is the most active, and likewise with the flame of charity, for nothing can resist its power. "The charity of Christ presseth us." (2 Cor. V, 14.)

Secondly, just as fire is made to burn much from the fact that it is especially sensitive (and rapidly spreads) so also, charity produces the warmth of fervour (and burns away the dross of earth) so that man might pursue the ways of God and follow his destined course unto the end.

Thirdly, just as fire is led upwards, so also charity, inasmuch as it unites us with God. "He that abideth in charity, abideth in God, and God in him." (I John IV, 16.)

3. John was shining in intellect.

First, interiorly by a knowledge of truth for "the Lord filled his soul with brightness," (Isaias LVIII . . . II), that is, He made, He caused John to shine with heaven's splendor.

Secondly, John shone exteriorly by his preaching the word of God. "Blameless and sincere . . . among whom you shine as lights in the world: holding forth the word of life, to My glory in the day of Christ." (Phil. II; 15).

Thirdly, John was a shining light by the examples of his good works. "So let your light shine before men, that they may see your good works, and glorify your Father Who is in heaven." (Math. V, 16).

DECEMBER 4

The Manner of Repairing Human Nature

1. The manner of repairing had to be such that it was suitable to the nature repaired and to the disease. I say suitable to nature, for since man has a rational nature, endowed with free will, he had to be brought back to a state of uprightness, not necessarily by external force, but according to his own will. I say also that the manner of repairing human nature had to be suitable to the disease, because when a sick person is considered in regard to the weakness of his will, it is necessary that his will be led back to the path of rectitude.

But rectitude or uprightness of will consists in the regulation of love which is the will's chief affection. But if we are to place spiritual things ahead of things material our love must be so regulated that we love God above all things as our highest good (the summum bonum) and secondly, that we refer whatever we love—to God—as our final end; so that a proper order might be observed by us in other things loved. Now, to win our love for God, the Word of God, by Whom all things were made, could do nothing more for the reparation of our nature than to assume it, so that He is God and Man.

2. First of all, it is especially proven in so far as God loves man; that for man's salvation, God willed to become man, nor is there anything inspires more to love than to know that we are being loved. But man could not easily raise himself to those things which are above him, since his intellect and affections were burdened with material things. However, it is easy for one man to know and love another man. But to realize the depth of Divine Love, and to be borne into it by the proper affection of love, is not in every man's power; but in the power of those who through God's help are raised with a great desire and labour from things material to things spiritual. Therefore, in order that the way to God might be opened and made clear to all men, God willed to become man; so that even little children, so like to God, might be able to know and love God; and thus by this means can all understand God, and gradually arrive at perfection.

From the fact also that God became man, hope was given to man, that man could arrive at the participation of perfect happiness which happiness God alone has naturally. For man realizing his own weakness, even if he had been promised to obtain that happiness which the Angels are scarcely capable of possessing, namely, the happiness of the Vision of God; man of himself could hardly ever hope for this; unless, from another standpoint, the dignity of his nature were shown to him; a dignity which God considered of such great importance that He willed to become man; and so through this blessing God became man; He gave to us the hope, that we also can obtain that perfection which will unite us to God in everlasting enjoyment.

The knowledge of man's dignity is accordingly important for man to realize, from the fact that God assumed human nature; so that man might subject his will to no creature, either by worshiping devils or any created things, or by debasing himself through the improper love of worldly things. For it is unworthy of a man that he should improperly subject himself to things inferior to God; since man is of such dignity according to Divine Wisdom, and so like to God, that God willed to become man (to make man God-like). (Saracens, V)

DECEMBER 5

The Wonderful Incarnation of the Son of God

1. Among Divine works, this mystery of the Incarnation, especially, exceeds the grasp of reason, for nothing can be thought of that is more wonderful than the Divine fact, that the true God, the Son of God, became true man. And because it is the most wonderful mystery, it follows that all other wonderful things are ordained especially to faith in this mystery, since that which exists also in one genus seems to be the chief cause of other things.

2. Moreover, we believe in this wonderful Incarnation of God on Divine Authority which has revealed it to us for it is written, "The Word was made flesh and dwelt amongst us." (John I, 14.)

The very words of our Lord Jesus Christ also prove this fact, "The Father is greater than I." (John XIV, 28). And again, "My soul is sorrowful unto death." (Matth. XXVI, 38). In these words our Lord speaks of things humble and human. These things were proper to Him according to His assumed humanity. Sometimes He speaks, on the other hand, of things sublime and Divine, namely, "I and the Father are one." (John X, 30). And again, "All things whatsoever the Father hath are mine." (John XVI, 15). It is certain that these things belong to Christ according to His Divine Nature.

The works of the Lord also prove the reality of the Incarnation, for we read concerning Him, that "He feared, became sad, was thirsty and died. These facts pertain to His human nature, but that by His own power He cured the sick, raised the dead to life, calmed the sea, cast out devils and finally ascended into heaven, these things demonstrate Divine Power in Christ."

3. Moreover, in all created things, nothing is found like unto this union of the Divine and human nature in the Incarnation; except the likeness of the union of the soul with the body. Hence, Athanasius says, that "just as the rational soul and the human body form one man, so God and Man are one Christ." But the likeness cannot consist in this, that the rational soul is united to the body as to matter, for then, one nature in God and Man would result.

Therefore, the likeness consists in this, that the soul is united to the body as to an instrument. In fact, some Doctors say, that the human nature in Christ is a certain organ of the Divinity; just as the body is considered the organ of the soul. Hence, in the Union of God and of man, all men are compared to God as instruments to whom He is united. "For He it is Who worketh in us and perfects us."

But some men are compared to God as external and separate instruments. For they are moved by God, not to works proper to themselves, but to deeds common to all rational nature, that is to know truth, to love good things, to perform just works. But the human nature assumed by Christ is such that instrumentally it does the things proper to the Son of God, just as it is proper to Him to forgive sins, to enlighten minds by His grace and to lead us to eternal life. Therefore, the human nature of Christ with God, is likened to one's own united instrument, as the hand in regard to its union with the soul. Still, the aforesaid example is not an exact likeness for it must be remembered that the Word of God is united to the human in a manner much more sublime and intimate. (Contr. Gent. IV, 41).

DECEMBER 6

If Man Had Not Sinned Would God Have Become Man?

Augustine explaining Luke XIX, says: " 'The Son of Man is come to seek and to save that which was lost':—Therefore, if man had not sinned, the Son of Man would not have come. And in I Tim. I, 15: 'Christ Jesus came into this world to save sinners,' the gloss says: There was no cause of Christ's coming into the world, except to save sinners. Take away diseases, take away wounds, and there is no need of medicine."

1. There are different opinions about this question. Some claim that even if man had not sinned the Son of God would have become incarnate. Others declare the contrary, and our assent ought rather to be given to this opinion.

For such things as come from God's will, and beyond the creature's due, can only be made known to us by being revealed in the Sacred Scripture, in which the Divine Will is made known to us. Hence, since everywhere in Sacred Scripture the sin of the first man is assigned as the reason of the Incarnation, it is more in accordance with this to say that the work of the Incarnation was ordained by God as a remedy for sin; so that, had sin not existed, the Incarnation would not have been. Although the power of God is not limited to this; even had sin not been, God could have become Incarnate.

2. All other things which are assigned to the Incarnation of Christ, namely, man's promotion in faith, hope and charity, have to do with a remedy for sin. For if man had not sinned, he would have been endowed with the light of Divine Wisdom and would have been protected by God with the righteousness of justice in order to know and execute everything needful. But because man on deserting God had stooped to corporeal things, it was necessary that God should take flesh, and by corporeal things should afford him the remedy of salvation. Hence, in John I, 14, "And the Word was made flesh," Augustine says: "Flesh had blinded thee, flesh heals thee; for Christ came and overthrew the vices of the flesh."

3. On the other hand, it is reasonable and fitting that human nature should have been raised to something greater after sin. For God allows evils to happen in order to bring a greater good therefrom; hence it is written (Rom. V, 20): "Where sin abounded, grace did more abound." Hence also, in the blessing of the Paschal candle, we say: "O happy fault,

that merited such and so great a Redeemer!" (Summa 3a, q. 1, a. 3).

DECEMBER 7

Should God Have Become Incarnate at the Beginning of the World?

It is written (Gal. IV, 4): "When the fulness of time was come, God sent His Son," concerning which the gloss says that "the fullness of the time—is when it was decreed by God the Father to send His Son." But God decreed everything by His wisdom. Therefore, God became incarnate at the most fitting time; and it was not fitting that God should become incarnate at the beginning of the human race.

Since the work of the Incarnation is principally ordained to the restoration of the human race by the removal of sin, it is manifest, that it was not fitting for God to become incarnate at the beginning of the human race before sin. For medicine is given only to the sick. Hence, Our Lord Himself says (Matth. IX, 12): "They that are in health need not a physician, but they that are ill. . . . For I am not come to call the just, but sinners" to repentance.

Nor was it fitting that God should become man—immediately—after sin.

First, on account of the manner of man's sin, which was the result of pride; hence, man was to be liberated in such a manner that he might be humbled, and see how he stood in need of a deliverer. Hence, on the words in Gal. III, 19: "Being ordained by angels in the hand of a mediator," the gloss says: "With great wisdom was it so ordered that the Son of Man should not be sent immediately after man's fall. For first of all God left man under the natural law, with the freedom of his will, in order that he might realize his natural strength; so that, having recognized his infirmity, he might cry out for a physician, and beg the help of grace."

Secondly, on account of the order of furtherance in good, whereby we advance from imperfection to perfection. Hence, the Apostle says (I Cor. XV, 46): "Yet that was not first which is spiritual, but that which is natural; afterwards that which is spiritual. . . . The first man was of the earth, earthly; the second man from heaven, heavenly."

Thirdly, on account of the dignity of the Incarnate Word, for on the words (Gal. IV, 4): "But when the fulness of the time was come," the gloss says: "The greater the Judge Who was coming, the more numerous was the band of heralds who ought to have preceded Him."

Fourthly, lest the fervor of faith should cool by the length of time, for the charity of many will grow cold at the end of the world. Hence (Luke, XVIII, 8), it is written: "But yet the Son of Man, when He cometh, shall He find, think you, faith on earth?"

Charity does not put off bringing assistance to a friend; for always keep in mind the circumstances as well as the condition of the persons. For if the physician were to give the medicine at the very outset of the ailment, it would do less good, and would hurt rather than benefit. And hence, our Lord did not bestow upon the human race the remedy of the Incarnation in the beginning, lest they should despise it through pride, if they did not already recognize their disease. (Summa 3a, q. 1, a. V).

DECEMBER 8

The Feast of the Immaculate Conception

"Thou art all fair, O my love, and there is not a spot in thee." (Cant. IV, 7.)

Mary was always immune from every sin. First of all in her very conception. For it is reasonably believed that Mary received greater gifts of grace than all others, since she gave birth to "the Only Begotten of the Father, full of grace and of truth." Hence, it is written, "The Angel said to her, 'Hail, full of grace, the Lord is with thee, Blessed art thou among women'." (Luke, I, 28).

Moreover, it is to be observed that it was granted by way of privilege to others, to be sanctified in the womb; for example, to Jeremias, to whom it is written (Jer. I, 5): "Before thou camest out of the womb, I sanctified thee"; and again to John the Baptist, of whom it is written (Luke, 1, 15), "He shall be filled with the Holy Ghost even from his mother's womb."

(Therefore, in order that Mary might receive more grace

than these, she had to be not only sanctified in the womb but also preserved from the original stain of sin.)

But this infusion of grace took place not before animation, but at the very first instant of animation. For the things of the Old Testament were figures of the New according to I Cor. XII: "All things happened to them in figure." Now the sanctification of the tabernacle, of which it is written, Ps. XLV, 5, "The Most High hath sanctified His own tabernacle," seems to signify the sanctification of the Mother of God who is called God's Tabernacle according to Ps. XVIII, 6: "He hath set His tabernacle in the Sun." But of the tabernacle it is written (Exod. XL, 31): "After all things were perfected, the cloud covered the tabernacle of the testimony and the glory of the Lord filled it." Therefore, also, the Blessed Virgin was not sanctified until after all in her were perfected, namely, her body and soul, that is, in the same instant.

Secondly, Mary's whole life was free from sin. For God so prepares and endows those whom He selects for some particular office, that they are rendered capable of fulfilling it, according to 2 Cor. III, 6: "Who hath made us fit ministers of the New Testament." Now the Blessed Virgin was chosen by God to be His Mother. Therefore, there can be no doubt that God, by His grace, made her worthy of that office, according to the words spoken to her by the Angel (Luke I, 30), "Thou hast found grace with God, behold thou shalt conceive in thy womb and shall bring forth a son and thou shalt call His Name Jesus." But she would not have been worthy to be the Mother of God if she had ever sinned. First, because the honor of the parents reflects upon the child, according to Prov. XVII, 6: "The glory of the children are their fathers"; and consequently, on the other hand, the Mother's shame would have reflected on her Son. Secondly, because of the singular affinity between her and Christ Who took flesh from her. And it is written (2 Cor. VI, 15): "What concord hath Christ with Belial?" Thirdly, because of the singular manner in which the Son of God, "Who is the Divine Wisdom" (1 Cor. I, 24), dwelt in her, not only in her soul but in her womb. And thus, it is written (Wisd. I, 4): "Wisdom will not enter into a malicious soul, nor dwell in a body subject to sins."

We must therefore confess simply that the Blessed Virgin committed no actual sin, either mortal or venial; so that what is written (Cant. IV, 7), is fulfilled: "Thou art all fair, O my love, and there is not a spot in thee." (3a, q. 27)

DECEMBER 9

The Departing Night

"The night is passed and the day is at hand. Let us, therefore, cast off the works of darkness and put on the armor of light." (Rom. XII, 13.)

1. "The night is passed and the day is at hand." This seems to be thus understood, that the entire time of the present life might be compared to night, because of the darkness of ignorance in which the present life is surrounded. On the contrary, the state of future blessedness is to be compared to "the day," because of the brightness of God by which the saints are enlightened.

In another way, it can be understood as meaning that the state of crime might be compared to "night," because of the darkness of crime; concerning which it is written, "They have not known, nor understood. They walk on in darkness." (Ps. LXXXI, 5). Moreover, the day is called the state of grace, because of the light of spiritual intelligence which the just have, but which the wicked have not. "Light is risen to the just, and joy to the right of heart." (Ps. XCVI, 11).

In another way, "the night is passed and the day is at hand," may be understood thus, that the time before the Incarnation of Christ might be compared to "night," because it was as yet clear and the world was under a certain cloud of darkness. On the contrary, the time from the Incarnation of Christ is compared to the day, because of the power of the spiritual sun which came into the world with the birth of Christ.

It can also be understood as the time of the grace of Christ, which even if that time of grace had already arrived according to the course of time, still it is said to approach us through faith and devotion. "The Lord is nigh." It can also apply to those who begin to repent of their sin and for whose souls "the day of grace" is approaching.

2. Honesty is, therefore, necessary for life.

First, in regard to the removal of vices. "Let us, therefore, cast off the works of darkness." With the departure of night, the works of night should cease. On the other hand, the works of darkness are called sins, because they are in themselves deprived of the light of reason with which human works should shine forth; for they are performed in darkness and because through works of darkness, man is led into darkness, according to Matth. XXII, 13, "Cast him into exterior darkness."

Secondly, honesty is necessary for putting on the virtues. "Put on the armour of light," that is, the virtues, which are termed "armour," inasmuch as they fortify us and they are called "the armour of light," because they beautify and perfect the light of reason and because by our works of virtue others are enlightened. "So let your light shine before men, that they may see your good works and glorify your Father Who is in heaven." (Matth. V. 16).

Thirdly, the Apostle exhorts us to the practice of and advancement in the virtues when he says, "Let us walk honestly as in the day." (Rom. XIII, 13). For these two things seem to be suitable for the day. First of all, honesty, for on each day we should so conduct ourselves, that our honesty is apparent unto others. Secondly, man usually walks in the daytime, not so much at night. Hence, it is said, "If a man walk in the day, he stumbleth not, because he seeth the light of this world, but if he walk in the night, he stumbleth, because the light is not in him." (John XI, 9). Therefore, because the day is at hand, it is necessary that we walk, that is, advance from what is good to what is best. Hence, it is written, "Walk while you have light and the darkness will overtake you not." And Jesus said, "Yet a little while, and the light is among you. Walk while you have the light." (John XII, 35). (In Rom. XIII).

DECEMBER 10

The Translation of the House of Our Lady of Loretto

"Holiness becometh Thy house, O Lord." (Ps. XCII., 5)

The Blessed Virgin received the fulness or perfection of grace.

She was full of grace. For in every genus, the nearer a thing is to the principle, the greater the part which it has in the effect of that principle. Hence, Dionysius says, that the angels being nearer to God have a greater share than men in the effects of the Divine goodness. Now, Christ is the principle of grace, authoritatively as to His Godhead, instrumentally as to His humanity. Whence (John I, 17) says, "Grace and truth came by Jesus Christ." But the Blessed Virgin Mary was nearest to Christ in His humanity because He received His human nature from her. Therefore, it was due to her to receive greater fulness of grace than others.

In like manner, there was a threefold perfection of grace in the Blessed Virgin. The first was a kind of disposition by which she was made worthy to be the Mother of Christ and this was the perfection of her sanctification. The second perfection of grace in the Blessed Virgin was through the presence of the Son of God Incarnate in her womb. The third perfection of the end is that which she has in glory.

That the second perfection excels the first, and the third the second, appears evident.

1. From the point of view of deliverance from evil, for at first, in her sanctification, she received grace inclining her to good, but in the conception of the Son of God she received consummate grace confirming her in good and in her glorification her grace was further consummated so as to perfect her in the enjoyment of all good.

2. Mary is the dispenser of grace to others.

God gives grace to each one according to the purpose for which He has chosen him. And since Christ as man was predestinated and chosen to be "predestinated the Son of God in power . . ., of sanctification" (Rom. I, 4), it was proper to Him to have such a fulness of grace that it overflowed from Him into all, according to John I, 16, "Of His fulness we have all received." But the Blessed Virgin Mary received such a fulness of grace that she was nearest of all to the Author of grace, so that she received with her Him Who is full of grace and by bringing Him forth she, in a manner, dispensed grace to all.

There is no doubt that the Blessed Virgin received, in a high degree, both the gift of wisdom and the grace of miracles and even of prophecy, just as Christ had them. But she did not receive them so as to put them and suchlike graces to every use, as did Christ; but according as they befitted her condition in life. For she had the use of wisdom in contemplation, according to Luke II, 19, "But Mary kept all these words pondering them in her heart." But she had not the use of wisdom as to teaching since this befitted not the female sex, according to 1 Tim. II, 12, "I suffer not a woman to teach."

The use of miracles did not become her while she lived because at that time the Teaching of Christ was to be confirmed by miracles, and hence, it was befitting that Christ alone and His disciples, who were the bearers of His Doctrine, should work miracles. Hence of John the Baptist it is written, "That he did no sign," (John X, 41); that is, in order that all might fix their attention on Christ. As to the use of prophecy, it is clear that Mary had it from the canticle spoken by her: "My soul doth magnify the Lord." (Luke I, 46). (3a, q. 27, a. v.)

DECEMBER 12

The Desire for Our Lord's Incarnation

The Sacrament of the Divine Incarnation was desired by the holy fathers. Hence, it is written, "The Desired of all nations shall come." (Aggeus II, 8). For this reason Augustine says, "The holy fathers knew that Christ would come, and all who believed in His coming, lived holy. O would that this birth of Christ might find me holy! O would that I may see with my eyes that which I believe in the sacred writings!"

There are three reasons why the ancients desired so much the Incarnation of Christ:

1. Because of the flood of earthly miseries from which they suffered. Hence, in Ps. XVII, 7, we read, "In my affliction, I called upon the Lord and I cried to my God." That is, they longed for the coming of the Body of Christ, in Whose Incarnation we behold the effect of prayer. "I beseech Thee, Lord, send whom Thou wilt send." (Ex. IV, 13). "Behold the affliction of Thy people. Come and free us, as Thou hast said." Here it is to be observed, that the affliction and liberation of the Israelites was a figure of the affliction and salvation of the whole human race.

2. They longed for the Incarnation of our Lord, because of the abundance of internal and external peace which abounded everywhere at His coming. Hence, it is written in Ps. LXXI, 7, "In His days shall justice spring up and abundance of peace, till the moon be taken away." And again, Canticles I, 1, says, "Let Him kiss me with the kiss of His mouth." For a kiss is a sign of peace. Therefore, the spouse prays for the Incarnation of the Son of God, which is, as it were, a foreshadowing of our union with God in which union truly exists the peace of our hearts.

3. The people of old desired the Incarnation of Christ,

because of the abundance of internal joy which they received. "Look about thee, O Jerusalem, towards the east, and behold the joy that cometh to thee from God." (Baruch IV, 36). In seeing and in believing in this joy, the holy fathers had tasted it before it arrived. "Abraham your father rejoiced that he might see My day. He saw it and was glad." (John VIII, 56). A gloss explains this thus, "Abraham understood about the day of My Incàrnation." Wherefore, Augustine beautifully says, "What joy of heart came at seeing the Word dwelling amongst us, the splendor of the Father shining in holy minds. The joy that God dwelling with the Father, and still not departing from the bosom of the Father, would one day be in the flesh, as Christ the Saviour, the Prince of Peace." (Humility of Christ.)

DECEMBER 13

It Was Fitting for the Son of God to Assume Human Nature from the Stock of Adam

Augustine says: "God was able to assume human nature elsewhere than from the stock of Adam who by his sin had enslaved the whole human race; yet God thought it better to assume human nature from the conquered race and thus to overcome the enemy of the human race." And this for three reasons: first because it would seem but justice that he who sinned should make amends and hence that from the nature which had been corrupted should be assumed that by which satisfaction was to be made for the whole nature. Secondly, it redounds to man's greater dignity that the conqueror of the devil should spring from the stock conquered by him; and thirdly, because God's power is made more manifest since, from a corrupt and weakened nature, He assumed that which was raised to such power and dignity.

Therefore it is rightly said: "He came unto His own and His own received Him not." (John I, 11.) The Light of the World, although present in the world and manifest by its effects, is nevertheless not recognized by the world. Thus "He came unto His own" so that He might be recognized, through the assumption of human nature. He Who was invisible came that he might become visible to all mankind. He came unto His own, that is unto Judea, which was in truth in a special manner His own. But it is better to say that He came into the world created by His own power.

"And they received Him not"; that is mankind, formed by Him and made to His image and likeness. But here too it is better to say, the Jews who were His own received Him not for they should have believed in Him and worshiped Him.

The Jews were indeed "His own" because they were chosen by Him to be His own special people. "The Lord has chosen thee to be His peculiar people." (Deut. XXVI, 18.) His own because they are His kinsmen; "my kinsmen according to the flesh." (Rom. IX, 3) Likewise His own because of the many and great favors God has conferred upon them. "I have brought up children, and exalted them; but they have despised me." (Isaias I, 2)

DECEMBER 14

It Was More Fitting That the Person of the Son Rather Than Any Other Divine Person Should Assume Human Nature

Damascene says, "In the mystery of the Incarnation the wisdom and the power of God are made known; the wisdom, for He found a most suitable solution for a most heavy debt; the power, for He made the conquered conquer." But power and wisdom are proper to the Son, according to 1 Cor. I, 24. "Christ, the power of God and the wisdom of God." Hence it was fitting that the Person of the Son should become incarnate.

First, on the part of the union; for such as are similar are fittingly united. Now the Person of the Son, Who is the Word of God, has a certain common agreement with all creatures, because the word of the craftsman, that is, his concept —is an exemplary likeness of whatever is made by him. Hence the Word of God, Who is His eternal concept is the exemplar of all creatures. And therefore as creatures are established in their proper species, though movably, by the participation of this likeness, so by the non-participated and personal union of the Word to a creature, it was fitting that the creature should be restored in order to its eternal and unchangeable perfection; for the craftsman by the intelligible form of his art, whereby he fashioned his handiwork, restores it when it has fallen into ruin.

In another way, He has a particular agreement with human nature, since the Word is a concept of the eternal Wisdom, from Whom all man's wisdom is derived. And hence man is perfected in wisdom (which is his proper perfection, as he is rational) by participating in the Word of God, as the disciple is instructed by receiving the word of his master. Hence it is said (Eccles. I, 5), "The Word of God on high is the fountain of wisdom." And hence for the complete perfection of man it was fitting that the very Word of God should be personally united to human nature.

Secondly, the reason for this fitness may be taken from the end of the union, which is the fulfilling of predestination—that is, of such as are preordained to the heavenly inheritance, which is bestowed only on sons, according to Rom. VIII, 17. "If sons, heirs also." Hence it was fitting that by Him Who is the eternal Son, men should share His likeness of sonship by adoption, as the Apostle says in the same chapter (VIII, 29), "For whom He foreknew, He also predestined to be made conformable to the image of His Son."

Thirdly, the reason for this fitness may be taken from the sin of our first parent, for which the Incarnation supplied the remedy. For the first man sinned by seeking knowledge, as is plain from the words of the serpent, promising to man the knowledge of good and evil. Hence it was fitting that by the Word of true knowledge man might be led back to God, having wandered from God through an improper thirst for knowledge. (3a, Q. 3. A. VIII)

DECEMBER 15

No Merits Preceded the Union of the Incarnation

First, with regard to Christ Himself, it is clear that no merits of His preceded the union. For we do not hold that He was first of all a mere man, and that afterwards by the merits of a good life it was granted Him to become the Son of God, as Photinus held; but we hold that from the beginning of His conception this man was truly the Son of God, seeing, that He had no other hypostasis but that of the Son of God, according to Luke I, 35. "The Holy which shall be born of thee shall be called the Son of God."

Neither could the deeds of any other man whatsoever have

availed to merit this union condignly;—first, because the meritorious works of man are properly ordained to beatitude, which is the reward of virtue, and consists in the full enjoyment of God. Whereas the union of the Incarnation, inasmuch as it is in the personal being, transcends the union of the beatified mind with God, which is by the act of the soul in fruition; and therefore it cannot merit.

Secondly, because grace cannot fall under merit, for the principle of merit does not fall under merit and hence neither does grace, for it is the principle of merit. Therefore, still less does the Incarnation fall under merit, since it is the principle of grace, according to John I, 27. "Grace and truth came by Jesus Christ."

Thirdly, because the Incarnation is for the reformation of the entire human nature, and therefore it does not fall under the merit of any individual man, since the goodness of a mere man cannot be the cause of the good of the entire nature. Yet, the holy Fathers merited the Incarnation, congruously by desiring and imploring; for it was becoming that God should hearken to those who obeyed Him.

The Blessed Virgin is said to have merited to bear the Lord of all; not that she merited His Incarnation, but because by grace bestowed on her she merited the degree of purity and holiness, which fitted her to be the Mother of God. (3a, Q. II, a. XI)

DECEMBER 16

The Gift of the Son of God in the Incarnation

"In this the charity of God has appeared to us, that God sent His only Begotten Son into the world, that we might live through Him." (I John IV, 9).

"In this," as by a most certain proof, "the charity of God appeared to us," that is, the charity of God was shown to us; because God sent His Son, and not a servant. Gregory says, "Is not this love of charity indescribable that in redeeming the slave, God sacrificed His Son, consubstantial with Himself, not an adopted Son, but His Own Son by nature. God sent His Only Begotten Son, not one from many sons; but He Who is infinitely great amongst the greatest—God sent Him into the world—to save the world"; so that we might live—"that we who were first dead, might live—being vivified through Him." But God Who is rich in mercy, because of His exceeding charity wherewith He loved us, even when we were dead in sins—quickened us together in Christ—that He might show in the ages to come the abundant riches of His grace; for by grace you are saved through faith, for it is a gift of God." (Ephes. II).

Observe that the Apostle states four reasons whereby the gift (of the Incarnation) should be pleasing and acceptable:

First because of the Person giving the gift; since He Who gives, gives from the greatest love and affection. Hence, sometimes care is taken not so much concerning that which is given, as concerning the love of the person giving a gift. But surely, this gift of God to us was given from the greatest love or charity of the Father: "In this the charity of God appeared to us."

The second reason (why the gift of the Incarnation should be pleasing and acceptable to us) is on the part of the gift given or sent. When that which is given is great and precious, it should be all the more welcome and acceptable and pleasing. And certainly this gift to us of God the Son Incarnate was the greatest. Wherefore it is noted: "He sent His Only Begotten Son."

The third reason is on the part of the person receiving the gift; particularly when the person to whom the gift is given needs it in the worst way. And certainly we needed in the worst manner such a gift from God to vivify us, because we were dead in our sins, and this fact is noted in the words: "That we might live through Him."

The fourth reason (why we should appreciate the God-given gift of the Incarnation) is on the part of the person bringing that gift. For sometimes, because of the beauty, graciousness, and pleasingness of the person bringing a gift—as in the case of a beautiful lady—the gift presented is rendered all the more pleasing. And so because of the beauty and grace of the Virgin bearing that Divine gift, it should be most acceptable to us, and this is implied in the words: "God sent His Son, made of a woman." (Gal. IV). "Now therefore, you are no more strangers and foreigners; but you are fellow citizens with the saints and domestics of God." (Ephes. II, 19.) (1 John IV.)

DECEMBER 17

The Work of the Incarnation Is Proper to the Holy Spirit

"The Holy Ghost shall come upon thee and the power of the most High shall overshadow thee." (Luke I, 35.)

1. The formation of the body of Christ, which was perfected by Divine power, is properly attributed to the Holy Spirit, although it is a work common to the Three Persons of the Blessed Trinity. This seems to be suitable to the Incarnation. For just as our word conceived in the mind is invisible, but is perceived when orally or externally expressed; so too, the Word of God, according to eternal generation, invisibly existed in the heart of the Father, but through the Incarnation, the Word of God became visible to us. Hence, the Incarnation of the Word of God is, as it were, the vocal expression of our word. On the other hand, the vocal expression of our word is formed. Therefore, it is properly said, that the formation of the flesh of the Son of God was formed by the Holy Spirit.

It is also proper to lay down a cause for the existing Incarnation of the Word made flesh. Indeed, there can be no other cause than God's love for man, whose nature He wished to assume in the unity of Person. Moreover, among the Divine Persons, the Holy Spirit is such that love proceeds from Him. Therefore, it was suitable that the work of the Incarnation should be attributed to the Holy Ghost.

2. Indeed, in every work denoting an effect in a creature, things appropriate to the Divine Persons shine forth; just as in the Incarnation, according to Saint John Damascene, the goodness and wisdom and power of God shine forth. The goodness of God, in so far as God did not despise the weakness of our nature; the power of God, in so far as He united the extremes between heaven and earth; and His wisdom, in so far as He found a suitable manner for doing this which seemed impossible. Still, each work is said to be more appropriate to a certain Person, in as far as, what is proper to that Person is more manifested in that work.

On the other hand, inasmuch as any work surpasses the merit of the creature, by so much the more is the grace and goodness of God manifested in it. Therefore, since the work of the Incarnation is of this nature, it is attributed in its beginning to grace, namely to the Holy Spirit.

In truth, it is also attributed to the power of the Father,

but it must be remembered that although power shines forth in the Incarnation, still the nature of goodness is more apparent here, because power is in the work, but goodness is in the execution or end of the work and the end is the cause of the things produced. (3 dist. 4, q. a. 1.)

DECEMBER 18

The Feast of the Expectation of the Blessed Virgin Mary

"Blessed is the womb that bore Thee." (Luke XI, 27.)

The womb of the Blessed Virgin is called blessed on account of many things.

1. Because it bore Him Who is blessed in Himself in the highest degree possible. "Our Lord Jesus Christ, Who is the Blessed and only Mighty, the King, to Whom be honour and empire everlasting." (1 Tim.)

2. Her womb is blessed, because of the highest blessedness and Trinity which it bore. For Mary was the spouse of the Father, the Mother of the Son, the Tabernacle of the Holy Ghost. Hence, we address her: "Hail, Mother of sanctity and of the whole Trinity, the magnificent dwelling."

3. Because it conceived without corruption.

4. It bore without labour.

5. It gave birth to Him without experiencing pain. Concerning these things it is written, "The Holy Ghost shall come upon thee, and therefore, thou wilt conceive without pain and corruption, and the power of the most High shall overshadow thee, and hence, you will bring forth without labour. Therefore, also, the Holy which shall be born of thee, shall be called the Son of God. Hence, thou wilt bear without pain." (Luke I, 35.)

6. The womb of the Blessed Virgin is blessed, because it bore the price of our redemption. "O Lord God, hear the cry of this people and open to them Thy treasure, a fountain of living water, that being satisfied, they may cease to murmur. And the glory of the Lord appeared to them." (Numbers XX, 6.)

7. Mary had virtues from every state: from the state of virgins she had purity; from the state of wedlock, fecundity; from the state of continency, chastity.

8. Finally Mary is blessed, because she must be frequently blessed or praised and preached by all. "All generations shall call me blessed." (Luke I, 48.) (Discourse 46.)

DECEMBER 19

Penance

"Do penance, for the kingdom of heaven is at hand." (Matth. III, 2.)

1. "Do penance," John the Baptist thus announces a certain life. As St. Augustine says, "No one, who is the master of his own will, can begin this new life, unless he repents of his old life." Therefore, he first advises us to do penance and secondly, he announces salvation. "The kingdom of heaven is at hand." Likewise, "do penance," by which the remission of sin is accomplished. Hence, Chrysostom says, "With the birth of the Son of God, God sent a precursor into the world."

It must be observed that it is one thing to do penance and another thing to repent. One repents who turns away from sin, but weeps not for having committed them. It must be realized that everything is referred to the intention of the mind, that is, a person must resolve not to commit sin again, and for this penance is required. To do penance, moreover, is to satisfy for sins committed. "Bring forth fruits worthy of penance." (Luke III, 8.) This refers to penance for sins committed after baptism. Hence Peter (Acts II, 38) says, "Do penance and be baptized every one of you in the name of Jesus Christ for the remission of your sins, and you shall receive the gift of the Holy Ghost," that is so you may be ready to obtain salvation.

2. "The Kingdom of Heaven." Nowhere in the Old Testament is there found a promise of the kingdom of heaven. But John the Baptist was the first to announce it, for this pertained to his dignity. Moreover, the kingdom of heaven may be considered in four ways:

First, it is called Christ Himself living in us through His grace. "The Kingdom of God is within you" (Luke XVII, 21), for through the indwelling of grace the heavenly life is begun in us.

Secondly, Sacred Scripture is sometimes called the Kingdom of Heaven. "The Kingdom of God shall be taken away from you" (Matth. XXI, 43), that is, Sacred Scripture. It is called the kingdom because its law leads to the kingdom.

Thirdly, the Church militant on earth is called the kingdom of heaven. "The kingdom of heaven is like unto a net cast into the sea and the gathering together of all kinds of fishes." (Matth. XIII, 47.) It is called the kingdom of heaven because it was instituted after the manner of the heavenly church.

Fourthly, the kingdom of heaven is called the heavenly curia or celestial building. "They shall come from the east, and from the west and shall sit down with Isaac, Abraham and Jacob in the kingdom of heaven." Moreover, before the time of John the Baptist, there was mention made only of the Kingdom of Jebusites, but now the kingdom of heaven, the Church of God, is promised. (Matth. III.)

DECEMBER 20

Fruit Worthy of Penance

"Who hath showed you to flee from the wrath to come? Bring forth, therefore, fruit worthy of penance." (Matth. III, 7.)

1. There are two things which lead to penance, namely, a realization of our own sins and a fear of the Divine judgment. "By the fear of the Lord, everyone declineth from evil." (Prov. XV, 27.) "Know ye that there is a judgment." (Job XIX, 29.) Ambrose and Chrysostom explain concerning the future, namely, "Who hath showed you, so that you might abandon evil? Who, but God? Show to us, O Lord, Thy mercy and grant to us Thy salvation." (Ps. LXXXIV, 8.) Rabanua also explains concerning the future wrath thus: "It is good that you do penance, otherwise who shall show you to flee from the wrath to come?" Psalm CXXXVIII, 8, says, "Whither shall I go from Thy spirit? or whither shall I flee from Thy face?" The anger of God must not be taken as an affection of His mind, but as an effect. Hence His anger is His just revenge.

There are two classes of people who are unwilling to do penance, namely, those who disbelieve in the judgment and those who delay their repentance. "Set not thy heart upon unjust possessions, and say not, I have enough to live on." (Eccle. V, 1.) And again, Job XIX, 29, advises to "flee ye from the face of the sword, for the sword is the avenger of iniquities."

The other class delay to do penance, and concerning these it is said, (2 Peter, III, 9) : "The Lord delayeth not His promise, as some imagine, but dealeth patiently for your sake, not willing that any should perish, but that all should return to penance." But John excludes both reasons saying, "Now, the axe (of penance) is laid to the root of the trees; every tree, therefore, that bringeth not forth good fruit (of penance) shall be cut down and cast into the fire." (Luke, III, 9.) As if the Evangelist had said, "Let us not delay to do penance."

2. "Bring forth, therefore, fruit worthy of penance." On the fruit tree the fruit appears after the blossoms (or flowers) appear and if there are no blossoms on the tree no fruit will follow. The flower, indeed, of penance appears in sorrow for sin, but the fruit of penance appears in good works. "My flowers are the fruit of honor and riches." (Eccles. XXIV, 23.) It must be observed that there is one fruit of justice and another fruit of penance; for more is demanded from the penitent than from a person who does not commit sin.

There is a threefold fruit worthy of penance. The first is that the sinner do penance according to the judgment of the priest, "After thou didst convert me, I did penance. . . . I am confounded and ashamed because I have borne the reproach of my youth." (Jerm. XXXI, 19), "that is, I have afflicted my flesh."

The second fruit worthy of penance is that the sinner flee from sin and the occasions of sin. Hence it is said that to satisfy for sin is to shun the causes of sin. "My son hast thou sinned? Do so no more, but for thy former sins also pray that they may be forgiven thee." (Eccle. XXI, 1.) "Flee from sins as from the face of a serpent, for if thou comest near them they will take hold of thee. The teeth thereof are the teeth of a lion, killing the souls of men." (Eccle. XXI, 2.)

The third fruit worthy of penance is that the sinner exert himself as much in doing good as he did in committing sin. "For as you have yielded your members to serve uncleanness and iniquity, so now yield your members to serve justice unto sanctification." (Rom. VI, 19.) (Matth. III.)

DECEMBER 21

The Voice of One Crying in the Desert

"I am the voice of one crying in the wilderness. Prepare ye the way of the Lord." (John I, 23.)

John says that he is a voice, because the voice is posterior to the word, but knowledge is prior to the word. For the word conceived in the heart (or mind) we know through the spoken word (or voice), since it is the sign of the word conceived in the mind. God sent the precursor, John, so that His Word, eternally conceived, might be made known; John said: "I am the voice."

"Of one crying," that is of John crying and preaching in the desert, or crying of Christ in him.

John, therefore, is crying for four reasons:

1. A cry introduces a manifestation, and therefore, to show that Christ speaks publicly through John and in him, John cries: "On the last and great day of the festivity, Jesus stood and cried, saying: 'If any man thirst, let him come to Me and drink.'" (John VII, 37.)

2. A cry is sounded to those who are distant. But the Jews were far away from God, and hence it was necessary that John should cry. "Friend and neighbor thou hast put far from Me." (Ps. LXXXVII, 19.)

3. He cries because they are deaf to the voice of God. "Who is deaf, but he to whom I have sent My messengers." (Isaias, XLII, 19.)

4. He cries because he speaks with righteous indignation; for these unbelievers had merited the anger of God. "He spoke to them in his anger." (Ps. II, 5.)

"One crying in the wilderness," so that, remaining in the desert, John might be immune from all sin and thus become more worthy to bear testimony to Christ, and from the example of his life in the desert, his testimony of Christ might be more readily believed by men.

But what does John cry? "Prepare the way of the Lord." Moreover, the way to receive God is the way of justice, ready and straight. "The way of the just is right." (Isaias XXVI, 7.)

For the way of the just man is right when the entire man is subjected to God; namely, when man's intellect is subjected to Him through faith, man's will through love, and man's actions through willing and holy obedience. (John I.)

DECEMBER 22

The Heavenly Dew

"Drop down dew, ye heavens, from above, and let the clouds rain the just. Let the earth be opened, and bud forth a Saviour." (Isias XLV, 8.)

1. Here the prophet Isaias points out three prophetic things about the birth of Christ, namely, the principle of His birth, the beginning of His birth, and the fruit of His birth. The principle of His birth is threefold:

First, the heavens descending as if an effective principle, namely, the nativity, is the work of the three Persons, for which reason the plural "heavens" is used. It is the work of the Father Who sent His Son, the work of the Son Who assumed human nature, and the work of the Holy Spirit in causing the conception.

The second principle is the raining clouds, which is a preparative principle, in which the work of the Angelic messenger is indicated. "Thou, O Lord, makest the clouds Thy chariot." (Ps. CIII, 3.)

The third principle is the earth budding forth, which is the conception principle; namely, the Blessed Virgin, concerning whom it is written in Ps. LXXXIV, 13, "Our earth shall yield her fruit; and whose virgin mind was opened and disposed to welcome the privilege of grace." "Do not be afraid, Mary hast found grace"; the grace of understanding, so believe the message of the Angel; the grace of the womb, to conceive the Son of God.

2. The beginning of the birth of Christ is truly compared to the dew, to the rain, and to the buds, for Christ is the dew that makes the earth cool, and the rain that enriches the earth. "He shall come down as rain upon the fleece. And as the rain and the snow come down from heaven and return no more thither, but soak the earth, and water it and make it to spring and give seed to the sower and bread to the eater; so shall My word be which shall go forth from My mouth. It shall not return to Me void, but it shall do whatsoever I please, and shall prosper in the things for which I sent it. (Isaias LV, 10.) And, "I will raise up to David a just branch." (Jer. XXIII, 5.)

The fruit of Christ's birth is justice, which sprang forth with His nativity and which was fulfilled in three ways; namely, by work, by word, and by gifts. By work, "Thus, it became us to fulfill all justice." By word, "I that speak justice, and am a defender to save." (Isaias LXIII, 1.) Fulfilled by gifts, which God gave to the world, "Of Him are you in Christ Jesus, Who of God is made unto us wisdom, and justice, and sanctification, and redemption. That, as it is written, He that glorieth, may glory in the Lord." (1 Cor. I, 30.) (Isaias C, 45.)

DECEMBER 23

Four Advantages of the Incarnation

There are four advantages arising from our Lord's Incarnation, namely, the exaltation of human nature; secondly, the adoption of sons; thirdly, the interior repairing of the mind; fourthly, the increase of happiness.

1. The exaltation of human nature. "Who shall give Thee to me for my brother that I may find Thee without, and kiss Thee, and now no man may despise me?" (Cant. VIII, 1.) The Beloved was at one time within. "In the beginning was the Word." At another time the Beloved was outside, when "the Word was made Flesh, and dwelt amongst us." "That I may kiss Thee," that is, that I may see Thee face to face, and speak to Thee, mouth to mouth; "and now no man may despise me." Afterwards, Christ came pouring His spirit of liberty into His own. Likewise the Church which Christ founded was honored by Angels. Hence, it is written in Apoc. XXII, 9, "I, John, who have heard and seen these things . . . fell down to adore, before the feet of the Angel, who showed me these things." Wherefore, Pope Leo also wrote: "O Christian, know thy dignity, that thou art made a companion with the Divine nature. Wherefore, thou shouldst be unwilling to return to your former worthlessness to become degenerated by your old vileness."

2. "The adoption of Sons." God sent His Son that we might receive the adoption of sons. (Gal. IV, 4.) Hence, Saint Augustine says, "The Son of God became the Son of man, so that He might make men sons of God. The Only Begotten Son of God made many sons of God; for He bought to Himself brethren by His own Blood. He reclaimed the outcast. He redeemed the slave, honored the undeserving, gave life to the dead. Without a doubt He who scorned not to receive evil things at thy hands will give thee His own good gifts."

Moreover, it must be observed that this adopted sonship has a certain likeness to natural sonship. The Son of God naturally proceeds from the Father as One intellectual Word existing in the Father, unto the Eternal Word, according to the unity which it has with the Father, which is caused through grace and charity. Hence, the Lord prayed, "I pray that they all may be one in Us as Thou Father, in Me, and I in Thee; so that the world may believe that Thou hast sent Me." (John XVII, 21.) And such likeness perfects the nature of our adoption because heirship is due to the heirs.

3. The interior repairing of the mind followed from the Incarnation. For, as Augustine says, "So that man might eat the Bread of Angels, the Creator of the Angels became Man." Likewise, Saint Bernard says, "The manna descended from heaven so that the hungry may rejoice." "She brought forth her first born, and wrapped Him up in swaddling clothes" (Luke II, 7), so that He might satisfy us with His own most precious food.

4. An increase of happiness resulted from the Incarnation. "I am the door. By me, if any man enter in, he shall be saved, and he shall go in, and go out, and shall find pastures." (John X, 9.) Wherefore Augustine says, "God became man, so that He might make all mankind happy in Him, and that the entire love of man might be centered in Him, and that the entire conversion of man might be towards Him; since, from an observation of the Flesh, He might be seen by flesh, and by a perception of the mind, He might be seen through the contemplation of His Divinity. All this is for man's good, so that whether man goes in, or goes out, he might find pastures in his work; outside, in the Flesh of his Saviour; inside, in the Divinity of his Creator." (The Humanity of Christ.)

DECEMBER 24

The Incarnation Is a Help for Man Striving for Happiness

If anyone diligently and piously considers the mysteries of the Incarnation, he will find such depth of wisdom that it exceeds all human knowledge. Hence, it happens to one piously meditating on this truth, that always more and more admirable reasons for a mystery of this nature reveal themselves. It must, therefore, be remembered that the Incarnation of

God was the most efficacious help for man tending to happiness.

1. The perfect happiness of man consists in the immediate vision of God. But this vision seemed to be impossible of attainment, because of the immense distance of the human nature from the Divine. Through this, that God willed to unite our human nature to Himself in Person, He most clearly proved to men that man can be united to God by his intellect seeing Him directly. It was, therefore, most suitable that God should assume human nature to raise man's hope to eternal happiness. Hence, after the Incarnation, men began to aspire more and more to celestial happiness. "I am come that they may have life, and have it more abundantly." (John X, 10.)

2. Because perfect happiness consists in such a knowledge of God that it exceeds the power of every created intellect, it was necessary that there should be a certain sacrifice of this Divine knowledge to man, so that he might be directed to that plenitude of ever blessed knowledge which is obtained through faith. Moreover, the knowledge by which man is directed to his ultimate end, must be most certain from the fact that it is the principle of all the things which are ordained to the ultimate end.

Therefore, in order that man might obtain perfect certitude concerning the truth of faith and receive Divine instruction in a human way, it was necessary that he be instructed by God Himself, made Man. Wherefore, we see that after the Incarnation of Christ, men were instructed more clearly and with greater certitude in Divine knowledge. "The earth is filled with a knowledge of the Lord." (Isaias XI, 9.)

3. Since perfect knowledge consists in the Divine enjoyment, it was necessary that the affections of man be disposed to desire the Divine fruition. Just as we know that there is in man a natural desire for happiness, and the desire for the enjoyment of anything is caused by a love for that thing; so it was necessary that man tending to perfect happiness be led to Divine love. But nothing so inspires us with love for someone as an example of their love for us. But God's love for man could not be shown in a more powerful way than that He willed to be united to man in Person. For it is characteristic of love to unite the lover with the beloved. Hence, it was necessary for man tending to perfect happiness that God should become man.

More than this, since friendship consists in a certain equality, those persons or things are very unequal which seem not to be capable of being united in friendship. In order, therefore, that the friendship between man and God might be more intimate, it was expedient that God should become man.

4. It is clear that happiness is the reward of virtue, and so it was necessary that those tending to happiness be disposed to virtue. But we are inspired to virtue by word and example. Inasmuch as the words and example of anyone are the more powerful, by so much the more are men led to practice virtue and hold in greater esteem the goodness of the person giving good example. But even in the holiest of men some defects are found, hence, it was necessary for man, so that he might be most firmly established in virtue, that he receive the doctrine and examples of virtue from God, made Man. (Contr. IV, 54.)

DECEMBER 25

The Goodness and Usefulness of Christ's Birth

"The goodness and kindness of God, our Saviour, appeared." (Titus III, 4.)

1. It must be remembered that Christ showed to us His goodness in communicating His Divinity, but He showed His mercy in assuming our nature. Hence, Saint Bernard says, "The power of God appeared in the creation of things, His wisdom, in the government of things, but His goodness especially appeared in His assumption of our nature." For God revealed a wonderful sign of His goodness when He willed to add the name of God to humanity, for "Not from works of justice which we did, but by His mercy are we saved." Did He not show forth His mercy, when He received and took upon Himself our misery? What was so full of holiness as the Word of God, which was made flesh for us and dwelt amongst us? Hence, the Church sings, "Oh Christ, the Redeemer of all, the Only God of the Father." And Isaias LXIII, 16, says, "Thou, O Lord, art our Father, our Redeemer, from everlasting is Thy Name."

Moreover, concerning the blessings and usefulness of our Saviour's birth, Isaias XI, 6, says, "A child is born to us," that is for our benefit and welfare. In truth, there are four great blessings which have come down to us from the birth of Christ, which we may consider from the four special virtues which children possess; namely, purity, humility, lovableness and pleasingness. These are found in the Christ Child in a most excellent manner.

First, we find in Him the greatest purity because He is the brightness of eternal light, and the unspotted mirror of God's majesty, and the image of His goodness. (Wis. VI, 26.) Moreover, He demonstrated His purity in being conceived and born without sin. Hence, Alcuin observes that, "The Maker of all men, in order that He might become Man for the sake of men, had to select such a mother for Himself, and He knew that it was becoming that she should be Immaculate and most pleasing to God. Therefore, He willed that she should be a Virgin Immaculate, and from the Immaculate was born the Immaculate Child, Who will purge the sins of all mankind."

Secondly, in this Child, we find the greatest humility, for, "He, God, emptied Himself, taking the form of a slave." (Phil. II, 7.) He showed this humility, as Bernard says, in being born in a stable, wrapped in swaddling clothes, and laid in a manger.

Thirdly, we find in the Christ Child the highest kind of lovableness. He was the most beautiful of the sons of men and the delight of the Angels. The union of His Divinity with the humanity caused this lovableness in a certain manner. Hence, Bernard said, "Behold the Man, the Maker of Man, filled with every manner of sweetness."

Fourthly, we find in the Christ Child the greatest pleasingness for, "He is gracious and merciful, patient and rich in mercy, and ready to repent of evil." (Joel II, 13.) Wherefore, Bernard says, "Christ is a Child and is easily pleased. Who does not know that a child easily gives? Behold if Christ were not great and kind to us, we could never be reconciled to Him in the least thing; but the least thing, I say, done for Him is pleasing to Him." And just as the kindness of God appeared as something beyond all hope and expectation, so we can, if we repent, hope for a similar manifestation of God's mercy at the judgment. (The Kindness of Christ.)

DECEMBER 26

Christ Was Born Subject to Suffering and Death

"God sent His Own Son, in the likeness of sinful flesh ... hath condemned sin in the flesh." (Rom. VIII, 3.)

It was not fitting that God should take impassible and immortal flesh, but rather that He should assume a flesh that was subject to suffering and death.

First, because it was necessary for man to know of the blessing bestowed upon him through the Incarnation, in order that he might be inflamed with Divine love. Now, that the truth of the Incarnation might be evident to man, it was necessary that God should assume flesh like that of other men—namely, passible and mortal. For, had He taken impassible and immortal flesh, men who were unacquainted with flesh of that kind would have considered it to be imaginary and not real.

Secondly, it was necessary for God to assume human flesh in order to atone for the sin of mankind. Now, one man can atone for another; on the condition, however, that he take upon himself willingly the punishment due to another and not due to himself. But the punishment resulting from the sin of the human race is death as well as other sufferings of the present life. Wherefore, the Apostle says (Rom. V, 12): "That by one man sin came into the world, and by sin, death." Hence, it was expedient that God should take suffering and mortal flesh without sin, so that by suffering and dying for us He would make atonement and take sin away. "He hath condemned sin in the flesh," by the pain He endured in His flesh.

Thirdly, since his flesh was subject to suffering and death. He was the better able to give us an example of virtue by His fortitude in conquering the sufferings of the flesh and by the godly use He made of them.

Fourthly, we are the more raised to the hope of immortality, seeing that He was transformed from the state of suffering and mortal flesh, to that of a flesh that knows neither suffering nor death; and so, we also hope that it will be the same with us, who are now clothed in flesh, passible and mortal. Whereas, had He assumed impassible and immortal flesh from the very first, we who know ourselves to be mortal and corruptible would have had no reason to hope for immortality.

Moreover, His office of Mediator required that He should be a partner with us in suffering and mortal flesh, and with God in power and glory, so that He might take away from us that which He shared with us, namely, suffering and death and lead us to that which he shared with God; since for this He was the Mediator, that He might unite us to God. (Contra Gentiles IV, 55.)

DECEMBER 27

Saint John the Evangelist

"Now there was leaning on Jesus' Bosom, one of His disciples, whom Jesus loved." (John XIII, 23.) This disciple was John, the Evangelist, who spoke of himself in the person of another, as he wished to avoid vain glory, and follow the custom of others who had written the Sacred Scriptures. For thus, Moses, in his writings, spoke of himself as of a certain other person, saying, "The Lord spoke to Moses." And thus did Matthew speak, "Jesus saw a man, sitting at the receipt of custom by the name of Matthew." Likewise did Saint Paul speak, "I know a man."

1. Moreover, John here treats of three things concerning himself. First, the love with which he rested in Christ saying, "Now there was leaning on Jesus' bosom," that is resting. "Then shalt thou abound in delights in the Almighty and shall lift up thy face to God." (Job. XXII, 26.) And (Ps. XXII, 3), says, "He hath brought me up on the water of refreshment. He hath converted my soul."

Secondly, John mentions the knowledge of the secrets which Christ revealed to him, especially in the writing of this Gospel. Hence, he said that he was "leaning on the bosom of Jesus." By "bosom" is meant "secret." "The only begotten Son, Who is in the bosom of the Father, He hath declared him." (John I, 18.)

Thirdly, John speaks of the special love with which Christ loved him. Hence, he said, "One of His disciples, whom Jesus loved"; not indeed that Jesus loved John only, but that He loved him, as it were, in a more excellent manner than the others.

2. We must realize that John was loved by Christ more than the other disciples because of his purity of heart, for he was a virgin chosen by God and a virgin he remained forever.

"He that loveth cleanness of heart, for the grace of his lips shall have the King for his friend." (Prov. XXII, 11.)

DECEMBER 28

Concerning Four Blessings of Christ's Birth

"A Child is born to us, that we might imitate His purity and humility, that we might be attracted by His lovableness, and that we might have confidence in His Mercy."

1. This Divine Child is born to us as an example of holy purity. Hence, Saint Matthew (I, 21) says, "He shall save His people from their sins." And Bernard further observes, "In Christ Himself, Who maketh the purification of our sins, behold He cometh to cleanse the dregs of humanity." Here also, Augustine declares, "O Blessed Infancy, by which the life of our race is repaired. O most gracious and delightful cry of an Infant, by which we may escape the eternal weeping and gnashing of teeth. O happy garments, by which the horrible wounds of our sins are healed."

2. "A Child is born to us," for an example of humility. Hence, Bernard says, "Let us strive to become as this Child. Let us learn from Him, for He 'is meek and humble of heart,' for this Child namely, the great God, became man, not without cause."

3. "A Child is born to us," to bring us an increase of charity. "I am come to cast fire upon the earth, and what will I but that it be kindled." (Luke XII, 49.) Bernard says, "Great Lord, Thou hast become a Child, exceedingly to be loved and praised." A Child, it is said "is born," He Himself is everything lovable to us, for He is Our Father, Brother, Lord Servant, Reward and Example. Inasmuch as He humbleth Himself in becoming man, by so much the more does He show Himself greater in manifesting His goodness."

4. "A Child is born to us," as a consolation to our hope and security. Hence, Saint Paul (Heb. IV, 16) says, "Let us go, therefore, with confidence to the throne of grace," that is, to Christ in Whom grace reigns supreme, "so that we may obtain mercy," that is, the remission of our previous sin, "and find grace in seasonable aid." Augustine says, "O sweetest day, the day of Christ's birth, in which compunction came

even to unbelievers, mercy to the wicked, pardon to the sorrowful, a release to the captive, a remedy to the wounded. O blessed day, in which was born "the Lamb of God, Who takest away the sins of the world; in Whose birth, whosoever has a good conscience, rejoices sweetly; whosoever is good, prays fervently, supplicates most devoutly. Sweet day and truly sweet for those doing penance and seeking pardon. I promise you, my beloved children, and I am certain that on this day, if anyone repents from his heart, and returns not to the vomit of sin, whatsoever he or she asks, will be granted to you." (The Kindness of Christ.)

DECEMBER 29

The Repentant Soul

We can mystically observe that the offspring of the Blessed Virgin Mary signifies the good works of a repentant soul, concerning which it is written: "In Thy fear, O Lord, we shall conceive and bring forth the Spirit of salvation." (Isaias XXVI, 17.) The place of Christ's birth spiritually represents the bringing forth from the soul, true penance. Hence, Bernard says, "Would that you also by the pure condition of your heart—were Bethlehem (which means house of bread), so that your tears might be for you, bread both day and night, and that you were delighted in the nourishment of those tears of repentance. Would that you were *Juda*, by your confession, or the city of David by your satisfactory good works, Christ might then be born in you, and give to your heart, joy through His grace in this life, and glory hereafter!"

Moreover it must be noted that after the bringing forth or performance of true penance, the soul of the penitent ought to be clothed in the garments of charity as a shield against the disgrace and ugliness of sinning again—sin which consists in the interior debasement of the mind. The repentant soul ought to be inclined by the love of humility as a protection against pride—pride which consists in an aversion of whatever is humble. The repentant soul should be placed in the front line of austerity through worthy penance as a safeguard against pleasure in sin; for by such penance the soul turns to God, and through delight in sin it turns away from God.

It is written (Prov. X, 12): "Charity covereth a multitude

of sins." Now, we ought to be covered on all sides with this garment of charity. First, so that we might love God, Who is above us; secondly, because God created and redeemed us; thirdly, that He may be with us; fourthly, that He might live in us through His grace and His Charity.

It is likewise written: "A contrite and humble heart, O God, Thou wilt not despise." (Ps. L, 19.) Humility commends us to God, for it makes us subject to God and pleasing unto Him; as it did for the Blessed Virgin of whom it is said: "The Lord regarded the humility of His handmaid."

It is further written (Luke III, 8): "Bring forth fruit worthy of penance." Hence, Bernard says: "Flee carnal pleasures, because they are the death of the soul wherever they enter in and delight the soul. Do penance, for through this means, the kingdom draws near unto you. The stable of Bethlehem preaches penance to you, the manger exhorts you, and these tiny hands of the Infant Jesus cry out to you—'Do penance, or you shall all likewise perish'." (The Humanity of Christ.)

DECEMBER 30

The Circumstances of Christ's Birth

1. Christ willed to be born at Bethlehem because of two reasons. First, because "He was made ... of the seed of David according to the flesh, to whom also a special promise was made concerning Christ." (Rom. I, 3.) Hence, He willed to be born at Bethlehem, where David was born, in order that by the very birthplace, the promise made to David might be fulfilled. The Evangelist points out this by saying, "Because He was of the house and of the family of David."

Secondly, because as Gregory says, "Bethlehem is interpreted 'the house of bread'." It is Christ Himself, Who said, "I am the living Bread which came down from heaven."

As David was born in Bethlehem, so also did he select Jerusalem to set up His throne and to build there the Temple of God, so that, Jerusalem was at the time a royal and priestly city. Now, Christ's priesthood and kingdom were consummated principally in His Passion. Therefore, it was becoming, that He should choose Bethlehem for His birthplace and Jerusalem for the scene of His Passion.

Likewise, also, He silenced the vain boasting of men who

take pride in being born in great cities, where also they desire especially to receive honour. Christ, on the contrary, willed to be born in a mean city and to suffer reproach in a great city.

2. Christ was born at a suitable time.

"When the fullness of time was come, God sent His Son, made of a woman, made under the law." (Gal. IV, 4.) There is this difference between Christ and other men; that, whereas they are born subject to the restrictions of time, Christ as Lord and Maker of all time, chose a time in which to be born, just as He chose a mother and a birthplace. And hence, since "What is of God is well ordered," and becomingly arranged, it follows that Christ was born at a most fitting time.

Christ came to bring us back from a state of bondage to a state of liberty, and therefore, as He took our mortal nature in order to restore us life, so as Bede says, "He deigned to take flesh at such a time that, shortly after His birth, He would be enrolled in Caesar's census and thus submit Himself to bondage for the sake of our liberty."

Moreover, at that time, when the whole world lived under one ruler, peace abounded on the earth. Therefore, it was a fitting time for the birth of Christ, for "He is our peace, Who hath made both one," as it is written. (Eph. II, 14.)

Again it was fitting that Christ should be born while the world was governed by one ruler, because "He came to gather His own, Children of God, together into one" (John XI, 52), so "that there might be one fold and one Shepherd." (John X, 16.)

Christ wished to be born during the reign of a foreigner, that the prophecy of Jacob might be fulfilled (Gen. XLIX, 10), "This sceptre shall not be taken away from Juda, nor a ruler from his thigh, till He come that is to be sent." Because as Chrysostom says, "as long as the Jewish people were governed by Jewish kings, however wicked, prophets were sent for their healing. But now, that the Law of God is under the power of a wicked king, Christ is born; because a grave and hopeless disease demanded a more skillful physician."

Christ wished to be born when the light of day begins to increase in length, so as to show that He came in order that man might come nearer to the Divine Light, according to Luke I, 79: "To enlighten them that sit in darkness and in the shadow of death."

In like manner, He chose to be born in the rough winter season, that He might begin from then to suffer in body for us. (3 a. q. 35 a. V and VIII.)

DECEMBER 31

Divine Sonship

"But as many as received Him, He gave them power to be made the sons of God, to them that believe in His Name." (John I, 12.)

Men become sons of God through likeness of God, and therefore, according to a threefold likeness of men to God, men are the sons of God.

1. By infusion of grace; for whosoever has grace, namely, sanctifying grace which makes us pleasing to God, such a person becomes the son of God. "And because you are the sons of God, God hath sent the Spirit of His Son into your hearts." (Gal. IV, 6.)

2. We become like unto God by the perfection of our actions, for he who does the works of justice is the child of God. "Love your enemies, so that you may be the children of your Father, Who is in Heaven." (Matth. V, 44.)

3. We become like unto God by the adoption of glory, and as to the soul, by the light of glory; for John III, 2 says: "When He shall appear, we shall be like Him," and Phil. III, 21, declares, "He will reform the body of our lowness." Hence, concerning these two references, it is written Rom. VIII, 23, "Waiting for the adoption of the sons of God."

If moreover, power to become the sons of God is understood in as far as perfection of our actions is concerned, then there is no difficulty, for it is written, "He gave them power" but if it is understood of the power of grace, by which virtue is possessed, then man can do the works of perfection, and possess eternal glory.

If on the other hand, power is understood to mean an infusion of grace, God then "gave them power to become the sons of God, for He gave them power of receiving grace." Even this can be taken in two ways:

1. By preparing us beforehand for grace and placing it before men for their acceptance, just as the author who writes a book and places it before man to read, is said to give man an opportunity of reading.

2. It can be understood of God as moving the will of man to consent to the reception of grace. This is clear from Lam. V, 21, "Convert us, O Lord, to Thee" (by moving our wills to Thy love), "and we shall be converted." In this manner, power

may be called the interior call, concerning which it is said, Rom. VIII, 30, "Them also He called" (by exteriorly moving their wills to accept grace), "them He also justified" (by infusing grace into their souls).

For in truth, by this grace of God, man has power of preserving himself in the Divine Sonship. And in another way it can be said, "He gave them power," that is, to those who "received Him, power to become the sons of God," that is, "grace" by which they are to be preserved powerful in the Divine Sonship. "Everyone, who is born of God, sins not, but the grace of God preserves him." (1 John III, 9.) For through the grace of God, we become regenerated into sons of God.

So, therefore, "He gave them power to become the sons of God," through sanctifying grace, through the perfection of good works, through the adoption of glory, and all this through God, preparing them, moving them, and preserving them in His grace, as the sons of God. (John I.)

JANUARY 1

Christ's Circumcision

"After eight days were accomplished, that the child should be circumcised." (Luke II, 21.)

For several reasons Christ ought to have been circumcised. First, in order to prove the reality of His human nature, in contradiction to the Manicheans, who said He had an imaginary body, and also, so that by His example, He might exhort us to be obedient to the Law. And to show His approval of circumcision, which God had instituted of old.

Secondly, that "He Who had come in the likeness of sinful flesh might not reject the remedy, whereby sinful flesh was wont to be healed." For circumcision signified the passing away of the old generation from the decrepitude of which we are freed by Christ's Passion.

Thirdly, that by taking upon Himself the burden of the Law, He might liberate others. Therefore, according to Gal. IV, 4: "God sent His Son . . . made under the Law, that He might redeem them who were under the Law."

As Christ voluntarily took upon Himself our death, which is the effect of sin, whereas He had no sin Himself, in order to deliver us from death, and to make us to die spiritually unto sin; so also, He took upon Himself circumcision, which was a remedy against original sin, whereas He contracted no original sin, in order to deliver us from the yoke of the Law, and to accomplish a spiritual circumcision in us; that is to say, that by taking upon Himself the shadow, He might accomplish the reality.

Moreover, Origen says: "As we died when He died and rose again when Christ rose from the dead, so were we circumcised spiritually through Christ; wherefore we need no carnal circumcision." And this is what the Apostle says (Col. II, 11): "In Whom (that is in Christ), you are circumcised with circumcision not made by hand in despoiling of the body of the flesh, but in the circumcision of our Lord Jesus Christ." (3 a. q. 37, a. I.)

JANUARY 2

The Suitableness of the Holy Name

"After eight days were accomplished, that the Child should be circumcised, His Name was called Jesus." (Luke II, 21.)

It is related in Gen. XVII that Abraham received from God both his name and the commandment of the circumcision. For this reason, it was customary among the Jews to name children on the very day of circumcision, as though before being circumcised, they had not as yet perfect existence; just as now also the children receive their names in Baptism.

Now, the names of individual men are always taken from some property of men to whom they are given. Either in regard to time, thus men are named after the Saints on whose feasts they are born; or in respect to some blood relation, thus a son is named after his father or some other relation; and thus, the kinsfolk of John the Baptist wished to call him by his father's name, Zachary, not by the name of John.

But names given to men by God always signify some gratuitous gift bestowed on them by Him, thus it was said to Abraham (Gen. XVII, 5): "Thou shalt be called Abraham, because I have made thee a father of many nations," and it was said to Peter (Matth. XVI, 18): "Thou art Peter, and upon this rock I will build My Church."

Since, therefore, this gift of grace was bestowed on the

Man Christ that through Him all men might be saved, therefore, He was suitably called Jesus, that is, Saviour; the angel having foretold this name not only to His mother but also to Joseph, who was to be His foster-father.

It is written (Isaias LXII, 2), "Thou shalt be called by a new name, which the mouth of the Lord hath named." But this Name, Jesus, is not a new name but was given to several in the Old Testament. But the Name, Jesus, could be suitable for some other reason to those who lived before Christ; for example, because they were saviours in a particular and temporal sense. But in the sense of spiritual and universal salvation, the name is proper to Christ and in this sense it is called a new Name. (3 a. q. 38, a. 2.)

JANUARY 3

The Usefulness of the Name—Jesus

We must realize that the Name, Jesus, possesses great and manifold power, for it is to those repenting, a refuge; to those who are sick, a remedy; to those fighting life's battle, a shield of defense; to those praying, a help and consolation; because It obtains pardon for sins, strength of body and of mind; victory for those tempted; power and confidence in securing the salvation of our souls.

Concerning the first (pardon for sins), it is written (1 John II, 12): "I write unto you, little children, because your sins are forgiven you for His Name's sake." Hence Augustine says, "What does the Name Jesus signify, unless Saviour? Therefore, because of Thyself, O Lord, be to me a Jesus. Do not O Lord, so consider my sins, as to forget Thine own goodness. But we must bear in mind, that this Name, which was imposed at the Circumcision, from this very fact means that they are saved who are spiritually circumcised." Wherefore, Bernard says, "Brethren, we must be circumcised spiritually, and thus receive the lifesaving Name, circumcised not in the letter, but in spirit and in truth."

Concerning the second (strength of body and of mind), we read in Canticles I, 2, "Thy Name, O Lord, is as oil poured out." For just as oil soothes pain, so does the Name Jesus. Hence Bernard writes: "My soul, thou hast a hidden remedy in a little vessel, named Jesus, which has proven Itself to be a powerful cure for every disease." And Peter Ravenna remarks that, "This Name Jesus is the Name which gave sight to the blind, hearing to the deaf, walk to the cripples, speech to the speechless, and life to the dead."

Concerning the third (victory for those tempted), we read in Prov. XVIII, 10, "The Name of the Lord is a strong tower, the just runneth to It and shall be exalted." And Mark XVI, 17, "In My Name they shall cast out devils." While Luke X, 17, says, "The seventy-two returned with joy, saying, Lord, the devils also are subject to us in Thy Name." Peter Ravenna concludes thus, "The power of this Name, Jesus, has put to flight the entire power of the devil, from bodies possessed of diabolical power."

Concerning the fourth (power and confidence in securing the salvation of our souls), it is said in John XIV, 14, "If you ask the Father anything in My Name, He will give it to you." Wherefore, Augustine explains, "In My Name, that is in the Name of Jesus, we ask in the Name of the Saviour, and whenever we ask in the Name of Jesus, we ask in the Name of the Saviour; and still, Jesus is the Saviour Himself, not only when He grants what we ask but also when He refuses, for He sees that we ask perhaps something not conducive to our salvation. He shows Himself our Saviour by not granting what we ask. For a wise physician knows what is good for his patient and does not allow the sick person to have something injurious to health; so that he might restore the patient to health."

Observe carefully the words of Bernard concerning the Circumcision of Christ and the bestowal of His Name, "Great and wonderful sacrament. The Child is circumcised, and His Name is called Jesus. What does this connection will to Him? Recognize the Mediator of God and of man from the very beginning of His birth, sharing even in the highest degree, His Divine gifts with humanity. He is born of a woman, but the fruit of her womb takes place in such wise, that the flower of her virginity dies not. He is wrapped in swaddling clothes, but these swaddling clothes are honored by Angelic praises. He is hidden in a stable, but a radiant star in the heavens above announced His birth. So too, His circumcision proved the truth of His assumed nature, and the Name which is above every name indicates the glory of His Majesty." (The Humanity of Christ, C. 26.)

JANUARY 4

The Virginity of Mary

1. Without any doubt, we must assert that the Mother of Christ was a virgin even in His Birth; for the prophet says not only: "Behold a virgin shall conceive," but also adds, "and shall bring forth a son." This indeed was suitable because of three reasons:

First, because this was in keeping with a property of Him Whose Birth is in question, for He is the Word of God. For the word is not only conceived in the mind without corruption, but also proceeds from the mind without corruption. Wherefore, to show that Body to be a Body of the very Word of God, it was fitting that it be born of a virgin incorrupt. Whence, in the sermon on the Council of Ephesus we read: "Whosoever brings forth mere flesh ceases to be a virgin. But since she gave birth to the Word made flesh, God safeguarded her virginity so as to manifest His Word, by which Word he thus manifested Himself; for neither does our word, when brought forth, corrupt the mind; nor does God, the substantial Word, deigning to be born, destroy virginity."

Secondly, this is fitting as regards the effect of Christ's Incarnation; since He came for this purpose, that He might take away our corruption. Wherefore, it is unfitting that in His Birth He should corrupt His Mother's virginity. Thus Augustine says in a sermon on the Nativity of our Lord: "It was not right that He Who came to heal corruption, should by His advent violate integrity."

Thirdly, it was fitting that He Who commanded us to honor our father and mother should not in His Birth lessen the honor due to His Mother.

For this reason, therefore, Christ mingles wonderful things with lowly things. Therefore, to show that His body was real He was born of a woman; but in order to manifest His Godhead He was born of a virgin, for such a birth befits God. And therefore, the Blessed Virgin without pain gave birth to the Saviour. For the pain of childbirth is caused by an opening of the womb through which the infant comes forth. "But Christ coming forth did not violate the abode of her sacred womb, which His entrance therein had hallowed," writes Venerable Bede. Wherefore, in this birth there was no pain and no corruption, but there was the greatest joy, because of the fact that God born into the world became man, according to Isaias XXXV, 2: "It shall bud forth and blossom, and shall rejoice with joy and praise . . . and they shall see the glory of the Lord and the beauty of our God."

2. Mary remained a virgin after Christ's Birth, for it is written (Ezech. XLIV, 2): "This gate shall be shut, it shall not be opened, and no man shall pass through it; because the Lord, the God of Israel hath entered in by it." Explaining these words, Augustine says in a sermon on the Annunciation. "What means this closed gate in the House of the Lord, except that Mary is to be forever inviolate? What does it mean that 'no man shall pass through it,' save that Joseph shall not know her? And what is this, 'the Lord alone enters in and goeth out by it,' except, that the Holy Ghost shall impregnate her and the Lord of Angels shall be born of Her? And what means this, 'it shall be shut forever,' but that Mary is a virgin before His Birth, a virgin in His Birth, and a virgin after His Birth?"

This indeed was befitting Christ's perfection, for just as according to His Divine nature Christ is the Only Begotten of the Father, and being thus His Son in every respect, perfect; so it was becoming that He should be the only begotten Son of His Mother, as being her perfect offspring. (3 a. q. 28, a. 2, 3.)

JANUARY 5

The Fruit of the Womb of the Blessed Virgin Mary

"Blessed is the fruit of thy womb." (Luke I, 42.)

Sometimes a sinner asks for something which he cannot obtain, but the just man obtains it. "The substance of the sinner is kept for the just." (Prov. XIII, 32.) Thus Eve desired the fruit, but she did not find in it all the things which she wished. But the Blessed Virgin in her fruit found all the things which Eve desired. For Eve in her fruit longed for three things:

1. That which the devil falsely promised to her, namely, that they would be as gods, knowing good and evil. "The deceiver said to them: "You will be as gods." He lied, for the devil "is a liar, and the father thereof." (John VIII, 44.) For Eve, on account of eating the forbidden fruit, did not become like unto God, but more unlike Him, because the sinner by sinning departs from God, his salvation. But the Blessed Virgin

found this likeness and all Christians will find it in the fruit of her womb, Jesus; because through Christ we become united and likened unto God. "When He appears, we will be like unto Him, for we will see Him, as He is." (1, John III, 2.)

2. In her fruit, Eve desired delight because it was good to eat the forbidden fruit or seemed so to her; but she did not find delight, for immediately she realized her misery and experienced pain and sorrow. But in the fruit of the Virgin we will find salvation. "He that eateth My flesh, hath everlasting life." (John VI, 55.)

3. Eve's fruit was beautiful to the eye, but more beautiful was the fruit of the Blessed Virgin upon Whom the Angels love to gaze. "Thou art beautiful above the sons of men. Grace is poured abroad on Thy lips, therefore, hath God blessed Thee forever" (Ps. XLIV, 2), because He is the brightness of Eternal glory.

Eve, therefore, found in her fruit only that misery which every sinner finds in sin. Consequently, we should seek those things which we desire, seek them in the fruit of the Blessed Virgin, from Her Son Jesus.

Moreover, this fruit was blessed by God, because God so filled Him with every grace and richness, and came to us to teach us love and reverence for this blessed fruit of the Virgin's womb. "Blessed be the God, and the Father of our Lord Jesus Christ, Who hath blessed us with every spiritual blessing, in Christ." (Eph. I, 3.) Blessed by Angels, blessed by men. Likewise, the Apostle says, "Every tongue shall confess, that the Lord Jesus Christ is in the Glory of the Father." (Phil. II.) "Blessed is He Who cometh in the Name of the Lord." (Ps. CXVII, 26.)

Accordingly, therefore, the Blessed Virgin is blessed, but even more blessed is the fruit of her womb. (Angelical Salutation.)

JANUARY 6

The Epiphany of Christ

"The Gentiles shall walk in Thy light, and kings in the brightness of Thy rising." (Isa. XL, 3.)

The Magi are the first fruits of the Gentiles that believed in Christ; because their faith was a forerunner of the faith and devotion of the nations who were to come to Christ from afar. And therefore, as the devotion and faith of the nations is without any error through the inspiration of the Holy Ghost, so also, we must believe that the Magi, inspired by the Holy Ghost, did wisely in paying homage to Christ.

As Augustine says in a sermon on the Epiphany: "The Star which led the Magi to the place, where the Infant was with His Virgin Mother, could bring them to the town of Bethlehem, in which Christ was born. Yet it hid itself until the Jews also bore testimony of the city in which Christ was born; so that being encouraged by a two-fold witness, as Pope Leo says, they might seek with more ardent faith Him, Whom both the brightness of the star and the authority of prophecy revealed. Thus, they proclaim that Christ is born and inquire where; they believe and ask, as it were, betokening those who walk in faith and desire to see. But the Jews, by pointing out to them the place of Christ's birth, are like the carpenters who built the Ark of Noe, who provided others with the means of escape, and themselves perished in the flood. Those were they who asked, heard and went their way, the teachers spoke and stayed where they were; like milestones that point out the way and walk not."

It was also by God's will that when they no longer saw the star, the Magi, by human instinct, went to Jerusalem to seek in the royal city the newborn King, in order that Christ's birth might be publicly proclaimed first in Jerusalem, according to (Isaias II, 3): "The Law shall come forth from Sion, and the Word of the Lord from Jerusalem;" and also in order that by the zeal of the Magi who came from afar, the indolence of the Jews who live near at hand might be proved worthy of condemnation.

The faith of the Magi was marvelous. For as Chrysostom says: "If the Magi had come in search of an earthly king, they would have been confused at finding that they had taken the trouble to come such a long way for nothing." Consequently, they would neither have adored nor offered gifts. But since they sought a heavenly King, though they found in Him no sign of royal pre-eminence, yet, content with the testimony of the star alone, they adored; for they saw a man, and acknowledged a God. Moreover, they offer gifts in keeping with Christ's greatness: Gold, as to the great King; incense, as to God, because it is used in the Divine Sacrifice; and myrrh, which is used in embalming the bodies of the dead, is offered as to Him, Who is to die for the salvation of all.

"And falling down they adored Him." (Matth. II, 11.) Hence, Augustine says, "Oh Infancy, which even the stars obey! Whose supernatural glory and magnitude is this? that even the Angels rejoice at Thy swaddling clothes and kings fear and wise men adore? Who is this that is so worshipped and so great? I am astonished when I see the swaddling clothes and behold heaven. I am inflamed with love and amazed when I see Thee, poor in a manger and resplendent above the stars of Heaven. May faith help us, O Lord, where reason fails us." (The Humanity of Christ.)

JANUARY 7

The Order of Christ's Manifestation

1. Christ's birth was first made known to the shepherds on the very day that He was born. For as it is written (Luke II, 8, 15), "There were in the same country shepherds watching, and keeping the night watches over their flock. And it came to pass, after the angels departed from them into heaven, the shepherds said one to another: 'Let us go over to Bethlehem and they came with haste.'"

2. In order were the Magi who came to Christ on the thirteenth day after His birth, on which day the feast of the Epiphany is celebrated. For if they had come after a year, or even two years, they would not have found Him in Bethlehem, since it is written (Luke II, 39) that, "after they had performed all things according to the Law of the Lord—that is to say, after they had offered up the Child Jesus in the Temple—they returned into Galilee, to their own city, namely, Nazareth."

3. In the third place, it was made known in the Temple to the righteous on the fortieth day after His birth, as related by Luke II, 22.

The reason of this order is that the shepherds represent the Apostles and other believers of the Jews, to whom the faith of Christ was made known first, among whom there were "not many noble," as we read (1 Cor. I, 26). Secondly, the faith of Christ came to "the fulness of the Gentiles," and this is foreshadowed in the righteous. Wherefore, also, Christ was manifested to them in the Jewish Temple.

That manifestation of Christ's birth was a kind of foretaste of the full manifestation which was to come. And as in the later manifestation the first announcement of the grace of Christ was made by Him and His Apostles to the Jews and afterwards to the Gentiles, so the first to come to Christ were the shepherds, who were the first fruits of the Jews as being near to Him; and afterwards came the Magi from afar, who were "the first fruits of the Gentiles."

Augustine says in a sermon on the Epiphany: "The shepherds were Israelites, the Magi were Gentiles. The former were nigh to Him, the latter far from Him. Both hastened to Him together as to the corner-stone;" for "in Christ there is neither male or female, neither Gentile nor Jew, bond nor free; but Christ is all and in all." (3a. q. 36, a. VI and 3.)

JANUARY 8

The Diligence of the Magi

The diligence with which the Magi sought the Christ Child is shown in three ways. Hence, Augustine says, "O my soul, if thou dost diligently seek, thou wilt show this in signs. First, thou must seek the light, lest thou be blinded by darkness; secondly, inquire from those who know, lest in seeking you go astray; thirdly, rest in no place, until you have found, the Beloved."

Concerning the first, (thou must seek the light), it is written in Ps. LXVI, 1, "May God have mercy upon us. May He cause the light of His countenance to shine upon us. That we may know Thy way, O Lord, upon earth," that is, the way to heaven. "For the path of the just, as a shining light, goeth forward and increaseth, even to perfect day." (Prov. IV, 18.) Hence the works of the just are done by the light of knowledge and lead to eternal life, which is the perfect day.

Hence the Magi sought the Lord through the light of a star and we must observe that this light, namely, the light of grace, is lost by sin. Hence, Remigius says, that, "the star is the grace of God, but Herod signifies the devil. For he who subjects himself to the devil immediately loses grace; but if he repents he immediately recovers grace which if he retains, will lead him to the home of the Child, namely, to the Church of God; as the star which led the Magi to the Crib at Bethlehem.

Concerning the second (inquire from those who know), it is said (Jer. VI, 16), "Thus saith the Lord. Stand ye on the ways, and see, and ask for the old paths; which is the good way and walk ye in it, and you shall find refreshment for your souls." Wherefore the "Magi came to Jerusalem inquiring and saying where is He that is born King of the Jews?" Augustine says, "The Magi proclaim and inquire, they believe and seek, representing those who walk by faith and desire the Beautiful One. But alas! there are many leaders, who even though the fountain of life is shown to them as to the Magi, yet are dead with dryness of soul. Some of them even show the way to others, and they themselves are not able to walk in the way of the Lord."

Concerning the third, (rest not until you have found the Beloved), it is mentioned in Cant. III, 1: "In my bed by night, I sought Him, Whom my soul loveth." On this Gregory remarks, "We seek the Beloved in bed, when after a little rest of the present life, we long with a desire for our Saviour. We should seek Him by night, because even though the eyes are closed in sleep, the mind can watch for Him. But whosoever does not find his Beloved, should go about the city, that is, to His Holy Church, with the mind of the elect, seek Him, inquire about Him, and rest not until you find Him."

Thus the Magi sought Christ, the Beloved, and finally found Him.

We must bear in mind that a fervent desire of Divine Love permits not the faithful soul to rest until it finds its Beloved; because a true desire when fulfilled delights the soul. Therefore, inasmuch as the desire is more fervent, by so much the more is the Beloved found to be the more delightful to the soul. Hence the Magi who sought Christ with a more fervent desire found Him to be more delightful. Wherefore, Matth. II, 10, says: "seeing the star, they rejoiced, with exceeding great joy." Thereupon, Bernard says, "We rejoice with great joy, when we rejoice for the sake of God and this is true joy." (The Humanity of Christ.)

JANUARY 9

Gifts of the Magi

"Opening their treasures, they offered Him gifts: gold, frankincense, and myrrh." (Matth. II, 11.)

(Ever since the birth of Christ, and perhaps before the Saviour's birth, gold was considered precious and as something greatly to be prized.) St. Matthew II, 11, tells us of the wise men who offered the Saviour gifts of gold, frankincense, and myrrh. "Entering into the house, they found the Child with Mary, His Mother, and falling down they adored Him. Opening their treasures, they offered Him gifts: gold, frankincense and myrrh."

In a spiritual sense gold means heavenly wisdom. The wise men were called wise because they followed the star, found the Saviour, gave Him their gold (in place of hoarding it), for they recognized Jesus as the Giver of all good gifts and realized that whatever good things they had were from God. To recognize that important fact and to appreciate it is the highest wisdom and more precious to us than gold and silver.

The Magi also brought frankincense to the Crib of Bethlehem and offered it to the world's Redeemer. Frankincense is a fragrant inflammable resin, burnt as incense, producing a sweet smelling odor. In the spiritual order it signifies a devout prayer. Hence King David, the royal Psalmist says, "O Lord, hear my voice, and let my prayer be directed as incense in Thy sight." (Ps. CXL, 2.) To have our prayers thus directed to God, they must be fervent and inflamed with the fire of charity.

Myrrh is the aromatic gummy resin of Balsamodendron Myrrh that grows in Arabia and Abyssinia and is of an agreeable or spicy nature. By myrrh, in the spiritual sense, is understood the mortification of the flesh (so much needed in this age of luxury, ease and up-to-date comfort). Wherefore, we read in Canticles V, 5, "I arose up to open to My Beloved. My hands dropped with myrrh and my fingers were full of the choicest myrrh." In these words the Church mystically describes Christ to those who know Him not, that is, to infidels; in order to convert them to the true faith. For by the visible things (of God) namely, gold, frankincense and myrrh when considered in a spiritual manner, we rise to a knowledge of the invisible things of God; and only then do we realize how much we need heavenly wisdom, devout prayer and mortification of the flesh. These three are the spiritual gold of the human soul. (The Humanity of Christ.)

JANUARY 10

Searching for God

"Thy Father and I have sought Thee, sorrowing." (Luke II, 48.)

From these words we learn to seek God and Sacred Scripture often advises us to search for Him. Moreover, three things are here to be observed: Those searching; a manner of searching; and, God Whom we must seek.

First, those searching are Mary and Joseph. "I and the Father," by whom two kinds are meant who seek the Lord. He is sought for by contemplatives in meditation and men of action in their works. By Mary is represented the enlightened and she also signifies the contemplatives who in meditation receive Divine illuminations. Joseph signifies an increase of the works of mercy and represents the active (those living an active life) who should have an increase of the works of mercy. The Lord is sought by these two classes of people. Concerning both classes, Ps. CIV, 3, says, "Let the heart of them rejoice, that seek the Lord. Seek ye the Lord and be strengthened. Seek His face evermore." The first part of this scriptural quotation pertains to contemplatives who are in possession of continual joy and delight; the second part refers to those of the active life who sometimes need to be greatly strengthened.

Or by Mary, the Star of the Sea, faith is meant and through Joseph is meant an increase of charity. Faith seeks God in as far as God is our Father. Charity seeks God in as far as He is our Highest Good. Concerning these two, Canticles V, 6, says: "My soul melted when He spoke. I sought Him and found Him not"; that is, in as far as He spoke, in as far as I desired Him; for Faith comes from hearing. In as far as He is the Beloved, charity seeks Him; for He is Life uniting the lover with the Beloved. But if He is sought through charity, He is afterwards completely found.

Secondly, concerning the manner of seeking the Lord note that He should be sought in six ways as can be concluded from the text. 1. With purity of mind, so that we should be free from every stain of sin. "All had separated themselves from the filthiness of the nations of the earth to seek the Lord." (Esdr. VI, 21.) 2. With simplicity of intention, "Seek Him in simplicity of heart," (Wis., 1) with the whole heart, so that we may think of God only. 3. With thy will, so that you may desire God only. "With all their heart and with all their will they sought Him and they found Him and the Lord gave them rest." (2, Paral. XV, 15.) 4. With haste before the time passes in which God cannot be found. "Seek the Lord, while He can be found." (Is. LV, 6.) 5. With perseverance and 6. without ceasing and with sorrow for sin. "Seek His face evermore." (Ps. CIV, 4.)

Thirdly, we should seek God since it is written, "Thy Father and I have sought Thee."

Moreover, He must be sought by us for four reasons, because He is just, meek, good and He is Life. Just, for He offers Himself to those seeking Him and in this way His justice is manifested; for no one seeks God as He should be sought but finds Him. Meek, for those seeking God, He receives them kindly. Good, as those who seek Him He magnifies and rewards. "The Lord is good to them that hope in Him, to the soul that seeketh Him." (Lam. III, 25.) Life, because those who seek God, He makes them live eternally. "Seek ye the Lord and your soul shall live." (Ps. LXVIII, 33.)

JANUARY 11

Where Jesus Dwelleth

"The disciples said to Him, 'Rabbi (which means Master) where dwellest Thou?' He said to them, 'Come and see.'" (John I, 38.)

1. Literally, the disciples sought the home of Christ. For because of the wonderful and great things which they had heard of it from John, they desired to ask the Master about it, to ask Him not perfunctorily, nor even once, but often and seriously. Therefore, they wished to know His home so that they might frequently come there, according

to the counsel of the wise. "If thou see a man of understanding, go to him early in the morning and let thy foot wear the steps of his door." (Eccles. VI, 36) and (Prov. VIII, 34) "Blessed is the man that heareth Me and watcheth daily at my gates."

Allegorically, the home of God is in Heaven. Therefore, they naturally sought where Christ dwells because to this home we ought to follow Christ, so that by Him we might be led to heaven, that is, to our celestial glory.

Morally, they inquired, "Where dwellest Thou?" as if they wished to know what men ought to be who are worthy that Christ dwell in them. Concerning this indwelling of God in men, it is written, "You also are built together into an inhabitation of God in the Spirit." (Ephes. II, 22.)

2. He saith to them, "Come and see." Mystically He said, that the dwelling of God either of glory or of grace, can be known only by experience. For it cannot be explained in words, and therefore Christ said, "Come," through faith and good works, "and see," from experience and knowledge.

Moreover, we must remember, there are four ways of acquiring this knowledge:

1. Through the performance of good works. Hence, Christ said, "Come." "When shall I come and appear before the face of God." (Ps. XLI, 3.)

2. Through peace or spiritual freedom of mind. "Be still and see, that I am God." (Ps. XLV, 11.)

3. Through a taste of Divine sweetness. "Taste and see, that the Lord is sweet." (Ps. XXXIII, 9.)

4. Through the practice of devotion. "Let us lift up our hearts with our hands to the Lord in the heavens." (Lam. III, 41.) "Handle and see." (Luke XXIV, 39.)

Immediately it follows, that "they came and saw," because in coming they saw, and in seeing they were not forsaken by God. Hence, it is written, "they remained there"; for those who leave Christ do not see Him as they should see Him. Moreover, those who perfectly believed saw Him and remained there with Him that day, hearing Him speak, seeing Him and enjoying a blessed day. "They went adoring back to Jerusalem with great joy." (Luke XXIV, 52.) "Blessed are they, and blessed are Thy servants, who stand before Thee always and hear Thy wisdom." (Kings X, 8.) Hence, Augustine beautifully says, "May we ourselves build and make in our own hearts, a home, into which He may come and teach us." (John I.)

JANUARY 12

Spiritual Marriages

"There was a marriage in Cana of Galilee and the mother of Jesus was there. Jesus and His disciples were also invited to the marriage." (John II, 1.)

1. Mystically, by these nuptials is understood, the union of Christ and His Church, because as the Apostle says, "This is a great sacrament, but I speak in Christ and in the Church" (Ephes. V, 32); that matrimony, or union, was instituted in the virginal womb, when God the Father united in His Son human nature in the unity of the Person. Of this union, the bed was the virginal womb. "He placed His tabernacle in the sun." (Ps. XVIII, 6.) It was published when the Church was united to it through faith. The marriage was consummated when the spouse, that is, the Church, was introduced into the bed of my spouse, namely, into heavenly glory. "I will espouse thee to Me, in faith and thou wilt know that I am the Lord." (Osee. II, 20.)

Moreover, the place was suitable for the mystery, for Cana means zeal, the transmigration of Galilee. Therefore, with the zeal of the transmigration, these nuptials were celebrated, so that it especially made known those worthy to live in union with Christ, namely, those who, fervent with the zeal of holy devotion, transmigrate from a state of sin to the grace of the Church, and from death to life, that is, from a state of mortality and misery to a state of immortality and of glory.

2. At the spiritual nuptials is the mother of Jesus, the Blessed Virgin, as the Consoler of the married couple; for through Mary's intercession they are united to Christ through grace, and Mary is the mother of Divine grace. "In me is all grace of the way and of the truth. In me is all hope of life and of virtue." (Eccles. XXIV, 25.) Moreover, just as it is said, that Christ is the true spouse of the soul, "He that hath the bride is the bridegroom," (John III, 29), so, too, the disciples are, as it were, the espousers uniting the Church with Christ, concerning whom it was said: "I have espoused you to one husband, that I may present you, as a chaste virgin to Christ." (2 Cor. XI, 2.)

JANUARY 13

Mary Interceding with Jesus

The wine failing, the mother of Jesus said to Him: "They have no wine." (John II, 3.)

1. In Mary's intercession three things must be considered. First, her piety and mercy. For it pertains to mercy that a person has compassion for the defects or misery of another and regards them as one's own; for one is called merciful who has a merciful heart in regard to the distress of others. "Who is weak, and I am not weak." (2 Cor. II, 29.) Because the Blessed Virgin was full of mercy she wished to relieve the distress of others present at the marriage in Cana and hence she said to Jesus as the wine was failing, "They have no wine."

2. Secondly, observe Mary's reverence for Christ. For from the reverence we have for God it is enough for us just to mention our defects or needs to Him, according to Ps. XXXVII, 10: "Lord, all my desire is before Thee, and my groaning is not hidden from Thee." Moreover, as God is ever ready to aid us, it is not proper for us to investigate into His purposes, as it is written, "For we know not what we should pray for as we ought." (Rom. VIII, 26.) Therefore, His Blessed Mother simply mentioned the needs of the other guests saying, "They have no wine."

3. Thirdly, observe the solicitude and diligence of the Virgin Mary. She did not wait to mention their needs until extreme necessity demanded but, "as the wine was failing," she took occasion to mention the fact to her Divine Son to relieve the marriage guests from an evident embarrassment. She realized that the "Lord is become a refuge for the poor, a helper in due time, in tribulation." (Ps. IX, 10.)

· But why did Mary not urge Christ to perform a miracle before that time? For she had been instructed by the Angel concerning His power and convinced of His power by the many wonderful things which she had seen Him accomplish and remembering all these things, pondered them in her heart. Moreover, the time did not seem to her as yet opportune, and hence, Mary prudently refrained from asking Jesus to perform the miracle. But after the reply from John and after the conversion of the disciples, she confidently urged Christ to perform miracles, showing that the Mother of Christ is the figure of the synagogue; for it is characteristic of the Jews to require miracles. "The Jews require miracles and the Greeks seek after wisdom." (1 Cor. I, 22.) (John II.)

JANUARY 14

Good Wine

"Every man at first setteth forth good wine, but thou hast kept the good wine until now." (John II, 10.)

St. Thomas Aquinas, explaining these words, says, that in a spiritual sense a person sets forth at first good wine when, at the beginning of his conversion to God, he lives a holy and spiritual life, and later degenerates into a carnal mode of living. Whereupon it is said: "Are you so foolish, that, whereas you began in the Spirit, you will now be made perfect by the flesh?" (Gal. III, 3.)

Christ does not at first set forth good wine for us, but sets forth the bitter and trying things; "Straight is the way that leadeth to life." (Matth. IV, 14.) But in so far as a man advances in God's faith and doctrine, in so far does his life become sweetened and he perceives sweetness; "I will show thee the way of wisdom, and I will lead thee by the paths of equity." (Prov. IV, II.)

So in this world, all who wish to live in Christ suffer bitterness and tribulations; "Amen, amen, I say to you that you shall lament and weep." (John XXI, 20). But in the Kingdom of God they will receive joys and delights. Hence, it is written: "Your sorrow will be turned into joy." (Rom. VII.) Again, Scripture says: "I reckon that the sufferings of this world are not worthy to be compared to the future glory which shall be revealed to us." (John II.)

JANUARY 15

The Holy Name of God

The Name of God is a wonderful, a lovable, a venerable, and an inexplainable Name.

1. A wonderful name, because it accomplished remarkable things in every creature. "In My Name they (the Apostles) shall cast out devils. They shall speak with new tongues. They shall take up serpents and if they shall drink any deadly thing, it shall not hurt them." (Mark XVI, 17.)
2. A lovable Name, "for there is no other name under heaven given to men, whereby we must be saved." (Acts IV, 12.) But salvation must be loved by all men; hence the most holy Name of Jesus should be loved by all mankind. We have the example of Saint Ignatius the martyr, who so loved the Name of Jesus, that when Trajan demanded from him to deny the Name of Christ, Ignatius answered that it was impossible to remove that adorable Name from his lips. And when the cruel Emperor threatened to cut off the saint's head and remove the Name of Jesus from his tongue, Ignatius bravely replied: "Even if you take It from my mouth, you can never remove It from my heart, for I have the Name of Jesus inscribed in my heart and consequently I cannot cease invoking It." Trajan on hearing these words and anxious to see a proof of what Ignatius said, ordered his heart to be brought to him, and found that the Name of Jesus was written on it in letters of gold. Ignatius had placed this wonderful and lovable Name as a seal upon his heart.
3. A venerable Name, for "At the Name of Jesus every knee should bow, of those who are in heaven, on earth, and under the earth." (Phil. II, 10.) Those who are in heaven, namely, the angels and saints venerate that Name because they have obtained glory through His Name; those who are on earth should venerate that Name because of their desire to possess eternal glory or to avoid punishment and those in hell must bow in fear forever at the mention of Jesus' Name.
4. It is an inexplainable Name, in so far as every tongue fails to adequately express Its power, and hence Its power is sometimes explained by analogy to created things. Wherefore, this Name of God is called a rock—a fire—a light. A rock because of Its stability. "Upon this rock I will build My Church." A fire, because of Its purifying power, for just as fire purifies metals, so God purifies the hearts of sin-

ners. It is called a light, for as light illuminates the darkness so does the Name of God shine through the darkness of the mind.

Moreover let it be known that in the Name of God, we must walk, pray, speak, work and hope. "Some trust in chariots, and some in horses; but we will call upon the Name of the Lord." (Ps. XIX, 8) and again it is written: "If you ask the Father anything in My Name, He will give it to you." (John XVI, 23) "Whatsoever you do in word or in work, do all in the Name of our Lord Jesus Christ." (Col. III, 17.) For, "Blessed is the man whose trust is in the name of the Lord." (Ps. XXXIX, 5.).

Remember that the Name of God must be retained in the heart because of Its joy; held on the tongue, for It affords greater joy; heard in the ear, because of Its sweetness; carried in the hand because of Its power; written on the forehead because of Its charm.

Remember, also, that the Name of Jesus has a manifold power, for by Its power all things are created. Through Its power the demons are put to flight, sinners are sanctified, grace is increased in the just; and finally through the Holy Name of God we are all called to be saved.

JANUARY 16

The Threefold Wine

"They have no wine." (John II, 3.)

Before the Incarnation of Christ, there was need of a threefold wine, namely, the wine of justice, the wine of wisdom and the wine of charity or grace.

1. Because wine stings and in regard to this justice is called wine. The good Samaritan poured wine and oil into the wounds of the poor man who fell among robbers, (Luke X, 30) that is, they poured on the severity of justice the sweetness of mercy. "Thou hast made us drink the wine of sorrow." (Ps. LIX, 5.)

Wine also rejoices the heart, according to Ps. CIII, 15, "Wine rejoiceth the heart of man." As to this, wisdom is called wine, because meditating on wisdom especially rejoices the heart of man. "Her conversation hath no bitterness, nor her company any tediousness, but joy and gladness." (Wisdom VIII, 16.)

Wine likewise inebriates. "O friends, drink and be inebriated, my dearly beloved." (Cant. V, 1.) As to this, charity, is called wine. "I have drunk my wine with my milk." (Cant. V, 1.) Charity is also called wine because of its fervor. "The Lord of hosts will protect them. What is the good of Him, but wine (charity) springing forth virgins." (Zach. IX, 17.)

2. And in truth the wine of justice was lacking in the old law, during which justice was imperfect. But Christ perfected it. "Unless your justice abounds more than that of the Scribes and Pharisees, you shall not enter the kingdom of heaven." (Matth. VII, 2.)

The wine of wisdom was also lacking which was hidden and figurative. But Christ manifested wisdom. "For He was teaching them as one having power." (Matth. VII, 2.)

But above all the wine of charity was lacking before the Incarnation of Christ, for they recevied the spirit of servitude only in fear. But Christ changed the water of fear into the wine of charity, when "He gave the Spirit of adoption of sons, whereby we cry Father and when the charity of God was diffused in our hearts." (Rom. V, 5.) (John II.)

JANUARY 17

Christ's Conversation and Associations

"Afterwards He was seen upon earth and conversed with men." (Baruch III, 38.)

Christ's manner of life had to be in keeping with the purpose of His Incarnation by reason of which He came into the world.

1. Now He came into the world, first, that He might publish the truth; thus He says Himself (John XVIII, 37): "For this was I born and for this came I into the world, that I should give testimony to the truth." Hence, it was fitting, not that He should hide Himself by leading a solitary life but that He should appear openly and preach in public. Wherefore, (Luke IV, 42) He says to those who wished to stay Him, "To other cities also I much preach the kingdom of God; therefore am I sent."

2. Secondly, He came into this world in order to free men from sin, according to 1 Tim. XV: "Christ Jesus came into this world to save sinners." And hence, as Chrysostom says: "Although Christ might, while staying in the same place, have drawn all men to Himself, to hear His preaching, yet He did not do so; thus giving us an example to go about and seek those who perish; like the shepherd in search of the lost sheep and the physician in his attendance on the sick."

3. Thirdly, He came that by Him "we might have access to God," as it is written (Rom. V, 2.) And thus it was fitting that He should give men confidence in approaching Him by associating familiarly with them. Wherefore it is written (Matth. IX, 10): "It came to pass as He was sitting in the house, behold many publicans and sinners came and sat down with Jesus and His disciples." On which Jerome comments as follows: "They had seen the publican who had been converted from a sinful to a better life and consequently, they did not despair of their own salvation."

Christ wished to make His Godhead known through His human nature, therefore since it is proper to man to do so, He associated with men, at the same time manifesting His Godhead to all, by preaching and working miracles and by leading among men a blameless and righteous life. (3a. q. XL, a. I.)

JANUARY 18

It Was Becoming That Christ Should Have Led an Austere Life

It was in keeping with the end of the Incarnation that Christ should not lead a solitary life, but should associate with men. Now, it is most fitting that He, Who associates with others, should conform to their manner of living; according to the Apostle (I Cor. IX, 22): "I became all things to all men." And therefore, it was most fitting that Christ should conform to others in the matter of eating and drinking.

In His manner of living, our Lord gave an example of perfection as to all those things which of themselves relate to salvation. Now abstinence in eating and drinking does not of itself pertain to salvation, according to Rom. XIV, 17: "The kingdom of heaven is not meat and drink." And Augustine says, that "in all such things, it is not the use of them but the abuse of the user that is sinful."

Now both these lives are lawful and praiseworthy, namely, that a man withdraw from the society of other men and observe abstinence and that he associate with other men and live like them. And, therefore, our Lord wished to give men an example of either kind of life.

As Chrysostom says: "That thou mightest learn how great a good is fasting, and how it is a shield against the devil and that after Baptism thou shouldst give thyself up, not to luxury but to fasting, for this cause did Christ fast, not as needing it Himself, but as teaching us. And for this did He proceed no further than Moses and Elias, lest His assumption of our flesh might seem incredible."

On the other hand there was no inconsistency in Christ's returning to the common manner of living after fasting and retiring into the desert. For it is becoming to that kind of life which we hold Christ to have lived wherein a man delivers to others the fruits of his contemplation, that he devote himself, first of all to contemplation, and that afterwards, he come down to the publicity of active life by associating with other men. Hence Bede says: "Christ fasted that thou mightest discern His sanctity and acknowledge His power." (3a. q. XL, a. 2.)

JANUARY 19

The Active Life of Christ

"He was seen upon earth and conversed with men." (Baruch III, 38.) Our Lord not only lived a life of contemplation, retirement and prayer, but also a life of action. [Christ was and is the greatest and highest exponent of Catholic Action.] "Christ's manner of life," writes St. Thomas Aquinas, "had to be in keeping with the purpose of His Incarnation, because of which He came into the world. Now, He came into the world, first, that He might publish the truth." (John XVIII, 37.) Hence, it was fitting, not that He should hide Himself by leading a solitary life, but that He should appear openly and preach in public. Wherefore, He says to those who wish to stay Him: "To other cities also I must preach the Kingdom of God, for this therefore am I sent." (Luke IV, 42.)

Secondly, He came in order to free men from sin, according to 1 Tim. I, 15: "Christ Jesus came into this world to save sinners." And hence, St. Chrysostom says: "Although Christ might, while staying in the same place, have drawn all men to Himself to hear His preaching, yet He did not do so, thus, giving us the example to go about and seek those who perish, like the shepherd in his search of the lost sheep, and the physician in his attendance on the sick."

Thirdly, Christ came that by Him we might have access to God. (Rom. V, 2): "By whom we have access through Faith into this grace and glory in the hope of the glory of the sons of God." Thus, it was fitting that Christ should give men confidence in approaching Him by associating familiarly with them. Thus, it was a righteous life, concludes St. Thomas Aquinas.

Christ's purpose then in leading both an active and contemplative life was for our instruction and edification, that we might give to other less fortunate souls the benefits of our prayers and contemplations and become worthy exponents of Catholic Action, by living Godly lives, in diffusing truth and goodness always and everywhere. (3a, q. XL, a, 1, 2, 3.)

JANUARY 20

Christ's Poverty

In this day when there is so much poverty in the midst of so much wealth, it may be well for us to think on the poverty of our Lord and see why He was so poor and accepted His poverty as a blessing from heaven. We have heard much of the goodness, the kindness, mercy, humility, charity, and wisdom of the Saviour, but are we familiar with the reasons why Jesus led a life of poverty in this world? St. Thomas Aquinas asks this important question: "Should Christ have led a life of poverty in this world?" This learned saint states four reasons showing how fitting it was for Christ to have lived a life of poverty.

First, because this was in keeping with the duty of preaching, for which purpose He says He came (Mark I, 38): "Let us go into the neighboring towns and cities, that I may preach there also; for to this purpose am I come." Now, in order that the preachers of God's word may be able to give all their time to preaching, they must be wholly free from care of worldly matters; which is impossible for those who are possessed of wealth. Wherefore, the Lord Himself when sending the Apostles to preach said to them (Matth. X, 9): "Do not possess gold or silver." And the Apostles say (Acts VI, 2): "It is not reasonable that we should leave the Word of God to serve tables."

Secondly, because just as He took upon Himself the death of the body in order to bestow spiritual life upon us, so did He bear bodily poverty in order to enrich us spiritually, according to (2 Cor. VIII, 9): "You know the grace of our Lord Jesus Christ that He became poor for our sakes, that through His poverty we might be rich."

Thirdly, lest if He were rich His preaching might be ascribed to cupidity. Wherefore, Jerome says on Matt. X, 9, that "if the Apostles had been possessed of wealth they had seemed to preach for gain, and not for the salvation of mankind. And the same reason applies to Christ."

Fourthly, that the more lowly He seemed by reason of His poverty, the greater might the power of His Godhead be shown to be.

Hence, in a sermon of the Council of Ephesus we read: "He chose all that was poor and despicable, all that was of small account and hidden from the majority, that we might recognize His Godhead to have transformed the terrestrial sphere. For this reason did He choose a poor maid for His mother, a poorer birthplace, and live in want. Learn this from the manger."

It was not expedient then, that the Incarnate God should live in wealth and luxury in this world, and be crowned with worldly honors and dignities, because He came to withdraw the minds of men absorbed in earthly things and raise them up to divine things. Moreover, if Christ had abounded in riches and surrounded Himself with the greatest of worldly dignities, that which He did through His divine power would have been attributed more to worldly power than to the power of His divinity. Hence, a most powerful argument for His Divinity is that without an iota of worldly power Christ changed the whole world for better.

JANUARY 21

Christ Conformed His Conduct to the Law

It is written (Matth. V, 17): "Do not think that I am come to destroy the Law or the Prophets." Commenting on these words Chrysostom says: "He fulfilled the Law, in one way, by transgressing none of the precepts of the Law; secondly, by justifying us through faith, which the Law, in the letter, was unable to do."

Christ conformed His conduct in all things to the precepts of the Law. In proof of this He wished even to be circumcised; for the circumcision is a kind of confession of man's purpose of keeping the Law; according to Gal. V, 3: "I testify to every man circumcising himself, that he is a debtor to do the whole Law."

And Christ, indeed, wished to conform His conduct to the Law, first to show His approval of the Old Law; secondly, that by keeping the Law He might perfect it and bring it to an end in His own self, so as to show that it was ordained to Him; thirdly, to deprive the Jews of an excuse of slandering Him; fourthly, in order to deliver men from subjection to the Law, according to Gal. IV, 4: "God sent His son, made under the Law, that He might redeem them who were under the Law."

Christ, in truth, healed a man on the Sabbath and commanded him to take up his bed; and therefore, the Jews (wishing to accuse Him of breaking the Sabbath) said: "This man is not of God, who keepeth not the Sabbath." (John IX, 16.) But the Lord excused Himself on this ground from transgression of the Law in three ways:

First, because the precept of keeping the Sabbath holy forbids not Divine work but human work, that is, unnecessary manual labor; for though God ceased on the seventh day from the creation of new creatures, yet He ever works by keeping and governing His creatures. Now that Christ wrought miracles was a Divine work. Hence says (John V, 17): "My Father worketh until now and I work."

Secondly, Christ excused Himself on the ground that this precept does not forbid works which are necessary for bodily health. Wherefore, He says (Luke XIII, 15). "Doth not every one of you on the Sabbath day loose his ox or ass from the manger and lead them to water? And further on: "Which of you shall have an ass or an ox fall into a pit, and will not immediately draw him out on the Sabbath day?" Now it is clear, that the miraculous works done by Christ related to health of body and soul.

Thirdly, because this precept does not forbid works pertaining to the worship of God. Wherefore, Christ says (Matth. XII, 5): "Have ye not read in the Law, that on the Sabbath day the priests in the Temple break the Sabbath and are without blame?" Now, when Christ commanded the paralytic to carry his bed on the Sabbath day this pertained to worship of God, that is, to the praise of God's power. And thus it is clear, that He did not violate the Sabbath; although the Jews threw this false accusation in His face saying (John IX, 16): "This Man is not of God, who keepeth not the Sabbath." (3a. q. LX, a. IV.)

JANUARY 22

Christ's Humility and Obedience

"He humbled Himself, becoming obedient unto death." (Phil. II, 8.)

1. In order to give us an example of humility, Christ willed to suffer the death of the cross. It is true, that humility is not in God; since the virtue of humility consists in this, that a man keeps to his own place and does not reach out to things above him but is subject to his superior. Hence it is clear that humility is not becoming to God Who has no superior but is above all. If however, someone out of humility subjects himself at times either to an equal or to an inferior, this is because he looks upon as superior to himself in some respect one who is simply his equal or inferior. Even though the virtue of humility is not becoming to Christ in His Divine nature, it is becoming to Him is His humanity. And His humility is rendered the more praiseworthy by reason of His Divine nature; because personal worth enhances the praise of humility, as for example, when a great man has through necessity to suffer an indignity. Now no man is of greater worth than One Who is God; and consequently most praiseworthy was the humility of the Man-God, Who suffered the infamies which it behoved Him to suffer for man's salvation, for pride had made men lovers of worldly glory. Wherefore, that He might transform man's mind from the love of worldly glory to the love of Divine glory, He was willing to suffer death, not any kind, but the most humiliating death. There are those who,

though they fear not death, abhor an ignominous death, and it was that men might despise even this that our Lord encouraged men by the example of His death.

Again, although men might have been taught humility by divine discourses, nevertheless deeds inspire more to action than words, and all the more effectively, as the goodness of the deed is known with great certainty. So that however many other men might be examples of humility, it was still most expedient that we should be inspired by the example of a Man-God, Who certainly could not err, and Whose humility is all the more wonderful as His majesty is the more sublime.

2. The Incarnate Son of God, according to the Apostle's teaching, suffered death in obedience to His Father's command. God's commands to men concern acts of virtue; and according as a man's virtuous acts are more perfect, the more is he obedient to God. Now the greatest of the virtues is charity, to which all the others are referred. Hence Christ, Whose act of charity was most perfect, was most obedient to God; for no act of charity is more perfect than that a man die for the love of another, as our Lord Himself declared (Jo. XV, 13): *Greater love than this no man hath, that a man lay down his life for his friends. You are My friends, if you do the things I have commanded you."* Therefore, Christ, by dying for the salvation of man, and for the glory of God the Father, performed an act of perfect charity, and was most obedient to God. (Contra Gentiles IV, 55.)

JANUARY 23

The Espousals of the Blessed Virgin Mary

"Now the generation of Christ was in this wise: When as His Mother Mary was espoused to Joseph, before they came together, she was found with child of the Holy Ghost." (Matth. I, 18), and (Luke I, 26): *"The Angel Gabriel was sent, to a virgin espoused to a man whose name was Joseph."*

1. Was not this a true marriage between Mary and Joseph? We must say that the marriage of the Virgin Mother and Joseph was absolutely true; because there were present the three blessings of matrimony, namely, God Himself, secondly, offspring; and thirdly, faith. There was the Sacrament of matrimony and an inseparable union of souls.

But how was it a marriage? Now marriage or wedlock is said to be true by reason of its attaining its perfection. Although Mary had vowed her virginity to God, this did not constitute an impediment to her marriage, for she had done this before she espoused Joseph and only under condition that her vow was pleasing to God, yet she submitted her will in this regard to the Divine will. Afterwards, however, having taken a spouse according to the customs of the time and after she had accepted this to be the will of God together with her husband and from common consent, she vowed her virginity to God and this was before it was made known by the Angel, for she said to the Angel: "How can this be since I know not man?" This she could not have said unless she had vowed her virginity to God. Hence, the Mother of God is not believed to have taken an absolute vow of virginity before being espoused to Joseph, although she desired to do so, yet yielding her own will to God's judgment.

2. It was fitting that Christ should be born from an espoused virgin; first, for His own sake; secondly, for His Mother's sake; and thirdly, for our sake.

For the sake of Christ Himself, for four reasons: First, lest He should be rejected by unbelievers as illegitimate. Secondly, in order that in the customary way His genealogy might be traced through the male line. Thirdly, for the safety of the new-born child, lest the devil should plot serious evil against Him. Hence Ignatius says that Mary was espoused that "the manner of His Birth might be hidden from the devil." Fourthly, that He might be fostered by Joseph, who is therefore called His Father as provider.

It was fitting for the sake of the Virgin: First, because she was rendered free from punishment, that is, as Jerome says, "Lest she should be stoned by the Jews as an adulteress." Secondly, that thus she might be protected from ill fame. Whence Ambrose says: "She was espoused lest she be wounded by the ill-fame of violated virginity, in whom the pregnant womb would betoken corruption." Thirdly, so that Joseph might administer to her wants, as in their flight into Egypt and their return home.

It was fitting for our sake: First, because Joseph is thus a witness to Christ's being born of a Virgin. Hence Ambrose says: "Belief in Mary's words is strengthened, the motive for a lie is removed. Being espoused she had no motive for lying, since, a woman's pregnancy is the reward and gives grace to the nuptial bond. Secondly, her husband is the more trustworthy witness of her purity, in that he would deplore the dishonour and avenge the disgrace, were it not that he acknowledged the mystery." These two reasons add strength to our faith.

By the espousals of Mary the Universal Church is typified, which is a virgin and yet is espoused to one Man, Christ.

Since the Mother of the Lord being both espoused and a virgin, both virginity and wedlock are honored in her person, in contradiction to those heretics who ridiculed one or the other. (3a. q. 28, a. 4 and q. 29 a. I.)

JANUARY 24

The Infinite Grace of Christ

"God does not give the Spirit by measure." (John III, 34.)

The purpose why something is given to us is that we might have it. But to have the Holy Spirit is proper to Christ, both in as far as He is God and in as far as He is Man—in as far as He is Man, for the purpose of sanctifying us, and in as far as He is God, as a manifest proof that the Holy Spirit proceeds from Him and in both ways Christ has the Holy Spirit in an unlimited or infinite degree.

In Christ, grace is threefold, namely, the grace of union, the grace of the individual person, and the grace as Head, which is for influence, and Christ has received each of these immeasurably.

The grace of union is given to Christ in as far as the human nature of Christ was united to the Son of God personally. But the Divine nature is infinite. Hence from this very union, Christ received an infinite gift.

It is called habitual grace in so far as the soul of Christ was full of grace and wisdom. Christ is said to have received habitual grace immeasurably, from a threefold reason:

1. Because of the recipient. When to any nature is given a natural capacity of its own species as long as it lasts, it seems to be given by measure, but on the other hand, when the entire natural capacity is filled, it seems to be given to nature not by measure. Although it may be by measure from the part of the receiver, still it is not by measure from the part of the One giving, namely God, Who is ready to give all. Just as someone bringing a vase to the river to be filled,

finds there water ready without measure, although he or she receives it by measure, according to the determined size or quantity of the vase.

2. From the part of the gift received. The habitual grace of Christ according to its essence is endless and immeasurable, for whatever can belong to the nature of grace, Christ has received completely. Other persons do not receive completely, but one receives so much and another in a lesser or greater degree.

3. From the part of the cause. For in a certain manner an effect is contained in its cause. Whatever, therefore, is presently flowing from a cause of infinite power that cause is said to have that which flows without measure, and in a certain infinite manner. For example, if any one should have a fountain which contains an infinite supply of water, he would be said to have water infinitely and immeasurably. Thus the soul of Christ has grace, infinite and without measure, from this very fact that He has the Word united to Him; Which is the Infinite and Unfailing Principle of all creatures emanating from this Principle.

From these reasons, it is clear that the grace of Christ which is of the Head or Principle is infinite in regard to its influence. For from this that Christ (or grace) has the gifts of the Spirit without measure and has received the power of diffusing these gifts without measure, so that namely, the grace of Christ, not only suffices for the salvation of each individual, but for all mankind, and even for the salvation of many worlds, if there should be such. (John III.)

JANUARY 25

The Conversion of Saint Paul the Apostle

"This man is to Me a vessel of election to carry My Name before the Gentiles and kings of the earth and the children of Israel." (Acts IX, 15.)

1. That Blessed Paul was such a vessel of election is clear from that which is written Eccles. L, 10: "A massy vessel of gold, adorned with every precious stone." In truth, he was a golden vessel because of the brilliancy of his wisdom. "The gold of that land is very good." (Gen. II, 12.) He was

a solid vessel, solid in the vessel of charity. "I am certain," said he, "that neither death, nor life, can separate us from the love of God, which is in Christ Jesus, our Lord." (Rom. VIII) He was a vessel adorned with every precious stone, namely, adorned with all virtues.

That Saint Paul was such a distinguished vessel, is also clear from this that he carried in his mind and preached from his heart such remarkable doctrine. He taught in a most excellent manner the mysteries of the Divinity, which reveals his wonderful wisdom. He recommended too, in a most powerful manner, the practice of charity and instructed men in the different virtues.

2. It seems to pertain to vessels that they are made to be filled with certain kinds of liquids and among vessels is found a diversity. For some vessels are for wine, some for oil, things of various kinds. Likewise also men are divinely filled with diverse graces, as if with diverse liquids.

But this vessel of which we are now speaking was filled with precious liquid, namely, with the Name of Christ; concerning which Name, Canticles 11, says: "My Name is as oil poured out." Hence, it is said of Paul that he is, "to carry My Name." For it seems that he was wholly filled with a strong love for this Name. For he held this Name uppermost in the knowledge of his intellect, according to his own word: "I do not judge myself to know anything among you, but Jesus Christ and Him crucified." (1 Cor. II.) He also kept this Name foremost in the love of his affections, according to Rom. VIII: "Who shall separate us from the love of Christ?" He also used this adorable Name in his every conversation. Hence, he said to the Galatians: "I live, now not I, but Christ liveth in me."

3. In regard to the use of a vessel, we must remember that all vessels are made for a certain specific purpose; some for more honorable and some for less honorable purposes. But this vessel was fashioned for a noble purpose. It is the vessel carrying the Divine Name. Fashioned "to carry My Name." Moreover, Saint Paul carried the Name of Christ, first, in his body by imitating the conversation and Passion of Christ: "I bear the marks of the Lord Jesus in my body." (Gal. VI, 17.) Secondly, on his lips; for in his Epistles, he most frequently mentioned the Name of Jesus, because from the abundance of the heart the mouth speaketh. Hence, Paul can be called by the name of dove; for "he came to the ark bearing the olive branch in his mouth." (Gen. VIII.) For the olive signifies mercy. "Thou shalt call His Name Jesus, for

He shall save His people from their sins." (Matth. I.) Moreover, Paul carried this olive branch with blooming foliage to the ark, the Church of God; when he in many ways preached its power and meaning by pointing out the grace and mercy of Christ.

4. In regard to results, some vessels are useless because of sin or because of ignorance or error. But Saint Paul was pure, free from sin and error. Hence, he was a useful vessel of election, and the usefulness or good results of this vessel is expressed by our Lord when He said, "to carry My Name, before the Gentiles, and kings, and the children of Israel." (Prolog. ad Rom.)

JANUARY 26

The Priesthood of Christ

"We have therefore a great high-priest Who hath passed into the heavens, Jesus, the Son of God." (Heb. IV, 14.)

1. Christ is a priest.

The office proper to a priest is to be a mediator between God and the people, namely, inasmuch as He bestows Divine things on the people. Hence sacerdos (priest) means a giver of sacred things (sacra dans), according to Mal. II, 7: "They shall seek the Law at his mouth," that is the priest's mouth; and again, forasmuch as he offers up the people's prayers to God, and, in a manner, makes satisfaction to God for their sins; wherefore the Apostle says Heb. V. I: "Every high-priest taken from among men is ordained for men in the things that appertain to God, that he may offer up gifts and sacrifices for sins."

Now this is most befitting to Christ. For through Him are gifts bestowed on men, according to 2 Peter I, 4: "By Whom (that is, Christ), He hath given us most great and precious promises, that by these you may be made partakers of the Divine nature. Moreover, He reconciled the human race to God, according to Col. I, 19: "In Him (that is Christ) it hath pleased the Father that all fullness should dwell, and through Him to reconcile all things to Himself." Therefore it is most fitting that Christ should be a priest.

2. Christ is both priest and victim.

Augustine says: "Every visible sacrifice is a sacrament, that is a sacred sign of the invisible sacrifice." Now the invisible sacrifice is that by which a man offers his spirit to God, according to Ps. I, 19, "A sacrifice to God is an afflicted spirit." Wherefore, whatever is offered to God in order to raise man's spirit to God may be called a sacrifice. Now man needs to offer sacrifice for three reasons:

First, for the remission of sin, since through sin he is turned away from God. Hence the Apostle says (Heb. V, 1): "That it appertains to the priest to offer gifts and sacrifices for sins."

Secondly, that man may be preserved in a state of grace by ever adhering to God in Whom his peace and salvation consist. Hence under the Old Law the sacrifice of peace-offerings was offered for the salvation of the offerers, as prescribed in the third chapter of Leviticus.

Thirdly, in order that the spirit of man might be perfectly united to God which will be most perfectly realized in glory. Hence under the Old Law the holocaust was offered up, so called because the victim was wholly burnt up, as we read in the first chapter of Leviticus.

Now these effects were conferred on us by the humanity of Christ.

First, our sins were taken away, according to Rom. IV, 25: "He was delivered up for our sins."

Secondly, through Him we received the grace of salvation, according to Heb. V, 9: "He became to all that obey Him the cause of eternal salvation."

Thirdly, through Him we have acquired the perfection of glory, according to Heb. X. 19: "We have a confidence in the entering into the Holies (that is, the heavenly glory) through His blood."

Therefore Christ Himself, as man, was not only priest but also a perfect victim, being at the same time victim for sin, victim for a peace-offering, and a holocaust. (3a, q. XXII, a 1 and 2.)

JANUARY 27

A Compendium of Christ's Preaching

The Word of the Eternal Father embracing all things by its immensity, in order that the Word might bring back man degenerated by sin to the heaven of Divine glory, willed to become little, in fact assumed our lowness, without however lowering His majesty.

And in order that no one might be exempted from acquiring the doctrine of the heavenly Word, God gave it to us clearly and copiously in the different books of sacred scripture and for those who are exceedingly busy He has compressed the doctrine of human salvation under the briefest compendium.

For fear the human intellect might become obscured by various errors in the intention of a proper end, or fail in reaching true happiness by pursuing improper ends rather than by the observation of justice and for fear man's intellect might become blinded and contaminated by different vices, God has made human salvation consist in a knowledge of Truth. Moreover, Christ has compressed the knowledge of Truth necessary for salvation under a few brief articles of faith. Hence it is that the Apostle speaking to the Romans, IX, 28, said: "A short word shall the Lord make upon the earth," and again, "this is the word of faith which we preach." (Rom. X, 8.)

In truth, Christ rectified the human intention with a brief prayer. For while He taught us how to pray, He showed us how our intention and hope should tend. He showed that human justice consists in the observance of the Law, and finally He concluded under one precept, that "Love is the fulfilling of the Law." (Rom. XIII.)

Wherefore, the Apostle (1 Cor. XIII, 13) says: "Now, there remain these three, faith, hope and charity," as if under these brief headings of our salvation, consisted the entire perfection of the present life. "Now there remain faith, hope and charity." "Behold these three," says Saint Augustine, "by which God is worshipped."

And right reason demands this order. For love cannot be right unless at first a proper end is determined for hope, nor can hope be right if a knowledge of the truth is lacking. First of all then, faith is necessary for salvation, by which one knows the truth, secondly, hope, by which your intention is directed to its proper end, and thirdly, charity is necessary, by which your love and affections are completely regulated. (Ad. Regin.)

JANUARY 28

The Delightful Well

"The woman said to Him: 'Sir, thou hast nothing wherein to draw and the well is deep'." (John IV, 11.)

1. By the depth or deepness of the well is understood the depth of sacred scripture or of Divine wisdom. "Wisdom is a great depth, and who shall find it out?" (Eccles. VII, 25.) Moreover, those who draw the water of lifesaving wisdom, draw it through prayer. "If any of you want wisdom, let him ask of God, Who giveth to all men abundantly." (James I, 5.)

The well of sacred doctrine is recommended for three reasons: First, for it is great from authority because it was given by the Holy Spirit. Secondly, it is delightful by reason of its sweetness. "How sweet are Thy words to my palate more than honey to my mouth." (Ps. CVIII, 103.) Thirdly, the well of sacred scripture is abounding in wealth, because it communicates freely not only to the wise but also to the unwise.

2. The properties of sacred doctrine.

It is running water. Since our Lord says: "The water that I will give him, shall become in him a fountain of water, springing up into everlasting life." (John IV, 14.) He shows that His doctrine is living water from the motion of this water. Hence, He says that it is "A fountain of running water." "The stream of the river maketh the city of God joyful." (Ps. XLV, 5.)

The sacred doctrine is water ascending. The course of earthly water is downwards while the course of spiritual water is upwards. Therefore, Jesus said to the woman: Whosoever drinketh of this water (of the earth) shall thirst again; but he that shall drink of the water that I will give him, shall not thirst forever." (John IV, 13.) Because it is living water and united to its Fountain Head. Hence Christ says: "It will become in him a fountain."

The sacred doctrine will be water ascending into heaven. "It shall become in him, a fountain of water, springing up into everlasting life." A fountain leading us by good works into eternal life. Therefore, Christ calls it, "a fountain of water springing into everlasting life", where there is no thirst. "He who believeth in Me, out of him shall flow rivers of living water." (John VII, 38.)

Namely, rivers of good desires: "For with Thee is the fountain of Life" (Ps. XXXV, 10), namely, the Holy Spirit Who is the Spirit of Life. (John IV.)

JANUARY 29

How We Should Be Disposed Towards the Word of God

1. If the Word of God is the Son of God and all the words of God are a certain likeness of this Word, we ought then, first of all, willingly hear the words of God; for this is a sign that we love God, if we willingly hear His words.

First, we should believe in the words of God because of the fact that the Word of God dwells in us, that is, Christ, Who is the Word of God. "That Christ may dwell by faith in your hearts." (Ephes. III, 17.) "You have not His Word abiding in you, for Him Whom the Father hath sent, Him you believe not." (John V, 38.)

Secondly, we should continually meditate on the Word of God abiding in us because it is necessary for us not only to believe but to meditate, otherwise, we advance not spiritually. A meditation against sin will profit us greatly in a spiritual way. "Thy words have I hidden in my heart that I may not sin against Thee." (Ps. CXVIII, 11.) "On His law he shall meditate day and night." (Ps. I, 2.) Hence it is said of the Blessed Virgin (Luke II, 51): "She kept all these words, pondering them in her heart."

Thirdly, we should also communicate the Word of God to others by recalling the word of God to their minds; seconly, by preaching the word of God; thirdly, by enkindling hearts with love for the word of God. "Let no evil speech proceed from your mouth, but that which is good, to the edification of the faith, that it may administer grace to the hearers." (Ephes. IV, 29.) "Let the word of Christ dwell in you abundantly in all wisdom, teaching, and admonishing one another." (Coloss. III, 16.) "Preach the word of God. Be instant in season and out of season. Reprove, entreat, rebuke in all patience and doctrine." (2 Tim. IV, 2.)

Fourthly, we are commanded to put the word of God in practice in our daily lives. "Be ye doers of the Word and not hearers only; deceiving yourselves." (James I, 22.)

2. The Blessed Virgin observed five things in bringing to life the Word of God. First of all, she listened. The Angel

said to her: "The Holy Ghost shall come upon thee, and the power of the Most High shall overshadow thee." (Luke I.) Secondly, she consented through faith to become the Mother of God. "Behold the handmaid of the Lord." Thirdly, she preserved and carried the Word of God in her womb. Fourthly, she brought forth and gave birth to the Word of God. Fifthly, she nourished and fed the Word Made Flesh. Hence the Church sings:

"Ipsum Regum Angelorum, sola Virgo lactabat ubere de caelo pleno," which we might paraphrase in translating—"The only Virgin fed the very King of the Angels with the abundant richness of heaven." (Opus. VII, in Symbol.)

JANUARY 30

Keeping the Word of God

"If any man hear My words and keep them not, I do not judge him." (John XII.)

1. It must be remembered that those people are blessed who hear the Word of God and keep it. Blessed are they who believe the Word of God with their whole heart and are doers of the Word. On the other hand, those who hear the Word of God and do not trouble themselves to keep it, because of this, become more deserving of condemnation. "For not the hearers of the law are just before God, but the doers of the law shall be justified." (Rom. II, 13.) And James (I, 22) says: "Be ye doers of the word and not hearers only, deceiving yourselves."

"If any man hear my words, and keep them not, I do not judge him." The reason is, because anyone can judge another in two ways: either as judge or as the cause of the condemnation. For the judge condemns the murderer to be hanged and pronounces the sentence, while the murderer himself who committed the murder is the cause of his own condemnation. Therefore, our Lord says: "I do not judge him," that is, "I am not the cause of his condemnation but the culprit himself is the cause." "Destruction is thy own, O Israel. Thy help is only in Me." (Osee XIII, 9.) And this because, "I came not to judge the world," (John XII, 47) that is, "I am sent not to condemn, but to save the world."

2. "He that despiseth Me, and receiveth not My words,

hath one that judgeth him; the word that I have spoken, the same shall judge him on the last day." (John XII, 48.) As if our Lord had said: "Those who do not keep My words, by believing, obeying and fulfilling the law, will not go unpunished; whomsoever they may be." And the reason is because if they received not His words they despised the commandment of God, Which is the Word of God. Just as he who does not obey the commandment of his Master, Job XIX, 29, says, "Flee from the face of the sword, for the sword is the revenger of iniquities; and know ye that there is a judgment."

3. "The word that I have spoken, the same shall judge him." "This means as much," says Saint Augustine, "as if Christ has said, 'I will judge him.'" Inasmuch as Christ has expressed Himself in His words He has made Himself known to the world. He is therefore the Word which He has spoken, for He has spoken of Himself in unmistakable language. "Although I give testimony of Myself, My testimony is true; for I know whence I came and whither I go." (John VIII, 14) As if our Lord had said: "This very word which I have spoken of them, will judge them, even as they despised it." (John XII.)

JANUARY 31

The Usefulness of Meditating on the Mysteries of Christ

"I meditated on all thy works." (Ps. CXLII, 5), and, *"In my meditation a fire shall flame forth."* (Ps. XXXVIII, 4.)

1. Matters concerning the Godhead are, in themselves, the strongest incentive to love and consequently to devotion because God is supremely lovable. Yet such is the weakness of the human mind that it needs a guiding hand, not only to the knowledge, but also to the love of Divine things by means of certain sensible objects known to us. Chief among them is the humanity of Christ, according to the words of the Preface, "that through knowing God visibly, we may be caught up to the love of things invisible."

Wherefore, matters pertaining to Christ's humanity are the chief incentive to devotion, leading us thither as a guiding hand, and frequently, greater devotion is caused by a consideration of Christ's Passion and other mytseries of His humanity than by a consideration of His Divine greatness; although devotion itself has for its object chiefly matters concerning the Godhead.

2. Christ, after having washed the feet of His Apostles, said to them: "Know you what I have done to you?" (John XIII, 12); as if He had said: "You indeed see, what I have done, but still you do not understand why I did these things." And therefore, Christ proceeds to show the greatness of His action and leads the Apostles to reflect upon it.

For the works of God must be meditated on because they are profound, "O Lord, how great are Thy works? Thy thoughts are exceedingly deep." (Ps. XCI, 6.) And Ecclesiastes VIII, 17: "I understood that man can find no reason of all these works of God that are done under the sun."

The mysteries of God and His works are also delightful for meditation, and frequent reflection. "Thou hast given me, O Lord, a delight in Thy doings, and in the works of Thy hands I shall rejoice." (Ps. XCI, 5.)

The works of God and His mysteries are also useful to us as subjects for contemplation because they lead us to a knowledge of their Author. "I have greater testimony than that of John; for the works which the Father hath given Me to perfect—the works themselves which I do, give testimony of Me, that the Father hath sent me." (John V, 36.)

3. If anyone from a devout intention meditates on the suitableness of Christ's Passion and death, he will find such depth of wisdom, that certain things will always suggest more and greater things to every reflecting mind; so that (from devout and frequent meditation on the works and mysteries of Christ) we can truly experience what the Apostle says: "We preach Christ crucified unto the Jews indeed a stumbling block, and unto the Gentiles, foolishness. But unto them that are called, both Jews and Greeks, Christ the power of God and the wisdom of God. For the foolishness of God (that is what appears foolish to the world, but most wise in the eyes of God) is wiser than men, and the weakness of God (that is, what appears weak to sinful men) is stronger than men." (I Cor. XXIII.)

FEBRUARY 1

Jesus at the Door

"Behold I stand at the gate and knock." (Apoc. III, 20.)

"I stand," waiting for you to do penance. The Lord is patient and waits for us to repent so that He might show mercy. He stands at the door of the heart, which is our free will. The door of our heart is closed against Christ as long as we have a desire to do evil, so that the Lord cannot enter our hearts. "Wisdom will not enter into a malicious soul, nor dwell in a body subject to sin." (Wisdom I, 4.)

"I knock," at the door of the human heart by inspiration, by sickness, by preaching, by conferring favors. "The voice of my beloved knocking. Open to me, my sister, my love, my dove, my undefiled." (Canticles V, 2.)

"If any one should hear My Voice," namely with one ear of the heart which is intelligence and the other ear which is obedience, the Lord will draw such a one to Himself, but alas few are they who hear and listen to the Voice of the Lord. And if man will open to the Lord the door of his heart, which is his free will, the Lord will enter the soul of that man, for the soul is said to be open to Christ through a good will and open to Satan through a perverse will or evil consent.

"I will enter into him," by giving to him grace and strength. For just as the sun enters into a house through the open window, spreading its rays everywhere, but if the windows and doors are closed the sun cannot enter that home; neither can the sunshine of God's grace enter the human soul if the door of the heart is closed by sin.

"I will dine with him," that is the Lord will increase our faith and good works, from which will result joy unspeakable. God dines with us when He operates in us by His grace and inclines our will to do good and we dine with God when we cooperate with His grace and follow His inspirations. Hence St. Paul (Heb. XII, 15) says: "Follow peace with all men and holiness, without which no man shall see God. Look diligently, lest any man be wanting to the grace of God."

God dines with man in this life and man with God in paradise, but the banquet which God makes for man is better than that which man makes for God. "The sufferings of this life are not worthy to be compared with the glory that shall be revealed in us." (Rom. VIII, 18.) "Blessed therefore, are they that are called to the marriage supper of the Lamb." (Apoc. XIX, 9.)

FEBRUARY 2

The Purification of the Blessed Virgin

"After the days of her purification, according to the law of Moses were accomplished, they carried Him to Jerusalem, to present Him to the Lord." (Luke II, 22.) In this Gospel, seven virtues are to be observed in the Blessed Virgin. First, humility in her purification since she did not need purification; second, love of purity in her superabundant purification; third, love of obedience according to the law; fourth, reverence to her Son in bringing Him to Jerusalem; fifth, devotion in visiting the Holy place; sixth, thanksgiving in the oblation of her Son, "So that they might present Him to the Lord," "We offer Him to Thee O Lord, Him Whom Thou hast given to us." Seventh, poverty in the offering, namely two doves, which was the offering of the poor.

But in so far as the Blessed Virgin wished to be purified, even though she did not need purification, she teaches us that men who need to be purified should be purified. Moreover we ought to be purified in eight ways as can be understood from the text: 1. From the contamination of sin. "The Lord took away his sins." (Eccl. XLVII, 13.) 2. In knowledge, as to the intellect. "From a pure heart." (1 Tim. I, 5.) 3. In affection, as to love. "Those who call upon the Lord with a pure heart." (2 Tim. II, 22.) 4. In mind, by right intention. "Purge out the old leaven," that is, hypocrisy. "Beware of the leaven of the Pharisees which is hypocrisy." (Luke I, 12.) 5. Purification of mouth, as to speech. "Evil thoughts are an abomination to the Lord, and pure words most beautiful shall be confirmed by Him." (Prov. V, 26.) 6. In hands, as to operation. "I will therefore, that men pray in every place, lifting up pure hands without anger, and contention." (1 Tim. II.) 7. In the whole body, as to conversation. 8. In things, as to the removal of superfluities. "I am the true vine; and My Father is the husbandman. Every branch that beareth not fruit, He will take away, and every one that beareth fruit, he will purge it." (John XV, 1.)

FEBRUARY 3

The Presentation of Christ in the Temple

"Christ wished to be made under the law, that He might redeem them who were under the Law," (Gal. IV, 4,) and that "the justification of the Law" might be spiritually fulfilled in His members. Now the Law contained a two-fold precept relating to children born.

One was a general precept which referred to all—namely, that "when the days of the mother's purification had expired," a sacrifice was to be offered either "for a son or for a daughter," as laid down in Lev. XII, 6. And this sacrifice was for the expiation of the sin in which the child was conceived and born and also for a certain consecration of the child, because it was then presented in the Temple for the first time. Wherefore one offering was made as a holocaust and another for sin.

The other was a special precept in the Law concerning the first-born of both "man and beast"; for the Lord claimed for Himself all the first-born in Israel, because in order to deliver the Israelites, He "slew every first-born in the land of Egypt, both men and cattle," (Exod. XII, 12) the first-born of Israel being saved; which law is set down in Exod. XIII. Here also Christ was foreshadowed, Who is the First-born amongst many brethren." (Rom. VIII, 29.)

Therefore, since Christ was born of a woman and was her first-born and since He wished to be "made under the Law," the Evangelist Luke shows that both these precepts were fulfilled in His regard. First, as to that which concerns the first-born when he says (XI, 22): "They carried Him to Jerusalem to present Him to the Lord; as it is written in the Law of the Lord, 'Every male opening the womb shall be called holy to the Lord.' Secondly, as the general precept which concerned all, when he says (I ibid; 24): "And to offer a sacrifice according as it is written in the Law of the Lord, pair of turtle doves or two young pigeons."

As the Son of God "became man, and was circumcised in the flesh, not for His own sake, but that He might make us to be God's through grace, and that we might be circumcised in spirit; so, again, for our sake He was presented to the Lord that we may learn to offer ourselves to God." (Athanasius on Luke II, 23.) And this was done after His circumcision, so "that no one who is not circumcised from vice is worthy of Divine regard." (Bede, on Luke II, 23.)

The Law of Lev. XII, 6, 8, commanded "those who could, to offer for a son or daughter, a lamb and also a turtle dove or a pigeon; but those who were unable to offer a lamb were commanded to offer two turtle doves or two young pigeons." (Bede XV, in Purif) And so the Lord, "Who being rich," as is written 2 Cor, VIII, 9, "wished the poor man's victim to be offered for Him;" just as at His birth He was "wrapped in swaddling clothes and laid in a manger." (3a. q. 37, a. 3.)

FEBRUARY 4

How to Offer Ourselves to God

Four things are necessary which are mystically designated concerning the oblation of ourselves to Christ. They are purity of mind, humility of heart, peace of soul, and an abundance of good works.

The first, namely, purity of mind is designated through the time of the oblation of ourselves; "the days of our purgation being completed," by which is mystically meant that we cannot offer ourselves to God unless we are first purified of every uncleanliness of mind and of body. "The Eyes of the Lord are far brighter than the sun, and they cannot look favourably upon iniquity." (Eccl. XXIII, 28) And Matth. XVIII, 3, says, "Unless you be converted, and become as little children, you will not enter the kingdom of heaven." And Apoc. XXI, 27, declares, "There shall not enter into heaven anything defiled." But there are two things in us which must be purified, namely, the intellect that knows and the will which desires.

The second, namely, humility of heart is demanded for this reason that Christ, Who was not subject to the law, willed to be offered according to the law; for the Word of God became flesh, not by the seed of man, but through a Mystical breathing. Wherefore, Christ willed to be thus offered as a sign of humility; so that by the merit of humility He might teach us to become worthy of Divine favour. "My Eye hath seen every precious thing," that is, Christ looks with pleasure upon the soul, humbled under the influence of His wisdom and grace; because inasmuch as anyone is more precious in the Eyes of God by so much the more should such a person be humbler in his own eyes. "When you were a little one in your own eyes, were you not made the head." (I Kings XV, 7.)

The third, namely, peace of soul is required from the fact that Christ was offered in Jerusalem, which is interpreted—peaceful—or vision of peace. "Follow peace with all men, and holiness; without which no man shall see God." (Heb. XII, 14.) Augustine says that, "peace is serenity of mind, tranquility of soul, simplicity of heart, a bond of love, the companion of charity, and whosoever is unwilling to observe this testimony of peace, cannot enjoy the possession of the Lord." Nor can one have peace with Christ, if he is at strife with his neighbor, "For he who rests peacefully hereafter, must here refrain from every evil action."

The fourth, namely, an abundance of good works is required for the oblation of ourselves to God for the reason that Christ was offered up with all His gifts to His Eternal Father. "Thou shalt not appear empty before Me." (Ex. XXIII, 15.) That is, empty of good works. Wherefore Gregory says, "the hand will not be empty of gifts, if the ark of the heart is filled with a good will." (The Humanity of Christ.)

FEBRUARY 5

The Temple of God

"Presently the Lord whom you seek, shall come to His holy temple." (Malach. III, 1.)

This statement can be understood as the coming of the Lord into the womb of the Blessed Virgin, for she was the wonderful temple of God—wonderful above all the saints.

1. This Virginal temple was wonderfully great because of the length and depth of Mary's charity. For just as she had more faith, hope, and charity, than any other creature, so she had more of greatness. "The house which Solomon built was sixty cubits long." (3 Kings IV.)

2. Wonderfully great is this temple because desiringly beautiful. "There was nothing in the temple, which was not covered with gold." (3 Kings IV) For there was nothing in the Virgin Mary but was full of sanctity. "O thou most beautiful among women! Thou art all fair, O My love, and there is not a spot in thee." (Cant. IV, 7.)

3. Wonderfully great is this temple because covered with

various pictures, that is, it was adorned with all the virtues of the saints and angels. "He made in the temple figures of Cherubims, and carvings." (3 Kings VI, 29.)

4. Wonderfully great is this temple because it was adorned by great and marvelous columns. "Wisdom hath built herself a house. She hath hewn her out of seven pillars." (Prov. IX, 1.) By the seven pillars can be understood seven virtues which are noted in the Gospel for the Feast of the Purification of the Blessed Virgin.

5. Wonderfully great is this temple for it was consecrated by the work of the three persons of the Blessed Trinity. "The Most High hath sanctified His own tabernacle." (Ps. XLV, 5.) "The Holy Ghost shall come upon thee." (Luke I, 35.)

6. Wonderfully great is this temple because it was privileged with great dignity; so that every creature, yea even every malefactor who runs to it with his whole heart, will be saved and every prayer poured forth in it will be heard.

7. Wonderfully great is this temple because it was built so that the Son of God might therein become man.

"Let us go therefore, with confidence to the throne of grace; that we may obtain mercy, and find grace in seasonable aid." (Heb. IV, 16.) (Sermon XXIII.)

FEBRUARY 6

Following the Lord

"A great multitude followed Him." (John VI, 2.) We should follow Christ for three reasons: First, because nothing is easier to do than this before death; secondly, nothing is more secure at death; and thirdly, nothing more beneficial after death.

1. Nothing easier before death because Christ has taught us the way to follow Him. "Christ suffered for us, leaving us an example that we should follow His footsteps." (1 Peter II, 21.) And behold His way: "He committed no sin." Behold His way of purity: "Neither was guile found in His mouth." Behold His way of truth: "Who when He suffered, did not revile." Behold His way of final patience. It would be small for us to follow Christ for a long time by way of penance and then turn away from Him through sin.

2. Nothing is more secure at death. For those who are

His companions in life will be protected by Him in death. The good and faithful traveler does not reject his companion in sickness but carefully guards him, wherefore it is said: "My sheep hear My voice, and I know them, and they follow Me, and I give them life everlasting, and they shall not perish forever, and no man shall pluck them out of My hand." (John X, 27.) The devil is like a wolf, who lies in wait for the sheep as they are entering and leaving the sheepfold, but the Lord is the good Shepherd who, when the sheep are going out, goes before them and leads them to pasture. Hence when souls are leaving this world Christ goes before them to open heaven's gate for them and lead them into eternal life. Wherefore St. John X, 4, says: "And when He (the Lord) has led out His own sheep, He goes before them, and the sheep follow Him, because they know His voice. But a stranger they follow not, but fly from him."

3. Nothing is more beneficial after death. Therefore it is written: "If you wish to be perfect, go and sell all that you have, and give it to the poor, and come and follow Me, and you will have treasures in Heaven." (Luke XVIII, 28.) Again Jesus said: "Amen I say to you, that you who have followed Me . . . and left all things for My Name's sake, shall receive a hundred fold, and shall possess life everlasting." (Matt. XIX, 28.)

FEBRUARY 7

The Yoke of Christ

"Take up My yoke upon you, and learn of Me; because I am meek and humble of heart, and you shall find rest to your souls. For My yoke is sweet, and My burden light." (Matth. XI, 29.)

1. "Take My yoke," namely, the Evangelical counsels or the law. In truth, the entire law consists in two things, in meekness and humility. By meekness man is disposed towards his neighbour. By humility man is properly disposed in regard to himself and to his God. "To whom shall I have respect, but to him that is poor and little, and of a contrite heart?" (Isaias LXVI, 2.) Hence humility makes a man worthy to possess and hold God.

2. Concerning the usefulness of bearing the yoke, Christ has said, "Come to Me, and I will refresh you." What is this

refreshment? It is such that, "You will find rest to your souls." For the body is not refreshed as long as it is afflicted with pain but sometimes when the body is not afflicted in a worse way, it is said to be refreshed. Just as hunger in the body, so is desire in and to the mind; wherefore, the satisfying of our desires is refreshment. "Bless the Lord, O my soul, Who satisfieth thy desire with good things." (Ps. CII, 5) This means rest for the soul. "I have laboured a little, and have found much rest to myself." (Eccles. LI, 31.) In the world, the meek do not find rest, hence Christ says, "you will find rest," eternal rest, namely, in the fulfillment of all your desires.

3. "For My yoke is sweet, and My burden light."

In all things, the doctrine or law of Christ which changes the heart is actually very light and easy of fulfillment; because it makes us love not earthly but spiritual things. For whosoever loves temporal things loses in a little while a great deal more than he who loves spiritual things loses in a long time. The law does not prohibit us loving temporal things but advises against becoming too much attached to them. "I will show thee the way of wisdom. I will lead thee by the paths of equity; which when thou hast entered, thy steps shall not be straightened, and when thou runnest thou shalt not meet a stumbling block." (Prov. IV, 11.)

Likewise in regard to actions, the law was burdensome in relation to external actions. But our law is in the will only. Hence Rom. XIV, 17, says, "the kingdom of God is not meat and drink; but justice and peace, and joy in the Holy Ghost."

Likewise the law of Christ rejoiceth the heart of man. Wherefore, Saint Paul says, "justice, joy, and peace in the Holy Ghost."

Indeed many and great are the adversities of life. For, "all who will live Godly, in Christ Jesus, shall suffer persecution." (2 Tim. III, 12.) But these persecutions are not too severe because they are made pleasant with the spice of love; for when anyone loves another he is not annoyed by what he suffers for his friend. Hence love makes all burdensome and even impossible things a joy and a pleasure. Wherefore, if anyone truly loves Christ, nothing will be a burden to him and therefore, the new law is not burdensome. "My yoke is sweet and My burden light."

FEBRUARY 8

The Imitation of Christ

"I have given you an example, that as I have done to you, so do you also." (John XIII, 15.)

1. In the actions of men example is more powerful than words. For man does this and chooses that which seems good to him. Hence he shows that what he chooses is good rather than what he teaches. Hence it is, that sometimes a person says something and still does the opposite, persuades others more by this, than that which he teaches. Therefore, from this very fact, it is especially necessary to give an example, a good example.

But the example of a pure man was not sufficient for the human race to imitate, both because human reason fails in due reflection and is deceived in the very consideration of things. And therefore, an example is given to us, an example of the Son of God which is infallible and sufficient for all things and for all men. For He is the Image of the Father and just as He is the Exemplar of creation, so should He be the Exemplar of our justification. "For unto this (justification) are you called, because Christ also suffered for us, leaving you an example that you should follow His steps" (1 Peter II, 21.) "My foot hath followed His steps. I have kept His way, and have not declined from it." (Job XXII, 11.)

2. Christ is the infallible Example, for He can be considered as the Wayfarer, or as the Knower, or as God.

As Wayfarer, He is the Leader directing us on the right way. For in every journey there must be a leader who can not be led astray, otherwise there would be error in all things regulated by him. Therefore, Christ Himself had such fullness of grace and wisdom, that even inasmuch as He was a Wayfarer, He could not sin. Hence also, those who were united to Him by grace were so confirmed, for example, the Apostles, that they could not sin mortally although they could sin venially.

Secondly, Christ was the Knower or Perceiver, for His mind was completely united to the end so that He could not act otherwise than in relation to the end.

Moreover, as far as He was God, both His soul and body had been, as it were, an organ of the Deity, according as the Deity ruled His soul and His soul ruled His body. Wherefore, sin could not touch Christ's soul, just as no sin could contaminate God.

We, too, can share in a certain way, in this inability to sin if we walk in this way wherein our Leader walked, if we strive to unite our mind to the proper end and if we permit God to govern our souls. (3 Dist. 12 Q. 2, a.1.)

FEBRUARY 9

The Vine and Its Branches

"I am the true vine, and My Father is the husbandman." (John XV, 1.)

The Lord Himself is the vine. Hence He says, "I am the vine," by a certain likeness (to the vine). For just as the vine, although disregarded or despised, nevertheless, excels all trees in the sweetness of its fruit; so with Christ, although He seemed despised and overlooked because He was poor and appeared ignoble, even bearing ignominy; still He bore the sweetest fruits, according to Canticles II, 3, "His fruit was sweet to my palate." And therefore, Christ is the vine, bearing the wine which inebriates spiritually, namely, the wine of compunction. Likewise He is the consoling wine, namely, the wine of true refreshment for our souls.

"And My Father is the husbandman." God Himself takes care of us, so that we might become better under His care, in so far as He removes evil germs from our heart. He opens the ground of our hard hearts by the plough of His word, plants there the seeds of His commandments and reaps the fruit of piety.

But the vine concerning which we here treat was perfect. It needed not the cultivation of the husbandman. Hence all the labour of the husbandman which had to be done was around the branches. But the branches are of the nature of the vine, hence the branches of this vine of which we speak are those adhering closely to Christ.

"Every branch in Me, that beareth not fruit, He will take away." (John XV, 2.) Here is indicated the work of the husbandmen around the evil branches they cut off from the vine. Hence Christ says, "Every branch," that is every Christian, "not bearing fruit" namely in the vine, "in Me," without

Whose aid no one or no thing can bear fruit; "He will take away," take him away from the vine. From which it appears, that not only will some who because they commit evils be cut away from Christ, but also because they neglect to do good. Wherefore, the Apostle used to say of himself, "By the grace of God, I am what I am, and His grace in Me hath not been void." (1 Cor. XV, 10.) And Matth. XXV, 28, says "that the talent was taken away by the master from the man who did not increase it but buried it." "Thou wicked and slothful servant. Take ye away from him the talent, and give it to him who has ten talents." Likewise, the Lord commanded the barren tree to be cut down and cast into the fire.

And everyone that beareth fruit, He will purge it, that it may bring forth more fruit." (John XV, 2.) Here is laid down the work which the husbandman does for the good branches so that they might be nourished to produce more fruit. For it really happens in the natural vine that the branch which has many sprouts or suckers produces less fruit by reason of the diffusion of the sap to all; and therefore the husbandmen or cultivators, so that the branch might be more fruitful, purge it of superfluous suckers or sprouts.

Thus it is with man. For although a man is well disposed and united to God, still if his affections are bent on diverse and trifling things his power is weakened and he is rendered less effective to do good. And hence it is, that God, to make us productive of good, often cuts off from us and purges us of similar impediments by sending us tribulations and temptations, which if we overcome we become stronger in the performance of good and therefore, it is rightly said, "He purges man," even if a man should be pure, for no man in this life is so pure but he may be more and more purified. And this, "so that he may bring forth more fruit," that is, increase in virtue; so that in so far as we are the more fruitful or productive of good by so much the more we need to be purified. (John XV, 1, 2.)

FEBRUARY 10

The Study of Wisdom—Especially of Incarnate Wisdom

1. Among all the studies to which man might devote himself, the study of wisdom is the more perfect, the more sublime, the more useful, and the more pleasing.

In truth, the study of wisdom is the more perfect because in so far as a man devotes himself to a study of wisdom, so far has he already a certain share of true happiness. Hence the wise man says, "Blessed is the man that shall continue in wisdom." (Eccl. XIV, 22.)

The study of wisdom is, moreover, the more sublime because through it man chiefly approaches the Divine likeness, which does all things from wisdom. Hence because the likeness is the cause of love, the study of wisdom then, chiefly unites us to God; for which reason it is written that, "Wisdom is an infinite treasure to me, and they that use it become the friends of God, being commended for the gift of discipline." (Wis. VII, 14.)

It is the more useful study because through it man arrives at the kingdom of immortality. "The desire of wisdom bringeth you to the everlasting kingdom. Love wisdom, therefore, that you may reign forever." (Wis. VI, 21.)

It is on the other hand a most pleasing study, because, "her conversation hath no bitterness, nor her company any tediousness, but joy and gladness." (Wis. VIII, 16.)

2. There is a difference between the knowledge we acquire of God by science and by faith. The knowledge of God possessed by a study of the sciences enlightens our intellect only, by showing that God is the first cause, that He is One and All-Wise. But the knowledge of God had by faith both enlightens the intellect and delights the heart; because that knowledge not only tells us that God is the First Cause but that He is our Saviour, that He is the Redeemer, that He loves us and became man for us. Therefore, it must be said, that this knowledge of God's goodness, "like the vine, brings forth a pleasant odor," in the person "believing in Him in every place," because this odor of His sweetness and goodness is diffused far and wide and perceived by faith. (Eccl. XXIV.) "Behold the odor of My Son is as the odor of a plentiful field, which the Lord hath blessed." (Gen. XXVII, 27.) "Now thanks be to God, Who always maketh us to triumph in Christ Jesus, and manifesteth the odor of His knowledge by us in every place." (2 Cor. II, 14.)

3. Always advance in the study of wisdom.

Since the perfection of man consists in union with God it should be that man, from all things which are in him and around him, be introduced to and led to Divine things, to study of Divine things, in as far as he can study them; so that his intellect might devote itself to a contemplation of

Divine things and his reason to an investigation of things Divine; according to Ps. LXXII, 27; "It is good for me to adhere to God."

Since moreover, God is infinitely distant from the creature, no creature, either in receiving from Him or in knowing Him, is so moved towards God as to be equal to Him. But each creature is moved in this respect that he becomes more and more like unto God, as far as that is possible. And thus the human mind should always be moved to know more and more about God, in His own way. Hence Hilary says, "he who piously pursues infinite and Divine things, even if he does not reach them, nevertheless advances by pursuing them." (In Boet. de Trinit.)

FEBRUARY 11

The Feast of the Apparition of the Blessed Virgin

"The goodness and kindness of God our Saviour appeared." (Titus III, 4.)

1. The goodness and kindness of the Saviour appeared in the Saviour Himself and in the Blessed Virgin, for the Blessed Virgin was full of grace.

First, with regard to the overflow of grace from her soul to her body. It is a wonderful thing in the saints that they have sufficient grace to sanctify their souls but the soul of the Blessed Virgin was so full of grace that from it overflowed grace to her body; so that from her might be born the Son of God. And therefore, Hugh of Saint Victor says, "that in Mary's heart the love of the Holy Ghost was so extraordinarily ardent that it accomplished wonderful things in her body, so that from her God and Man might be born." "Therefore the Holy which shall be born of thee, shall be called the Son of God." (Luke I, 35.)

Secondly, Mary was full of grace in so far as she had an abundance of grace for all mankind. For it is a great thing in each saint when he or she has such grace as suffices for their own salvation but greater when a saint has so much grace that it is sufficient for the salvation of many; but when a saint has such an abundance of grace that it suffices for the salvation of all mankind this indeed is the greatest of all. And this plenitude of grace is in Christ and in His Blessed Mother.

For in every danger you can obtain salvation from this glorious Virgin. "Thy neck is as the tower of David, which is built with bulwarks. A thousand bucklers hang upon it, all the armour of valiant men." (Cant. IV, 4.) "A thousand bucklers," remedies against evils, "hang upon it." Likewise in every work of virtue you can have Mary as your helper and therefore, she truly says of herself, "I am the Mother of fair love, and of holy fear, and of knowledge, and of holy hope. In me is all hope of life and of virtue." (Eccl. XXIV, 24.)

2. "There shall come forth a rod out of the root of Jesse, and a flower shall rise up out of this root." (Isaias XI, 1.) The Blessed Virgin is our beloved Lady because of her many blessings which are principally six:

First, because she has divided the sea for us, that is the world, so that we might safely pass through it. "Lift up the rod, and stretch forth thy hands over the sea, and divide it; so that thy children . . . may go through the midst of the sea on dry ground." (Ex. XIV, 16.)

Secondly, because she has brought to us the water of grace from the rock Christ so that we may drink freely of this life-saving water. "Take the rod . . . and speak to the rock before them, and it shall yield waters, and all the multitude shall drink." (Num. XX, 8.)

Thirdly, Mary is our beloved favour bearing Queen for she gives us the honey of devotion so that we might be refreshed. "She put forth the end of the rod, and dipped it in a honeycomb." (1 Kings XIV, 27.)

Fourthly, she is our beloved because we ask grace and mercy through her divine clemency. "The King held out to her the golden sceptre." (Esth. V, 2); in which was shown the sign of mercy.

Fifthly, because through her we conquer the devil. "He went down to him with a rod, and forced the spear out of the hand of the Egyptian," (2 Kings XXIII, 21); that is out of the hand of the devil.

Sixthly, Mary is our beloved Queen, for through her power we are set free from the hands of all our enemies. "The Lord will send forth the sceptre of thy power. Rule thou in the midst of thy enemies." (Ps. CIX, 2.) (Annunciation of the Blessed Virgin.)

FEBRUARY 12

The State of Sinners

Lent is a very opportune time for all of us to perform some little sacrifice or do some penance for sin; either in atonement for our own sins or as an act of reparation for the crimes perpetrated by others. In the 23rd chapter of St. Matthew, Our Lord employs some very forceful language against sinners and denounces in no uncertain terms the hypocrisy, blindness, insincerity, and bad example of the scribes and Pharisees. Jesus said: "Woe to you scribes and Pharisees, and hypocrites; because you are like to white sepulchres, which outwardly appear to men beautiful, but within are full of dead men's bones, and of all filthiness."

We know that a sepulchre is a place where a corpse is laid to rest. The bodies of saints are the temples of God in which God dwells. "The temple of God is holy, which you are." (1 Cor. III, 17.) The body is the dwelling place of the soul and the soul is the throne of God; just as the body is the temple of the soul, so the soul is the home of God. "The Lord is in His Holy temple." (Psalm X, 6.) But the body of a sinner is a sepulchre, because it contains the dead. In a sepulchre there is a dead body, but sometimes on the outside there is a certain image which seems to live; hence it is written in the Apocalypse (III, 1), "Thou hast the name of being alive, and thou art dead." Therefore our Lord said of sinners that "outwardly you appear beautiful," because of beauty which is put on and wholly external; but "inwardly they are full of dead men's bones, and all filthiness," that is filled with all rottenness and corruption. Hence Christ continues: "And so outwardly you appear to men as just," that is men think you are just, "but inwardly you are full of hypocrisy, and iniquity." And again the Saviour says: "Thou blind Pharisee, first make clean the inside of the cup and of the dish that the outside may become clean." (Matthew XXIII.) Every one of us can now do what the Saviour commands, through prayer, purity, repentance, and devout reception of the Sacraments. Now is the acceptable time for us to cleanse our hearts, become spiritualized and sincere with God and honest with ourselves. Now especially, when the Church during Lent offers us so much spiritual help, courage, and consolation, we should strive to become truly converted to God and live with Him forevermore.

FEBRUARY 13

Our Conversion Must Not Be Put Off

"Be at agreement with thy adversary, whilst thou art in the way with Him, lest perhaps the adversary deliver thee to the judge, and the judge deliver thee to the officer, and thou be cast into prison." (Matth. V, 25.)

1. Our adversary is God. "I the Lord, abhor the wicked." (Ex. XXIII, 7.) Or His Divine Word may be our adversary which opposes those desiring to sin. "All scripture, inspired of God, is profitable to teach, to reprove, to correct, to instruct in justice." (2 Tim. III, 16.) Or our conscience accusing us may be our adversary, according to Ps. XLIX, 21, "I will reprove thee, and set before thy face." Thus in all these ways, we may be accused by our Adversary.

Hence, "Be at agreement with thy adversary," that is with God and with His Divine Word with which we should agree because of the hope of His promise, the fear of punishment, the force of His commandment, and the necessity of avoiding evil. "Whilst," that is, as long as, "you are with Him on the way," namely, in a state of meriting. "I must work the works of Him that sent me whilst it is day, for the night cometh when no man can work." (John IX, 4.) "With Him," that is with Whom you can rightly advance, "on the way," namely, "the way of Christ." "Lest," that is without delay. "Delay not to be converted to the Lord, and defer it not from day to day." (Eccles. V, 8.)

2. "Lest perhaps the adversary deliver thee," that is, lest sometimes a just cause should arise for delivering thee to the judge. He says, "perhaps," that is, for fear your opportunity to repent might be taken away from you. "Lest the adversary deliver thee," that is, the Divine Law, or God or your accusing conscience hand thee over to the hands of Christ—your Judge. "And the judge," that is Christ, "deliver thee to the officer," that is to the Angel who will gather the cockle to be burned; or "to the officer," that is to the exactor—the devil.

"And thou be cast into prison," that is, into the depths of hell. "They shall be gathered together as in the gathering of one bundle into the pit, and they shall be shut up there in prison." (Isaias XXII, 24.) "He cast him into the bottomless pit." "Amen I say to thee, thou shalt not go out from thence, until thou repay the last farthing;" (Matth. V, 26) that is—never. Hence Augustine says, "until," does not mean the end of punishment but a continuance of misery, as if Christ has said, "you will pay forever and never will you repay."

"Until you repay the last farthing," that is, be punished for the smallest sins because nothing will go unpunished. (Matthew V.)

FEBRUARY 14

We Must Cling to Christ

"I am the Way, the Truth, and the Life." (John XIV, 6.)

1. Christ Himself is the Way for through Him we have access to the Father. But because this way is not distant from the end but united to it Christ adds, "the Truth and the Life." And so Christ Himself is at the same time the Way and the End—the Way according to His humanity, the End according to His Divinity. So therefore, in as far as He is man He says, "I am the Way," and in as far as He is God He adds the words, "the Truth and the Life." By these two the end of this life is fittingly pointed out. For the end of this life is the finish of all human desires. But man chiefly desires two things, namely, a knowledge of Truth and a continuation of his own existence. But Christ is the Way by which we arrive at a knowledge of the Truth, since He is Truth and He is the Way by which we arrive at life, since He is the Life.

2. So therefore, Christ designated Himself the Way which united to the end for He is the end, having in Himself whatever can be desired by the human heart, namely living truth and life. If therefore, you are seeking for that by which you may safely pass through this world, take Christ as your guide for He is the Way. "This is the way. Walk ye in it." (Isaias XXX, 21.) And Augustine says, "Walk by Man, and you come to God." For it is better to walk blindly in the Way than to walk strongly outside the Way. For he who walks blindly in the Way, although he advance but a little, still he is approaching his destined end, but on the other hand whosoever walks outside the Way, even if he runs rapidly is so much the more removed from his proper end.

If in truth you are seeking information by which road to

travel cling to Christ, because He is the Truth to which we all desire to come.

If you are looking for a place in which to rest, adhere to Christ, for He is life and peace and rest. "He that shall find Me, shall find life, and shall have salvation from the Lord." (Prov. VIII, 35.)

3. He is security. Adhere to Christ if you wish to be secure and safe. You cannot go astray with Christ for He is the Way. Hence those who cling to Christ do not walk in impassable places but by the right and straight way. Likewise, He cannot be deceived for He is Truth and teacheth all truth. Likewise He cannot be confused for He is Life and the Giver of Life. "I am come that they may have life, and have it more abundantly." (John X, 20.) Wherefore, Augustine declares, "The Lord says of Himself, I am the Way, the Truth and the Life; as if He had said, Do you wish a way by which to go? I am the Way. Do you wish a place to remain at rest? I am Life. Do you wish that by which you can walk? I am the Truth."

Or another explanation can be this. There are three things in man which pertain to sanctity, namely, action, contemplation and intention and these are perfected by Christ. For Christ is the Way to those advancing in the active life. He is the Truth for those persevering in the contemplative life; but He directs the intention of those in the active and contemplative life unto Eternal Life. Accordingly, the Lord is for us the Way by which we go to Him and through Him to the Father. (John XIV.)

FEBRUARY 15

Christ's Love for His Disciples

"As the Father hath loved Me, I also have loved you. Abide in My love." (John XV, 8.)

1. The word "as" sometimes denotes equality of nature and sometimes likeness of action. But here, "as" means likeness of grace and of love. For the love with which the Son loves His disciples is a certain likeness of that love whereby the Father loves His Son. For since to love anyone is to wish good to him, the Father loves the Son according to His Divine Nature in so far as He wishes for Him His infinite good; which

He has. "The Father loveth the Son, and showeth all things to Him, which Himself doth." (John V, 20.)

The Father also loves the Son in so far as he has human nature and also for this reason, that Christ is at the same time both God and Man.

But for none of these reasons does the Son love His disciples. For He does not love them so that they may be God by nature nor that they may be united to God in person but He loves them because of a certain likeness in these things; so that they might be God's by participation of grace. "I have said, You are God, and all of you Sons of the Most High." (Ps. LXXXI, 6.) "By Whom He hath given us most great and precious promises, that by these you may be made partakers of the Divine nature." (2 Peter I, 4.) That likewise they may become one in love, "for he who is joined to the Lord, is one spirit with Him." (1 Cor. VI, 17.) "Whom He foreknew, He also predestinated to be made comformable to the image of His Son; that He might be the firstborn among many brethren." (Rom. VIII, 29.)

So therefore, God the Father has placed greater good in His Son than the Son has placed in His disciples and this because of the Son's twofold nature; whereas Christ loves His disciples because we are made like to Him by grace.

2. "Abide in My love," as if He had said, "Abide in My love, because you will receive such a blessing from My love that you will love Me." Or, "abide in My love" because I will love you, because of my grace in you. "Abide in My love," so that you may not be deprived of the good things which I have prepared for you. And this explanation is more fitting as the sense of "Abide in My love," is "Persevere in this holy state, so that you may be loved by Me, through the effect of grace in your soul." "Let every man abide in the same calling in which he was called." (1 Cor. VII, 20.) "He that abideth in charity, abideth in God, and God in him." (1 John IV, 16.) (John XV.)

FEBRUARY 16

Abiding in Christ

"Abide in Me, and I in you. As the branch cannot bear fruit of itself, unless it abide in the vine, so neither can you unless you abide in Me." (John XV, 4.) 21.)

1. Here is shown that abiding with Christ is necessary if we wish to bear fruit of virtue and good works. As if Christ had said, "You ought to abide in Me, so that you may be productive of good works because, "as the branch," literally, the material branch, "cannot bear fruit of itself, unless it abide in the vine (from whose root, moisture ascends to the growth of the branches), so neither can you do good, nor bring forth fruit of virtue unless you abide in Me." Abiding therefore, in Christ is the reason of fructification (of making our life-work meritorious). Hence it is written concerning those who abide not in Christ, "What fruit hath you therefore, in those things, of which you are now ashamed?" (Rom. VI, 21.) "The congregation of the hypocrite is barren, and fire shall devour their tabernacles." (Job. XV, 34.)

Moreover, this likeness is fitting because, "I am the vine, and you are the branches." As if Christ had said, "such is the comparison between you and Me, the comparison of the branch with the vine." Concerning these branches it is written in Ps. LXXIX, 12, "It stretched forth its branches unto the sea. The branches thereof, the cedars of God."

2. "He who abideth in Me, and I in him, the same beareth much fruit." (John XV, 5.)

Here it is proven that abiding in Christ is efficacious. Not only is it therefore necessary for man "to abide in Me," so that he might do good consistently but also it is efficacious; because, "he that abideth in Me," through faith, obedience and perseverance and "I in him," by giving him enlightenment, assistance, and perseverance he, and none other, beareth much fruit. He beareth, I say, a threefold fruit in this life. The first is to abstain from sin; the second is to devote oneself to works of sanctity and the third is to edify others. "The earth shall be filled with the fruit of the works." (Ps. CIII, 13.) Such a person shall bear fruit, the fruit of eternal life. This is the final and perfect fruit of our labours.

The reason for this efficiency is, "because without Me you

can do nothing." Therefore, the Lord says that without Him, without His Divine help, we are not only powerless to do great things, but even small things. Nor is this wonderful, for God Himself did nothing without Divine assistance. "Without Him was made nothing that was made." For our works are either performed by the power of nature or of Divine grace. If by the power of nature, since all the movements of nature are caused by the very Word of God, then no nature can be moved to do anything without God. If, on the other hand, our works are the result of Divine grace and God is the Author of grace, "because grace and truth came through Jesus Christ," it is then clear that no meritorious work can be done by us without God's help. "Not that we are sufficient to think anything of ourselves, as of ourselves, but our sufficiency is from God." (2 Cor. III, 5.)

If therefore, we cannot think even one good thought without God's help, in a much less degree can we do other things. "Without Me you can do nothing," nothing advantageous for your salvation. (John XV.)

FEBRUARY 17

Life in Christ

"To me, to live is Christ, and to die is gain." (Phil. I, 21.)

1. Christ is life, for He is the beginning of our every operation. For things are said to be alive which move of themselves. And hence it is that, what seems to be fundamentally the life of man is the principle of motion in him. But this principle, is that to which love is united as to an end because man is moved to all things from love. Hence some people say that from this principle of love they are moved to love their life as hunters love hunting and friends love friends. So therefore, Christ is our life, since Christ is the entire Principle of our life and operation and hence the Apostle says, "To me, to live is Christ," because Christ alone moved him. Christ alone was the Author of his life—his first beginning and his last end.

And Paul further remarked, "to die is to gain," and here he wisely spoke. For each one may consider it a gain for himself when he has imperfect life, which can be perfected. Thus the former sick man considers health a gain or advantage and rightly so. Our life is Christ. "Your life is hid, with Christ, in God." (Col. III, 3.) But here life is imperfect for, "While we are in the body, we are absent from the Lord," and therefore, when the body dies our life in us will be perfected, namely, perfected in the life of Christ to Whom we will then be present face to face.

2. Christ is our life because in Him is our entire love. "And I live, now not I; but Christ liveth in Me." (Gal. II, 20.) Man is said to live for that in which he chiefly centers his love and in which he is especially delighted. And hence, men who are especially delighted in study or in hunting say this is life for them. But each man has a certain personal love by which he seeks what is his own. As long, therefore, as anyone lives, seeking only that which is his, he lives to himself (or for himself) but when he seeks good things for others he is also said to live for them. Because therefore, the Apostle fixed his love on the Cross of Christ he used to say he was dead to himself, dead to his own selfish love. "With Christ I am nailed to the Cross" (Gal. II, 19), that is, "through the Cross of Christ, my own personal love is removed from me." Wherefore, Paul used to say, "I live, now not I, but Christ liveth in me, that is, I possess Christ to such a degree, through His love, that Christ Himself is my very life."

3. Christ is life for He is the end of our life. "Christ died for all; that they also who live, may not now live to themselves, but unto Him Who died for them, and rose again." (2 Cor. V, 15.)

Each one of us ought to consider himself dead unto himself, "that they also who live," may not live for themselves but live on account of the good only. "Live . . . unto Him Who died for them, and rose again," namely, Christ; so that they might consecrate their whole life to the service and honor of Christ.

The reason for this is because each one labouring takes the rule of his work according to the end. Hence if Christ is the end of our life we ought to regulate our life, not according to our own will, but according to the will of Christ. Observe that Saint Paul mentions two things, namely, that Christ died and rose for us and because of this, two things are required of us. For because Christ died for us, we ought also to die to ourselves, that is, we ought to deny ourselves for the sake of Christ. On the other hand, because Christ rose again for us, we ought to so die to sin, to our old manner of living and to our own selfishness, that finally we may rise to a new life with

Christ. Wherefore our Lord has not only said, "Deny thyself, and take up thy cross," but He has also added, "and follow Me"; namely, in the newness of life by advancing in virtue. (2 Cor. V.)

FEBRUARY 18

Peace and Victory Through Jesus

"These things I have spoken to you, that in Me you may have peace. In the world you shall have distress. But have confidence (in Me). I have overcome the world." (John XVI, 33.)

1. All these things which I have told you personally or of which I have spoken to you through My entire Gospel are for this purpose, that you return to Me, "so that in Me you may have peace." For the end or purpose of the Gospel is peace—in Christ. "Much peace to them that love Thy law. To them there is no stumbling-block." (Ps. CXVIII, 165.) The reason is because peace is opposed to disturbance, which arises from evils, oncoming and increasing. If moreover, someone has grief at times, and at the same time has joy exceeding these evils, it is evident that disturbance does not remain. And hence it is, that worldly men who are not united to God through love have tribulations without peace, but the Saints who possess God in their hearts through love, although they may have tribulations from the world, still they have peace in Christ. "God hath placed peace in thy borders." (Ps. CXLVII, 14.) For our end or purpose here in this world should be that we have peace in God. "My soul refused to be comforted," namely by worldly things; "but I remembered God, and was delighted." (Ps. LXXVI, 3.)

2. The need of this peace of Christ arises from this, that by it vexation from the world is taken away from us. Hence Christ says "In the world you shall have distress," that is, distress from worldly things, from persecutions. "Do not wonder if the world hate you." (1, John III, 19.) "Because I have chosen you out of the world, the world hateth you." (John XV, 19.)

3. Against this future and predicted distress Christ gives us His confidence as a remedy. "In Me have confidence. I have overcome the world." For He Himself will save us. As if

Christ said, "Hasten to Me, and you will find peace," and this because, "I have overcome the world," which persecutes you.

Christ conquered the world. First, by taking away from it the arms by which the world fights (or attacks us), namely greed and avarice. For Christ overcame worldly riches by poverty, worldly honors by His humility and death, sensual pleasures by His sufferings and labors.

Whosoever therefore so overcomes these evils conquers the world and this is what true faith does. "This is the victory which overcometh the world, your faith." (1 John V, 4), for since "faith is the substance of things to be hoped for," which things are spiritual and eternal, it makes us despise carnal and fleeting pleasures.

Secondly, Christ conquered the world by casting out Satan —the prince of the world and of the world's darkness. "Now shall the prince of this world be cast out." (John XII, 31.) Despoiling the principalities and powers, He hath exposed them confidently in open show, triumphing over them in Himself." (Col. II, 15.) From which fact (or victory of Christ over the devil and the world) it is clear, that the world and the devil must be overcome by us. "Shalt thou play with Him as with a bird, or tie Him up with thy handmaids?" (Job XL, 24.) Literally, after the Passion and victory of Christ, the young handmaids of Christ and the little children play with Him.

Thirdly, Christ conquered men of the world by converting them to Himself. The world rebelled (and still rebels) by provoking seditions among men of the world whom Christ has won to Himself. "The Pharisees therefore said among themselves, "Do you see that we prevail nothing? Behold the whole world is gone after Him!" (John XII, 19.)

Therefore, we need not fear worldly distress because Christ, our Helper and Leader, has conquered the world for us. (John XVI.)

FEBRUARY 19

The Narrow Gate

"Enter ye in at the narrow gate, for wide is the gate, and broad is the way that leadeth to destruction; and many there are who go in thereat." (Matth. VII, 13.)

1. Lest anyone should believe from what the Lord said, "Ask and you shall receive," that man receives everything from God, without good works, He also teaches that we receive through the performance of good works. Therefore, Christ said, "Enter ye in."

Augustine explains this in two ways. "Christ is the gate." "I am the door. By Me if any man enter in, he shall be saved." (John X, 9.) Without Him, without His Divine help, we cannot enter the kingdom of heaven. This gate is narrow through humility, for He humbled Himself unto the death of the cross. "The Lord spoke a brief word upon the earth." (Isaias X, 23.) Hence, He said, "Enter ye in by the narrow gate," that is, through the humility and the Passion of Christ. "For it behooved Christ to suffer, and so enter into His glory." (Luke XXIV, 26.) Hence through many tribulations we also must enter the kingdom of God.

This gate is likewise called charity. "This is the gate of the Lord. The just shall enter into it." (Ps. CXVII, 20.) This gate is narrowed by Divine Law and through it we must enter and can enter only by obeying God's Law and Commandments.

2. Our Lord assigns a reason for our entering in at the narrow gate, "because, wide is the gate, and broad the way that leadeth to destruction." He describes two gates, one wide, the other narrow. The gate is called wide because it is the devil's gate, widened by pride and presumption and ready to receive all, "unto destruction," but satisfying no one who enters. This gate is called the gate of iniquity and vice. It is wide because of the many vices which enter there. "Cursing, and lying, and killing, and theft, and adultery have overflown, and blood hath touched blood there." (Osee IV, 2.)

The gate is likewise wide because it is the work of sin. "Broad is the way," because at its beginning it seems to be wide but afterward it is narrowed, for it leads to destruction because, "the wages of sin is death, and many there are who enter thereat." Here our Lord mentions a number, "many," for truly, "the number of fools is infinite." (Eccle. I, 15.)

3. "How narrow is the gate, and straight is the way, that leadeth to life, and few are they that find it." (Matt. VII, 14.) This gate is the opposite of the wide gate because it is narrowed according to the regulation of Divine Law and it is a way opposed to the broad way. It seems that the way of charity is not wide. "I will show thee the way of wisdom, and I will lead thee by the paths of equity" (Prov. IV, 11), which way is contrary to the unjust and crooked way of sinners. "We have walked in difficult ways." We must remember there is the way of the flesh and the way of right reason. The way of charity or the way of right reason is the narrow way which leads to life eternal.

"And few are they who find it." The finding of the spirit or the way of the Spirit is rare and difficult but going the way of the flesh is easy and the reason is because the way of the flesh is selfish pleasure, and this pleasure is always at hand, but the way of the Spirit is hidden. "O how great is the multitude of Thy sweetness, O Lord, which Thou—hast hidden—from them that fear Thee." (Ps. XXX, 20.) Because this sweetness is hidden, few therefore are they who find it. But concerning the few that find it, and those who turn back in the search, Jesus says, "No man putting his hand to the plough, and looking back is fit for the kingdom of God." (Luke IX, 62.) (Matt. VII.)

FEBRUARY 20

The Renunciation of Worldly Things

"Denying ungodliness and worldly desires, we should live soberly, and justly, and Godly in this world." (Titus II, 12.)

1. Man is placed between the things of this world and spiritual goods wherein eternal happiness consists so that the more he cleaves to the one, the more he withdraws from the other and vice versa. Wherefore he that cleaves wholly to the things of this world, so as to make them his God and to regard them as the reason and rule of all he does, falls away altogether from spiritual goods. Hence this disorder is removed by the Commandments.

Nevertheless, for man to gain the aforesaid end, it is not necessary for him to renounce the things of the world entirely, since he can by using them properly attain to eternal happiness, that is, he must not make them his God; but he will attain more speedily to eternal happiness by renouncing the goods of this world entirely. Wherefore the evangelical counsels are given for this purpose.

Now the goods of this world which come into use in human life consist in three things, namely, in external wealth pertaining to the concupiscence of the eyes; carnal pleasures pertaining to the concupiscence of the flesh; and honors which pertain to the pride of life, according to 1 John II, 16; and it is for renouncing these altogether, as far as possible, that the evangelical counsels exist. Moreover, every form of the religious life that professes the state of perfection is based on these three—since riches are renounced by poverty, carnal pleasures by perpetual chastity, and the pride of life by the bondage of obedience.

2. Now if a man observes these absolutely, this is in accordance with the counsels as stated. But if a man observes any one of them in a particular case, he is taking that counsel in a restricted sense, namely, as applying to that particular case. For example, when anyone gives an alms to a poor man, not being bound so to do, he follows the counsels in that particular case. In like manner, when a man for some determined time refrains from carnal pleasures that he may give himself to prayer, he observes the counsel for that particular time. . . . And again, when a man follows not his own will as to some deed which he might do lawfully, he follows the counsel in that particular case; for instance, if he should do good to his enemy when he is not bound to or if he forgives an injury of which he might justly seek to be avenged. In this way, also, all particular counsels may be reduced to these three general and perfect counsels. (Ia., 2ae, q. 108, a. IV.)

SEPTUAGESIMA SUNDAY

We Must Labour in the Lord's Vineyard

"Going out about the third hour, he saw others standing in the marketplace idle. And he said to them, 'Go you also into my vineyard, and I will give you what shall be just'." (Matt. XX, 3.)

1. In these words of sacred Scripture four things are pointed out. First, the goodness of our Lord in "Going out," to save His people. For Christ went out to lead men into the vineyard of His justice and this was an act of His infinite goodness. Moreover, it is said, He went out in five ways. First, at the beginning of the world, secondly, at His birth, thirdly, at the time of His Passion as the Father of His Children, fourthly, as a merciful and just Judge and fifthly, as a severe Judge.

1. At the beginning of the world, Christ went out as the sower, by sowing the seed of His Divine Word among His creatures. 2. At His nativity, He went out illuminating the world. "I will not rest until her just One come forth as brightness, and her Saviour be lighted as a lamp." (Isaias LXII, 1.) "I came forth from the Father, and I am come into the world. Again I leave the world, and I go to the Father." (John XVI, 28.) 3. In His Passion, Christ again went forth by saving His own from the power of the devil and from all vices. "My just One is near at hand. My Saviour is gone forth." (Isaias LI, 5.) 4. Christ went forth as a householder, providing good things for His children. "The kingdom of heaven is like unto an householder who went out early in the morning to hire labourers into his vineyard." (Matt. XX, 1.) 5. He went out finally in judgment, as a visitator, passing severe judgment upon the wicked and like a most brave fighter, conquering His rebels, punishing them justly, like a just judge for evil deeds committed.

2. The second point in the above is the foolishness of man. For nothing is more foolish in this life than that a man should live in idleness, who ought to so work for himself that he might live eternally. "He saw others standing in the market place idle." That market place is the present life. A market place is that place at which things are bought and sold and resembles the present life which is full of quarrels in buying and selling and during which advancement in grace and possession of heavenly glory are sold for good works. These

are idle because they have lost part of their life. And they are called idle, not only those who do evil, but also those who neglected to do good. And just as the idle do not follow the end for which they are destined, so neither do those who deliberately neglect to do good. The end of man is eternal life. Therefore, whosoever works in the manner in which God has commanded him to work, such a person will obtain eternal life but idleness and laziness contribute nothing to the possession of life everlasting.

Therefore, it is great foolishness to live in idleness because from idleness as from a bad woman teacher, bad knowledge is acquired and because the need of eternal good is forfeited through idleness and an eternal reward is lost for a little laziness.

3. The third point evident is the necessity of working in the Lord's vineyard. "Go you also into My vineyard." This vineyard into which they are sent to labour is the vineyard of justice in which there are as many branches as there are virtues. In this vineyard we should labour in five ways. First, by planting in it good works and virtues, secondly, by eradicating and getting rid of the thorns, that is our vices. Thirdly, by cutting off superfluous branches. "Every branch that beareth not fruit, He will purge it, that it may bring forth more fruit." (John XV, 2.) Fourthly, by driving away from the vineyard the little foxes, that is, the devils, and fifthly, by guarding it from thieves, namely, the flattery and distractions of man.

4. The reward of labour is pointed out in these words: "I will give to you that which is just." The reward for those labouring in this vineyard is a penny each, which represents a thousand pieces of silver. And that is what is meant by "The peaceable had a vineyard . . . and every man bringeth forth the fruit thereof a thousand pieces of silver." (Cant. VIII, 11.) A thousand pieces of silver are the thousand joys of eternity which are signified by a penny.

MONDAY WITHIN SEPTUAGESIMA

Good Works

"If any man build upon this foundation, gold, silver, precious stones, wood, hay, stubble; every man's work shall be manifest." (1 Cor. III, 12.)

1. The works by which man becomes initiated into spiritual and Divine things are compared to gold, silver and precious stones which are solid, brilliant and precious; so that at least by gold is meant those things by which man tends toward His God through contemplation and love. "I counsel thee to buy of me gold, fire tried, that thou mayest be made rich" (Apoc. III, 18), that is, wisdom with charity. By silver is meant the actions through which man clings to the spiritual things which he must believe, love, and contemplate. Hence, silver represents the love of our neighbor, but by precious stones are designated the works of the different virtues by which the human soul is adorned.

On the other hand, the human works by which man tends to procure temporal things are compared to "stubble" which is worthless, for stubble is light and easily burned. But there are certain grades of stubble and according as they are more substantial are the less easily burned. So men themselves, among carnal creatures are also more worthy and are preserved through succession and hence they are compared to "wood." But the flesh of man is more easily corrupted than stubble, by sickness and death, wherefore, it is compared to "hay". Moreover those things which pertain to the glory of earthly honors are compared to stubble, because they very easily pass away.

So therefore, to build upon this foundation of gold, silver, and stones is to build upon the foundation of faith; upon those things which pertain to the contemplation of Divine wisdom, the love of God and of our neighbor, the devotion of the saints and the cultivation of the virtues. On the other hand, to build upon "wood, hay or stubble" is to build upon those things which pertain to the plan and fancy of human affairs, care of the flesh and vain glory.

2. Moreover, it happens that man craves for temporal things in three ways. First, in so far as he fixes his heart on them and makes them his end, and because of this he sins mortally. In this way, man does not build, but with the foun-

dation reversed he places the wrong foundation. For the end is the foundation in things desired.

Secondly, anyone who strives to use temporal things for the glory of God does not build upon wood, hay, and stubble but upon gold, silver and precious stones.

Thirdly, anyone, even though he does not set his heart on temporal things nor wish because of them to act contrary to God but still loves temporal things more than he should, so that by them he is drawn away from the things of God, sins venially. This means building upon wood, hay and stubble because the works pertaining to the care of earthly things have little aids to venial sins, because of the more vehement love for temporal things—which affection according as it inheres more or less in us is compared to wood, hay and stubble. (1 Cor. III.)

TUESDAY WITHIN SEPTUAGESIMA

Our Reward

"Every man shall receive his own reward, according to his own labor."

1. This reward is common to all and proper to each one. Common to all because all will see the same Object and all will enjoy the same Object, namely God. "Thou shalt abound in delights in the Almighty, and shall lift up thy face to God." (Job XXII, 25.) "In that day the Lord of hosts shall be a crown of glory, and a garland of joy to the residue of His people." (Isaias XXVIII, 5.) Therefore, Matt. XXVIII, says that all laborers in the vineyard received an equal reward.

2. On the other hand, there will be a special reward for each one because one person will see the Beatific Vision more clearly than another and one will enjoy this Vision more fully than another according to the measure determined for each one. Hence it is written, "In My Father's house there are many mansions." (John XIV, 2), on account of which Christ said: "Every man shall receive his own reward."

Our attention is indirectly directed to the measure of each one's reward when He adds, "according to his own labour." Still the equality of the reward is not designated according to the quantity of the labour to the reward, but according to equality of proportion, so that where there is greater work done for God's sake, there the reward will be greater. "For that which is at present momentary and light of our tribulation, worketh for us above measure exceedingly, an eternal weight of glory." (II. Cor. IV, 17.)

3. But labour can be understood to be more preferable or greater in three ways.

First, according to the form of charity to which the essential reward of merit corresponds, namely, the reward of the enjoyment of the Divine Vision. Hence it is said, "He who loves Me will be loved by My Father, and I will love him and manifest Myself to him." (John XIV, 23.) Hence he who labours from the greater charity, or love of God, although he produces lesser labour receives more of the essential reward.

Secondly, labor can be understood from the nature of the labour and may be the more preferable. For just as one is rewarded the more who is engaged in the nobler work, as the architect, although he does less physical labour than the workman in his building, receives a greater reward, so also in Divine things he who is engaged in a nobler undertaking receives a greater, though accidental, reward.

Thirdly, from the quantity of the labor the reward may be the greater and this indeed can happen in two ways. For sometimes the greater labor receives the greater reward, chiefly in regard to the remission of punishment, for example, he who fasts longer and travels farther, and also in regard to the joy which he receives from the greater labour. On the other hand, sometimes a work is greater from action of the will. For in those things which we do from our own will, or selfishness, we receive the smaller reward. And such greatness of work increases not but lessens the reward. Hence it is said "that they who hope in the Lord shall renew their strength, they shall take wings as eagles, they shall run and not be weary, they shall walk and not faint." (Isaias XL, 31.) Herein is a reward. (1 Cor. III.)

WEDNESDAY WITHIN SEPTUAGESIMA

The Necessity of Carefulness

"Wherefore he that thinketh himself to stand, let him take heed lest he fall." (1 Cor. X, 12.)

1. From the example of the Jews who because of punishment were prostrated in the desert, we are advised by the Apostle to be on our guard against a fall. Hence Scripture implies four things of interest to the wise man. First, the multitude of those falling, when St. Paul says, "wherefore." Secondly, the uncertainty of those standing, when he adds, "he that thinketh himself to stand." Thirdly, the necessity of being careful, when he advises, "let him take heed." Fourthly, the ease with which we fall and ruin ourselves, when he declares, "lest he fall." The Apostle says, "wherefore," as if he said, "Those, and many are they, who blessed with favors from God, still perish on account of their sins." Wherefore, from a consideration of these, who think from a certain conjecture that they can stand, that is that they are secure in the grace and charity of God, "let man take heed," pay careful attention, "lest he fall, by sinning, or by leading others into sin." "How art thou fallen from heaven, O Lucifer?" (Isaias XIV, 12.) "A thousand shall fall at thy side." (Ps. XC, 7.) "See, therefore, brethren, how you walk circumspectly, not as unwise." (Ephes. V, 15.)

2. It must be observed that many things incite us to fall. First, the weakness of nature, secondly, the weight of our sins, thirdly, the multitude of those falling, fourthly, the dangers of the way, fifthly, the variety of the offenses, sixthly, the ignorance of those falling, seventhly, the bad example of those who fall, and finally, the lusts of the flesh.

First, the weakness of nature causes a fall, just as children, the aged, the infirm, easily fall. "Youths shall faint, and young men shall fall by infirmity." (Isaias XL, 30.) "The Lord is the everlasting God. . . . It is He that giveth strength to the weary, and increaseth force and might." (Isaias XL, 28.) This fall happens through tepidity and instability in the performance of good works.

Secondly, the burden of our sins causes us to fall; just as the beast of burden falls under a very heavy load. "The workers of iniquity are fallen." (Ps. XXXV, 13.)

Thirdly, the multitude of those falling contributes to our fall, just as the tree, or the house in falling, pulls many other things down with it, and this happens through the attack of the enemy.

Fourthly, the dangers of the way incite to a fall just as those who are not careful while walking fall on the slippery street. "Take heed lest thou slip with thy tongue, and fall in the sight of thy enemies, who lie in wait for thee; and thy fall be incurable unto death." (Eccles. XXVIII, 30.) This happens through careless guard of the senses.

Fifthly, the variety of snares, as the bird is caught in the middle of the trap. "A just man shall fall seven times." (Prov. XXIV, 7.) This happens through the wickedness of creatures. "Seek not to be like men, neither desire to be with them." (Prov. I, 1.)

Sixthly, the ignorance of those falling causes us to fall just as the blind fall easily. "They are blind, and leaders of the blind. And if the blind lead the blind both fall into the pit." (Matt. XV, 14.) This happens through negligence in learning what is necessary. Therefore ignorance of fundamentals is a certain blindness which causes us to fall.

Seventhly, the bad example of those falling incites to a fall, just as the angels who fell because of Lucifer. "A just man falling down before the wicked, is as a fountain troubled with the foot, and a corrupted spring." (Prov. XXV, 27.)

Finally, the lusts of the flesh contribute to our ruin. For the body which is corrupted pulls down the soul, as a stone around the neck of a drowning man. "A mountain falling cometh to nought . . . so in like manner thou shalt destroy man. His flesh while he shall live, shall have pain, and his soul shall mourn over him." (Job. XIV, 18.) This fall of man happens through the superfluous and unbridled lusts of the flesh. (1 Cor. X.)

THURSDAY WITHIN SEPTUAGESIMA

Interior Reformation

"Be not conformed to this world, but be reformed in the newness of your mind, that you may prove what is the good, and the acceptable, and the perfect will of God." (Rom. XII, 2.)

1. Conformity to this world is forbidden. "Be not conformed to this world," that is, to the things of this world, which pass away with time. For the present world is a cer-

tain measure of those things which perish in time. Moreover, man becomes conformed in mind to temporal things by loving them. He is also conformed to this world when he imitates the life of those living in a worldly fashion. "This then I say and testify in the Lord. That henceforth you walk not as also the Gentiles walk in the vanity of their mind." (Ephes. IV, 17.)

2. Interior reformation of the mind is commanded when it is said: "Be reformed in the newness of your mind." The mind of man here means reason, in so far as through reason man judges the things which must be done, but man has this mind entire and vigorous from his creation. "God created man of the earth, and made him after His own image. He created of him a helpmate . . . and filled their hearts with wisdom; and showed to them both good and evil." (Eccles. XVII, 1, 6.) But through sin man's mind became corrupted as if it had grown old long before its time. And consequently man lost through sin his beauty and sense of propriety.

Therefore, the Apostle advises that "we be reformed," that is that we assume again that form and beauty of mind which our mind gracefully possessed; which indeed takes place through the grace of the Holy Spirit, in which through participation man ought to have such a good will; that those who do not yet possess that grace may possess it in perceiving it in man; and those who have this grace of God already may further advance in it and in God's friendship. "Be reformed in the newness of your mind." "Be renewed in the spirit of your mind." (Ephes. IV, 23), namely, in your exterior actions, "in the newness of your mind," that is, according to newness of grace which you percieve in your soul.

3. The reason for that aforesaid advice is, "that you may prove what is the will of God." We must remember that just as a man who has an infected taste has not a right judgment concerning delicacies; but those things which are sweet, he despises as long as his bad taste endures; on the other hand, those things which are abominable he desires; but the man who has a sound, healthy taste has right judgment concerning delicacies. So too, a man who has a corrupted love, as if conformed to worldly things, has not a correct judgment concerning goodness; but he who has a right and healthy love has a right judgment about goodness, for his mind is renewed through God's grace. Therefore, Saint Paul says, "Be not conformed to this world, but be reformed in the newness of your mind, that you may prove, 'that is, that you may realize from

experience' taste and see that the Lord is sweet." (Ps. XXXIII, 9.)

"What is the will of God," by which He wishes you to be saved. "This is the will of God, your sanctification" (1 Thess. IV), that is, God wishes us to be good and honorable and to this end He leads us by His commandments. "I will show to thee, O man, what is good, and what the Lord requires of thee." (Mich. VI.) "And pleasing," namely, a good will is delightful in this that God wishes us to be well disposed for the reception of His grace. And not only useful to reach our destined end but also "the perfect will of God," uniting us to our end which is God.

Therefore, they who are not conformed to this world but reformed in the newness of their mind, experience the good and the acceptable and the perfect will of God. "But those who remain in their old evil ways are conformed to this world, and judge the will of God not to be good, but burdensome and useless. (Rom. XII.)

FRIDAY WITHIN SEPTUAGESIMA

Do Good Always

"In doing good, let us not fail, for in due time we shall reap (a reward) not failing." (Gal. VI, 9.)

The great Apostle St. Paul mentioned three things in the above words which he spoke to the Galatians. He advises us to do good. We should do good because all things naturally teach us to do good.

1. Because all things are good. "God saw all the things that He had made and they were very good." (Gen. I, 34.) Sinners, therefore, can be sufficiently ashamed of themselves in such a multitude of creatures who are good, whereas sinners themselves are evil.

2. We ought to do good because all things are naturally intended to do good and whenever a person sacrifices himself, that is a sign of Divine goodness. The goodness of God is poured forth in all things. It is a great indication of Divine goodness that each creature is compelled to make some sacrifice. Now especially during the holy season of Lent, when we should all do penance, we have excellent opportunities to do good by making many little sacrifices; sacrifices of our free time by attending daily Mass and Lenten devotions.

3. We ought to do good because all things naturally desire goodness and tend to what is good. Goodness is that which is desired by all, even the sinner seeks goodness but it is only a fictitious good and not the real good which he seeks. The evil looks good to the sinner and for that reason he longs for it.

4. The Apostle advises that we should not fail in doing good. There are three things which help a man to persevere in doing good. First, frequent and devout prayer by which man implores God's help, lest he succumb to temptation . . . "Watch and pray, lest you enter into temptation." (Matt. XXVI, 41.) Secondly, a continual wholesome fear, for as soon as man thinks that he is so secure that he cannot fall he then and there fails to perform good works. "Unless you hold yourself diligently in the fear of the Lord, thy house will be quickly overthrown." (Eccl. XXVII, 4.) The fear of the Lord is the safeguard of life. Thirdly, avoid venial sins which are the occasion of mortal sins which frequently destroy your building of good works. "He who despises little things shall fall little by little." (Eccl. X, 1.)

5. The Apostle also mentions a reward, a suitable, plentiful and eternal reward. "In due time," said he, "we shall reap without failing." That is, an unfailing reward.

First, the reward will be suitable, that is, a reward in its own time, in a suitable and convenient time, namely, in the day of judgment when each one will receive the reward of his labor, for just as the farmer does not immediately reap the benefit from the seed which he sows, but in a suitable time, so we also will be rewarded for our labor at the proper time. "Be patient therefore, until the coming of the Lord. Behold, the husbandman waits for the precious fruit of the earth, patiently bearing until he receives the early and latter rain." (St. James V, 7.)

Secondly, we will receive a plentiful reward. "We shall reap." In reaping, an abundance is included. "He who soweth in blessings, shall also reap blessings." (2 Cor. IX, 6), and St. Matthew (V, 12), says: "Your reward is very great in heaven."

Thirdly our reward will be eternal, "not failing." We shall reap without failing. Therefore, we should do good, not for a short time only, but always. Let us therefore not fail in doing good to others because we will never fail in reaping a reward, which will be suitable, abundant, everlasting. "Whatever thy hand can do, do it quickly." (Eccl. IX.) Hence we must not fail in acquiring merit by our good works, since we expect an eternal reward. If man does not do good from a supernatural motive, neither does God grant him a reward. "Therefore, whilst we have time, let us work good to all men, but especially to those who are of the household of the faith." (Galatians V, 10.)

SATURDAY WITHIN SEPTUAGESIMA

Our Lord's Prayer in the Garden

"And going a little further, He fell upon His face, praying and saying, My Father, if it be possible, let this chalice pass from Me. Nevertheless not as I will, but as Thou wilt." (Matt. XXVI, 39.)

Here a threefold condition for prayer is recommended by Our Divine Lord, namely, carefulness, humility, devotion. First, carefulness, in going a little further, because He withdrew even from those whom He had chosen. "When you pray, enter your room, and having closed the door, pray to thy Father in secret." But observe that Our Lord advanced not a great deal, but a little, so that He might prove He is not far from those calling upon Him and also that they (the Apostles) might see Him praying and might acquire a method of praying.

Second, humility. "He fell upon His face." By this, Christ left us an example of humility. First, because humility is necessary for prayer, and because Peter had said: "If I should die with Thee, I will not deny Thee." Therefore the Lord continued to pray so that neither the Apostles, nor we, might depend too much upon our own power.

Third, devotion is shown when He said: "My Father," etc. It is necessary for a person praying to pray devotionally. Hence He said, "My Father," because Christ is the Son of the Father by nature, and we are sons by adoption.

"If it be possible, let this chalice pass from Me. Nevertheless not as I will, but as Thou wilt." Here is set forth the power of every good and persevering prayer. Christ prayed according to His affection, in as far as His prayer expressed the affections of His sensitive nature. He did this to teach us three things:
1. That He might prove He assumed a true human nature

with all its natural affections. 2. That He might show that it is not lawful for man to wish what the Lord does not wish. 3. That He might teach us to subject our affections to the Divine Will.

Christ, acting as man, manifested a human will when He said: "Let this chalice pass from Me," for He was then wishing for something human. But because He wished His desire to be directed to God, Christ added: "However, not as I will, but as Thou wilt." Christ had two wills, one from the Father, as He was God; the other a human will as He was man, and He submitted to the Father this will in all things so that we might submit our wills to the holy Will of God in all things. "I came down from Heaven, not to do My own will, but the will of the Father Who sent Me." (John VI, 38.)

SEXAGESIMA SUNDAY

The Seed

"The sower went out to sow his seed." (Luke VIII, 5.)

1. The zeal of the Sower is to be observed first of all. It is Christ who went out. He went out in three ways, namely, from the bosom of the Father, not changing His place, secondly, from Judea to the people, and thirdly, from the depths of His wisdom to the open street of His public teaching. Christ sowed the seed of His doctrine in the hearts of men. For the seed is the beginning of the fruit. Hence every good work is from God. What did Christ sow? The seed of His own doctrine. That seed is the Word of God. And what did it do? It made sons of God, like unto Him, from Whom the Word of God came.

2. The obstacles to the seed. The seed is interfered with in three ways, for three things are required for its effectual growth; namely, that it be preserved in the memory, secondly, that it be planted in love and that it be kept with great and tender care. On the other hand these three things are destroyed by three things, memory by vanity, love by hardness of heart, care or solicitude by the germination of vices.

First of all, "some (seed) fell by the wayside." The way is open to every traveller, just like the heart which is exposed to each thought. Hence, when the word of God falls into a vain and unsteady heart (or mind), it falls by the wayside, and is subjected to a twofold danger. Matthew mentions only one namely, "the birds of the air devour it." But Luke speaks of two dangers, namely, "it is trampled down and devoured by the birds." Because the vain receive the Word of God it is trampled down by proud thoughts and by society. Wherefore the devil rejoices greatly when he can trample down, destroy and snatch from the hearts of men this Divine seed—which is the Word of God.

Secondly, hardness of heart interferes with the seed of God's word and this is opposed to charity, because hardness of heart weakens charity. For hard is that which is fettered in itself and narrowed in its own fears, while love causes the lover to be transformed into the Beloved, whence His love is diffused. "Other some fell among rocks." Therefore Christ says, "I will give you a new heart, and put a new spirit within you, and I will take away the stony heart out of your flesh. I will put My spirit in the midst of you, and I will cause you to walk in the ways of My commandments, and to keep My judgments, and do them." (Ezech. XXXVI, 26.) For there are some people whose hearts are privately open to every love but lack true love; while there are others who have good love but very little of it; hence they have no profound love. Profound love is present when the affection is profound. Therefore, he has a profound or deep love who loves all things for God's sake and places nothing prior to the love of God. Some there are who are well delighted in God but more delighted with other things. These are not entirely attracted by the love of God and such lovers have not much ground for the Divine seed to grow in their hearts—such have no solid foundation.

It follows, "that other (seed) fell upon stony ground, where they had not much earth and they sprang up immediately because they had no deepness of earth and when the sun was up they were scorched and because they had not root they withered away." (Matth. XIII, 5.) For those who think deeply, think long, but those who think not deeply break forth immediately into action, hence they depart quickly. So it is with those who hear quickly, but are not firmly established in the word of God, they have "no deepness of earth," no depth of love and charity.

Thirdly, the destruction of the fruit (of the word of God) results because if man loves riches more, when the time of tribulation comes he receives that which he loves the more.

Hence, "when the sun was up, they (the seed) were scorched," by extravagant passion. "And because they had no root they withered away," for their root was not God. "Other seeds fell among thorns," which are worldly anxieties, anger, "and the thorns grown up with it, choked it." (Matth. XIII.)

MONDAY WITHIN SEXAGESIMA

The Goodness of God

"If God be for us, who is against us? He that spared not even His own Son, but delivered Him up for us all, how hath He not also, with Him, given us all things?" (Rom. VIII, 31.)

1. When the Apostle had made mention of many sons, saying, "You have received the Spirit of adoption of sons," he separated from all these sons, this Son, saying, "His own Son," that is, not adopted but the natural and co-eternal Son, of Whom the Father said: "This is My Beloved Son, in Whom I am well pleased, hear ye Him." (Matth. III, 17.)

Moreover, he says, "that God spared not His own Son," which must be understood that God did not exempt Him from pain and punishment. Although God could have spared Him and exempted Him for there was no fault in His beloved Son. Still God the Father did not spare His Son, Who is above all things, perfect God, but for our advantage He subjected His Son to the Passion and death of the Cross.

And this is what Saint Paul has in mind, when he says, "He delivered Him up for us all," that is, He sacrificed His Son in the Passion for the expiation of our sins. "He was wounded for our iniquities. He was bruised for our sins. The Lord has laid upon Him the iniquity of us all." (Isaias LIII, 5.) God the Father delivered Him up to death by deciding that His Son should become Man and suffer, by inspiring His human will with the love of charity, whereby the Son willingly consented to His Passion and death. Hence it is written He gave Himself. "He hath delivered Himself for us. . . . Be ye therefore, followers of God as most dear children, and walk in love, as Christ also hath loved us, and hath delivered Himself for us, an oblation and a sacrifice to God for an odour of sweetness. (Ephes. V, 1.) He delivered Himself, sacrificed Himself even for Judas.

Moreover it must be observed that Saint Paul emphasizes the words, "He spared not even His own Son," as if Paul had said, "God the Father delivered up to suffering and tribulation not only other saints for the salvation of mankind but also His own Son."

2. Hence, having delivered Him up for us and given all things to us, Paul adds, "How hath He not also, with Him given us all things," namely, superior things, things of the Divine Person, for our enjoyment, all inferior things to use, not only prosperous but also adverse things. "All things are yours and you are Christ's, and Christ's is God's." (Cor. III, 22.) Hence it is evident, that "Nothing is wanting to those who fear (love) the Lord." "The Lord is a firmament to them that fear (love) Him, and His covenant shall be made manifest to them." (Ps. XXIV, 14.) (Rom. VIII.)

TUESDAY WITHIN SEXAGESIMA

The Commemoration of Our Lord's Passion

"Think diligently upon Him that endured such opposition from sinners against Himself, that you be not wearied, fainting in your minds." (Heb. XII, 3.)

1. The Apostle advises us to diligent consideration. "Think diligently upon Him," that is, think upon our suffering and crucified Saviour again and again. "In all thy ways, think of Him, and He will direct thy steps." (Prov. III, 6.) The reason is, because in your every tribulation you will find a remedy in the cross of Christ, for there on the cross is obedience to God, "He humbled Himself becoming obedient unto death." There on the cross, is the affection of piety and respect for parents, for from the cross Christ took care of His mother. There too, on the cross is the most remarkable example of charity; when Christ prayed for His persecutors, saying: "Father, forgive them, for they know not what they do." (Luke XXIII.) Likewise there on the Cross, Christ taught us to be patient in time of trials. "I was dumb, and was humbled, and kept silence from good things, and My sorrow was renewed." (Ps. XXXVIII, 3.) Likewise and above all things, Christ on the cross teaches us final perseverance; wherefore

He persevered unto death. "Father, into Thy hands, I commend My spirit." (Luke XXIII.)

Therefore, on the cross is found the example of every virtue. Hence Saint Augustine says, "The cross was not only the instrument of Christ's suffering, but also the pulpit of His teachings."

2. But what must we think diligently upon? Three things.

First, the nature of Christ's Passion. "He endured such opposition," that is, affliction and opposition from words, when His enemies shouted, "Vah, Thou that destroyeth the temple of God, and in three days dost rebuild it, save Thy own self. If thou be the Son of God, come down from the cross." (Matth. XXI, 40.) "Thou wilt deliver Me from the contradictions of the people." (Ps. XVII, 44.) "For a sign, He will be contradicted." (Luke III.) "He endured such opposition," that is, such serious and shameful insults. "Oh all you who pass by the way, attend, and see, if there be any sorrow like unto My sorrow." (Lam. I, 12.)

Secondly, think of what Christ suffered, and for whom did He suffer. He suffered the death of the cross and that for sinners. "Christ died once for our sins, the just for the unjust, that He might offer us unto God, being put to death indeed in the flesh, but enlivened in the spirit." (1 Peter III, 11.)

Thirdly, think diligently upon the person suffering. Before His passion even from the beginning of the world Christ suffered in His members, for the vision of His Passion was ever present to His Divine mind, but during the Passion, Christ suffered in His own Person. Hence it is written, "He delivered Himself to him, who judged Him unjustly, His own self bore our sins in His body upon the tree, that we being dead to sins, should live to justice; and by Whose stripes you were healed." (1 Peter II, 24.)

3. The usefulness of this reflection is revealed by Saint Paul in these words, "that you be not wearied." For devout and frequent reflection on Christ's Passion will cause us not to become wearied, "but enlivened in spirit." Gregory says, "if the Passion of Christ is recalled to mind, nothing will be so hard, but will be patiently endured." Hence you will not fail, since you will not be wearied in mind, you will not fail in your love for the true faith and you will not be wanting in good works.

Saint Paul places the reason saying, "You have not as yet resisted unto blood, striving against sin." (Heb. XII, 4.) As if he had said, "you should not fail in your tribulations for yourselves, because you have not yet endured such opposition as Christ endured. For He shed His blood for us." (Hebr. XII.)

WEDNESDAY WITHIN SEXAGESIMA

The Necessity of Vigilance

"Watch, for you know not at what hour the Lord will come." (Matth. XXIV, 42.)

1. The Lord warns us to be vigilant because of the uncertainty of the hour of our death. He says therefore, that the day is uncertain and that no one can trust in his present state, for wheresoever you go, one person is suddenly taken away by death, and another remains. Therefore, you ought to be diligent and vigilant. "Watch therefore." And as Jerome says, "the Lord willed to make the end of our life uncertain; so that we might always expect it." For man fails in three things especially: he fails to think, he fails to act, he fails in vigilance, therefore, the Lord says, "Watch," so that your minds might be raised up to God through contemplation. "I sleep, and my heart watcheth. The voice of My beloved knocking." (Cant. V, 3.) Likewise, "watch," lest you be taken in death. For He who watches for the Lord is diligent in the performance of good works. "Be sober, and watch, because your adversary the devil, as a roaring lion, goeth about, seeking whom he may devour." (1, Peter V, 8.) "How long wilt thou sleep, O sluggard?" (Prov. VI, 9.) "Go to the ant, O sluggard, and consider her ways, and learn wisdom." (Prov. VI, 6.)

2. "Because you know not at what hour the Lord will come." Augustine says that this is necessary for us and for those who have gone before us, and even necessary for the Apostles because the Lord comes in two ways. He will come at the end of the world to all in general. Likewise He comes to each one at the end of life. Therefore, His coming is twofold, at the end of the world and also at death, and both comings He wishes to be uncertain in regard to the hour.

These comings complement one another. They are both proper because as a person is found (spiritually or otherwise) at the first coming of our Lord, so will he be found at His second coming. Wherefore, Augustine says, "The last day of the world will find that man unprepared, whom the last day of life found unprepared."

Likewise, mention is made in sacred scripture of another coming of the Master, namely, His invisible coming, when the Lord comes to the mind with His inspirations and grace. "If He comes to me, I shall not see Him." (Job IX, 11.) Thus He comes to many but they do not see Him. Hence, you ought to watch a great deal and carefully, so that if He should knock at the door of your heart you may open it unto Him. "Behold, I stand at the gate, and knock. If any man shall hear My voice, and open to Me the door, I will come to him, and will sup with him, and he with Me." (Apoc. III, 20.) (Matth. XXIV.)

THURSDAY WITHIN SEXAGESIMA

Watch Always

"Watch ye therefore, because you know not at what hour your Lord will come.

"But this know ye, that if the good man of the house knew at what hour the thief would come, he would certainly watch, and would not suffer his house to be broken open." (Matth. XXIV, 42.)

Because the good man of the house knows not at what hour the thief will come, it is necessary that he watch all night long.

The house is the human soul. In this house of the soul, man should be at rest. "When I go into my house," that is into my conscience, "I shall repose myself with her." (Wis. VIII, 16.) The good man of this house is right reason. "The king that sitteth on the throne of judgment, scattereth away all evil with his look. But who can say, My heart is clean, I am pure from sin?" (Prov. XX, 8.)

Sometimes the thief breaks open the house. The thief is a certain persuasion by false doctrine or a certain temptation. He is called a thief because, "He that entereth not by the door into the sheepfold, but climbeth up another way, the same is a thief and a robber." (John X, 1.) The door is properly called natural knowledge or natural right. Therefore whosoever enters the house of his soul through right reason, enters by the door but he who enters by bad desires, impurity, anger and sins of this nature is a thief.

Thieves are accustomed to come and break into homes at night. Hence if they come in the daytime, they may not be so much feared. Thus when man is in the contemplation of Divine things, then temptation does not assail him, but when he leaves off work and gives himself to idleness; then the devil tempts him, and temptation attacks or perhaps overcomes him. Therefore the Psalmist wisely makes this prophecy and prayer: "When my strength shall fail me, do not Thou, O Lord forsake me." (Ps. LXX, 9.)

Hence we ought to watch, for we know not when the Lord will come to judge us. Or we can refer to the day of our death. "For when they shall say peace, and security; then shall sudden destruction come upon them. Therefore be ye ready, for at what hour you know not, the Son of Man will come. Therefore, let us watch, and be sober . . . having on the breastplate of faith and charity, and for a helmet the hope of salvation." (1 Thess. V, 3.) Hence Chrysostom says, that men anxious about their temporal affairs lie awake and watch at night. And if they watch for their worldly things by so much the more must we watch for spiritual possessions.

We must here take notice of a certain comparison which Augustine makes concerning three servants. He speaks of three servants who love and watch the coming of the Lord. One servant says, "My Lord will come quickly (or soon), and therefore I will watch." A second servant says, "The Lord will delay in coming, and therefore, I desire to watch." A third servant says, "I do not know, when he will come, and so I will watch." Which of these three servants speaks the more wisely? Augustine says that the first servant may be badly deceived, for if he thinks the Lord may come speedily and the Lord is slow in coming, he is in danger, as he might fall asleep from weariness. The second servant may be deceived but is not in danger. But the third servant acts wisely, for being in doubt, he watches always for the coming of his Lord. Therefore it is unwise to set or determine any special time. "Of the times and the moments, brethren, you need not that we should write to you. For yourselves know perfectly, that the day of the Lord shall so come, as a thief in the night. Therefore, let us not sleep, as others do; but let us watch, and be sober. We beseech you brethren to rebuke the unquiet, comfort the feeble-minded, support the weak, be patient towards all men—ever following that which is good towards each other, and towards all men." (1 Thess. V, 1, 6, 14.) (Matth. XXIV.)

FRIDAY WITHIN SEXAGESIMA

On Serving God

"Thou shalt not have strange Gods before me." (Ex. XX, 3.)

We are commanded to worship One God and we are encouraged to do this for five reasons. First, because of the dignity of God, secondly, because of His generosity to us, thirdly, because of the certainty and strength of His promise, fourthly, because of the misfortunes in serving the devil, fifthly, because of the greatness of our gain or reward in serving God.

1. Because of the dignity of God which if it is taken away an injury is done to God. For to each dignity, reverence is due. Hence the betrayer of a king is he who robs the king of that honor which belongs to him; and some do this to God. "They changed the glory of the incorruptible God, into the likeness of a corruptible man." (Rom. I, 23.) And this is extremely displeasing to God.

2. Because of God's generosity to us, we should serve Him. For every good which we possess has come to us from God; and this also pertains to the dignity of God, since He is the Maker and Giver of all good things. "When thou openest Thy hand, they shall all be filled with good." (Ps. CIII, 28.) Thou art exceedingly ungrateful, therefore, if you do not recognize God's gifts to you; moreover you are ungrateful, if you worship any other God, but Him; as the children of Israel who after being led out of Egypt through God, that is when we seek aid from man which we should ask from God. "Blessed is the man, whose hope is in the Name of the Lord." (Ps. XXXIII, 5.) "But now, after you have known God, or rather been known by God, how turn you to the weak and needy elements; which you desire to serve again?" (Gal. IV, 9.)

3. Because of the certainty and strength of God's promise, we should serve Him. For we renounced the devil (when we were baptized) and we promised faith to God alone. Hence we should not break faith with God and violate our promise. "A man making void the law of Moses dieth without any mercy under two or three witnesses. How much more, do you think he deserveth worse punishments, who hath trodden under foot the Son of God, and hath esteemed the blood of the testament unclean, by which he was sanctified, and hath offered an affront to the Spirit of grace." (Hebr. X, 28.)

"Therefore, whilst, her husband liveth, she shall be called an adulteress, if she be with another man" (Rom. VII, 3); and such a person (according to the old law) ought to be burned or stoned to death. Woe therefore, to the sinner, walking the earth by two ways, and to those wavering in two paths, serving or trying to serve two masters. "You cannot serve two masters. You will either love the one, or despise the other. You cannot serve God and Satan." "I am a jealous God," saith the Lord. "Thou shalt love the Lord, Thy God, with thy whole heart, and Him only shalt thou serve."

4. We should serve God, because of the diabolical slavery and misfortunes in serving satan. "I will cast you forth out of this land, into a land which you know not, and there you shall serve strange gods day and night; which shall not give you any rest." (Jer. XVI, 13.) For no one rests in sin but rather he exerts himself to commit another sin, or lead someone else into sin. "Whosoever sins, is the servant (slave) of sin. Whosoever committeth sin, committeth also iniquity, and sin is iniquity. He that committeth sin, is of the devil, for the devil sinneth from the beginning. For this purpose the Son of God appeared that He might destroy the works of the devil." (John III, 6, 8.) Therefore, it is not easy for the habitual sinner to renounce sin and the devil. Hence Gregory says, "A sin which is not washed away by the tears of repentance drags the sinner by its weight, on to commit another sin." Sin is opposed to the Divine rule, for the commandments of God are not hard to observe. "My yoke is sweet and My burden light." (Matth. XI, 30.) Wherefore, anyone who puts forth as much effort in serving God as in committing sin, he is judged worthy by Almighty God. "For as you have yielded your members to serve uncleanness and iniquity, unto iniquity; so now yield your members to serve justice, unto sanctification. What fruit had you therefore, in those things of which you are now ashamed? For the end of them is death." (Rom. VI, 19.) But of the servants of the devil it is written, "We wearied ourselves in the way of iniquity and destruction, and have walked through hard ways; but the way of the Lord we have not known. What hath pride profited us? All those things are passed away like a shadow . . . and as a ship that passeth through the waves." (Wis. V, 7.) Of the servants of sin and of satan, Jeremias (IX, 2) says, "They have laboured to commit iniquity."

5. We should serve God, because of the greatness of the reward that He has for us. For in no law were such rewards

promised as in the Law of Christ. To the Saracens were promised rivers of milk and honey and to the Jews the land of promise, but to Christians is promised the glory of the Angels. "They shall be as the Angels of God in heaven." (Matth. XXII, 30.) Peter reflecting upon this glory exclaimed: "Lord, to whom shall we go? Thou hast the words of eternal life." (John VI, 69.) (Decalog XII.)

SATURDAY WITHIN SEXAGESIMA

How We Must Worship God

1. God must be worshipped with the interior devotion of our minds and the external adoration of the body. Since we are composed of a twofold nature, intellectual and sensible, we offer God a twofold adoration; namely, a spiritual adoration, consisting in the exterior humbling of the body. And since in all acts of adoration that which is external is referred to the interior as being of greater import, it follows that exterior adoration is offered because of interior adoration, in other words we show signs of humility in our bodies in order to arouse our affections to submit to God, since it is connatural to us to proceed from the sensible to the intellectual.

2. In regard to external acts, discretion should be adhered to. For the just man has different ways of worshipping God both in respect to his internal and external acts of worship. For the good of man and his justice chiefly consists in interior actions by which man believes, hopes and loves. Hence it is written (Luke XVII): "The Kingdom of God is within you." Now the kingdom of God consists not in external actions, for it is written: "The kingdom of heaven is not meat and drink." Hence the interior actions are referred to the end, which is sought in itself, while the external actions by which the body subjects itself to God are related as those things leading to the end. In all our actions whether they are interior acts of devotion or external acts of adoration, God should be the end and purpose of all our thoughts and deeds; so that all things may cooperate unto God's glory and our own and our neighbor's welfare.

3. And likewise a man should apply no measure in regard to his faith, hope, and charity; but inasmuch as he believes, hopes, and loves the more, in so far is his spiritual condition

better. Wherefore it is written Duet, VI: "Thou shalt love the Lord, thy God, with thy whole heart, with thy whole soul, and with all thy strength." But in external actions the rule of discretion by comparison with charity should be observed. (Rom. XII.)

QUINQUAGESIMA SUNDAY

How We Should Serve God on Sundays

"Remember that thou keep holy the sabbath day." (Ex. XX, 8.)

Man ought to sanctify the Sunday for indeed it is truly called holy in two ways, namely, because it is sacred and because it was consecrated by God. On such a holy day we ought to abstain from certain unnecessary works and occupy ourselves with certain spiritual good works.

First, we should offer sacrifices to God. It is commanded in Numbers XXVIII, 3, that God ordered that on each day a lamb should be offered in the morning, another in the evening but on the Sabbath that this offering be doubled and this means that on Sunday we should offer a special sacrifice to God, a sacrifice of all the things which we have. "These are the sacrifices which you shall offer. Two lambs of a year old without blemish every day for the perpetual sacrifice. One you shall offer in the morning, the other in the evening. It is the continual holocaust which you offered on Mount Sinai, for a most sweet odour by fire to the Lord." Numbers XXVIII, 2.)

1. Moreover and of our own accord, we ought to offer our soul to God, by repenting of our sins and by praying for favours. "Let my prayer, O Lord, be directed as incense in Thy sight; the lifting up of my hands, as evening sacrifice." (Ps. CXL, 2.) For the Sunday was established that we may obtain spiritual joy which is obtained through prayer.

2. We should offer the sacrifice of our body to God, not only on Sundays, but every day. "I beseech you, brethren, by the mercy of God, that you present your bodies a living sacrifice, holy, pleasing unto God, your reasonable service." (Rom. XII, 1.) "The sacrifice of praise shall glorify Me." (Ps. XLIX, 23.) Hence on Sundays and holy days our spiritual Hymns of praise should be multiplied and sung with great devotion in gratitude to our Saviour.

3. We should make an offering of our possessions to God by giving alms, and this twice as much on Sundays as on other days because then there is universal joy.

4. On Sundays you should especially study the word of God. "The voices of the Prophets which are read every Sabbath." (Acts XIII, 27.) Hence Christians, whose justice ought to be more perfect should on Sunday gather to hear the word of God and join in the official prayers of the Church. For these two spiritual aids are useful for the soul of the sinner because they change his or her heart for the better. The word of God enlightens the ignorant and arouses the lukewarm from their lethargy.

5. We should devote ourselves to a study of Divine things for this belongs to the perfect. "Taste and see, that the Lord is sweet" (Ps. XXXIII, 9), and this for the sake of rest for your soul. For just as the fatigued body desires and needs rest, so does the soul. Moreover the resting place of the soul is God. "Be Thou, unto me a God, a protector, and a house of refuge, to save me." (Ps. XXX, 3.) "There remaineth therefore, a day of rest, for the people of God. For He that entered into His rest, the same also hath rested from His words, as God did from His." (Heb. IV, 9.) "When I go into my house (that is my conscience) I shall repose myself with her." (Wis. VIII, 16.)

But before the soul arrives at this degree of quietude, it must remove three disturbances. First, it must remove the disturbances caused by sin. "The heart of the wicked is like a raging sea, which cannot rest; and the waves thereof cast up dirt and mire." (Isaias LVII, 20.)

Secondly, the disturbances caused by the passions must be removed because the flesh lusteth against the spirit and the spirit against the flesh.

The third disturbance to be removed is the cares and anxieties of the world. "Martha, Martha, thou art solicitous about many things, but only one thing is necessary." (Luke X, 41.)

Then after these internal and external disturbances to our peace of mind are removed the soul freely and calmly rests in God. "If thou call the sabbath delightful, and dost not thy own will, and glorify the Lord; thou shalt then be delighted in the Lord; and I will lift thee above the high places of the earth, and I will feed thee." (Isaias LVIII, 14.) Moreover the Saints sacrificed all things, because, "the kingdom of heaven is like unto a treasure hidden in a field. Which a man having found, hid it, and for joy thereof, selleth all that he hath, and buyeth that field." (Matth. XIII, 44.) For this rest is eternal life and everlasting joy.

"This is my rest forever and ever. Here will I dwell, for I have chosen it." (Ps. CXXXI, 14.) (Decalog XVII.)

MONDAY WITHIN QUINQUAGESIMA

Sanctity

It is written (Luke I, 74, 75): "That we serve Him without fear. In holiness and justice before Him all our days." Now to serve God belongs to religion. Therefore religion is the same as sanctity.

The word sanctity seems to have two meanings. In one sense it denotes purity and this meaning seems to fit in with the Greek (agios), for agios means unsoiled, unworldly or unearthly. In another sense it signifies firmness, wherefore in older times the term—sancta—was applied to such things as were established by law and were not to be violated. Hence a thing is said to be sacred when it is ratified by law.

In either case the meaning requires sanctity to be ascribed to those things that are applied to the Divine worship so that not only men, but also the temple, vessels and such like things are said to be sanctified through being applied to the worship of God.

For purity is necessary in order that the mind be applied to God, since the human mind is soiled by contact with inferior things, even as all things depreciate by admixture with baser things, for instance, silver being mixed with lead. Now in order that the mind be united to the Supreme Being it must be withdrawn from inferior things and hence it is written (Heb. XII, 14): "Follow peace with all men and holiness, without which no man shall see God."

Again,—firmness—is required for the mind to be applied to God, for it is applied to Him as to its last end and first beginning, and such things must be most immovable. Hence the Apostle said (Rom. VIII, 38): "I am certain that neither death, nor life . . . shall separate us from the love of God."

Accordingly, it is by sanctity that the human mind applies itself and its acts to God so that it differs from religion not essentially but only logically. For sanctity is called religion according as it gives God due service in matters pertaining especially to the Divine worship, such as sacrifices, oblations and so forth; while it is called sanctity, according as man refers to God not only these but also the works of the other virtues or according as man by means of certain good works disposes himself to the worship of God. (2a, 2ae, q. 81, a. 8.)

TUESDAY WITHIN QUINQUAGESIMA

The Scourging of Christ

"Then Pilate released Barabbas, and having scourged Jesus, delivered Him to them to be crucified." (Matth. XXVII, 26.)

Why did Pilate deliver Jesus to be crucified after He had been scourged? Jerome says, "it was the custom among the Romans; that anyone sentenced to death, should first be scourged." Hence, is fulfilled that which the Psalmist XXXVII, 18, says, "I am ready for the scourges, and My sorrow is continually before Me." Some say that Pilate scourged Jesus to move the multitude to compassion so that the rabble in seeing Jesus scourged, might let Him go free. "Then, therefore, Pilate took Jesus and scourged Him." (John XIX, 1.) He scourged Him, not with His own hands, but through the rough hands of unmerciful soldiers. "And the soldiers platting a crown of thorns, put it on His head, and put on Him a purple garment (of mockery) and said, Hail King of the Jews, and they gave Jesus blows." (John XIX, 2.) This was ordered done, so that the Jews observing His injuries, might be satisfied and might desist from putting Jesus to death. For it is natural that angry persons cease from their rage when they see him humiliated and punished, against whom their anger is aroused. It is characteristic of anger that it desires an injury to its neighbor with moderation; but not so with actual hate, which desires the complete destruction of the person held in hatred. "An enemy if he find an opportunity, he will not be satisfied with blood." (Eccles. XII, 16.) Moreover, the enemies of Christ were moved with actual hatred against Christ. "I have been scourged all the day." (Ps. LXXII, 14.) "I have given My body to the strikers." (Isaias L, 6.)

But does this intention excuse Pilate from his crime in the scourging of Christ? By no means, because of all things which are directly bad in themselves, none can become entirely good by a good intention. Moreover to punish the innocent, and especially to punish the Son of God, is in itself the greatest evil and therefore in no wise can it be excused or exonerated from blame. (John XIX.)

ASH WEDNESDAY

Death

"By one man sin entered into this world, and by sin death." (Rom. V, 12.)

1. If anyone through his own fault be deprived of a favour bestowed on him, the privation of that favour is a punishment of that fault. Now God bestowed this favour on man in his primitive state, that as long as his mind was subject to God, the lower powers of his soul would be subject to his rational mind and his body to his soul. But inasmuch as through sin man's mind withdrew from subjection to God, the result was that neither were his lower powers wholly subject to his reason and from this there resulted so great a rebellion of the carnal appetite against reason that neither was the body entirely subject to the soul; whence arose death and other bodily defects. For life and soundness of body depend on the body being subject to the soul, as perfectible is subject to its perfection. Hence, on the other hand death, sickness and all the defects of the body are due to the lack of the body's subjection to the soul.

It is therefore clear that as the rebellion of the carnal appetite against the spirit is punishment of our first parents' sin, so also are death and all the defects of the body.

2. In truth the rational soul is of itself immortal and therefore death is not natural to man on the part of his soul but on the part of his body, which is composed of contraries, of which corruptibility is a necessary consequence. In this respect death is natural to man, but God conferred upon him the favour of being exempt from death which favor, however, was withdrawn through the sin of our first parents. Accordingly death is natural on account of a condition attaching to matter, and it is penal on account of the loss of the Divine favour preserving man from death.

3. Both original and actual sin are removed by Christ by the same cause that removes also corporal defects; according to the Apostle (Rom. VIII, 11), "He . . . shall quicken . . . your mortal bodies because of His spirit that dwelleth in you." But each is done according to the order of Divine wisdom, at a fitting time.

It is right that first of all we should be conformed to Christ's sufferings, before attaining to the immortality and impassibility of glory which was begun in Him and by Him acquired for us. Hence it is necessary that our bodies should remain, for a time, subject to suffering in order that we may merit the impassibility of glory in conformity with Christ. (1a, 2æ, q. 85, a. 5, 2nd, obj. R.)

THURSDAY AFTER ASH WEDNESDAY

Fasting

1. Fasting is practiced for a threefold purpose. First, in order to bridle the lusts of the flesh, wherefore the Apostle says (2 Cor. VI, 5), "In fasting, in chastity," because through fasting chastity is preserved. For according to Jerome, "Venus is cold, when Ceres and Bacchus are not there," that is to say, "lust is cooled by abstinence in meat and drink." Secondly, we have recourse to fasting in order that the mind may arise more freely to the contemplation of heavenly things. Hence it is related of Daniel (Dan. X) that he received a revelation from God after fasting three weeks.

Thirdly, in order to satisfy for our sins. Wherefore, it is written, (Joel XII, 12), "Be converted to Me with all your heart, in fasting, and in weeping, and in mourning." The same is emphasized by Augustine in a sermon on prayer and fasting. "Fasting cleanses the soul, raises the mind, subjects one's flesh to the spirit, renders the heart contrite and humble, scatters the clouds of concupiscence, quenches the fire of lust, and kindles the true light of charity."

2. Fasting is a matter of precept. For fasting is useful for the removal and prevention of sin and for raising the mind to spiritual things. And everyone is bound by the natural dictates of reason to practice fasting as far as it is necessary for the aforesaid purposes. Wherefore fasting in general is a matter of precept becoming and profitable to the Christian people, is a matter of precept of positive law estab-

lished by church authority, and this is the fast of the church, the former is the fast prescribed by nature.

3. The times for the Church fastings are fittingly appointed. Fasting is directed to two things, the removal of sin and the raising of the mind to heavenly things. Wherefore fasting ought to be appointed especially for those times when it behooves a man to be cleansed from sin and the minds of the faithful to be raised to God by devotion; and these things are particularly required before the feast of Easter, when sins are loosed by Baptism which is solemnly conferred on Easter-eve; on which day our Lord's burial is commemorated "because we are buried together with Christ by baptism unto death." (Rom. VI, 4.)

Moreover at the Easter festival the mind of man ought to be devoutly raised to the glory of eternity which Christ restored by rising from the dead and so the Church ordered a fast to be observed immediately before the Easter feast and for the same reason, on the eve of the chief festivals because it is then that we ought to prepare to keep the coming feast devoutly. (2a, 2æ. q. 147, q. 1, 3, 5.)

FRIDAY AFTER ASH WEDNESDAY

The Crown of Thorns

"Go forth, ye daughters of Sion, and see King Solomon in the diadem, wherewith his mother crowned him in the day of his espousals, and in the day of the joy of his heart." (Canticles III, 11.)

Listen to the voice of the Church, in the Canticles, inviting the souls of the faithful to contemplate how wonderful and precious is Christ, her Spouse. For the daughters of Sion are those daughters of Jerusalem, holy souls, citizens of that heavenly kingdom who with the Angels will enjoy eternal peace and consequently will enjoy the glory of the Lord.

1. "Go forth," that is, depart from the turbulent conversation of this world, so that with enlightened mind you may contemplate Him, Whom you should love. "And see King Solomon," that is Christ, the true peacemaker. See Him "in the diadem, wherewith his mother crowned Him"; as if it were said, "Behold Christ clothed with flesh for us," which

flesh He assumed from the flesh of the Virgin Mary. For the flesh which Christ assumed for us is called "the diadem," in which he died and destroyed the empire over death, and also in which he arose from the dead and brought us the hope of resurrection.

Concerning this diadem the Apostle says (Heb. XI, 9), "We see Jesus, for the suffering of death, crowned with glory and honour." Moreover, His Mother is said to have crowned Him because the Virgin Mary presented to Him the material from her flesh for His flesh.

"In the day of His enemies," that is during the time of His Incarnation when He united to Himself the Church without spot or stain or when God united man to Himself.

"And in the day of the joy of His heart," for the joy and happiness of Christ is the salvation and redemption of the human race. "And coming home, call together his friends and neighbors, saying to them, Rejoice with Me, because I have found My sheep that was lost." (Luke XV, 6.)

2. Moreover, the words of the Canticles can be absolutely referred to the Passion of Christ; for Solomon long before beheld in spirit the Passion of the Saviour and advised ahead of time the daughters of Sion, that is the Israelite people. "Go forth ye daughters of Sion, and see King Solomon," that is Christ, "in the diadem," that is in the thorny crown wherewith His mother, the Synagogue, crowned Him; "in the day of His espousals," in which He rejoiced at redeeming the world through His Passion from the power of the devil.

Therefore, "go forth," and depart from the darkness of infidelity, "and see," that is, realize in your heart, that He Who has suffered is true God and true Man. Or also, "go forth," outside the gate of your city so that you may see Him crucified on Mount Calvary. (Cant. III.)

THE SATURDAY AFTER ASH WEDNESDAY

The Grain of Wheat

"Amen, amen, I say to you, unless the grain of wheat falling into the ground die; itself remaineth alone. But if it die, it bringeth forth much fruit." (John XII, 24.)

1. We use a grain of wheat for a twofold purpose, namely, for bread and for seed. Here wheat is to be understood in as

far as it is a seed, not as it is the material for bread; because in as far as it is the material for bread the seed never spreads out so as to produce fruit. Scripture moreover says, "Unless the grain of wheat . . . die," that it does not lose its producing power, but it does when it is changed into another species. "Senseless man, that which thou sowest, is not quickened except it die first." (I Cor. XV, 36.)

Moreover, just as the Word of God is the seed in the soul of man, in as far as it is planted by the human voice of the preacher, to produce the fruit of good works, "for the seed is the Word of God" (Luke VIII, 2); so the Word of God clothed with flesh is the seed sent by God the Father into the world; from which the greatest harvest should be produced, and therefore the Word of God is likened to a grain of mustard seed. "Behold the sower went forth to sow . . . and some fell upon good ground, and they brought forth much fruit, some a hundredfold, some sixtyfold, and some thirtyfold. I have come that the seed might bear fruit, and therefore, I say to you: Unless the grain of wheat falling into the ground die, itself remaineth alone; that is unless I die, the fruit of the conversion of the nations will not follow." (Matth. XIII.)

2. "But if it die, it bringeth forth much fruit."

The usefulness of the Passion of Christ is here indicated, as if Christ had said: "Unless humiliated through My Passion, and buried in the earth (like the grain of wheat) no usefulness will result"; because itself remaineth alone. "But if it die," that is if mortified and killed by the Jews, "it (the Passion) bringeth forth much fruit."

The fruit (or good effect of the Passion) is threefold, the fruit of the remission of sin, the conversion of the Gentiles to God, and the fruit of glory.

1. The fruit of the remission of sin. "This is all the fruit that the sin thereof should be taken away." (Isaias XXVII, 9.) This fruit is produced by the Passion of Christ, according to Peter (III, 18), "Christ died once for our sins, the just for the unjust, that He might offer us unto God."

2. The fruit of the conversion of the people (of the Gentiles) to God. "I have chosen you, and have appointed you that you should go, and bring forth fruit, and your fruit should remain." (John XV, 16.) This fruit the Passion of Christ produced. "If I be lifted up from the earth, I will draw all things to Myself. Now this He said, signifying what death He should die." (John XII, 32.)

3. The fruit of glory. "The fruit of good labours is

glorious." (Wis. III, 15.) And this fruit was the result of Christ's Passion. "Have therefore, brethren, confidence in the blood of Christ, for the new and living way which He hath dedicated through the veil, that is to say, His flesh." (Heb. X, 19.) "Let us go therefore, with confidence to the throne of grace, that we may obtain mercy, and find grace in seasonable aid." (Heb. IV, 16.) (John XII.)

FIRST SUNDAY OF LENT

Was It Becoming that Christ Should be Tempted?

"Jesus was led by the Spirit into the desert to be tempted by the devil." (Matth. LV, 1.)

Christ willed to be tempted.

First, that He might strengthen us against temptations. Hence Gregory says: "It was not unworthy of our Redeemer to wish to be tempted, Who came also to be slain; in order that by His temptations He might conquer our temptations, just as by His death He overcame our death."

Secondly, on account of our safety Christ willed to be tempted; that we might be warned so that none, however holy, may think himself safe or free from temptation. Wherefore, He willed also to be tempted after His baptism, because, as Hilary says, "The temptations of the devil assail those principally who are sanctified, for he desires above all, to overcome the holy." Hence also it is written (Eccles. II, 1), "Son, when thou comest to the service of God, stand in justice and in fear, and prepare thy soul for temptation."

Thirdly, Christ wished to be tempted in order to give us an example, so that He might teach us how to overcome the temptations of the devil. Hence Augustine says, "that Christ allowed Himself to be tempted by the devil, that He might be our Mediator in conquering temptations; not only by helping us, but also by giving us an example."

Fourthly, Christ wished to be tempted in order to fill us with confidence in His mercy. Hence it is written (Hebr. IV, 15), "Who have not a highpriest who cannot have compassion on our infirmities, but One tempted in all things like as we are, without sin." (3a, q. XII, a. 1.)

MONDAY WITHIN THE FIRST WEEK OF LENT

Should Christ Have Been Tempted—"in the Desert"?

"Jesus was in the Desert forty days and forty nights, and was tempted by Satan." (Mark I, 13.)

1. Christ of His own will allowed Himself to be tempted by the devil; just as by His own free-will He submitted to be killed by His enemies; otherwise the devil would not have dared to approach Him. Now the devil prefers to attack a man who is alone, for, as it is written (Eccles. IV, 12), "if a man prevail against one, two shall withstand him." And so it was that Christ went into the desert, as to a field of battle, to be tempted there by the devil. Hence Ambrose says, "that Christ was led into the desert for the purpose of provoking the devil. For had the devil not fought, Christ would not have conquered."

He adds other reasons saying "that Christ in doing this set forth the mystery of Adam's delivery from exile, who had been expelled from paradise into the desert, and set an example to us that the devil envies those who strive for better things."

2. Christ indeed exposed Himself to temptation, as Chrysostom says, "so that then the devil might when seeing Christ alone, especially tempt Him. Thus did he tempt the woman in the beginning when he found her apart from her husband. Still it does not follow from this that man should lead himself into temptation, as this is a dangerous thing to do, but rather we should avoid the occasion of being tempted.

The occasions of temptations are twofold. One is on the part of man, for example, when a man causes himself to be near to sin by not avoiding the occasion of sinning. And such occasions of temptation should be avoided, as it is written of Lot (Gen. XIX, 17), "Neither stay thee in all the country about Sodom."

Another occasion of temptation is on the part of the devil, who always envies those who strive for better things, as Ambrose says. And such occasions of temptation cannot be avoided. Hence Chrysostom says, "Not only Christ was led into the desert by the Spirit, but all God's children who have the Holy Ghost. For it is not enough for them to sit idle; the Holy Ghost urges them to do something great, which is for them to be in the desert from the devil's standpoint, for no unrighteous, in which the devil delights, is there. Again, every good work, compared to the flesh and to the world, is the desert; for it is not according to the will of the flesh and of the world."

Now, there is no danger in giving the devil such an occasion of temptation, because of the help of the Holy Ghost, Who is the Author of the perfect deed and is more powerful than the assault of the envious devil. (3a, Pars. q. 41, 2.)

TUESDAY OF THE FIRST WEEK OF LENT

Christ Endured All Suffering

Human sufferings may be considered under two aspects. In one way, specifically, and in this manner it was not necessary for Christ to endure them all, since many species of suffering are mutually opposed; as burning and drowning; besides we are now speaking of sufferings inflicted from without, for it was not becoming for Him to endure those arising from within, such as bodily ailments.

But speaking generically, He did endure every human suffering and this can be understood in three ways.

First, sufferings on the part of men, for Christ endured something from Gentiles and from Jews; from men and from women, as is clear from the women servants who accused Peter. He suffered from the rulers, from their servants, and from the mob; according to (Ps. II, 1), "Why have the Gentiles raged, and the people devised vain things? The kings of the earth stood up, and the princes met together, against the Lord and against His Christ." He suffered from friends and acquaintances, as is clear from Judas betraying, and Peter denying Him.

Secondly, the same is evident from the part of the sufferings which a man can endure. For Christ suffered from His friends abandoning Him; in His reputation from the blasphemies hurled at Him; and in His honor and glory, from the mockeries and insults heaped upon Him; in things, for He was despoiled of His garments; suffered in His soul, from weariness, sadness, and fear; in His body, He suffered from wounds and scourgings.

Thirdly, His sufferings may be considered in regard to His bodily members. In His head He suffered from the crown of piercing thorns; in His hands and feet, from the fastening of the nails; on His face from the blows and spittle; and from the lashes over His entire body.

Moreover, He suffered in all His bodily senses. In touch, by being scourged and nailed; in taste, by being given vinegar and gall to drink; in smell by being fastened to the gibbet in a place reeking with the stench of corpses which is called Calvary; in sight, by beholding the tears of His mother, and of the disciple whom He loved.

The very least one of Christ's sufferings was sufficient of itself to redeem the human race from all sins; but as to fittingness, it sufficed that He should endure all classes of sufferings. (3a. q. 46, a. V.)

WEDNESDAY OF THE FIRST WEEK OF LENT

The Pain of Christ's Passion Was Greater than All Other Pains

"O all ye who pass by the way attend, and see if there be any sorrow like unto My sorrow." (Lam. I, 12.)

There was true and sensible pain in the suffering Christ, which is caused by something hurtful to the body, also, there was internal pain, which was caused from the apprehension of something hurtful, and this is called "sadness." And in Christ each of these was the greatest in this present life. This arose from four causes.

1. First of all, from all the sources of His pain. For the cause of the sensitive pain was the wounding of His body; and this wounding had its bitterness, both from the extent of the suffering, and from the kind of sufferings, since the death of the crucified is most bitter, because they are pierced in nervous and highly sensitive parts—namely, the hands and feet. Moreover, the weight of the suspended body intensifies the agony; and besides this there is the duration of the suffering, because the crucified do not die at once, like those slain by the sword.

The cause of the interior pain was, first of all, all the sins of the human race, for which He made satisfaction by suffering. Hence, He ascribes them so to speak, to Himself, saying (Ps. XXI, 2), "the words of My sins."

The second cause of His interior pain was especially the fall of Judas and of the others who sinned in His death, chiefly of the Apostles, who were scandalized at His Passion.

The third cause of His interior pain was the loss of His bodily life, which is naturally horrible to human nature.

2. Secondly, the magnitude of His suffering may be considered—considered from the susceptibility of the suffered as to both soul and body. For His body was endowed with a most perfect constitution, since it was fashioned miraculously by the operation of the Holy Ghost; just as some other things made by miracles are better than others. And consequently Christ's sense of touch, the sensitiveness of which is the reason for our feeling pain, was most acute. His soul likewise, from its interior powers, apprehended most vehemently all the causes of sadness.

3. Thirdly, the magnitude of Christ's sufferings can be estimated from the singleness of His pain and sadness. In other sufferers the interior sadness is lessened, and even the exterior suffering from some consideration of reason, by some derivation of redundance from the higher powers into the lower; but it was not so with the suffering Christ because "He permitted each one of His powers to exercise its proper function," as Saint John Damascene says.

4. Fourthly, the greatness of the pain of Christ's suffering can be arrived at by this, that the pain and sorrow were accepted voluntarily, to deliver men from sin; and consequently He embraced the amount of pain proportionate to the magnitude of the fruit which resulted therefrom. Wherefore, the Apostle (2 Cor. VII, 10) says, "The sorrow that is according to God worketh penance, steadfast unto salvation." And (Isaias LIII, 4) declares, "Surely He hath borne our infirmities, and carried our sorrows . . . He was wounded for our iniquities, and bruised for our sins . . . and by His bruises we are healed." (3a, pars. q. 46, a. 6.)

THURSDAY OF THE FIRST WEEK OF LENT

Was It Fitting for Christ To Be Crucified with Thieves?

"He was reputed with the wicked." (Isaias LIII, 12.)

Christ was crucified between thieves from one intention on the part of the Jews, and from quite another on the part of God's ordaining it. As to the intention of the Jews, Chrysostom remarks that, "they crucified two thieves, one on either side, that he might be made to share their guilt. But it did not happen so, because mention is never made of them; whereat His cross is honored everywhere. Kings lay aside their crowns to take up the cross. On their purple robes, on their diadems, on their weapons, on the consecrated table, everywhere the cross shines forth."

Secondly, as to God's ordinance, Christ was crucified with thieves, as Jerome says, "As Christ became accursed of the cross for us, so for our salvation He was crucified as a guilty one among the guilty."

Thirdly, Pope Leo observes in his sermon on the Passion, "The two thieves were crucified, one on His right, ond one on His left, to set forth by the very appearance of the gibbet that separation of all men which shall be made in His hour of judgment." And Augustine on John VII, 36, says, "The very cross, if thou mark it well, was a judgment seat, for the judge being set in the midst, the one who believed was delivered, the other who mocked Him was condemned. Already He has signified what He shall do to the quick and the dead; for some He will set on His right, others on His left hand."

Fourthly, according to Hilary, "Two thieves are set, one upon His right, and one upon His left, to show that all mankind is called to the sacrament of his Passion. But because of the cleavage between believers and unbelievers, the multitude is divided into right and left, those on the right being saved by the justification of faith."

Fifthly, because, as Bede says, "The thieves crucified with our Lord denote those who, believing and confessing Christ, either endure the conflict of martyrdom or keep the laws of stricter observance. But those who do the like for the sake of everlasting glory are denoted by the faith of the thief on the right; while others who do so for the sake of human applause imitate the mind and conduct of the one on the left."

Just as Christ was not obliged to die, but willingly submitted to death so as to vanquish death by His power, so neither deserved He to be classed with thieves, but willed to be reputed with the ungodly that He might destroy ungodliness by His power. Accordingly Chrysostom says, "That to convert the thief upon the cross and lead him into paradise, was no less a wonder than to shake the rocks." (3a, q. 46, a. 11.)

FRIDAY OF THE FIRST WEEK OF LENT

In the Feast of the Lance and Nails of Our Lord

"One of the soldiers with a spear opened His side, and immediately there came out blood and water." (John XIX, 34.)

1. Significantly does Sacred Scripture say that the side of Jesus was "opened," instead of "wounded," because through this, that His side was opened, is meant that the door of eternal life is opened for us through Christ's death. "After these things I looked, and behold a door was opened in heaven." (Apoc. IV, 1.) This door signifies the door in the side of the ark, through which entered the animals which did not perish in the flood.

2. But this door or opening in the side of Christ, which was made by the soldier's spear, is for the sake of our salvation. Hence, "immediately there came out blood and water," which is very wonderful that from the dead body in which the blood had congealed, blood issued forth.

This fact is to show that through the Passion of Christ we obtain the full remission of our sins, and even the removal of the stains of sin through the Blood, which is the price of our redemption. "You were not redeemed with corruptible things as gold or silver, from your vain conversation, but with the precious blood of Christ, as of a lamb unspotted and undefiled." (1 Peter I, 18.) From the very stains of sin, moreover, are we cleansed, through "the water," which is the bath of our salvation. "I will pour upon you clean water, and you shall be cleansed from all your filthiness." (Ezech. XXXVI, 25.) "There shall be a fountain open to the house of David, and to the inhabitants of Jerusalem, for the washing of the sinner, and the unclean woman." (Zach. XIII, 1).

And therefore, these two, namely, the blood and water, pertain especially to two Sacraments. The water pertains to the sacrament of baptism, the blood to the sacrament of the Blessed Eucharist. Or both pertain to the Eucharist, for in the sacrament of the Eucharist is mingled water with wine; although water is not of the substance of this sacrament.

This is also proper to the figure, because just as from the side of Christ resting on the cross, there came forth blood and water, by which the Church is consecrated, so from the side of Adam while sleeping, woman was formed, which prefigured the same Church. (John XIX.)

SATURDAY OF THE FIRST WEEK OF LENT

The Charity of God in the Passion of Christ

"God commendeth His charity to us; because when as yet we were sinners, Christ died for us." (Rom. V, 8.)

1. Christ died for the wicked. This is wonderful if we consider Who has died for us, and wonderful also, if we consider for whom He died. "For scarce for a just man will one die, yet for a good man some one would dare to die." (Rom. V, 7); that is, scarcely will anyone die for a just man, to set him free.

As on the contrary, it is said, "The just perisheth, and no man layeth it to heart," (Isaias LVII, 1). That is, someone unusual because of zeal for virtue, might perhaps dare to die for a good man. For it is unusual, and because of this it is the greatest act of self-sacrifice; and hence it is written, "Greater love than this no man hath, than that he lay down his life for his friends." (John XV, 13.) But never has anyone died for the criminal, the wicked or unjust; but that is exactly what Christ did. And therefore we must admire the reason why Christ died for sinners, "the just God for unjust man."

2. If on the other hand anyone should inquire why Christ died for the wicked the answer is this, because "God commendeth His charity to us," that is, by this act Christ proved that He loved us in the highest degree possible; "because when as yet we were sinners (and therefore His enemies) Christ died for us." (Rom. V.)

Moreover, the death of Christ showed the charity of God for us, because God gave His own Son to be crucified, so that by His death He might make complete satisfaction for us. "God so loved the world, that He gave His only begotten Son." (John III, 16.) Just as the charity of God for us is shown through the fact that He gave to us His Holy Spirit, so God commendeth His charity to us when He gave us His Son.

But when Saint Paul says, "God commendeth His charity," he assigns a certain immensity of Divine charity, which in truth is revealed from two facts. First of all, from the fact that God gave His Son to die for us, and secondly, from the part of our condition, because Christ was not inspired to die for us by reason of our merits, "because as yet we were sinners, and therefore His enemies." (Rom. V, 8.) "But God Who is rich in mercy for His exceeding charity wherewith He loved us; even when we were dead in sins, hath quickened us together in Christ, by Whose grace you are saved." (Ephes. II, 4.)

3. All these things seem scarcely believable. "Behold ye among the nations, and see, wonder, and be astonished. For a work is done in your days, which no man will believe when it shall be told." (Habac. I, 5.) For the very fact that Christ died for us, it is so hard to believe that our intellect can scarcely grasp its full significance. Moreover in no wise does this great mystery fall under the grasp of our intellect, and this is what the Apostle says, "He Whom God hath raised from the dead saw no corruption. . . . Beware, therefore, lest that come upon you which is spoken in the prophets. Behold, ye despisers, and wonder, and perish; for I work a work in your days, a work which you will not believe, if any man shall tell it to you." (Acts XIII, 37, 41.)

For so great is God's grace and love for us, that it does more for us than we can believe or understand. (Creed.)

THE SECOND SUNDAY OF LENT

Did God the Father Deliver Up Christ to the Passion?

"God hath not spared His own Son, but delivered Him up for us all." (Rom. VIII, 32.)

Christ suffered voluntarily, out of obedience to the Father. Hence in three respects God the Father did deliver up Christ to the Passion.

1. In the first way, because by His eternal will He pre-ordained Christ's Passion for the deliverance of the human race, according to the words of Isaias (LIII, 6), "The Lord hath laid on Him the iniquities of us all"; and again (verse 10) "The Lord was pleased to bruise Him in infirmity."

2. Secondly, inasmuch as, by the infusion of charity, He inspired Him with the will to suffer for us; hence it is written in the same passage of Isaias, "He was offered because it was His own will. (Verse 7.)

3. God the Father delivered up Christ by not shielding Him from the Passion, but abandoning Him to His persecutors. Thus we read (Matth. XXVII, 46) that Christ, while hanging upon the cross, cried out: "My God, My God, why hast Thou forsaken Me," because He left Him to the power of His persecutors, as Augustine says.

It is indeed a wicked and cruel act to hand over an innocent man, to hand him to torment and to death against his will. Yet God the Father did not so deliver up Christ, but inspired Him with a will to suffer for us. God's severity is thereby shown, for He would not remit sin without penalty; and the Apostle indicates this when He says, "God spared not even His own Son." (Rom. VIII, 32.) Likewise His goodness shines forth (Rom. XI, 22), since by no penalty endured could man pay Him enough satisfaction, and the Apostle denotes this when he says, "He delivered Him up for us all"; and again (Rom. III, 25), "Whom, that is to say, Christ,—God hath proposed to be a propitiation through faith in His blood."

The same act, for good or evil, is adjudged differently, accordingly as it proceeds from a different source. The Father delivered up Christ, and Christ surrendered Himself, from charity, and consequently we give praise to both the Father and the Son. But Judas betrayed Christ from greed, the Jews from envy, and Pilate from worldly fear, for he stood in fear of Cæsar; and these are accordingly guilty.

Christ therefore, was not a debtor to death from necessity, but from charity to mankind, by which he willed the salvation of man; and from charity to God, by which He desired to fulfill His Divine will, as Matth. XXVI, 39, says, "He fell upon His face, praying and saying 'My Father, if it be possible, let this chalice pass from Me. Nevertheless not as I will, but as Thou wilt.'"

MONDAY OF THE SECOND WEEK OF LENT

It Was Fitting for Christ to Suffer at the Hands of the Gentiles

"They shall deliver Him to the Gentiles to be mocked and scourged, and crucified, and the third day He shall rise again." (Matth. XX, 19.)

The effect of Christ's Passion was foreshown by the very manner of His death. For Christ's Passion wrought its effect of salvation first of all among the Jews, very many of whom were baptized in His death. Afterwards by the preaching of the Jews, Christ's Passion passed on to the Gentiles. Consequently, it was fitting that Christ should begin His sufferings at the hands of the Jews, and, after they had delivered Him up, finish His Passion at the hands of the Gentiles.

Christ in order to show the fulness of His love, on account of which He suffered, prayed upon the cross for His persecutors. Therefore, that the fruits of His petition might accrue to Jews and Gentiles, Christ willed to suffer from both.

Now it was not the Gentiles but the Jews who offered the figurative sacrifice of the Old Law. On the other hand, Christ's Passian was the offering of a sacrifice, inasmuch as He endured death of His own free will out of charity. But in so far as He suffered from His persecutors it was not a sacrifice, but a most severe sin.

Moreover, the Jews said that, "it is not lawful for us to put any man to death," for they understood that it was not lawful for them, owing to the sacredness of the feast-day, which they had already begun to celebrate. Or as Chrysostom observes, because they wanted Him to be slain, not as a transgressor of the Law, but as a public enemy; since He had made Himself out to be a King, of which it was not their place to judge. Or again, because it was not lawful for them to crucify Him (as they wanted to), but to stone Him, as they did to Stephen. Better still is it to say, that the power of putting to death was taken from them by the Romans, whose subjects they were. (3a. q. 47, a. IV.)

TUESDAY OF THE SECOND WEEK OF LENT

Christ's Passion Brought About Our Salvation by Way of Merit

1. Grace was bestowed on Christ not only as an individual, but inasmuch as He is the Head of the Church; so that it might overflow into His members; and therefore Christ's works are referred to Himself and to His members in the same way as the works of any other man in a state of grace are referred to himself.

But it is clear that whosoever suffers for the sake of justice, provided he be in a state of grace, merits his salvation thereby, according to Matth. V, 10, "Blessed are they who suffer persecution for justice sake, for theirs is the kingdom of heaven." Consequently, Christ by His Passion merited salvation not only for Himself, but likewise for all His members.

From the beginning of His conception Christ merited our eternal salvation; but on our part there were certain obstacles by which we were prevented from obtaining the effect of His preceding merits. Consequently, in order to remove such hindrances, "it was necessary for Christ to suffer."

Moreover, Christ's Passion has a special effect, which His preceding merits did not possess, not on account of greater charity, but because of the nature of the work, which was suitable for such an effect; as is clear from the arguments set forth on the fittingness of Christ's Passion.

The members and the head pertain to the same person. Hence since Christ is our Head, because of the Divinity and plenitude of His grace overflowing to others, and therefore His merit does not actually belong to us, since we are not His actual members; but it flows to us because of our unity with the Mystical Body of Christ. (3 Dist. 18, a. VI.)

2. We must realize that although Christ merited sufficiently for the human race, by His death, still there are certain remedies which must be secured for each one's salvation; for the death of Christ is, as it were, a certain universal cause of our salvation; just as the sin of Adam was a universal cause of damnation. But it is necessary that the universal cause be applied in a special way to each one, so that each one might share in the effect of the universal cause.

Therefore, the effect of our first parents' sin comes to each one through the origin of the flesh; but the effect of Christ's death reaches each one of us by spiritual regeneration; through which man, in a certain manner, becomes united to and incorporated in Christ.

Consequently, it is necessary that each one of us seek to be regenerated through Christ, and receive other things in which the power of Christ's death operates. (Contra. Gen. IV, 55.)

WEDNESDAY OF THE SECOND WEEK OF LENT

Christ's Passion Brought About Our Salvation by Way of Atonement

"He is the propitiation for our sins, and not for ours only, but also for those of the whole world." (I John II, 2.)

1. He properly atones for an offense who offers something which the offended one loves equally, or even more than

he detested the offense. But by suffering, out of love and obedience, Christ gave more to God than was required to compensate for the offense of the human race. First of all, because of the exceeding charity from which He suffered; secondly, on account of the dignity of His life which He laid down in atonement, for it was the life of One Who was God and man; thirdly, on account of the extent of the Passion and the greatness of the grief endured.

And therefore, Christ's Passion was not only a sufficient but a superabundant atonement for the sins of the human race; according to 1 John II, 2, "He is the propitiation for our sins, and not for ours only, but also for those of the whole world."

The head and members are as one mystic person; and therefore Christ's satisfaction belongs to all the faithful as being His members. Also, in as far as any two men are one in charity, the one can atone for the other. But the same does not hold good of confession and contrition, because atonement consists in an outward action, for which helps may be used; among which friends are to be reckoned.

2. Although by His death Christ satisfied sufficiently for original sin, still it is not unfitting that punishments consequent on original sin remain as yet in all who also become sharers in Christ's redemption. For this was done suitably and usefully, namely, that the punishment for sin should remain, even though the crime was taken away. That was done for three reasons.

First, so that there might be conformity between the faithful and Christ, just as the conformity of members to a head. Hence just as Christ at first endured many sufferings, and thus won the glory of immortality; so it is fitting that His faithful servants should at first undergo sufferings, and thus win immortality; as if bearing in themselves the insignia of Christ's Passion, so that they might secure the likeness of His glory.

Secondly, because if men coming to Christ should immediately obtain immortality and impassibility (incapable of suffering), many men would come to Christ, attracted more through these corporal favours than by reason of spiritual goods; which is contrary to the intention of Christ coming into the world; so that men might be removed from the love of bodily things to the love of things spiritual and everlasting.

Thirdly, because if those coming to Christ were rendered immediately incapable of suffering and immortal, this in a certain way, might compel men to embrace the faith of Christ and thus the merit of faith would be diminished. (Contr. Gen. IV, 55.)

THURSDAY OF THE SECOND WEEK OF LENT

Christ's Passion Operated by Way of Sacrifice

1. A sacrifice properly so called is something done for that honor which is properly due to God, in order to appease Him; and hence it is that Saint Augustine says, "A true sacrifice is every good work done in order that we may cling to God in holy fellowship, yet referred to that consummation of happiness wherein we can be truly blessed. But Christ offered Himself up for us in His Passion, and this voluntary enduring of the Passion was most acceptable to God as coming from charity. Therefore, it is manifest that Christ's Passion was a true sacrifice."

Moreover, as Augustine says later on in his book "The City of God," the primitive sacrifices of the holy Fathers are many and various signs of this true sacrifice, one being prefigured by many, in the same way as a single concept of thought is expressed in many words, in order to commend it without tediousness, and Augustine further observes, "since there are four things to be noted in every sacrifice—namely, to whom it is offered, by whom it is offered, what is offered and for whom it is offered—that the same One True Mediator reconciling us with God through the peace-sacrifice continues to be One with Him to Whom He offered it, might be one with them for whom He offered it, and might Himself be the Offerer and what He offered."

2. Indeed in the Sacrifices of the old law, which prefigured Christ, never was human flesh offered, but it does not follow from this that the Passion of Christ was not a sacrifice. For although the truth answers to the figure in some respects, yet it does not in all; since the truth must go beyond the figure. Therefore the figure of this sacrifice, in which Christ's flesh is offered for us, was flesh right fittingly, not the flesh of men, but of animals, as denoting Christ's. And this is a most perfect sacrifice.

First of all, since being flesh of human nature, it is fittingly offered for men, and is partaken by them under the Sacrament.

Secondly, because being passible and mortal, it was for immolation.

Thirdly, because being sinless it had virtue to cleanse from sins.

Fourthly, because being in the offerer's own flesh, it was acceptable to God on account of His charity in offering up His own flesh.

Hence it is as Augustine says, "What else could be so fittingly partaken of by men, or offered up for men, as human flesh? What else is there so appropriate for this immolation as mortal flesh? What else is there so clean for cleansing mortals as the flesh born in the womb without fleshly concupiscence, and coming from a virginal womb? What could be so favorably offered and accepted as the flesh of our sacrifice which was made the body of our Priest?"

FRIDAY OF THE SECOND WEEK OF LENT

The Feast of the Holy Cloth

"And Joseph taking the body (of Jesus), wrapped it up in a clean cloth." (Matth. XXVII, 59.)

1. By this cloth, according to the mystery, three things are indicated. First of all that the flesh of Christ was clean, secondly, His Church is stainless, and thirdly, a clean conscience is signified.

First, the flesh of Christ was clean. For just as linen is washed by much pressure, and becomes clean, so the flesh of Christ through much pressure and sufferings attained the dazzling whiteness of His Resurrection. "Thus it behoved Christ to suffer, and to rise again from the dead, on the third day." (Luke XXIV, 46.)

Secondly, the church without stain or wrinkle, is signified, by this clean cloth in which the body of Jesus was wrapped. This is signified from the fact that the linen cloth (like the church), is interwoven from diverse threads.

Thirdly, "the clean cloth," represents a pure conscience, for only where there is a clean conscience, does Christ rest.

2. "And laid the body in his own new monument." (Matth. XXVII, 60.)

First of all, Saint Matthew says, that Joseph laid the body

in "his own" monument, which he had hewed out in a rock. And this was rightly becoming, because He Who died for the sins of others should rightly be buried in the tomb of another.

Likewise, he says, "in a new monument," because if any other bodies were buried with Christ it would not be known who had risen. Another reason is, because, He Who was born from a spotless Virgin, it was fitting that He should be buried "in a new monument"; for just as in the womb of Mary, there was no one before Jesus, so also, no one was buried after Him in this new monument. Likewise, that we might understand that Christ is hidden (becomes buried) in a mind renewed through faith. "That Christ may dwell by faith in your hearts." (Eph. III, 17.)

And Saint John (XIX, 41) also adds, "Now there was in the place where Jesus was crucified, a garden; and in the garden a new sepulchre, wherein no man yet had been laid." Herein must be noted, that Christ was arrested in a garden, seized in a garden and suffered in a garden and was buried in a garden; to show that through the power of His Passion we are set free from the sin, which Adam committed in the garden of Paradise, and that through Christ the Church is consecrated; which is like an enclosed garden (of delights). (Matth. XXVII.)

SATURDAY IN THE SECOND WEEK OF LENT

Christ's Passion Brought About Our Salvation by Way of Redemption

It is written (1 Peter I, 18), "you were not redeemed with corruptible things as gold or silver from your vain conversation of the tradition of your fathers; but with the precious blood of Christ, as of a lamb unspotted and undefiled." And (Gal. III, 13), "Christ hath redeemed us from the curse of the Law, being made a curse for us." Now He is said to be "a curse for us," inasmuch as He suffered upon the tree. Therefore, He did redeem us by His Passion.

Man was held captive on account of sin in two ways.

First of all, by the slavery of sin, because (John VIII, 34), "Whosoever committeth sin is the servant of sin"; and (2 Peter II, 19), "By whom a man is overcome, of the same also he is the slave." Since then, the devil had overcome man by inducing him to sin, man was subject to the devil's bondage.

Secondly, as to the debt of punishment, to the payment of which man was held fast by God's justice; and this, too, is a kind of bondage, since it savours of bondage for a man to suffer what he does not wish, just as it is the free man's condition to apply himself to what he wills.

Since, then, Christ's Passion was a sufficient and a superabundant atonement for the sin and the debt of the human race, it was as a price at the cost of which we were freed from both obligations. For the atonement by which one satisfies for self or another is called the price, by which he ransoms himself or someone else from sin and its penalty; according to Daniel (IV, 24), "Redeem thy sins with alms." Now Christ made satisfaction, not by giving money or anything of the sort, but by bestowing what was of greatest price—Himself—for us. And therefore Christ's Passion is called our Redemption.

Man by sinning became the bondsman both of God and of the devil. Through guilt he had offended God, and put himself under the control of the devil by consenting to him. Consequently, man did not become God's servant on account of his guilt, but rather, by withdrawing from God's service, he, by God's just permission, fell under the devil's servitude on account of the offense committed. But as to the penalty, man was chiefly bound to God as his sovereign judge, and to the devil as his torturer; according to Matth. V, 25, "Lest perhaps the adversary deliver thee to the judge, and the judge deliver thee to the officer"—that is, to the relentless avenging angel, as Chrysostom says.

Consequently, although after deceiving man, the devil, so far as in him lay, held him unjustly in bondage as to both sin and penalty, still it was just that man should suffer it, God so permitting it as to the sin, and ordaining it as to the penalty. And therefore, justice required man's redemption in regard to God, but not with regard to the devil. Because, with regard to God, redemption was necessary for man's deliverance, but not with regard to the devil, for the price had to be paid not to the devil but to God. And therefore, Christ is said to have paid the price of our redemption—His Own Precious Blood—not to the devil but to God. (3a q. 48, a. IV.)

THIRD SUNDAY OF LENT

We Were Delivered from Sin Through Christ's Passion

"He loved us, and washed us from our sins in His own blood." (Apoc. I, 5.)

Christ's Passion is the proper cause of the forgiveness of sins, in three ways.

First of all, by way of exciting our charity, because as the Apostle says (Rom. V, 8), "God commendeth His charity towards us; because when as yet we were sinners, according to the time, Christ died for us." But it is by charity that we procure pardon for our sins, according to Luke (VII, 47), "Many sins are forgiven her because she hath loved much."

Secondly, Christ's Passion causes forgiveness by way of redemption. For since He is our Head, then by the Passion which He endured for us from love and obedience, He delivered us as His members from our sins, as by the price of His Passion. In the same way as if a man by the good industry of his hands were to redeem himself from a sin committed with his feet. For just as the natural body is one, though made up of diverse members, so the whole Church, Christ's mystic body, is reckoned as one person with its head, which is Christ.

Thirdly, Christ's Passion causes forgiveness of sins, by way of efficiency, inasmuch as Christ's flesh, wherein He endured the Passion, is the instrument of the Godhead, so that His sufferings and actions operate with Divine power for expelling sin.

Christ by His Passion delivered us from our sins causally—that is, by setting up the cause of our deliverance, from which cause all sins whatsoever, past, present, or to come, could be forgiven. Just as if a Doctor was to prepare a medicine by which all sickness can be cured even in the future.

But because Christ's Passion preceded, as a kind of universal cause of the forgiveness of sins, it needs to be applied to each individual for the cleansing of personal sins. Now this is done by Baptism and Penance and the other sacraments, which derive their power from Christ's Passion.

Christ's Passion is also applied to us through faith, that we may share in its fruits, according to Rom. (III, 25), "Whom God hath proposed to be a propitiation—through faith in His blood." But the faith with which we are cleansed from sin is not lifeless faith, which can exist even with sin, but faith living through charity; that thus Christ's Passion may be applied to us—not only as to our minds, but also as to its effects. And even in this way sins are forgiven through the power of the Passion of Christ. (3a. q. 49, a. 1.)

MONDAY OF THE THIRD WEEK OF LENT

We Were Delivered from the Devil's Power Through Christ's Passion

Our Lord said (John XII, 31), when His Passion was drawing near, "Now shall the prince of this world be cast out; and I, if I be lifted up from the earth, will draw all things to myself." Now He was lifted up from earth by His Passion on the cross. Therefore by His Passion the devil was deprived of his power over man.

There are three things to be considered regarding the power which the devil exercised over man previous to Christ's Passion.

The first, is on man's own part, who by his sin deserved to be delivered over to the devil's power, and was overcome by his tempting. Another point is on God's part, whom man had offended by sinning, and Who with justice left man under the devil's power. The third, is on the devil's part, who from his most wicked will hindered man from securing his salvation.

As to the first point, by Christ's Passion man was delivered from the devil's power, in so far as the Passion is the cause of the forgiveness of sins. As to the second, it must be said that Christ's Passion freed us from the devil's power, inasmuch as it reconciled us with God. But as to the third, Christ's Passion delivered us from the devil, inasmuch as in Christ's Passion he exceeded the limit of power assigned him by God, by conspiring to bring about Christ's death, Who, being sinless did not deserve to die. Hence Augustine says, "The devil was vanquished by Christ's justice; because, while discovering in Him nothing deserving of death, nevertheless he slew Him. And it is certainly just that the debtors whom he held captive should be set at liberty, since they believed in God, Whom the devil slew, though He was no debtor."

The devil is said even now to exercise such power over men, that with God's permission, he can still tempt men's souls and assault their bodies; yet there is a remedy provided for man through Christ's Passion, whereby he can safeguard himself against the enemy's assaults, so as not to be dragged down into the destruction of everlasting death. And all who resisted the devil previous to the Passion were enabled to do so through faith in the Passion, although it was not as yet accomplished. Yet in one respect no one was able to escape the devil's hands—that is, so as not to descend into hell. But after Christ's Passion, men can defend themselves from hell by the Power of our Lord's Passion.

God permits the devil to deceive men by certain persons, and in time and places, according to the hidden motives of His judgments; still, there is always a remedy provided through Christ's Passion, for defending themselves against the wicked snares of the demons, even in Antichrist's time. But if any man neglected to make use of this remedy, it detracts nothing from the efficacy of Christ's Passion. (3a. q. 49, a. 2.)

TUESDAY OF THE THIRD WEEK OF LENT

Christ—Our True Redeemer

"You are redeemed with the Precious Blood of Christ, as of a lamb unspotted and undefiled." (1 Peter I, 19.)

Through the sin of our first parents the entire human race was separated from God. "You were at that time without Christ, being aliens from God" (Eph. II, 12), not indeed alienated from the power of God, but from the vision of God's face, to which the children and servants of God are admitted to enjoy. Again and again we fell into the usurped power of the devil, for by consenting to satan, man subjected himself to the devil's diabolical control.

And therefore, Christ through His Passion did two things. He set us free from the enemy's power, by conquering the enemy, by the contrary weapons with which the enemy had conquered man, namely, humility, obedience, austerity of penance, which are opposed to the sinful pleasure resulting from eating the forbidden fruit. And secondly, by His Passion, satisfied for our sins, united us to God, and made us the friends and children of God.

Hence, this liberation included two reasons for our purchase. For in as far as Christ liberated us from the devil's power, it is said that He redeemed or purchased us; just as a king regains his kingdom through the pains of battle, from the adversary who had usurped his kingdom. On the other hand, in as far as Christ appeased the anger of God for us, He is said to have redeemed us; just as one paying the price of our ransom, to free us from punishment and from sin.

Moreover the price of "His precious blood," was not paid to the devil, but to God, so that He might satisfy for us; but He snatched us from the devil by the victory of His Passion.

And although the devil had unjustly usurped us, still we had justly fallen into his power, in as far as he had overcome us; and therefore, it was also necessary, that the devil should be conquered by the opposite of those vices with which he subdues us; for he does not conquer us by violence, but by deceitfully inducing us to sin. The devil overcomes us by causing us to yield to pride, impurity, selfishness, while Christ wins us to Himself by the practice of humility, purity, unselfishness, faith, hope, and love of God.

"Therefore, I will put my trust in God, for in that wherein He Himself hath suffered and been tempted, He is able to help them also that are tempted." (Hebr. II, 13, 18.) (3 Dist. 19 q. 1, a. IV.)

WEDNESDAY OF THE THIRD WEEK OF LENT

The Price of Our Redemption

"You are bought with a great price." (1, Cor. VI, 20.)

An injury or suffering of anyone is reckoned according to the dignity of the person upon whom the suffering is inflicted. A king if he is struck in the face, suffers a greater injury than a private citizen. But the dignity of the Person of Christ is Infinite, because He is a Divine Person. Therefore each suffering of Our Lord, even the slightest, is infinite. Hence each one of His sufferings, even without His death, would have sufficed to redeem mankind.

The smallest drop of His Most Precious Blood would have redeemed the human race. Any drop of the Blood of Christ, without His death, would have paid the price of our salvation. Hence the price of mankind's redemption was not only infinite in value, but also of an infinite nature, since Christ redeemed us from death through His death.

Secondly, the death of Christ was not only the price of our redemption, but also an example of virtue for us, so that we might not fear death. St. Paul (Hebrews II, 14) assigns these two reasons for the Saviour's death saying: "That through death, He might destroy him (namely the devil) who had the empire of death, and might deliver them, who through the fear of death were all their lifetime subject to servitude."

Christ also died, so that His death might be for us a sacrament of salvation, in so far as we by virtue of His death, die to sin, and to carnal lusts, and improper affections. Hence St. Peter (III, 18) says: "Christ died once for our sins, the just for the unjust, that He might offer us to God, being put to death indeed in the flesh, but enlivened in the spirit."

Hence the human race was not redeemed by any other suffering, but by the death of Christ. In truth, Christ not only in sacrificing His life, but also in enduring the least suffering would have paid a sufficient price for our redemption, because of the Infinite dignity of the Person of Christ. (Quod. 1, 2 q. 1, a. 2.)

THURSDAY OF THE THIRD WEEK OF LENT

The Samaritan Woman Preaching Christ

"The woman left her water-pot, and went her way into the city." (John IV, 28.)

This woman of Samaria who came to Jacob's well for water, after she had been enlightened there by Christ, assumes the work of an apostle, and from her words and actions, three things are evident. Firstly, a manifestation of devotion, secondly, a method of preaching, thirdly, the good result of preaching.

A manifestation of devotion appears from two things, first from this that the Samaritan woman, because of this great devotion, left the well, and the water which she had so eagerly sought. Hence it is said: "The woman left her water-pot, and went into the city," to announce the wonderful things about Christ, not caring for her own bodily comfort, because of the help she might be to others, and in this incident we have an example of the Apostles, who "left their fishing nets, and followed Christ." Secondly, the effect of her conversation with Christ appears from the multitude of those to whom she announced the glad tidings of His power and dignity; for she preached not merely to one, or two, or three people but to the entire city. "She went into the city."

Secondly, a method of preaching is set forth by the Samaritan woman. " She said to the men there: Come and see, a man, Who has told me all things whatsoever I have done. Is not He the Christ?" (John IV, 28.) She invites them, as guests, into Christ's presence. "Come and see a man." She did not immediately say, "Come to Christ," lest she might cause them to blaspheme, but she said of Christ what things were true. She did not say, "believe," but "come, and see," because she realized, if they would but taste of that Living Fountain, in seeing Him, they would believe the same things as she now believed. She therefore imitated the example of a true preacher of the Gospel, by attracting men not to herself, but to Christ.

Secondly, she makes known a sign of Christ's Divinity, when she says: "He has told me all things whatsoever I have done," namely that she had many unlawful husbands. Christ told her this in such a manner that her soul became enkindled with love divine.

Thirdly, she concludes her sermon with references to the Majesty of Christ saying: "Is not He the Christ?" She dares not assert He might be Christ, lest she might seem to wish to teach others, and those angered on account of this, might refuse to come to Christ. However she is not entirely silent, about Christ's Divinity, and so by way of a question, she leaves the matter to their judgment, for this is the better manner of persuading her audiences.

Fourthly, the good result of preaching is here seen in these words: "They went out of the city and came to Christ" (John IV, 30), from which it can be concluded, that if we wish to go to Christ, we must leave the city, that is cast aside the love of the flesh, and live by the spirit of God. And many of the Samaritans said to the woman: "We now believe, not for thy saying, for we ourselves have heard Him, and know that this is indeed the Saviour of the world." (John IV, 42.) (John IV.)

FRIDAY OF THE THIRD WEEK OF LENT

We Were Freed from the Punishment of Sin Through Christ's Passion

"Surely He hath borne our iniquities and carried our sorrows." (Isaias LIII, 4.)

Through Christ's Passion we have been delivered from the debt of punishment, in two ways. First, directly, namely, inasmuch as Christ's Passion was sufficient, and superabundant satisfaction for the sins of the whole human race; but when sufficient satisfaction has been paid, then the debt of penalty is abolished. In another way, indirectly, that is to say, in so far as Christ's Passion is the cause of the forgiveness of sin, to which a debt of punishment is due.

The lost in hell are not delivered by and cannot avail themselves of the effects of Christ's Passion, because, the Passion of Christ secures its effect in them only to whom it is applied, through faith, and charity, and the sacraments of faith. And consequently, the lost in hell cannot avail themselves of its effects, since they are not united to Christ in the aforesaid manner.

And although we are freed from the debt of punishment, still, satisfactory punishment is imposed upon all penitents. For in order to secure the effects of Christ's Passion, we must be likened unto Him. Now we are likened unto Him sacramentally in Baptism, according to (Rom. VI, 4), "For we are buried together with Him by Baptism unto death." Hence no punishment of satisfaction is imposed upon men at their Baptism, since they are fully delivered by our Lord's satisfaction. But because it is written (1 Peter II, 18), "Christ died but once for our sins," therefore, a man cannot a second time be likened unto Christ's death by the sacrament of Baptism. Hence it is necessary, that those who sin after Baptism be likened unto Christ suffering, by some form of punishment or suffering which they endure in their own person; yet, by the coöperation of Christ's satisfaction, much higher penalty suffices than one that is proportionate to the sin.

If, on the other hand, death, which is a punishment for sin, still continues, this is, because Christ's satisfaction produces its effect in us, inasmuch as we are incorporated with Him, as members with their head. Now the members must be conformed with their head. Consequently, as Christ first had grace in His soul with bodily possibility; and through the Passion attained to the glory of immortality, so we likewise, who are His members, are freed by His Passion, from all debt of punishment, yet so that first we receive in our souls, "the spirit of adoption of sons," whereby our names are written down for the inheritance of immortal glory, "being made conformable to the sufferings and death of Christ, we are brought into immortal glory, according to the words of the Apostle (Rom. VIII, 17), "And if sons, heirs also, heirs indeed of God, and joint heirs with Christ; yet so if we suffer with Him, that we may be also glorified with Him."

SATURDAY OF THE THIRD WEEK OF LENT

We Were Reconciled to God Through Christ's Passion

"We were reconciled to God by the death of His Son." (Rom. V, 10.)

1. Christ's Passion is in two ways the cause of our reconciliation to God. In the first way, inasmuch as it takes away sin by which men became God's enemies, according to Wisdom XIV, 9, "To God the wicked and his wickedness are hateful alike"; and Ps. V, 7: "Thou hatest all the workers of iniquity." In another way, inasmuch as His Passion is a most acceptable sacrifice to God. Now it is the proper effect of sacrifice to appease God, just as man likewise overlooks an offense committed against him on account of some pleasing act of homage shown to him. Hence it is written (1 Kings XXVI, 19), "If the Lord stir thee up against me, let Him accept of sacrifice." And in like manner, Christ's voluntary suffering was such a good act that, because of its being found in human nature, God was appeased for every offense of the human race with regard to those who are united to the crucified Christ in the aforesaid manner.

Christ's Passion is not said to have reconciled us with God, as if God had begun anew to love us, since it is written (Jer. XXXI, 3), "I have loved thee with an everlasting love"; but because, the source of hatred was taken away by Christ's Passion, both through sin being washed away, and through compensation being made in the form of a more pleasing offering.

2. The Passion of Christ on the part of those who cruci-

fied Him, was indeed a cause of indignation. But the charity of Christ suffering, was greater than the wickedness of His murderers. And therefore, the Passion of Christ availed more to reconcile the entire human race to God, than to provoke to anger.

For the love of God for us is shown by its effect. One is said to love others, in so far as he makes them sharers in his goodness. But the final and most complete participation in God's goodness, consists in a Vision of His Essence; according to which we will sweetly and sociably live with Him, since happiness consists in this sweetness of union. Hence it is said that Christ loves those absolutely, whom He admits to this aforesaid Vision of Himself, to whom He gave His Holy Spirit as a pledge of this Vision.

Therefore, from this participation in the Divine goodness, namely, participation in the Vision of His Own Essence, man had been removed through sin, and on this account, man was said to have been deprived of the love of God.

Consequently, in as far as Christ by His Passion satisfied for us, He obtained for us admission to the Vision of God, and in this way He is said to have reconciled us to God.

FOURTH SUNDAY OF LENT

Christ Opened the Gate of Heaven to Us by His Passion

"We have confidence in the entering into the Holies, through the blood of Christ." (Hebr. X, 19.)

The closing of the gate is the obstacle which prevents men from entering in. But it is on account of sin that men were prevented from entering into the heavenly kingdom, since, according to Isaias XXXV, 8, "It shall be called the Holy way and the unclean shall not pass over it."

Now there is a twofold sin which prevents man from entering into the kingdom of heaven. The first is common to the whole human race, for it is our first parents' sin, and by that sin heaven's entrance is closed to man. Hence we read in Gen. III, 24, that after our first parents' sin, "God placed . . . cherubim and a flaming sword, turning every way, to keep the way of the tree of life." The other is the personal sin of each one of us, committed by our personal act.

Now by Christ's Passion we have been delivered not only from the common sin of the whole human race, both as to its guilt and the debt of penalty, for which He paid the penalty on our behalf; but, furthermore, from the personal sins of individuals who share in His Passion by faith and charity, and the sacraments of faith. Consequently, then, the gate of heaven's kingdom is thrown open to us by Christ's Passion. This is precisely what the Apostle says (Hebr. IX, 11, 12), "Christ being come a high-priest of the good things to come . . . by His Own blood entered once into the Holies, have obtained eternal redemption." And this is forshadowed (Num. XXXV, 25, 28), where it is said that the slayer, "shall abide there," that is to say in the city of refuge—"until the death of the high-priest, that is anointed with the holy oil; but after he is dead then shall he return home."

The holy fathers by doing works of justice, merited to enter into the heavenly kingdom, through faith in Christ's Passion, according to Heb. XI, 33, "The saints by faith conquered kingdoms, wrought justice," and each of them thereby was cleansed from sin, so far as the cleansing of the individual is concerned. Still the faith and righteousness of them sufficed for removing the barrier arising from the guilt of the whole human race; but this was removed at the cost of Christ's blood. Consequently, before Christ's Passion no one could enter the kingdom of heaven by obtaining everlasting beatitude which consists in the full enjoyment of God.

Christ by His Passion merited for us the opening of the kingdom of heaven, and removed the obstacle; but by His ascension He, as it were, brought us to the possession of the heavenly kingdom. And therefore it is said that by ascending He opened the way before them. (3a. q. 49, a. V.)

MONDAY OF THE FOURTH WEEK OF LENT

By His Passion Christ Merited to Be Exalted

"He became obedient unto death, even the death of the cross; for which cause God also exalted Him." (Phil. II, 8.)

Merit implies a certain equality of justice, and hence the Apostle says (Rom. IV, 4), "Now to him that worketh the reward is not reckoned according to grace, but according to debt." But when anyone by reason of his unjust will ascribes to himself something beyond his due, it is only just that he be deprived of something else which is his due; thus "when a man steals a sheep he shall pay back four." (Exod. XXI, 1.) And he is said to deserve it, inasmuch as his unjust will, is chastised thereby. So when any man by his just will has deprived himself of what he ought to have, he deserves that something further be granted to him as the reward of his just will. And hence it is written (Luke XIV, 11), "He that humbleth himself shall be exalted."

Now in His Passion Christ humbled Himself beneath His dignity in four ways.

In the first place, as to His Passion and Death to which he was not bound.

Secondly, as to the place, since His body was laid in a sepulchre, and His soul in hell.

Thirdly, as to the shame and mockeries He endured.

Fourthly, as to His being delivered up to man's power, for He Himself said to Pilate (John XIX, 11), "Thou shouldst not have any power against Me, unless it were given thee from above." And consequently He merited a fourfold exaltation, from His Passion.

First, as to His glorious Resurrection. Hence it is written (Ps. CXXXVIII, 1), "Thou hast known my sitting down—that is the lowliness of my Passion—and My rising up—that is My Resurrection."

Secondly, as to His Ascension into heaven. Hence it is written (Eph. IV, 9), "Now that He ascended, what is it, but because He also descended first into the lower parts of the earth? He that descended is the same also that ascended above all the heavens."

Thirdly, Christ has merited exaltation, as to His sitting at the right hand of the Father, and the showing forth of His Godhead, according to (Isaias LII, 13), "He shall be exalted and extolled, and shall be exceeding high. As many have been astonished at thee, so shall His visage be inglorious among men." Moreover (Phil. II, 8), declares, "He humbled Himself becoming obedient unto death, even to the death of the cross; for which cause also God hath exalted Him and hath given Him a Name that is above all names—that is to say, so that He shall be hailed as God by all; and all shall pay Him homage as God. And this is implied in what follows, "That in the Name of Jesus, every knee should bow, of those that are in heaven, on earth, and under the earth."

Fourthly, as to His judiciary power, Christ merited to be exalted; for it is written (Job XXXVI, 17), "Thy cause hath been judged as that of the wicked, cause and judgment Thou shalt recover." (3a. q. 49, a. 6.)

TUESDAY OF THE FOURTH WEEK OF LENT

The Example of Christ Crucified

Christ assumed human nature to restore man to the dignity from which he had fallen through sin. Therefore, it was necessary that Christ suffer and do those things which could be applied to human nature, as a remedy against the fall of man into sin.

But man's sin consists in this, that clinging to material things, he neglects spiritual good things. Therefore, it was fitting that the Son of God, in assuming the nature of man, show by those things which He did, and suffered, that material goods or evil deeds would lead men to ruin, unless their inordinate desire for worldly things were checked, and at least that men might desire spiritual things.

Hence Christ selected poor parents, but nevertheless perfect in virtue; lest anyone might glory only in nobility of blood and in the riches of wealthy parents.

He lived a life of poverty. Hence He has taught us how to regard wealth and how to make proper use of riches.

He lived a life deprived of dignity, so that He might recall men from their disorderly love of honors.

He endured hard work, thirst, hunger, scourgings, lest men given to lustful desires and sinful pleasures, might because of the trials of this life be drawn away from the good of virtue.

He endured death to the end, death in its most painful form; lest some because of their fear of death might abandon the truth. And lest anyone might fear to endure death in behalf of the truth, Christ selected the most reproachful kind of death, namely, the death of the cross.

Consequently, it was also fitting that the Son of God, made man, should endure such a death; so that by His example He might inspire men to practice virtue; and likewise so that it might be truly verified that which Peter said: "Christ suffered for us, leaving you an example that you should follow His steps." (1 Peter II, 21.)

On the other hand, "Christ suffered for us, leaving an example," the example of tribulation, of insults, of scourgings, the example of the cross and of His death; so that we might follow His steps. If we will endure trials and sufferings now for the sake of Christ, we will afterwards live with Him in eternal happiness. Bernard says, "How few, O Lord desire to follow after Thee, and still no one may come to Thee who is unwilling to follow Thee. Yet delights, are in Thy right hand unto the end. Moreover all wish to enjoy Thee, but all do not wish to so imitate Thee as to live with Thee. They desire to reign with Thee, but not to suffer with Thee. They do not care to seek Thee Whom they desire to find at last. They desire to receive Thy reward, but not to follow Thy example. (The Humanity of Christ Chapter 47.)

WEDNESDAY OF THE FOURTH WEEK OF LENT

The Divine Friend

"There was a certain man sick, named Lazarus. His sisters therefore sent to Jesus saying: Lord, behold, he whom Thou lovest is sick." (John XI, 1, 3.)

Here three things took place, which must be considered.

The first thing is that the friends of God are sometimes afflicted in body. Hence it is not a proof that someone who is afflicted physically, is not a friend of God; just as Eliphaz who argued falsely against Job, and pretended that God never afflicts the innocent, saying: "Remember, I pray thee, who ever perished being innocent? Or when were the just destroyed?" (Job IV, 7.) And therefore Proverbs (III, 12) declareth, "Whom the Lord loveth He chastiseth and as a father in the son he pleaseth himself." Wherefore, the sisters of Lazarus wisely said, "Behold, he whom Thou lovest is sick."

The second thing to be observed is what the sisters did not say. They did not say, "O Lord, come and cure him"; but mentioning only the illness of Lazarus, they simply said, "he whom Thou lovest is sick." In this statement is signified that it suffices to mention to their Friend, the need of His friend, without adding any request. For a friend is one who wishes good to a friend as if to himself, and is as anxious to remove the evil of his friend as if it were his own evil. And this is especially true of Him who is the truest Friend, and most truly loves. "The Lord keepeth all them that love Him." (Ps. CXLIV, 20.)

The third thing to be noted, is that these two sisters, desiring the cure of their sick brother, did not come personally to Christ; as did the paralytic and the centurion; and this because of the confidence which they had in Christ, resulting from the special love and familiarity which Christ showed them; and perhaps because they were detained by grief from coming to Christ, as Chrysostom says. "A friend if he continue steadfast, shall be to thee as thyself, and shall act with confidence among them of their household. A faithful friend is a strong defense, and he that hath found him hath found a treasure. For a faithful friend is the medicine of life and immortality, and they that fear the Lord shall find Him." (Eccles. VI, 11.) (John XI.)

THURSDAY OF THE FOURTH WEEK OF LENT

Lazarus' Death

1. *"Lazarus our friend sleepeth; but I go that I may awake him out of sleep."* (John XI, 11.)

"Our friend," by reason of the many favours and grace which Christ has conferred on us, and therefore, we should not be in need of spiritual help.

"He sleepeth." Hence it is necessary that he receive assistance. "He that is a friend loveth at all times, and a brother is proved in distress." (Prov. XVII, 17.) "Sleepeth," as Augustine remarks, "sleepeth to the Lord; but dead to men who were not able to restore life to the dead Lazarus."

Sleep may be considered in many ways, namely, for the sleep of nature, for negligence, for the sleep of fault, for the calm of contemplation, for the rest of future glory, and sometimes sleep is taken to mean death. "We will not have you ignorant, brethren, concerning them that are asleep; that you be not sorrowful, even as others who have no hope." (1 Thess. IV, 12.)

Moreover, death is called sleep, because of the hope of our resurrection, and therefore, death is accustomed to be referred to as sleep, from that time when Christ died and arose from the grave. "I have slept and have taken My rest; and I have risen up, because the Lord hath protected Me." (Ps. III, 6.)

2. "But I go that I may awake him from sleep." In this action Jesus gives us to understand that He was able to raise Lazarus to life from the grave with as much easiness as you might awaken one sleeping in a bed. Nor is this to be wondered at since He Who gives life can as easily restore life to the dead. Hence it is written, "The hour cometh in which all who are in their graves will hear the voice of the Son of God."

3 "Then Jesus said to them plainly. Lazarus is dead. And I am glad for your sakes, that I was not there, so that you may believe. But let us go to him." (John XI, 14.) In these words, the mercy of God is revealed; in as far as men living in sin are as if dead and cannot of themselves come to Christ; and thus He mercifully goes to them and attracts them, according to Jerm. XXXI, 3, "I have loved thee with an everlasting love, therefore, have I drawn thee, taking pity on thee."

4. "Jesus therefore came and found that he (Lazarus) had been already four days in the grave." (John XI, 17.) According to Augustine, the four days that Lazarus was in the grave signifies the sinful man, held captive by the death of a fourfold sin. First by the death of original sin, secondly, by the death caused from actual sin, which is contrary to the law of nature, thirdly, the death caused by actual sin, contrary to the written law, and fourthly, death caused by actual sin, contrary to the law of the Gospel and of grace.

Or again, the first day, represents the sin of the mind, "Take away the evil of your devices." (Isaias I, 16.) The second day represents the sins of the tongue. "Let no evil speech proceed from your mouth." (Eph. IV, 29.) The third day is the sin of action, "Cease to do perversely." (Isaias I, 16.) The fourth day represents the sin resulting from perverse habit.

Finally it may be said that the Lord sometimes cures those dead four days that is those who have transgressed the law of the Gospel, and are enslaved by a long habit of sinning. (John XI.)

FRIDAY OF THE FOURTH WEEK OF LENT
The Most Precious Blood of Our Lord

1. By the blood of Christ the new testament was confirmed. "This chalice is the new testament in My blood." (1 Cor. XI, 25.) A testament may be considered in two ways. In one way, as a certain covenant. Moreover, God entered into such a covenant with the human race, in two ways. In one way by promising temporal goods and by liberating us from temporal evils; and this is called the Old Testament. In another way, by promising spiritual goods, and by freeing us from conflicting evils, and this covenant is called the New Testament. "I will make with the house of Israel and with the house of Juda a new covenant, not according to the covenant which I made with their fathers, that I might lead them out of the land of Egypt. I will give My law into their hearts, and they shall be My people and I will be their God." (Jerm. XXXII, 40.) Among the ancients it was customary to sprinkle the blood of certain victims for the confirmation of the covenant. Thus Moses took the blood, and sprinkled it upon the people, and said: "This is the blood of the covenant which the Lord hath made with you." (Exod. XXIV, 8.) Just as the old testament was therefore, confirmed in the blood of animals, so the new testament or covenant was confirmed in the blood of Christ, which was shed in His Passion.

In another way, testament may be considered more strictly, namely, for the disposal of possessions received. But a testament considered thus, is confirmed only through death, as the Apostle says: "For a testament is of force, after men are dead, otherwise it is of no strength, while the testator liveth." (Heb. IX, 17.) Moreover, God at first made a disposal of the eternal possessions to be received but under the figure of temporal goods, which pertains to the Old Testament. But afterwards He made a new testament, expressly promising us an eternal kingdom, which in very truth was confirmed, written with the blood of Christ's death. And therefore the Lord Himself said of this covenant: "This chalice is the New Testament—in My Blood," as if He had said, through this (sacrifice) which is continued in the chalice, the new testament is confirmed by the blood of Christ.

2. There are other blessings which have flowed to us from the blood of Christ.

First, the cleansing of our sins, and removal of wounds caused by sin. "From Jesus Christ Who is the faithful witness, the first begotten of the dead, and the Prince of the kings of the earth, Who hast loved us, and washed us from sins in His own blood." (Apoc. I, 5.)

Secondly, our Redemption. "Thou hast redeemed us, O Lord, to God in Thy blood." (Apoc. V, 9.)

Thirdly, our peace with God and the Angels, is assured through Christ's blood. "Through Him . . . making peace through the blood of His cross, both as to the things that are on earth, and to the things that are in heaven." (Col. I, 20.)

Fourthly, Christ's blood is drink and nourishment to all receiving it. "Drink ye all of this" (Matth. XXVI, 28), "that they might drink the purest blood of the grape." (Deut. XXXII, 14.)

Fifthly, the gates of heaven were opened to us by the blood of Christ. "Having therefore, brethren, a confidence in the entering into the holies by the blood of Christ" (Hebr. X, 19), that is, the blood of Christ, is a continual prayer for us to God, for His blood cries daily for us to the Father, "And you have access to Jesus the Mediator of the new testament, and to the sprinkling of blood, and to the company of many thousands of Angels, which speaketh better than that of Abel." (Hebr. XII, 24.) The blood of Abel cried for vengeance, the blood of Christ pleads for mercy.

Sixthly, the deliverance of the souls from purgatory is affected through Christ's blood, "Thou also by the blood of Thy new testament, has sent forth Thy prisoners out of the pit, wherein is no water." (Zach. IX, 11.) (Sermon on Passion Sunday.)

SATURDAY OF THE FOURTH WEEK OF LENT

"There Was No More Suitable Way of Delivering the Human Race Than by Christ's Passion"

Among means to an end that one is the more suitable whereby the various concurring means employed are themselves helpful to such an end. But in this that man was delivered by Christ's Passion, many other things besides deliverance, from sin, concurred for man's salvation.

In the first place, man knows thereby how much God loves him, and is thereby aroused to love Him in return; in which the perfection of human salvation consists. Hence the Apostle says, "God commendeth His charity towards us; for when as yet we were sinners . . . Christ died for us." (Rom. V, 8.)

Secondly, because by His Passion, He set us an example of obedience, humility, constancy, justice, and the other virtues displayed in the Passion, which are necessary for man's salvation. Hence it is written, "Christ also suffered for us leaving you an example that you should follow in His steps." (Peter II, 21.)

Thirdly, because Christ by His Passion not only delivered man from sin, but also merited justifying grace for him and the glory of bliss promised him.

Fourthly, because man is all the more bound to refrain from sin, when he bears in mind that he has been redeemed by Christ's blood, according to 1 Cor. V, 20, "You are bought with a great price, glorify and bear God in your body."

Fifthly, because it redounded to man's greater dignity, that as man was overcome and deceived by the devil, so also it should be a man that should overthrow the devil; and as man deserved death, so a man by dying should vanquish death. Hence it is written (1 Cor. XV, 57), "Thanks be to God Who hath given us the victory through our Lord Jesus Christ."

Consequently, it was accordingly more fitting that we should be delivered by Christ's Passion than simply by God's will. Wherefore, Augustine says, "There was no other suitable way of healing our misery than by the Passion of Christ." (3a. q. 46, a. 3.)

PASSION SUNDAY

The Passion of Christ

"*As Moses lifted up the serpent in the desert, so must the Son of man be lifted up. That whosoever believeth in Him, may not perish; but may have life everlasting.*" (John III, 14.)

Here three things must be considered, namely, the figure of the Passion, secondly, the manner of the Passion, and thirdly, the fruit or effect of our Lord's Passion.

First, the figure of the Passion, "As Moses lifted up the serpent in the desert." Speaking of the Jewish people, it is written: "Our soul now loatheth this very light food." (Numbers XXI, 5.) And in revenge the Lord sent serpents, but afterwards commanded a brazen serpent to be made as a remedy against serpents and as a figure of His Passion. It is characteristic of a serpent to have poison, but the brazen serpent possessed no poison, but was a figure of a poisonous serpent. Likewise, Christ had no sin, sin as it were poison to the soul, but He had the likeness of sin. "God sent His Son in the likeness of sinful flesh." (Rom. VIII, 3.) Therefore, Christ produced the effect of the serpent against the motion of the enkindled lusts of the flesh.

Secondly, the manner of the Passion must be considered. "So must the Son of man be exalted," and this is understood of the exaltation of the cross. Moreover Christ wished to die —lifted up, or exalted. First, so that He might cleanse the things above, for already He had cleansed the earth, by the sanctity of His life. It remained for Him now to purge the very atmosphere by His death on the Cross.

2. He wished to die lifted up, so that He might triumph over the demons, who were fighting in the sky.

3. He wished to die lifted up, so that He might draw our hearts to Himself. "I when I am lifted up from the earth, will draw all things to Myself." Since Christ was exalted by His death on the Cross, in as far as He triumphed on the cross over His enemies, His death is rightly called an exaltation. "He shall drink of the torrent in the way. Therefore shall He lift up the head." (Ps. CIX, 7.)

4. Because the cross was the cause of His exaltation. "He became obedient, unto death. For which cause God exalted Him." (Phil. II, 8.)

Thirdly, the fruit of the Passion must be considered. The fruit is eternal life. "That whosoever believeth in Me (and doth good works), will not perish but will have everlasting life, and I will raise him up on the last day." And this fruit or effect corresponds to the effect of the figurative serpent. For whosoever looked upon the brazen serpent, were freed (cured) of the poison, and their life was preserved. But whosoever looks upon the Son of man, lifted up on the cross, and believes in Christ crucified, and follows His steps, will be accordingly liberated from the serpent satan and from sin; and preserved unto life everlasting. (John III.)

MONDAY OF PASSION WEEK

Christ's Passion Is a Remedy Against Sins

Against all the evils which we incur through sin, we have a remedy in Christ's Passion. But we fall heir to five evils through sinning, namely, first the stain of sin, secondly, we commit an offense against God, thirdly, weakness of our wills, fourthly, a debt of punishment, and fifthly, banishment from the kingdom of God.

First, the stain. For when man sins he soils, debases his soul; because just as the virtue of the soul is its beauty, so sin is its stain. "How happeneth, O Israel, that thou art in thy enemies' land. Thou art defiled with the dead." (Baruch III, 10.) But the Passion of Christ removes this defilement of the soul, for Christ in His Passion made a bath of His blood, in which He cleanses sinners of their defilement. But the soul is washed in the blood of Christ in Baptism, because Baptism has a regenerating power from the blood of Christ. And therefore, when anyone defiles himself by sin, he does an injury to God, and sins more than before.

Secondly, the offense against God. For just as a carnal man loves carnal beauty so God loves spiritual beauty, that is the beauty of a virtuous soul. When therefore, the soul is defiled by sin, God is offended, and the sinner becomes God's enemy. But Christ's Passion removes this defilement; since it made satisfaction to God the Father for sin; which satisfaction man himself was not able to make; for the charity and obedience of Christ were greater than the sin and disloyalty —of the first man.

Thirdly, weakness of the will follows from sin for man in sinning once, thinks he can sin again, and easily sins again; because by the first sin his will becomes weakened, and is more prone to sin. Likewise sin controls man all the more, both because man subjects himself to it, and places himself in such a state that he cannot rise, unless aided by Divine power; just like one who throws himself into a very deep well. Hence after man sinned, our nature became weakened and corrupted; as a result that man became more prone to sin.

But Christ lessened this weakness and debility, although He did not take the weakness away entirely; still man is so strengthened by the Passion of Christ, that the impetus to sin is decreased, and he is not so much controlled by sin as before, and man aided by God's grace which comes to him from the sacraments and prayer, and which receive their efficacy from Christ's Passion, man thus divinely assisted can try to avoid sin, and even hate sin, but after the Passion there are many souls who have lived and many who are now living entirely free from mortal sin by virtue of the Saviour's Passion and death.

Fourthly, the debt of punishment. For the justice of God demands this that whosoever sins should be punished. But punishment is reckoned according to the crime and should be proportioned to the crime committed. Hence since the crime of a mortal sin is infinite, in as far as it is a crime against the Infinite Good, namely against God, Whose commandments the sinner despises, the punishment due to one mortal sin is infinite.

But Christ by His Passion took away from us this punishment and even endured it for us. "He Himself bore our sins," that is the punishment for our sins, "He bore it in His own body on the tree of the cross." (1 Peter II.) For the Passion of Christ was of such great virtue that it sufficed to expiate every sin of the whole world, yea even thousands of worlds. And hence it is that the baptized are freed from all sins, hence it is also, that the priest forgives sins in Christ's name; hence it is that whosoever conforms oneself more to the Passion of Christ, loves it the more, obtains greater pardon and merits more grace.

Fifthly, we incur banishment from the kingdom of God because of sin. For those who offend kings, are compelled to leave the kingdom or are sent into exile sometimes and thus man because of sin was expelled from Paradise. Hence it is that Adam immediately after he had sinned was driven out of paradise, and the gates of heaven were closed against him and his posterity. But Christ by His Passion opened that gate and recalled the exiles to His kingdom. For when the side of Christ was opened with the spear, the gate of heaven opened wide, and when His blood was shed on Calvary's cross the stains of our sins were removed, the anger of God was appeased, punishment was expiated, and the exiles were recalled to the kingdom of God. And hence it is that Christ immediately said to the repentant thief, who cried for mercy and pardon, "This day thou shalt be with Me in Paradise." (Luke XXIII, 43.) This was not said of old. For it was not said to anyone else, not to Adam, not to Abraham, not to David. But "today," namely, when heaven's gate is opened, does the thief seek and find pardon. "Having therefore, brethren, a confidence in the entering into the holies by the blood of Christ." (Hebr. X, 19.) (The Creed.)

TUESDAY OF PASSION WEEK

The Burial of Christ

Our Lord said to the woman who anointed Him, *"She has wrought a good work upon Me, for she, in pouring this ointment upon My body hath done it for My burial."* (Matth. XXVI, 10.)

It was fitting for Christ to be buried.

First, to establish the truth of His death, for no one is laid in the grave unless there is certainty of death. Hence we read (Mark XV, 44), that Pilate by careful inquiry assured himself of Christ's death before granting permission for His burial.

Secondly, because by Christ's rising from the grave, to them who are in their graves, hope is given of rising again through Him, according to John V, 25: "All that are in their graves shall hear the voice of the Son of God . . . and they that hear shall live."

Thirdly, as an example to them who dying spiritually to their sins are "hidden away from the disturbance of men." (Ps. XXX, 21.) Hence it is written, "You are dead, and your life is hid with Christ in God." (Col. III, 3.) Wherefore, the baptized likewise, who through Christ's death die to sins, are as it were buried with Christ by immersion, according to Rom. VI, 4, "We are buried together with Christ by baptism unto death."

As Christ's death efficiently wrought our salvation, so likewise did His burial. Hence Jerome says, "By Christ's burial we rise again," a gloss adds, "He shall give to God and the Father, the Gentiles who were without godliness, because He purchased them by His death and burial."

Likewise, it is written, "I am become as a man without help, free among the dead." (Ps. LXXXVII, 6.) Although buried, Christ proved Himself "free among the dead," since, although imprisoned in the tomb, He could not be prevented from going forth by rising again. (3a. q. 51, a. 1.)

WEDNESDAY OF PASSION WEEK

Spiritual Burial

Heavenly contemplation is signified by burial. Hence, commenting on (Job III, 22), "They rejoiced exceedingly when they found the grave." Gregory says: "Just as a body in the grave, so is the soul dead to the world that is hidden in Divine contemplation, where it rests secure from the disturbance of the world as if in a threefold immersion for a period of three days buried in the Lord." "Thou shalt hide them (contemplative souls) in the secret of Thy face, from the disturbance of men." (Ps. XXX, 21.) Those contemplating the face of God are not disturbed, vexed or annoyed, by the reproaches of men.

But three things are necessary for us to become spiritually buried in God. Our mind must be exercised in the virtues, secondly, the mind must become entirely clean and candid, and thirdly, we must die completely to this world; which things are mystically demonstrated in the burial of Christ.

The first point is shown (Mark XIV, 8) where we read that Mary Magdalen came to anoint the body of Jesus for His burial, for the sweet smelling ointment designates virtues, because of its preciousness, and there is nothing in this life so precious as virtue. Therefore, a holy soul should first of all be anointed by the practice of virtue; if the soul desires to become buried in Divine contemplation. Hence Job V, 26, says: "Thou shalt enter into the grave in abundance (of divine contemplation), as a heap of wheat is brought in its season." A gloss says, "because the time of action is the reward of eternal contemplation, it is necessary first of all, that the mind be exercised perfectly, in every virtue, and afterwards hide itself in the mansion of rest."

The second point is suggested in Mark (XV, 46) where we read that Joseph bought fine linen; because linen is fine white cloth, and produced with great labour in regard to its whiteness. Hence it represents the interior purity of the mind, at which we must arrive with great labour on our part if we wish to become perfect, and "be buried with Christ in God." Wherefore (Apoc. XXII, 11), says, "He that is just let him be justified still, and he that is holy, let him be sanctified still." And the Apostle (Rom. VI, 4) exhorts us thus, "Let us walk in newness of life," by advancing in a state of goodness to that which is better—advancing through the justice of faith into the hope of glory. Therefore, men ought to be hidden in the sepulchre of Divine contemplation by the dazzling whiteness of their interior cleanliness of heart and of mind. Hence Jerome commenting on, "Blessed are the clean of heart for they shall see God" (Matth. V, 8), says, "The pure Lord looks with favour upon a clean heart."

The third point is signified in (John XIX, 39), where it is written that "Nicodemus came to Jesus at night, bringing a mixture of myrrh and aloes, with the spices, about a hundred pound weight," because through the hundred pounds of myrrh and aloes the dead body might be preserved incorruptible, and likewise, by this is signified the perfect mortification of the exterior senses, so that the mind or soul dead to the world is preserved, lest it become corrupted by worldly vices. Wherefore the Apostle says (2 Cor. IV, 6), "Though our outward man is corrupted, yet the inward man is renewed day by day," that is by diligently becoming purer and more free from vices through the fire of trial and tribulation.

Therefore, the mind of man should first of all become mortified and dead with Christ to this world's vices, and afterwards be buried with Him in the hidden recess of Divine contemplation. Hence it is written (Col. III, 30), "You are dead with Christ (to vain and perishable things), and your life is hid with Christ in God." (The Humanity of Christ—Chapter 42.)

THURSDAY OF PASSION WEEK

The Greatest Manifestation of Christ's Love for Us

It seems that Christ showed greater love for us in giving His body to us for food than in suffering for us. For the charity of heaven is greater than giving His Body to us as food, is more likened to the charity of heaven by which we will completely enjoy God. But the Passion which He suffered for us is more akin to the charity of this life, whereby He endured suffering for the sake of Christ. Therefore, it is a greater sign of love, that Christ gave us His body for food, than that Christ suffered for us. More He could not do than give Himself to us.

But on the contrary, it is written, "Greater love than this no man hath than that a man lay down his life for his friends." (John XV, 13.)

Now among the various kinds of love of man, the most powerful is the love whereby he loves himself. Consequently, from this love it is necessary to take the measure of all love by which anyone loves another. Moreover, it pertains to the love whereby anyone loves oneself, that he wish good to himself. Therefore, inasmuch as anyone proves that he loves another more, in so far does he wish more good to that person, and suffers loss because of his friend; according to Prov. XII, 26, "He that neglecteth a loss for the sake of a friend is just."

On the other hand, man wishes for himself a special threefold good, his body and external good things. It is therefore, a certain sign of love if some one willingly suffers a loss of external goods in behalf of another. But it is a greater manifestation of love if he suffers even the loss of his own body, by enduring hardships and scourging for the sake of his friend.

But it is the greatest sign of love when one sacrifices and wills to give his own soul or life for a friend by dying for him. But Christ in suffering for us offered His own soul in sacrifice, His very life; and this was the greatest manifestation of love. On the other hand, when He gave His Body as food for our souls in the Blessed Sacrament, He suffered no loss in Himself. Hence it is clear that the first, namely the Passion of Christ, if we consider the loss He endured, is a greater sign of love. On the other hand, the Sacrament of the altar is a certain memorial and figure of Christ's Passion. But the truth is more excellent than the figure, and the virtue more than the memorial.

In truth, the reality of the Body of our Lord in the Blessed Eucharist reveals a certain likeness of the charity whereby God loves us in heaven, but the Passion of Christ pertains also to the very love of God bringing us back from perdition to heaven. However the love of God is no greater in heaven than on earth. (Quodl, V. Q. 3, 2.)

FRIDAY OF PASSION WEEK

The Compassion of the Blessed Virgin

"Thy own soul a sword shall pierce." (Luke II, 35.)

In these words is noted the great compassion of the Blessed Mother for Christ. We must also observe four things which made the Passion of Christ most painful for the Blessed Virgin. First of all the love of God, secondly, the cruelty of His crucifiers, thirdly, the shamelessness of the punishment, and fourthly, the unmercifulness of His sufferings.

1. The goodness of Her Son "Who committed no sin." (Peter II, 22.)

2. The cruelty of His crucifiers pierced Mary's heart, which is clear from the fact that they would not permit her to moisten with a drop of water, the parched and feverish lips of her dying son, nor even allow her to console her child in any manner. She who would have gladly given her own life to save His.

3. The shamelessness of the punishment endured by her Son was another sword of sorrow that pierced the compassionate heart of Mary Immaculate. "Oh, all ye who pass by the way, attend and see, if there be any sorrow like unto my sorrow." (Lam. I, 12.)

Origen and certain other doctors explain those words of Simeon, "Thy own soul a sword shall pierce," as referring to the sorrow which she suffered at the time of our Lord's Passion. Ambrose says that "The sword signifies Mary's prudence which carefully observed the heavenly mystery." "For the word of God is living and effectual, and more piercing than any two-edged sword." (Hebr. IV, 12.)

Others again take the sword to mean doubt. This is to be understood, of the doubt, not of unbelief, but of wonder and discussion. Thus Basil says that the, "Blessed Virgin while standing by the cross and observing every detail, after the message of Gabriel, and the indescribable knowledge of the Divine Conception, after that wondrous manifestation of miracles, was troubled in mind," that is to say, on the one side seeing Him suffer such humiliation and on the other considering His marvelous works.

Although Mary knew through faith, that God willed that Christ should suffer, and that His will should be conformed to the Divine will, just as the blessed are conformed, still the sadness which the Blessed Virgin experienced at the death of

Christ, in as far as the inferior will is concerned, was repugnant to a particular desire, but not contrary to perfection.

SATURDAY OF PASSION WEEK

How We Should Wash One Another's Feet

"If I then being your Lord and Master, have washed your feet; you also ought to wash one another's feet." (John XIII, 14.)

The Lord desires that His disciples imitate His example. Therefore He says, "If I Who am greater than you, because I am your Lord and Master, have washed your feet, by so much the more should you, who are My disciples and servants wash the feet of one another." "Whosoever will be the greater among you, let him be your minister. And he that shall be first among you shall be your servant. For the Son of man came not to be ministered to, but to minister, and to give His life for the redemption of many." (Matth. XX, 26, 28.)

According to Augustine every man ought to wash the feet of another either actually or spiritually. It is much better and without doubt more genuine, if one actually washes the feet of another, so that he might be worthy to do what Christ did. But if we do not actually wash the feet of another, at least we ought to do it spiritually. For in the washing of the feet of the disciples, our Lord also wished to convey to our minds the washing away of the stains of sin. Therefore then, you spiritually wash the feet of your brother, when in as far as you can you wash away the stains of his sins.

This may be done in three ways.

1. By forgiving him his offense against you according to Col. III, 13. "Bearing with one another, and forgiving one another, if any have a complaint against another; even as the Lord hath forgiven you, so do you also."

2. By praying for the forgiveness of your neighbor's sins, according to James V, 16. "Pray for one another, that you may be saved." And this two-fold manner of washing is the duty of everyone of us, and can easily be performed by all, since we all can and should forgive others and pray for others.

3. This manner of spiritual washing in a special way pertains to priests who from the authority invested in them by our Divine Lord, ought to wash away the sins of their penitents, by forgiving them in the sacrament of confession, according to the command of the Saviour Who has said to them: "Receive ye the Holy Ghost whose sins you shall forgive they are forgiven them." (John XX, 23.)

We can also conclude that in this great act of humility, of washing His disciples' feet, our Lord showed all the works of mercy. For He gave bread to the hungry, He washed the feet of His disciples. He clothed the naked, visited the sick. Likewise whosoever receives Christ as a guest into his heart does the works of Christ, and whosoever from a spirit of Christlike charity performs the spiritual and corporal works of mercy, does the work of Christ; for he "communicates to the necessities of the saints." (Rom. XII, 13.) (John XIII.)

PALM SUNDAY

The Usefulness of Christ's Passion in Regard to Our Example

The Passion of Christ suffices to reform completely our entire life. For whosoever desires to live perfectly, need do nothing more than despise those things which Christ on the cross despised, and love the things which Christ loved. For no example of virtue is absent from the cross.

If you seek an example of charity here it is, "Greater love than this no one hath, that he lay down his life for his friends." (John XV.) Christ did this very thing on the Cross. Therefore, if Christ gave His life for us, we ought to endure every hardship and every trial for the sake of Him. "What shall I render to the Lord, for all the things that He hath rendered to me." (Ps. CXV, 12.)

If you are looking for an example of patience, behold there on the cross the most excellent example of patience. For great patience is shown in two ways. Either when anyone endures great pain with resignation or when anyone endures that which he was able to avoid and did not avoid. But Christ endured great sufferings upon the cross. "Oh all ye who pass by the way, attend and see, if there be any sorrow like unto My sorrow" (Lam. I, 12), and this suffering He endured resignedly, "Who when He was reviled, did not revile. When he suffered, He threatened not, but delivered Himself to him that judged Him unjustly." (1 Peter, II.) "He shall be led as a sheep to the slaughter, and as a lamb before His shearer, He shall not open His mouth." (Isaias LIII, 7.) Likewise Christ was able to avoid these sufferings, but did not avoid them. "Thinkest thou that I cannot ask My Father, and He will give Me presently more than twelve legions of Angels?" (Matth. XXVI, 53.) Therefore, the greatest patience of all times was exemplified by Christ on His death-bed of the Cross. "Therefore, let us run by patience to the fight proposed to us, looking on Jesus, the Author and Finisher of faith, who having joy set before Him, endured the cross, despising the shame, and now sitteth at the right hand of the throne of God." (Hebr. XII, 1. 2.)

If you are seeking an example of obedience, follow Him Who "became obedient unto death." (Rom. V, 19.) "Just through the disobedience of one man, many became sinners, so through the obedience of One, Jesus Christ—many shall be made just." (Rom. V, 18.)

If you are seeking an example of humility, gaze upon the crucifix. For God willed to be judged by Pontius Pilate and to die at his hands. "Thy cause hath been judged as that of the wicked." (Job XXXVI, 17.) Truly that of the wicked, because Wisdom (II, 20) declares, "Let us condemn Him to a most shameful death."

If you are seeking an example of despising earthly things, follow Him Who is the King of Kings and the Lord of Lords; in Whom are all the treasures of wisdom; yet behold Him naked on the cross, mocked, spit upon, struck, crowned with thorns, given gall and vinegar to drink, God dead upon the cross. If you wish to be unaffected by dress and by riches, behold Christ, "They parted My garments, and upon My vesture, they cast lots." (Ps. XXI, 19.) Unaffected by honors, behold how Christ endured mockery and scourging. "They pierced My hands and My feet, and they have numbered all my bones." Behold how Christ was crowned with thorns, if you wish to be uninfluenced by false dignities. "Platting a crown of thorns they placed it upon My head." (Matth. XXVII, 29.) If you wish to remain unaffected by false pleasures, behold Christ on the cross, saying "They gave Me gall for My food, and in My thirst they gave Me vinegar to drink." (Ps. LXVIII, 22.) Behold the greatness of His sufferings and the malice of His persecutors, if you wish to profit by Christ's example, of humility, patience, charity, forgiveness, and love of suffering! (The Creed.)

THE MONDAY FOLLOWING PALM SUNDAY

The Necessity of Perfect Cleanliness

1. Jesus answered and said to Peter, "If I wash thee not, thou shalt have no part with Me." (John XIII, 8.) For no one can share in the eternal kingdom and be an heir of Christ, unless he is spiritually cleansed and wholly purified of every stain of sin, for this is what Apoc. XXI, 27 says, "Nothing defiled shall enter the kingdom of God." And again the Psalmist (Ps. XIV, 1) says, "Lord, who shall dwell in Thy tabernacle?" The innocent in hands, and clean of heart. (Ps. XXIII, 4.) As if therefore, Christ should have said, "If I wash thee not, you will not be clean, and if you are not clean, you will have no part with Me."

2. Simon Peter said to Him, "Lord (wash) not only my feet, but also my hands and my head." (John XIII, 9.) Peter being terrified, and aroused by love and fear, thereupon offered himself entirely to the Lord, to be purified. For Clement writes in his Itinerario that, "Peter was so deeply attracted to the bodily presence of Christ that his heart was inflamed with the most fervent love, so that after Christ's Ascension, when he recalled the adorable Presence and holy conversation of Christ, he so completely burst into tears, that the eyes of his soul seemed inflamed with love of God."

We must remember there are three things in man which serve his purpose. The head, which is the highest, the feet, which are the lowest members of the body, and the hands which are midway. And likewise in the interior man, namely in the soul, is the head or superior reason (the intellect), by which the soul clings to God; moreover, there are the hands, resembling the inferior powers which devote themselves to works of the active life; and finally the feet, in which are the powers of sensitiveness. But the Lord knew that His disciples were clean in regard to the head, for they were united to God by faith and charity; and clean in regard to their hands, because their works were holy, but regarding the feet, some as yet entertained certain affections for earthly things and this resulted from sensitiveness rather than from right reason. They were, in their affections for certain earthly things, swayed by sensitiveness rather than guided by right reason.

On the other hand, Peter fearing the threat of Christ, consented not only to the washing of his feet, but also that his hands and head be washed by the Saviour of his soul, saying: "Lord (wash) not only my feet, but also my hands and my head." As if he had said, I do not know that I need cleansing of my hands and head, "for I am not conscious to myself of anything, yet am I not hereby justified." (Cor. IV, 4.) And therefore, I am now ready to have washed not only my feet, that is my interior affections, but also my hands, that is, my works, and likewise my head, that is the superior powers of my soul.

3. "Jesus said to Peter: He that is washed, needeth not but to wash his feet, for he is clean wholly, and you are clean but not all." (John XIII, 10.) Origen says that the disciples were clean, but there was yet need of greater cleanliness; because reason should always strive to attain superior gifts from above and ought always to mount higher in virtue, and shine forth with the heavenly brightness of justice. "He that is holy, let him be sanctified still." (Apoc. XXII, 11.) (John XIII.)

THE TUESDAY AFTER PALM SUNDAY

The Washing of the Apostles' Feet by the Saviour

"Jesus riseth from supper, and layeth aside His garments, and having taken a towel, girded Himself." (John XIII, 4.)

1. Christ with the willingness of His humility, proved Himself to be a servant of the people, according to the words of Matth. XX, 28, "The Son of man is not come to be ministered to, but to minister, and to give His life a redemption for many."

Moreover three things are essential for every good minister or servant of the people.

First of all, he should be sufficiently wise to see all the things which may need his ministrations or services, but this is especially hindered if he should remain seated, or lie down on his obligations by neglecting them in any way. Hence, it is expected of servants to stand while rendering service; and therefore it is written, "Jesus riseth from supper." "For who is the greater, he that sitteth at table or he that serveth? But I am in the midst of you, as He that serveth." (Luke XXII, 27.)

Secondly, that servant or minister must be prepared to serve, so that he can properly do whatever things are necessary for him to do, but this proper execution of duty is impeded greatly by too much garments; and consequently, "The Lord layeth aside His garments." It is also written in Gen.

XVII, that Abraham bought unimpeded servants who were prepared to do their work promptly and efficiently.

Thirdly, the minister should be prompt in serving, so that he has all things necessary for the service. Luke X, 40, says of Martha that "she was busy about much serving." Hence it is that the Lord "having taken the towel, girded Himself," so that He might be fully prepared not only to wash the disciples' feet, but also to dry them. By this very act of humility, the Lord trampled under foot all swellings of pride, since He Who came from God and returned to God, stooped to wash the feet of His disciples. We too must be humble, if we wish to return to God from Whom we came.

2. "After that He put water into a basin and began to wash the feet of His disciples." (John XIII, 5.) Here the willingness of Christ is expressed, so that His humility is commended in regard to three things.

First of all, in regard to the nature of His willingness, which was profoundly humble; so much so that the Lord of power and majesty stooped to wash the feet of His servants.

Secondly, His humility is commendable in regard to the the extent of His compliance, for He Himself put water into the basin, washed their feet and dried them.

Thirdly, His humility is to be commended (and imitated by us) in regard to His mode of action, for He did not act through others, or with help from others, but with His hands He performed this great act of humility. "For great is the power of God alone, and He is honored by the humble. The greater thou art, the more humble thyself in all things, and thou shalt find grace before God." (Eccles. III, 20, 21.) (John XIII.)

THE WEDNESDAY AFTER PALM SUNDAY

Three Things Which Must Be Understood Mystically in Christ

"He putteth water into a basin, and began to wash the feet of His disciples, and to wipe them with the towel wherewith He was girded." (John XIII, 5.)

Through this action on Christ's part, three things can be mystically understood.

First of all, from the fact that Christ put water into a basin, may be understood the pouring out of His blood upon the earth. For the blood of Jesus can be called water, since it has cleansing power. And hence it is that blood and water flowed together from the side of Christ, so that we might understand that the blood of Christ would be for the washing away or remission of sins. Or the water can signify the Passion of Christ. Therefore, "He putteth water into a basin," that is, Christ impressed upon the minds of the faithful, through faith and devotion, the memory of His Passion. "Remember my poverty, and transgression, the wormwood and the gall." (Lam. III, 19.)

Secondly, through this, that Christ "began to wash the feet of His disciples," is meant human imperfection. For the Apostles after the washing were more perfect, even though they had yet certain imperfections; so that no matter how perfect a man may be, he can still become more perfect and contract certain impurities; according to Prov. XX, 9, "Who can say, My heart is clean. I am free from sin." But nevertheless impurities of this kind are in the feet only.

Moreover, some people are not only impure in regard to the feet; they are completely infected. For those who are totally contaminated by earthly impurities live for the things of earth entirely; hence those who devote themselves wholly to sensual love and give their affections entirely to things of this earth are absolutely unclean.

But those who stand firmly, that is, those who in heart and desire strive to obtain heavenly things, contract uncleanliness in respect to the feet. For just as it is necessary for a man standing on the ground to touch the earth with his feet, so as long as we live in this mortal life we need earthly things for the upkeep of the body, and on this account we contract samething of sensuality. And hence the Lord commanded His disciples "to shake the dust off their feet." (Luke IX.)

Moreover it is written, "He began to wash the feet of His disciples," because the cleansing of our affections from things of earth begins here, and is perfected in the life to come.

Consequently, the pouring out of Christ's blood is signified through His placing of water in a basin, and the remission of sins is prefigured through His washing the feet of His disciples.

Thirdly, there appears the receiving of our punishment by Christ Himself. For not only did Christ wash away our stains of sin, but He took upon Himself the punishments due to them. For our punishments and penances are not sufficient unless they are established and strengthened by the merits and power of Christ's Passion; which fact appears from this, that Christ dried the feet of His disciples with a towel, namely, with the towel of His own body. (John XIII.)

THURSDAY OF HOLY WEEK

The Lord's Supper

The sacrament of our Lord's Body was suitably instituted at the last Supper.

First of all, because of the contents of this Sacrament, for it contains Christ Himself. When Christ was about to say farewell to His disciples, when He was about to withdraw His Presence from their midst forever, He left them—Himself—in the Sacramental Species; just as in the absence of a Commander or Leader, His image is exhibited or presented. Wherefore Eusebius says, that, "It was necessary that Christ at the last supper, should consecrate, the Sacrament of His Body and Blood, since His Body was about to be taken up, and borne into Heaven, so that for all time His Body might be worshipped in faith, that body which he sacrificed and offered up as the price of our salvation."

Secondly (the Sacrament of the Blessed Eucharist was suitably instituted at the last supper), because, without faith in the Passion of Our Lord no one can be saved; consequently it was necessary that there should be for all time among men, a representation or memorial of the Saviour's Passion, the beginning of which, in the Old Law, was the Paschal Lamb, for it is a perpetual reminder of Our Lord's Passion, just as the Paschal Lamb prefigured it. Hence with the Passion at hand, and having at first celebrated the Sacrament, it was fitting for Christ then to institute a new Sacrament.

Thirdly (at the last supper was the suitable time to institute the Sacrament of the Blessed Eucharist), because those things which He spoke to His friends in His farewell address would be all the more deeply and gratefully impressed on their memories, especially because, then their affections would be the more lovingly enkindled, and on the other hand, those things which are the more loved are the more profoundly impressed on the mind. Therefore, among sacrifices there can be no sacrifice greater than the Body and Blood of Christ nor no oblation more powerful than this, consequently, in order that His Body and Blood might be held in the greatest veneration, our Lord instituted this Sacrament at His final departure from His disciples. Wherefore, Augustine says, "The Saviour so that He might the more lovingly recommend the depth of this mystery, willed to impress it as the last thing upon the hearts and memories of His disciples, from whom He was about to depart because of His Passion and death."

Moreover, it must be remembered that this Sacrament has a threefold signification.

First of all, in regard to the past, secondly, in respect to the present, and thirdly, in regard to the future.

1. In regard to the past, in so far as it is a reminder of our Lord's Passion, which was a true sacrifice; and in this way, it is called a sacrifice—the Sacrifice of the Mass.

2. In respect to the present, the Sacrament represents the bond of Church Unity; so that by means of this Sacrament men the world over might be united, and in this way it is called Communion of Saints. John Damascene says, "It is called Communion, because we communicate with Christ through Himself, and because we share in His Body and Divinity, and because through Him, we will share with one another and be united in Christ."

3. In regard to the future, in so far as this Sacrament is a pledge of our glory with God, which will take place in heaven, it is called Viaticum; for it shows us the way of reaching our heavenly home. In this way it is also called the Eucharist, that is grace, "for the grace of God is life eternal; or because it really contains Christ, Who is full of grace, through which we receive the divinity of the Son of God. (The Humanity of Christ.)

GOOD FRIDAY

The Death of Christ

It was expedient that Christ should die.

First of all, for the completion of our redemption, because even though the Passion of Christ possessed infinite power, still the redemption of the human race was not completed by each suffering of the Passion, but through His death. Hence the Holy Ghost says through the lips of Caiphas, "It is expedient for you that one man should die for the people." (John XI, 50.) Hence Augustine says, "Let us admire, congratulate, rejoice, love, praise, adore; because through the death of Our Redeemer we are called from darkness to light, from death to life, from exile to home, from grief to everlasting joy."

Secondly (it was expedient that Christ should die), to increase our faith, our hope and charity. Concerning our increase in faith, it is written, Ps. CXL, 10: "I am alone until I pass from the world to the Father. Moreover, when I pass from the world to the Father, then I shall increase immeasurably. "Unless the grain of wheat falling into the ground die, itself remaineth alone." (John XII, 24.) Concerning the increase of our hope, it is written (Rom. VIII, 32), "He that spared not even His own Son, but delivered Him up for us all, how hath He not also, with Him, given us all things?" No one can deny this, namely that Christ gave us all things, since for our sake He delivered Himself up to death. Hence, Bernard says, "Who is the man that is not filled with hope of obtaining confidence and courage when he gazes trustfully upon the position of our Lord's Crucified Body. His head is bent to give us the kiss of peace. His arms extended to receive us, His hands pierced to pour His blessings upon us. His heart opened to love us. His feet nailed to the cross to soften our hearts, and remain with us." "Wherefore," Canticles II, 13, says, "Come, My dove, into the clefts of the rock." For on the wounds of Christ the Church rests and builds on solid foundation; since she places the hope of our salvation on the Passion of our Saviour, and assures us that because of Christ's Passion our hope of salvation is safe from the snares of the devil.

Thirdly (it was expedient that Christ should die), because of the sacrament of our salvation, so that He might die to this world in regard to the likeness of His death. "My soul chooseth hanging and my bones death." (Job VII, 15.) Gregory says that "the soul is the power of the mind, and the bones the strength of the body. That which hangs is raised up. Therefore, the soul hangs on the Eternal, so that the bones may die, because with the love of eternal life in the soul, the soul kills in itself all strength of worldly life and sinful pleasures." But a sign of this kind of death appears when anyone despises this world. Hence Gregory says that, "the sea retains living bodies, but immediately expels its dead." (The Humanity of Christ, Chapter 47.)

HOLY SATURDAY

The Advantages of Our Lord's Descent into Hell

From the descent of Christ into hell, or limbo, we can gather four things for our instruction.

First of all, a firm hope in God should be enkindled in our hearts. For whenever we are suffering from trials and afflictions, we should always hope in God for help and confide in Him at all times. For there is nothing so painful as to be in hell. If therefore, Christ liberated those souls who were imprisoned there, by so much the more should he liberate each one of us if we are the friends of God and confide in Him. so that through Him we might be liberated from every evil and affliction. "She, namely, Wisdom herself, forsook not Him into the pit." (Wis. X, 13.) And because God in a very special manner helps His servants, how much more secure ought he be who serves God faithfully and trusts in His mercy. "He that feareth the Lord shall tremble at nothing, and shall not be afraid, for God is his hope." (Eccles. XXXIV, 16.)

Secondly, we ought to entertain fear, filial fear, and rid ourselves of presumption. For although Christ suffered for sinners and descended into hell, still he did not set free all, but only those who were free from mortal sin. On the other hand, those who were without mortal sin, He liberated them. And therefore, no one who because of mortal sin descends into hell can expect to be pardoned; for the duration in hell is as long as the duration of the saints in Paradise, namely—eternal.

Thirdly, we ought to be solicitous. For Christ descended into hell for our salvation and consequently we should be desirous to descend there often in spirit by considering the punishments of hell, as the holy Ezechias was accustomed to do, saying, "I said in the midst of my days, I shall go to the gates of hell." Isaias XXXVIII, 10.) For whosoever goes frequently in spirit during life to the gates of hell, will not at death easily descend into hell; because meditation of this nature, that is, frequent and devout meditation, prevents us from sinning, and withdraws us from hell. For since we see that men of the world refrain from committing evil deeds, because of temporal punishment, therefore, by so much the more should we fear and refrain from mortal sin, because of the punishment of hell, which is more terrible in regard to its duration, severity, and variety. "In all thy works remember thy last end, and thou shalt never sin." (Eccli. VII, 40.)

Fourthly, an example of love comes to us from Christ's descent into hell. For Christ descended into hell to set free His own loyal friends, and consequently we should often descend there in spirit so that we might help our own souls spiritually, and the souls in purgatory. For the suffering souls in purgatory are powerless to help themselves, and therefore we should from charity help them. For we would be considered exceedingly hard-hearted who, if he could, would not assist his own brother were he in a city prison; and therefore a great deal more hard-hearted are we if we do not help our friends in purgatory; especially since no earthly punishment can be compared with their's in any way. Hence (Job XIX, 21), cries out, "Have pity on me, have pity on me, at least you my friends, because the hand of the Lord hath touched me."

Moreover we can assist the suffering souls by our Masses, prayers, and alms-giving. Nor is this to be wondered at, because even in this world a friend can satisfy and make atonement for a friend.

Christ did not descend into the hell of the lost, but into limbo, the place of the just. He penetrated to all the lower parts of the earth, however, not passing through them locally with his soul, but by spreading the effects of His power in a measure to all parts of the lower regions; yet so that He enlightened only the just.

A thing is said to be in a place in two ways. First of all through its effect, and in this way Christ descended into each of the hells or lower regions, but in a different manner. For going down into the hell of the lost, through the effect of His power, He wrought this effect, that by descending there He put them to shame for their unbelief and wickedness; but to them who were detained in Purgatory He gave hope of attaining glory, while upon the Holy Fathers . . He shed the light of glory everlasting.

In another way a thing is said to be in a place through its essence, and in this way Christ's soul descended only into that part of hell (called limbo) wherein the just were detained; so that He visited them in place according to His soul, whom He visited interiorly by grace, according to His Godhead. Accordingly while remaining in one part of hell He wrought this effect in a measure in every part of hell; just as while suffering in one part of the earth He delivered the whole world by His Passion. (3a, q. 52, a. 2.)

EASTER SUNDAY

The Necessity of Christ's Resurrection

"Ought not Christ to have suffered these things, and so to enter into His glory?" (Luke XXIV, 26.)

It was necessary for Christ to rise again for five reasons. First of all for the commendation of Divine justice, to which it belongs to exalt them who humble themselves for God's sake, according to (Luke I, 52), "He hath put down the mighty from their seat, and hath exalted the humble." Consequently, because Christ humbled Himself even to the death of the cross, from love and obedience to God, it behooved Him to be uplifted by God to a glorious resurrection. Hence it is said of His Person (Ps. CXXXVIII, 2), "Thou hast known, that is approved, My sitting down, that is, My humiliation and Passion, and My rising up, that is, My glorification in the resurrection."

Secondly, for our instruction in the faith, since our belief in Christ's Godhead is confirmed by His rising again, because, according to (Cor. XIII, 4), "Although he was crucified through weakness, yet He liveth in the power of God and therefore it is written (1 Cor. XV, 14), "If Christ be not risen again, then is our preaching vain, and your faith is also vain." And (Ps. XXIX, 10), "What profit is there in My blood," that is, in the shedding of My blood, "while I go down," as by various degrees of evils, "into corruption." As though He were to answer, "There is no profit, for if I do not at once rise again, and My body be corrupted, I shall preach to no one, and I shall save no one."

Thirdly, (it was necessary for Christ to rise from the grave) for the raising of our hope, since through seeing Christ Who is our head, rise again, we hope that we likewise shall rise again. Hence it is written (I Cor. XIX, 12), "I know," that is with certainty of faith, "that My Redeemer," that is Christ, "liveth," having risen from the dead, "and therefore in the last day I shall rise out of the earth and see God my Saviour. This my hope is laid up in my bosom."

Fourthly, Christ rose from the grave to regulate the lives of the faithful, according to (Rom. VI, 4), "As Christ is risen from the dead by the glory of the Father, so we also may walk in newness of life," and further on, "Christ rising from the dead, dieth now no more; so do you also reckon that you are dead to sin but alive to God."

Fifthly, Christ arose from the dead to complete the work of our salvation, because just as for this reason did He endure evil in dying that He might deliver us from evil, so was He glorified in rising in order to advance us towards good things; according to (Rom. IV, 25), "He was delivered up for our sins, and He rose again for our justification." (Part 3a, Q. 53, a. 1.)

EASTER MONDAY

The Advantages of Our Lord's Resurrection

From the mystery of our Saviour's resurrection we can learn four things.

First of all we learn that we should strive to rise spiritually from the death of the soul which we have caused by sin, and rise to a life of justice which is acquired through penance. "Rise thou that sleepest and arise from the dead, and Christ shall enlighten thee." (Eph. V, 14.) And (Apoc. XX, 6), "Blessed and holy is he that hath part in the first resurrection. In these the second death has no power, but they shall be priests of God and of Christ, and shall reign with Him."

Secondly (from our Lord's resurrection we should learn) not to defer rising spiritually until death is upon us, but rise now and promptly; for Christ rose for our example, on the third day. "Delay not to be converted to the Lord, and defer it not from day to day." (Eccles. V, 8), because you will not be able even to think of those things pertaining to your salvation when serious illness comes upon you; and also because by delaying your conversion you lose part of all the good things which the Church accomplishes; and what is worse, you incur many evils because of your perseverance in sin. Likewise, inasmuch as the devil possesses you for a longer time, so much the more difficult will it be for you to rid yourself of satan.

Thirdly, we should learn to rise to an incorruptible life, so that we may not die again, that is, having firmly resolved to do penance, we may not sin again. "Christ rising from the dead, dieth now no more, death shall no more have dominion over Him." (Rom. VI, 9.) And further on, Rom. VI, 11, "So you also reckon that you are dead to sin but alive to God in Jesus Christ, our Lord. Let not sin, therefore, reign in your mortal body, so as to obey the lusts of the flesh. Neither yield ye your members as instruments of iniquity unto sin, but present yourselves to God, as those that are alive from the dead, and your members as instruments of justice unto God."

. Fourthly (from our Saviour's resurrection we should learn) to rise to a new and glorious life, so that we may avoid everything which was before the occasion and cause of our spiritual death and of sin. "That as Christ is risen from the dead by the glory of the Father, so we also may walk in newness of life." (Rom. VI, 4.) And this new life is a life of justice, which renews our souls and leads us unto a life of everlasting glory. (The Creed.)

TUESDAY WITHIN THE OCTAVE OF EASTER

The Wounds on the Body of the Risen Christ

Our Lord said to Thomas, *"Put in thy finger hither, and see My hands, and bring hither thy hand, and put it into My side, and be not faithless but believing."* (John XX, 27.)

It was becoming for Christ's soul at His Resurrection to resume the body with its scars.

In the first place, for Christ's own glory. For Bede says that Christ kept His scars not from inability to heal them but to wear them as an everlasting trophy of His victory. Hence Augustine says, "Perhaps in that Kingdom we shall see on the bodies of the Martyrs the traces of the wounds which they bore for Christ's Name; because it will not be a deformity, but a dignity in them; and a certain kind of beauty will shine in them, in the body, though not of the body."

Secondly, Christ rose with the scars on His body to confirm the hearts of His disciples as to the faith in His resurrection.

Thirdly, that when He pleads for us with the Father, He may always show the manner of death He endured for us.

Fourthly, that He may convince those redeemed in His blood how mercifully they have been helped, as He shows them the traces of the same death.

Fifthly, Christ arose with the scars on His body so that on Judgment day He may condemn the wicked with their just condemnation. Hence Augustine says, "Christ knew why He kept the scars in His body. For as He showed them to

Thomas who would not believe except he handled and saw them, so will He show His wounds to His enemies; so that He Who is the Truth may convict them saying: Behold the Man Whom you crucified, see the wounds you inflicted; recognize the side you pierced, since it was opened by you and for you, yet you would not enter this haven of rest."

Consequently, the scars that remained in Christ's body belong neither to corruption nor defect, but to the greater increase of glory, inasmuch as they are the trophies of His power; and a special comeliness will appear in the places scarred by His wounds." (3a, q. 54, a. 4.)

WEDNESDAY WITHIN THE OCTAVE OF EASTER

Christ the Resurrection and the Life

1. "I am the Resurrection and the Life." The Lord manifested His virtue and power and showed that it is a living and life-giving virtue and power. It must be remembered that some need to share in the effect of life, some because they have lost life, and some not because they have lost life but so that they might preserve the life which they now possess. So therefore, in regard to the first class of people, Christ says of Himself, "I am the Resurrection," for those who have lost life through death will regain it. In regard to the second class (namely those living), Christ says, "And the Life," so that those living might be preserved by Him, and so that they may realize it is by His power they are preserved both in this life and in the future life of glory.

Moreover, we must bear in mind that when Christ says, "I am the Resurrection," it is as if He said, I am the Cause of the Resurrection. Christ is in very truth the entire cause of our resurrection, both the resurrection of our souls and the resurrection of our bodies. And therefore, when He says, "I am the Resurrection," it is as if He said, "All that will rise in soul and in body will rise through Me." Hence it is written, "For by a man came death, and by a Man resurrection of the dead." (1 Cor. XV. 21.) "In Him was life, and the life was the Light of men." (John I, 4.)

2. A twofold effect follows. First, Christ Who is the Life, vivifies the dead. "Whosoever believeth in Me, although he be dead, shall live. I am the Resurrection," that is, the cause of the resurrection, and anyone may obtain the effect

of this cause by believing in Me. Hence Christ said, "he who believeth in Me, although he be dead, shall live." For from the fact that he believes in Me, he has Me in his heart. "That Christ may dwell by faith in your hearts." (Eph. III, 17.) Moreover whosoever has Me in his heart has the Cause of the Resurrection. Therefore, "Whosoever believeth in Me, shall live," namely, in the spiritual life, by rising through God's grace from death of sin, and even live in the natural life by rising from the death of punishment.

3. Because Christ is Life, He will preserve those living unto life everlasting. "For everyone that liveth and believeth in Me, shall not die forever. Believest thou this?" (John XI, 25.) "Such shall live in his faith, and will not die for ever," that is he, the just man, will not die an eternal death but will have eternal life. "And this is the will of My Father, Who sent Me, that everyone who seeth the Son and believeth in Him may have life everlasting, and I will raise him up on the last day." (John VI, 40.) (John XI.)

THURSDAY WITHIN THE OCTAVE OF EASTER

The Three Persons Restored to Life by Christ

1. Let us remember that Christ restored to life three dead persons, namely, the daughter of Jairus, the ruler; secondly, the son of the widow, who was being carried outside the city to be buried, and thirdly, Lazarus, who had been four days in the grave. But the daughter of Jairus was restored to life at home, the son of the widow outside the city, and Lazarus was restored to life in the grave. Likewise be it observed, that when Christ gave back life to this young woman only a few witnesses were with Him, namely, the parents of the girl, and three of His disciples: Peter, James and John. On the other hand a great crowd was present when Jesus restored life to the young man, while a very great multitude was at hand when Jesus raised Lazarus from the dead.

For through the three dead persons three classes of sinners are signified. For some people sin in their hearts, by consenting to mortal sin, and these are designated by the girl, dead at home.

On the other hand there are those who sin by external

signs and actions; and those are signified by the dead young man who was being carried out to be buried.

But when through sinful habit sinners become fixed in sin, then they are as if buried in the grave.

Nevertheless, the Lord resuscitates all classes of sinners. But those who sin only through consent, especially slight consent of the will, are easily restored to life. And because a sin is secret, it is sometimes removed by a secret remedy. But when sin is publicly committed, then it needs a public cure.

2. "The hour cometh, and is now at hand, when the dead shall hear the Voice of the Son of God, and they who hear shall live." This can be explained as referring to the resurrection of the body. "The hour cometh, and is now at hand," as if Christ had said, "It is true that all the dead will finally rise, but that hour is even now at hand when some whom the Lord will restore to life will hear His voice." Thus did Lazarus hear the Voice of Christ, when Christ said to him, "Lazarus come forth." Thus did the daughter of Jairus, and the son of the widow hear the Master's Voice. Consequently, it is significantly written, "The hour is now at hand," because through Me the dead have already begun to be restored to life.

3. Thirdly, it can be explained as referring to the resurrection of the soul. For resurrection is twofold. There will be the resurrection of our bodies after death, at the future judgment; and secondly, there is the resurrection of souls from the death of unbelief to a life of faith, and from the death of injustice to justice; and therefore, that resurrection "is now present." Therefore Christ says, "The hour cometh and is now at hand when the dead," namely, infidels and sinners, "will hear the voice of the Son of God, and they who hear shall live," according to the true faith. (John V.)

FRIDAY WITHIN THE OCTAVE OF EASTER

The New Life

"As Christ is risen from the dead by the glory of the Father, so we also may walk in newness of life." (Rom. VI, 4.)

We must bear in mind that the old life means a worldly life consumed by an age-long experience in sin, according to Lam. III, 4. "My skin and my flesh (sin) hath made old." Hence the soul sighs when the flesh exteriorly as it were, grows old, and the conscience interiorly wastes away, like the flesh, being corrupted by the putrefaction of sin. But the new life is the heavenly life, renewed from day to day by the grace of God; according to Ephes. IV, 23, "Be renewed in the spirit of your mind." And Rom. VI, 4, "As Christ is risen from the dead by the glory of the Father, so we also." Moreover since Christ is risen, it is added, Rom. VI, 9, "Christ rising from the dead dieth now no more. So you also reckon yourselves dead to sin, but alive unto Christ Jesus, our Lord."

Note well, that just as Christ died once, so we should die to sin once and for all time and never sin again. And just as Christ liveth forever, so also should we always live in virtue, and in Christ Jesus our Lord; in Whom alone rests our hope of salvation.

On the other hand we must remember that life is manifested through action, and hence the old life is revealed through works of a worldly nature, of which it is written, Ps. XVI, 11, "They have set their eyes bowing down to the earth." On the other hand the new life is declared through the actions of a heavenly operation, concerning which Saint Paul says (Col. III, 1), "If you be risen with Christ, seek the things which are above." Wherefore a commentary says, "Think on the new found spiritual things, hold fast to them with joy, and this is why," the Apostle adds, "seek the things which are above." (The Humanity of Christ.)

SATURDAY WITHIN THE OCTAVE OF EASTER

The Proof of Our Spiritual Resurrection

Just as Christ proved His Resurrection in three ways, namely, by sight, touch and taste, so also should our spiritual resurrection be demonstrated. By sight, "See My hands and feet, that it is I Myself." By touch, "Handle and see, for a spirit hath no flesh and bones, as you see Me to have." By taste, "And while they yet believed not and wondered for joy, He said, have you anything to eat?" (Luke XXIV, 39, 41.) So also should a spiritual resurrection be made known.

First of all, by a vision of our sanctity. "So let your light shine before men." (Matth. V, 16.) Augustine says, "man should not make this life his goal, but refer it to God, consecrate it to God," and hence Scripture says, "so that you may glorify your Father who is in Heaven." Moreover as the Lord showed His hands and feet, He thereby pointed out that our spiritual resurrection is made known through our affection for Divine love, and through the effect of our good works. "Thou hast the name of being alive, but thou art dead" (Apoc. III, 1), namely spiritually dead, because you are wanting in Divine Love and lacking in good works.

Secondly, by the touch of adversity (our spiritual resurrection appears). "As gold in the furnace, so is man tried, (Prov. XXVII, 21), "that I may feel thee and may prove whether thou art my son or not." (Gen. XXVII, 21.) Wherefore, a Gloss says, "The sorrowful things of this world are now my food for trials. But the sweet foods are for the love and desire of heaven." Moreover, the Lord said, "Taste and see, that a spirit has not flesh and bones." Here He points out that the spiritual man's heart is not fixed on carnal consolations, but is established and fixed in the hope of his heavenly home, even though he suffers hardships in arriving there. "That this may be my comfort, that afflicting me with sorrow, He spare not, and that I may not contradict the words of the Holy One. (Job VI, 10.)

Thirdly, by a taste of internal and external sweetness (our spiritual resurrection is revealed). "Seek the things which are above." (Col. III, 2.) Hence Bernard says, "Whosoever after doing penance returns not to carnal consolations, but advances with a certain confidence in the Divine mercy, and proceeds with a certain devotion and joy in the Holy Ghost, and is so sorrowful at the memory of past sins, that this memory is delighted and enkindled with a longing desire for eternal things, such a person has evidently risen with Christ; because a holy delight fills that soul which was before filled with worldly pleasures. Nor can this heavenly delight mingle with worldly vanities, nor the eternal with the transitory, nor the spiritual with the carnal; so that you partly seek the things which are above, and partly earthly things. "Seek ye first the kingdom of God, and His justice, and all these things will be added unto you."

Moreover, since the Lord ate part of the fish placed before Him, and part of the honey-comb, He mystically points out that those who have spiritually risen ought beforehand taste the sweetness of His divinity and humanity; and Gregory says, "What do we believe the fish there present to signify, unless the suffering Mediator between God and man. For from His side flowed the regenerating water that saved the human race. And He Who was worthy to be caught like a fish, might share in the sweetness of His divinity and humanity." (The Humanity of Christ, 57.)

SUNDAY IN THE OCTAVE OF EASTER

The Apparition of Christ in the Octave of Easter

"When . . . the doors were shut, where the disciples were gathered together, for fear of the Jews, Jesus came and stood in the midst of them and said: 'Peace be to you'." (John XX, 19.)

1. According to some, to enter a place with the doors closed is proper to a glorified body; because they claim that by reason of a certain condition inherent in it, that it can be with another body at the same time in the same place in so far as it is a glorified body; and furthermore, they claim this can be and can happen without a miracle. But this opinion cannot stand. And therefore we must say that Christ did this miraculously by the power of His Divinity, (namely, He appeared to His disciples and stood in the midst of them, when the doors were closed).

Augustine says: "Do you seek to know how Christ entered through the closed doors? If you understand how He did it, it is not a miracle. Where reason fails, there begins the building of faith. Certainly He was able to enter when the doors were shut, Who at His birth preserved the virginity of His Mother—inviolate." Therefore, just as His Birth from His Virgin Mother was miraculous by the power of His Divinity, so was this entrance into the midst of His disciples miraculous.

Through this incident we may understand in a mystical sense that Christ appears to us sometimes when the doors are shut, that is, when our external senses are closed in prayer. "But thou when thou shalt pray, enter into thy chamber, and Thy Father Who seeth in secret will repay thee." (Matth. VI, 6.)

Moreover the disposition of the disciples that must be imitated by us, is also described, which indeed is mysterious, because "they were gathered together." Mysterious for Christ came to those disciples who were gathered together. The Holy Ghost descends on those gathered together because of Christ and the Holy Spirit is present only to those united in charity: "For where there are two or three gathered together in My Name, there I am in the midst of them." (Matth. XVIII, 20.)

2. "Jesus came and stood in the midst of the disciples." He Himself came personally, just as He had promised them. "I go away and I come unto you." (John XIV, 28.) "Jesus stood in the midst of them," so that all might certainly recognize Him, and recognize the likeness of the human nature which He had in common with them. "He stood in their midst," through courtesy and condescension; for He lived with them as One of them. And likewise to point out to us that we should be in the midst of virtue.

3. "And said: 'Peace be to you'." This salutation was necessary, for their peace was disturbed in many ways, first in regard to God; secondly, in regard to themselves, thirdly, in regard to the Jews.

In regard to God, against Whom they had sinned, some by denying Him, others by flight from Him. "All you shall be scandalized in Me this night. For it is written: I will strike the Shepherd and the sheep of the flock shall be dispersed." (Matt. XXVI, 31.) And against this trial Jesus proposed to them the peace of reconciliation with God. "We are reconciled to God by the death of His Son." (Rom. V, 10), for Christ won this reconciliation for us through His Passion.

Likewise their peace was disturbed in regard to themselves, for they were sad and weak in faith; and hence Christ spoke peace to them. "Much peace to those loving Thy Law." (Ps. CXVIII.)

Likewise their peace was disturbed by persecutions from the Jews and in opposition to these persecutions and fears, Jesus said to His disciples: "Peace be to you." (John XX.)

MONDAY AFTER OCTAVE OF EASTER

"The Peace of Christ"

"Peace I leave with you. My peace I give unto you; not as the world giveth, do I give unto you." (John XIV, 27.) These words from Christ, the Prince of Peace, should appeal to us today more than ever before, especially when we see in the world unusual and uncalled for distress, strife, contention and general disturbances of the peace among individuals, and among nations. Peace is nothing more than a tranquility of order. Man is said to be peaceful when the order of peace is threefold. First in regard to himself, secondly in regard to his God, and thirdly in regard to his neighbor, and so there is a threefold peace in man, namely, that peace by which he is at peace with God, entirely subjected to His ordination, secondly at peace with himself, and a third, peace with his fellowman.

It must be noted that in us three things should be regulated to obtain peace, namely: the intellect, the will, and the sensitive appetite, so that the will might be directed according to the mind, and the will. Augustine therefore describing the peace of the saints says: "Their peace is serenity of mind, calmness of soul, simplicity of heart, a bond of love, a union of charity," so that serenity of mind refers to right reason, which is free, and not enslaved, nor absorbed by any inordinate affection. Tranquility of soul refers to the sensitive appetite which should be at rest from disturbance of the passions. Simplicity of heart refers to the will, which should be centered on God, its object; entirely centered on God. The bond of love has to do with our neighbor, while union by charity unites us to God. Here in this life we can possess this peace but imperfectly, because we are not entirely free from disturbance by other people, never wholly free from the snares of our enemies, the disturbers of our peace of mind. But in the kingdom of God we will enjoy perfect peace, for there our enemies cannot disturb or molest us. Hence Christ, the Prince of Peace, said: "My peace I give unto you, not as the world giveth do I give unto you." Thus Christ distinguishes His peace from worldly peace. The peace of God, or peace of the saints, differs from the peace of the world in three ways. First in regard to intention. For the peace of the world is ordained to the quiet and peaceful enjoyment of temporal things, and sometimes sin and crime cooperate with the enjoyment of these things. But the peace of the saints is ordained to eternal things. It is in this sense therefore, Christ said "not as the world giveth do I give unto you," that is, not for the same end does He give us peace, because the world gives peace for the quiet possession of external things, but Christ giveth peace to His own for the enjoyment of things eternal.

Secondly the peace of the world is a pretended or external peace. The nations are talking peace, but secretly and actively preparing for war. "They speak of peace with their neighbor, but evil designs are in their hearts." Psalm XXVII, 3.) On the contrary the peace Christ giveth is true peace, both interiorly and exteriorly. "Not therefore as the world giveth, do I give," pretended peace, no, but true peace.

Third the peace of Christ differs from worldly peace in regard to its perfection, because the peace of the world is imperfect and fleeting, since it is for the quiet of the exterior man and not for the interior man. But the peace of Christ calms us interiorly and exteriorly. "Much peace to those loving His law." (Psalm CXVIII.) (John XIV, 27.)

TUESDAY AFTER THE OCTAVE OF EASTER

Heavenly Things Must Be Sought

"If you be risen with Christ, seek the things that are above; where Christ is sitting at the right hand of God. Mind the things that are above, not the things that are upon the earth." (Col. III, 1.)

It is a favour from God when we rise with the risen Christ, and this resurrection is twofold. In one way through the hope of a corporal resurrection. Secondly, if we rise with Christ we are restored to the way of justice. "He was delivered up for our sins, and rose again for our justification." (Rom. IV, 25.)

1. Consequently, we are instructed to have a right intention in regard to the final end, and first of all the Apostle

wishes that each one chiefly intend the end (by always keeping the end in mind). Hence he says: "If we be risen with Christ, seek the things that are above"; for here is the end. "Seek first the Kingdom of God and His justice" (Matth. VI); for this is the end. "One thing I have asked of the Lord, this will I seek after; that I may dwell in the house of the Lord all the days of my life." (Ps. XXVI, 4.) And therefore, seek this, "where Christ is sitting at the right hand of God." Christ sitteth at the right hand of God, in as far as He is Man, and shares in the spiritual possessions of the Father; but in as far as Christ is God, sitting at the right hand means that Christ is equal to God (in power and glory). And thus that there might be a well-regulated order for you, namely, that just as Christ died and rose and ascended to the right hand of God, so also may you die to sin to live the life of justice and afterwards be taken to glory.

Or again we rise through Christ, but Christ Himself sitteth at the right hand of God. Therefore our every desire should be directed towards Him. "Wheresoever the body shall be there shall the eagles also be gathered together" (Matth. XXIV, 28), and, "Where thy treasure is, there is thy heart also." (Matth. VI, 21.)

2. It is necessary to judge other things in relation to the end; and therefore, the Apostle says: "Seek the things which are above." Now a man seeks the things that are above, who regulates his life according to reasons from above, and judges all things in accordance with these heavenly reasons, "For this is wisdom, descending from above." (James III, 15.) On the other hand, the man who seeks those things which are above, but who ordains and regulates the highest good things according to all earthly things; such a man's "glory is in his shame for minding earthly things." (Phil. III, 19.)

And the Apostle states the reason (why you should seek heavenly things) when he says: "You are dead, and your life is hid with Christ in God." As if he had said: "Seek not those things which are worldly, for you are dead to earthly communication. For a man who is dead to this life, seeks not the things of this world;" and so you also, "if you be dead with Christ," you will be dead to the elements of this world; "So do you also reckon that you are dead to sin, but alive unto God, in Christ Jesus our Lord." (Rom. VI, 11.)

Therefore, there is another life, a hidden life. Hence the Apostle says: "Your life is hid with Christ in God." We acquire this hidden life through Christ. "Christ died for our sins." (Peter III.) Moreover because this life is through Christ, Christ is now hidden from us; for He is in the glory of God the Father; and likewise the life given through Christ is hidden; namely, hidden there where He is in the glory of the Father: "O how great is the multitude of Thy sweetness, O Lord, which Thou hast hidden from them that fear Thee." (Ps. XXX, 20.) And therefore, when the Apostle says: "Christ our life appeared," he shows how this life is manifested, namely, just like Christ Himself.

Now "when Christ our life shall appear, because He is the Author of our life, and because our life consists in knowing and loving God, then you also will appear": "When He shall appear, we shall be like to Him." (1 John III, 2.) (Coll. 3.)

WEDNESDAY AFTER THE OCTAVE OF EASTER

The Beginning of the New Life (or the Life of Grace)

1. Because the ultimate end of every rational creature, which is to see God in His essence, exceeds the power of the rational creature's nature, those things which are directed to the end must be proportioned to the end, according to the proper order of Providence. It follows then, that Divine assistance must be given to the rational creature; not only in regard to those things which are proportioned to nature, but also those things which exceed the power of nature. Hence over and above the natural power of reason, the light of grace is Divinely conferred on man by which he is perfected interiorly in regard to virtue and in regard to knowledge; while man's mind is elevated and enlightened by this Divine Light to know those things which exceed the grasp of his reason. And in regard to action and love, man's affections by means of this Divine assistance are raised above all created things so that man might love God, hope in Him and do those things which Divine love requires.

2. Now the gifts or assistance of this nature, which are supernaturally bestowed on man, are called gratuitous for two reasons.

First because they are divinely and freely granted. For nothing can be attributed to man by which he condignly merits these divine gifts; since they exceed the power of human nature to merit them.

Secondly, because through gifts of this nature, man is

rendered in a certain special manner pleasing unto God. For since the love of God is the cause of the goodness in things (caused not by any pre-existing goodness as our love is caused), it is necessary that the special effects of the Divine goodness be considered in regard to those on whom God bestows certain special effects of His goodness. Hence it is that God especially and absolutely loves those on whom He bestows such effects of His goodness, by means of which these privileged souls arrive at their ultimate end, which is God Himself—the Fountain Head of all goodness. (Ad Regim.)

3. God alone causes grace. "The Lord will give grace and glory." (Ps. LXXXIII, 12.) For the gift of grace surpasses every capability of created nature, since it is nothing short of a partaking of the Divine Nature, which exceeds every other nature. And therefore, it is impossible that any creature should cause grace. For it is as necessary that God alone should deify, bestowing a partaking of the Divine Nature by a participated likeness, as it is impossible that anything save fire should enkindle.

Moreover Christ's humanity is "an organ of His Godhead." Now an instrument does not produce the action of the principal agent by its own power, but in virtue of the principal agent. Hence Christ's humanity does not cause grace by its own power, but by virtue of the Divine Nature joined to it, whereby the actions of Christ's humanity are saving actions.

So in the Sacraments of the New Law, which are derived from Christ, grace is instrumentally caused by the sacraments, and principally by the power of the Holy Ghost working in the sacraments; according to John III, 5; "Unless a man be born again of water and the Holy Ghost he cannot enter into the kingdom of God." (I a. 2æ, q. II 2, a. 1.)

SATURDAY AFTER OCTAVE OF EASTER

Thirsting for the Living Water

"Whosoever drinketh of this water shall thirst again; but he that shall drink of the water that I will give him, shall not thirst forever." (John IV, 13.)

The opposite of these scriptural words seems to be expressed in Eccl. XXIV, 29: "They that drink Me, shall yet thirst." How therefore, does one "not thirst forever, who drinks of this water," which Christ will give us? namely, Divine Wisdom, since Wisdom itself says: "They that drink Me, shall yet thirst."

Both statements are true, because whosoever drinks of the water which Christ gives, both thirsts again and does not thirst, but whosoever drinks of earthly water, thirsts again. And this because of two reasons:

First, because earthly water is not everlasting, neither has it a perpetual cause, but only a failing, defective cause. Consequently its effect also must necessarily cease. "All those things are passed away like a shadow." (Wisdom V, 9.) On the contrary, the spiritual water has a perpetual cause, namely, the Holy Spirit, Who is the unfailing fountain of life. Therefore, he who drinks of this spiritual fountain will not thirst forever; just as he who has the Fountain of living water in him will not thirst forever.

Secondly, because of the difference between a thing that is temporal and something that is spiritual. For although both produce thirst, still they produce it in different ways. For the temporal when possessed causes a thirst, not of itself, but because of another thing; whereas the spiritual takes away the thirst for another thing, and causes thirst of itself. The reason for this is because the temporal thing before being possessed, is considered to be of great and sufficient value; but after it has been obtained, because it is found from experience to be neither so great nor sufficient to satisfy our desires, our hearts' desires are moved to another Object, higher and more completely satisfying than the temporal object for which we thirsted.

On the other hand, the spiritual thing is recognized only when it is possessed . . . "No man knoweth, but he that receiveth it." (Apoc. II, 17.) And hence when the spiritual is not possessed, the heart's desire remains unmoved; but when it is possessed and recognized, then the spiritual delights the affection and moves the desire; not indeed to possess another, but because imperfectly recognized by reason of the imperfection of the receiver, it moves the heart so that it might perfectly possess the spiritual. And concerning this (spiritual) thirst it is written: "My soul hath thirsted after the strong living God." (Ps. XLI, 3.)

But this thirst is never wholly satisfied in this world, for we are not able to possess spiritual good things sufficiently in this life; and hence, whosoever drinks of this (spiritual) water, thirsts as yet for his perfection; but will not thirst forever, as if this water should fail, because it is written: "They shall be inebriated with the plenty of Thy house" (Ps. XXXV, 9.) But in the life of glory, where the blessed will perfectly drink of the water of Divine grace, they will not thirst forever. "Blessed are they who hunger and thirst after justice," namely, in this world, "for they shall have their fill"; in the life of glory. (Matth. V, 6.) (John IV.)

THE SECOND SUNDAY AFTER EASTER

Our Divine Adoption

"God sent His Son, . . . that we might receive the adoption of sons." (Gal. IV, 4.)

1. Adoption is transferred to Divine things because of a likeness in human things. For a man is said to adopt another as his child, in as far as he gives him gratuitously, the right of sharing in his inheritance, which did not belong to the adopted by nature. Moreover the inheritance of man is called that possession, by which a man becomes wealthy. But that by which God is rich, is the enjoyment of Himself; because of this He is blessed and infinitely happy; and so this is His inheritance. Hence in regard to men who cannot by natural right (or by natural power) achieve this enjoyment, He gives His—grace—by which man can merit this eternal happiness; so that man has a right to this everlasting inheritance; in so far as God is said to have adopted man as His son. "You have received the Spirit of adoption of sons, whereby we cry, Father. . . . For the Spirit Himself giveth testimony to our spirit, that we are the sons of God, and if sons, heirs also— heirs indeed of God, and joint heirs with Christ." (Rom. VIII, 15, 17.)

On the other hand, it happens in legal adoption, that by it the inheritance is divided among the heirs; in so far as the entire inheritance cannot be possessed at the same time by many. But on the contrary, the heavenly inheritance is possessed entirely and at the same time by the Father and by all His adopted children. Wherefore there is no division nor succession (in the eternal inheritance).

2. Our adoption is through grace. Man indeed, by his creation, excels in the participation of intellect, and as it were,

bears the image of God Himself; because the last of those things in which our created nature shares is intellectuality, like unto the uncreated nature (of God), and therefore, the rational creature alone bears the image of the Creator. Hence the rational, through creation, has received the name of Sonship or adoption of "heirs of God, and joint heirs with Christ."

But adoption requires that the adopted acquire a right to the inheritance of the person adopting. But the inheritance of God Himself is His Own Blessedness, which only the rational creature is capable of possessing; and this right belongs to the rational creature, not from creation itself, but from the gift of the Holy Ghost. And therefore, it is plainly evident, that creation does not give to irrational creatures adoption nor sonship, but only on rational creatures is this gift of God bestowed.

For participation in any kind of good things does not suffice for adoption, but participation in the inheritance—in the rightful inheritance. Hence, a creature is not said to be adopted from the fact that certain good things come to him from God, but from the fact that God gives to us our inheritance, which is Divine happiness.

Moreover, in no wise must it be said, that Christ is the adopted Son of the Father, because by His nature Christ is eternal with the Father, having by reason of His nature a right to the Paternal inheritance, because all things which the Father has, are the Son's also. Hence this right to the eternal inheritance did not come to Christ by grace bestowed on Him; but by nature the eternal inheritance or everlasting happiness belongs to Christ. (3 Dist. X, q. 2, a. 1 and 2.)

MONDAY WITHIN THE SECOND WEEK AFTER EASTER

The Indwelling of the Divine Persons in the Soul

1. It is said of Divine Wisdom (Wis. IX, 10), "Send her from heaven to thy saints, and from the throne of thy greatness."

The Whole Trinity dwells in the mind by sanctifying grace, according to John XIV, 23, "We will come to him, and we will make Our abode with him." But that a Divine Person be sent to anyone by invisible grace signifies that both this Person dwells in a new way within him, and that He has His origin from another. Hence, since to the Son and to the Holy Ghost it belongs to dwell in the soul by grace, and to be from another, it therefore belongs to both of them to be invisibly sent. As to the Father, though He dwells in us by grace, still it does not belong to Him to be from another, and consequently He is not sent.

The soul is made like to God by grace. Hence for a Divine Person to be sent to anyone by grace, there must needs be a resemblance of the soul to the Divine Person Who is sent by some gift of grace. Because the Holy Ghost is love, the soul is assimilated to the Holy Ghost by the gift of charity. Hence the mission of the Holy Ghost is according to the mode of charity. Whereas the Son is the Word, not any sort of word, but one who breathes forth Love. Hence Augustine, says, "The Word we speak of, is knowledge with Love." Thus the Son is sent not in accordance with every and any kind of intellectual perfection, but according to the intellectual illumination, which breaks forth into the affection of love (of God), as it is said (John VI, 45), "Everyone that hath heard from the Father, and hath learned, cometh to Me," and (Ps. XXXVIII, 4), "In my meditations a fire shall flame forth." Thus Augustine plainly says, "The Son is sent, whenever, He is known and perceived by anyone." Now perception implies a certain experimental knowledge; and this is properly called wisdom (sapientia) as it were a sweet knowledge (sapida scientia), according to Ecclus. VI, 23, "The wisdom of doctrine is according to her name."

2. How this mission takes place. Mission in its very meaning implies that he who is sent either begins to exist where he was not before, as occurs to creatures; or begins to exist where he was before, but in a new way, in which sense mission is ascribed to the Divine Persons. Thus, mission in regards to the one to whom it is sent implies two things, the indwelling of grace, and a certain renewal by grace. Thus the invisible mission is sent to all in whom are to be found these two conditions.

The invisible mission takes place also as regards progress in virtue or increase of grace. Such invisible mission, however, chiefly occurs as regards anyone's proficiency in the performance of a new act, or in the acquisition of a new state of grace; as, for example, the proficiency in reference to the gift of miracles or of prophecy, or in the fervour of charity leading a man to expose himself to the danger of martyrdom.

or to renounce his possessions, or to undertake an arduous work.

3. "The Holy Ghost proceeds temporally for the creature's sanctification," writes Augustine. Since then the creature's sanctification is by sanctifying grace, it follows that the mission of the Divine Person is only by sanctifying grace.

For God is in all things by His essence, power and presence, according to His one common mode, as the cause existing in the effects which share in His goodness. Above and beyond this common mode, however, there is one special mode belonging to the rational nature wherein God is said to be present as the object known is in the knower and the beloved in the lover. And since the rational creature by its operation of knowledge and love attains to God Himself, according to this special mode God is said not only to exist in the rational creature, but also to dwell therein as in His Own temple. So no other effect can be put down as the reason why the Divine Person is in the rational creature in a new mode, except sanctifying grace.

Again we are said to possess what we can freely use or enjoy, and to have the power of enjoying the Divine Person results only from sanctifying grace. Hence the Holy Ghost is sent and given to man as a gift of God's Grace. (1 a, Q. 43, a. 5, 6 and 3.)

THURSDAY WITHIN THE SECOND WEEK AFTER EASTER

Spiritual Regeneration Through Baptism

1. Baptism takes away every sin. As the Apostle says (Rom. VI, 3), "All we who are baptized in Christ Jesus are baptized in His death." And further on he concludes (verse 11), "So do you also reckon that you are dead to sin, but alive unto God, in Christ Jesus our Lord." Hence it is clear that by Baptism, man dies unto the oldness of sin, and begins to live unto the newness of grace. But every sin belongs to the primitive oldness. Consequently every sin is taken away by baptism.

2. Baptism liberates from all debt of punishment due to sin. By Baptism a man is incorporated in the Passion and death of Christ, according to Rom. VI, 8, "If we be dead with Christ, we believe that we shall live also together, with Christ." Hence it is clear that the Passion of Christ is com-

municated to every baptized person, so that he is healed just as if he himself had suffered, and died. Now Christ's Passion is a sufficient satisfaction for all the sons of all men. Consequently, he who is baptized, is freed from the debt of all punishment due to him for his sins, just as if he himself had offered sufficient satisfaction for all his sins.

3. Baptism confers grace and virtues. The Apostle says (Tit. III, 5, 6), "He saved us by the laver of regeneration—that is, by Baptism, and renovation of the Holy Ghost, Whom He had poured forth upon us abundantly, that is, unto the remission of sins, and the fulness of virtues. Therefore, the grace of the Holy Ghost and the fulness of virtues are given in Baptism. For the effect of Baptism, is that the baptized are incorporated in Christ as His members. Now the fulness of grace and virtues flows from Christ, the Head of all His members; according to John I, 16, "Of His fulness we all have received."

4. Baptism confers the fruitfulness of all good works. By Baptism man is born again unto the spiritual life, which is proper to the faithful of Christ, and comes through faith in Christ. Now life (spiritual life) is only in those members who are united to the head from which they derive sense and movement. And therefore, it follows of necessity that by Baptism man is incorporated in Christ, as one of His members. Again just as the members derive sense and movement from the material head, so from their spiritual Head, that is Christ, do His members derive spiritual sense, consisting in the knowledge of truth, and spiritual movement which results from the operation of grace. Hence it is written, (John I, 14, 16), "We have seen Him . . . full of grace and truth; and of His fulness we all have received." Therefore, it follows from this, that the baptized are enlightened by Christ as to the knowledge of truth, and made fruitful by Him with the fruitfulness of good works by the infusion of grace. (3a, Q. 69, a. 1, 2, 4, 5.)

FRIDAY WITHIN THE SECOND WEEK AFTER EASTER

The Penalties of Sin That Belong to This Life

Baptism has the power to take away penalties of the present life; yet it does not take them away during the present life, but by its power they will be taken away from the just in the resurrection, when "this mortal hath put on immortality" (1 Cor. XV, 54). And this is reasonable.

First, because by Baptism man is incorporated in Christ, and is made His member. Consequently it is fitting that what takes place in the Head should take place also in the member incorporated. Now from the very beginning of His conception, Christ "was full of grace and truth," yet He had a passible body, which through His Passion and death was raised up to a life of glory. Wherefore a Christian receives grace in Baptism, as to his soul; but he retains a passible body, so that he may suffer for Christ therein; yet he will finally be raised up to a life of impassibility. Hence the Apostle says (Rom. VIII, 11), "He that raised up Jesus Christ from the dead, shall quicken also our mortal bodies, because of His Spirit that dwelleth in us," and further on in the same chapter (ver. 17); "Heirs indeed of God, and joint heirs with Christ; yet so, if we suffer with Him, that we may be also glorified with Him."

Secondly, this is suitable for our spiritual training, namely, in order that by fighting against concupiscence and other defects to which he is subject, man may receive the crown of victory. Hence, on Rom. VI, 6, "that the body of sin may be destroyed," a gloss says, "If a man after baptism live in the flesh, he has concupiscence to fight against, and to conquer by God's help." In sign of which it is written (Judg. III, 1, 2), "These are the nations which the Lord left, that by them He might instruct Israel . . . that afterwards their children might learn to fight with their enemies, and to be trained up to war."

Thirdly, this was suitable lest men might seek to be baptized for the sake of impassibility (escaping suffering and strife) in the present life, and not for the sake of the glory of life eternal. Wherefore, the Apostle says (Cor. XV, 19), "If in this life only we have hope in Christ, we are of all men most miserable."

The punishment of sin is twofold, the punishment of hell and temporal punishment. Christ entirely abolished the punishment of hell, so that those who are baptized and truly repent should not be subject to it. He did not, however, entirely abolish temporal punishment yet awhile. For hunger, thirst and death still remain. But He overthrew its kingdom and power in the sense that man should no longer be in fear of it, and at length He will altogether exterminate it on the last day. (3a, q. 69, a. 3.)

SATURDAY WITHIN THE SECOND WEEK AFTER EASTER

The Sacrament of Confirmation

1. Confirmation is a Sacrament. The sacraments of the New Law are ordained unto special effects of grace, but where there is a special effect of grace, there we find a special sacrament ordained for the purpose. But from what takes place in the life of the body, we can perceive that which is special to the spiritual life. Now it is evident that in the life of the body a certain special perfection consists in man's attaining to the perfect age, and being able to perform the perfect actions of a man. Hence the Apostle says (1 Cor. XIII, 11), "When I became a man I put away the things of a child." And hence it is that besides the movement of generation whereby man receives life of the body, there is the movement of growth, whereby man is brought to the perfect age. So therefore, does man receive spiritual life in Baptism, which is a spiritual regeneration, while in Confirmation man arrives at the age, as it were, of the spiritual life.

2. Chrism, that is oil mixed with balm, is the fitting matter of this Sacrament of Confirmation.

In this sacrament the fulness of the Holy Ghost is given for the spiritual strength which belongs to the perfect age. Now when man comes to the perfect age he begins immediately to communicate with others; whereas until then he lives an individual life, as it were, confined to himself. Now the grace of the Holy Ghost is signified by oil; hence Christ is said to be "anointed with oil of gladness" (Ps. XLIV, 8). Consequently, oil is a suitable matter of this sacrament. Christ is said to be anointed with oil of gladness, because He is filled with the gifts of the Holy Ghost; which gifts receive a strengthening in our souls in confirmation.

Balm is mixed with the oil because of its fragrant odour, which spreads about unto others. Hence the Apostle says (2 Cor. II, 15), "We are the good odour of Christ." And though many other things be fragrant, yet preference is given to balm, for it confers incorruptibility. Hence it is written (Eccles. XXIV, 21), "My odour is as the purest balm."

3. Confirmation imprints a character on the soul. A character is a spiritual power ordained to certain sacred actions. Now just as Baptism is a spiritual regeneration unto Christian life, so also is Confirmation a certain growth bring-

ing man to perfect spiritual age. But it is evident, from a comparison with the life of the body, that the action which is proper to man immediately after birth, is different from the action which is proper to him after he has arrived at perfect age. And therefore, by the Sacrament of Confirmation man is given a spiritual power in regard to sacred actions other than those in respect to which he receives power in Baptism. For in Baptism man receives power to do things which pertain to his own salvation; for as much as he lives to himself; in Confirmation he receives power to do those things which pertain to the spiritual combat with the enemies of the Faith. This is evident from the example of the Apostles, who, before they received the fulness of the Holy Ghost, were in "the upper room . . . persevering . . . in prayer" (Acts I, 13, 14); whereas afterwards they went out and feared not to confess their faith publicly, even in the face of the enemies of the Christian Faith. And therefore, it is evident, that a character is imprinted in the soul in the Sacrament of Confirmation. (3a, q. 72, a. 1, and 5.)

THE THIRD SUNDAY AFTER EASTER

Why the Sacrament of Confirmation Is Conferred on the Forehead

In this sacrament man receives the Holy Ghost for strength in the spiritual combat that he may bravely confess the faith of Christ even in the face of the enemies of that faith. Wherefore, he is fittingly signed with the sign of the cross on the forehead with chrism for two reasons.

First, because he is signed with the sign of the cross as a soldier with the sign of his leader, which should be evident and manifest. Now, the forehead which is hardly ever covered is the most conspicuous part of the human body. Wherefore, the confirmed is anointed with chrism on the forehead, that he may show publicly that he is a Christian. Thus, too, the Apostles after receiving the Holy Ghost showed themselves in public, whereas before they remained hidden in the upper room.

Secondly, because man is hindered from confessing Christ's Name because of two things—by fear and by shame. Now both these betray themselves principally on the forehead, on account of the nearness of the imagination, and because the vital spirits mount directly from the heart to the forehead; hence those who are ashamed blush and those who are afraid become pale, confessing the name of Christ

The principle of courage (or fortitude) is in the heart, but its sign appears on the forehead. Wherefore it is written (Ezech. III, 8), "Behold I have made thy forehead harder than their foreheads." Hence the Sacrament of the Eucharist, whereby man is confirmed in himself belongs to the heart, according to Ps. CIII, 15, "That bread may strengthen man's heart." But the Sacrament of Confirmation is required as a sign of fortitude against others, and for this reason it is conferred on the forehead. (3a, q. 72, a. 9.)

MONDAY WITHIN THE THIRD SUNDAY AFTER EASTER

The Sacrament of the Eucharist

"He who eats My flesh, and drinks My blood, hath everlasting life." (Jo. VI, 55.)

1. This spiritual food is likened unto bodily nourishment in this respect that without it spiritual life in the soul cannot exist; just as without food for the body, bodily life will not exist. But it means more than bodily food, for the Sacrament of the Eucharist causes everlasting life in the person receiving it worthily, which is not caused through corporal food; since he who eats bodily food lives not forever. For as Augustine says, "it frequently happens that many who live sumptuously, and partake of much food, die either from old age, sickness, or some other cause." On the other hand, he who receives this Divine food and drinks of the Body and Blood of the Lord, "hath everlasting life," and is therefore, compared to the tree of life. "She is a tree of life to them that lay hold on her, and he that shall retain her is blessed." Prov. III, 18. Hence the Blessed Eucharist is called the "Bread of Life." "With the Bread of Life and understanding she shall feed him." (Eccles. XV, 3.) And therefore, John says, "everlasting Life." This is because, he who eats this (Divine) Bread has Christ within him, Who is the true God and Life eternal.

Moreover he has life everlasting who eats and drinks not only sacramentally, but also spiritually; that is by receiving not only the Sacrament but the very virtue of the Sacrament.

For the worthy receiver is united by faith and charity to Christ Who is contained in this Sacrament of the altar; so that the communicant becomes transformed into Christ, and becomes His member. For this Divine Food is not converted into the receiver, but It converts the receiver into Christ; according to Augustine, "Thou shalt not convert Me into thee, but thou shalt be converted into Me." Consequently, this Food of the Blessed Eucharist is capable of making men Divine, and of filling them with the Divinity.

2. But this Sacrament is also great, for it gives eternal life likewise to the body, and therefore, Christ says, "I will raise thee up on the last day." For whosoever eats and drinks of this food spiritually, becomes a sharer in the gifts of the Holy Ghost, through Whom we are united to Christ, in a union of faith and charity, and through Whom we are made members of His Church. Moreover, the Holy Spirit causes us to merit the Resurrection, according to Rom. VIII, 11, "If the Spirit of Him that raised up Jesus Christ from the dead, dwell in you, He that raised up Jesus Christ from the dead shall quicken also your mortal bodies, because of His spirit that dwelleth in you."

And therefore, the Lord says, that he who eats and drinks worthily of the Body of the Lord, will be raised up to glory, not to condemnation, because this resurrection does not deceive. And in truth, a spiritual effect of this nature is suitable and sufficiently attributed to the Sacrament of the Eucharist, for the Word resuscitates souls, but the Word made flesh also vivifies bodies. Moreover in this Sacrament is not only the Word according to His Divinity, but also according to His Humanity; and therefore, Christ is not only the Cause of the resurrection of souls, but likewise of the resurrection of our bodies. Consequently, the Spiritual advantages of receiving this Divine Food (frequently and devotionally) is plainly evident. (John VI.)

TUESDAY WITHIN THE THIRD WEEK AFTER EASTER

The Attraction of God and the Cooperation of Man with God

1. "No man can come to Me, unless the Father Who sent Me, draw him." (John VI, 44.) Truly no one can come to God, except he is first drawn to God by the Father. For just as a heavy weight cannot naturally rise of itself, unless moved

by another, so the human heart which by nature tends to inferior things, cannot of itself lift itself to heavenly things, unless it is moved by God the Father.

On the other hand, the Father without injury to man draws men to His Son in many ways. First, by persuading their reason, and in this manner the Father draws men to the Son; by demonstrating to them that He is His Son. This He does in two ways, either by interior revelation or by His own power. By interior revelation, as Matth. XVI, 17, says, "Blessed art thou Simon Barjona, for flesh and blood has not revealed it to thee, but My Father Who is in Heaven."

Secondly, the Father attracts men to His Son through His power by the work of miracles, which the Son performs in the Father's Name. "She (Wisdom) drew man away with the speech of her lips" (Prov. VII, 21). And in this way, those who come to Jesus are drawn by the Father, by the authority of His Paternal Majesty, attracted by His Divine power. But souls are also attracted by the Son, by His admirable delight in and love of—Truth—which is the Son of God Himself. "I am the way, the truth, and the life. If any man come to Me, My Father will love him, and we will come to him, and make our abode with him." For if man is attracted by pleasures, by so much the more, should he be attracted to Christ if he is delighted with happiness, justice, truth, eternal life; which are completely in Christ. Therefore, if we must be drawn to Christ, let us be drawn by a love of Truth. "Delight in the Lord, and He will give thee the requests of thy heart." (Ps. XXXVI, 4.) Hence the spouse of the Canticles (aspiring to an union with Christ) says, "Draw me. We will run after Thee to the odour of the ointments." (Cant. 1, 3.)

Thirdly, the Father draws many souls to the Son, by the inspiration of a Divine operation interiorly moving the heart of man, to believe and to love. "The heart of the king is in the hand of the Lord, whithersoever He will He shall turn it." (Prov. XXI, 1.)

2. The response or cooperation of man with God. "They shall all be taught of God. Everyone that hath heard of the Father, and hath learned, cometh to Me." (John VI, 45.) "Everyone that hath heard of the Father," through His teaching and revelation, "hath learned," and by accepting His doctrines and revelation, "man comes to Me. Everyone in this way, I say, cometh to Me." Everyone then cometh to God in three ways, namely, through a knowledge of the truth, through the love of God and imitation of His works.

And it behooves each one to hear and to learn. For, whosoever comes to God, through a knowledge of the truth, it behooves him to listen to God's inspirations. "I will hear what the Lord will speak in me, for He will speak peace unto His people" (Ps. LXXXIV, 9), and to learn by love and affection for God's word.

On the other hand, he who comes to God through love and desire must hear the Word of the Father, and so receive it, that he might increase in knowledge and in the love of God. For he who truly learns the Word of God, accepts it according to the mind of the Divine Speaker. Moreover the Word of God the Father breathes forth Love; so that he who accepts the Word of God, learns it with fervent love. For that Word, "reneweth all things, and through nations conveyeth itself into holy souls, and maketh the friends of God and prophets." (Wis. VII, 27.)

Thirdly, through the imitation or performance of good works we journey to Christ. And in this way also, whoever comes to Christ, must likewise learn. For just as a conclusion is to things knowable, so also are good works in relation to things done. In sciences whoever learns perfectly, arrives at the right conclusion; and therefore in actions also, whosoever perfectly learns the Word of God (and puts it into practice in his daily life) performs the right work. (John C. VI.)

WEDNESDAY WITHIN THE THIRD WEEK AFTER EASTER

Should Man Be Able to Know That He Has the Grace of God?

1. Sometimes it is expedient for us that we should not know of God's Presence in us by His grace.

First of all, that the fear of the future judgment might keep us humble. "Blessed is the man that is always fearful. But he that is hardened in mind, shall fall into evil," (Prov. XXVIII, 14). This fear keeps a man humble, for which reason it is sometimes expedient that we are ignorant of God's grace in us. Gregory says, "God at times wishes that our good things be uncertain to us, so that we might always have one certain grace, namely humility."

Secondly, lest presumed security might cause us to fall. "For when they shall say, peace and security; then shall sudden destruction come upon them." (1 Thess. V, 3.) Jerome says, "Fear is the custodian of our virtues, security easily leads to destruction."

Thirdly, so that we might await the Grace of God with vigilance and longing desire. "Blessed is the man that heareth Me, and watcheth daily at My gates, and waiteth at the posts of My doors," (Prov. VIII, 34).

2. Sometimes God reveals as a special favour, to certain individuals that they have grace and are in His friendship; so that the joy of security may begin in them even in this life, and so that they might continue to perform magnificent works with greater confidence and zeal, and endure more bravely the trials of the present life. On the other hand, a person can know by conjecture that he has grace; in as far as he perceives that he is delighted in God, and despises worldly things (for God's sake); and inasmuch as man is conscious to himself of not having committed a mortal sin (or is not here and now in mortal sin). In this manner, it can be understood what is written in Apoc. II, 17, "To him that overcometh, I will give the hidden manna, . . . which no man knoweth, but he that receiveth it," because he that receives the grace of God, realizes its sweetness from actual experience, which sweetness is not experienced by the man who receives not God's grace.

There are especially three signs by which the Presence of grace in our souls might be known, namely, the testimony of a good conscience, secondly, a devout reception and practise of the Word of God, and thirdly, an interior taste of Divine Wisdom.

First, the testimony of a good conscience. "Our glory is this, the testimony of our conscience, that in simplicity of heart, and sincerity of God, and not in carnal wisdom, but in the grace of God, we have conversed in this world." (2 Cor. I, 12.) Hence Bernard says, "Nothing is clearer than this Light, nothing more glorious than this conscience; since the mind truly sees itself; but how? Pure, reverent religiously fearful, cautious, in no wise conscious to itself, of being ashamed in the Presence of Truth. For this is plainly evident, that above all the good of the soul, the power of vision is most delighted in things Divine."

Secondly, we must not only listen devoutly to the Word of God, but also put it into practice in our daily lives. "He who is of God heareth the Word of God." (John VIII, 47.) Hence Gregory says, "We are commanded to long for the land of truth, to renounce worldly glory, to seek not another's goods, to be generous with our own. Therefore, let each one think within himself, if this Voice of the Lord sound strong within his own ears, and if now we know, it is the Voice of God."

Thirdly, an interior taste of Divine Wisdom, as it were, a certain foretaste of our everlasting future happiness. "Taste and see that the Lord is sweet," (Ps. XXXIII, 9), namely, taste through His grace in us. Hence Augustine says, "As long as we are in the body, we are journeying to the Lord; may we then at least taste His sweetness, for the Lord is sweet, since He has given us the pledge of the Holy Spirit, in Whom we experience His heavenly sweetness, and in Whom we desire to see His Fountain of grace and glory, wherein we shall be filled with the plenitude of God's house, and increase as the tree planted beside the river of many waters. Grant, I beseech Thee, O Lord, that I may taste through love, what I now taste through knowledge, that I may experience by love, what I now perceive through my intellect; for I owe more to Thee than my entire self, but Thou mayst not have more, since I am not able to give Thee my whole self, by myself. Therefore, draw me O Lord, into Thy Love. Draw this whole self of mine, all that I am—into Thy love." (The Humanity of Christ.)

THURSDAY WITHIN THE THIRD WEEK AFTER EASTER

Gifts of the Holy Ghost

"The Spirit of the Lord shall rest upon Him, the spirit of wisdom, and of understanding, the spirit of counsel and of fortitude, the spirit of knowledge and of Godliness, and He shall be filled with the spirit of the fear of the Lord." (Isaias XI, 2.)

Gifts are certain perfections of man by which he is disposed, so that he becomes promptly moved by Divine inspiration, to act above a human manner and motives.

First of all, the human mind proceeds in a human way in regard to a knowledge of the necessary and eternal things; when the intellect is perfected by virtue, and possesses an insight into things Divine. But when spiritual things are understood from a simple truth, this is above the natural powers, and this takes place through the gift of understanding, for example, when a man's mind is become enlightened by faith from listening to the word of God.

Secondly, the human mode of procedure (in acquiring knowledge) is this, that man from an inspection of the first principles and of the highest causes, judges and regulates concerning inferior things. And this happens through wisdom which is an intellectual gift. But when a man is united to these first causes (or First Cause), and transformed into their likeness, so that he clings to God with his whole soul; he then judges concerning the lowest things in their relation to the highest, and ordains not only things knowable, but also human conduct and passions in relation to God—(the First Cause). This mode of procedure is above the human way of doing things, and is accomplished by the gift of wisdom.

Thirdly, on the part of man's actions, there ought to be counsel. In fact the human way is that which proceeds by inquiry and conjecture from those things which are accustomed to happen; but this mode of procedure is perfected by means of good counsel. But when a man accepts wholeheartedly what must be done, and is taught with certainty by the Holy Spirit, this is above the human way, and the gift of counsel does this very thing for us.

Fourthly, on the part of the things done, the human way is that from those things which are accustomed to happen often man, concerning new things, judges probably through counsel, and furthermore, he places the order of this judgment on inferior things. But when a man knows with certainty those things which must occur, this is above man's power, and is achieved through the gift of knowledge.

Fifthly, in regard to the operations by which communication is made to another, they are regulated either by justice or by liberality. But as the nature of the communication is considered from the good of the person communicating or from the good of the person receiving the communication, man should give to another as much as he ought to give, or as much as it is expedient for him to give. But inasmuch as the Divine goodness is received from God and shines forth in God Himself, or from our neighbor, this also, is something above the human way, and is attributed to the gift of piety.

Sixthly, when a man in all these things receives divine virtue or power, so that he exercises himself in the most difficult works of virtue, which exceed his own powers, and overcomes dangers which he could overcome only by Divine help, this is also above the human way, and is accomplished by the gift of fortitude.

Seventhly, isasmuch as man is attracted to temporal needful good, this is done through temperance. But when a man from a spirit of Divine reverence considers all things as trash (in comparison with God), this is something above the human way, and is perfected by the gift of filial fear. (3 Dist. 34, q. 1, a. 2.)

FRIDAY WITHIN THE THIRD WEEK AFTER EASTER

The Gift of Piety

All moral material is divided into three parts, namely, into the agreeable, the difficult, and the communicable. Into the agreeable, which the carnal affections pursue, into the difficult from which we flee and into the communicable to others, and which consist more in action than in passivity.

Therefore, in each of these the moral material directs both the gift and virtue, but differently. For the virtue in relation to moral affairs directs, while taking the rule of conduct as something human; but the gift (of God) directs us to take the rule of conduct as something Divine.

Consequently, in agreeable things we are directed by the virtue; from the dignity of our human nature, whose disgrace we flee from through temporal pleasures. But by the gift we are directed as if by a Divine rule and Divine dignity, from which we fear to be separated by disgrace and this pertains to the holy gift of fear. Likewise, it is clear from what has been said, that the gift of fortitude directs us differently than the other virtues; for fortitude or courage is ordained to aid us in overcoming and enduring trials and difficulties.

Wherefore the gift of the Holy Ghost, which we receive, enables us to consider the rule of conduct, the rule of God Himself; so that as has been said here of fortitude, man uses the Divine power as his own, and this through confidence in God, to conquer difficult things, communicates this power to another, who in turn uses this God-given power or virtue as his own. Hence (Matth. V, 45) says, "God maketh His sun to rise upon the good and bad." And because the communication of virtue which pertains to divine things is called piety, hence the gift which has a Divine measure, is likewise called piety.

Although piety as a virtue, was manifested by God Himself, still it carried something human in measure, namely the favour received from God, in as far as this favour was for man's edification. But piety which is a gift of the Holy Ghost, receives something Divine for a measure; so that thereby honor is attributed to God, not simply because honor and reverence are due to God, but because God is worthy of honor and reverence from His very nature. In this wise, God should be honored and worshiped by us through the cultivation and manifestation of all the virtues.

Piety, as a gift, is not the same as mercy; because mercy strives to relieve the miseries of our neighbors from the fact that they are united to us either by the ties of blood or friendship, or at least by a likeness of nature; and in all these respects we take something human as our guide or measure just as we do in the manifestation of other virtues. But piety, as a gift from God, inspires us to relieve the miseries of others from a Divine motive, namely, in as far as they are the children of God, or marked with the Divine likeness. Hence the more becoming name of piety, as a gift, is something Divine.

"The gifts are bestowed to assist the virtues, and to remedy certain attacks, so that seemingly, they accomplish what the virtues cannot. Hence, the gifts (of the Holy Ghost) are more excellent than the virtues.

"There are three kinds of virtue, theological, intellectual and moral. The theological are those whereby man's mind is united to God; the intellectual, whereby reason itself is perfected; and the moral virtues are those which perfect the powers of appetite in obedience to reason. On the other hand the gifts of the Holy Ghost dispose all the powers of the soul to obey the Divine inspiration." (1a 2ae. q. 68, a. 8.)

SATURDAY WITHIN THE THIRD WEEK AFTER EASTER

The Enumeration of the Beatitudes

Some have held, that beatitude, or happiness, consists in one of three things, for some have ascribed it to the sensual life, some to the active, and some to the contemplative. Hence the Lord spoke of removing the obstacle to happiness. For a life of pleasure consists in two things.

1. First in the affluence of external goods, whether

riches or honors; from which man is withdrawn by virtue—so that he uses them moderately, and by a gift, in a more excellent way, so that he despises them altogether. Hence the first beatitude is "blessed are the poor in spirit," which may refer either to the contempt of riches or to the contempt of honors which results from humility.

Secondly, the sensual life consists in following the bent of one's passion whether irascible or concupiscible. From following the irascible passions, man is withdrawn by virtue, so that they are kept within the bounds appointed by the ruling of right reason, and by a gift, in a more excellent manner; so that man according to God's will, is altogether undisturbed by them. Hence the second beatitude is, "Blessed are the meek."

From following the concupiscible, man is withdrawn, by a virtue, so that man uses these passions in moderation, and by a gift, so that, if necessary, he casts them aside altogether; nay more, so that, if needs be, he makes a deliberate choice of sorrow. Hence the third beatitude is, "Blessed are they that mourn."

2. The active life consists chiefly in man's relations with his neighbor, either by way of duty or by way of spontaneous gratuity. To the former we are disposed by a virtue, so that we do not refuse to do our duty to our neighbor, which pertains to justice; and by a gift, so that we do the same thing more heartily, by doing works of justice with an ardent desire, even as a hungry and thirsty man eats and drinks with eager appetite. Hence the fourth beatitude is, "Blessed are they that hunger and thirst after justice."

Concerning spontaneous favours we are perfected, by a virtue, so that we give where reason dictates we should give, for example, to our friends or others united to us; which pertains to the virtue of liberality; and by a gift, so that through reverence for God, we consider only the needs of those on whom we bestow our gratuitous bounty. Hence it is written (Luke XIV, 12, 13), "When thou makest dinner or supper, call not thy friends, nor thy brethren—but call the poor, the maimed, and the blind," which properly, is to have mercy. Hence the fifth beatitude is, "Blessed are the merciful."

3. Those things which concern the contemplative life, are either final happiness itself, or some beginning of it, and therefore, they are included in the beatitudes, not as merits, but as rewards. Yet the effects of the active life, which dispose man for the contemplative life, are likewise contained in the beatitudes.

Now the effect of the active life, as regards those virtues and gifts by which man is perfected in himself, is the cleansing of man's heart so that it is not defiled by the passions. Hence the sixth beatitude is, "Blessed are the clean of heart, for they shall see God."

But as regards the virtues and gifts whereby man is perfected in relation to his neighbour, the effect of the active life is peace, according to Isaias, XXXII, 17, "The work of justice shall be peace." Hence the seventh beatitude is, "Blessed are the peacemakers, for they shall be called the children of God." (1a, 2ae, q. 69, a. 3.)

THE FOURTH SUNDAY AFTER EASTER

The Rewards of the Beatitudes

1. The reward for the first three beatitudes corresponds to those things which some persons seek to find in earthly happiness. For men seek to excel and abound in external things, namely, riches and honours; and each of these correspond to the kingdom of heaven, whereby man attains to excellence and abundance of good things in God. Hence our Lord promised the kingdom of heaven to the poor in spirit. Again cruel and selfish men seek by wrangling and fighting to destroy their enemies so as to gain security for themselves. Hence our Lord promised the meek a secure and peaceful possession of the land of the living, whereby the solid reality of eternal goods is signified. Again, men seek consolation for the toils of the present life in the lusts and pleasures of the world. Hence our Lord promised comfort to those who mourn.

2. Two other beatitudes belong to the works of active happiness, which are the works of virtues directing man in relation to his neighbour; from which operations some men withdraw through inordinate love of their own good. Hence our Lord assigns to these beatitudes, rewards in correspondence with the motives with which men withdraw from them. For there are some who recede from acts of justice, and instead of rendering what is due, lay hands on what is not theirs so that they may abound in temporal goods. Wherefore, our Lord promised those who hunger after justice, that they shall have their fill.

Some again depart from works of mercy, lest they be busied with other people's misery. Hence our Lord promised the merciful that they should obtain mercy, and be delivered from all misery.

3. The last two beatitudes belong to contemplative happiness or beatitude. Hence the rewards are assigned in correspondence with the dispositions included in the merits. For cleanness of the eye disposes one to see clearly; and hence the clean of heart are promised that they shall see God.

Again to make peace either in oneself or among others, shows a man to be a follower of God, Who is the God of unity and peace. Hence, as a reward, he is promised the glory of Divine Sonship, consisting in perfect union with God through consummate wisdom.

4. All these rewards will be perfectly consummated in the life to come, but meanwhile they are, in a manner, begun even in this life. Because the kingdom of heaven as Augustine says, can denote the beginning of perfect wisdom, in so far as the spirit begins to reign in men. The "possession," of the land, denotes the well-ordered affections of the soul that rest by their desire, on the solid foundation of the eternal inheritance, signified by the "land." They are comforted, in this life, by receiving the Holy Ghost, Who is called the Paraclete, that is, the Comforter. They have their fill, even in this life, of that food of which our Lord said (John IV, 34), "My meat is to do the will of Him that sent Me." Likewise, the (mind's) eye being cleansed by the gift of understanding, we can so to speak, see God. Likewise also, in this life, those who are the peacemakers of their own movements, approach to the likeness of God, and are called "the children of God." Nevertheless, these things will be more perfectly fulfilled in heaven." (1a, 2ae, q. 69, a. 4, and a 2, Reply to Obj. 3.)

MONDAY WITHIN THE FOURTH WEEK AFTER EASTER

The Fruits of the Spirit

"My flowers are the fruits of honour and riches." (Eccles. XXIV, 23.)

1. The word "fruit," has been transferred from the material to the spiritual world. Now fruit among material things, is the produce of a plant when it comes to perfection, and has some attraction in taste. This fruit has a twofold relation, namely, to the tree that produces it, and to the man that gathers the fruit from the tree. Accordingly, in spiritual matters we may take the fruit in two ways, as acquired, from labour and study, or produced, as the fruit is produced from the tree; so that the fruit of man, who is likened to a tree, is that which he produces, and secondly, that man's fruit is what he gathers. Now the works of the spirit are called fruits, not as if possessed or acquired, but as produced. Moreover the fruit which is possessed has the nature of the last end, but not the fruit produced. For not all that man gathers is fruit, but only that which is last and gives pleasure. For a man has both a field and a tree and yet these are not called fruits; but that only which is last, namely, that which man intends to derive from the field and from the tree. In this sense man's fruit is his last end which is intended for enjoyment. "His fruit was sweet to my palate." (Cant. II, 3.)

Likewise, the works of virtue and of the spirit, are something final in us. For the Holy Spirit is in us through grace, by which we acquire the habit of virtue, and from this we become powerful in performing virtuous actions. The works of the Holy Ghost are likewise delightful. "You have your fruit unto sanctification, and the end life everlasting" (Rom. VI, 22), that is, in sanctified works; which are therefore, rightly called "fruits".

And so our works, in so far as they are produced by the Holy Ghost working in us are called fruits, but in so far as they are referred to the end, which is eternal life, they should rather be called "flowers." Hence it is written, "My flowers are the fruits of honour and riches." (Ecclus. XXIV, 23.) For just as from flowers spring the hope of the fruit, so from virtuous works there comes to us the hope of eternal life and happiness. And just as in the flower, is the beginning of the fruit; so in the works of virtue, there is here a certain beginning of that everlasting blessedness, which we will reap when knowledge and charity are perfected in us.

Consequently, virtuous works, on account of their very nature, must be desired by us for two reasons, both because they contain in themselves sweetness and because of the happiness, which is their final end. Just as tasty medicine is desired formally because of its sweetness, still it is desired on account of an end, namely, for the sake of health.

2. From these things it is clear why the Apostle speaks of "the works of the flesh," but refers to "the operations of the spirit," as "the fruit of the spirit." For fruit is said to be something final and sweet produced of itself, as something is said to be the fruit of a person's reason, but if it proceeds from him in respect of a higher power, which is the power of the Holy Ghost, then man's operation is said to be the fruit of the Holy Ghost, as of a Divine seed; for it is written, "Whosoever is born of God, committeth no sin, for His seed abideth in him." (1 John III, 9.)

On the other hand the works of the flesh are sinful, but God has given us the gift of His grace, to conquer all sinful desires of the flesh. And therefore, because the works of virtue are naturally produced in us through God's grace, they are properly called "fruits," not works of the flesh, "but the fruits of the spirit, which rise in the soul from the spiritual seed of grace."

Hence Ambrose says, "that virtuous deeds are called fruits, because they refresh those that have them with a holy and genuine delight." (1a. 2ae. q. 70, a. 1.)

TUESDAY WITHIN THE FOURTH WEEK AFTER EASTER

The Number of the Fruits of the Holy Spirit

"On both sides of the river was the tree of life, bearing twelve fruits." (Apoc. XXII, 2.)

The number of the twelve fruits enumerated by the Apostle (Gal. V,) is suitable. For since a fruit is something that proceeds from a source as from a seed or root, the difference between these fruits must be gathered from the various ways in which the Holy Ghost proceeds in us, namely, that the mind of man is set in order, first of all in regard to itself, secondly, in regard to things that are near it, thirdly, in regard to things that are below it.

1. Accordingly, man's mind is well disposed in regard to itself, when it has a good disposition towards good things and towards evil things.

Now the first disposition of the human mind towards the good is effected by love, which is the first of our emotions and the root of them all. Wherefore among the "fruits," of the Holy Ghost we reckon "charity," wherein the Holy Ghost is given in a special manner, as in His own likeness, since He Himself is love. Hence it is written (Rom. V, 5.) "The charity of God is poured forth in our hearts by the Holy Ghost, Who is given to us." The necessary result of the love of charity is "joy," because, every lover rejoices at being united to the beloved. Now charity has always the actual presence of God Whom it loves according to (1 John IV, 16,) "He that abideth in charity, abideth in God, and God in him." Wherefore, the result of charity is joy.

Now the perfection of joy is peace in two respects.

First, as regards freedom from outward disturbance; for it is impossible to rejoice perfectly in the beloved good, if one is disturbed in the enjoyment thereof, and again, if a man's heart is perfectly set at peace in one object, he cannot be disturbed by another, since he regards all others as nothing. Hence it is written (Ps. CXVIII, 165,) "Much peace have they that love Thy Law, and to them there is no stumbling-block," because, external things do not disturb those who enjoy God.

Secondly, as regards the calm (or control) of the restless desire. For he does not perfectly rejoice, who is not satisfied with the object of his joy. Now peace, implies these two things, namely, that we do not be disturbed by external things, and secondly, that our desires rest altogether in one object. Hence after charity and joy, peace is given the third place.

In evil things the mind has a good disposition, in regard to two things. First, by not being disturbed whenever evil threatens; which pertains to patience. Secondly, by not being disturbed whenever good things are delayed, which belongs to long-suffering; since to lack good has the nature of evil.

2. Secondly, man's mind is well disposed as regards to what is near him, for example, his neighbour, first as to the will to do good, and to this belongs goodness, secondly, as to the execution of well-doing; and to this belongs benignity,

for the benign are those in whom the salutary flame of love (bonus ignis), has enkindled the desire to be kind to their neighbour.

Thirdly, as to his suffering with equanimity the evils his neighbour inflicts on him. To this belongs "meekness," which curbs anger.

Fourthly, in regard to our refraining from doing harm to our neighbour, not only through anger, but also through fraud or deceit. To this pertains "faith," if we take it as denoting fidelity. But if we take it for the faith, whereby we believe in God, then, man is directed thereby to that which is above him, so that he subjects his intellect, and consequently, all that is his, to God.

Fifthly, man is well disposed in respect to that which is below him, as regards external actions, by "modesty," whereby we observe the proper mode in all our words and actions, and as regards internal desires by "continency and chastity." These two differ because chastity withdraws man from unlawful desires, continency, also from lawful desires; because the continent man is subject to concupiscence, but is not led away, whereas the chaste man is neither subject to, nor led away by unlawful desires. (1a. 2ae. q. 70, a. 3.)

WEDNESDAY WITHIN THE FOURTH WEEK AFTER EASTER

A Man in Grace Can Merit Eternal Life Condignly (or Deservedly)

What is granted in accordance with a fair judgment, would seem to be a condign, or well-deserved reward. But life everlasting is granted by God, in accordance with the judgment of justice, according to 2 Tim. IV, 8, "As to the rest there is laid up for me a crown of justice, which the Lord, the just Judge, will render to me on that day." Therefore, man merits everlasting life condignly, or deservedly.

Man's meritorious work may be considered in two ways —first, as it proceeds from free-will; secondly, as it proceeds from the grace of the Holy Ghost. If it is considered as regards the substance of the work, and inasmuch as it springs from free-will, there can be no condignity or deservedness, because of the very great inequality (between our meritorious work and everlasting life). But there is congruity, or suitableness on account of an equality of proportion. For it would seem congruous (or suitable) that, if a man does what he can, God should reward him according to the excellence of his power.

If, however, we speak of a meritorious work, inasmuch as it proceeds from the Holy Ghost moving us to everlasting life, it is meritorious of life everlasting condignly. For thus the value of its merit depends upon the power of the Holy Ghost moving us to eternal life; according to John IV, 14, "Shall become to him a fount of water springing up into life everlasting." And the worth of the work depends upon the dignity of grace, whereby a man, being made a partaker of the Divine Nature, is adopted as the son of God, to whom the inheritance is due by right of adoption, according to Rom. VIII, 17, "If sons, heirs also."

The grace of the Holy Ghost which we have at present, although unequal to glory in act, is equal to it virtually as the seed of a tree, wherein the whole tree is virtually. So likewise, by grace the Holy Ghost dwells in man; and He is a sufficient cause of life everlasting; hence, He is called "the pledge," of our inheritance. (2 Cor. I, 22) (1a, 2ae, q. 114, a. 3.)

THURSDAY WITHIN THE FOURTH WEEK AFTER EASTER

We Merit More Especially Through Charity

Our Lord said (John XIV, 21), "He that loveth Me, shall be loved by My Father; and I will love him, and manifest Myself to him." Now, everlasting life consists in the clear knowledge of God, according to John XIII, 3, "This is eternal life, that they may know Thee, the only true and living God." Hence the merit of eternal life rests chiefly with charity.

1. Human acts have the nature of merit from two causes, first and chiefly from the Divine ordination, inasmuch as acts are said to merit that good to which man is divinely ordained. Secondly, on the part of free-will, inasmuch as man, more than other creatures, has the power of voluntary acts by acting of himself. And in both these ways does merit chiefly depend on charity. For we must first bear in mind, that everlasting life consists in the enjoyment of God. Now the movement of the human mind to the fruition of the Divine good is the proper act of charity, where all the acts of

the other virtues are ordained to this end, since all the other virtues are commanded by charity. Hence, the merit of life everlasting pertains first to charity, and secondly, to the other virtues, inasmuch as their acts are commanded by charity.

So, likewise, is it clear, that what we do from love we do most willingly. Hence even inasmuch as merit depends on voluntariness, merit is chiefly attributed to charity.

2. A work moreover, has not always more merit, because it is laborious and difficult. For a work can be toilsome and hard in two ways; first, from the greatness of the work, and thus the greatness of the work pertains to the increase of merit; and thus charity does not lessen the labour, rather, it makes us undertake the greatest toils, "for it does great things, if it exists," as Gregory says. Secondly, from the defect of the worker; for what is not done with a prompt will is hard and difficult to all of us, and this toil lessens merit and is removed by charity.

Especially deserving of merit are the acts of faith, patience and fortitude as appear in the martyrs, who fought for the faith patiently and bravely even till death. But acts of faith, patience, and fortitude are not meritorious unless a man does them from charity, according to 1 Cor. XIII, 3, "If I should deliver my body to be burned, and have not charity, it profiteth me nothing." (1a, 2ae, q. 114, a. IV.)

FRIDAY OF THE FOURTH WEEK AFTER EASTER

Were the Actions of the First Man in a State of Innocence, Less Efficacious Than Ours Are?

The degree of merit may be considered in two ways. In one way, in its root, which is grace and charity. Merit thus measured corresponds in degree to the essential reward; which consists in the enjoyment of God; for the greater the charity whence our actions proceed the more perfectly shall we enjoy God. Secondly, the degree of merit can be measured by the degree of the action itself. This degree is of two kinds, absolute and proportional. The widow who put two mites into the treasury performed a deed of absolutely less degree than others who put great amounts therein. But in proportionate degree the widow gave more, as Our Lord said; because she gave more in proportion to her means.

In each of these cases the degree of merit corresponds to the accidental reward, which consists in rejoicing for created good.

Consequently, we must conclude, that in the state of innocence man's works were more meritorious than after sin was committed, if the degree of merit on the part of grace be considered; which would have been more copious, as meeting with no obstacle in human nature; and in like manner, if we consider the absolute degree of the action; because as man could attain to greater virtue, he would perform greater actions. But if we consider the proportionate degree, a greater reason for merit exists after sin, on account of man's weakness; for a small deed is more beyond the capacity of one who works with difficulty than a great deed is beyond one who performs it easily.

Difficulty and struggle belong to the quantity of merit according to the proportionate degree of the action performed. It is also a sign of the will's promptitude striving after what is difficult to itself. But the promptitude of the will is caused by the intensity of charity. Yet it may happen that a person performs an easy action with as prompt a will as another performs an arduous action; because he is ready to do what may be even difficult to him. But the actual difficulty, in as far as it is penal, assists the doer in satisfying for sin. (1a. q. 95, a. 4.)

SATURDAY WITHIN THE FOURTH WEEK AFTER EASTER

Man Can Merit an Increase of Grace

Just as to a crime belongs a twofold punishment—one which is inflicted for the crime itself, namely, remorse of conscience, and other things of this nature—because the sinful and disordered mind is a punishment to itself. The other punishment is that which is inflicted by the Divine or human judge—so also, there is a twofold reward corresponding to merit. One reward is that which belongs to the meritorious act, namely, the sheer delight resulting from the good work done. The other reward is that which is rendered by God, namely, eternal life, or by man, for example, some recompense for the good accomplished.

Hence, a man possessing the grace of God can advance

more in grace, not as if he himself increased it in his soul, since the increase of grace must come from God, but because man can by reason of the grace accepted by him, merit an increase of grace, by disposing himself in such ways that he become more suitable for greater grace.

The increase of grace in fact, comes from God, just as its infusion comes from God. But our actions are differently related in regard to the infusion of grace and the increase of grace. For before the infusion of grace, man is not as yet a sharer in the Divine Being, hence his actions are out of proportion to merit something Divine, since something Divine exceeds the power of nature. But by the infusion of grace, man is established in the Divine Being, and shares in the gifts of God. Hence his acts become now, through God's grace, proportioned to merit an increase of grace or perfection in grace.

Nevertheless, by every meritorious act a man merits the increase of grace, equally with the consummation of grace, which is eternal life. But just as eternal life is not given at once, but in its own time, so neither is grace increased at once, but in its own time, namely, when a man is sufficiently disposed for the increase of grace. (1a, 2ae, q. 114, a. 8, Reply to 3rd Obj.)

THE FIFTH SUNDAY AFTER EASTER

Prayer

"Jesus lifting up His eyes," said: "Father I give Thee thanks that Thou hast heard Me." (John XI, 41). St. John speaks here of two things. First, a proper method of praying, namely, "the lifting of the eyes towards Heaven," that is, raising up the intelligence, and leading it through prayer to the Father above. If we wish to pray according to the examples of Christ, we must lift the eyes of our mind towards Christ, by removing them from material distractions. We raise the eyes to God, when not trusting on our own merits, we hope on the mercy of God alone. "To Thee have I lifted up my eyes who dwellest in Heaven. And as the eyes of the handmaid are on the hands of her mistress, so are our eyes unto the Lord our God, until He has mercy on us." (Psalm CXXII.) "Let us lift up our hearts with our hands to the Lord in Heaven." "We do not cease praying and beseeching God for you," writes St. Paul. Prayer then, is a lifting up of the mind towards God. Petition is a request or demand for certain things. Prayer should go before petition, so that the person devoutly praying might be heard; for just as those seeking to win others to their side, put forth persuasion, so should we first send up meditation on God and on divine things, so that we may raise ourselves towards Him.

Secondly, St. John mentions the power of prayer, when he says: "Father I give Thee thanks because Thou hast heard Me." In this statement we have proof, that God is generous and quick to grant our petitions: "The Lord has heard the desire of the poor," (Psalm IX, 17); and so, even the desire which precedes words may be heard. "At the sound of thy cry, as soon as He will hear, He will answer thee." (Isaias XXX, 19.) Therefore, it is much more helpful for us to remember that God the Father heard the forthcoming prayer of the Saviour, for the tears which Christ shed at the death of Lazarus took the place of prayer. It was at the grave of Lazarus Jesus wept and prayed, and gave thanks to God the Father. In this, Christ teaches us an exemplary lesson, namely, before we ask God for future needs, we should thank Him for past favors. "In all things give thanks to God." (I Thess. V, 18.) (John XI.)

ROGATION DAYS. 1

The Advantages of Prayer

Devout prayer obtains for us a threefold good. It is an efficacious and useful remedy against evils, secondly, it is powerful and useful in obtaining what we ask, and thirdly, it is useful, because prayer makes us the friends of God.

First of all, prayer is an efficacious and useful remedy against evils for it frees us from sins committed. "Thou hast forgiven the wickedness of my sin; for this shall everyone that is holy pray to Thee in a seasonable time." Ps. XXXI, 5.) Thus the repentant thief prayed on the cross, and obtained forgiveness, for Christ said to him, "this day thou shalt be with Me in Paradise." Thus did the poor Publican pray, and "he went down into his home justified."

Prayer also protects us against the fear arising from future sins, mental disturbances and sadness. "Is any of you sad? Let him pray ... cheerful in mind." (James V, 13.)

Prayer also liberates us from persecutions and from our enemies. "Instead of making Me a return of love, they detracted Me, but I gave Myself to prayer." (Ps. CVIII, 4.)

Secondly, prayer is powerful and useful in obtaining for us all our requests. "Therefore, I say unto you, all things whatsoever you ask when ye pray, believe that you shall receive, and they will come unto you." (Mark XI, 24.) On other hand, we shall not be heard, either because we do not persevere in prayer, or because we do not ask for that which is more expedient for our salvation. Hence it is written, "We ought always to pray and not to faint." (Luke XVIII, 1.) "Pray without ceasing." (1 Thess. V. 17.) Augustine says, "The good Lord often refuses what we ask, so that He might grant us what we need." This is clear from the example of Paul, who prayed that the "sting of the flesh might be taken away from him," yet his prayer was not heard, for it was not expedient to his salvation, that the sting of the flesh should be taken away.

Thirdly, prayer is useful since it makes us friends of God. "Let my prayer be directed as incense in Thy sight" (Ps. XCI, 2.) For prayer is an act of religion, whereby man shows reverence to God, in so far as he subjects himself to Him (as the Author of good,) and by praying confesses that he needs Him, as the Author of all good.

By praying, man surrenders his mind to God, since he subjects it to Him with reverence, and so to speak, presents it to Him. Wherefore, just as the human mind excels exterior things, whether bodily members, or those external things that are employed for God's service, so too, prayer surpasses other acts of religion.

God, in very truth bestows many things on us out of His liberality even without our asking for them; but that He wishes to bestow certain things on us at our asking, is for our good, namely, that we may acquire confidence in having recourse to God, and that we may recognize in Him the Author of our good. Hence Chrysostom says, "think what happiness is granted thee, what honour bestowed on thee, when thou conversest with God in prayer, when thou talkest with Christ, when thou askest what thou wilt, whatever thou desirest."

TUESDAY WITHIN THE FIFTH WEEK AFTER EASTER
ROGATION DAY 2
The Lord's Prayer

The Lord's Prayer has five excellent merits, required in every prayer. For prayer should be confident, straightforward, regulated, devout and humble.

Confident—so that we might approach the throne of God's grace, with confidence. In faith also not failing: "Let him ask in faith, nothing wavering. For he that wavereth is like a wave of the sea, which is moved and carried about by the wind" (James I, 6.) But the Lord's Prayer is most secure, for it was formulated by Our Advocate, Who is a most prudent Petitioner, "in Whom are all the treasures of wisdom." Hence St. Cyprian says: "We have Christ as an Advocate with the Father, for the remission of our sins, and when we petition Him, we speak the words of Our Advocate."

Further, His prayer appears more secure from this that He Himself has taught us to pray. He has heard the prayer with the Father. "He has cried to me and I have heard him." (Psalm XC, 15.) Hence St. Cyprian says: "that the Lord asks for us with His own prayer—a friendly, familiar, and devout prayer." Hence this prayer is never said in vain, for through its devout recitation venial sins are remitted.

Our prayer should be straghtforward (coming from the heart), suitable, so that the one praying asks of God, things which are suitable for him. But to know what we should seek is most difficult since it is most difficult to know what we should desire. "We know not what we should pray for as we ought, but the Spirit himself asketh for us with unspeakable groanings" (Romans VIII, 26.) But Christ Himself is the Giver of the Holy Spirit, and He it is who teaches what to pray for.

Our prayer, like our desire, should be proper, since prayer is the messenger of our desire. Prayer delivers the message, so that in desiring and in praying, we should prefer the spiritual to the temporal, heavenly things to terrestrial. The Lord teaches us this in the prayer "Our Father," in which heavenly things are asked first, and afterwards earthly things.

Our prayer should be devout, because the essence of devotion is to make of prayer, a sacrifice most acceptable to God. "In Thy Name, I will lift up my hands. Let my soul be filled as with marrow, and fatness" (Psalm LXII, 5.) But devotion for the most part is weakened by the length of the prayer, hence the Lord has taught us to avoid prayer of a superfluous length: "When you are praying, speak not much" (Matt. VI, 7.) Hence St. Augustine says: "Let much loquacity be removed from prayer, but let a fervent appeal be present, and let a fervent intention persevere." Hence the Lord Himself institutes this brief prayer—the Our Father. But devotion arises from charity, which consists in the love of God and of our neighbor, both of which are shown in the Lord's prayer. To gain divine love we call God, Father, and to win the love of our neighbor we pray for all in general saying, "Our Father," and "Forgive us our trespasses." The love of our neighbor should induce us to do this.

Our prayer should also be humble. "He has regarded the prayer of the humble, and He has not despised their petition." (Psalm CI, 18.) "Thy power, O Lord, is not in a multitude, nor is Thy pleasure in the strength of horses, nor from the beginning have the proud been acceptable to Thee, but the prayer of the humble and the meek have always pleased Thee. O God of the heavens, Creator of the waters, and Lord of all creation, hear me a poor wretch, making supplication to Thee, and presuming on Thy mercy" (Judith IX, 16.) This humility is in truth contained in the Lord's prayer, for true humility exists, when we presume nothing upon our own powers, but place all our confidence upon a power—divine.

WEDNESDAY WITHIN THE FIFTH WEEK AFTER EASTER

MEDITATION FOR ROGATION DAY 3

Why Prayers Remain Unanswered Sometimes

"Whatsoever you ask the Father in My name, that will I do" (John XIV, 13.) What is it that the Lord says? "Whatsoever you ask, that will I do." Why then do we so frequently ask favors from God and yet not always receive them? We must remember that our Lord says, "in My name," and then He adds, "that will I do." The name of Christ is a lifesaving name. "She shall bring forth a Son, and thou shalt call His name Jesus. For he shall save His people from their sins" (Matt. I, 21.) Consequently, whosoever asks of God something pertaining to his salvation, asks in the Name of Christ. Do we always ask something pertaining to the good of our souls, or do we sometimes seek only material things, which if granted might ruin our souls, because of the improper use we might possibly make of God's gifts? It happens then, that one might ask something from God, which does not pertain to his salvation. We might do this in two ways. First, from a wrong disposition of mind, for example, when we seek something which we like, but still if we obtained it, it might be injurious to our salvation. And therefore he who asks in this manner is not heard. "You ask and you receive not; because you ask wrongly" (James IV, 3.) Hence, when anyone from a depraved desire will use badly the gift which he wishes to receive, he does not receive it; because the Lord being most merciful, does not hear that prayer, but preserves it for greater usefulness. For the good Lord sometimes refuses to grant that which we ask, so that He may grant something more beneficial to us later on. Secondly, we might ask something from ignorance, as when we ask that which we think is useful for us, and still is not useful. God who is more wise than we are, does not grant those things which He foresees would be a disadvantage to us. St. Paul who labored more than any of the other Apostles, asked three times that the sting of the flesh might leave him. Still he did not obtain that which he sought, for it was not expedient for him to obtain it. "For we know not what we should pray for as we ought; but the Spirit Himself asketh for us with unspeakable groanings" (Cor. IX, 26.) "You know not what you ask," said Jesus to the mother of the sons of Zebedee, when she asked that her two boys might sit in the kingdom of heaven, one on the right hand of Christ and the other on the left. This was a praiseworthy request, but it was a little too much.

It is clear therefore, that when we ask in the name of Christ, He will hear our prayer. But Christ says, "this will I do," in the future. He does not say I will do it right away, because sometimes Christ puts off granting what we ask, to increase our desire to pray, and so that He might grant our request at a more suitable time. "I will give you rain in due seasons" (Leviticus XXVI, 3.)

It also happens sometimes, that we ask from God a favor for another, but we are not heard because of the sins of that person. Human perversity, a desire to continue in sin, and actual perseverance in sin on the part of that person stand in the way of our prayer and of our request being granted. Saint Monica had to pray many years for her wayward son Augustine, before she saw him converted, or before the desired effect of her prayers was really granted. Hence, we must pray perseveringly, humbly, confidently, fervently and in the name of Christ, leaving it to Him to grant or not grant our requests as He sees fit, and in His own time and manner. (John XIV.)

THE ASCENSION OF CHRIST

1. The Ascension of Christ was exalted on high, because He ascended into heaven.

First of all, He ascended above all the terrestrial heavens. "He that descended is the same also that ascended above all the heavens, that He might fill all things" (Ephes. IV, 10). And Christ was the first to ascend into heaven.

Secondly, He ascended above all the spiritual heavens, namely above all things of a spiritual nature. "Raising Jesus up from the dead, and setting Him on His right hand in the heavenly places, above all principalities and powers, and virtue, and dominion, and every name that is named, not only in this world, but also in that which is to come" (Ephes. I, 20).

Thirdly, Christ ascended to the throne of His Father. "He ascended into Heaven and sitteth at the right hand of God, the Father Almighty." This is to be understood metaphorically, because when it is said that "God sitteth at the right hand of the Father," it means His equality with the Father in the possession of spiritual goods.

On the other hand, the devil pretended to ascend, "I will exalt my throne above the stars of God. I will ascend into heaven." But Christ alone made good His promise, and entered the Kingdom of God.

2. The Ascension of Christ was reasonable, because it took place in Heaven.

First of all, because heaven was due to Christ from His very nature. For it is only natural that a thing return to the place whence it received its origin. But the principle of Christ's origin is from God, Who is above all things. And although the saints ascended into heaven, their ascension is not, however, the same as Christ's; for Christ ascended by His own power, the saints, on the contrary, are drawn thither by the aid of Christ. Or it can be said that only Christ ascended into heaven, because they ascend there only in as far as they are members of Christ, the Head of the Church.

Secondly, heaven belonged to Christ, was owed to Him because of His Victory. For Christ was sent into the world to fight against the devil and to conquer him, and therefore He merited to be exalted above all things. "He who humbleth himself shall be exalted." But Christ humbled Himself unto the death of the cross. "Wherefore God has exalted Him."

Thirdly, heaven was due to Christ by reason of His humility. For no humility is so great as the humility of Christ, since He Who was truly God willed to become man, and since He Who is our Lord and Master willed to assume the form of a servant. "He became obedient unto death, and descended into hell." And therefore, Christ deserved to be exalted in heaven, at the very throne of God. For humility is the royal road to exaltation.

3. The Ascension of Christ is useful to us, especially in regard to three things, namely, in regard to leadership, security and the winning of our love.

First, in regard to leadership. For Christ ascended into heaven to lead us there; for we did not know the way, but He has shown it to us, and He ascended so that He might make us secure in the possession of the heavenly kingdom.

Secondly, in regard to our security. He likewise ascended for this very purpose, that He might plead for us with the Father and render us eternally safe.

Thirdly, He ascended so that He might win our hearts to Himself, "Where thy treasure is, there is thy heart also." (Matt. VI, 21), and so that we might despise temporal possessions. "If you be risen with Christ, seek the things which are above, not the things . . . upon the earth." (Col. III, 1.) (Creed.)

FRIDAY WITHIN THE OCTAVE OF ASCENSION

The Usefulness of Our Lord's Ascension to Us

In the Apostles' Creed we say of Our Saviour: "He ascended into heaven." The fact then, that Our Lord arose from the dead, and ascended into heaven is for all Catholics an explicit and clearly defined article of faith, concerning which there is no room for doubt. We might, however, ask this question: "Of what use is the Ascension of Our Lord to us?" The Ascension of Christ is useful to us, first to increase our faith, which is of things unseen, secondly, to uplift our hopes, and thirdly, to direct the fervor of our charity to heavenly things.

1. To increase our faith. Hence Our Lord said that the Holy Ghost shall come and convince the world . . . of justice, that is, of the justice of those who believe, "for blessed are they who see not, yet believe." Hence it is just that because of our faith in God, our faith be increased and rewarded.

2. To uplift our hope. Hence Our Lord said before He ascended into heaven: "If I shall go, and prepare a place for you, I will come again, and will take you to Myself, that where I am, you also may be." (John XV, 13.) For by placing in heaven the human nature which He assumed, Christ gave us the hope of going thither, since, "wheresoever the body shall be, there shall the eagles also be gathered together." (Matt. XXIV, 28.) Hence it is written likewise: "He shall go up that shall open the way before them." (Mich. II, 13.)

3. The Ascension is useful in directing the fervor of our charity to heavenly things. Hence St. Paul (Cor. III, 1) says: "Seek the things that are above, where Christ is sitting at the right hand of God. Mind the things that are above, not the things that are upon the earth." (St. Matt. VI, 21.) And since the Holy Ghost is love drawing up to heavenly things, therefore our Lord said to His disciples (John XVI, 7): "It is expedient to you that I go; for if I go not, the Paraclete will not come to you; but if I go I will send Him to you." Hence, although a heavenly place befitted Christ when He rose to immortal life, nevertheless He delayed the Ascension in order to confirm the truth of His Resurrection. Hence it is written (Acts 1, 3) that "He showed Himself alive after His passion, by many proofs, for forty days appearing to them." And when the Master of life and of death was about to ascend into heaven He said: "I ascend to My Father and to your Father, to My God, and to your God." (John XX, 17.) "Christ then by once ascending into heaven," writes the Angelic Doctor, "acquired for Himself and for us in perpetuity the right and worthiness of a heavenly place." (3a. q. 58, a. 1.)

SATURDAY WITHIN THE OCTAVE OF ASCENSION

Christ's Ascension Is the Cause of Our Salvation

"It is expedient to you that I go; for if I do not go, the Paraclete will not come unto you; but if I go, I will send Him unto you." (John XVI, 7.)

Christ's Ascension is the cause of our salvation in two ways. First of all, on our part; secondly, on His.

1. On our part, in so far as by the Ascension our souls are uplifted to Him: for His Ascension fosters, first, faith; secondly, hope; thirdly, charity. Fourthly, our reverence for Him is thereby increased, since we no longer consider Him an earthly man, but the God of Heaven. Thus the Apostle says (2 Cor. V, 16), "If we have known Christ according to the flesh" that is as mortal, whereby we reputed Him as a mere man, as the gloss interprets the word,—"but now we know Him so no longer."

2. On His part, in regard to those things which, in ascending He did for our salvation.

First, He prepared the way for our ascent into heaven, according to His own words (John XIV, 2), "I go to prepare a place for you," and the words of Micheas (II, 13), "He shall go up that shall open the way before them." For since He is our Head the members must follow whithersoever the Head has gone. Hence He said (John XIV, 13), "That where I am you also may be." In sign thereof He took to heaven the souls of the saints delivered from Limbo, according to Ps. LXVII, 19, and (Eph. IV, 8); "Ascending on high, He led captivity, captive," because He took with Him to heaven, those who had been held captive by the devil,—to heaven, to a place foreign to human nature; captives indeed of a happy taking, since they were won by His victory.

Secondly, because as the high-priest under the Old Testament entered the holy place to stand before God for the people, so also Christ entered heaven, "to make intercession for us," as is said in Hebr. VII, 25. Because the very appearance of Himself in the human nature which he took with him to heaven is a pleading for us; so that for the very reason that God so exalted human nature in Christ, He may take pity on them for whom the Son of God took human nature.

Thirdly, that being established in His heavenly throne as God and Lord, He might send down gifts upon men, according to Eph. IV, 10. "He ascended above all the heavens, that He might fill all things," that is, fill all things with His gifts.

Christ's Passion is the cause of our ascending to heaven, properly speaking, by removing the hindrance which is sin, and also by way of merit; whereas Christ's Ascension is the direct cause of our ascension; as by beginning it in Him Who is our Head, with Whom the members must be united.

Christ by once ascending into heaven acquired for Himself and for us in perpetuity the right and worthiness of a heavenly home; which worthiness suffers in no wise, if, from some special dispensation, He sometimes comes down in body to earth; either in order to show Himself to the whole world, as at the judgment; or else, to show Himself particularly to some individual; for example, in Paul's case, as we read in the Acts IX. And lest any man may think that Christ was not bodily present when this occurred, the contrary is proven from what the Apostle says in 1 Cor. XV, 8, to confirm faith in the Resurrection.—"Last of all He was seen also by me, as by one born out of due time," which vision would not confirm the truth of the Resurrection except he had beheld Christ's very body. (3a. q. 57, a. VI.)

SUNDAY WITHIN THE OCTAVE OF ASCENSION

Conversation in Heaven

"Our conversation is in Heaven." (Phil. III, 20.)

The Apostle, St. Paul, teaches us in these words to the Philippians, that the conversation of the just is in Heaven; and, wherefore, if we wish to be like them, our conversation must not be entirely upon the miserable things of Earth, but on Heavenly things.

The Saints converse about Heaven, because of three things: First, because of its security, secondly, because of its happiness, thirdly, because their need of all earthly things has vanished.

1. On account of its security, for he whose conversation is in Heaven, is safe from the dangers of this nerve-wrecking life.

2. On account of Heaven's happiness for whosoever converses about Heaven will have as it were, continual joy and

happiness. "His conversation has no bitterness, nor tediousness, but joy and happiness." (Wisdom VIII, 16.)

3. Their need of earthly things has passed away. The Saints realize that all worldly things will quickly vanish (like smoke before our eyes). "The day of the Lord shall come as a thief, in which the Heavens shall pass away with great violence, and the elements shall be melted with heat, and the earth and the works which are in it shall be burnt up. Seeing then, that all these things are to be dissolved, what manner of people ought we to be in holy conversation and Godliness. Looking for and hastening unto the coming of the Lord, on account of which the Heavens being on fire shall be dissolved, and the elements shall melt with the burning heat? But we look for new heavens and a new earth, according to His promises, in which justice dwelleth." (2 Peter III, 10.)

The Saints converse in a threefold manner, First, by thinking always on the blessedness of Heaven. Second, by desiring it always. Third, by living according to Heaven's law. In three ways then, the conversation of the Saints resembles the conversation of the Angels. These three are especially proper to the angels—namely: simplicity in essence, purity in nature, charity in grace. In these three, also, consists the conversation of the Saints.

MONDAY WITHIN THE OCTAVE OF ASCENSION

The Heavenly Father

"Our Father Who Art in Heaven." (Matth. VI, 9.)

Among other things which are necessary for a person praying, confidence is absolutely essential. Hence the Lord in teaching us how to pray, announces beforehand those things by which confidence is produced in us; namely, the kindness of the Father. Hence Christ says, "Our Father." Secondly, the greatness of the Father's power is mentioned to arouse our confidence in the God the Father. Hence Christ says, "Who art in heaven." Moreover, "Who art in heaven," can refer to three things.

First, preparation of the person praying, secondly, facility of Christ hearing our prayers, thirdly, the power of God listening to our prayers.

First, in regard to the preparation of the person praying it is written, "Before prayer prepare thy soul, and be not as a man that tempteth God" (Eccles. XVIII, 23), so that your prayer may be understood and acceptable in heaven, namely, in the glory of heaven. Wherefore, Matth. V, 2, says, "Your reward is very great in heaven."

And this preparation ought to be by our imitation of heaven because the son should imitate the father. "Therefore, as we have borne the image of the earthly, let us also bear the image of the heavenly." (1 Cor. XV, 49.)

Likewise, this preparation should be made by our meditation on heavenly things, because men are wont to direct their attention to things in which they share, and to other things which they love." "Where thy treasure is, there is thy heart also." (Matth. VI, 24.) Hence the Apostle frequently said, "Our conversation is in heaven; from whence we look for the Saviour, our Lord Jesus Christ." (Philip III, 20.)

Secondly, our preparation for prayer should be the result of earnestness and intention on celestial things, so that from Him, Who is in heaven, we seek only heavenly gifts, according to the saying of the Apostle, "Seek those things which are above, where Christ is." (Col. III, 1.)

Thirdly, our preparation for prayer should result from love of God. "For he who abideth in charity, abideth in God, and God in him." (1 John IV, 16.)

Secondly, in regard to the facility of Christ hearing our prayers. It is easy for Him to hear us, for He is near to us, and this is clear from the words, "Who art in heaven," that is, He is in the holy, in whom God dwells. "Thou, O Lord, art amongst us, and Thy Name is called upon us. Forsake us not." (Jer. XIV, 9.) For the saintly are called heavenly, according to Ps. XVIII, 2, "The heavens declare the glory of God." But God dwells in His holy ones through faith. "That Christ may dwell by faith in your hearts." (Ephes. III, 17.)

Thirdly, in regard to the power of God listening to our prayers, so that by the words "in heaven," we understand the corporeal heavens. Not that God is inclosed by the heavenly bodies, but it means that God is perfect, and All-seeing in His consideration of things; in so far as He sees from on High, and that He is most sublime in power, and eternally unchangeable. (The Lord's Prayer.)

Fourthly, through the fulfillment of His commandments. "If any man love Me, he will keep My word; and the Father will love him, and We will come to him, and We will make our abode with him." (John XIV, 23.)

TUESDAY WITHIN THE OCTAVE OF ASCENSION

Our Confidence in the Heavenly Father

Since Christ has taught us to say, "Our Father Who Art in Heaven," He has inspired us with confidence in prayer, in regard to three things; namely, in regard to the power of Him to Whom we pray, secondly, in regard to the friendship between God and us and thirdly, in regard to the suitableness of our petitions.

1. The power of God, from Whom we ask favours, is included in the Our Father, even if by the word "heaven," is understood the terrestrial heavens; for it is written, "I fill heaven and earth, saith the Lord." (Jer. XXIII, 24.) Therefore, Christ is said to be in heaven; so that He is the Highest among all things, since His Divine power is above all things exceeding even the desire and intellect of man. Hence whatever can be thought or desired is less than God. For this reason it is written, "Behold God is great, exceeding our knowledge. The number of His years is inestimable." (Job XXXVI, 26.)

2. Moreover God's friendship is shown towards us, from the fact that the Saints are received by Him into heaven. Some commentators erred in saying that God on account of His greatness, cares not for things human. In support of their error they quote Job XXII, 14, "The clouds are His covert and He doth not consider our things; and He walketh about the poles of heaven." The contrary, however, is true, for God is more intimate with us than we are with ourselves, and cares more for us than we do for ourselves. This very fact of God's love and friendship for us should arouse confidence in those praying, because of two things especially. First, in regard to God's closeness to us; "for the Lord is nigh to all calling upon Him." (Ps. CXLIV, 18.) Hence Matth. VI, 6 says (using our Lord's own words), "Thou when thou shalt pray, enter into thy chamber, namely the chamber of thy heart, and having shut the door, pray to thy Father in secret, and Thy Father Who seeth in secret will repay."

Secondly, our confidence in prayer should be aroused in regard to the intercession of the saints who plead for us before God, and in whom God dwells. For from this very fact alone, new confidence should arise in our hearts, in asking God for favours through the merits of His saints.

3. The suitableness of prayer is shown, from this that in

heaven spiritual and eternal good things are clearly understood; for in these consist everlasting blessedness; and this happens because of two things.

First, because through this eternal happiness, our desire for heavenly things is aroused and sustained. For our desires ought to tend to those things in which we share—our hearts should be where our inheritance is. "Unto an inheritance incorruptible, and undefiled, and that cannot fade, reserved in heaven for you." (1 Peter I, 4.) "Seek therefore, the things which are above." (Col. III, 1.)

Secondly, because through prayer and an earnest desire for eternal happiness, we are reminded that our future life is to be a celestial life, and that we are to be made like to the eternal Father according to (1 Cor. XV, 48), "Such as is the heavenly, such also are they that are heavenly."

These two things therefore, render it fitting for us to ask God for favours, namely, a heavenly desire and a heavenly life. From which two things, we see the suitableness and reasonableness of prayer. (The Lord's Prayer.)

WEDNESDAY WITHIN THE OCTAVE OF ASCENSION

The Source of All Consolation

"Blessed be the God and Father of our Lord Jesus Christ, the Father of mercies, and the God of all comfort." (2 Cor. I, 3.)

1. We bless God, and God blesses us, but differently. For to speak of God is to act. "I sought the Lord and He heard me, and He delivered me from all my troubles." (Ps. XXXIII, 5.) Hence to bless God, or to pray to God, is to do good and to be infused with goodness. Moreover, our blessing is not something causal or of little consequence, but something recognized and expressive. Hence our blessing is a recognition of good. Wherefore, when we give thanks to God, we bless God, that is, we proclaim His goodness, and recognize Him to be the Author of all good.

Rightly therefore, does the Apostle give thanks to the Father, because He is merciful and because He is the God of all comfort. For there are especially two things in which all mankind needs Divine help; first of all, that evils be taken away, and secondly, that we be sustained when evils do come.

1. That evils be taken away from us, belongs to mercy, the mercy of God, which removes our miseries, and has compassion upon our weaknesses. And to be merciful is an attribute of God Himself. Mercy belongs to God the Father.

2. That we obtain strength against oncoming evils, and properly speaking this means to be consoled; because unless man has something on which to rest his heart when evils press heavily upon him he cannot exist for any long time or endure misfortunes bravely. It is then, therefore, man needs consolation and spiritual strength. And although in certain trials one man can console another, and sustain him, still only God can console us in all our trials. Therefore, it is written, "Blessed be the God . . . of all comfort, Who comforteth us in all our tribulations, that we also may be able to comfort them who are in all distress, by the exhortation wherewith we also are exhorted by God." (2 Cor. I, 3, 4.) For when you sin, it is God who later consoles you, because He is merciful . . . and when you are afflicted, may He console you, either by removing your affliction by His power, or by judging it through His justice. If you labour for Him, He will console you with a reward. Therefore, it is written, "Your reward is very great in heaven," and again, "Blessed are they who mourn, and thirst after justice. Fear not I am thy protector, and thy reward exceeding great." (Gen. XV, 1.)

2. That we also may be able to comfort them who are in all distress.

In all divine things, God comforts them, this is the sense of the words of the Apostle. For this purpose God gives special gifts to some; so that they might pour them out unto the usefulness and edification of others. For God did not give light, that it might shine for itself alone, but for the whole world. Hence God desires that a certain usefulness come to others from all our God-given gifts, whether they are riches or power or knowledge or wisdom. Wherefore, the Apostle says, "Blessed be the God and Father of our Lord Jesus Christ, Who consoles us in every tribulation," but why? Not that this consolation might be good for us only, but of advantages to others also. Hence the Apostle also says, "that we also may be able to comfort them who are in all distress."

For we are able to console others through the strength of our Divine consolation, but he who is not thus consoled knows not how to console rightly. "The Spirit of the Lord is upon me, to comfort all that mourn." (Isaias LXI, 1.)

We are able to console (and to be consoled) by exhortation in enduring sufferings, because of the promise of eternal rewards. And thus our consolation abounds unto the consolation of others. (2 Cor. I, 3.)

THURSDAY WITHIN THE OCTAVE OF ASCENSION

Preparation for the Reception of the Holy Spirit

"If you love Me, keep My commandments, and I will ask the Father, and He shall give you another Paraclete, that He may abide with you forever." (John XIV, 15.)

1. Amongst the disciples of our Lord, a twofold preparation was necessary, namely, pure love of the heart and obedience in action. One of these essentials the Lord supposes the disciples to have, and therefore, He says, "If you love Me," and this is evident, because you are saddened at My departure. The other thing necessary refers to the future, and this Christ lays down as a command saying, "Keep My commandments," as if He said; "You will show the love you have for a manifest proof of your love." Therefore, these two things, love and obedience, prepared them for the reception of the Holy Spirit. For since the Holy Spirit is Love, He is given only to those who love God. "I love them that love Me." (Prov. VIII, 17.) Likewise the Holy Spirit is given to those who obey God's Law. "The Spirit of the Lord shall rest upon them, the Spirit of wisdom, and of understanding, the spirit of counsel, the spirit of knowledge, and of godliness." (Isaias XI, 2.)

2. But why are obedience and love necessary for the reception of the Holy Spirit? It would seem that both are essential. For the love by which we love God comes through the Holy Spirit. But obedience also comes to us from the Holy Ghost.

It must be observed that this condition is in the gifts of God, namely, that he who makes good use of God's gifts, merits more the reception of grace and the reception of God's gifts; but who makes bad use of God's gifts, they will be taken away. The talent which the lazy servant had received was because of his laziness, taken away from him by the Master, and given to the man who had five talents. Consequently true obedience to work is also a gift of the Holy Spirit.

For no one can truly love God, unless he has the Holy Spirit abiding in his soul, for we do not come to God before the grace of God, but it comes to us first. Hence it must be concluded that the Apostles first of all and in very truth received the Holy Spirit so that they through Him might love God, and obey His commandments. But for this end, it was necessary that they should receive the Holy Spirit with greater plenitude; so that by love and obedience they might make good use of the gifts of the Holy Ghost, which they had previously received. And according to this manner are the words, "If you love Me," to be understood, "If you love Me, through the Spirit which you have and obey My commandments, you will receive in greater abundance the Holy Spirit which you now possess." (John XIV.)

FRIDAY AFTER THE OCTAVE OF ASCENSION

The Holy Spirit Is Not Given to the World (or to the Worldly)

"The Spirit of Truth Whom the world cannot receive, because it seeth Him not, nor knoweth Him; but you shall know Him, because He shall abide with you, and shall be in you." (John XIV, 17.)

1. The Lord here calls "the world," those who love this world and its sinful pleasures. Indeed these worldly lovers, as long as they love the world, cannot receive the Holy Spirit, for He is the Love of God. Moreover one cannot love with his whole heart, God and the world at the same time. "If any man loveth the world, the charity of the Father is not in him." (1 John II, 15.) Hence Gregory says, "The Holy Spirit fills everything, even the invisible things to be desired, and although worldly hearts love visible things solely, the worldly person then, does not receive this Holy Spirit, because the worldly person does not rise to the love of the Invisible. For worldly minds in as far as they indulge themselves in worldly desires, by so much the more do they narrow the entrance of their hearts to the reception of this Holy Spirit."

2. The Holy Spirit which is not given to the worldly, assigns the reason for this, when He says, because, "the world seeth Him not, nor knoweth Him not." For spiritual gifts are not received unless desired. "Divine Wisdom preventeth them

who covet her." (Wis. VI, 14.) But only those things which are known in some degree are coveted or desired.

Moreover, that these things are not even known, by the worldly, results from two causes. First indeed from this, that man does not fix his mind on a knowledge of these things, and secondly, the worldly man is not capable of receiving this knowledge of the Holy Spirit. The world as such, does not possess the Holy Spirit, and hence cannot give what it does not have.

First of all, the worldly do not intend to desire the Holy Spirit. And on this point the Lord says, "the world seeth Him not," that is, the world or the worldly is not concerned about knowing Him. "They have cast Me forth, and now they have surrounded Me. They have set their eyes bowing down to the earth." (Ps. XVI, 11.)

Again. The worldly cannot know or recognize the gifts of the Holy Spirit. Hence our Lord says, "nor does the world know Him." For as Augustine declares, "worldly love has no invisible eyes, by which means only, the Holy Spirit can be invisibly seen." For the sensual man perceiveth not those things which are of the Spirit of God, for it is foolishness to him, and he cannot understand, because it is spiritually examined." (1 Cor. II, 14.) Just as an infected tongue does not perceive sweet flavour, because of the corruption of this member of the body, so also the soul, infected with worldly corruption, tastes not the sweetness of things heavenly.

3. "But you shall know Him, because He shall abide with you, and shall be in you." Here our Lord shows to whom the Holy Spirit is given, namely, to His faithful servants. Hence Christ says, "But you," who are inspired by the Holy Spirit, "you shall know Him." Now we have received not the spirit of this world, but the Spirit that is of God; that we may know the things that are given us from God." (1 Cor. II, 12.) And this, therefore, because you despise the world. "Looking not at the things which are seen, but at the things which are not seen. For the things which are seen are temporal; but the things which are not seen are eternal." (2 Cor. IV, 18.)

Moreover the reason for this is, "because He shall abide with you." In these words of our Lord, note well the familiarity of the Holy Spirit towards the Apostles, "because He shall abide with you," that is, for your usefulness; and secondly, observe the intimate indwelling of the Holy Spirit in their souls, "because He shall be in you," namely, in the secret chamber of our hearts. (John XVI.)

SATURDAY IN THE VIGIL OF PENTECOST

The Workings of the Holy Spirit

"The Paraclete, the Holy Ghost, whom the Father will send in My Name, He will teach you all things." (John XIV, 26.)

Here three things are indicated.
1. The Holy Ghost Himself is described, and in several ways, for He is called Paraclete, Spirit and holy. He is the Paraclete, for He consoles us, when sadness arising from worldly disturbances afflicts us. He consoles us, in so far as He is the Love, which causes us to love God, and to have Him for our greatest friend; on account of Whom we joyfully endure calumnies and sufferings. Because of the strength and consolation received from the Holy Spirit, "the Apostles went forth from the presence of the council, rejoicing that they were accounted worthy to suffer reproach for the Name of Jesus." (Acts V, 41.) For since the Holy Spirit is Love, He causes us to despise earthly things and to cling to God. Wherefore, He drives away grief and sadness from us, and gives us joy in Divine things. Likewise, He consoles us against sadness arising from our past sins, and He does this in so far as He obtains for us the hope of pardon.

The Holy Ghost is a Spirit, because He moves our hearts to obey God. And because this name—Spirit—implies a certain impulse or movement, and every movement or impulse produces an effect suitable to its principle, for example, heat produces warmth, it follows that the Holy Spirit is sent to those whom He makes like unto His own Spirit; and therefore, since, "He is the Spirit of Truth, He teaches all truth. He will teach you all things." Likewise, because He is the Spirit of the Son, He will make us the children of God.

Moreover, the Spirit is holy, because He consecrates us to God; and all things consecrated are called holy.
2. The Mission of the Holy Ghost is also described in our next, namely, "Whom the Father will send in My Name." The Holy Spirit is said to be sent, not as if He changes His place, for He truly fills every place, but because in a new manner He begins to dwell by grace in the hearts of those whom he consecrates and sanctifies, temples of God. "The Father will send in My Name," because the mission of the Holy Spirit is from the Father and the Son, which is in-

dicated in Apoc. XXII, 1, "He showed me a river of water of life, clear as crystal, proceeding, from the throne of God and of the Lamb," that is, the Holy Spirit, "proceeding from the throne of God and of the Lamb." And therefore, concerning the mission of the Holy Spirit, mention is made of the Father and of the Son, by Whom He is sent equal to them in power and in virtue.

3. The effect of the Holy Spirit is also described. "He will teach you all things." For just as the effect of the mission of the Son was to lead mankind to the Father, so the effect of the Holy Spirit is to lead the faithful to the Son. Moreover, the Son since He is Wisdom itself, is Truth itself, and therefore, the effect of a mission of this nature, is to make men sharers in the Divine Wisdom and knowers of the Truth. Consequently, the Son gives His doctrine to us, since He is the Word, but the Holy Spirit disposes us to receive His teachings; and therefore, our Lord says, "He will teach you all things," because whatever things a man learns without His aid, he learns in vain if the Holy Spirit enlightens not his intellect; for unless the Holy Ghost is present in the heart of the person listening, the sermon of the teacher will be burdensome and fruitless to the listener, as the Son speaking to humanity avails nothing, unless God Himself operates interiorly on the mind of man through the medium of the Holy Ghost.

"Come, O Holy Ghost, enlighten our minds, and enkindle in us the fire of Thy Divine Love." (John XIV, 26.)

THE FEAST OF PENTECOST

The Gift of the Most High God

1. It is proper to a Divine Person to be a "gift," and to be given. But the Holy Ghost receives this proper name from the fact that He proceeds from the Father and Son. Therefore, "gift," is a name proper to the Holy Ghost, for Augustine says, "As the body of flesh is nothing but flesh; so the gift of the Holy Ghost is nothing but the Holy Ghost." For what is given has an aptitude or relation both to the giver and to that to which it is given. For it would not be given by anyone, unless it were his to give; and it is given to someone to be his. Now a Divine Person is said to belong to

another, either by origin, as the Son belongs to the Father or as possessed by another. But we are said to possess what we can freely use or enjoy as we please, and in this way a Divine Person cannot be possessed, except by a rational creature united to God.

Other creatures can be moved by a Divine Person, not, however, in such a way as to be able to enjoy the Divine Person and to use the effect thereof. The rational creature does sometimes attain thereto; as when it is made partaker of the Divine Word and of the Love proceeding, so as to freely know God, and to love God rightly. Hence the rational creature alone can possess the Divine Person. Nevertheless, in order that it may possess Him in this manner, its own power avails nothing. Hence this must be given it from above; for that is said to be given us which we have from another source. Thus a Divine Person can be "given" and can be "a gift." The Holy Ghost is therefore, God's gift to us.

2. The Holy Spirit is indeed God's gift. For since the Holy Spirit proceeds through a mode of love, by which God loves Him, but while God loves Himself and other things by reason of His own goodness, it is clear that the Love by which God loves us, pertains to the Holy Ghost; and likewise, also, the love by which we love God, since the Holy Spirit makes us lovers of God. And in regard to both kinds of love, it is proper to the Holy Spirit to be given as God's gift of love to us, because of two reasons.

First, because of the love by which God loves us, for one is said to give his love to another when one begins to love another. Although God began to love none in point of time, if we speak of the Divine will by which He loves us, still the effect of His love in us is caused in time, since He draws us to Himself.

Secondly, because of the love with which we love God (it is proper that the Holy Ghost be given to us), because the Holy Spirit causes this love in us. Hence in as far as this love dwells in us we possess Him; so that we might enjoy His Divine assistance.

3. The proper name for the Holy Ghost is "Gift." A gift is an unreturnable giving (or donation), that is, a thing which is not given with the intention of return and it thus contains the idea of a gratuitous donation. Now the reason for donation being gratuitous is love, since we give something to anyone gratuitously because we wish him well. So what we first give him is the love whereby we wish him well. Hence it is clear that love has the nature of a first gift,

through which all free gifts are given. So since the Holy Ghost proceeds as love, He proceeds as the first gift. Hence Augustine says, "By the gift, which is the Holy Ghost, many particular gifts are portioned out to the members of Christ." (1a, q. 38, a. 2.)

MONDAY WITHIN THE OCTAVE OF PENTECOST

How We Are Moved by the Holy Ghost to do Good

It seems to be especially proper to friendship to converse with a friend. But the conversation of man with God is through contemplation of Him, as the Apostle states: "Our conversation is in Heaven." Because the Holy Ghost makes us lovers of God, it follows that through the Holy Spirit we become contemplators of God. "We all beholding the glory of the Lord with open face, are transformed into the same image from glory to glory, as by the Spirit of the Lord." (2 Cor. III, 18.)

It is also proper to friendship that one is happy in the presence of a friend, rejoices in his words and deeds, and finds consolation in him in the midst of all anxieties and cares. Hence in sadness we fly to friends for comfort. Because, therefore, the Holy Spirit makes us friends of God, and makes Himself to live in us and we in Him, it follows that through the Holy Spirit we receive joy and consolation from God, against all the adversities and strife of the world. Therefore the Lord calls the Holy Spirit the Paraclete, that is Consoler.

It must be remembered then, that through the Holy Ghost, we as children of God act, . . . not as slaves, but as free men. We do those things freely, which we do of our own free will. But the Holy Spirit so inclines us to act, that He makes us act willingly, in as far as He makes us lovers of God. Consequently, children of God are acted upon freely by the Holy Spirit, . . . from love, and not through slavish fear. Hence the Apostle says: "You have not received the spirit of bondage again in fear, but you have received the adoption of sons, whereby we cry Father. For the Spirit Himself giveth testimony to our spirit that we are the sons of God." (Rom. VIII, 15.) (Contr. Gent. IV, 22.)

TUESDAY WITHIN THE OCTAVE OF PENTECOST

The Properties and Power of the Holy Ghost

"The Spirit breatheth where he will and thou hearest his voice, but thou knowest not whence he cometh, and whither he goeth. So is everyone that is born of the Spirit." (John V, 8.)

Four things are here mentioned by Saint John, concerning the Holy Ghost. First, his power. "The Spirit breatheth where he will." By his freedom of power He not only breathes where he wills but when he wills; enlightening minds and inflaming hearts with Divine love.

Since the Holy Spirit is the sanctifier of the human soul and comes from the Father and the Son; he breathes wheresoever the Father and the Son commands.

Secondly, the sign of the Holy Spirit is mentioned in the words, "thou hearest his voice." The voice of the Spirit is two-fold. One voice which speaks to man's heart; according to Psalm LXXXIV, 9, "I will hear what the Lord God will speak in me." Another voice, is that by which the Holy Ghost speaks to us in Sacred Scripture and through God's missionaries; for it is also written, "It is not you that speak, but the Spirit of your Father that speaketh in you." (Matt. X, 19.) Even infidels and sinners hear this Voice of the Spirit.

Thirdly, the origin of this Voice is hidden. "Thou knowest not whence he cometh." Even though you hear His Voice, you do not know whence it comes; and the reason is because it comes from the Father and the Son. But the Father and the Son dwell in light inaccessible; which no living man can see or is able to behold.

Fourthly, the departure of the Holy Spirit is likewise hidden from human eyes, "Thou knowest not whither he goeth." But we do know that he leads us to eternal happiness; for Saint Paul tells us, "the eye has not seen, nor the ear heard, neither has it entered into the heart of man, what things God has prepared for them that love Him." (1 Cor. II, 9.)

"Thou knowest not whence He cometh," that is, we do not know how the Holy Spirit enters our hearts, "or whither he goeth," that is, to what degree of perfection he may lead us.

"So is everyone that is born of the Spirit," born of the Holy Spirit. Nor is this wonderful, because the power of the Holy Ghost is in the heart of the spiritual man; just as the flame of fire is in the burning fire.

The Holy Spirit first comes to us in baptism with his grace, to make us free children of God and worthy of eternal life. Hence it is written, "Where the Spirit of the Lord is, there is liberty," (2 Cor. III, 17), because the Spirit of God leads us to do what is right and frees us from the slavery of sin and from the slavery of the law.

WEDNESDAY IN THE OCTAVE OF PENTECOST

The Manifold Blessings Flowing from the Holy Spirit

The blessings that come to us from the Holy Spirit are manifold and great. First of all, He washes away our sins; secondly, He enlightens our intellects; thirdly, He strengthens our hope in life everlasting; fourthly, He helps us to keep the commandments; fifthly, He counsels us in regard to the will of God.

1. The Holy Spirit washes away our sins. The reason for this is, because it is the work of the Holy Ghost to renew and sanctify, as it is His work to establish us in the friendship of God. Now the soul is created by the Holy Spirit, for all things which God does, He does through the Spirit. For God created all things by loving His Own goodness: "Thou lovest all things that are, and hatest none of the things which Thou hast made." (Wis. XI, 25.) Dionysius says that "Divine love was not diffused without producing its effects. Therefore, it was necessary that the hearts of men destroyed by sin, should be renewed by the Holy Ghost." "Thou shalt send forth Thy Spirit, and they shall be created; and Thou shalt renew the face of the earth." (Ps. CIII, 30.) Nor is it surprising, that the Holy Spirit purges sin, for all sins are removed—forgiven—through love. . . . "Many sins are forgiven thee, because thou hast loved much," said Christ to the repentant Magdalen. "Charity covereth all sins." (Prov. X, 12.)

Secondly, the Holy Spirit enlightens our intellects, because all things which we know, we learn from the Holy Spirit. "But the Paraclete, the Holy Ghost, Whom the Father will send in My Name, He will teach you all things, and bring all things to your mind, whatsoever I will have said to you." (John XIV, 26.) Likewise, 1 John II, 27: "Let the unction which you have received from Him abide in you, for His unction teacheth you all things."

Thirdly, the Holy Spirit aids us and encourages us to observe the commandments. For no one can keep the commandments of God, unless he loves God. "If any man love Me, he will keep My word." (John XIV, 23.) Therefore, the Holy Spirit causes us to love God. "I will give you a new heart, and put a new spirit within you; and I will take away the stony heart out of your flesh, and will give you a heart of flesh; and I will put My Spirit in the midst of you; and I will cause you to walk in My Commandments, and to keep My judgments, and to do them." (Ezech. XXXVI, 26.)

Fourthly, the Holy Ghost strengthens our hope in life everlasting, because He is as it were, the pledge of our eternal inheritance. "You were signed with the Holy Spirit, Who is the pledge of our inheritance" (Ephes. I, 13.) For He is our safeguard to eternal life. The reason for this is, because eternal life is due to man inasmuch as the Son of God has won it for him, and He did this because man is like unto Christ. Now we become like unto Christ, when we have the Spirit of Christ—the Holy Spirit. "You have not received the spirit of bondage again in fear; but you have received the Spirit of adoption of sons, whereby we cry: (Abba) Father. For the Spirit Himself giveth testimony to our spirit, that we are the sons of God." (Rom. VIII, 13.) And Gal. IV, 6, says: "Because you are sons, God hath sent the Spirit of His Son into your hearts, crying: Abba, Father."

Fifthly, the Holy Ghost counsels us concerning what is the will of God in regard to us. "He that hath an ear, let him hear what the Spirit saith to the churches." (Apoc. II, 7.) And Isaias L, 4, says of the Holy Spirit: "That I may hear Him as a master." (The Creed.)

THURSDAY WITHIN THE OCTAVE OF PENTECOST

The Apparition of the Holy Ghost in the Form of a Dove

"I saw the Spirit coming down, as a dove from Heaven, and He remained upon Him." (John I, 32.)

Why does the Holy Ghost appear in the form of a dove rather than in any other form? (To show the possessions of the baptized.)

First, because of the simplicity of the dove. "Be ye therefore wise as serpents and simple as doves." (Matth. X, 16.) Now the Holy Spirit, because He makes us reflect upon One Object (of our love), makes us morally simple and upright (in our way of thinking and acting), and therefore, He appears in the form of a dove. According to Augustine, "He also appears in the shape of fire, as He did to the Apostles gathered together, for some souls are simple, but lukewarm, others fervent, but resentful. Therefore in order that the sanctified might be freed from guile, and lest simplicity might become cold through remissness, the Holy Spirit appears in the form of a dove, or in the form of fire."

Secondly, because of the unity or bond of charity; for the dove nourishes love exceedingly. "One is My dove. My perfect one is but one." (Cant. VI, 8.) Therefore the Holy Spirit appears in the form of a dove, that He might also show the unity of the Church.

Thirdly, because of His unspeakable cry (of intercession for us). For the dove has a cry like unto chanting. Accordingly, "The Holy Spirit Himself asketh for us with unspeakable groanings." (Rom. VIII, 26.)

Fourthly, because of His fruitfulness, for the dove is a most fruitful animal. Hence to show the fruitfulness of spiritual grace in the Church, the Holy Ghost appears in the shape of a dove.

Fifthly, because of His prudence. For the dove sits beside the river banks, whence it can see the falcon (and other birds of prey) flying around, and thus protect itself from these vultures. "Thy eyes as doves upon the brooks of waters." (Cant. V, 12.) Hence, because in baptism He is our safeguard and defender, it is suitable that the Holy Spirit should appear in the form of a dove.

Finally, because it corresponds to the figure of the Old Testament. For just as the dove bearing the branch of the olive tree, was a sign of the mercy of God to those who were saved from the waters of the flood, so also the Holy Spirit coming to us at Baptism in the form of a dove, is a sign of Divine mercy to the baptized, since their sins are forgiven and God's grace bestowed. (John I.)

FRIDAY WITHIN THE OCTAVE OF PENTECOST

The Spirit Descending and Remaining

"I saw the Spirit coming down from heaven, and remaining upon Him." (John I, 32.)

That the Holy Spirit was present when Christ was baptized was suitable to the Baptized, namely to Christ, and suitable to the Sacrament of Baptism. Suitable to the Baptized, for just as the Son existing in the Father manifested the Father (John XVII, 6), "I have manifested Thy Name," so the Holy Spirit existing in the Son manifested the Son: "He shall glorify Me, because He shall receive of Mine." (John XVI, 14.)

It was suitable to the Sacrament of Baptism, because the Baptism of Christ was the beginning of our baptism. Now our Baptism is consecrated by the invocation of the Blessed Trinity. Therefore, in order that we might call upon the Blessed Trinity at our baptism, the three Persons were present at the Baptism of Christ. The Father was there in the Word, the Holy Spirit in the form of a dove, the Son in human nature.

Moreover, Saint John speaks of "the Spirit coming down." For there is a twofold spirit. One the spirit of the world, the other the Spirit of God. Now the spirit of the world means love of the world, which is not upwards but rises from below unto man and causes man to descend; whereas, the Spirit of God, namely the love of God, comes down to man and makes man ascend higher. "Now we have not received the spirit of this world but the Spirit of God, that we may know the things that are given us from God." (1 Cor. II, 12.)

Secondly, Saint John speaks later on of "the Spirit remaining upon Christ," because by remaining, or abiding, rest is designated. And if the Holy Spirit rests not in anyone—abides not with anyone—it is due to two causes. One cause is the result of sin. For all men, Christ excepted, are wounded by the wound of mortal sin, by reason of which the Holy Spirit is put to flight, or they are soiled by the stain of venial sin on account of which a certain operation of the Holy Spirit is impeded (in the soul). Now in Christ there was neither mortal nor venial nor original sin. Therefore, in Him there was no resistance against the Holy Spirit. But "He remained upon Him," that is, the Spirit of God abided with Christ.

A second reason (why the Holy Spirit remains not with us), because the power of working through sanctifying grace is not always with us, just as the power of working miracles is not all the time present to the saints, nor the gift of prophecy present always to the prophets. On the contrary, Christ had power always in regard to every operation of virtue and of grace; and therefore to prove this fact (and designate that power) the Holy Spirit "remained upon Him." Hence that was the proper sign of recognizing Christ (of acknowledging Him as the Saviour). ".The Spirit of the Lord shall rest upon Him." (Isaias XI, 2), which saying must be understood of Christ in as far as He was man. (John I.)

THE FEAST OF THE BLESSED TRINITY

The Coming of the Trinity Into the Mind

Not only the Son, but also the Father and the Holy Spirit come and dwell in the human mind by grace, according to John XIV, 23, Jesus said, "If any one love Me he will keep My word, and My Father will love him and We will come to him and will make Our abode with him."

The Father comes comforting us by His power. "It is He that giveth strength to the weary." (Isaias XL, 29.)

The Son comes enlightening us with His wisdom, "for He is the true Light that enlighteneth every man."

The Holy Spirit comes through His goodness, filling our hearts with His Love.

For truly, whatever good is in us is from the Holy Spirit. since He comes to us with His love; because the love of God is the fountain of all goodness. Therefore then, the Spirit chiefly communicates Himself to us; but very sweetly is He in us when He rejoices us with the interior taste of His sweetness. Wherefore on this point the Psalmist says: "The Lord is sweet to all, and His tender mercies are over all His works." (Ps.CXLIV, 9.) But especially sweet is He to those tasting Him. Bernard speaking of the Holy Spirit says: "He is the One Consoler. He Who is God and Love. . . . Thus the devout soul who intimately tastes the sweetness of the Divine goodness is to be admired because it finds no such sweetness in created things." Wherefore Anselm says: "Imagine how great is that good which contains the sweetness of all good things and which we cannot find in things created, and differs (from all natural good) as much as the Creator differs from the creature."

The sweetness of this Divine goodness is so great no tongue and no words are capable of expressing it; only grace can fittingly praise it. "To him that overcometh I will give the hidden manna," Apoc. II, 17; for it is revealed in no discourses. Hence Bernard says: "O whosoever is anxious to know what it means to enjoy the Word, let him prepare, not his ear, but his mind; for not the tongue, but grace teaches it."

More than this, the sweetness of Divine goodness excels every desire and all knowledge. It is so great that we are not only incapable of finding words to express its greatness, but also we fail in investigating its true power. Wherefore in Psalm LXXVI, 4, we read: "I remembered God, in Whom is sweetness, and I was delighted, and was exercised, and my spirit swooned away." Hence Bernard says: "The intellect does not grasp this, except in so far as the soul experiences it."

Therefore, the words of the prophet are plainly evident, namely: "Wonderful are Thy works, O Lord, and my soul knoweth right well. I will praise Thee, for Thou art fearfully magnified." (Ps. CXXXVIII, 14), that is, so exceedingly great is the power of the Father, the wisdom of the Son and the sweetness of the Holy Spirit, that we fail to realize the magnitude of that power, the depth of the wisdom and the abundance of that overflowing sweetness. (The Humanity of Christ.)

MONDAY WITHIN THE OCTAVE OF TRINITY

The Image of God Is Found in Every Man

"God created man to His own image." (Gen. I, 27.)

1. As man is said to be the image of God, because of his intellectual nature, he is most especially like God according to that in which he can best imitate God in his intellectual nature. Now the intellectual nature imitates God chiefly in this, that God understands and loves Himself. Wherefore we see that the image of God is in man in three ways.

Firstly, inasmuch as man possesses a natural aptitude for understanding and loving God, which aptitude consists in the very nature of the mind which is common to all men.

Secondly, inasmuch as man actually or habitually knows and loves God, though imperfectly; which kind of image is by the conformity of grace.

Thirdly, inasmuch as God knows and loves God perfectly, which is from the likeness and conformity of glory. Wherefore, on the words "The Light of Thy countenance, O Lord, is signed upon us" (Ps. IV, 7), the gloss distinguishes a threefold image, namely, the image of creation, of re-creation and of likeness. The first is found in all men, the second only in the just and the third in the blessed.

2. The image of God is especially in us when we actually know and love God. For the intellectual creature is chiefly like unto God from the very fact that he is intellectual. For man has this likeness in preference to other creatures, and this includes all other created things. From the fact that man understands, he is chiefly likened unto God, for God in understanding Himself understands all other things.

Therefore, first and chiefly, the image of the Trinity is to be found in the acts of the soul, that is, inasmuch as from the knowledge we possess by actual thought, we form an internal word, and thence break forth into love. But since the principles of acts are the habits and powers, and everything exists virtually in its principle, so, secondarily and consequently, the image of the Trinity may be considered as existing in the powers and still more in the habits as much as the acts virtually exist therein.

3. The image of God abides ever in the soul; whether this image of God be so obscure, as if it were clouded so as to amount almost to nothing, as in those who have not the use of reason, or obscured and disfigured, as in sinners, or clear and

beautiful as in the just, as Augustine says. (1a, q. 93, a. 8, Reply to 3rd. Obj.)

TUESDAY WITHIN THE OCTAVE OF TRINITY

The Greatest Love and Highest Worship Belong to God

1. "Let us love God, since He first loved us," (1 John IV, 10). We ought to love God in three ways. First, we should use our whole heart in loving Him. "Thou shalt love the Lord, thy God with thy whole heart." (Deut. VI.) Secondly, we should love nothing except for the sake of God. Augustine says, "A person loves you less, who loves something with you which he does not love on account of you." Thirdly, no adversity should turn us away from the love of God. "Who shall separate us from the love of Christ?"

We should love God because of three things in particular. First, because of his goodness, secondly, on account of His love and thirdly, because of the advantages to ourselves.

First of all, because of His goodness. Hence Saint Bernard says, "the reason for loving God, is God." For the goodness of God is so great that if nothing were ever done by the goodness of man, still man should always love the goodness of God.

Secondly, we should love God because of His immense love. "Let us love God," writes Saint John, "since God first loved us." Hence Augustine says, "Wretched man that I am. How I ought to love my God, who made me, redeemed me when I was perishing because of my sins. He came for me and loved only me, and paid the price of His blood for me."

Thirdly, we should love God, because of the great advantages it will bring to ourselves. For no tongue can adequately describe the wonderful things which God has prepared for those who love Him. "Eye hath not seen, nor ear heard, neither hath it entered into the heart of man, what things God hath prepared for them that love Him. . . . But to us God hath revealed them by His Spirit. For the Spirit searcheth all things, yea, the deep things of God." (1 Cor. II, 10.)

2. Worship, moreover, acknowledges the service and obedience which we owe to God, who created us. Hence, worship is due to God in so far as He is our Creator, and secondly because He is our last end, as well as the first beginning of

our existence. And because He is the Creator, all-good, all-wise and by Him all things were made and are preserved.

And because the Father and Son and Holy Spirit are one Creator, one worship is therefore owed to them; since worship is due to God in as far as He is the Creator.

All things in fact proclaim that we owe God worship. For in us there is a threefold good, namely, spiritual, bodily and extrinsic. And because all these things which we have are from God, therefore, according to all things we ought to pay worship to God. In regard to our soul, we should manifest to Him the proper love; in regard to our bodies, by prayers, prostrations, genuflections, mortifications, penance and spiritual hymns. Finally, in regard to external goods, we should offer to God many and great sacrifices. Hence we should show worship to God, not because He needs it, but in order that thereby we may gratefully acknowledge that all things which we have came from God. And just as we recognize Him in all things, so also will we honor Him in all things. (3 Dist. 9, q. I, a. 3.)

WEDNESDAY WITHIN THE OCTAVE OF TRINITY

A Sin Against the Father and the Son and the Holy Ghost

1. To sin against the Father is to sin from weakness of will. To sin against the Son is to sin from ignorance and to sin against the Holy Ghost is to sin from a certain malice; so that it is called a sin against the Father when that is lacking which should be attributed to the Father, namely, power, and a sin against the Son is committed when wisdom is lacking in the sinner, which wisdom is attributed to the Son; and a sin against the Holy Spirit is committed when the opposite of goodness, namely vice, is sought, which goodness is attributed to the Holy Ghost.

For a sin may be committed in three ways, either from ignorance or from passion or from deliberate choice. From ignorance when one is ignorant of those things, a knowledge of which would prevent the sinner from sinning (which knowledge he could have acquired and should have acquired). Hence that kind of ignorance is there and then the cause of sin is present. And this is said to be a sin against the Son. Secondly, one sins from passion when on account of the force of the passion the judgment of the reason is destroyed. And this is proper to sins committed from weakness of the will, which is a sin against the Father. Thirdly, a sin from deliberate choice takes place when man deliberately clings to sin, not as if he were conquered by any special temptation, but because of sin he has a corrupt appetite for sin, so that sin in itself pleases him. And this is to sin from malice, which is a sin against the Holy Spirit.

2. The above species are fittingly assigned to the sin against the Holy Ghost taken in the third sense, because they are distinguished in regard to the removal or contempt of these things whereby a man can be prevented from sinning by choice. These things are either on the part of God's judgment or on the part of His gifts or on the part of sin.

First, by the consideration of Divine judgment wherein justice is accompanied with mercy, man is hindered from sinning through choice, both by hope arising from consideration of the mercy that pardons sins and rewards good deeds, which hope is removed by despair; and by fear, arising from the consideration of Divine justice that punishes sins, which fear is removed by presumption when a man presumes that he can obtain glory without merits or pardon without penance.

Secondly, God's gifts whereby we are withdrawn from sin are two. One is the acknowledgment of the truth, against which there is the resistance of the known truth, when a man resists the truth which he has acknowledged in order to sin more freely; while the other is the assistance of inward grace, against which there is envy of a brother's spiritual good when a man is envious not only of his brother's person, but also of the increase of Divine grace in the world.

Thirdly, on the part of sin there are two things which may withdraw man therefrom. One is the impropriety and shamefulness of the act the consideration of which is wont to arouse man to repentance for the sin he has committed, and against this there is impenitence, not as denoting permanence in sin until death, but as denoting the purpose of not repenting. The other thing (which may withdraw us from sin) is the smallness or brevity of the good which is sought in sin, according to Rom. VI, 21, "What fruit therefore had you then in those things of which you are now ashamed?" The consideration of this is wont to prevent man's will from being hardened in sin, and this is removed by "obstinacy," thereby man hardens his purpose by clinging to sin. Of these two it is written, "There is none that doth penance for his sin saying, What have I done? They are all turned to their own course, as a horse rushing to the battle." (Jer. VIII, 6.) (2a, 2a, q. 14, a. 2.)

THE FEAST OF CORPUS CHRISTI

The Blessed Eucharist Bestows Grace

"The bread which I will give, is My flesh for the life of the world." (John VI, 52.)

The effect of this Sacrament ought to be considered.

1. First of all and principally from what is contained in this Sacrament, which is Christ; Who just as by coming into the world He visibly bestowed the life of grace upon the world, according to John I, 17, "Grace and Truth came by grace," according to John VI, 58, "He that eateth Me the same also shall live by Me." Hence Cyril says on Luke XXII, 19, God's life-giving Word by uniting Himself with His own flesh, made it to be productive of life. For it was becoming that He should be united somehow with bodies through His sacred flesh and blood, which we receive in a life-giving blessing in the bread and wine.

2. Secondly, this Sacrament should be considered on the part of what is represented by this Sacrament, which is Christ's Passion. And therefore this sacrament works in man the effect which Christ's Passion produced in the world. Hence Chrysostom says on the words, "Immediately there came out blood and water." (John XIX, 34), "Since the sacred mysteries derive their origin from thence, when you draw nigh to the awe-inspiring chalice, so approach as if you were going to drink from Christ's own side. Hence our Lord Himself says (Matt. XXVI, 28), "This is My blood . . . which shall be shed for many unto the remission of sins."

3. Thirdly, the effect of this sacrament is considered from the way in which this sacrament is given, for it is given by way of food and drink. And therefore this sacrament does for the spiritual life all that material food does for the bodily life, by sustaining, giving increase, restoring and giving delight. Accordingly, Ambrose says, "This is the bread of everlasting life, which supports the substance of our soul," and Chrysostom says, "When we desire it, He lets us feel Him and eat Him, and embrace Him." And hence our Lord says

(John VI, 56), "My flesh is meat indeed, and My blood is drink indeed."

4. Fourthly, the effect of this sacrament should be considered from the species under which it is given. Hence Augustine says, "Our Lord betokened His body and blood in things which out of many units are made into some one whole; for out of many grains is one thing made, namely bread, and many grapes flow into one thing, namely, wine." And therefore, Augustine observes elsewhere, "O Sacrament of piety, O sign of unity, O bond of charity!"

And since Christ and His Passion are the cause of grace and since spiritual refreshment and charity cannot be without grace, it is clear from all that has been set forth that this sacrament bestows grace. (3a, q. 79, a. 1.)

FRIDAY WITHIN THE OCTAVE OF CORPUS CHRISTI

How Grace Is Bestowed Through the Blessed Eucharist

1. This Sacrament has of itself the power of bestowing grace; nor does anyone possess grace before receiving this sacrament except from some desire thereof, from his own desire, as in the case of the adult; or from the Church's desire in the case of children. Hence it is due to the efficacy of its power that even from desire thereof a man procures grace whereby he is enabled to lead the spiritual life. It remains then, that when the sacrament itself is really received grace is received and the spiritual life perfected; yet in different manner from the Sacrament of Confirmation, in which grace is increased and perfected for resisting the outward assaults of Christ's enemies. But by this Sacrament of the Eucharist grace receives an increase and the spiritual life is perfected, so that man may stand perfect in himself by union with God.

2. This Sacrament confers grace spiritually together with the virtue of charity. Hence Damascene compares this sacrament to the burning coal which Isaias saw (VI, 6), "For a live ember is not simply wood, but wood united to fire; so also the bread of Communion is not simply bread, but bread united with the God-head." But as Gregory observes in a Homily for Pentecost, "God's love is never idle; for, wherever it is it does great works." And hence through this sacrament, as far as its power is concerned, not only is

the habit of grace and of virtue bestowed, but it is furthermore aroused to act according to 2 Cor. V, 14, "The charity of Christ presseth us." Hence it is that the soul is spiritually nourished through the power of this sacrament by being spiritually gladdened and as it were inebriated with the sweetness of the Divine goodness, according to Canticles V, 1, "Eat, O friends, and drink, and be inebriated, My dearly beloved."

3. Because the sacraments operate according to the similitude which they signify, therefore, by way of assimilation it is said that in this Sacrament, "the body is offered for the salvation of the body, and the blood for the salvation of the soul," although each works for the salvation of both, since the entire Christ is under each. And although the body is not the immediate subject of grace, still the effect of grace flows into the body, while in the present life we "present our members as instruments of justice unto God." (Rom. VI, 13), and in the life to come our body will share in the incorruption and the glory of the soul. (3a, q. 79, a. i.)

SATURDAY WITHIN THE OCTAVE OF CORPUS CHRISTI

An Effect of the Eucharist Is the Possession of Glory

"If any man eat of this bread he shall live forever." (John VI, 52.) In this sacrament we may consider both that from which it derives its effect, namely, Christ contained in it, as also His Passion represented by it, and that through which it works its effect, namely, the use of the sacrament and its species.

Now as to both of these it belongs to this sacrament to cause the attainment of eternal life. Because it was by His Passion that Christ opened to us the approach to eternal life, according to Heb. IX, 15. "He is the Mediator of the New Testament; that by means of His death . . . they that are called may receive the promise of eternal inheritance." Accordingly, in the form of this sacrament it is said: "This is the chalice of My blood, of the New and Eternal Testament."

In like manner, the refreshment of spiritual food and the unity denoted by the species of the bread and wine are to be had in the present life, although imperfectly; but perfectly in the state of glory. Hence Augustine says on the words "My flesh is meat indeed," (John VI, 56) : "Seeing that in meat and drink, men aim at this, that they hunger not, nor thirst, this effect nothing can everlastingly afford, except only this meat and drink, which maketh them who partake worthily thereof to be immortal and incorruptible, in the fellowship of the saints where there shall be peace, and unity, full and perfect."

And although this sacrament is for our use in this life, it follows that an effect of this sacrament means for us the possession of glory. As Christ's Passion, in virtue whereof this sacrament is accomplished, is indeed the sufficient cause of glory, yet not so that we are thereby immediately admitted to glory, but we must first "suffer with Him in order that we also may be glorified afterwards with Him," Rom. VIII, 17, so this sacrament does not at once admit us to glory, but bestows on us the power of coming unto glory. And therefore it is called Viaticum, (that is Bread for the journey to eternal life), a figure whereof we read in 3 Kings XIX, 8: "Elias ate and drank, and walked in the strength of that food forty days and forty nights unto the mount of God, Horeb." (3a, q. 79, a. 2.)

SUNDAY WITHIN THE OCTAVE OF CORPUS CHRISTI

The Effect of the Sacrament of the Eucharist Is Hindered by Venial Sin

Damascene says, "The fire of that desire which is within us, being kindled by the burning coal, that is, this sacrament, will consume our sins, and enlighten our hearts, so that we shall be inflamed and made God-like." But the fire of our desire or love is hindered by venial sins, which impede the fervour of charity. Therefore, venial sins hinder the effect of this sacrament.

Venial sins can be considered in two ways. First of all as past, secondly, as in the act of being committed. Venial sins considered in the first way do not in any way hinder the effect of this sacrament. For it can happen that after many venial sins a man may approach devoutly to this sacrament and fully secure its effect.

Considered in the second way, venial sins do not entirely hinder the effect of this sacrament but merely in part. For the effect of this sacrament is not only the obtaining of habitual grace or charity, but also a certain actual refreshment of spiritual sweetness which is indeed hindered if anyone approach to this sacrament with mind distracted through venial sins; but the increase of habitual grace or of charity is not taken away.

He that approaches this sacrament with actual venial sin on his soul, eats spiritually indeed, in habit but not in act, and therefore he shares in the habitual effect of the sacrament but not in its actual effect.

Venial sins do not indeed hinder the effect of Baptism, but we must not speak of the Eucharist as of Baptism. For Baptism is not ordained, as this sacrament of the Eucharist is, for the fervour of charity as its actual effect. Because Baptism is spiritual regeneration, through which the first perfection is acquired, which is a habit or form; but this sacrament of the Eucharist is spiritual eating which has actual delight. (3a, q. 79, a. 8.)

SATURDAY AFTER THE OCTAVE OF CORPUS CHRISTI

Christ's Love

"Jesus knowing that His hour was come, that He should pass out of this world to the Father, having loved His own who were in the world He loved them unto the end." (John XIII, 1.)

Here the fervent love of Christ is commended with regard to four things.

1. First of all it was a prevenient love, secondly, it was suitable, thirdly, necessary, and fourthly, perfect. It was a prevenient or anticipated love, according to 1 John IV, 10, "Not as though we had loved God, but because He had first loved us." And in regard to this John says, "having loved His own," that is, Jesus loved us before we loved Him. He loved us before He created us. "Thou lovest all the things that are, and hatest none of the things which Thou hast made." (Wis. XI, 25.) He loved all things before they were named. "Yea I have loved thee with an everlasting love, therefore, have I drawn thee, taking pity on thee." (Jer. XXXI, 3). Jesus loved us before he redeemed us.

2. Christ's love was a suitable love, because He loved His own. As some are His own in a different manner, according to this they are loved differently by Almighty God. More-

over some persons are His in a threefold way, namely, by creation, by consecration or dedication and thirdly, by special devotion. By creation Jesus loves them by preserving for them the goods of nature. "He came unto His own," (John I, 2), by creation, "and His own received Him not." Some are His own by consecration or dedication to His Service, who are born by faith through the power of God the Father. "Now all things which Thou, O Father, hast given Me are from Thee." (John XVII, 7). And He loves these by preserving them in the blessings of His grace. Thirdly, some are His own chosen ones by reason of a special devotion. "We are, O David, thy bone and thy flesh." (1 Paral, XI, 1.) He loves those by consoling them in a special manner.

3. Christ's love was necessary since "He loved His own who were in the world." For some are His own who are now in the glory of the Father; because the holy fathers are also his own, as they hoped to be liberated through Christ. But these also in the world needed the love of Christ, and hence He says, "having loved His own who were in the world," in the world but not of the world.

4. Christ's love is commended in as far as it is perfect. Hence it is said, "He loved them unto the end." The end of the intention to which our intention should be ordained is eternal life. I repeat that an end of this nature should be Christ. And these two, eternal life and Christ, are really one need, for eternal life is nothing else than the enjoyment of Christ according to His Divinity. "This is eternal life, that they might know Thee, the only true God, and Jesus Christ, Whom Thou hast sent. (John XVII, 3.)

Secondly, John says, "Jesus loved them unto the end," so that He might lead them to the end, namely to Himself, or unto eternal life which is nothing less than Christ Himself.

Another explanation is this, that death may be called an end, and thus it may be said that "Jesus loved His own unto the end," that is, unto death. But considered in this way, Christ loved His own only unto death and not beyond death. But it would be false to say this. Far be it from Christ that His love should end in death, for His love is not finite like death, but infinite.

"Unto the end," may also be explained in another way, since up to the end, up to His death, He showed to His own many proofs of His love for them, yet His death showed them a proof of greater love. "I told you not these things from the beginning, because I was with you." (John XVI, 5), as if He had said, "It was not necessary that I should show you how much I loved you, except that at My death My love and My remembrance might be more deeply impressed on your hearts." (John XIII.)

MONDAY WITHIN THE OCTAVE OF CORPUS CHRISTI

By the Eucharist Man Is Preserved from Future Sins

"This is the bread which cometh down from heaven, that if any man eat of it, he may not die." (John VI, 50.)

Sin is the spiritual death of the soul. Hence man is preserved from future sin in the same way as the body is preserved from future death, and this happens in two ways. First of all, in so far as man's nature is strengthened inwardly against inner decay, and so by means of food and medicine he is preserved from death. Secondly, by being guarded against outward assaults, and thus he is protected by means of arms by which he defends his body.

Now this sacrament preserves man from sin in both of these ways. For first of all, by uniting man with Christ through grace, it strengthens his spiritual life, as spiritual food and spiritual medicine, according to Ps. CIII, 5. "That bread strengthens man's heart." Augustine likewise says, "Approach without fear. It is bread, not poison."

Secondly, inasmuch as it is a sign of Christ's Passion, whereby the devils are conquered, it repels all the assaults of demons. Hence Chrysostom says, "Like lions breathing forth fire. thus do we depart from that table, being made terrible to the devil."

Indeed it is also true that many after receiving this sacrament worthily fall again into sin, but it is due to changeableness of free will that a man sins after possessing charity, for his free-will can be easily fixed on good or evil. Hence, although this sacrament of itself has the power of preserving us from sin, yet it does not take away from man the possibility of sinning. And the same must be said of charity. For charity in itself preserves man from sin, but because of the weakness of free-will, it happens that one sins after possessing charity just as one does after receiving this sacrament.

Although this sacrament is ordained directly to lessen the inclination to sin, yet it does lessen it as a consequence, inasmuch as it increases charity, because as Augustine says, "the increase of charity is the lessening of concupiscence." But it directly strengthens man's heart in good, whereby he is also preserved from sin. (3a, q. 79, a. 6.)

TUESDAY WITHIN THE OCTAVE OF CORPUS CHRISTI

How Punishment for Sin Is Forgiven by the Eucharist

This sacrament is both a sacrifice and a sacrament. It has the nature of a sacrifice inasmuch as it is offered up, and it has the nature of a sacrament inasmuch as it is received. And therefore it has the effect of a sacrament in the recipient and the effect of a sacrifice in the offerer, or in them for whom it is offered.

If then, it be considered as a sacrament, it produces its effect in two ways. First of all, directly through the power of the sacrament; secondly, as by a kind of concomitance. Through the power of the sacrament it produces directly that effect for which it was instituted. Now it was instituted not for satisfaction but for nourishing spiritually through union between Christ and His members, as nourishment is united with the person nourished. But because this union is the effect of charity from the fervour of which man obtains forgiveness, not only of the guilt but also of the punishment, but according to the measure of his devotion and fervour.

But in so far as it is a sacrifice, it has a satisfactory power. Yet in satisfaction, the affection of the offerer is weighed rather than the quantity of the offering. Hence our Lord says (Mark XII, 43) and (Luke XXI, 4), of the widow who offered "two mites," that she cast in "more than all." Therefore, although this offering suffices of its own quantity to satisfy for all punishment, yet it becomes satisfactory for them for whom it is offered, or even for the offerers, according to the measure of their devotion, and not for the whole punishment.

Christ's power which is contained in this sacrament is infinite. If part of the punishment and not all be taken away by this sacrament, it is due to a defect not on the part of Christ's power, but on the part of man's devotion. (3a, q. 79, a. 6.)

WEDNESDAY WITHIN THE OCTAVE OF CORPUS CHRISTI

Venial Sins Are Forgiven Through the Eucharist

Two things may be considered in this sacrament, namely, the sacrament itself and the reality of the sacrament; and it appears from both that this sacrament has the power of forgiving venial sins. For this sacrament is received under the form of nourishing food. Now nourishment from food is necessary for the body to make good the daily waste caused by the action of natural heat. But something is also lost daily of our spirituality from the heat of concupiscence through venial sins, which lessen the fervour of charity. And therefore it belongs to this sacrament to forgive venial sins. Hence Ambrose says that his daily bread is taken "as a remedy against daily infirmity."

The reality of this sacrament is charity, not only as to its habits but also as to its act, which is kindled in this sacrament; and by this means venial sins are forgiven. Consequently, it is clear that venial sins are forgiven by the power of this sacrament.

By the power of this sacrament a certain transformation of man to Christ is effected through love and this is its proper effect. And because of the fervor venial sins are removed, it follows that by the power of this sacrament venial sins are forgiven.

Moreover, inasmuch as the fervor of devotion can be such as to remove all venial sins, neither is it improper to say that man is sometime free from every venial sin: still, he cannot continue on account of difficulties, for a long time without committing some venial sins. But only according to the measure of our devotion does the sacrament take away all venial sins, for the removal of venial sins is not the proximate effect of this sacrament, but the consequent effect.

Venial sins, although not opposed to the habit of charity, are nevertheless opposed to the fervor of its act, which act is kindled by this sacrament by reason of which act venial sins are removed. (3a, q, 79, a. 4 Reply to Obj. 1.)

THURSDAY WITHIN THE OCTAVE OF CORPUS CHRISTI

The Use of the Eucharist

1. The Eucharist should be received frequently.

Those things which are produced in this sacrament bear a likeness to those things which happen in bodily nourishment. For since a constant loss of physical strength takes place through the action of natural heat and the practice of hard work, it is therefore necessary for a person to take bodily nourishment often to regain the loss; lest continual physical loss bring on death.

Likewise also, from an innate concupiscence and anxiety about worldly things, results a loss of devotion and fervour by which man is united to God. Hence it is necessary that man's spiritual loss be frequently restored, lest he might become completely separated from God.

2. Should we receive Holy Communion daily?

In this sacrament two things are required on the part of the recipient, a desire to be united with Christ which is caused through love of God, and secondly, a deep reverence for this Sacrament which belongs to holy fear. The first requisite encourages us to receive holy Communion daily, but the second, namely, reverence, draws us away from daily reception.

Hence, if anyone knows from experience, that by receiving this Sacrament daily, the fervour of his love of God has increased and his reverence has not lessened, such a person should receive holy Communion daily. But if anyone knows that through daily reception of this Sacrament, his reverence has decreased and his fervour has not been increased, such a person should now and then refrain from frequent reception, so that afterwards he might approach the sacrament with greater reverence and devotion.

However in regard to this matter, each person must be left to his own judgment. And this is the opinion of Augustine, who says, "If anyone should say that the Eucharist should not be received daily and another affirms it should be received daily, let each one do that which according to his faith, he piously believes should be done. And proof of this is shown by the examples of Zachaeus and the Centurion, one of whom received the Lord rejoicing, the other said: 'Lord, I am not worthy that Thou shouldst enter under My roof,' and both received mercy, both honored the Saviour, yet not in the same way."

Nevertheless love and hope, to which Sacred Scripture always exhorts us, are preferable to fear. And hence when Peter exclaimed, "Depart from me, O Lord, for I am a sinful man," Jesus responded, "Fear not."

Let us approach Jesus (in this sacrament) especially through humility. But it does not follow, that it is more praiseworthy to abstain from receiving this sacrament, inasmuch as it is more meritorious. For charity is that virtue which directly unites us with God, but humility disposes us to this union, in so far as it wins man to God. Hence merit consists more in charity than in humility. (4, Dist. 12, q. 3, a. 2.)

THE FEAST OF THE SACRED HEART OF JESUS

The Most Sacred Heart of Jesus

1. *"My heart has become as wax melting in the midst of My bowels."* (Ps. XXI, 15.)

We must say that melting is characteristic of love. "My soul melted when He spoke." (Canticles V, 6.) Before a thing melts, it is hard and bound together in itself. If it melts, it is diffused and extends itself to another thing. Fear also becomes hard at times when it is not great, and likewise love; because when love conquers, then man extends himself to another thing which was before in him. And concerning this kind of melting it can be applied to Christ, according as He is our Head. For to be melted in this wise, is the work of the Holy Spirit who is in the midst of us, that is in our affections—for He is Love, and our affections tend to love.

Or by the heart of Christ may be understood Sacred Scripture which reveals the heart of Christ. Moreover this Heart was closed before the Passion, for it was unknown, but was opened after the Passion, that now thinking persons might meditate on it and realize how the prophecies were fulfilled. (Ps. XXI.)

2. "What is man that Thou shouldst magnify him? Or why dost Thou set Thy heart upon him?" (Job VII, 17.)

What is man? That is, how small and weak in body! And that Thou shouldst magnify him, with great honor amongst other created things. Why shouldst Thou set Thy heart upon him?" by showing him special love, and protecting him with special care. Although all things exist by Divine Providence, still all things are differently disposed by God, according as they have order in the universe. Those things which lack perpetuity tend accidentally to the perfection of the world, and are not governed on account of themselves but on account of the preservation of the species. But man is perpetual, both as to species and as to the individual, and therefore, God has set His heart on him, providing for him through His own goodness. Moreover the manner in which God regards man and has set His Heart on him, is shown when Job says, "Thou visitest him early in the morning," that is at the beginning of his birth, God gives to man from His Providence, the things which are necessary for life and honour, both corporal and spiritual, "an dThou provest him suddenly," through adverse circumstances, in which appear the virtues which man possesses. "The furnace trieth the potter's vessels, and the trial of affliction just men." (Eccles. XXVII, 6.) But it is said that God tries man, not that He might learn man's condition, but that He might make man to know himself and others. (Job VII.)

SUNDAY AFTER THE OCTAVE OF CORPUS CHRISTI

The Most Pure Heart of Mary

1. The Blessed Virgin had to be most pure. For it behoved the Mother of God to shine with the greatest purity, since nothing is worthy to receive God unless it be pure, according to Ps. XCII, 5, "Holiness becometh Thy House, O Lord."

2. The Mother of God took a vow of virginity.

Works of perfection are most praiseworthy when performed in fulfillment of a vow. Now virginity had a special place in the Mother of God. It was therefore fitting that her virginity should be consecrated to God by vow. Hence Augustine says, "Mary answered the announcing angel; how shall this be done, because I know not man? She would not have said this unless she had already vowed her virginity to God." Just as the fulness of grace was in Christ perfectly, yet some beginning of this fulness preceded in His Mother; so also the observance of the counsels which is an effect of God's grace, began its perfection in Christ, but was begun in certain manner in His Virgin Mother.

The Mother of God is not believed to have taken an absolute vow of virginity before being espoused to Joseph, although she desired to do so yet yielding her own will to God's judgment . . . Afterwards, however, having taken a husband, according to the custom of the time together with him she took a vow of virginity.

3. The Blessed Virgin won the aureola of virginity.

The aureola is a certain privileged reward corresponding to a privileged victory. And therefore, according to privileged victories won in three battles, which are waged against every man, three aureolas are awarded. In the fight against the flesh, he or she obtains a most powerful victory who refrains from indulging in the lusts and sins of the flesh. Such a person is a virgin. Second—there is the battle against the world. That is the chief victory, especially when someone not only removes the enemy from oneself, but also from the hearts of others; and this is done by teaching and preaching (the Word of God). And hence the aureola is due to virgins, martyrs and preachers. Therefore the aureola belongs to the Blessed Virgin, in whom was the most perfect virginity; and hence she is called "the Virgin of Virgins."

Some however object, and claim that the aureola was not due to Mary since she endured no battle in being pure. For this reason, some say that the Blessed Virgin has not the aureola, as a reward of virginity. If moreover, we speak of aureola absolutely, in so far as it refers to a battle, still she has something greater than an aureola, because of her most perfect desire to preserve her virginity. On the contrary, others say that she has a most excellent aureola, for although she did not experience a fight, still she had a certain battle of the flesh with which to contend, but from the power of her virtue, she kept the desires of the flesh subdued and hence she was insensible to this fight.

But this seems to be incorrectly said, since it is believed that the Blessed Virgin was entirely free from the inclination to sin, because of her perfect sanctification. It is pious to say that she experienced no battle in herself in this regard. But we must hold that she properly has the aureola, so that in this also, she might be in conformity with the other members of the Church, in whom virginity is found; and although she experienced no fight against carnal temptation, nevertheless, she had to fight against temptation from the devil, who even tempted Christ Himself. (4 Dist. 49, q. 5, a. 3.)

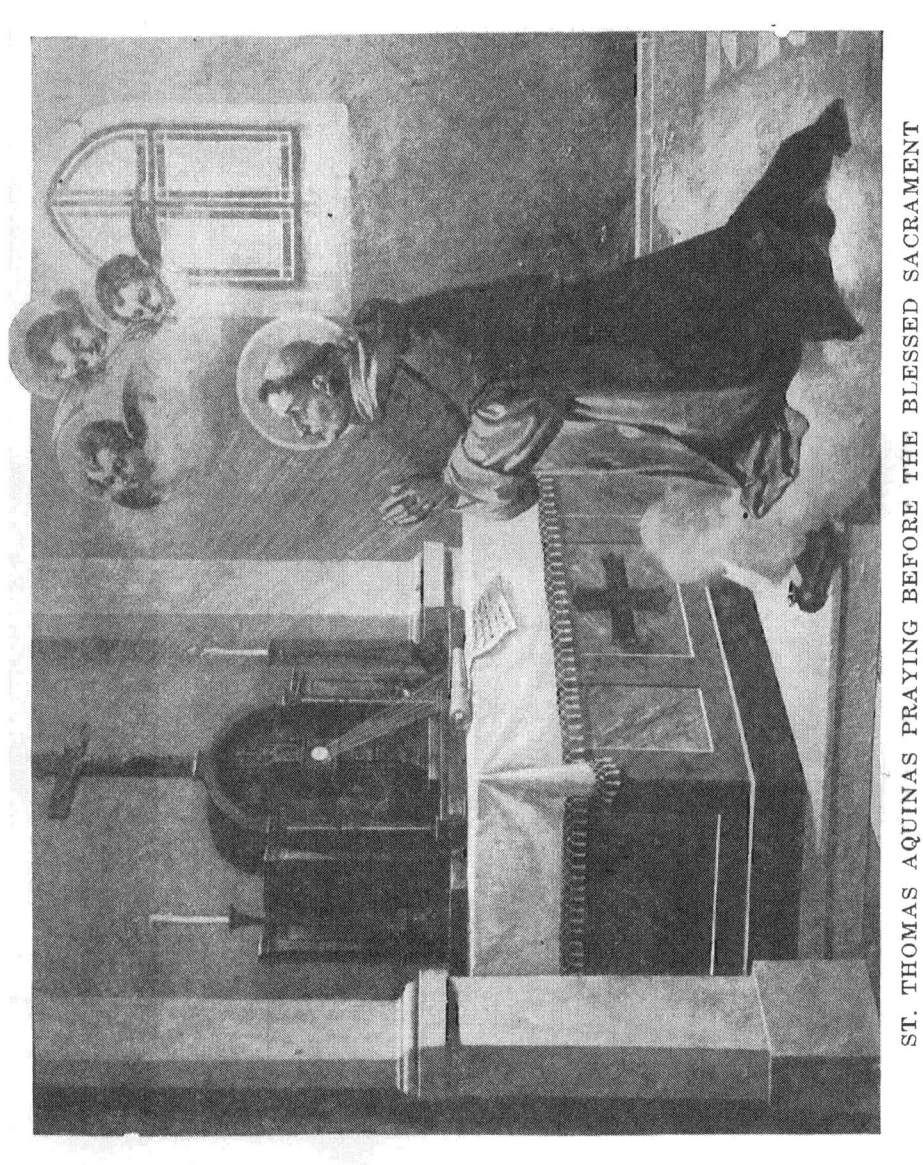

ST. THOMAS AQUINAS PRAYING BEFORE THE BLESSED SACRAMENT

SECOND PART

"Prayer is the wing wherewith the soul flees to God, and meditation the eye, wherewith we see God."
—Saint Ambrose.

JULY 1

The Excellence of the Divine Nature

1. God is not limited by time. He is Eternal, for He is without beginning and end; and also His Being is changed neither by the past nor by the future. Nothing is taken away from Him, neither can anything new come to Him. Hence He said to Moses. "I am who am," because His existence does not depend upon the past and future, but is present always.

2. His greatness incomparably exceeds the greatness of all creatures, for it is immense. Even if a thing exceeds in greatness, it can be measured by something else, when the excess is according to a certain proportion, just as 2 is the measure of 6, in so far as, three multiplied by two make six. Six moreover, exceeds two by a certain proportion, in so far as two is the measure of six. But God infinitely exceeds and excels every creature in the greatness of His power. Therefore, He is called infinite, because there is no commensuration or proportion between Him and any creature. Hence, it is said in Psalm (CXLIV, 3), "Great is the Lord and greatly to be praised, and of His greatness there is no end."

3. God exceeds all change, for He is immutable; immutable because in Him there is no alteration, as Saint James (I, 17) says, "With God there is no change or shadow of alteration."

4. God's power transcends everything, for He can do all things. Hence the Lord said to Moses (Gen. XVII, 1), "I am the Almighty God."

5. He exceeds the reason and understanding of all, for He is incomprehensible. We are said to comprehend a thing, when we know it perfectly, in as far as things are knowable. But no creature can know God in as far as He is knowable, that is, in as far as it is possible to know Him; and for this reason no one can comprehend God perfectly. Hence Job (XI, 7) says, "Perhaps thou wilt comprehend the steps of God, and wilt find out the Almighty perfectly?" As if he had said. "Never wilt thou comprehend God perfectly." And Jeremias (XXXII, 18) exclaims, "O most mighty, great, and powerful, the Lord of hosts is Thy name. Great in wisdom, and incomprehensible in thought, Whose eyes are open to all the ways of the children of Adam, to render unto everyone according to his ways, and according to the fruit of his devices."

6. God's nature exceeds all description, for it is indescribable and no one can sufficiently praise it. Hence Eccl. (XLIII, 33), declares, "Exalt Him as much as you can, for He is above all praise." (1 Decretals.)

JULY 2

Visitation of the Blessed Virgin

The Blessed Virgin after conceiving Christ did three things, by which three things are mystically understood what every holy soul should do after a spiritual conception of the word of God. She hastened to the mountain, saluted Elizabeth, and magnified the Lord. By hastening to the mountain is meant the perfection of virtues, in saluting Elizabeth, fraternal love is shown, while in magnifying the Lord, Mary poured forth her praise and exaltation of the Saviour.

1. "Mary rising up went into the hill country with haste, into a city of Juda." (Luke I, 39.) The consent of the Blessed Virgin to become the Mother of God being received, the Angel asked for heavenly things. Mary followed the Angel and hastened to the mountain. Likewise the soul which receives the word of God ascends to the top of perfection by the steps of love, so that it might enter the city of Juda, that is the citadel of confession and praise, and remain in it almost three months, for the perfection of faith, hope and charity. But in this ascent there are three things, namely the valley of fear and humility, acquired by labor and retained by love."

2. "Mary entered the house of Zachary, and saluted Elizabeth." (Luke I, 40.) Salutation is the desire of salvation. Moreover it pertains to fraternal love to wish the salvation of our neighbor; because this is the true manner of loving our neighbor as expressed by Saint Matthew (XXII, 29), "Thou shalt love thy neighbor as thyself." Therefore in this love, each holy soul, after it spiritually conceives the word of God, should remain steadfast, as recommended by Saint John (1, IV, 12), "If we love one another, God abideth in us, and His charity is perfected in us!" Likewise it can be said, that where true love is, what is there that can be wanting to us? On the other hand, where true love is lacking, what is there that can profit us?

3. Mary said, "My soul doth magnify the Lord." That canticle is a canticle of praise and exultation, which each holy

soul, after conceiving the word of God, can sing. Hence Saint Ambrose says, "It may be that for each one of us the soul of Mary is magnifying God. What does it mean to magnify God? The Lord is magnified, not that human praise adds anything to Him; but that He may be praised in us, and our souls created to the image of God, may through justice conform themselves to Christ, Who is the likeness of the Father. Thus while Mary imitates Christ, she magnifies Him, and becomes more sublime by participating in His greatness; so that she seems to express in herself His image, by the splendid manifestation of her good works and by emulation of virtue. Hence Origen says, "Wherever I magnify my soul, by work, thought, or speech, then the Image of the great God is produced, and the Lord Himself Whose Image I am, is magnified in my soul." Saint Bede beautifully says, "Mary's soul magnifies God, because her every affection for man is transferred to God, by divine praise and service. Her spirit rejoices in God, her Saviour. Her spirit which nothing on earth can injure, no abundance of perishable things can soften, no adversity break; delights in the memory of her Creator, from Whom she alone hopes for eternal salvation." (The Humanity of Christ.)

JULY 3

The Fruit of the Knowledge of God

John, the Precursor, said of Christ, "The latchet of Whose shoe I am not worthy to lose." As if he wished to say, "You do not understand Him, Who excels me in dignity, just as one man is preferred to another, but so excellent is Christ that 1 am nothing in comparison with Him. And this is clear, because I am not worthy to loose the latchet of His shoe, which is the least favor that can be done by man."

From this, it is evident that John acquired much knowledge of God, that from a consideration of God's infinite greatness, He esteemed himself as absolutely nothing. Like Abraham when he actually knew the Lord, he said, "I will speak to my Lord, whereas (in comparison with Whom) I am dust and ashes." (Gen. XVIII, 27.) Likewise Job (XLII, 5) when he had seen the Lord, he said, "Now my eyes seeth Thee. Therefore I reprehend myself, and do penance in dust and ashes." Likewise Isaias (XL, 17) after he had seen the glory of the

Lord, said, "All nations are before Him as if they had no being at all." Hence Pope Gregory once exclaimed, "The human mind in so much as it more perfectly knows heavenly things, by so much the more should it humble itself. And every saintly man in so far as he raises himself higher to contemplate the Divinity, by so much the more does he fall lower in the estimation of himself."

Moreover, by the word, "shoe," which is made from the hides of animals, is understood our mortal human nature which Christ assumed. The latchet of His shoe is the union of His divinity with His humanity which neither John nor anyone else can solve, or fully investigate, since it was such that God became man, so that man might become Godlike, and therefore John says, "The latchet of Whose shoe I am not worthy to loose," that is, not worthy to explain the mystery of the Incarnation. Be it fully and perfectly understood therefore, that only in an imperfect manner does John, and all other preachers of God's words, "loose the latchet of His shoe." (John I.)

JULY 4

God's Presence Everywhere

1. God is in all things, not indeed, as part of their essence, nor as an accident; but as an agent is present to that upon which it acts. For an agent must be joined to that wherein it acts immediately, and touch it by its power. Now, since God is very being by His own essence, created being must be His proper effect; as to ignite is the proper effect of fire. Now, God causes this effect in things, not only when they first begin to be, but as long as they are preserved in being, as light is caused in the air by the sun as long as the air remains illuminated. Therefore as long as a thing has existence, God must be present to it, according to its manner of existence. But existence is innermost in each thing and most fundamentally inherent in all things since it is formal in respect of everything found in a thing. Hence, it must be that God is in all things and innermostly.

2. God is in every place. He is everywhere. "I fill heaven and earth." (Jer. XXIII, 24.) Just as God is in all things as giving them being, power and operation, so He is in every place as giving it existence and locative power. Moreover God

fills every place, by the very fact that He gives being to the things which fill that place. To be everywhere primarily and absolutely is proper to God, and belongs to Him alone; because whatever number of places are supposed to exist, God must be in all of them, not as a part of Himself, but as to His very self.

3. God is everywhere by His essence, presence and power. God is said to be in a thing in two ways; in one way, after the manner of an efficient cause, and thus He is in all things created by Him; in another way, He is in things as the object of operation is in the operator, and this is proper to the operations of the soul; according as the thing known is in the one who knows, and the thing desired in the one desiring. In this second way, God is especially in the rational creature, which knows and loves Him actually or habitually. And because the rational creature possesses this prerogative by grace, He is said to be thus, in the Saints by grace.

But how He is in other things created by Him, must be considered from human affairs. A king, for example, is said to be in the whole kingdom by his power, although he is not everywhere present. Again, a thing is said to be by its presence in other things which are subject to its inspection; as things in a house are said to be present to anyone; who nevertheless may not be in substance in every part of the house. Lastly, a thing is said to be by way of substance or essence in that place in which its substance may be.

So therefore, God is in all things by His power inasmuch as all things are His creation and open to His eyes; He is in all things, by His essence; inasmuch as His substance is present to all things as the cause of their being. (1a. Q. 8.)

JULY 5

The Immutability of God

1. It is the nature or perfection in God which is immutable in His nature. God Himself has testified to this. "I am the Lord and I change not." (Mal. III, 6.) Everything which is moved acquires something by its movement, and attains to what it had not attained previously. But since God is infinite, containing in Himself all the plenitude of perfection of all being, He cannot acquire anything new, nor extend Himself to

anything whereto He was not extended previously. Hence, movement in no way belongs to God.

Furthermore it is said of Wisdom, that it is more mobile than all things active (Wisd. VII, 24). But wisdom is called mobile by way of a similitude, according as it diffuses its likeness even to the uttermost of things; for nothing can exist which does not proceed from the divine wisdom by way of some kind of imitation, as from the effective and formal principle, as also works of art proceed from the wisdom of the artist. And so in the same way, inasmuch as the similitude of the divine wisdom proceeds in degrees from the highest things, which participate more fully of its likeness, to the lowest things which participate of it in a lesser degree, there is said to be a kind of procession or movement of the divine wisdom to things; as when we say that the sun proceeds to the earth, inasmuch as the ray of light touches the earth.

But it is said in Scripture, "Draw nigh to God, and He will draw nigh to thee." (James IV, 8.) This is said metaphorically. For as the sun is said to enter a house, or to go out, according as its rays reach the house, so God is said to approach us, or withdraw from us when we receive the influx of His goodness, or decline from Him. (1a. Q. 10, a. 1.)

2. And so we must acquire constancy of mind, in order that we might be immutable to good, and not broken by adversities, nor puffed up by prosperity, nor turned from the way of righteousness. But alas, we are very inconstant in holy meditations, in well regulated affections, in security of conscience, in good will. Alas, how quickly we change from good to evil, from hope into unholy fear, and vice versa, from joy into oppressive grief, from silence into too much talking, from charity into hatred or envy, from fervor into lukewarmness, from humility into vain glory or pride, from meekness into anger, from spiritual joy or spiritual love into carnal pleasures; so that never for one moment do we remain steadfast in the same state, except when we are steadfast in changeableness, in infidelity, in ingratitude, in spiritual defects, in imperfection, in abuse of time, in fickleness, steadfast in impure thoughts and affections. Moreover, instability of the external senses and mutability of bodily members indicate an internal condition and motion.

In regard to these things, let us shine in virtues and conduct ourselves with equanimity in our every thought and action. (De Divinis Moribus.)

JULY 6

Advantages of Reflecting on God as Creator

1. From a consideration of God as Creator, man is led to a knowledge of the Divine Majesty, for the Maker excels the things which He makes. Wherefore, because God is the Maker of all things, it is clear that He is more excellent than all things. And hence it is that whatever can be understood or thought, is less than God Himself. Job (XXXVI, 26) exclaims, "Behold God is great, exceeding our knowledge. The number of His years is inestimable."

2. From considering God as Creator, man is led to thank Him. From the fact that God is the Creator of all things, it is certain that whatever we are, and whatever good we possess, is from God. "What have you (of good) which you have not received?" (1 Cor. IV, 7.) And again the Psalmist (XXIII, 1) declares, "The earth is the Lord's, and the fulness thereof. The world, and all they that dwell therein." And therefore we ought to give thanks to God.

3. From a consideration of God the Creator, man is led to be patient under adversities. For although every creature is from God, and because of this every creature is good according to its nature, still if He inflicts punishment on us, or if injury comes to anyone, we should believe that this punishment is from God, not however as an evil; because no evil as such comes from God, but only that which is ordained to good. And therefore, if every affliction that man suffers is from God, he should patiently endure it. For afflictions purge sins, humiliate sinners, and encourage the good to love God. "If we have received good things at the hand of God, why should we not receive evil?" (Job II, 10.)

4. From considering God as the Creator, we are inspired to use created things rightly. For we should use created things for the purpose for which they were created by God. But things were created for a twofold purpose, namely for the glory of God, because all things are on account of Him; that is for God's glory, and for our usefulness. "The Lord thy God created all things for the service of all nations, that are under heaven." (Deut. IV, 19.) Therefore, we should use things for God's glory, so that in this we might please God, and for our own service; so that in using them, we do not sin. "All things are Thine O Lord, and all things which we have received from Thy hand we will return to Thee." Whatever you have there-

fore, be it knowledge, or beauty, you should attribute all of it to God and use it entirely for the glory of God.

5. From considering God the Creator, we are led through this, to a knowledge of human dignity. For God made all things for man, as mentioned in Psalm (VIII, 8), "Thou hast subjected all things under his feet," and man, after the Angels, is greater than all other creatures, since he is like unto God. Hence it is said in Genesis (I, 26), "Let us make man to Our image and likeness." This indeed the Lord did not say of the heavens, nor of the stars, but of man; not however in reference to his body, but to his soul, which possessing free will, and immortality, is in this, more like unto God than other creatures.

Therefore we should regard man, after the Angels; more noble than other creatures, and in no way lessen our dignity by sin and by sinful desires for bodily things, which are injurious to us, and yet made for our service; but we ought to keep ourselves in the manner in which God created us. For God made us to control all things which are on the earth, and subject ourselves to God. Therefore, we should rule and preside over things, but be subject to God, obey and serve Him; and by our obedience and service, come to the enjoyment of God." (The Creed.)

JULY 7

The Governor of All Things

"I believe in God." The name of God means nothing less than the Ruler and Provider of all things. Consequently, whosoever believes that God exists, believes that all things of this world are governed and provided for by Him. But whoever believes that all things are the result of chance, does not believe that God exists. But there is no one so foolish, who does not believe that the things of nature are governed, cared for and regulated, since they proceed in a well-regulated order, and at certain fixed times. For we see the sun, moon and stars, and all other natural things observing a determined course, which would not happen if they were from chance.

Therefore, we must firmly believe that God exists, rules and regulates not only the things of nature, but also the good actions of men. "They (the foolish) have said: "The Lord shall not see, neither shall the God of Jacob understand." Understand, ye senseless among the people, and you fools be wise at last. God that planted the ear, shall He not hear? Or He that formed the eye, does He not consider? The Lord knoweth the thoughts of men." (Psalm XCIII, 7.) Consequently, God sees all things, even the thoughts and hidden things of the human mind and will. Hence, God has imposed upon men especially, the obligation of doing good, because all things which men think and do are manifest to His Divine Eye. (The Creed.)

JULY 8

God Is Our Father

God is called our Father because of a special creation. He created us to His own image and likeness, which He did not impress upon other inferior creatures. He is also called our Father by reason of His government or Providence. In as far as He governs other things as His servants, He governs or treats us as masters. He treats us with great reverence. He is our Father by reason of adoption. We are His adopted children, to whom He has promised a kingdom. "You have not received the spirit of bondage again in fear, but you have received the spirit of adoption of sons, whereby we cry Father." (Rom. VIII, 15.)

Since God is our Father, we therefore owe Him four things: honor, imitation, obedience and patience. Honor. "If I then be a Father, where is My honor?" (Mal. I.) That honor consists in three things, namely, in giving praise to God. "The sacrifice of praise shall glorify Me," which should be not only done with the lips but also with the heart. (Psalm XLIX, 23), "These people honor Me with their lips, but their heart is far from Me." (1 Cor. VI, 20.) Secondly, we honor Him with purity of body; wherefore it is written: "Glorify and bear God in your body." Thirdly, we honor the Father in rendering justice to our neighbor. "The King's honor loveth justice and a good judgment." (Psalm XCVIII, 3.)

2. Imitation—Because God is our Father. "Thou shalt call Me Father, and shall not cease to walk after Me." (Jer. III, 19.) This imitation is perfected in us in three ways: by love, by mercy and by perfection. By love, "Be imitators of God, as very dear children and walk in His love." (Eph. V, 1.) In mercy, for love should be with merciful. "Be ye merciful." (Luke VI, 36.) By perfection, because love and mercy should

be perfect. "Be perfect as your Heavenly Father is perfect." (Matt. V, 48.)

3. Obedience, and subjection. (Heb. IX, 12): "We have had fathers of our flesh for instructors and we reverenced them, shall we not much more obey the Father of spirits and live?" Because of His dominion over us, God is our Master, and therefore, we owe Him obedience and also because He became for us obedient unto the death of the cross, leaving us a most perfect example of obedience.

4. We honor God through patience under afflictions, "My son reject not the correction of the Lord and do not faint when thou art chastised by Him." (Prov. III, 11.) (The Lord's Prayer.)

JULY 9

The Love of God

"Thou lovest all the things that are, and hatest none of the things which Thou hast made." (Wisdom XI, 25.)

1. God loves all existing things. For all existing things, in so far as they exist are good, since the existence of a thing is itself a good, and likewise whatever perfection it possesses. Now God's will is the cause of all things. It must needs be, therefore, that a thing has existence, or any kind of good, only inasmuch as it is willed by God. To every existing thing, then, God wills some good. Hence, since to love anything is nothing else than to will good to that thing, it is clear that God loves everything that exists. Yet not in the same manner as we love. Because, since our will is not the cause of the goodness of things, but is moved by it as by its object, our love then, whereby we will good to anything, is not the cause of its goodness, but conversely its goodness, whether real or imaginary, calls forth our love, by which we will that it should preserve the good it has, and receive besides, the good which it has not, and to this end we direct our actions; whereas the love of God infuses and creates goodness.

A lover is placed outside himself, and is made to pass into the object of his love, inasmuch as he wills good to the beloved; and works for that good by his providence even as he works for his own. Hence Dionysius says, "On behalf of the truth we must make bold to say even this, that God Himself, the cause of all things, by His abounding love and goodness, is placed outside of Himself by His providence for all existing things." (1a, Q. XX, a. 2.)

2. God loves the members, or children of His only begotten Son with a wonderful love. "The world knows that Thou lovest them, even as Thou lovest Me." (John XVII.) It must be remembered that God loves all things which He has made, by giving them existence, but in a special manner He loves His only Begotten Son, to Whom He gave His entire nature for an eternal generation. But in the middle way, so to speak, God loves the members of His Son, namely the faithful of Christ; by giving to them His grace, through which Christ lives in us.

"Thou hast loved them, even as Thou hast loved Me," not that this means an equality of love, but rather nature and likeness. As if the Lord said, "The love with which You have loved Me, is the nature and cause why You loved them. For because of that by which Thou lovest Me, loving Me, Thou lovest My members also." Hence Saint John (XVI, 27) says, "The Father loves you, because you love Me."

It follows then, that we cannot know now how great the love of God for us really is, because the good things which He will give to us exceed our every desire and longing, and their greatness cannot be conceived by the human mind. "The eye has not seen, nor the ear heard, neither has it entered into the heart of man, to conceive what things God has prepared for them that love Him." (1 Cor. II, 9.) The believing world therefore, that is the saints of God, know through experience how much God loves us, but the lovers of the world, namely sinners, know this also, in seeing and admiring the glory of the saints. "Saying within themselves, these are they, whom we had for some time in derision, and for a parable of reproach. We fools esteemed their life madness, and their end without honour. Behold how they are numbered among the children of God, and their lot is among the saints." (Wisdom V, 3.) (Com. in John, XVIII.)

JULY 10

The Threefold Banquet

We can distinguish a threefold banquet of Christ, namely, a sacramental, spiritual and eternal. Concerning the sacramental banquet, mention is made in the Apocalypse of Saint John the Apostle (XIX, 9), "Blessed are they who are called to the marriage supper of the Lamb." Truly blessed are they now, by grace, and in the future life by glory. "All good things came to me together with her." (Wisdom VII, 11.) Whosoever receives Christ in his heart, he especially receives a knowledge of all three, and possesses virtue and grace here, and hereafter eternal life. This is the supper at which Christ washed the feet of His disciples, that is, the affection of their minds for venial sins was washed away, because in this Sacrament the reformation of man to Christ is effected through love. Because venial sins are opposed to a fervent love, he then whose fervor is increased by the Blessed Sacrament, his venial sins as a consequence will be lessened. Hence Saint Bernard says, "In the Sacrament of the altar, the soul is filled with a heavenly sweetness, venial sins are washed away, and man is strengthened in grace."

Concerning the spiritual marriage supper, Saint John writes (Apoc. III, 20), "I stand at the gate and knock." Knock at the human heart closed by sin. "If any man shall hear My voice, and open to Me the door, I will come into him, and sup with him, and he with Me." (Apoc. III, 20.) That is, "I will make him rejoice in faith, and good works." This banquet is mystically described by Saint John (XII, 1), "Jesus therefore, six days before the pasch, came to Bethania, where Lazarus had been dead, whom Jesus raised to life. They made Him a supper there, and Martha served, and Lazarus was one of them that were at table with Him." Hence Alcuin writes, "The supper of the Lord mystically means the faith of the Church, which operates through love. Martha served with faith for her soul is filled with words of devotion. Lazarus was one of those sleeping; for those who are resurrected to justice after their death from sin, remain in His justice, they may well rejoice in the presence of Truth, and are nourished by the heavenly gifts of God's grace.

Saint Luke (XIV, 16) speaks of the third, or eternal supper, "A certain man made a great supper, and invited many." Great because He has prepared an abundance of internal delight for us. This is the supper at which John, that is each chosen one rests like John through grace on the Heart of the Saviour, away from the noise of the present life; because as Saint Bernard says, "There is rest from labors, peace from the enemy, security in eternity, sweetness and joy in the vision of God." (De humanitate Christi.)

JULY 11

The Vocation of Mankind

"God wishes all men to be saved." (1 Tim. II, 4.)

God wishes three things for us.
1. He wills that we have eternal life. For whenever God makes something for a definite end, He wills for that thing that for which He made it. But God made man for a purpose, a very specific purpose. "Hast Thou, O Lord, made all the children of men in vain?" (Psalm LXXXVIII, 48.) Saint Augustine answers, "Our hearts were made by Thee, and for Thee O Lord, and they will never rest until they rest in Thee." Therefore, God made man for some purpose, not however for sensual pleasures, because even the beasts of the fields have these pleasures, but in order that man might possess life eternal.

When moreover, anything lives for that purpose for which it was made, it is said to be saved. When it does not, it is said to be lost. Hence when man pursues eternal life, he is said to be saved, and the Lord wills this. "This is the will of My Father, that sent Me; that everyone who seeth the Son, and believeth in Him; may have life everlasting." (John VI, 40.)

But this will is already fulfilled in the Angels and Saints in heaven, because they see God and recognize Him and enjoy Him. We then, should desire that just as the will of God is fulfilled in the blessed, who are in heaven, so may it be fulfilled by us who are on earth. This we ask when we pray. "Thy will be done," in us who are on earth, just as it is done by the saints in heaven.

2. God wills that we obey His commandments. For when anyone desires something, not only does he will that which he desires, but all the things by which he might obtain that thing, just as a doctor who wishes to procure good health, wills also the diet and medicine that will secure health. Because there-

fore, through the observance of the commandments we will secure eternal life, God wills that we obey His commandments.

3. God wills that man be restored to the state and dignity in which the first man was created, which was such that the mind and soul felt no opposition from the flesh and sensuality. For as long as the soul was subjected to God, the flesh was likewise subject to the spirit, so that the flesh felt no corruption of death or of sickness or sting of any of the other passions. But because the will and the soul, which are the medium between God and the flesh, rebelled against God through sin, then the body rebelled against the soul, and then man began to experience death, and sickness, and a continual rebellion of sensuality against the spirit. So there is a continual fight between the flesh and the spirit, as a result that man is constantly weakened by sin. Consequently it is the will of God, that man be restored to his first state, so that actually, there might be nothing in the flesh fighting against the spirit. "This is the will of God, your sanctification, that every one of you should know how to possess his vessel in sanctification and honour." (1 Thess. IV, 3.) (The Lord's Prayer.)

JULY 12

Darkness and the Shadow of Death

"The Lord brought them out of darkness, and the shadow of death." (Psalm CVI, 14.)

1. There is a threefold darkness, namely the darkness of ignorance, of sin and of eternal damnation. The Psalmist (LXXXI, 5) says of the darkness of ignorance, "They have not known, nor understood. They walk on in darkness." Likewise the darkness of sin. "You were heretofore darkness, but now light in the Lord. Walk then as children of the light." (Eph. V, 8.) This darkness is not directly the result of human reason, but comes from a wrong desire, inasmuch as man being sinfully disposed through passions or habit, seeks something as good; which is not really good. Likewise, there is the darkness of eternal damnation. "The unprofitable servant cast out into exterior darkness." (Matt. XXV, 30.) The darkness of ignorance and of sin, are in this life, while the darkness of damnation is at the end of life.

Moreover it is written that Christ "brought them out of darkness," for He is the Light of the world, not the sun, but Him by Whom the sun was made; or as Saint Augustine says, "He is the Light which made the sun, and because this Light is universal, It therefore expels every darkness in every place." "Whosoever therefore, follows Me, walketh not in the darkness of ignorance, because I am the Truth, not in the darkness of sin, because I am the Way, not in the darkness of eternal damnation, because I am the Life." (John VIII, 12.)

2. Death is twofold. One kind of death is caused through the removal of actual grace, which removal leads us into mortal sin. When this spiritual death comes, no one can perform works meritorious for eternal life.

Another death is completed death, when one is not only deprived of actual grace through mortal sin, but even of the very power of possessing it, deprived through eternal damnation in hell; where everlasting death is awaiting those of whom it is written, "Depart from Me, ye cursed into everlasting fire." (Matt. XXV, 41.) Then on that day, no one can work, for the time of meriting is passed, except the time of receiving the merits of our actions. Therefore, while you are living, do as you, at death, will wish you had done. "Whatsoever thy hand is able to do, do it earnestly, for neither work, nor reason, nor wisdom, nor knowledge, shall be in hell." (Eccle. IX, 10.)

3. There is a third death, namely damnation in hell. "They are laid in hell like sheep. Death shall feed upon them." (Psalm XLVIII, 15.) The *umbra mortis*, "shadow of death," is the likeness of future damnation reserved for sinners. The terrible punishment of those who are now in hell, is separation from God, and because sinners are now separated from God in this life, they also have therefore, the likeness of future damnation; just as the saintly possess the likeness of future blessedness. (Matth. LI.)

JULY 13

The Wounds of Nature Consequent Upon Sin

"The imagination and thought of man's heart are prone to evil from his youth." (Gen. VIII, 21.)

As a result of original justice, the reason had perfect control over the lower parts of the soul, while reason itself was perfected by God and was subject to Him. Now this same original justice was forfeited through the sin of our first parents, so that all the powers of the soul are left, as it were, destitute of their proper order, whereby they are naturally directed to virtue; which destitution is called a wounding of nature.

Again there are four powers of the soul that can be the subject of virtue, namely the reason, where prudence resides, the will, where justice is the irascible, the subject of fortitude, and the concupiscible, the subject of temperance. Therefore, in so far as reason is deprived of its order to the true, there is the wound of ignorance; in so far as the will is deprived of its order to good, there is the wound of malice; in so far as the irascible is deprived of its order to the arduous, there is the wound of weakness; and in so far as the concupiscible is deprived of its order to the delectable, moderated by reason, there is the wound of concupiscence.

Accordingly, these are the four wounds inflicted on all of human nature as a result of our first parents' sin. But since the inclination to the good of virtue is diminished in each individual on account of actual sin, these four wounds are also the result of other sins, in so far as through sin, the reason is obscured, especially in practical matters, the will hardened to evil, good actions become more difficult, and concupiscence more impetuous. (1a. 2ae. Q. 85, a. 3.)

JULY 14

The Infirmities of Sin

"Jesus went up to Jerusalem. Now there is at Jerusalem a pond, called Probatica, having five porches. In these lay a great multitude of sick, of blind, of lame, of withered; waiting for the moving of the water." (John V, 1.)

Here Saint John describes the infirmities of sin.
 1. In regard to position, namely the sinners lay prostrate, "jacebant,". for by sin they clung to earthly things. For who soever lay prostrate, clings wholly to earth. "And seeing the multitudes He had compassion on them, because they were distressed, and lying like sheep that have no shepherd." (Matt. IX, 36.) The just, or saintly, do not lie prostrate in sin, but stand upright, steadfastly for heavenly things. "These," namely sinners, "are bound, and have fallen," but we, namely the just, "are arisen, and are set upright." (Psalm XIX, 9.)
 2. As to the number, they were many. Hence Saint John says, "a great multitude." "For the perverse are hard to be corrected, and the number of fools is infinite." Eccl. I, 15.) Likewise Saint Matthew (VII, 13) remarks, "Broad is the way which leadeth to destruction and many there are who go in thereat."
 3. As to the condition or habit of those sick, spiritually sick, Saint John mentions four things which man incurs through sin.
 1. Man, from the fact that he subjects himself to the predominating passions of his sins, becomes sick, and therefore John speaks of the "sick" (languentium). Hence it is that Cicero calls the passions of the soul, namely anger and concupiscence, certain infirmities of the soul. Likewise also the Psalmist (VI, 3) declares, *Miserere mei Domine, quoniam infirmus sum.* "Have mercy on me, O Lord, for I am weak."
 2. From the control and victory of the passions over man, reason becomes blinded by consent to sin, and in this regard John speaks of the "blind," "caecorum," blinded namely, by sin. "Their own malice blinded them." (Wis. II, 21.) "Fire hath fallen on them, and they shall not see the sun" (Psalm LVII, 9), namely the fire of anger and concupisence.
 3. Man weakened and blinded through sin, becomes unsteady, shiftless in his labors and as one lame. Hence it is said in Proverbs (XI, 18), "The wicked maketh an unsteady

work," and in regard to them John speaks of the "lame," *claudorum*. "How long do you halt between two sides? If the Lord be God, follow Him." (3 Kings XVIII, 21.)

4. Therefore the man who is spiritually sick, is blinded in reason, unsteady in work, becomes arid in affection, because he is deprived of all that heavenly richness of devotion; which King David prayed for saying, "Let my soul be filled with marrow and fatness, and my mouth shall praise Thee with joyful lips." (Psalm LXII, 6.) In regard to this John speaks of "the withered" *aridorum*, "My strength is dried up as a potsherd, and my tongue hath cleaved to my jaws, and Thou hast brought me down into the dust of death." (Psalm XXI, 16.)

But some are so affected by the infirmity of sin, that they await not the moving of the water, remaining undisturbed in their sins; "living in a great war of ignorance, they call so many and so great evils peace." (Wis. XIV, 22.) Concerning whom Proverbs (II, 14) exclaims: "They are glad when they have done evil, and rejoice in most wicked things." The reason of this is, because they do not hate sin, nor do they sin from ignorance or weakness, but from a certain malice.

But those spiritually sick, who sin not from malice, do not remain undisturbed in their sins, on the contrary, they hopefully await the motion of the water (of God's grace). Hence John speaks also of those "waiting for the motion of the water," *expectantium*.

Probatica was a pond where miracles were wrought. This is evident from the sacred text. "An angel of the Lord descended at certain times into the pond; and the water was moved. And he that went down first into the pond, was cured of whatsoever infirmity he lay under." (John V, 4.)

JULY 15

The Stain of Sin

1. A stain is properly ascribed to corporeal things. A stain results, when a comely body loses its comeliness through contact with another body, for example, a garment, gold or silver or the like. Accordingly a stain is ascribed to spiritual things in like manner. Now, man's soul has a twofold comeliness, one from the refulgence of the natural light of reason,

whereby he is directed in his actions; the other from the refulgence of the Divine Light, namely, of wisdom and grace, whereby man is also perfected for the purpose of doing good and becoming actions. Now when the soul clings to things by love, there is a kind of contact in the soul; and when man sins, he cleaves to certain things against the light of reason and of the Divine Law. Wherefore the loss of comeliness occasioned by this contact, is metaphorically called a stain of the soul.

2. From this, something is said to be stained, when it suffers a loss of its proper beauty. The beauty of the soul consists in a likeness to God Himself, to Whom the soul should be formed through the brightness of grace received from Him. Just as, the vision of corporeal brightness is obstructed from us by the sun, so also the brightness of God's grace is restrained from the soul by sin committed, which stands between us and God.

Now the light of grace both directs the intellect and moves the will, but sin leads to a twofold defect. A defect in the intellect because every sin arises from error, but the defect is principally in the will, because every sin is in the will. (4, Dis. 18, q. 1, a. 2.)

3. The stain of sin remains in the soul even when the act of sin is past. The reason for this is that the stain denotes a blemish in the brightness of the soul, on account of its withdrawing from the light of reason or the Divine Law. And therefore so long as man remains out of this light, the stain of sin remains in him; but as soon as, moved by grace, he returns to the Divine Light and to the light of reason, the stain is removed. For although the act of sin ceases, whereby man withdrew from light of reason and of Divine law, man does not at once return to the state in which he was before, and it is necessary that his will should have a movement contrary to the previous movement. Thus, if one man be parted from another on account of some kind of movement, he is reunited to him as soon as the movement ceases, but he needs to draw nigh to him and to return by a contrary movement. (1a. 2ae. Q. 86, a. 2.)

JULY 16

Can Sin Be the Punishment of Sin?

We may speak of sin in two ways, first, essentially, secondly, accidentally. Sin can in no wise be the punishment of another essentially. Because sin considered essentially is something proceeding from the will, for it is from this part that it derives the character of guilt. Whereas punishment is essentially something against the will. Consequently it is evident that sin can nowise be essentially the punishment of sin.

1. On the other hand sin can be the punishment of sin in three ways. First, when one sin is the cause of another, by removing an impediment thereto. For passions, temptations of the devil and the like are the causes of sin, but are impeded by the help of Divine grace which is withdrawn on account of sin. Wherefore since the withdrawal of grace is a punishment and is from God, the result is that the sin which ensues from this is also a punishment accidentally. It is in this sense that the Apostle speaks (Rom. I, 24) when he says, "Wherefore God gave them up to the desires of their heart," namely, to their passions, because when men are deprived of the help of Divine grace, they are overcome by their passions. In this way sin is always said to be the punishment of a preceding sin.

2. Secondly, by reason of the substance of the act, which is such as to cause pain, whether it be an interior act, as is clearly the case with anger or envy, or an exterior act, as is the case with one who endures considerable trouble and loss in order to achieve a sinful act, according to Wisdom (V, 7), "We wearied ourselves in the way of iniquity."

3. From the part of the effect so that one sin is said to be a punishment by reason of its effect. In the last two ways, a sin is a punishment not only in respect of a preceding sin, but also with regard to itself.

Even when God punishes men by permitting them to fall into sin, this is directed to the good of virtue. Sometimes indeed it is for the good of those who are punished, when men arise from sin more humble and more cautious. But it is always for the amendment of others, who seeing some men fall from sin to sin, are more fearful of sinning. With regard to the two other ways, it is evident that the punishment is intended for the sinner's improvement, since the very fact that man endures toil and loss in sinning, this should withdraw man from sin. (1a. 2ae. Q. 87, a. 2.)

JULY 17

Sin Calls for Punishment

"Tribulation and anguish upon every soul of man that worketh evil." (Rom. II, 9.) But to work evil is to sin. Therefore sin incurs a punishment which is signified by the words "tribulation and anguish."

It has passed from natural things to human affairs that whenever one thing rises up against another, it suffers some detriment therefrom. For we observe in natural things that when one contrary supervenes, the other acts with greater energy, for which reason hot water freezes more rapidly. Wherefore we find that the natural inclination of man is to repress those who rise up against him. Now it is evident that all things contained in an order, are, in some manner, one, in relation to the principle of that order. Consequently, whatever rises up against an order, is put down by that order or by the principle thereof. And because sin is an inordinate act, it is evident that whoever sins, commits an offense against an order, which repression is punishment.

Accordingly, man can be punished with a threefold punishment corresponding to the three orders to which the human will is subject. In the first place a man's nature is subjected to the order of his own reason; secondly, it is subjected to the order of another man who governs him either in spiritual or in temporal matters, as a member either of the state or of the household; thirdly, it is subjected to the universal order of the Divine government. Now each of these orders is disturbed by sin, for the sinner acts against his reason, and against human and Divine law. Wherefore he incurs a threefold punishment, one, inflicted by himself, remorse of conscience; another, inflicted by man; and a third inflicted by God. (1a. 2ae. Q. 87, a. 1.)

JULY 18

The Difference Between Venial and Mortal Sin

1. The difference between venial and mortal sin is consequent on the diversity of that inordinateness which constitutes the notion of sin. For inordinateness is twofold, one that destroys the principle of order, and another which, without destroying the principle of order, implies inordinateness in the things which follow the principle; thus in an animal's body, the frame may be so out of order that the vital principle is destroyed; that is the inordinateness of death; while, on the other hand, saving the vital principle, there may be disorder in the bodily humors; and then there is sickness.

2. Now the principle of the entire moral order is the last end, which stands in the same relation to the matters of action, as the indemonstrable principle does to matters of speculation. Therefore when the soul is so disordered by sin as to turn away from its last end, namely God, to Whom it is united by Charity, there is mortal sin, but when it is disordered without turning away from God, there is venial sin. For even as in the body, the disorder of death which results from the destruction of the principle of life, is irreparable according to nature, while the disorder of sickness can be repaired by reason of the vital principle being preserved, so is it in matters concerning the soul. Because, in speculative matters, it is impossible to convince one who errs in the principles, whereas one who errs, but retains the principles, can be brought back to the truth by means of the principles.

Likewise in practical matters, he who, by sinning, turns away from his last end, if we consider the nature of his sin, falls irreparably, and therefore, is said to sin mortally and to deserve eternal punishment; whereas when a man sins without turning away from God, by the very nature of his sin, his disorder can be repaired, because the principle of the order is not destroyed; wherefore he is said to sin venially, because he does not sin so as to deserve to be punished eternally. (1a. 2ae. Q. 72; a 5.)

JULY 19

Mortal Sin Incurs Eternal Punishment

"These (the wicked) shall go into everlasting punishment, but the just, into everlasting life." (Matt., XXV, 46.)

1. The reason why mortal sin incurs eternal punishment, can be understood from three things. First from the part of Him against Whom one sins, namely God; Who is infinitely great. Hence an offense of this nature, deserves infinite punishment; because inasmuch as he is more worthy, against whom a sin is committed, by so much the more should the sin be punished.

2. Mortal sin deserves everlasting punishment, from the will of the person sinning. For it is clear that one who sins mortally places the object of his delight in that in which he sins mortally; so that he even despises God for that object or loves a fleeting sinful pleasure. Moreover, it is evident that whosoever loves anything extremely, as to make it the end of his will, wishes from this very fact to adhere to it always. Therefore, the one sinning mortally, with that act of the will by which he chooses mortal sin, he chooses also to cling to sin always; unless he is accidentally prevented, either by fear of punishment or by something else. But if he can cling to sin indefinitely he will do so always, and hence, he sins eternally. Therefore, on account of this, mortal sin deserves eternal punishment.

3. From the very state of the person sinning mortally, who through sin is deprived of God's grace. Since therefore, the remission of punishment cannot be effected without grace, if then he should die in mortal sin, he will always remain in punishment, since he is by no means susceptible to grace.

4. Since sin is temporal, it does not follow that it should be punished only with temporal punishment, because punishment is proportionate to sin in point of severity, both in Divine and in human judgments. In no judgment, however, as Augustine says (De Civ. Dei. 21) is it requisite for punishment to equal fault in point of duration. For the fact that adultery or murder is committed in a moment does not call for a momentary punishment. In fact they are punished sometimes by imprisonment or banishment for life, sometimes even by death; wherein account is not taken of the time occupied in killing, but rather of the expediency of removing the murderer from

the fellowship of the living, so that this punishment, in its own way, represents the eternity of punishment inflicted by God.

Now it is just, according to Saint Gregory, that he who has sinned against God in his own eternity should be punished in God's eternity. A man is said to have sinned in his own eternity, not only as regards continual sinning throughout his whole life, but also because, from the very fact that he fixes his end in sin, he has the will to sin everlastingly. Wherefore, Gregory says (Moral. 34) that "the wicked would wish to live without end, that they might abide in their sins for ever." (1a. 2ae. q. 87, a. 3.)

JULY 20

Spiritual Sins

Spiritual sins are of greater guilt than carnal sins, yet this does not mean that each spiritual sin is of greater guilt than each carnal sin; but that, considering the sole difference between spiritual and carnal, spiritual sins are more grievous than carnal sins, other things being equal.

Three reasons may be assigned for this.

The first is on the part of the subject, because spiritual sins belong to the spirit, to which it is proper to turn to God, and to turn away from Him; whereas carnal sins are consummated in the carnal pleasure of the appetite, to which it chiefly belongs to turn to goods of the body; so that carnal sin, as such, denotes more a turning to something, and for that reason, implies a closer cleaving; whereas spiritual sin denotes more a turning from something, whence the notion of guilt arises; and for this reason it involves greater guilt.

A second reason may be taken on the part of the person against whom sin is committed; because carnal sin, as such, is against the sinner's own body which he ought to love less, in the order of charity, than God and his neighbor, against whom he commits spiritual sins, and consequently spiritual sins, as such, are of greater guilt.

A third reason may be taken from the motive, since the stronger the impulse to sin, the less grievous the sin. Now carnal sins have a stronger impulse, namely our innate concupiscence of the flesh. Therefore spiritual sins, as such, are of greater guilt.

The devil is said to rejoice chiefly in the sin of lust, because it is of the greatest adhesion, and man can, with difficulty, be withdrawn from it. For "the desire of pleasure is insatiable," as Aristotle states.

It does not follow that carnal sins are greater, because they are more shameful. The reason why it is more shameful to be incontinent in lust than in anger, is that lust partakes less of reason; and sins of intemperance are most worthy of reproach, because they are about those pleasures, which are common to us and irrational animals. Hence, by these sins man is, so to speak, brutalized, for which reason Gregory says, that they are more shameful. (1a. 2ae. Q. 73, a. 5.)

Anger is a spiritual sin, while lust pertains to carnal sins. Hence Gregory says that carnal sins are of less guilt, but of more shame than spiritual sins.

JULY 21

To Sin Through Malice Is More Grievous Than to Sin Through Passion

A sin that is committed on purpose, for this very reason deserves heavier punishment, according to Job (XXXIV, 26), "He hath struck them as being wicked, in open sight, who, as it were, on purpose, have revolted from Him." Now punishment is not increased except for a graver fault. Therefore a sin is aggravated through being done on purpose, that is, through certain malice.

A sin committed through certain malice is more grievous than a sin committed through passion, for three reasons.

1. First, because as sin consists chiefly in an act of the will, it follows that, other things being equal, a sin is all the more grievous, according as the movement of the sin belongs more to the will. Now when a sin is committed through certain malice, the movement of sin belongs more to the will, which is then moved to evil of its own accord, than when a sin is committed through passion, when the will is impelled to sin by something extrinsic, as it were. Wherefore a sin is aggravated by the very fact that it is committed through certain malice, and so much the more as the malice is greater; whereas it is diminished by being committed through passion, and so much the more as the passion is stronger.

2. Secondly, because the passion which incites the will to

sin, soon passes away, so that man repents of his sin and soon returns to his good intentions; whereas, the habit through which a man sins, is a permanent quality, so that whosoever sins through malice abides longer in his sin. For this reason, Aristotle (Ethics. 7) compares the intemperate man who sins through malice, to a sick man who suffers from a chronic disease, while he compares the impure man who sins through passion, to one who suffers intermittently.

3. Thirdly, because he who sins through certain malice is ill disposed to the end itself, which is the principle in matters of action; and so the defect is more dangerous than in the case of the man who sins through passion, whose purpose tends to a good end, although this purpose is interrupted on account of the passion for the time being. Now the worst of all defects is defect of principle. Therefore, it is evident that a sin committed through malice is more grievous than one committed through passion.

The impulse due to passion, is as it were, due to a defect which is outside the will, whereas, by a habit, the will is inclined from within.

He who sins through passion, sins while choosing but not through choosing; because his choosing is for him the first principle of his sin; for he is induced through passion to choose what he would not choose, were it not for the passion. On the other hand, he that sins through certain malice, chooses evil of his own accord and therefore his choosing, of which he has full control, is the principle of his sin; and for this reason he is said to sin through choosing. (1a. 2ae. Q. 78, a. 4.)

JULY 22

The Excellence or Condition of the Person Sinned Against Aggravates the Sin

Sacred Scripture censures especially those sins that are committed against the servants of God. Likewise much blame is attached to sin committed by a man against those who are akin to him, or against persons constituted in dignity or high office.

The person sinned against is, in a certain manner, the object of the sin. In truth the primary gravity of the sin is derived from its object; so that a sin is considered to be so much the more serious, as its object is a more principal end. But the principal ends of human acts are God, man himself and his neighbour; for whatever we do, it is on account of one of those that we do it, although one of them is subordinate to the other. Therefore the greater or lesser gravity of a sin, in regard to the person sinned against, may be considered on the part of these three.

First, on the part of God, to Whom man is the more closely united, as he is more virtuous or sacred to God; so that an injury inflicted on such a person redounds on to God, according to Zacharias (II, 8), "He that toucheth you, toucheth the apple of My eye." Wherefore a sin is the more grievous, according as it is committed against a person more closely united to God by reason of personal sanctity or official station.

On the part of man himself, it is evident that he sins all the more grievously, according as the person against whom he sins is more united to him, either through natural affinity or kindness received or any other bond, and for this very reason sins all the more grievously, according to Ecclus. (XIV, 5), "He that is evil to himself, to whom will he be good?"

On the part of his neighbour, a man sins the more grievously, according as his sins affect more persons; so that a sin committed against a public personage, for example, a Sovereign, Prince, Governor of the State or President, who represents the whole people, is more grievous than a sin committed against a private person. Hence it is expressly forbidden (Exod. XXII, 28), "The prince of thy people thou shalt not curse." It would also seem that an injury done to a person of prominence is all the more grave, because of the scandal and the disturbance it would cause among the people. (1a. 2ae. Q. 73, a. 9.)

JULY 23

The Excellence of the Person Sinning Aggravates the Sin

Sin is twofold. There is a sin which takes us unawares on account of the weakness of human nature, and such like sins are less imputable to one who is more virtuous, because he is less negligent in checking those sins, which nevertheless human weakness does not allow us to escape altogether.

But there are other sins which proceed from deliberation, and these sins are all the more imputed to a man according as he is more excellent. Four reasons may be assigned for this.

1. First, because a more excellent person, for example, one who excels in knowledge and virtue, can more easily resist sin; hence our Lord said (Luke XII, 47), "that the servant who knew the will of his Lord, . . . and did it not . . . shall be beaten with many stripes."

2. Secondly, on account of ingratitude, because every good in which a man excels, is a gift from God to Whom man is ungrateful when he sins; and in this way any excellence, even in temporal goods, aggravates a sin, according to Wisdom (VI, 7), "The mighty shall be mightily tormented."

3. Thirdly, on account of the sinful act being especially inconsistent with the excellence of the person sinning; for example, if a prince were to violate justice, whereas he is appointed as the guardian of justice or if a priest were to be a fornicator, whereas he has taken the vow of chastity.

4. Fourthly, on account of the example or scandal; because, as Gregory says, "Sin becomes more scandalous, when the sinner is honoured for his position," and the sins of the great are much more notorious and men are accustomed to bear them with more indignation. Moreover, if God punishes the mighty more for one and the same sin, He does not make Himself then a respector of persons; because their excellence increases the gravity of their sin. (1a. 2ae. Q. 73, a. 10.)

JULY 24

The Happiness Which Must Not Be Sought in This Life

1. Happiness cannot be found in sin, for sin wearies you like a heavy burden. "Your burdens of heavy weight even unto weariness." (Isaias, XLVI, 1.) Sin wearies one, (a) on account of the mental disturbance in thinking of sin, for "the sinful sleep not unless they have done evil, and drink the wine of iniquity." (Prov. IV, 16); (b) on account of the labor in pursuing sin. "We wearied ourselves in the way of iniquity and destruction" (Wis. V, 7); (c) on account of the confusion in evil thinking. "What fruit therefore had you in those things of which you are now ashamed?" (Rom. VI, 21); (d) on account of the disappointment in awaiting. "The expecta-

tion of the wicked shall perish." (Isaias, XLVI.) Hence happiness is not found in sin.

2. Neither is happiness found in sinful bodily pleasures. For the highest perfection of man cannot consist in uniting himself to inferior things but in that he is united to something higher; for the end is better when our activities are for a good end. But bodily pleasures consist in this that man unites himself to inferior things of the senses.

Therefore, if bodily pleasures were good in themselves, it would be best to use these in the highest degree possible. But this appears to be false. For the least use of these bodily pleasures is reputed dangerous, and is also proven injurious to the body. Sensual pleasures therefore, are not essential for man's happiness.

Likewise, God is our last end. It must needs be therefore, that the ultimate purpose of man should be to fix his affections on that which brings him closer to God. But by undue attachment to sensual delights man is prevented from approaching God; which approach is accomplished through contemplation. The aforesaid pleasures especially impede and immerse man in delights of the flesh, and withdraw him from intellectual pursuits. It is not therefore in these corporeal pleasures that human happiness should be sought.

3. In this life happiness (perfect happiness) is not found. Two reasons may be assigned for this.

(a) First from the general notion of happiness. For since happiness is perfect and sufficient good, it excludes every evil and fulfills every desire. But in this life every evil cannot be excluded. For this present life is subject to many unavoidable evils, to ignorance on the part of the intellect, to inordinate affection on the part of the appetite and to many penalties on the part of the body. Likewise neither can the desire for good be satiated in this life. For man naturally desires the good which he has, to be abiding. Now the goods of the present life pass away; since life itself passes away, which we naturally desire to have and would wish to hold everlastingly; for man naturally shrinks from death. Wherefore it is impossible to have true happiness in this life.

(b) Secondly, from a consideration of the specific nature of happiness, the vision of the Divine Presence, which man cannot obtain in this life. Hence it is evident that none can attain true and perfect happiness in this life.

Some are said to be happy in this life, either on account of the hope of obtaining happiness in the life to come, according to Rom. (VIII, 24), "We are saved by hope"; or on account of a certain participation of happiness, by reason of a kind of enjoyment of the Supreme Good. (1a. 2ae. Q. 5, a. 3.)

JULY 25

The Sacrament of Penance

Our Lord said (Luke XIII, 3) "Unless you shall do penance, you shall all likewise perish."

A thing is absolutely necessary for salvation, if no one can obtain salvation without it, the grace of Christ and the sacrament of Baptism, whereby a man is born again in Christ. The sacrament of Penance is necessary on a supposition, for it is necessary, not for all, but for those who are in sin. For it is written (2 Paral. XXXVII), "Thou, Lord, God of the righteous, hast not appointed repentance to the righteous, to Abraham, Isaac, and Jacob, nor to those who sinned not against Thee." But "sin, when it is completed, begeteth death." (James I, 15.) Consequently, it is necessary for the sinner's salvation that sin be taken from him; which cannot be done without the sacrament of Penance, wherein the power of Christ's Passion operates through the priest's absolution and the acts of the penitent, who co-operates with grace unto the destruction of his sin. For Augustine says, "God Who created thee without thee, will not justify thee without thee" (that is He will not justify you without your penitential cooperation). Therefore it is clear that after sin the sacrament of Penance is necessary for salvation, even as bodily medicine is necessary after a man has contracted a dangerous disease.

Saint Jerome says that "Penance is a second plank after shipwreck." For just as the first help for those who cross the sea is to be safeguarded in the whole ship, while the second help when the ship is wrecked is to cling to a plank, so, too, the first help in this life's ocean is that man safeguard his integrity, while the second help is, if he lose his integrity through sin, that he regain it by means of Penance.

Hence it is said in Prov. XXVIII, 13, "He that hideth his sins shall not prosper." And again "Charity covereth all sins." (Prov. X, 12). Likewise it is written, "By mercy and faith sins are purged away." Prov. XV, 27. But, once a man falls into sin, charity, faith and mercy do not deliver him from sin without penance. Because charity demands that a man should grieve for the offence committed against his friend and that he should be anxious to make satisfaction to his friend. Faith requires that he should seek to be justified from his sins through the power of Christ's Passion which operates in the sacraments of the Church and well ordered pity necessitates that man should aid himself by repenting of the pitiful condition into which sin has brought him; for according to Proverbs XIV, 34, "Sin maketh nations miserable." Wherefore it is written Eccles. XXX, 24, "Have pity on thy own soul, pleasing God." (3a. Q. 84, a. 5 et 6.)

JULY 26

The Remnants of Sin

We read (Mark VIII) that the blind man whom our Lord enlightened was restored first to imperfect sight, wherefore he said (verse 24), "I see men, as it were trees, walking"; and afterwards he was restored perfectly, "so that he saw all things clearly." Now the enlightenment of the blind man signifies the deliverance of the sinner (from sin). Therefore after the first remission of sin, whereby the sinner is restored to spiritual sight, there yet remain in him some remnants of his past sin.

Mortal sin, in so far as it turns inordinately to a changeable good produces in the soul a certain disposition, or even a habit, if the acts be repeated frequently. Now the guilt of sin is pardoned, as the aversion of the mind from God is removed through grace.

Nevertheless, when that which is on the part of the aversion has been removed through grace, that which is on the part of the inordinate turning to a changeable good can remain, since this may happen to exist without the other. Consequently, there is no reason why, after the guilt has been forgiven, the dispositions caused by preceding acts should not remain which are called the remnants of sin. Still they remain weakened and diminished so as not to control man and they follow the manner of dispositions rather than habits, like the temptation to sin which remains after Baptism.

Saint Augustine says, "Our Lord never healed anyone without delivering him wholly; for He wholly healed the man on the Sabbath, since He delivered his body from all disease, and his soul from all stain." Now God heals the whole man perfectly, but sometimes suddenly, as Peter's mother-in-law was restored at once to perfect health, so that "rising she ministered to them" (Luke IV, 38), and sometimes God heals gradually, as was said of the blind man who was restored to sight. (Matt. VIII.) And so too, He sometimes spiritually turns the heart of man with such power, that it receives at once spiritual health, not only is the guilt pardoned, but all remnants of sin are removed as was the case with Magdalen (Luke VII); whereas at other times He first pardons the guilt by operating grace, and afterwards by cooperating grace removes the remnants of sin by degrees. (3a. Q. 86, a. 5.)

JULY 27

Contrition

1. Our contrition should be the greatest. In contrition there is a twofold sorrow. One is in the will and is essentially that very sorrow which is nothing other than a grief for past sin and such sorrow should exceed all other sorrows by way of contrition for inasmuch as something pleases one, in so far should its opposite displease, since all things are desired for an end; and therefore sin which turns us away from our ultimate end, namely God, should be most displeasing to us.

There is another sorrow on the sensitive part of our nature and this contrition need not be the greatest. For sorrow in the sensitive part arises more from a sensitive injury than from reason. Hence sorrow for sin in the sensitive part arising from an intellectual displeasure of sin, is not greater than other sorrows, both because the inferior affection does not obey at will the superior power, so that the passion is led by the inferior appetite and also because the passions in actions of virtue use reason, whereas, sometimes there is unreasonable sorrow, which serves not reason but exceeds reason.

2. How this sorrow can be too great.

Contrition on the part of sorrow which exists in the reason, namely displeasure by which sin is displeasing in as far as it is an offense against God, cannot be too great, just as the love of charity cannot be too great, namely a love by which a displeasure for sin is intended. But in regards to sensitive sorrow, contrition can be too great just as even the external affliction of the body can be too excessive. In all these things the preservation of the individual as a rule should be followed and sufficent good sense in regard to those things which we must do; and therefore this is said in Romans XII, 1, "I beseech you therefore, brethren, by the mercy of God, that you present your bodies, a living sacrifice, holy, pleasing unto God, . . . your reasonable service."

3. Our sorrow should be greater for one sin than for another.

We may speak of contrition in two ways. In one way according as it corresponds to (or suffices for) each individual sin and so in regard to the sorrow of the superior affection it is required that one grieve more over the greater sin, because the reason for sorrow is greater in one than in another, namely the offense against God, for by a more unbecoming act God is the more offended. Likewise also to a greater guilt, greater punishment is due. Hence the sorrow of the sensitive part should be greater concerning the greater sin.

In another way contrition can be considered in as far as it is partly for all sins, just as in the act of justification, it is to a degree habitually or virtually greater in one than in another. For he who grieves because he has offended God, grieves implicitly concerning different things differently, according as by these things he has more or less offended God. Although each mortal sin separates us from God and deprives us of His grace, still a certain sin separates us farther from Him than another in so far as it possesses greater wickedness from its disorder to the order of Divine goodness. (4, Dist. 16, a. 3.)

JULY 28

The Duration of Contrition

1. Our contrition should last unto the end of life.

In contrition there is a twofold sorrow, one a rational sorrow which is a hatred of sin committed by us, another arises from the sensitive part of our nature and follows the rational or sensible sorrow. But in regard to both kinds, the duration of contrition is the entire period of the present life. For as long as anyone is on life's journey he should detest those evils by which he is retarded or prevented from arriving at the end of the journey. But since through past sin the course of our life towards God has been retarded, for that time was given to us to run to God and that time cannot now be regained, it is necessary that a state of contrition remain with us all through life to affect a hatred of sin. The fact that man has sinned should be always displeasing to him, for if it should please him to have sinned, by this very fact he incurs sin and loses the joy of pardon.

Likewise also as to sensible sorrow which is assumed by the will as a punishment, for man deserves eternal punishment in sinning, and since he has sinned against the Eternal God and the eternal punishment is changed to temporal, surely then sorrow should continue during the entire eternity of man that is during his life on earth. On this account Hugh of Saint Victor says that "God in absolving man from guilt and from eternal punishment, binds him with the bond of overlasting hatred of sin."

Contritional sorrow corresponds to the guilt on the part of aversion, wherefore it has a certain kind of infinity and hence contrition should always endure.

To perform interior penance by which one repents of sin committed and external penance by which one manifests exterior signs of sorrow, pertains to the state of beginners who relapse into sin. But interior penance has also a place among these advancing in perfection and amongst the perfect; according to the Psalmist (LXXXIII, 7), "Blessed is the man whose help is from Thee. In his heart he has disposed to ascend by steps, in the vale of tears. They shall go from virtue to virtue." Hence also the great Apostle, Saint Paul says, "I am not worthy to be called an Apostle, because I have persecuted the Church of God." (1 Cor. XV, 9.)

2. In what manner our contrition should be continued.

Since contrition, in as far as it is a certain detestation (for sin) in the rational appetite, is a penitential act of virtue, thereupon it can never be superfluous, either in regard to intensity or in regard to duration, unless that one act of virtue should impede another act more necessary for that time. Hence inasmuch as man can continually perform acts of detestation for sin, by so much the more will it be better for him.

But the passions can have superfluity and diminution both in regard to intensity and duration. Therefore, just as the passion of sorrow which the will assumes should be moderately intensified, so it should moderately endure, lest it might continue to excess and man should fall into despair and weakness and vices of this nature. (4, Dist. 17, q. 2.)

JULY 29

Concerning Solicitude and the Solicitous

"Martha, Martha, thou art careful, and art troubled about many things. But one thing is necessary" (Luke V, 41.)

1. Solicitude about temporal things may be unlawful in three ways.
(a) First on the part of the object of solicitude, that is if we seek temporal things as an end.
(b) Secondly, solicitude about temporal things may be unlawful through too much anxiety in endeavoring to obtain the temporal, the result being that a man is drawn away from spiritual things which ought to be the chief object of his search, wherefore it is written (Matt. XIII, 22) that, "the care of this world chokes up the word of God."
(c) Through over much fear, when a man fears to lack necessary things if he should do what he ought to do. Now our Lord gives three motives for laying aside this fear. First on account of the yet greater favours bestowed by God on man independently of his solicitude, for example, his body and soul (Matt. VI, 26); secondly, on account of the care with which God watches over animals and plants without the help of man, according to the requirements of their nature; thirdly, because of Divine Providence, through ignorance of which the gentiles are solicitous in seeking temporal goods before all others.
Therefore, He concludes that we should be solicitous most of all about spiritual goods, hoping that temporal goods also may be granted us according to our needs if we do what we ought to do.
2. Concerning the person seeking temporal things. "One thing is necessary," said the Lord. As Martha was solicitous about many things, the Lord wished to attract her to one thing. For the perfection of man consists in this that his heart is centered in one thing, because inasmuch as something is more one, by so much the more is it like unto God Who is verily One. "I have sought one thing from the Lord." On the contrary the search for this one thing, namely salva-

tion, suffers when one is over anxious for riches and things of this world, because then we become immersed in many desires of a worldly nature and the heart of man is drawn to diverse things.

Consequently, the Holy Ghost effected a twofold purification in the Blessed Virgin. The first was, as it were, preparatory to Christ's conception which did not cleanse her from the stain of sin, but rather gave her mind a unity of purpose and disengaged it from a multiplicity of things. The second purification effected in her by the Holy Ghost was by means of the conception of Christ which was the operation of the Holy Ghost. And in this respect, it may be said that He purified her entirely. (3a. Pars. Q. 27, a. 3 ad 3um.)

JULY 30

How Remarkable a Divine Favour When One Rises from Sin!

Man by himself can in no wise rise from sin without the help of grace.

1. For since sin is transient as to the act and abiding in its guilt, to rise from sin is not the same as to cease the act of sin; but to rise from sin means that man has restored to him what he lost by sinning. Now man incurs a triple loss by sinning, stain, corruption of natural good and debt of punishment. He incurs a stain, inasmuch as he forfeits the brightness of grace through the deformity of sin. Natural good is corrupted, inasmuch as man's nature is disordered by man's will not being subject to God's; and this order being overthrown, the consequence is that the whole nature of sinful man, remains disordered. Lastly, there is the debt of punishment, inasmuch as by sinning man deserves everlasting damnation.

2. Now, it is manifest that none of these three can be restored except by God. For since the lustre of grace springs from the shedding of divine light, this lustre cannot be brought back, except God sheds His light anew. Hence, a habitual gift is necessary and this is the light of grace.

Likewise the order of nature can only be restored, that is, man's will can only be subject to God when God draws man's will to Himself.

So, too, the guilt of eternal punishment can be remitted

by God alone, against Whom the offence was committed and Who is man's Judge.

And thus in order that man arise from sin there is required the help of grace both as regards a habitual gift and as regards the internal motion of God (on the soul).

Hence when it is said, "Arise and Christ will enlighten thee," we are not to think that the complete rising from sin precedes the enlightenment of grace; but that man when by his free-will, moved by God, strives to rise from sin he receives the light of justifying grace.

When nature is perfect, it can be restored by itself to its befitting and proportionate condition; but without exterior help it cannot be restored to what surpasses its measure. The natural reason is not the sufficient principle of the health that is in man by justifying grace. This principle is grace, which is taken away by sin. Hence, man cannot be restored by himself; but he requires the light of grace to be poured upon him anew as if the soul were infused into a dead body for its resurrection. And thus human nature undone by the act of sin, remains no longer perfect, but corrupted; nor can it be restored by itself to its connatural good, much less to the supernatural good of justice. (Ia. 2a. q. 109, a. 7.)

JULY 31

The Necessity of Keeping Our Hearts United to God Through Grace

1. In the state of corrupt nature man needs grace to heal his nature in order that he may entirely abstain from sin. And in the present life this healing is wrought in the mind, the carnal appetite being not yet restored. Hence, the Apostle (Rom. VII, 25) says in the person of one who is restored, "I myself with the mind, serve the law of God, but with the flesh, the law of sin."

And in this state man can abstain from all mortal sin, which consists in his reason; but man cannot abstain from all venial sin because of the corruption of his lower appetite of sensuality. For men can indeed repress its movements, but not all, because whilst he is resisting one, another may arise and also because the reason is not always alert to avoid these movements.

2. So, too, before man's reason wherein is mortal sin, is restored by justifying grace, he can avoid each mortal sin and for a time, since it is not necessary that he should be always actually sinning. But it cannot be that he remains for a long time without mortal sin. Hence, Gregory says that, "a sin not at once taken away by repentance, by its weight drags us down to other sins," and this because, as the lower appetite ought to be subject to the reason so should the reason be subject to God and should place in Him the end of its will. Now it is by the end that all human acts ought to be regulated, even as it is by the judgment of the reason that the movements of the lower appetite should be regulated. And thus, even as inordinate movements of the sensitive appetite are not subject to reason, so, too, since man's reason is not entirely subject to God, the result is that many disorders occur in the reason. For when man's heart is not so fixed on God as to be unwilling to be parted from Him for the sake of finding any good or avoiding any evil, many things happen, for the achieving or avoiding of which a man strays from God and breaks His commandments, and thus sins mortally; especially since, when surprised, a man acts according to his preconceived end and pre-existing habits; although with premeditation of his reason a man may do something outside the order of his preconceived end and the inclination of his habit.

But because a man cannot always have this premeditation, it may occur that he acts in accordance with his will turned aside from God, unless, by grace, he is quickly brought back to the proper order. (Ia. 2ae. Q. 109, a. 8.)

AUGUST 1

The Lack of Hope

1. Unbelief comes from this that man believes not in God's own truth, while hatred of God arises from man's will being opposed to God's goodness itself; whereas despair consists in a man ceasing to hope for a share of God's goodness. From this it is clear that unbelief and hatred of God are against God as He is in Himself, while despair is against Him, according as His goodness is partaken of by us. Wherefore strictly speaking it is a more grievous sin to disbelieve God's

truth, or to hate God, than not to hope to receive glory from Him.

If, however, despair be compared to the two other sins from our point of view, then despair is more dangerous, since hope withdraws us from evils and induces us to seek for good things, so that when hope is given up, men rush headlong into sin and are drawn away from good works. Wherefore, a gloss on Prov. XXIV, 10, "If thou lose hope being weary in the day of distress, thy strength shall be diminished." "Nothing is more hateful than despair, for the man that has it loses his constancy both in the every day battles of this life, and what is worse, in the battle of faith." Saint Isidore likewise declares (De Cum. Bono), "To commit a crime is to kill the soul, but to despair is to fall into hell."

2. Consequently, the hope of obtaining happiness may be lacking in a person in two ways. First, through his not considering it an arduous good, secondly, through his deeming it impossible to obtain either by himself or by another.

Now, the fact that spiritual goods taste good to us no more or seem to be goods of no great account, is chiefly due to our affections, being infected with the love of bodily pleasures, among which sexual pleasures hold the first place; for the love of those pleasures leads man to have a distaste for spiritual things and not to hope for them as arduous goods.

On the other hand, the fact that a man·deems an arduous good impossible to obtain, either by himself or by another, is caused by over dejection, for when this state of mind controls his affections it seems to him that he will never be able to rise to any good. And since sloth is a sadness that casts down the spirit, in this way despair is born of sloth and lust.

Hope, in fact, seems to arise from a consideration of Divine favours and especially from a consideration of the birth of our Lord. This very neglect to consider the Divine favours arises from sloth. For when a man is influenced by a certain passion, he considers chiefly the things which pertain to that passion; so that a man who is full of sorrow does not easily think of great and joyful things but only of sad things, unless by a great effort he turns his thoughts away from sadness. (2a. 2ae. Q. 20, a. 3 et 4.)

AUGUST 2

Concerning the Improper Love of Oneself

"He that loveth iniquity, hateth his own soul." (Ps. X, 6.)

1. Man is said to be something in respect to some predominance, but the predominating principle in man is the rational mind while the sensitive and corporeal nature takes the second place; the former of which the Apostle calls the inward man and the latter the outward man. (2 Cor. V.) Now, good men look upon their rational nature or the inward man as being the chief thing in them, wherefore they think themselves to be what they are. On the other hand, the wicked consider their sensitive and corporeal nature or outward man to hold the first place; wherefore not knowing themselves rightly, they do not love themselves aright but love what they think themselves to be.

2. But the good knowing themselves truly, love themselves properly and this is proved from five things which are proper to friendship. For in the first place, every friend wishes his friend to be and to live; secondly, he desires good things for him; thirdly, he does good things to him; fourthly, he takes pleasure in his company; fifthly, he is of one mind with him, rejoicing and sorrowing in almost the same things. In this way the good love themselves as to the inward man because they wish their preservation in its integrity and they desire good things for man, namely spiritual goods, indeed they do their best to obtain them and they take pleasure in entering into their own hearts because they find there good thoughts in the present, the memory of past good and the hope of future good, all of which are sources of pleasure. Likewise they experience no clashing of wills because their whole soul tends to one thing.

3. On the other hand, the wicked have no desire to be preserved in the integrity of the inward man nor do they desire spiritual goods for him nor work for that end, nor take pleasure in their own company by entering into their own hearts, because whatever they find there, present, past and future, is evil and horrible; nor do they agree with themselves because of the gnawings of conscience, according to Psalm XLIX, 21; "I will reprove thee and set before thy face." In the same manner it can be proved that the wicked love them-

selves, as to the corruption of the outward man whereas the good do not love themselves thus.

Therefore, the love of self which is the principle of sin is that which is proper to the wicked and reaches to the contempt of God, because the wicked so desire external goods as to despise spiritual goods. (2, 2ae. Q. 25, a. 7.)

AUGUST 3

Folly

1. Folly causes a dullness of the heart and a blindness of the senses. For dullness is contrary to sharpness, since an intellect is said by comparison to be sharp, when it is able to penetrate into the heart of things that are proposed to it. Hence it is dullness of mind that renders the mind unable to pierce into the heart of a thing. A man is said to be a fool if he judges wrongly about the common end of life, hence folly is properly opposed to wisdom which makes us judge aright about the universal cause. (2a. 2ae. Q. 8, a. 6, ad 1 um.)

2. Folly is a sin, for it denotes a certain dullness of sense in judging and chiefly as regards the highest cause, which is the last end and the sovereign good. Now a man may in this respect contract dullness in judgment in two ways. First, from a natural indisposition, as in the case of idiots, and such like folly is no sin. Secondly, by plunging his sense into earthly things whereby his sense is rendered incapable of perceiving Divine things, according to (1 Cor. II, 14). "The sensual man perceiveth not these things which are of the Spirit of God," even as sweet things have no taste for a man whose taste is infected with an evil humour, and such like folly is a sin.

3. Folly is the daughter of lust. For folly in so far as it is a sin is caused by the spiritual sense being dulled, so as to be incapable of judging spiritual things. Now man's sense is plunged into earthly things chiefly by lust, which is about the greatest pleasures, and these absorb the mind more than any others. Therefore, the folly which is a sin arises chiefly from lust.

It pertains to folly that a man should have a distaste for God and His gifts. Hence Gregory mentions two daughters of lust pertaining to folly, hatred of God and despair of the life to come, thus he divides folly into two parts.

AUGUST 4

Sloth

1. Sloth is a sin. For it is an oppressive sorrow which so weighs upon man's mind that he wants to do nothing. Hence sloth implies a certain weariness of work, as appears from a gloss on Psalm CVI, 18: "Their soul abhorred all manner of meat," and from the definition of some who say that sloth is a sluggishness of the mind which neglects to begin good.

Now, this sorrow is always evil, sometimes in itself, and sometimes in its effect. Sorrow is evil in itself when it is about that which is apparently evil but good in reality, even as pleasure is evil, if it is about that which seems to be good but is in truth evil. Since then, spiritual good is a good in very truth, yet sorrow about a spiritual good can be evil in itself. And yet that sorrow which is also about a real evil is evil in its effect, if it so oppresses man as to draw him away entirely from good deeds. Therefore sloth, which is sorrow at a spiritual good, is a sin. Hence the Apostle (2 Cor. II, 7) did not wish those who repented to be "swallowed up with overmuch sorrow."

Sin is ever to be shunned, but the assaults of sin should be overcome sometimes by flight, sometimes by resistance; by flight when a continued thought increases the incentive to sin as in lust; for which reason it is written, (1 Cor. VI, 18), "Fly fornication"; by resistance when perseverance in the thought diminishes the incentive to sin, which incentive arises from some trivial consideration. This is the case with sloth, because the more we think about spiritual goods the more pleasing they become to us and immediately sloth dies away.

2. Sloth is a special vice, not because one is sorrowful for a spiritual good in a general way for every vice shuns the spiritual good of its opposite virtue, nor in so far as it shuns a spiritual good as toilsome or troublesome to the body or as a hindrance to the body's pleasure, for this again would not sever sloth from carnal desires whereby man seeks bodily comfort and pleasure, but sorrow in the Divine good, about which charity rejoices, belongs to a special vice which is called sloth.

Wherefore, we must say that a certain order exists among spiritual goods, since all the spiritual goods that are in the acts of each virtue are directed to one spiritual good, which is the Divine good about which there is a special virtue, namely, charity. Hence, it is proper to each virtue to rejoice in its own spiritual good which consists in its own act, while it belongs especially to charity to have that spiritual joy whereby one rejoices in the Divine good. In like manner, the sorrow whereby one is displeased at the spiritual good which is in each act of virtue belongs, not to any special vice, but to every vice, but sorrow in the Divine good about which charity rejoices belongs to a special vice which is called sloth.

3. Sloth is a mortal sin. Mortal sin is so called because it destroys the spiritual life which is the effect of charity, whereby God dwells in us. Hence any sin which by its very nature, is contrary to charity is a mortal sin by reason of its genus. Such is sloth, for the proper effect of charity is joy in God, while sloth is sorrow about spiritual good inasmuch as it is a Divine good.

But if the movement of sloth is in sensuality only, by reason of the opposition of the flesh to the spirit, then it is a venial sin. But if sloth reaches to the reason which consents in the dislike, horror and detestation of the Divine good, on account of the flesh prevailing over the spirit, then sloth is a mortal sin. Sloth therefore, is an aversion of the mind from the Divine good, to which the mind is obliged to adhere; wherefore sloth becomes sinful when one is sorry to have to do something for God's sake. (2, 2ae. Q. 35, A. 1, 2, 3.)

AUGUST 5

Imprudence

"There is a treasure to be desired, and oil in the dwelling of the just, but the imprudent man shall spend it." (Prov. XXI, 20.)

1. The spiritual treasure of grace is not taken away except by sin. But it is destroyed or taken away by imprudence, therefore imprudence is a sin. Imprudence is so called in so far as it denotes a lack of that prudence which a man can and ought to have, and in this sense imprudence is a sin by reason of man's negligence in striving to have prudence.

Imprudence can be also taken as a contrary, in so far as the movement or act of reason is in opposition to prudence. Wherefore, if this should happen through aversion from the

Divine Law it will be a mortal sin, as when a man acts precipitately through contempt and rejection of the Divine teaching; whereas if he acts beside the Law and without contempt, and without detriment to salvation, it will be a venial sin.

2. Imprudence is a general sin through participation, for just as prudence shares in all the virtues in a certain way in so far as it directs them, so have all vices and sins a share of imprudence, because no sin can occur without some defect in an act of the directing reason, which defect belongs to imprudence.

Imprudence is also a general sin in so far as it contains in itself many species of sin and this happens in three ways.

(a) First, by opposition to the various subjective parts of prudence, for just as we distinguish a monastic prudence which guides the individual, and other species which govern a number of people, so also imprudence is of various kinds.

(b) Secondly, in respect to the quasi potential parts of prudence, which are virtues connected with it and correspond to the several acts of reason. Thus from defect of counsel, results, precipitation or temerity which is a species of imprudence, to defect of judgment corresponds thoughtlessness; while inconsistency and negligence correspond to the command which is the proper act of prudence.

(c) By opposition to those things which are required for prudence, which are the quasi integral parts of prudence. Since however all these things are intended for the direction of the aforesaid three acts of reason, it follows that all the opposite defects are reducible to the four parts mentioned above. Thus incautiousness and incircumspection are included in thoughtlessness, lack of docility, memory or reason pertain to precipitation; while improvidence, lack of intelligence and of shrewdness belong to negligence and inconstancy. (2a, 2ae, q. 53, a. 1 et 2.)

AUGUST 6

Christ's Transfiguration

It was fitting that Christ should be transfigured. Our Lord after foretelling His Passion to His disciples, had exhorted them to follow the path of His sufferings. Now, in order that anyone go straight along a road he must have some knowledge of the end; thus an archer will not shoot an arrow straight unless he first see the target. Hence Thomas said (John XV, 5), "Lord, we know not whither Thou goest; and how can we know the way?" This is especially necessary when hard and rough is the road, difficult the going but delightful the end.

Now by His Passion Christ achieved glory, not only of His soul which He had from the first moment of His conception, but also of His body; according to (Luke XXIV, 26), "Ought not Christ to have suffered these things, and so enter into His glory?" To which glory He brings those who follow the footsteps of His Passion, according to Acts XIV, 21; "Through many tribulations we must enter into the kingdom of God."

Therefore it was fitting that He show His disciples the glory of His clarity (which is to be transfigured), to which He will configure those who are His; according to Phil. III, 21, "He will reform the body of our lowness, made like to the body of His glory." Hence Bede says on Mark VIII,, 39, "By His loving foresight He allowed them to taste for a short time the contemplation of eternal joy, so that they might brave persecution bravely."

"He led them into a high mountain apart." In this He teaches that it is necessary for all desiring to contemplate God, that they do not lie prostrate in the valley of sensual pleasures, but that they raise themselves to heavenly things by a love for things Divine. He showed to His disciples the glory of His Divine clarity, not that they might seek it in the riches of this world, but in the kingdom of eternal blessedness. We read that He led them "apart," because holy men with their whole heart and with strong faith shun evils here and will be completely separated from them hereafter.

"O Lord it is good for us to be here." If Peter in beholding the glorified humanity of Christ, desired never to be separated from this vision, what must be thought of the joy of those who merit to see His Divinity? It is related that Peter did not realize what he said because of the astonishment of human weakness. But he realized this that man's sole good is to enter into the joy of the Lord. (The Humanity of Christ.)

AUGUST 7

Precipitation

Precipitation, or inordinate haste is a sin and is included in imprudence. It is written in Proverbs IV 19. "The way of the wicked is darkness, they know not where they fall." Now the darksome ways of ungodliness belong to imprudence. Therefore imprudence leads a man to fall or to be precipitated.

Precipitation is ascribed metaphorically to acts of the soul, by way of likeness to bodily movement. Now a thing is said to be precipitated as regards bodily movement when it is brought down from above by the impulse either of its own movement or of another's, and not in orderly fashion by degrees.

Now the summit of the soul is reason and the base is reached in the action performed by the body; while the steps that intervene by which one ought to descend in orderly fashion are memory of the past, intelligence of the present, shrewdness in considering the future outcome, reasoning which compares one thing with another, docility in accepting the opinions of others; by which steps he that takes counsel descends in proper order. Whereas, if a man is rushed into action by the impulse of his will or of a passion, without taking these necessary steps, it will be a case of precipitation. Since then, inordinate counsel pertains to imprudence, it is evident that the vice of precipitation is contained under imprudence.

Things are said to be done rashly when they are not directed by reason, and this may happen in two ways; first through the impulse of the will or of a passion, secondly through contempt of the directing rule and this is what is meant by rashness properly speaking. Wherefore it seems to proceed from that root of pride, which refuses ot submit to another's ruling. But precipitation refers to both, so that rashness is contained under precipitation. (2a. 2ae. q. 53, a. 3).

AUGUST 8

Negligence

1. Negligence is a special sin.

Negligence denotes lack of due solicitude. Now every lack or defect of a due act is sinful. Wherefore it is clear that negligence is a sin, and that it must needs have the character of a special sin, insofar as solicitude is the act of a special virtue. For in each sin it is necessary that the defect be about a certain act of reason; for example the defect of counsel and the like. Hence just as precipitation is a special sin on account of a special act of reason which is omitted, although it may be found in any kind of sin; so negligence is a special sin on account of the lack of a special act of reason, (solicitude) although it is found more or less in all sins.

Properly speaking, the matter of negligence is a good that one ought to do, not that it is a good when it is done negligently, but because on account of negligence one incurs a lack of goodness, whether a due act be entirely omitted through lack of solicitude or some due circumstance be omitted.

2. Negligence is opposed to prudence.

Negligence is directly opposed to solicitude. Now solicitude pertains to the reason and rectitude of solicitude to prudence. On the contrary, negligence pertains to imprudence. Negligence is not the same as laziness or idleness which pertains to sloth, for negligence is a defect in the internal act to which also choice belongs; whereas laziness and idleness denote slowness of execution, in such wise, that idleness denotes slowness in setting about the execution, while laziness denotes remissness in the execution itself.

Hence it is written in Eccles. VII, 19; "He that feareth God, neglecteth nothing." For the fear of God helps us to avoid all sins, as stated in Proverbs XV, 27: "by the fear of the Lord everyone declineth from evil." Therefore, fear makes us avoid negligence, yet not as negligence directly opposed to fear, but in so far as fear incites man to acts of reason. Wherefore it has been said that "fear makes us take counsel."

3. Negligence can be a mortal sin.

Hence it is written (Prov. XIX, 16), "He that neglecteth his own life shall die." Negligence arises from a certain remissness of the will, the result being a lack of solicitude on the part of the reason in commanding what it should command or as it should command. Accordingly, negligence may happen to be a mortal sin in two ways. First, on the part of that which is omitted through negligence. If this be either an act or a circumstance necessary for salvation, it will be a mortal sin. Secondly, on the part of the cause it can be a mortal sin, for if the will is so remiss about Divine things as to fall away altogether from the charity of God, such negligence is in truth a mortal sin and this happens when negligence is due to contempt.

But if negligence consists in the omission of an act of circumstance that is not necessary for salvation, it is not a mortal but a venial sin, provided the negligence arises, not from contempt, but from some lack of fervor to which venial sin is an occasional obstacle. (2a. 2ae. q. 54, a. 1 et 2, et 3.)

AUGUST 9

Intemperance

1. Intemperance is a childish sin. For the sin of intemperance is one of unchecked concupiscence, which is likened to a child in three ways. First as regards that which they both desire, for like a child, concupiscence desires something disgraceful. This is because in human affairs a thing is beautiful according as it harmonizes with reason. Now a child does not attend to the order of reason and in like manner concupiscence does not listen to reason.

Secondly, they are alike as to result, for a child, if left to his own will, becomes more self-willed. Hence it is written Eccles. XXX, 8, "A horse not broken becometh stubborn, and a child left to himself will become headstrong." So also concupiscence, if indulged gathers strength. Wherefore Saint Augustine says, "Lust served became a custom, and custom not resisted became a necessity."

Thirdly, as to the remedy which is applied to both the child and to concupiscence. For a child is corrected by being restrained. Hence it is said, "Withhold not correction from a child. . . . Thou shalt beat him with a rod, and deliver his soul from hell." (Prov. XXIII, 13.) In like manner by resisting concupiscence we moderate it according to the demands of virtue. Augustine means this when he says that "if the mind be lifted up to spiritual things, and remain fixed thereon, the impulse of custom, that is carnal concupiscence, is broken, and being suppressed is gradually weakened; for it was stronger when we followed it, and though not wholly destroyed, it certainly is less strong when we curb it." Hence the Philosopher says "that as a child ought to live according to the direction of his teacher, so ought the concupiscible to accord with reason."

2. Intemperance is the most disgraceful sin.

It is most disgraceful for two reasons. First, because it is most repugnant to human excellence, since it is about pleasures common to us and the lower animals, as stated in Psalm XLVIII, 21, "Man when he was in honor, did not understand, and he has been compared to senseless beasts and made like unto them."

Secondly, because intemperance is most repugnant to man's clarity or beauty, in so far as the pleasures which are the matter of intemperance dim the light of reason, from which all the brightness and beauty of virtue arises. Wherefore these pleasures are described as being most slavish or disgraceful. (2a. 2ae. q. 142, a 2 et 4.)

AUGUST 10

The Daughters of Lust

The daughters of lust are rightly said to be blindness of mind, thoughtlessness, rashness, inconstancy, self love, hatred of God, love of this world and abhorrence of a future world. For when the lower powers are strongly moved towards their objects, the result is that the higher powers are hindered and disordered in their acts. Now through the vice of lust especially, the lower appetite, the concupiscible, is most vehemently intent on its object, namely, pleasure, on account of the vehemence of the passion and pleasure. Hence the higher powers, the reason and the will, are most grievously disordered by lust.

Now the reason has four acts in matters of action, First, there is simple understanding, which apprehends some end as good and this act is hindered by lust; according to Daniel, XIII, 56, "Beauty hath deceived thee and lust hath perverted thy heart." In this respect we have blindness of mind.

Secondly, the act of counsel concerning those things which are to be done for an end and this is also retarded by the concupiscence of lust. Hence, Terence says, speaking of lecherous love, "This thing admits neither of counsel nor moderation. You cannot control it by counsel." In this respect there is rashness which is absence of counsel.

Thirdly, there is the act of judgment concerning things to be done and this again is hindered by lust. It is said of the lustful man (Dan. XIII, 9), "They turned away their own mind, so that they might not remember just judgments." In this respect there is thoughtlessness.

The fourth act is the reason's command about the thing to be done and this also is impeded by lust, in so far as being carried away by concupiscence, a man is hindered from doing what his reason ordered to be done. In this way inconstancy results. Hence Terence says of a man who declared he would leave his mistress, "One little false tear will undo these words."

On the part of the will there follows a twofold inordinate act. One is the desire for the end, to which we refer self love which regards the pleasure a man desires inordinately, while on the other hand there is hatred of God, by reason of the fact that God forbids the desired pleasure. The other act is the desire for the things directed to the end. With regard to this, there is love of this world whose pleasures a man desires to enjoy, while on the other hand there is despair of a future world because through being held back by carnal pleasures, he desires not to obtain spiritual pleasures since they are distasteful to him. (2a. 2ae. q. 153, a. 5.)

AUGUST 11

Ways of Conquering Lust

It must be remembered that in fleeing from the sin of lust, it behooves man to labor much; since lust is internal, a familiar enemy is conquered only with great difficulty. Lust is overcome in four ways. First, by flight from the external occasions, for example, bad society and all occasions leading to sin. "Gaze not upon a maiden, lest her beauty be a stumblingblock to thee. Look not around about thee in the ways of the city, nor wander up and down in the streets thereof. Turn away thy face from a woman dressed up, and gaze not upon another's beauty. For many have perished by the beauty of a woman, and thereby lust is enkindled as a fire"

(Eccli. IX, 5.) Again Proverbs VI, 27, says, "Can a man hide fire in his bosom, and his garments not burn?" Hence Lot was commanded by the Angel to flee every region around Sodom. "Save thy life, look not back, neither stay thou in all the country about but save thyself in the mountain, lest thou be also consumed" (Gen. XIX, 17.)

Secondly, lust is overcome by resisting the approach of bad thoughts, for they are the occasions exciting lust, and this must be done by mortification of the flesh. "I chastise my body and bring it under subjection" (1 Cor. IX, 27.)

Thirdly, by perseverance in prayer, for "Unless the Lord guards the city, he watches in vain, who guards it. I knew that I could not otherwise be continent, except God gave it, and I went to the Lord, and besought Him" (Wisdom VIII, 21.) Saint Matthew likewise declares (XVII, 20), "This kind of devil is not cast out except by prayer and fasting." If two persons should engage in a fight and you wish to aid one of them and not the other; it behooves you to aid the first and to withdraw your help from the second. Now between the spirit and the flesh there is a constant battle. Hence, it is necessary, if you wish the spirit to win that you assist it by prayer, while on the other hand you withdraw support from the flesh, and this is done through fasting; for the flesh and the lusts of the flesh are weakened by fast and abstinence.

Fourthly by regular occupations. "Idleness hath taught much evil" (Eccli. XXXIII, 29.) Again Ezechiel XVI, 49, declares: "This was the iniquity of Sodom, namely, pride, fulness of bread, abundance, and idleness." Hence Saint Jerome advises us saying: "Always be found doing something good, so that the devil will find you ever well occupied. Among all occupations, the study of Sacred Scripture is the best. Love the study of the Scriptures, and you will not love the vices of the flesh." (Decalogue, c. 30.)

AUGUST 12

Pride

The sin of pride may be considered in two ways. First, in respect to its proper species which it has from the nature of its proper object; and in this way pride is a special sin for it has a special object because it is an inordinate desire of one's own excellence, which fact is not in accord with right reason. For in respect to those things which man naturally desires, reason is his guide and so when anyone departs from the rule of right reason, either in excess or defect, the desire will be so much the more corrupt, as is clear from the desire for food which man naturally desires. But pride seeks an excellence in excess of right reason. A man is said to be proud because he wishes to appear above what he really is.

Secondly, pride may be considered as having a certain influence towards other sins. In this way it has a certain generic character inasmuch as all other sins may arise from pride in two ways.

First directly, in so far as other sins are directed to the end of pride, which is one's own excellence to which may be directed anything that is inordinately desired.

Secondly, indirectly and accidentally as it were, as when a man through pride despises the Divine Law which hinders him from sinning; according to Jeremias II, 20, "Thou hast broken My yoke, and thou saidst, I will not serve." (2a. 2æ. Q. 162, a. 2.)

AUGUST 13

The Wickedness of Pride

Gregory says that "pride is a most evident sign of the reprobate, and contrariwise, humility of the elect." But men do not become reprobate on account of venial sins. Therefore pride is not a venial but a mortal sin.

Pride is opposed to humility, which properly regards the subjection of man to God. Hence pride properly regards lack of this subjection, as a man exalts himself above that which is appointed to him according to the Divine rule or measure. "We will not glory beyond our measure; but according to the measure of the rule which God has measured to us." (2 Cor. X, 13.) Wherefore it is written (Eccles. X, 14), "The beginning of the pride of man is to fall off from God," because the root of pride is found to consist in man not being, in some way, subject to God and His rule. Now it is clear that not to be subject to God is of its very nature a mortal sin, for this consists in turning away from God and consequently pride is of its genus a mortal sin. But it happens that certain motions of pride are venial sins when reason does not consent to them.

2. Pride is the most grievous of sins.

Two things are to be observed in sin, conversion to a mutable good and this is the material part of sin; secondly, aversion from the immutable good which is the formal and complete nature of sin. Now on the part of the conversion, there is no reason for pride being the greatest of sins, because exaltation which pride covets inordinately has not essentially the greatest repugnance to the good of virtue. But on the part of the aversion, pride has extreme wickedness, because in other sins man turns away from God either through ignorance or through weakness or through desire for any other good whatever; whereas pride denotes man's absolute aversion from God, because he is unwilling to be subject to God and His rule. Hence Bœthius says that, "while all vices flee from God, pride alone resists God," for which reason it is especially stated (James IV, 6), "that God resisteth the proud, . . . and gives His grace to the humble." Wherefore aversion from God and His commandments, which is a consequence as it were in other sins belongs to pride by its nature for its act is the contempt of God. And since that which belongs to a thing by its nature is always of greater weight than that which belongs to it by something else, it follows that pride is the most grievous of sins by its genus, because it exceeds in aversion which formally completes sin.

Pride from the part of aversion is the greatest sin, since it brings greatness or wickedness upon other sins, for unbelief if it arises from proud contempt, becomes more grievous than if it results from ignorance or weakness. (2a. 2æ. Q. 152, a. 5 et 6.)

AUGUST 14

Pride Is the Beginning of Every Sin

1. The beginning of every sin is pride.

Some say pride can be considered in three ways. First, as denoting an inordinate desire to excel and thus it is a special sin. Secondly, as denoting actual contempt of God, not being subject to His commandment, and thus they claim it is a generic sin. Thirdly, as denoting an inclination to this contempt, owing to the corruption of nature; and in this sense they say it is the beginning of every sin, and that it differs from covetousness, because covetousness regards sin as turning toward the mutable good, by which sin is, as it were, nourished and fostered, for which reason covetousness is called the root; whereas pride regards sin as a turning away from God, to whose commandment man refuses to be subject, for which reason it is called the beginning, because the beginning of evil consists in turning away from God.

Now all this is true, nevertheless it is not in keeping with the mind of the wise man who said, "Pride is the beginning of all sin." For it is clear he is speaking of pride as denoting an inordinate desire to excel. Wherefore pride, in so far as it is a special sin, is the beginning of every sin.

In voluntary actions such as sins are, a twofold order exists, the order of intention and of execution. In the former order the principle is the end. Now man's end in acquiring all temporal goods, is that through their means he may have some perfection and excellence. Therefore, from this point of view, pride which is the desire to excel, is said to be the beginning of every sin. But, from the part of execution, the first place belongs to that which by furnishing the opportunity of fulfilling all desires of sin has the character of a root, and such are riches; so that from this point of view, covetousness is said to be the root of all evil.

2. Pride is the queen and mother of all vices.

Pride may be considered in two ways; first in itself, as being a special sin; secondly, as having a general influence towards all sins. Now the capital vices are said to be certain special sins from which many kinds of sin arise. Wherefore some considering pride in the light of a special sin, numbered it together with the other capital vices. But Gregory, considering its general influence towards all vices, did not place it among the capital vices, but held it to be the queen and mother of all vices. Hence he says, "Pride, the queen of vices, when it has vanquished and captured the heart, immediately delivers it in the hands of its lieutenants the seven principal vices, that they may despoil it, and produce vices of all kinds." (2a. 2æ. Q. 162, a. 8.)

AUGUST 15

The Assumption of the Blessed Virgin Mary

1. *"I was exalted like a cedar in Libanus."* (Eccli. XXV, 17.)

The exaltation of the Blessed Virgin mentioned here can be understood as the six orders of the blessed by means of the six trees to which her exaltation is compared.

A cedar signifies angels because of its natural loftiness.

A cypress signifies patriarchs and prophets because of its sweet odor. Hence it is said of one, "Behold the odor of my son is as the odor of a plentiful field." (Gen. XXVII, 27.)

A palm tree signifies the apostles on account of their glorious victory over the world, for a palm is significant of triumph.

A rose signifies martyrs because of their effusion of blood which has a reddish color. "And as a rose plant in Jericho." (Eccli. XXIV, 27.)

The elm signifies virgins for it grows by the river banks and is immune like virgins from the cold or heat of lustful desires.

The olive tree signifies confessors by reason of its oil. "I, as a fruitful olive tree in the house of God, have hoped in the mercy of God forever." (Ps. LI, 10.)

2. It is therefore in this sense that the Blessed Virgin is exalted as the angels, patriarchs, prophets, Apostles, martyrs, confessors and virgins; even exalted above the choirs of Angels and all the Saints of heaven. Nor is this wonderful. For she by living as an angel possessed the merit of the angels. Jerome says, "that to live in the flesh, but not of the flesh, is not an earthly life, it is heavenly. Virginity is the sister of the Angels."

She possessed the merit of a prophet by her prophecy. "Behold all generations shall call me Blessed" (Luke I). She saw with a prophetic vision and prophesied that she would be blessed by all nations, and that all nations must receive the Son of God, and her Son.

She possessed the merit of the Apostles and Evangelists in teaching. For many things are written and preached which could not be known unless through her revelation, such as the visit of the Angel Gabriel to Mary and many other things.

She possessed the merit of a martyr by patiently enduring the death of the Cross with her Son. "Thy own soul, a sword shall pierce" (Luke II).

She possessed the merit of the confessors by devoutly acknowledging her Lord. "My soul doth magnify the Lord" (Luke I).

She possessed the merit of virgins in beginning and preserving her virginity. "And the Angel Gabriel came to the Virgin Mary" (Luke I, 27).

Consequently, just as Mary possessed the merit of all, so it was becoming that she should be exalted above all. (Discourse 58.)

AUGUST 16

The Way to Avoid Pride

1. A sin is difficult to avoid in two ways. First, on account of the violence of its attack, thus anger is violent in its attack because of its impetuosity, and still more difficult is it to resist concupiscence on account of its connaturality. A difficulty of this kind in avoiding sin lessens the seriousness of the sin, because a man sins the more grievously according as he yields to a less impetuous temptation.

Secondly, it is difficult to avoid pride, for it takes occasion even from good deeds. Hence Augustine says pointedly that "pride lies in wait for good deeds," and it is written (Psalm CXLI, 4), "In the way wherein I walked, the proud have hidden a snare for me."

Hence no very great gravity attaches itself to the movement of pride while creeping in secretly before it is discovered by the judgment of reason; but once discovered by reason, it is easily avoided both by considering one's infirmity, according to Eccles. X, 9, "Why is earth and ashes proud?" and by considering God's greatness, according to Job XV, 13, "Why doth thy spirit swell against God?" as well as by considering the imperfections of the goods on which man prides himself, according to Isaias XL, 6, "All flesh is grass, and all the glory thereof as the flower of the field."

2. In order to overcome their pride God punishes certain men by allowing them to fall into sins of the flesh, which though they may be less grievous are more evidently shameful. Hence Isidore says, "that pride is the worst of all vices; whether it is appropriate to those who are of highest or fore-

most rank, or because it originates from just and virtuous deeds, so that its guilt is less perceptible. On the other hand, carnal lust is apparent to all, because from the outset it is of a shameful nature; and yet, under God's dispensation, it is less grievous than pride. For he who is in the clutches of pride and feels it not, falls into the lusts of the flesh, that being thus humbled he may rise from his disgrace.

From this indeed the gravity of pride is made manifest. For just as a wise physician, in order to cure a worse disease, allows the patient to contract one that is less dangerous, so the sin of pride is shown to be more grievous by the very fact that, as a remedy, God allows man to fall into other sins. (2a. 2ae. Q. 162, a. VI, ad 1um. et 3um.)

AUGUST 17

Vain Glory

1. Glory properly so called, signifies a certain good which comes to the knowledge and approval of many. If the word is taken in a larger sense, it not only consists in the knowledge of many but also in the knowledge of few, or of one, or of oneself, as when one considers one's own good as worthy of praise. Now it is not a sin to know and approve one's own good; for it is written (1 Cor. II, 12), "Now we have received not the spirit of this world, but the Spirit that is of God, that we may know the things that are given us from God." Likewise it is not a sin to be willing to approve one's own good works; for it is written (Matt. V, 16), "Let your light shine before men." Hence the desire for glory does not, of itself denote a sin; but the desire for empty or vain glory denotes a sin for it is sinful to desire anything vain; according to Psalm IV, 3, "Why do you love vanity, and seek after lying?"

Now glory may be called vain in three ways. First, on the part of the thing for which one seeks glory as when a man seeks glory for that which is unworthy of glory, for example, when he seeks it from something frail and perishable. Secondly, on the part of him from whom he seeks glory for instance a man whose judgment is uncertain. Thirdly, on the part of the man himself who seeks glory, when he does not refer the desire of his own glory to its proper end, such as God's honour, or the spiritual welfare of his neighbour.

2. A sin of vain glory, that is contrary to charity, can be mortal in two ways. In one way, because of the matter about which one glories, for example, when one glories in something false that is opposed to the reverence we owe to God, according to Ezech. XXVIII, 2, "Thy heart is lifted up and thou hast said I am God," and 1 Cor. IV, 7, "What has thou which thou hast not received? And if thou hast received, why dost thou glory, as if thou hast not received it?" Or again when a man prefers to God the temporal goods in which he glories, for this is forbidden (Jerem. IX, 23, 24), "Let not the wise man glory in his wisdom, and let not the strong man glory in his strength, and let not the rich man glory in his riches. But let him that glorieth glory in this, that he understandeth and knoweth Me." Or again when a man prefers the testimony of man to the testimony of God, thus it is written in condemnation of certain people (John XII, 43), "For they loved the glory of men more than the glory of God."

In another way, vain glory may be contrary to charity on the part of the one who glories, as when he refers his intention to glory as to his last end, so that he even directs virtuous deeds thereto, and in order to obtain it refrains not from doing that which is against God. And so this is a mortal sin.

Therefore, vain glory is a dangerous sin not only on account of its gravity, but also because it disposes one to grave sins, as it makes man presumptuous and too self-confident; and so it gradually disposes man to lose his inward good. (2a. 2æ. Q. 132, a. 1 et 3.)

AUGUST 18

Vain Glory Is a Capital Vice

1. Some speak of capital vices in two ways. Some place pride as one of the capital vices, and these do not reckon vain glory among the capital vices. Gregory, however, considers pride to be the queen of all vices, and vain glory as the immediate offspring of pride, he reckons to be a capital vice and not without reason. For pride denotes an inordinate

desire of excellence. But whatever good one may desire, one desires a certain perfection and excellence therefrom. Wherefore the end of every vice is directed to the end of pride, so that this vice seems to exercise a kind of causality over the other vices and ought not to be enumerated among the special sources of vice, known as the capital vices. Now among the goods that are the means whereby man acquires honour, glory seems to be the most influential to that effect, inasmuch as it denotes the manifestation of a man's goodness, since good is naturally loved and honoured by all. Wherefore, just as by the glory which is in God's sight, man acquires honour in Divine things, so too by the glory which is in the sight of man, he acquires excellence in human things. Hence on account of its close connection with excellence, which men desire above all, it follows that glory is most desirable. And because many vices arise from the inordinate desire of glory, it follows that vain glory is a capital vice.

2. From vain glory arise boastfulness, love of novelties, hypocrisy, contention, obstinacy, discord and disobedience, which are the daughters of vain glory. These vices which by their very nature are such as are directed to the end of a certain capital vice, are called its daughters. Now the end of vain glory is the manifestation of one's own excellence and to this end a man may tend in two ways.

In one way directly, either by words, and this is boasting or by deeds, and then if they be true and call for astonishment, it is love of novelties, which men are wont to wonder at most, but if they be false it is hypocrisy.

In another way a man strives to make known his excellence by showing that he is not inferior to another and this in four ways.

First, as regards the intellect, and thus we have obstinacy by which a man is too much attached to his own opinion, being unwilling to believe one that is better.

Secondly, as regards the will and then we have discord, whereby a man is unwilling to give up his own will and agree with others.

Thirdly, as regards speech and then contention results, whereby a man quarrels noisily with another.

Fourthly, as regards actions and this is disobedience, whereby a man refuses to carry out the command of his superiors. (2a. 2æ. q. 132, a. 4 et 5.)

AUGUST 19

The Garments of Virtues

"Put on the garments of thy glory, O Jerusalem." (Isaias LII, 1.)

1. These garments are virtues by which man becomes good. The old law contained certain commandments concerning the actions of these virtues and this reasonably so. For just as the principal purpose of the human law is to cultivate the friendship of man for man, so the intention of the Divine Law is principally to cultivate the friendship of man for God. Since moreover likeness is the reason for love; according to Eccli. XIII, "Every beast loveth its like," it is impossible for men to have friendship for God unless men become good. Hence it is written, Lev. XIX, 2, "Be ye holy, because I the Lord your God am Holy." But the goodness of man consists in virtue, which makes a man good who has it. Therefore it is necessary to have commandments of the law concerning the actions of virtues and these are the moral precepts, such as "thou shalt not kill, thou shalt not steal." (1, 2, q. 99, a. XI.)

2. The Saints have the garments of virtues in which they glory, and these garments are for a threefold purpose, for protection, for warmth and for prayer.

1. For protection. "I will greatly rejoice in the Lord, and my soul shall be joyful in my God; for He has clothed me with the garments of salvation, and with the robe of justice He has covered me, as a bridegroom decked with a crown, and as a bride adorned with her jewels." (Isaias LXI, 10.)

2. For warmth. "She shall not fear for her house in the cold of snow, for all her domestics are clothed with double garments" (Prov. XXXI, 21), namely with the garments of temperance, chastity, mercy, which are the praise and garments of the wise.

3. For prayer. "That thou mayest be clothed in white garments of virtue, and that the shame of thy nakedness may not appear" (Apoc. III, 18).

But these garments should be white with the honesty of work. "At all times let thy garments be white" (Eccl. IX, 8.) Clean with the uprightness of intention. "Every garment mingled with blood, shall be burnt, and be fuel for the fire" (Isaias IX, 5). Sweet smelling, by the renown of their fame. "The smell of thy garments as the smell of frankincense" (Cant. IV, 11).

3. But the most glorious and precious garment is Christ Himself. "Put ye on the Lord Jesus Christ" Rom. XIII, in Whom are all the virtues in the greatest abundance. We moreover put on the Lord Jesus Christ, first, through the reception of His sacrament. "For as many of you as have been baptized in Christ, have put on Christ" (Gal. III, 27). Secondly, through imitation of Christ. "Stripping yourself of the old man with his deeds, and putting on the new, according to the image of Him Who created you. Put ye on therefore, as the elect of God, holy and beloved" (Col III, 9). And again St. Paul speaking to the Ephesians, IV, 23, says, "Be renewed in the spirit of your mind, and put on the new man, who according to God is created in justice and holiness of truth." But, one is said to put on Christ who imitates the virtues of Christ, for just as a man is clothed with a garment and under its color appears in public, so in him who imitates Christ and lives the life of Christ, the works of Christ shine forth.

Just as he who is clothed with any garment is protected and covered by it and appears under the color of that vesture, so too, he who has put on Christ is protected and covered and shielded by Christ Jesus against evil assaults and storms of life and in that man nothing else appears but the things of Christ. And just as the kindled wood is covered with fire and participates in its power, so the man who has the virtues of Christ is clothed with Christ.

But remember that some clothe themselves exteriorly with Christ through good conversation or clean speech and interiorly through a renewed mind, and in both ways through likeness of His sanctity. (Gal. III.)

AUGUST 20

Virtue True and Great

1. Concerning true virtue. An act of virtue may be considered in two ways. First, materially, thus an act of justice is to do what is just and such an act of virtue can be without virtue, since many without having the habit of justice do what is just, led by the natural light of reason or through fear or in the hope of gain.

Secondly, something done is said to be an act of justice formally, and thus an act of justice is to do what is just in the way in which a just man acts, for example, with readiness and delight. In this manner an act of virtue cannot be without virtue.

Accordingly almsgiving can be material, without charity being in the giver, but to give alms formally, that is, for God's sake with delight and readiness and altogether as one should is not possible without charity. Hence Saint Paul says, 1 Cor. XIII, 3, that it is possible to give alms without having true charity, "If I should distribute all my goods to feed the poor . . . and have not charity, it profiteth me nothing."

2. Concerning the great virtue.

In virtuous actions two things must be always considered, namely, the thing which is done, and secondly, the manner or purpose for which it is done. It happens moreover, that the same thing which should be done in accord with perfect virtue is oftentimes done not only by a person having little virtue or by one possessing no virtue. But if we consider the purpose or manner of performing a virtuous act, then he who has not the virtue cannot operate like the person with the virtue, neither can the person with little virtue work like the one with great virtue who acts with ease, promptness and delight. But whosoever lacks virtue or possesses little virtue cannot act thus.

Accordingly, were one to offer himself as a martyr or even suffer martyrdom, this act can be performed not only with perfect charity but even with imperfect, yea more, performed by one lacking in charity; according to the Apostle. "If I should deliver my body to be burned, and have not charity, I am nothing." But perfect charity acts promptly and delightfully as is clear from the examples of Lawrence and Vincent, who showed such remarkable cheerfulness during their torments and sufferings. This cannot be done by one having but imperfect charity, nor by one lacking in charity.

3. The example from faith. Can faith be greater in one person than in another? I answer affirmatively, for wherever there is found little and great, there is found greater and less. But in matters of faith we find great faith and little faith, for our Lord said to Peter, "O thou of little faith, why didst thou doubt?" (Matt. XIV, 31.) And to the woman Christ said, "Woman, great is thy faith." Therefore faith can be greater in one person than in another.

Moreover, an act of faith proceeds both from the intellect and from the will. Therefore faith in one person can be said to be greater in one way from the part of the intellect, because of greater certitude and conviction. In another way from the part of the will, because of greater promptness, greater devotion or greater confidence. It is of the very nature of Faith, that the First Truth (namely that God exists) be preferred above all, but among those who place this great truth above all truths, some persons more than others subject themselves to it (cling to it) with greater certainty, and greater devotion. (2a. 2æ. Q. 5, a. 4.)

AUGUST 21

The Advantages and Necessity of Faith

Faith accomplishes four things.
1. By faith the soul is united to God, for through faith the soul enters into a certain union or marriage with God. "I will espouse thee to Myself in faith." (Osee. II, 20.) Hence it is that a man when he is baptized, first professes faith when the Priest says to him, "Do you believe in God?" for baptism is the first sacrament of faith. Therefore the Lord said, "He who believes and is baptized, shall be saved." Baptism without faith availeth nothing, and therefore we must remember that without faith no one is acceptable to God. For this reason, Saint Augustine, while commenting on Rom. XV, 23, "All that is not of faith is sin," says, "Where there is no knowledge of the eternal and unchangeable Truth, there, virtue is false even in the best morality."
2. Through faith eternal life is begun in us, for eternal life is nothing more than to know God. Hence the Lord said, "This is eternal life that they might know Thee the Only true God." But this knowledge of God in us begins here through faith and is perfected in eternal life, where we will know God as He is in Himself. Therefore it is written (Heb. XI, 1), "Faith is the substance of things to be hoped for." Therefor no one can obtain eternal blessedness, which is the true knowledge of God, unless through faith here he first acknowledges God.
3. Faith directs our present life. In order that man might live well, he should know what is necessary to live well. But faith teaches these things; for it teaches there is One God, the Rewarder of the good and Punisher of the wicked; and that there is another life beyond the grave, and by the

knowledge of these things we love good and hate evil. "The just man liveth by faith." (Heb. X, 38.) And this is clear from the fact that none of the philosophers before the advent of Christ were able to know as much of God and eternal life, as an old and devout woman knew through faith after Christ came. And therefore Isaias XI, 9, says, "The earth is filled with the knowledge of the Lord."

Faith is that supernatural virtue by which we conquer temptations. "By faith the saints conquered kingdoms, wrought justice, obtained promises, stopped the mouths of lions, quenched the violence of fire, recovered strength from weakness, became valiant in battle and put to flight the armies of foreigners. Through faith women received their dead raised to life again. But without faith it is impossible to please God, for he who comes to God must believe that He exists and is a Rewarder to them that seek Him" (Heb. XI, 33). Through faith we overcome temptations. This is clear because every temptation is either from the devil, the world or the flesh. The devil tempts us so that we might not obey God nor subject ourselves to Him. This diabolical temptation is removed through faith, for through faith we know that God is the Lord of all and consequently we are obliged to obey Him. "Be sober and watch, because your adversary the devil, as a roaring lion, goeth about seeking whom he may devour" (1 Peter V, 8).

The world tempts us, either by seducing us with its vanities or by terrifying us with its misfortunes. But even these we can conquer through faith, which enables us to believe in another life superior to this and teaches us to believe that better things are awaiting us. Hence by faith, we conquer the vanities of this world and fear not its adversities. "This is the victory which overcometh the world, your faith" (1 John V, 4.)

The flesh tempts us by attracting us to the pleasures of the present life, which pleasures at most, are fast fleeting and perishable. But faith warns us that through these pleasures, if we cling to them improperly, we will lose eternal happiness. (The Creed.)

AUGUST 22

The Effects of Faith

1. Fear is an effect of faith.

Through faith there arises in us an apprehension of certain penal evils, which are inflicted according to the Divine judgment. In this way then faith is the cause of fear, whereby one dreads to be punished by God and this is slavish fear.

It is also a cause of filial fear, whereby one dreads to be separated from God or whereby one shrinks from equaling oneself to Him and holds Him in reverence, as faith makes us appreciate God, the unfathomable and supreme good, separation from Whom is the greatest evil and to Whom it is wicked to wish to be equalled.

Of the first fear, namely slavish fear, lifeless faith is the cause, while living faith is the cause of the second, namely filial fear, because it makes man adhere to God and to be subject to Him by charity.

Although it is said in Eccli. XI, 2, "That thou mayest fear God, believe in Him," it must not be concluded that fear of God altogether precedes faith, because if we knew nothing at all about Him with regard to rewards and punishments, concerning which faith teaches us, we should nowise fear Him. If, however, faith be presupposed in reference to certain articles of faith, for example the Divine excellence, then reverential fear follows, the result of which is, that man submits his intellect to God, so as to believe in all the Divine promises. And hence it is written "Your reward shall not be void" (Ecc. XI, 3).

2. The purification of the heart is an effect of faith. "Purifying their hearts by faith" (Acts XV, 9). The impurity of anything consists in being mixed with baser things, for silver is not called impure, when mixed with gold which improves it, but when mixed with lead or tin. Now it is clear that the rational creature is more excellent than all transient and corporeal creatures, so that he becomes impure through subjecting himself to transient things by loving them.

From this impurity the rational creature is purified by means of a contrary movement, namely, by tending to that which is above, namely God. The first beginning of this movement is faith, since "he that cometh to God must believe that He is," according to Heb. XI, 6. Hence the first beginning of the heart's purification is faith, by which the impurity of error is purified and if this be perfected through being quickened by charity the heart will be perfectly purified thereby. (2a, 2æ. Q. 7, a. 1 and 2.)

AUGUST 23

Hope

1. The proper object of hope is eternal happiness.
Hope reaches God by leaning on His help in order to obtain the desired good. Now, an effect must be proportionate to its cause. Hence the good which we ought to hope for from God properly and chiefly is the infinite good, which is proportionate to the power of our Divine Helper, since it belongs to an infinite power to lead anything to an infinite good. Such a good is eternal life, which consists in the enjoyment of God Himself. For we should hope from Him for nothing less than Himself since His goodness, whereby He imparts good things to His creatures is no less than His essence. Therefore the proper and principal object of hope is eternal happiness.

2. Hope is a theological virtue distinct from the other theological virtues. A virtue is said to be theological when it has God for its object. Now, one may adhere to a thing in two ways, first, for its own sake, secondly, because something else is attained thereby. Hence, charity makes us adhere to God for His own sake, uniting our minds to God by the emotion of love.

On the other hand, hope and faith make man adhere to God as to a principle wherefrom certain things come to us. Now we derive from God both knowledge of truth and the attainment of perfect goodness. Hence, faith makes us adhere to God as the source from whence we derive the knowledge of truth, since we believe that what God tells us is true, while hope makes us adhere to God as the source from whence we derive perfect goodness, that is, by hope we trust to the Divine assistance for obtaining happiness.

3. Hence in the order of generation, hope precedes charity. For just as a man is led to love God for fear of being punished by Him for his sins, so also, hope leads to charity inasmuch as a man through hope of being rewarded by God, is encouraged to love God and obey His commandments. On the other hand, in the order of perfection charity naturally

precedes hope, wherefore with the coming of charity, hope is made more perfect, because we hope chiefly in our friends. It is in this sense that Ambrose states that charity flows from hope.

4. Hope has certainty, for hope is a certain expectation of future happiness, as the Master states (3 Sent. D. 26) and this also can be concluded from 2 Tim. I, 12, "I know Whom I have believed, and I am certain that He is able to keep that which I have committed to Him." In this life we cannot know with certainty that we have grace. But hope does not trust chiefly on grace already received but on God's all Powerfulness and Mercy, whereby even he that has not grace can obtain it, so as to come to eternal life. Now whoever has faith is certain of God's Omnipotence and Mercy.

That some who have hope fail to obtain happiness is due to a fault of the free will in placing the obstacle of sin, but not to any deficiency in God's power or mercy in which hope places its trust. Hence this does not prejudice the certainty of hope. (2a. 2æ. q. 17, a. 2, 6, 8, and q. 18, a. 4.)

AUGUST 24

The Excellence of Charity

"Now there remain faith, hope, charity, these three; but the greatest of these is charity." (I Cor. XIII, 13.)

1. Charity is the greatest amongst the theological virtues.

The greatness of a virtue, as to its species, is taken from its object. Now, since the three theological virtues behold God as their proper object, it cannot be said that anyone of them is greater than another by reason of its having a greater object, but only from the fact that it approaches nearer than another to that object and in this way charity is greater than the others. Because the others in their very nature, imply a certain distance from the object; since faith is of what is not seen and hope is concerning what is not possessed. But the love of charity is about that which is already possessed, since the beloved is, in a manner, in the lover, and again the lover is drawn by desire to union with the beloved; wherefore it is written (1 John IV, 16), "He that abideth in charity, abideth in God, and God in him." (1, 2ae. q. 66, a. 6.)

2. Charity is the form and root of all the virtues. "Rooted and founded in charity." (3 ph. III, 17.)

Now it is clear that it is charity which directs the acts of all the other virtues to their last end; for the last and principal good of man is the enjoyment of God, according to, Psalm LXXII, 27, "It is good for me to adhere to God." But to this end man is directed through charity and in this way charity gives form to all the other acts of virtues.

Charity is compared to the foundation or root in so far as all other virtues draw their sustenance and nourishment therefrom. Charity is called the end of the other virtues, because it directs all other virtues to its own end. And since a mother is one who conceives within herself and by another, charity is called the mother of the other virtues, because by commanding them it conceives the acts of the other virtues by the desire of the last end.

3. Charity is caused in us by infusion.

Charity is a friendship of man for God, founded upon the fellowship of everlasting happiness. Now this fellowship is in respect, not of natural, but of gratuitous gifts, for according to Rom. VI, 23, "the grace of God is life everlasting." Wherefore, charity itself surpasses our natural faculties. Now that which surpasses the power of nature, cannot be natural or acquired by the natural powers, since a natural effect does not transcend its cause. Therefore, charity can be in us neither naturally nor through acquisition by the natural powers, but by the infusion of the Holy Ghost, Who is the love of the Father and the Son and the participation of Whom in us is created charity.

God is supremely lovable in Himself, inasmuch as He is the object of happiness. But He is not supremely lovable to us in this way, on account of the inclination of our appetite towards visible goods. Hence it is evident that for us to love God above all things in this way, it is necessary that charity be infused into our hearts. (2, 2ae. q. 24, a. 2.)

AUGUST 25

The Fear of the Lord

"The fear of the Lord is the beginning of wisdom." (Ps. CX, 10.)

A thing may be called the beginning of wisdom in two ways. In one way because it is the beginning of wisdom itself as to its essence, in another way, as to its effect. Now, since wisdom is the knowledge of Divine things it is considered by us in one way and in another way by philosophers. For, seeing that our life is ordained to the enjoyment of God and is directed thereto by a participation of the Divine nature conferred on us through grace, wisdom, as we look at it, is considered as not only being cognizant of God, as it is with the philosophers, but also as directing human conduct, since this is directed not only by human law but also by the Divine law.

Therefore, the beginning of wisdom as to its essence consists in the first principles of wisdom, that is, in the articles of faith and in this sense faith is said to be the beginning of wisdom. But, as regards the effect, the beginning of wisdom is the point where wisdom begins to work and in this way fear is the beginning of wisdom, yet, servile fear in one way and filial fear in another. For servile fear is like a principle disposing a man to wisdom from without, in so far as he refrains from sin through fear of punishment and is thus fashioned for the effect of wisdom, according to Eccles. I, 27, "The fear of the Lord driveth out sin." On the other hand chaste or filial fear is the beginning of wisdom, as being the first effect of wisdom. For since the regulation of human conduct by the Divine law belongs to wisdom, in order to make a beginning man must first of all fear God and submit himself to Him; for the result will be that in all things he will be ruled by God.

But it is written (Job XXVIII, 28), "The fear of the Lord is wisdom," that is, because the fear of God is compared to a man's whole life that is ruled by God's wisdom, as the root to the tree. Hence it is said (Eccles. I, 25), "The root of wisdom is to fear the Lord, for the branches thereof are longlived." Consequently, as the root is said to be virtually the tree, so the fear of God is said to be virtually wisdom.

2. Poverty of spirit properly corresponds to fear. Because since it belongs to filial fear to show reverence and submission to God, whatever results from this submission belongs

to the gift of fear. Now from the very fact that a man submits to God, it follows that he ceases to seek greatness either in himself or in another but seeks it only in God, wherefore it is written (Psalm XIX, 8), "Some trust in chariots and some in horses; but we will call upon the name of our God." Hence, it follows if a man fears God perfectly, he does not by pride seek greatness, either in himself or in external goods, honours and riches. In either case this proceeds from poverty of spirit, as poverty of spirit denotes the emptying of a puffed up and proud spirit or the renunciation of worldly goods, which is done in spirit, that is, by one's own will through the influence of the Holy Spirit. (2a. 2ae. q. 19, a. 7 and 8.)

AUGUST 26

The Cardinal Virtues

1. There are four cardinal virtues, prudence, justice, fortitude and temperance. The aforesaid four virtues are understood differently by various writers. For some take them as signifying certain general conditions of the human mind, to be found in all virtues; so that prudence is merely a certain rectitude of discretion in any actions or matters whatever; justice, a certain rectitude of the mind whereby man does what he should in any event; temperance, a disposition of the mind moderating passions or operations so as to keep them within bounds; and fortitude, a disposition whereby the soul is strengthened for that which is in accord with right reason against any assaults of the passions or the labor involved by any operations.

Others, however, with better reason, take these four virtues according as they have their special determinate matter; each its own matter, in which special commendation is given to that general condition from which the name of the virtue is taken. In this way it is clear that the aforesaid virtues are distinct habits, differentiated in regard to their diverse objects.

2. Now these four virtues differ by reason of a difference of movement and term, so that some are virtues of men who are on their way and tending towards the Divine likeness, and these are called perfecting virtues, in as far as man in using them publicly desires the solitude of contemplation. Thus prudence by contemplating the things of God, counts as nothing

all the things of the world and directs all the thoughts of the soul to God alone; temperance, so far as nature allows, neglects the needs of the body; fortitude prevents the soul from being afraid of neglecting the body and rising to heavenly things; and justice consists in the soul giving a whole-hearted consent to follow the way thus proposed.

Besides these virtues, there are virtues for those who have already attained the Divine likeness, which are called perfect virtues or purgative virtues of the soul. Thus prudence sees nought else but the things of God, temperance refrains from all earthly desires, fortitude conquers all passions, and justice, by imitating the Divine Mind, is united thereto by an everlasting covenant. Such are the virtues attributed to the Blessed, or in this life to some who are at the summit of perfection. (1, 2ae. Q. 61, a. 4 and 5.)

AUGUST 27

Prudence

1. *"Prudence is wisdom for man."* (Prov. X, 25.)

A prudent man is one who is capable of taking good counsel. He therefore, is wise in any particular genus who considers the highest cause in that genus. Now in the genus of human acts the highest cause is the common end of all human life, and prudence intends this end. For the Philosopher says that just as he who reasons well for the realization of a particular end, such as victory is said to be prudent, not absolutely, but in a particular genus, namely warfare, so that he who reasons well with regard to right conduct as a whole, is said to be prudent absolutely. Wherefore it is clear that prudence is wisdom about human affairs.

2. Prudence as such cannot be in sinners. Prudence is threefold. There is a false prudence which takes its name from its likeness to true prudence. For since a prudent man is one who disposes well of the things that have to be done for a good end, whoever disposes well of such things as are fitting for an evil end has false prudence, in so far as that which he takes for an end is good, not in truth but in appearance. Thus a man is called **a good robber** and in this way we may speak of a prudent robber by way of similarity, because he devises fitting

ways for committing robbery. This is the kind of prudence of which the Apostle speaks (Rom. VIII, 6), "The prudence of the flesh is death," because it places its ultimate end in the pleasures of the flesh.

The second prudence is indeed true prudence, because it plans fitting ways of securing a good end; and yet it is imperfect, from a twofold source. First, because the good which it takes for an end is not the common end of all human life but of some particular affair; thus when a man plans fitting ways of conducting business or of sailing a ship, he is called a prudent business man or a prudent sailor. Secondly, because he fails in the chief act of prudence, as when a man takes counsel aright and forms a good judgment even about things concerning life as a whole, but fails to command effectively.

The third prudence is both true and perfect, for it takes counsel, judges and commands aright in respect to the good end of man's whole life, and this alone is prudence simply so-called and cannot be in sinners, whereas the first prudence is in sinners alone, while imperfect prudence is common to good and wicked men, especially that which is imperfect, because it is directed to a particular end, for that which is imperfect on account of a failing in the chief act is only in the wicked.

3. Cicero rightly divides prudence into memory of the past, knowledge of the present and foreknowledge of the future. For prudence is concerned about particular works, and the prudent man reasons rightly concerning these things which he must do, so that from the things which exist and which he keeps in memory and from the things which his intellect considers, he provides for the future. For memory is that faculty by which the mind reflects or recalls those things which happen, intelligence that faculty by which one examines those things which exist, while foreknowledge is that by which some future event is seen before it happens. (3 Dist. 23, q. 3, a. 1.)

AUGUST 28

Justice

1. It seems to belong to justice that each one pays his debt. Hence all the mortal virtues which are about actions belong in a certain general way to justice, for they have in a certain manner the nature of a debt. But the debt is not of

the same nature in all for one may owe something to an equal, another to a superior, another to a subject, another may owe something because of a contract or promise or by reason of a favor received. Hence because of the diverse nature of the debt, different virtues are employed; for example, religion by which a debt is paid to God, loyalty by which a debt is rendered to our parents and to our country, thanksgiving by which we render a debt to our benefactors and so on concerning other virtues. And there is legal justice which is called a general virtue as it directs all the virtues to the common good.

But in addition to justice which intends the common good, there is another justice properly called, which is intended for the private good of each one, so that it might be rendered to each one what belongs to him.

2. Justice is the most excellent of all the virtues.

If we speak of legal justice it is clear that it stands foremost among all the moral virtues, inasmuch as the common good transcends the individual good of one person. In this sense Aristotle declares that "the most excellent of the virtues would seem to be justice, and more glorious than the star of eve or dawn."

But even if we speak of particular justice, it excels the other moral virtues for two reasons. A virtue is said to be greater in so far as from it shines forth a greater intellectual good. In this way justice excels in so far as it comes closer to right reason. The first reason may be taken from the subject and the second from the object. From the subject, because justice is in the more excellent part of the soul, for instance, in the rational appetite or will, whereas the other moral virtues are in the sensitive appetite to which pertain the passions, which are the matter of the other moral virtues. The second reason is taken from the object, because justice is concerned about actions by which a man is directed not only in regard to his own welfare, but also for the good of others and so justice is somewhat the good of another person. Hence Aristotle says, "The greatest virtues must needs be those which are most profitable to other persons, since virtue is a faculty of doing good to others. For this reason the greatest honours are accorded the brave and the just, since bravery is useful to others in warfare, and justice is useful to others both in warfare and in time of peace.

3. The precepts of the Decalogue are precepts of justice.

The precepts of the decalogue are the first principles of the Law and the natural reason assents to them at once as to principles that are most evident. Now it is altogether evident that the idea of duty, which is essential to a precept appears in justice which is towards another. Because in those matters which relate to himself it would seem at a glance that man is master of himself and that he may do as he likes, whereas in matters that refer to another it appears manifestly that a man is under obligation to render to another that which is his due. Hence the precepts of the decalogue must needs pertain to justice. Wherefore the first precepts are about acts of religion which is the chief part of justice, the fourth precept is about acts of piety which is the second part of justice, and the six remaining are about justice commonly so called which is observed among equals. (2a. 2ae. q. 122, a. 1.)

AUGUST 29

Fortitude

1. The word fortitude can be understood in two ways. First as simply denoting a certain firmness of mind, and in this sense it is a general virtue or rather a condition of every virtue, because it is a requisite of every virtue to act firmly and immovably. Secondly, fortitude may be understood to denote firmness only in bearing and withstanding those things wherein it is most difficult to be firm, namely, in certain grave dangers. Therefore Cicero says that "fortitude is deliberate facing of dangers and bearing of toils." In this sense fortitude is considered a special virtue because it has a special matter.

2. Fortitude is chiefly concerned around the dangers of death. It belongs to the virtue of fortitude to guard the will of man and remove any obstacle that withdraws the will from following the reason, withdraws it from the good of reason because of fear of corporal evil. Now it behooves one to hold firmly the good of reason against every evil whatsoever, since no bodily good is equivalent to the good of the reason. Hence fortitude of soul must be that which binds the will firmly to the good of reason in face of the greatest evils; because he that stands firm against great things will in consequence stand firm against less things but not conversely. Moreover it pertains to the notion of virtue that it should regard something extreme, and the most fearful of all bodily evils is death since it deprives us of all bodily goods.

Therefore the virtue of fortitude is about the fear of the dangers of death.

Fortitude therefore, consists in this that man does not depart from the good of virtue on account of the dangers of death which seem to hang over him. Now fortitude is a virtue; and it is essential to virtue ever to tend to good. Wherefore it is in order to pursue some good that man does not fly from the danger of death. The dangers of death which occur in battle come to a man directly on account of some good, because he is defending the common good by a just fight. Now a just fight is of two kinds. First, there is the general combat, for instance, of those who actually fight in battle; secondly, there is the private combat, as when a judge or even a private individual does not refrain from giving a just judgment through fear of the impending sword or any other danger though it threaten death; or when a man endangers his life on account of virtue, for example, when a man fails not to care for or wait on a sick friend through fear of deadly infection or does not refuse to undertake a journey for some Godly purpose, through fear of shipwreck or robbers. Wherefore martyrs face the fight that is waged against their own person and this for the sake of the sovereign good which is God and hence their fortitude is praised above all.

On the other hand, although fortitude is chiefly against the dangers of death, still it is secondarily against all other dangers because a brave man behaves well in bearing all manner of adversity.

3. The act of fortitude is not chiefly to attack difficult things but to endure them, that is to stand immovable in the midst of dangers rather than to attack them; to stand without the confusion resulting from irrational fear. First, because endurance seemingly implies that one is being attacked by a stronger person. Secondly, because he that endures already feels the presence of danger, whereas the aggressor looks upon danger as something to come and it is more difficult to be unmoved by the present than by the future. Thirdly, because endurance implies length of time, and it is more difficult to remain calm and unmoved for a long time than to be moved suddenly to something arduous. Hence Aristotle says, "that some hurry to meet danger, yet fly when the danger is present; this is not the behaviour of a brave man." (2, 2ae. q. 123, a. 6.)

AUGUST 30

Temperance

1. The word temperance has a twofold signification. First, in accordance with its common signification and thus temperance is not a special but a general virtue, because the word temperance means a certain temperateness or moderation which reason appoints to human operations and passions and this is common to every moral virtue. Yet temperance differs from fortitude even if we take them both as general virtues. For temperance withdraws man from things which seduce the appetite from obeying reason and the Divine Law; while fortitude encourages him to endure or withstand those things on account of which he forsakes the good of reason.

On the other hand, if we take temperance as withholding the appetite from those things which are most seductive to man, it is a special virtue, for thus, it has, like fortitude, a special matter. But temperance is, properly speaking, concerned chiefly about pleasures and desires of touch, secondarily, it is around other desires. For just as fortitude is about fear and daring with respect to the greatest evils, as are the dangers of death, so in like manner temperance must needs be about desires for the greatest pleasures. Now these pleasures result from the sense of touch. Wherefore it follows that temperance is about pleasures of touch. Hence Saint Augustine says that, "the function of temperance is to control and quell the desires which draw us to the things which withdraw us from the laws of God, and from the fruit of His goodness, and it is the duty of temperance to spurn all bodily allurements and popular praise."

2. The rule of temperance must be undertaken in accordance with the needs of this life. The good of moral virtue consists chiefly in the order of reason, because man's good is to be in accord with right reason. Now the principal order of reason is that by which it directs certain things to their end and the good of reason consists chiefly in this order, since good has the nature of end, and the end is the rule of whatever is directed to the end. Now all the pleasurable objects which are at man's use and disposal are directed to some necessity of this life as to their end. Wherefore temperance takes the need of this life as the rule of the pleasurable objects of which it makes use, and uses them only as much as the need of this life requires. Wherefore, Augustine says that, "in both Testa-

ments the temperate man finds an established rule, forbidding him to love the things of this life, or to deem any of them desirable for its own sake, commanding him to avail himself of those things with the moderation of a user, not the attachment of a lover, in so far as they are necessary for the needs of this life."

3. Although beauty is becoming to every virtue, it is attributed to temperance by way of excellence for two reasons. First, in regard to the general notion of temperance, which consists in a certain moderate and fitting proportion and this is what we understand by beauty. Secondly, because the things from which temperance withholds us, hold the lowest place in man and are becoming to him by reason of his animal nature, wherefore it is natural that such things should defile him. In consequence, beauty is a foremost attribute of temperance, which above all hinders man from being defiled, for temperance destroys the things which degrade man and withstands the vices that bring most dishonour on man. (2, 2ae. q. 141, a. 2, 3um.)

AUGUST 31

The Virtue of Religion

1. Religion directs man to God.

Saint Isidore says that "a man is said to be religious from 'religio'," which means "I ponder over," because he ponders over, and as it were, reads again (religit), the things which pertain to the worship of God; so that religion would seem to take its name from reading over those things which belong to Divine worship, for we should frequently ponder over such things in our hearts, according to Prov. III, 6, "In all thy ways think on Him"; although it may also take its name from the fact that "we ought to seek God, Whom we had lost through our neglect." Or again, religion may be derived from "religare" (to bind together), wherefore Augustine says, "May religion bind us to the one Almighty God."

However, whether religion takes its name from frequent reading or from a repeated choice of what has been lost by negligence or from being a bond, it denotes properly a relation to God. For it is He to Whom we ought to be bound as to our unfailing principle; to Whom also our choice should be resolutely directed as to our last end; and Whom we lose when we neglect Him by sinning and Whom we should recover by believing and practicing our faith.

2. Religion is a special virtue.

Wherever there is a special reason for good, there is a special virtue. Now the good to which religion is directed is to give due honour to God. Again honour is due to someone from the standpoint of excellence; but to God a singular excellence is proper, since He infinitely surpasses all things and exceeds them in every way. Wherefore to Him is special honour due.

3. Religion is a virtue which must take precedence over other moral virtues, because religion approaches nearer to God than the other moral virtues in so far as its actions are directly and immediately ordered to the honour of God. Therefore religion is the chief of the moral virtues.

4. Religion embraces both interior and external acts. In (Ps. LXXXIII, 3), "My heart and my flesh have rejoiced in the living God." Now just as internal actions belong to the heart, so do external actions belong to the members of the flesh. Therefore God should be worshipped not only by internal actions but also by external actions.

We pay God reverence and honour, not for His sake, but for our own sake, because by the very fact that we revere and honour God, our mind is subjected to Him, wherein its perfection consists, since a thing is perfected by being subjected to its superior, for example, the body is perfected by being animated by the soul and the air by being illuminated by the sun.

Now the human mind, in order to be united to God, needs to be guided by the sensible world; since "the invisible things of God are clearly seen, being understood by the things that are made," as the Apostle says (Rom. I, 20). Wherefore in the Divine worship it is necessary to make use of corporeal things, that man's mind may be aroused thereby, as by signs, to the spiritual acts by means of which he is united to God. Therefore the internal acts of religion take precedence over the others and belong to religion essentially, while its external acts are secondary and subordinate to the internal acts.

Consequently, these external things are offered to God, not as if He needed them, according to the Psalm XLIX, 13, "Shall I eat the flesh of bullocks? or shall I drink the blood of goats?", but as signs of the internal and spiritual works, which are of themselves acceptable to God. Hence Augustine says (De Civ. Dei X), "The visible sacrifice is the sacrament or sacred sign of the invisible sacrifice." (2a. 2ae. Q. 81, a. 1, 4, 6, 7.)

SEPTEMBER 1

Devotion and Prayer—the Two Interior Acts of Religion

1. Devotion.

Devotion is derived from "devote," from the Latin "devovere," which means "to vow." Wherefore those persons are said to be devout who in a way devote themselves to God so as to subject themselves entirely to Him. Hence devotion seems to be nothing other than the will to give oneself readily to things pertaining to the service of God. Wherefore it is written (Exod. XXXV, 20): "The multitude of the children of Israel . . . offered first fruits to the Lord with a most ready and devout mind." Now it is evident that the will to do readily what concerns the service of God is a special kind of act. Therefore devotion is a special act of the will.

Devotion is in truth an act of religion. For it belongs to the same virtue to will to do something and to have the will ready to do it, because both acts have the same object. Now it is evident that to do what pertains to the worship or service of God, belongs properly to religion. Wherefore it belongs to the same virtue to have the will ready to do such things, and that is to be devout. Hence it is clear that devotion is an act of religion.

Devotion however, is not an act of charity, for it belongs immediately to charity that man should give himself to God, adhering to Him by a union of the spirit; but it belongs immediately to religion, and through the medium of religion, to charity which is the principle of religion, that man should give himself to God for certain works of Divine worship.

Devotion seems to precede charity; since in the Scriptures, charity is represented by fire while devotion is signified by fatness which is the material of fire. Nevertheless, devotion is not an act of charity. For bodily fatness is produced by the natural heat in the process of digestion and at the same time the natural heat lives, as it were, on this fatness. In like manner charity causes devotion, inasmuch as love makes one ready to serve one's friend, and at the same time charity feeds on devotion. Even so, all friendship is safeguarded and increased by the practice and consideration of friendly deeds.

2. Prayer.

Prayer is an act of religion, for it is written in Psalm (CXL, 2), "Let my prayer be directed as incense in Thy sight." It belongs properly to religion to show reverence and honour to God, and therefore all those things through which reverence is shown to God, pertain to religion. Now man shows reverence to God by means of prayer, in so far as man subjects himself to Him, and by praying acknowledges that he needs Him as the Author of his good. Hence it is evident that prayer is properly an act of religion.

If it may be said that it belongs to religion that one offers worship and ceremonial rites to the Godhead and that prayer seems not to offer anything to God but rather to ask something from Him, we answer, that by praying man surrenders his mind to God, since he subjects it to Him and so to speak presents it to Him. Wherefore, just as the human mind excels exterior things, whether bodily members or those external things that are employed for God's service, so too, prayer surpasses other acts of religion.

The will moves the other powers of the soul to its end and hence religion which is in the will directs the acts of the other powers to the reverence of God. Now among the powers of the soul the intellect is highest and the nearest to the will; and consequently after devotion which belongs to the will, prayer which belongs to the intellective part is the chief of the acts of religion, for by prayer religion directs man's intellect to God. (2a. 2ae. q. 83, a. 3.)

SEPTEMBER 2

The Cause and Effect of Devotion

1. Concerning the cause of devotion.

"In my meditation a fire shall flame forth." (Psalm XXXVIII, 4.) But spiritual fire causes devotion. Therefore meditation is the cause of devotion. The extrinsic and chief cause of devotion is God. But the intrinsic cause on our part must be meditation or contemplation. For devotion is an act of the will to the effect than man surrenders himself readily to the service of God. Now every act of the will proceeds from some consideration, since the object of the will is a good understood. Wherefore Augustine says that "the will arises from the intelligence." Consequently meditation must needs be the cause of devotion, in so far as through meditation man conceives the thought of surrendering himself to God's service. Indeed a twofold consideration leads him to God's service.

The first is the consideration of God's goodness and loving

kindness, according to Psalm LXXII, 28, "It is good for me to adhere to my God, to put my hope in the Lord God"; and this consideration arouses love, which is the proximate cause of devotion.

The second consideration is that of man's own shortcomings on account of which he needs to lean on God, according to Ps. CXX, 1, "I have lifted up my eyes to the mountains, from whence help shall come to me. My help is from the Lord, Who made heaven and earth"; and this consideration excludes presumption whereby man is prevented from surrendering himself to God, because he leans on His strength.

Science and anything else conducive to greatness is to man an occasion of self-confidence, so that he does not wholly surrender himself to God. The result is that such like things sometimes occasion a hindrance to devotion while in simple souls and among women devotion abounds by repressing pride. If however a man perfectly submits to God his science or any other perfection, by this very fact his devotion is increased.

2. The effect of devotion—namely spiritual joy.

The direct and principal effect of devotion is the spiritual joy of the mind, though sorrow is its secondary and indirect effect. Devotion is caused by a twofold consideration, chiefly by the consideration of God's goodness because this consideration belongs to the term, as it were, of the movement of the will in surrendering itself to God, and the direct result of this consideration is joy, according to Ps. LXXVI, 4, "I remembered God, and was delighted"; but accidentally this consideration causes a certain sorrow in those who do not enjoy God fully, according to Ps. XLI, 3, "My soul hath thirsted after the strong living God," and afterwards verse 4 continues, "My tears have been my bread."

Secondarily devotion is caused by the consideration of one's own failings, for this consideration pertains to the term from which man withdraws by the movement of his devout will, that he should not be self-confident but subject himself to God. This consideration has an opposite tendency to the first, for it is of a nature to cause sorrow directly and joy accidentally through hope of the Divine assistance.

Consequently it is evident that the first and direct effect of devotion is spiritual joy, while the secondary and accidental effect is that sorrow which is according to God. (2a. 2ae. Q. 82, a. 3 and 4.)

SEPTEMBER 3

The Manner of Praying

1. Should prayer be vocal?
"I cried to the Lord with my voice, with my voice I made supplication of the Lord." (Ps. CXLI, 2.) Therefore prayer should be vocal. Prayer is twofold, common and individual. Common prayer is that which is offered by the ministers of the Church representing the body of the faithful, wherefore such like prayer should come to the knowledge of the faithful for whom it is offered, and this would not be possible unless it were vocal prayer. On the other hand, individual prayer is that which is offered by any single person, and it is not essential to such a prayer that it be vocal. Yet the voice is used in such like prayers for three reasons.

First, in order to excite interior devotion, whereby the mind of the person praying is raised to God, because by means of external signs, whether of words or of deeds, the human mind is moved as regards apprehension and consequently also as regards the affections. Hence Augustine says that "by means of words and other signs we arouse ourselves more sharply to an increase of holy desires." Hence, then alone should we use words and such like signs when they help to arouse the mind internally. But if they distract or in any way impede the mind we should abstain from them and this happens chiefly to those whose mind is sufficiently prepared for devotion without having recourse to those signs. Wherefore the Psalmist (Ps. XXVI, 8) said, "My heart hath said to Thee ... My face hath sought Thee," and we read of Anna (1 Kings I, 13), "that she spoke in her heart."

Secondly, the voice is used in praying as though to pay a debt so that man may serve God with all that he has from God, that is to say, not only with his mind but also with his body and this applies to prayer considered especially as satisfactory.

Thirdly, we have recourse to vocal prayer, through a certain overflow from the soul into the body, from an excess of feeling, according to Ps. XV, 9, "My heart hath been glad, and my tongue hath rejoiced."

2. Is Attention a Necessary Condition of Prayer?
A thing is said to be necessary in two ways. First, a thing is necessary because the end is better obtained, and thus attention is absolutely necessary for prayer. Secondly, a thing is

said to be necessary when without it something cannot obtain its effect. Now the effect of prayer is threefold.

The first is an effect which is common to all acts animated by charity, and this is merit. In order to realize this effect, it is not necessary that prayer should be attentive throughout because the force of the original intention with which one sets about praying renders the whole prayer meritorious.

The second effect of prayer is to ask God for some favor and again the original intention, to which God looks chiefly, suffices to obtain this effect. But if the original intention is lacking, prayer lacks both merit and impetration. God hears not the prayer of those who have no intention of praying.

The third effect of prayer is that which it produces at once, namely the spiritual refreshment of the mind, and for this effect attention is a necessary condition. Wherefore it is written (1 Cor. XIV, 14), "If I pray in a tongue ... my understanding is without fruit ... Thou indeed givest thanks, but the other person is not edified ... In the church then, I rather speak five words with my understanding, that I may instruct others also, than ten thousand words in a tongue," that is without attention.

Attention is threefold, one which attends to the words lest we say them wrong, another which attends to the sense of the words, and a third which attends to the end of prayer, namely, God, and to the things we are praying for. This last kind of attention is most necessary and even idiots are capable of it. Moreover there is this attention whereby the mind is sometimes fixed on God so strong that the mind forgets all other things. (2a. 2ae, Q. 83, a. 12 and 13.)

SEPTEMBER 4

Continual Prayer

Our Lord said, *"We ought always to pray, and not to faint."* (Luke XVIII, 1), and it is also written, *"Pray without ceasing."* (I Thess. V, 17.)

We may speak about prayer in two ways. First, by considering it in itself; secondly, by considering it in its cause. The cause of prayer is the desire of charity, from which prayer ought to arise and this desire should be in us continually, either actually or virtually, for the virtue of this desire remains in whatever we do from charity; and we ought "to do all things to the glory of God." (1 Cor. X, 31.) From this point of view prayer ought to be continual. Wherefore Saint Augustine says, "Faith, hope, and charity are by themselves a prayer of continual longing."

But prayer considered in itself cannot be continual, because we have to be busy about other works and as Augustine says, "We pray to God with our lips at certain intervals and seasons, in order to admonish ourselves by means of such like signs, to take note of the amount of our progress in that desire, and to arouse ourselves more eagerly to an increase thereof."

Now, the quantity of a thing should be commensurate with its end, for example the quantity of the dose should be commensurate with health. And so it is becoming, that prayer should last long enough to arouse the fervour of the interior desire and when it exceeds this measure, so that it cannot be continued any longer without causing weariness, it should be discontinued. Wherefore Augustine said, "It is said that the brethren in Egypt make frequent but very short prayers, rapid ejaculations as it were, lest that vigilant and erect attention which is so necessary in prayer slacken and languish, through the strain being prolonged. By so doing they make it sufficiently clear not only that this attention must not be allowed to stray, so long as we can keep it up, but also that if we are able to continue, it should not be broken off too soon."

Therefore, one may pray continually either through having a continual desire, as stated above, or through praying at certain fixed times, though interruptedly, or by reason of the effect whether in the person who prays (because he remains more devout even after praying), or in some other person (as when by his kindness a man incites another person to pray for him), even when he himself has ceased from praying and rests.

It seems that prayer should not be continual for it is written (Matth. VI, 2), "When you are praying speak not much." But it does not follow from these words that one should not pray for a long time. For Augustine says, "to pray with many words is not the same as to pray for a long time; to talk for a long time is one thing, to be devout for long is another." For it is written that even our Lord spent "the whole night in prayer," and then "He prayed the longer," in order to give us an example. Further on Augustine says, "When praying talk little, yet pray much so long as your attention is fervent. For to talk much in prayer is to discuss your need in too many words; whereas to pray much is to knock at the door of Him to Whom we pray, by the continuous and devout clamour of the heart. Indeed this work is frequently done with groans rather than with words, with tears rather than with speech."

Therefore the length of prayer consists, not in praying for many things but in the affections persisting in the desire of one thing. Hence it is written, "And leaving them, Jesus prayed the third time, saying the self-same words" (Matth. XXVI, 44), and "being in an agony He prayed the longer." (Luke XXII, 43.) (2a. 2ae. Q. 83, a. 14.)

SEPTEMBER 5

Sacrifices Should Be Offered to God

1. The offering of a sacrifice is made to represent something. Now the sacrifice that is offered outwardly represents the inward spiritual sacrifice, whereby the soul offers itself to God; according to the words of the Psalmist (Ps. I, 19), "A sacrifice to God is an afflicted spirit," because the outward acts of religion are directed to the inward acts. Again the soul offers itself in sacrifice to God as its beginning by creation and its end by beatification; and according to true faith God alone is the Creator of our souls, and in Him alone our happiness consists. Wherefore just as to God alone ought we to offer spiritual sacrifice, so too ought we to offer outward sacrifices to Him alone.

2. Sacrifice is indeed a special act deserving of praise when it is done because of reverence for God; and for this reason it belongs to a definite virtue, namely religion. But it happens that the acts of the other virtues are directed to the reverence of God, as when man gives alms from his own goods for God's sake, or when a man subjects his own body to some affliction out of reverence for God; and in this way the acts also of other virtues may be called sacrifices. On the other hand there are acts that are not deserving of praise except when performed out of reverence for God. These acts are properly called sacrifices and belong to the virtue of religion.

3. Man's good is threefold. There is first his soul's good which is offered to God in a certain inward sacrifice by devotion, prayer and other interior acts and this is the principal sacrifice. The second good is the good of man's body, which is,

so to speak, offered to God in martyrdom, abstinence or purity. The third is the good which consists of external things; and of these we offer a sacrifice to God, directly when we offer our possessions to God immediately, and indirectly when we share them with our neighbour for God's sake. (2a. 2ae. Q. 85, a, 2 and 3.)

Or, in another way it must be said we ought offer three sacrifices to God, the sacrifice of the heart with sorrow for sin *Sacrificium Deo spiritus contribulatus,* "the sacrifice of a contrite spirit." Secondly, the sacrifice of the tongue in confession and prayer—*sacrificium laudis honorificabit Me. — Holocausta medullata offeram tibi cum incenso arietum.* "A sacrifice to God is an afflicted spirit. A contrite and humbled heart, O God, Thou wilt not despise . . . The sacrifice of praise shall glorify Me. I will offer up to Thee, holocausts full of marrow with burnt offerings of rams." The marrow which is fatness and strength to the bones, is likened to devotion which is the fervour and power of prayer. Thirdly the sacrifice of the body as a sacrifice of satisfaction. "Then Thou shalt accept the sacrifice of justice." (Psalm L, 21.)

SEPTEMBER 6

The Necessity of Humility

"Jesus said, unless you be converted and become as little children, you shall not enter into the kingdom of heaven. (Matth. I.)

1. The Lord showed how we are to arrive at heavenly glory by the road of humility. "And Jesus calling unto Him a little child, set him in the midst of them." What example does this little child teach us? Saint John Chrysostom believes that the child was little, since He was free from passions. Secondly, Christ called a little child, stood him in the midst of His disciples and said, "unless you become as this little child (innocent, pure, good, free from all sin), you cannot enter the kingdom of Heaven." Thirdly, through the example of this little child is understood the Holy Spirit, because he is the spirit of humility. Wherefore the Lord remarked, "unless you become as little children," not in age, but in simplicity. "Do

not become children in sense, but in malice be children, and in sense perfect." (1 Cor. XIV, 20.)

The characteristics of children are many. They are immune from the lusts of the flesh. "Whosoever shall look on a woman to lust after her, hath already committed adultery with her in his heart." (Matth. V, 28.) But little children have no such sinful desires. Likewise, they are free from all malice and enmity. Hence Christ said, "unless you become as little children," namely imitators of the virtues and qualities of little children, "you shall not enter into the kingdom of heaven." For none but the humble enter there. "Humiliation followeth the proud, but glory shall uphold the humble of heart." (Prov. XXIX, 23.) And again, Christ teaches the necessity of humility saying, "whosoever therefore, shall humble himself as this little child, he is the greater in the kingdom of heaven. And he that shall receive one such little child in My Name, receiveth Me" (Matth. XVIII, 4); that is, whosoever is the imitator of childlike innocence, he is the greater, because inasmuch as one is more humble by so much the more will such a person be exalted; for "he who humbles himself shall be exalted." (Luc. XVIII, 14.)

2. But it seems then, that it is not true that perfection consists in charity. Yet where greater charity is, there is greater perfection.

It must be admitted that humility is necessarily united with charity and you can readily understand this if you carefully consider what it means to be truly humble. Just as in pride there are two things, improper love and improper estimation of oneself, so the contrary is true of humility, because the humble man boasts not of his own excellence, nor reckons himself worthy. Every man receives the excellence which he loves. Therefore, inasmuch as a man has the greater humility, by so much the more does he love God and despise more his own excellence in so far as he attributes less to himself. Consequently, inasmuch as man has greater charity has he more of humility. (Matth. XVIII.)

SEPTEMBER 7

Man Ought, by Humility, Subject Himself to All Men

"In humility let each esteem others better than themselves." (Philip II, 3.)

We may consider two things in man, namely that which is God's and that which is man's. Whatever pertains to defect is man's but whatever pertains to man's welfare and perfection is God's; according to the words of Osee (XIII, 9), "Destruction is thy own, O Israel; thy help is only in Me." Now humility, properly regards the reverence whereby man is subject to God. Wherefore every man in regard to that which is his own ought to subject himself to every neighbour in regard to that which the latter has from God. But humility does not require a man to subject what he has from God to that which may seem to be God's in another. For those who have a share of God's gifts know that they have them, according to 1 Cor. II, 12, "That we may know the things that are given us from God." Wherefore, without prejudice to humility they may set the gifts they have received from God above those that others appear to have received from Him. Thus the Apostle says (Ephes. III, 5), "(The mystery of Christ) was not known to the sons of men as it is now revealed to His Holy Apostles."

In like manner, humility does not require a man to subject that which he has of his own to that which his neighbour has from man, otherwise each one would have to esteem himself a greater sinner than anyone else; whereas the Apostle says without prejudice to humility (Gal. II, 15), "We by nature are Jews and not of the Gentiles sinners."

Nevertheless, a man may esteem his neighbour to have some good which he lacks himself or himself to have some evil which another has not by reason of which he may be subject to him with humility.

We must not only revere God in Himself but also in that which is His in each one, although not with the same measure of reverence that we revere God. Wherefore, we should subject ourselves with humility to all our neighbours for God's sake, according to 1 Pet. II, 13, "Be ye subject . . . to every human creature for God's sake," but to God alone do we owe the worship of latria.

Humility, like other virtues, resides chiefly inwardly in the soul. Consequently, a man by an inward act of the soul may subject himself to another, without giving the other man an occasion of detriment to his spiritual welfare. This is what Augustine means in his Rule. "With fear, the superior should prostrate himself at your feet in the sight of God." On the other hand, due moderation must be observed in the outward acts of humility even as of other virtues lest they lead to the detriment of others. Wherefore Augustine used to say, "Let not humility serve to excess, lest the authority of ruling be broken," and further on he asks, "Are you thinking of raising the great fabric of spirituality?" Attend first of all to the foundation of humility, because our Saviour has said, "Learn of Me, for I am meek and humble of heart." (2a. 2ae. Q. 161, a. 3.)

SEPTEMBER 8

Our Mother's Birthday

"Blessed Art Thou Amongst Women."

Mary is called "blessed":

1. God the Father blessed thee, O Mary, because thou didst prepare a worthy tabernacle for His Son. Thou wert blessed by the Holy Ghost, by Whose power you gave birth to the world's Saviour.

2. Thou wert blessed by the Angels, because you began the Angelic life on earth, repairing the ruin of the fallen angels and humiliating thyself.

3. Thou art blessed by sinners, because you liberate them from ruin, help them through dangers and obtain pardon for their sins.

4. Thou art blessed by the just, because you hear their prayers, free them from temptations and increase grace in their souls.

5. "Blessed art thou amongst women," because thou dost free them from their enemies. Through sin they are chained by the devil, separated from God, but the Blessed Virgin has freed them from their enemies, because her Son, Christ has conquered Satan. Thou art honored, O Mary, by God (Gal. IV, 4) for "God sent His Son made of a woman."

6. Blessed art thou amongst all creatures, because thou rejoicest the Creator of them all, freest them from contamination, that is, purifiest them from sin, and restorest them to

their original state of happiness. Thy Son Whom thou didst bring forth, created all creatures, purified them, and renovated them. Therefore, O Blessed Virgin, God the Father, God the Son and God the Holy Ghost has blessed Thee! Likewise, do the Angels and sinners, the just and unjust, men and women and all created things bless Thee. On account of this it is said in Judith, "Thou art the glory of Jerusalem, thou art the honor of our people. For thou hast done manfully, and they heart has been strengthened, because thou hast loved chastity, and after thy husband thou hast not known any other. Therefore, the hand of the Lord hast strengthened thee, and therefore, thou shalt be blessed forever."

SEPTEMBER 9

Our Lord's Humility Commands Us to Be Humble

"Let this mind be in you, which was also in Christ Jesus ... Who being in the form of God—emptied—Himself, taking the form of a servant." (Philip II, 5.)

1. "Let this mind be in you," that is from experience have that humility which was in Christ Jesus. We should let this be in us in five ways, by means of the five senses. 1. By realizing His brightness, so that we being enlightened may become conformed to Him. 2. By listening to His wisdom so that we might be blessed. "Blessed are Thy men, and blessed are Thy servants, who stand before Thee always, and hear Thy wisdom." (3 Kings X, 8.) 3. By tasting the sweetness of His meekness. "Draw me. We will run after Thee to the odour of Thy ointments." (Canticles I, 3.) 4. By tasting the sweetness of His Sanctity. "Taste and see that the Lord is sweet." (Psalm XXXIII.) 5. By touching His power. "If I shall touch only His garment, I shall be healed." (Matth. IX, 21.) Wherefore, let this likeness be in us in the imitation of His works.

2. We have the shining example of Christ's humility in His Incarnation, "Who being in the form of God, thought it not robbery to be equal to God; but emptied Himself, taking the form of a servant." It is said "He emptied Himself." But since He was the fulness of Divinity, did He therefore empty Himself of His Divinity? No, because that which He had remained and that which He had not He assumed. For just as He came

down from heaven, not that He ceased to be in heaven, but because He began to live a new way on earth, so He emptied Himself, not by setting aside His Divine Nature, but by assuming our human nature.

Beautifully indeed has it been said that "He emptied Himself," for emptiness is the opposite of fulness. The Divine Nature was sufficiently perfect. because it contains every perfection of goodness. "I will show thee all good." (Exod. XXXIII, 19.) But human nature and the soul do not possess fulness, but are in potency or in power to possess fulness; for they are as it were a *tabula rasa*, an empty tablet. Hence human nature is empty. Therefore, it is well said "He emptied Himself," for He assumed human nature.

"Taking the form of a servant." For man is by creation the servant of God and human nature is the form of a servant.

3. The example of Christ in His Passion is an example of humility. "He humbled Himself, becoming obedient unto death, even unto the death of the cross." Christ is man, but exceedingly great, because He is at the same time God and man and still He humbled Himself. "The greater thou art, the more humble thyself in all things, and thou shalt find grace before God." (Eccle. III, 20.) But the manner of humiliation and the sign of humility is obedience. It belongs to the proud to follow their own will, for the proud man seeks vanity and haughtiness, and it pertains to haughtiness not to be ruled or guided by another, and hence obedience is contrary to pride. Hence the Holy Spirit wishing to show the perfection of humility and the perfection of Christ's Passion, said that, "He became obedient," because if Christ had suffered not from obedience, it would not have been so praiseworthy because obedience gives merit to our sufferings.

But how did He become obedient? Not by His Divine will, for that is a rule, but by His human will which was ruled in all things according to the will of His heavenly Father. But great and praiseworthy though this obedience may be, it is clear, that obedience is great when it follows the will of another in preference to its own, especially where the law of God is concerned. But the movement of the human will tends to two things, to life and to honour. But Christ was not unwilling to die. Likewise He did not flee from the shameful death of the cross. Hence it is written, *Mortem autem crucis*, "even the death of the Cross," which is the most shameful even though Christ endured willingly, patiently. "Let us condemn Him to a most shameful death, for there shall be respect shown unto Him by His word." (Wis. II, 20.) Wherefore, God has exalted Him and given Him a Name which is above all Names.

SEPTEMBER 10

Patience

1. Patience is necessary.

The moral virtues are ordained to the good, inasmuch as they safeguard the good of reason against the impulse of the passions. Now among the passions sorrow is strong to hinder the good of reason, according to 2 Cor. VII, 10, "The sorrow of the world worketh death," and Eccles. XXX, 25, "Sadness hath killed many and there is no profit in it." Hence the necessity of a virtue to safeguard the good of reason against sorrow lest reason give way to sorrow, and this patience prevents. Wherefore Augustine says (De patientia 2), "A man's patience is that whereby he bears evil with an equal mind, that is, without being disturbed by sorrow, lest he abandon with an unequal mind the goods whereby he may advance to better things. It is therefore evident that patience is a virtue.

2. Patience nevertheless, is not the greatest of the virtues.

A virtue's superiority and preponderance over other virtues is the greater according as it inclines man to good more effectively and directly. Now these virtues which are effective of good, incline man more directly to good than those which are a check on the things which lead man away from good; and just as among those which are effective of good, the greater is that which establishes man in a greater good (thus faith, hope, and charity are greater than prudence and justice); so, too, among those which are a check on things that withdraw man from good, the greater virtue is the one which is a check on a greater obstacle to good. But dangers of death, about which is fortitude, and pleasures of touch with which temperance is concerned, withdraw man from good more than any kind of hardship, which is the object of patience. Therefore, patience is not the greatest of the virtues, but falls short not only of the theological virtues and of prudence and justice which directly establish man in good, but patience also falls short of fortitude and temperance which withdraw him from greater obstacles to good.

3. In what sense has patience "a perfect work"?

According to Saint James I, 4, "Patience hath a perfect work." Patience is said to have "a perfect work," by enduring evils, wherein it excludes not only unjust revenge, which is also excluded by justice; not only hatred, which is also suppressed by charity; not only anger, which is subdued by gentleness; but also inordinate sorrow, which is the root of all the above. Wherefore patience in this way is the more perfect and excellent through plucking up the root in this matter. It is not, however, more perfect than all the other virtues simply. Because fortitude not only endures trouble without being disturbed, but also fights against it if necessary. Hence, whoever is brave is patient, but the opposite is not true, for patience is a part of fortitude. (1, 2ae. q. 66, a. 4, ad 2um.)

SEPTEMBER 11

Advantages of Sorrow and Tribulations

"We glory in tribulations, knowing that tribulation worketh patience, and patience trial, and trial hope. And hope confoundeth not, because the charity of God is poured forth in our hearts." (Rom. V, 3.) Here St. Paul tells us of the advantages of sorrows and the power of hope by which we expect to win the prize of eternal glory and become the children of God. When we earnestly desire something, we freely endure whatever is difficult and disagreeable to obtain our heart's desire; just as a sick man, if he anxiously desires health, willingly drinks the bitter medicine so that he might be cured by it. Therefore a sign of the earnestness of our hope, which we have because of Christ, is revealed by us when we not only rejoice in the hope of everlasting glory, but also when we patiently endure evil things for the possession of that glory. Hence it is said: "We glory in tribulations," through which we may win the crown of deathless fame. "Through many tribulations we must enter the kingdom of God." (Acts XV, 21.) And St. James (I, 2) writes to the faithful: "Count it all joy when you fall into different temptations."

"Tribulation worketh patience," not that tribulation is the effective cause of patience, but because tribulation and trials and sorrows of every kind are the occasion and material of performing an act of patience.

"Patience worketh trial." Therefore, it is written in Ecclesiasticus (II, 5) "Gold and silver are tried in the fire, but acceptable men in the furnace of humiliation. Take all that shall be brought upon thee, and in thy sorrow endure, and in thy humiliation keep patience." We endure easily the loss of a person or thing if we love God and eternal things more than the loss which we have sustained. Hence, if anyone patiently endures corporal and temporal sufferings for the sake of possessing eternal happiness, it is sufficiently clear that such a person loves the eternal good things more than temporal treasures from which death separates us all.

"Trial worketh hope," for tribulation prepares the way for hope. Hence, if anyone earnestly rejoices in eternal hope, it follows that he must glory in tribulations from which there is no escape in this life.

"Hope confoundeth not," that is, hope does not abandon its object. Man falls into despair and loses hope, only when he fails to pursue the eternal Object of all his hopes, desires and natural aspirations.

"The charity of God is poured forth in our hearts." The charity of God can be twofold, namely the charity with which God loves us, and the charity with which we love God. When we love Him, it is a sign that He loves us. Now the love of God for us is ofttimes shown to us in the sorrows, tribulations and trials which enter our lives, our homes and our fortunes. Consequently we all need charity and prudence and patience, in order that we might turn to our advantages the crushing afflictions, deep rooted sorrows and heavy burdens of every day life.

SEPTEMBER 12

Precepts of Charity

1. It was necessary that precepts should be given about charity, which is the love of God.

The special end of the spiritual life is that man be united to God; and this union is effected by charity, while all things pertaining to the spiritual life are ordained to this union as to their end. Hence the Apostle says, "The end of the commandment is charity from a pure heart, and a good conscience, and an unfeigned faith." (1 Tim. I, 5.) For all the virtues, about whose acts the precepts are given, are directed either to the freeing of the heart from the disturbance of the passions—such are the virtues that regulate the passions—or at least to the possession of a good conscience, such are the virtues that regulate operations; or to the having of right faith; such are those which pertain to the worship of God; and these three things are required of man that he may love God. For an impure heart is withdrawn from loving God, because of the passion which inclines it to earthly things; an evil conscience gives a man a horror for God's justice, through fear of His punishments; and an untrue faith draws man's affections to an untrue representation of God and separates him from the truth of God. Now in every genus, that which is for its own sake takes precedence of that which is for the sake of another, wherefore the greatest precept is that of charity, as stated in Matth. XXII, 38, "Thou shalt love the Lord Thy God with thy whole heart, and with thy whole soul, and with thy whole mind. This is the greatest and first commandment. And the second is like unto this. Thou shalt love thy neighbour as thyself."

2. Not only should precepts have been given about the love of God, but also concerning the love of our neighbour on account of those who are less intelligent, who do not easily understand that one of these precepts is included in the other. (2a. 2ae. Q. 45, a. 1 and 2.)

And these two precepts suffice, because as the Apostle says, "He that loveth his neighbour, hath fulfilled the law." (Rom. XIII, 8.) For all the precepts of the law, ordained chiefly for our neighbour; seem to be ordained to this end that men might love one another.

Wherefore the Apostle 1 Tim. I, 5, says, "the end of the precept is charity." For every law tends to this end, that it might establish the friendship of man for man, or of man for God. Hence the whole law is fulfilled and contained in this one commandment, "thou shalt love thy neighbour as thyself." For in the love of our neighbour is contained the love of God, when we love our neighbour because of God. Hence the Apostle lays down this one commandment for the two, which concern the love of God, and the love of neighbour; about which the Lord says, "On these two commandments dependeth the whole law and the prophets." (Matth. XXII, 40.) (1a. 2ae. q. 99, a. 1, ad 2um.)

SEPTEMBER 13

The Fitting Precept on the Love of Neighbor

1. *"The second commandment is like unto this. Thou shalt love thy neighbor as thyself."* (Matth. XXII, 39.)

This precept is fittingly expressed, for it points out both the reason for loving and the mode of love. The reason for loving is indicated in the word "neighbour," because the reason why we ought to love others out of charity is because they are close to us, both as to the natural image of God, and as to the capacity for glory. Now does it matter whether we say "neighbour," or "brother," according to 1 John IV, 21, or "friend," according to Levit. XIX, 18, because all these words express the same affinity.

The mode of love is indicated in the words, "as thyself." This does not mean that a man must love his neighbour equally as himself, but in like manner as himself, and this in three ways. First, as regards the end, that he should love his neighbour for God's sake, even as he loves himself for God's sake; so that his love for his neighbour is a "holy" love. Secondly, as regards the rule of love, that a man should not give way to his neighbour in evil, but only in good things, even as he ought to gratify his will in good things alone; so that his love for his neighbour may be a "righteous" love. Thirdly, as regards the reason for loving, that a man should love his neighbour, not for his own profit or pleasure, but in the sense of wishing his neighbour well; so that his love for his neighbour may be a "true" love; since when a man loves his neighbour for his own profit or pleasure he does not love his neighbour truly, but loves himself. (2a. 2ae. q. 44, a. 7.)

2. Such are Christ's insignia, "By this shall all men know that you are My disciples, if you have love one for another." (John XIII, 35.) We must remember that whatever soldier is enlisted in the service of any king wears the insignia of his Majesty's service. But Christ's insignia is the insignia of Charity. Whoever, therefore, wishes to be numbered among the soldiers of Christ, should bear in his heart the sign of charity. And this is what our Lord means when He says, "By this shall all men know that you are My disciples, if you have love one for another," that is, holy love. "I am the mother of fair love, and of fear, and of knowledge, and of holy hope." (Eccle. XXIV, 24.)

But bear in mind that even though the Apostles received many gifts from Christ, such as life, knowledge, health and certain great spiritual gifts; such as the power of working miracles, as Saint Luke (XXI, 15) describes: "I will give you a mouth and wisdom, which all your adversaries shall not be able to resist nor gainsay," still all these things are not signs of Christ's disciples, since these can be common to the good and the evil. But a special sign of Christ's disciple, is charity and holy love. "God it is, Who has sealed us, and given the pledge of the Spirit in our hearts." (2 Cor. I, 22.)

SEPTEMBER 14

The Death of the Cross

"And I, if I be lifted up from the earth, will draw all things to myself." (John XII, 32.)

Our Lord willed to die the death of the cross for a twofold reason. First, indeed because of the shamefulness of this death. "Let us condemn Him to a most shameful death" (Wis. XI, 20). Wherefore Augustine also says, "in this manner therefore, the Lord wished to die, so that the very shamefulness of His death might not repel man from the perfection of justice." Secondly, because such a death is the road to exaltation. Hence the Lord said, "if I be lifted up, I will draw all things to myself." Wherefore the nature of His death was suitable to the effect, to the cause and to the figure of His Passion.

Suitable to the effect, because through His Passion He deserved to be exalted. "He humbled Himself, becoming obedient unto death, even to the death of the cross. For which cause God also hath exalted Him, and hath given Him a Name which is above all names" (Phil II, 8). And therefore, the Psalmist (XX, 14) says: "Be thou exalted, O Lord, in Thy own strength. We will sing and praise Thy power."

His death was a suitable cause of His Passion in two ways. First, from the part of mankind, and secondly from the standpoint of demons. From the standpoint of mankind because He died for the salvation of all men. But these would have perished, because they had fallen into and were swallowed up in the ocean of earthly things. "They have set their eyes bowing down to the earth" (Ps. XVI, 11). He willed therefore to die lifted up, so that He might raise our hearts to heavenly things. For His death is our royal road to heaven. Secondly, from the standpoint of demons, so that Christ when lifted up on the cross might crush their diabolical rule and power in the heavens above and on the earth below.

Thirdly, the nature of His death was befitting the figure of His Passion, because the Lord willed to become the brazen serpent in the desert. "And as Moses lifted up the serpent in the desert, so must the Son of Man be lifted up" (John III, 14). Therefore, being thus lifted, "I will draw all things through charity to Myself." "Yea, I have loved you with an everlasting love, therefore have I drawn thee, taking pity on thee" (Jer. XXXI, 3.) In this death of the cross, the greatest love of God for man is evident, as He was worthy and willing to die for man. In this death of the cross is fulfilled that divine favor which the spouse of Christ prays for in Canticles I, 3: "Draw me. We will run after Thee to the odor of thy ointment."

SEPTEMBER 15

Mutual Love

"A new commandment I give unto you. That you love one another, as I have loved you." (John XIII, 34.)

1. The obligation of the commandment is mutual love. Hence our Lord says, "that you love one another." For it is the nature of love that it be not hidden, otherwise it would not be friendship, but a certain kind of friendship. Therefore it is necessary for true and solid friendship that friends mutually love one another, because then friendship is just and well established, as if it were twofold. Therefore the Lord wishing that perfect friendship should exist among His faithful ones and His disciples, gave them a commandment of reciprocal love. "He that feareth God, shall likewise have good friendship" (Eccli. VI, 17).

2. Moreover our Lord gives us an example of love when He says: "As I have loved you." For Christ has loved us in a threefold way, namely freely, efficaciously, and rightly.

Freely, because He Himself began to love us, nor was He waiting for us to begin to love Him. "Not as though we had loved God, but because He had first loved us, and sent His

Son to be a propitiation for our sins" (I John X, 13). And so we ought to first love our neighbour and not expect him to come first and favour us.

Efficaciously. God loved us efficaciously, which is clear from His actions. For the proof of love is the manifestation of action. But the greatest thing a man can do for his friend is to give himself for his friend and Christ did this very thing. "He loved us and gave Himself for us" (Eph. V, 2). Therefore, following the example of our Saviour, may we love one another efficaciously and profitably. "My little children, let us not love in word, nor in tongue, but in deed and in truth" (I John II, 18).

Rightly. Indeed God loved us rightly. Likeness is the cause of love, for since every friendship is founded upon some communication or likeness, right friendship is that which is because of a likeness or communication in good. But Christ in so far as He has loved us by so much are we like to Him, through the grace of adoption. Christ loved us according to this likeness, to draw us to God. So, therefore, we ought to love our neighbour, not only because it brings us profit and pleasure, but because love is from God and in such like love of our neighbour is included also love of God.

SEPTEMBER 16

The New Commandment of Love

"A new commandment I give unto you. That you love one another." (John XIII, 34.)

Long ago, even in the old Testament or law there was a commandment on the love of neighbour. Christ when asked by the lawyer, what was the first commandment, responded: "Thou shalt love the Lord thy God," and He also added, "and thy neighbour as thyself." That same commandment was likewise mentioned in the old Testament, in Leviticus XIX, 18, "Thou shalt love thy neighbour as thyself."

Nevertheless, this commandment is called "new," especially because of three things.

First, because of the change which it produces. "Stripping yourselves of the old man with his deeds, and putting on the new, him who is renewed unto knowledge, according to the image of Him who created him" (Col. III, 9). This newness moreover, is through charity to which Christ has exhorted us.

Secondly, this commandment is called "new," by reason of the cause which produces it; for it is caused by a "new" spirit. For there is a twofold spirit, namely, the old and the new. In truth the old spirit is the spirit of bondage, whereas the new spirit is the spirit of love. The old spirit produces slaves, the new, produces children of adoption. "You have not received the spirit of bondage again in fear, but you have received the spirit of adoption of sons" (Rom. VIII, 15). And this spirit enkindles charity; "because the charity of God is diffused in our hearts, by the Holy Spirit."

Thirdly, this commandment is called "new," because of the effect which it produces; namely a new covenant. For a concise difference between the old law and the new is that the old engenders fear while the new causes love. "Behold the days will come, saith the Lord, and I will make a new covenant with the house of Israel, and with the house of Juda" (Jer. XXXI, 31). But moreover, that commandment which was in the old law from fear and holy love pertained to the new law. Wherefore that commandment was in the old law, not as belonging to it, but as a preparation for the new law.

SEPTEMBER 17

How Perfect Love of Our Neighbor Is Possible

As the state of the present life does not allow of a man always actually tending to God, so neither does it allow of his always tending actually (or loving) each individual neighbour; but it suffices for him to tend to all in common and collectively, and to each individual habitually and according to the preparedness of his mind.

Now in the love of our neighbor, as in the love of God, we may observe a twofold perfection. One perfection without which charity is impossible, and consisting in one's having in one's affections nothing that is contrary to the love of one's neighbour; and another perfection without which it is possible to have charity. The latter perfection may be considered in three ways.

First, as to the extent of love, by a man loving not only his friends and acquaintances but also strangers and even his enemies, for as Augustine says, "this is a mark of the perfect children of God."

Secondly, as to the intensity of love, which is shown by the things which man despises for his neighbour's sake, through his despising not only external goods for the sake of his neighbor, but also bodily hardships and even death, according to John XV, 13, "Greater love than this no man hath, that a man lay down his life for his friends."

Thirdly, as to the effect of love, so that a man will surrender not only temporal but also spiritual goods and even himself, for his neighbour's sake, according to the words of the Apostle (2 Cor. XII, 15), "But I most gladly will spend and be spent myself for your souls; although loving you more, I be loved less." (2a. 2æ. Q. 184, a. 2, ad 3um.)

SEPTEMBER 18

Why Love Our Enemies?

"Thou shalt love thy neighbor as thyself." (Matt. XXII, 30.)

It is clear that you sin if you do not grant pardon to the person who has injured or offended you. It is Christian Charity that we love such persons, attract them to God, and let them share in our friendship, and many reasons induce us to do this. First, the preservation of our own dignity; secondly, the winning of a victory; thirdly, the example of many advantages; fourthly, because our prayers are more easily heard, and fifthly, sin is avoided, which we should especially desire.

We should love our enemies in order to preserve our own dignity as Christians. Different dignities have different signs. But no one should throw away the signs of his own dignity. Amongst all the signs of dignity, the greatest is that we are children of God. The sign of this dignity is that you love your enemies. "Love your enemies ... so that you may be children of your Father Who is in heaven" (Matt. V, 44). If we love only our friends, that is not a sign of our Divine affiliation, for even sinners and heathens do this.

Secondly, there is the victory which we achieve from loving our enemies. Everyone naturally desires to be a winner and to secure the prize of victory. But to be victorious in this contest over self, you must attract him who has offended you; attract him to love by your own goodness; for if you entertain hatred against your offender you lose. "Be not overcome by evil, but overcome evil by good" (Rom. XII, 21).

Thirdly, there is the good and far reaching example resulting from the love we show our enemies. Through this means you make friends. "If thy enemy be hungry, give him to eat, if he thirst give him to drink . . . and the Lord will reward thee" (Rom. XII, 20). There can be no greater incentive to love than to love one's enemy for the love of God. No one is so hard-hearted, that even if he is unwilling to manifest love, still he is attracted by love.

Fourthly, our prayers are more easily and quickly answered if we forgive our enemies who may have offended, insulted or injured us. Hence it is written in Jeremias XV, 1: "The Lord said, if Moses and Samuel shall stand before me, my soul is not towards this people." Namely, they who pray for their enemies will win the friendship of God for themselves and for their persecutors. Likewise, Christ said, "Father forgive them," as He hung upon the Cross on Calvary. Likewise St. Stephen, the martyr, did a great service to the Church when he prayed for those who stoned him to death, because through his prayers Paul was converted from a persecutor of the Church to an Apostle of Christ.

Fifthly, by showing love towards our enemies we avoid a multitude of sins. Sometimes we sin when we do not seek God, and God often wishes to draw us to Himself, sometimes through sickness and again through persecution from our enemies. "I will hedge up the way with thorns" (Osee, II, 6). Thus was St. Paul treated . . . "I have gone astray as a sheep that was lost. Seek Thy Servant Oh Lord, for I have not forgotten Thy commandments" (Ps. CLXVIII). But we follow the way of the Lord if we forgive our enemies. "Forgive and you will be forgiven" (Matt. V, 7). And again Christ said: "Blessed are the merciful, for they shall obtain mercy," for there is no greater mercy than to pardon our enemies. "Do good to those who hate you. Bless those who curse you and pray for those who persecute and calumniate you." Such is God's Way and God's Law.

SEPTEMBER 19

Is Mercy the Greatest Virtue?

It would seem that mercy is the greatest of the virtues. But on the contrary, the Apostle says (Col. III, 14), "Above all things have charity, which is the bond of perfection." Hence, mercy is not the greatest of virtues. "Mercy," says Saint Augustine, "is a heartfelt sympathy for another's distress, impelling us to help him if we can."

1. Any virtue can be considered the greatest in two ways, first, in itself; secondly, in comparison with its subject. In itself, indeed mercy is the greatest, for it belongs to mercy to be generous to others and what is more to help others in their wants, which pertains chiefly to a superior. Hence mercy is properly attributed to God, and therein His Allpowerfulness is said to be chiefly manifested.

On the other hand, with regard to its subject, mercy is not the greatest virtue unless that the subject is greater than all others, surpassed by none and exceeding all. For whosoever has anyone above him, it is better for that person to be united to that which is above him than to supply the defect of that which is beneath. Hence, as regards man, who has God above him, charity which unites him to God is greater than mercy, whereby he supplies the defects of his neighbour. But of all the virtues which relate to our neighbour mercy is the greatest, even as its act surpasses all others, since it belongs to one who is higher and better to supply the defect of another inasmuch as the latter is deficient.

But mercy, according to the prophet Osee, VI, 6, is preferred it would seem, to the worship of God. "I have desired mercy and not sacrifice," because we worship God by external sacrifices and gifts not for His profit, but for that of ourselves and our neighbour. God, it is true, needs not our sacrifices but wishes them to be offered to Him in order to arouse our devotion and to help our neighbour. Hence mercy whereby we supply others' defects is a sacrifice more acceptable to God, as leading more directly to our neighbour's well-being, according to Heb. XIII, 16, "Do not forget to do good and to impart, for by such sacrifices God's favor is obtained."

Although the sum total of the Christian religion consists in mercy, as regards external works; but the inward love of charity, whereby we are united to God takes precedence over both love and mercy for our neighbour. From this results in us a better likeness to God. For charity likens us to God by uniting us to Him in the bond of love. Wherefore it is more powerful than mercy by which we are likened to God as regards similarity of works.

2. Three things especially should inspire us to have mercy, namely, its need, its usefulness, its suitableness.

First, its need, because he who does not show mercy will not find mercy. "Judgment without mercy to him who hath not done mercy." (James II, 13.)

Secondly, its usefulness, because he who shows mercy will find mercy. "Blessed are the merciful, for they shall obtain mercy." (Matth. V, 7.)

Thirdly, its suitableness, because since we receive mercy from all creatures, it is altogether fitting that we be merciful to others. For we are full of misery, and unless persons showed mercy to us by giving themselves and favours to us we could not live. For if the sun withdrew from us its light, and if fire deprived us of its heat, and the earth its riches, what would miserable man do? How wretched would be his condition? Therefore it is sufficiently suitable that man since he needs mercy, should show mercy unto others.

SEPTEMBER 20

The Fourfold Good of the Law of Love

Since all people cannot study science, a brief law has been given by our Lord, so that it can be known by all and no one because of ignorance can be excused from its observance; and this law is the law of Divine Love. "The Lord has placed a brief word upon all the world." (Rom. IX.) This law should be the rule of all human actions, so that every human deed might be right and virtuous. When our actions are in harmony with the Divine rule of love, they are truly good, right and perfect, but when they are not in harmony with it, they depart from the law of love Divine. Moreover the law of Divine love produces in man four very desirable things.

First, it causes spiritual life in him, for it is clear, that the one loved is naturally in (the mind of) the one loving, and therefore whoever loves God has God in him. "God is charity, and he that abideth in charity, abideth in God, and God in him." (1 John IV, 16.) Even the nature of love is such that it transforms the lover into the beloved. Wherefore if we love evil and earthly things, we become sinful and restless. But if we love God, we become divine, or Godlike; because, "he who is joined to the Lord, is one spirit." (1 Cor. VI, 17.) Hence Augustine says, "Just as the soul is the life of the body, so God is the life of the soul." Rightly then, do we say that the body lives because of the soul, when it has the proper actions of life, and when it is operated and moved by the soul; but when the soul departs from the body, the body is dead—it is neither operated nor moved. So also then, the soul operates virtuously and perfectly, when it operates through charity, by which God dwells in it, for without charity, the soul does not rightly operate."

Moreover if anyone should have all the gifts of the Holy Spirit, and have not charity, he has not life. He lacks spiritual life. Even if he should have the gift of tongues, or the gift of faith, or whatever else he may have, without charity he does not possess spiritual life; for if a dead body is clothed with gold, and precious diamonds, nevertheless it is a dead body.

Secondly, charity causes the divine commandments to be observed. Gregory says, "Never is the love of God a burden, for it does great things wherever it exists. Moreover if work is a failure, or despised, there divine love is not present. Hence, an evident sign of charity is promptitude in observing the Divine commandments. For we have seen that the lover does great and difficult things for the sake of the beloved."

The third thing which love accomplishes, is that it becomes a stronghold against adversities. For to the one having charity, no adverse circumstance can injure him, but on the contrary, adversities become useful to him. "To those loving God, all things cooperate unto good." (Rom. VIII, 28.) Moreover adversities and trials become delightful to the one loving God, as we clearly see from everyday examples among us.

The fourth thing which charity does for us, is that it leads us to happiness. For only to those having charity, is eternal happiness promised; yea more, without charity, all other things are as nothing. Be it remembered therefore, that according to our degree of charity, will be our degree of eternal happiness; and not according to any other virtue.

SEPTEMBER 21

Other Advantages of the Law of Love

1. Charity obtains the pardon of our sins. For if anyone offends another, and afterwards intimately loves the offended person, because of that the offender secures pardon for himself; and likewise God pardons the sins of those who truly love Him. From this, someone might say, "therefore charity suffices to remit sins, and penance is not necessary." But we must remember, that no one truly loves God who does not truly and sincerely do penance. For inasmuch as we love anyone the more, by so much the more should we grieve if we offend that person, and this is one effect of charity.

2. Charity causes enlightenment of heart as Job, XXXVII, 19, says, "We are all wrapped up in darkness." For very often we do not know what we should do or desire, but charity teaches all things necessary for salvation. Hence it is written in 1 John II, 27, "His unction teacheth you about all things." The reason for this is, because where charity exists, there is the Holy Spirit, Who knows all things and leads us on the right road. Wherefore it is said in Eccli. II, 10, "Ye that fear the Lord, love Him and your hearts shall be enlightened."

3. Charity produces in man perfect joy, for no one has true joy unless he who abideth in charity. Whosoever desires something rejoices not, is not happy, nor satisfied until he possesses that thing. But it happens in our search for things temporal, that our desires are not satisfied fully, our needs are despised, and disgust is generated. But it is not so in our search for things spiritual. On the contrary, he who loves God, possesses Him, and therefore the soul of the one loving and desiring God rests in Him, and is satisfied in Him.

4. Charity causes perfect peace. It happens in temporal things, that often they are desired, but in their possession the mind of the person desiring these things is not perfectly satisfied; even when he has what he desired, he still desires something more. "The wicked are like a raging sea which cannot rest, and the waves thereof cast up dirt and mire. There is no peace to the wicked, said the Lord God." (Isaias LVII, 20.) But such is not the case in charity concerning God. For he who loves God has perfect peace of soul. "Much peace have they that love Thy law, and to them there is no stumbling block." (Psalm CXVIII, 165.) The reason for this is there-

fore, because God alone satisfies the fulfillment of our every desire. For God is at His best in our hearts, and therefore Saint Augustine says, "Thou hast made us for Thyself, O Lord, and our hearts are restless until they rest in Thee."

5. Charity makes a man of great dignity. All created things serve the Divine Majesty, as artificial artisans serve their master, but charity makes of a slave, a free man and a friend. Hence the Lord said to the Apostles, "I will not now call you servants, but friends." Not only does charity make us free, but also sons, so that we are called and are the sons of God. For when a stranger becomes the adopted child of another, he acquires for himself a right to the possessions of the adopter, and so likewise charity acquires a right to a share of the inheritance of God, which is life eternal. "Behold how they are numbered among the children of God, and their lot is among the saints." (Wisdom V, 5.)

SEPTEMBER 22

The Love of God

"Thou shalt love the Lord thy God with thy whole heart, and with thy whole soul, and with all thy strength, and with all thy mind." (Luke X, 27.)

1. This precept is differently worded in various places of Sacred Scripture. For in Deut. VI; three points are enumerated, namely, "with thy whole heart, and with thy whole soul, and with thy whole strength." In Matth. XXII, we find two of these mentioned, namely, "with thy whole heart and with thy whole soul," while with thy whole strength is omitted, but "with thy whole mind," is added. Yet in Mark XII, we find all four, namely, "with thy whole heart, and with thy whole soul, and with thy whole mind, and with thy whole force" which is the same as "strength." Moreover, these four are indicated in Luke X; where in place of "force," we read "with all thy strength."

2. Hence a reason for these four must be assigned, for if one of them is omitted here or there, it is because one is implied in the others. We must therefore observe, that love is an act of the will which is here denoted by "the heart," because just as the bodily heart is the principle of all the

movements of the body, so, too, the will, especially as regards the intention of the last end which is the object of charity, is the principle of all the movements of the soul. Now there are three principles of action that are moved by the will, namely, the intellect which is signified by "the mind," the lower appetitive power, signified by "the soul," and the exterior executive power signified by "strength, force, or might." Therefore, we are commanded to direct our whole intention to God, and this is signified by the words "with thy whole heart," to submit our intellect to God, and this is expressed in the words "with thy whole mind," and to regulate our appetite according to God, in the words, "with thy whole soul"; and to obey God in our external actions, and this means to love God "with our whole strength, force, or might."

Saint John Chrysostom, on the other hand, takes "heart and soul" in the opposite sense, and Augustine refers "heart" to the thought, "soul" to the manner of life, and "mind" to the intellect. Again some explain "with thy whole heart," as meaning the intellect, "with thy whole soul" as signifying the will, "with thy whole mind" as referring to the memory. And again according to Gregory of Nyssa, "heart" signifies the vegetative soul, "soul" the sensitive, and "mind" the intellective soul, because our nourishment, sensation and understanding ought all to be referred by us to God.

3. In Divine Love, or in our love for God, no mode must be observed. ("God," writes Saint Bernard, "is the cause of our loving God, the measure of our love is to love Him without measure.") For the end of all human actions and affections is the love of God, whereby principally we attain our last end, wherefore the mode in the love of God must not be taken as in a thing measured in which there is more or less, but as in the measure itself, where there cannot be excess and where the more the rule is reached the better it is, so that the more we love God the better our love is. (2. 2ae. Q. 27, A. 6.)

SEPTEMBER 23

Four Things Necessary to Fulfill the Precept of the Love of God

Christ being asked before His Passion, what was the greatest and first commandment, answered, "thou shalt love the Lord thy God, with thy whole heart, and with thy whole mind; this is the greatest and first commandment." In truth, this commandment is the greatest, the most excellent and most useful of all the commandments, because in obeying this commandment, we obey all the commandments. But in order that it might be perfectly observed by us four things are required.

1. A remembrance of Divine favours, because all (the good) things which we have, either of body or soul, or external, we have received from God; and therefore, we should be grateful to Him for all things and love Him with a perfect heart. For he who thinks of the favours received from another, is exceedingly ungrateful if he does not love that person. King David reflecting on Divine favours, exclaimed, "All things are Thine, and we have given Thee what we have received of Thy hand. Now therefore, our God, we give thanks to Thee, and we praise Thy glorious Name." (1 Par. XXIX, 13.) Hence, in God's praise it is written again, "With his whole heart he praised the Lord, and loved God that made him, and God gave him power against his enemies." (Eccl. XLVII, 10.)

2. A consideration of the Divine Excellence is necessary. "For God is greater than our heart." (1 John III, 20.) Hence, if we should serve Him with our whole heart and with all our strength, we would not sufficiently praise Him. "Glorify the Lord as much as ever you can, for He will yet far exceed, and His magnificence is wonderful. Blessing the Lord, exalt Him as much as you can, for He is above all praise." (Eccle. XLIII, 32.)

3. A renunciation of worldly and earthly things. For he does a great injury to God, who likens something to God or loves something more than God. "To whom then have you likened God?" (Isaias, XL, 18.) But we do liken other things to God, when we love temporal and perishable things more than God or together with God. The latter is entirely impossible. "For the bed is straitened, so that one must fall out, and a short covering cannot cover both." (Isaias, XXVIII, 20.) Here the heart of man is likened to a straitened bed and a short covering. For the human heart is a bed in respect to God. Hence, when you receive other things into your heart in preference to Him, you expel Him, for He does not permit a consort or partner in the soul, not even as a man and wife; and therefore He Himself has said, "Thou shalt not have strange gods before Me. I am the Lord thy God, mighty, jealous." (Exod. XX, 5.) For He wishes that we love nothing as much as Him or more than Him.

4. The entire shunning of sin. For no one can love God who is living in sin. Hence if you are living in sin, you do not love God. But he loved God (namely Ezechias) who prayed thus, "I beseech Thee, O Lord, remember how I have walked before Thee in truth, and with a perfect heart, and have done that which is good in Thy sight." (Isaias, XXXVIII, 3.) In addition to this the prophet Elias exclaims, "How long do you halt between two sides? If the Lord be God, follow Him." (3 Kings, XVIII, 21.) Just as a blind man or as one halting now here and now there changes for the worse (way), so likewise does the sinner who now sins, and then strives to find God. Wherefore the Lord says: "Be converted to Me with all your heart, in fasting, and in weeping, and in mourning." (Joel. II, 12.) (In Decalog. C, V.)

SEPTEMBER 24

How It Is Possible to Have Perfect Charity in This Life

1. The perfection of charity may be understood in two ways. In one way, with regard to the object loved, and secondly, with regard to the person who loves. With regard to the object loved, charity is perfect if the object be loved as much as it is lovable. Now God is as lovable as He is good and His goodness is infinite, wherefore, He is infinitely lovable. But no creature can love Him infinitely, since all created power is finite. Consequently, no person's charity can be perfect in this manner; the charity of God alone can, whereby He loves Himself.

2. On the part of the person who loves, charity is perfect when he loves as much as he can. This happens in three ways.

First, so that man's whole heart is always actually borne towards God. This is the perfection of charity in heaven, and is not possible in this life, wherein, because of the weakness of human life, it is impossible to think always actually of God and to be moved by love towards Him.

Secondly, so that man makes an earnest endeavour to give his time to God and Divine things which scorning other things except in so far as the needs of the present life demand. This is the perfection of charity that is possible to a wayfarer; but it is not common to all who have charity.

Thirdly, so that a man gives his whole heart to God habitually, for example, by neither thinking nor desiring anything contrary to the love of God; and this perfection is common to all who have charity.

Therefore, perfect charity is possible in this life, but still perfection on the way (to heaven) is not absolute perfection, but is such that it can always increase.

The perfection of charity to which the Counsels are ordained consists in this, that man in as far as it is possible, renounce temporal things, even lawful things, which by occupying his mind, impede the actual motion of the heart toward God.

God intends by the precept, "thou shalt love the Lord thy God with thy whole heart, and with thy whole mind," that man be united wholly to Him, which happens in heaven, when "God will be all things to all men." Consequently, the above precept will be fulfilled fully and perfectly in heaven. On the way (to heaven) however, the precept of love of God is fulfilled, but imperfectly, and still while on the way, in so far as one person fulfills this precept more perfectly, by so much the more does his or her charity, through a certain likeness, resemble the perfection of heaven." (2a. 2ae. Q. 46, a. 6.)

SEPTEMBER 25

An Increase of Charity

1. The charity of a wayfarer can increase. For we are called wayfarers, because we are on the way to God, Who is the last end of our happiness. In this way we advance as we come closer to God, Who is approached "not by steps of the body but by affections of the mind," writes Augustine; and this approach is through charity, since it unites man's mind to God. Consequently, it is necessary to the charity of a wayfarer that it increase, for if it could not, all further advance along the way would cease. Hence the Apostle calls charity the way, when he says, "I will show you a more excellent way." (1 Cor. XII, 31.)

2. The charity of a wayfarer can be increased more and more. For in no manner is a limit imposed to the increase of man's charity, while he is in the state of a wayfarer. For charity, by its very nature, has no limit to its increase, since it is a participation of the infinite charity which is the Holy

Ghost. In like manner the cause of the increase of charity, namely, God, is possessed of infinite power. Furthermore, on the part of its subject, no limit to this increase can be determined, because whenever charity increases, there is a corresponding increased ability to receive a further increase. For the capacity of the rational creature is increased through charity, since the heart is enlarged thereby, according to 2 Cor. VI, 2, "Our heart is enlarged," so that no limit to the increase of charity can be fixed in this life. Charity can go on increasing here indefinitely.

3. Charity is not increased by the addition of charity to charity, but through this that the subject participates more and more of charity, that is, by his being more influenced by its act and more subjected to its power. The increase of charity means a change to having more from having less, so that there is need, not for anything to be there (in the soul) that was there before, but that something is there now in a greater degree than was there before. This is what God does when He increases charity, that is, He makes it to have a greater hold on the soul, and the likeness of the Holy Ghost to be more perfectly participated by the soul.

4. The spiritual increase of charity is somewhat like the increase of the body. Now bodily increase in animals and plants is not a continuous movement, but for a certain space of time nature works by disposing for the increase without causing any actual increase, and afterwards brings into effect that to which it had disposed, by giving the animal or plant an actual increase.

In like manner, charity does not increase through every act of charity, but each act of charity disposes us to an increase of charity, in so far as one act of charity makes man more ready to act again according to charity, and this readiness increasing, man breaks out into an act of more fervent love, and strives to advance in charity, and then his charity increases actually.

Every act of charity merits eternal life, which however, is not to be granted immediately, but at its proper time. In like manner, every act of charity merits an increase of charity; yet this increase does not take place at once, but when we strive for that increase. (2a. 2ae. q. 24, a. 4, 7.)

SEPTEMBER 26

Three Degrees of Charity

1. "Charity," says Augustine, "when it is born, is nourished, which refers to beginners, after being nourished, it grows strong, which pertains to those who are advancing, and when it becomes strong, it is perfected; which refers to the perfect." Therefore, there are three degrees of charity.

The spiritual increase of charity may be considered in respect of a certain likeness to the growth of the human body. For although this latter growth may be divided into many parts, yet it has certain fixed divisions according to those particular actions or pursuits to which a man is brought by this same growth. Thus, we speak of a man being an infant until he has the use of reason, after which we distinguish another state of man wherein he begins to speak and to use his reason, while there is a third state, that of puberty, when he begins to acquire the power of generation, and so on until he arrives at perfection. In like manner the different degrees of charity are distinguished according to the various pursuits to which a man is brought by the increase of charity.

2. For at first it is incumbent on man to occupy himself chiefly with avoiding sin and resisting his concupiscences, which move him in opposition to charity; and this concerns beginners, in whom charity has to be fed or fostered lest it be destroyed.

Secondly, man's chief pursuit is to aim at progress in good; and this is the pursuit of the proficient; whose chief aim is to strengthen their charity by adding to it. But man's third pursuit is to aim principally at union with and enjoyment of God. This belongs to the perfect who "desire to be dissolved and to be with Christ." In like manner, we observe in local motion that at first there is the departure from one place (or term), then approach to the other term, and thirdly, rest in this term.

Although those who are beginners in charity may progress, yet the chief care that hangs over them is to resist the sins which disturb them by their attack. Afterwards, however, when they come to feel this attack less, they begin to tend to perfection with greater security, yet with one hand doing the work, and with the other holding the sword as related in Esdras, IV, 17, concerning the builders of Jerusalem.

Even the perfect make progress in charity, yet this is not

their principal care, but their aim is chiefly directed towards union with God. And although the beginner and the proficient seek this, yet their solicitude is chiefly about other things, the beginner, about avoiding sin, the proficient, about advancing in virtue. (2a. 2ae. q. 24, a. 9.)

SEPTEMBER 27

Things Necessary to Acquire and Increase Charity

Since charity is so useful, we must earnestly strive to acquire it and increase it. Two things are especially necessary to acquire charity, and two things to increase the charity acquired.

1. To acquire therefore, charity, there must be first of all a loving attention to the word of God. For those listening to good things about some friend, their love is increased for that friend, and so, too, when we listen to the word of God, we should be enkindled with love for God and for His Holy Gospel. "Thy word is exceedingly refined, and Thy servant has loved it." (Ps. CXVIII, 140.) And likewise, the two disciples mentioned by Saint Luke, XXIV, 32, burned with Divine Love on hearing the word of God. "Was not our heart burning within us, whilst He spoke on the way, and opened to us the Scriptures."

2. Secondly, we must think continually of good things. "My heart grew warm within me, and in my meditation a fire shall flame forth." (Ps. XXXVIII, 4.) Consequently, if you wish to obtain Divine love, you must meditate on good things. It would be almost impossible for one who pursues Divine favours, avoids dangerous occasions of sin, if meditating upon the happiness promised to him by Almighty God, his heart would not burn with love Divine. Hence Augustine says, "Hard indeed is the heart of a man who even if he is unwilling to expand with this love, should be willing to return love. And just as all evil thoughts destroy charity, so, too, all good thoughts acquire it, nourish it and preserve it."

There are also two things necessary to increase charity already acquired.

1. First, the separation of the heart from earthly things. For the heart cannot be perfectly centered on diverse things. Hence, no one can love God and the world at the same time.

Consequently, inasmuch as our soul is divorced from the love of worldly things, by so much the more it becomes strengthened with Divine love. Hence Augustine says that, "the destruction of charity is the hope of possessing and of retaining worldly things, while the food of charity is the removal of avarice, and perfection of charity, means no avarice" (no passionate longing for earthly things). Whosoever therefore, wishes to nourish charity, must insist on removing sinful desires, or avarice. But avarice is a love of possessing or obtaining worldly things. The beginning of lessening this avarice is a holy fear of God, Who alone cannot be feared without love. For this purpose therefore, is religion, by which the mind is drawn away from mundane things, and directed to things Divine. This is signified where it is said, "The sun which was first in a little cloud, shone brightly." The sun, that is, the human intellect, is in a little cloud, when it is absorbed with earthly things, but it shines splendidly, when it is separated and removed from the love of worldly things. For then, Divine love shines in it and increases in it.

The second thing necessary to increase charity, is a firm patience in adversities. For when we endure hard things for one whom we love, love is not destroyed, but rather increased, and therefore the Saints and holy persons who endured trials for God's sake, became more strengthened in His love; just as the artist who loves more the masterpiece in which he has labored more. Hence it is that the faithful in so far as they suffer and endure more afflictions for God, by so much the more are they exalted in their love of Him. (Decalog. C, IV.)

SEPTEMBER 28

On the Love of the Highest and Most Delightful Good

"I remembered God, and was delighted." (Ps. LXXVI, 4.)

God, just as He excels every desirable thing, in like manner rejoices the heart more than all delightful things, and does this in three ways, namely, in a more general, a more intimate and more lasting manner.

1. Other things delight in a particular way, as flavour delights the taste, but not the sense of touch; sound rejoices the hearing, not the vision and so of each thing. But God

affords pleasure generally, because He is a universal good and the cause of every particular good (the source of true happiness and of genuine joy). Hence Saint Anselm says, "If singular good things are delightful and pleasing to us, how delightful is that Supreme Good (which contains in Itself the sweetness of all good things. A sweetness, the like of which we find not in things created, but a sweetness that differs as much as the Creator differs from the creature."

2. Other things afford us pleasure in a superficial manner, as if exteriorly, but God delights us intimately and therefore profoundly. For God alone substantially penetrates the very substance of our soul, and consequently, rejoices the marrow of our bones. Accordingly, Augustine says, "When I adhere to Thee with my whole mind, never will it be labour and grief, but filled will my whole life be; filled completely of Thee. O Lord God! what is it that I love when I love Thee? It is not the appearance of Thy Body, not the beauty of Thy countenance, not the brightness of Thy light so friendly to my eyes, not the sweet perfume of flowers, not manna, and honey, not something pleasing to the flesh. No, I do not love these when I love my God, and yet I love a certain Light, a certain Voice, and sweetness, a certain food, and certain embrace. I do not love my God, as I love light, voice, odor, food, embrace of the exterior man, but of my interior self, where God floods my soul, which no place embraces, and wherein He is heard everywhere, and everywhere emits a sweet odor which no blast can scatter, a sweetness which my entire soul partakes of, and nothing can lessen, which adheres to it, so that nothing can tear it away. This is what I love when I love my God."

3. Other things delight temporarily and limitedly, but God eternally. Hence Augustine says, "Wretched indeed, is every soul, shackled with friendship for inferior things, torn apart when it loses them, but no one loses Thee, O Lord, except he who abandons Thee." The reason is, because every created thing is changeable in itself. But whereas, "a soul that is filled (or satisfied) shall tread upon the honeycomb" (Prov. XXVII, 7), but a soul loving created things longs for them, because pursuing and possessing them, enjoys them and delights in them, so that the more he longs for the created good, the less he desires God—the increated Good. Consequently, hunger of soul results from a love of created things, according to the Psalmist, LXXVI, 3, "My soul refused to be comforted," by these temporary things. "But I remembered God, and was delighted." Wherefore Augustine writes, "The

creature despises other things, but the Creator sweetens (rejoices) the heart." (On the Love of God, IV.)

SEPTEMBER 29

On the Causes of Love

1. You are a friend of a certain man because you are present. But in this respect, God excels in a threefold manner, for He is present, within (the soul), present always and everywhere. Man is present because he is alongside of you, but God is more intimately present, because He is within you. Augustine says, "God is nearest to the heart, and yet the heart wanders away from Him. Man is present sometimes, and sometimes absent through necessity, but God is never absent from you, although sometimes you wander away and are absent from Him. Thou, O Lord, art within, and I am outside, and there I have sought Thee, and I deformed (by sin) rushed blindly upon Thy beautiful form. Thou wert with me, and I was not with Thee."

God is present everywhere. Hence when you are dying, then indeed, you will need the consoling presence of friends, yet you cannot have them; but you can have the consoling Presence of your best Friend. "If I walk in the midst of the shadow of death, I will fear no evils, for Thou art with Me." (Ps. XXII.)

2. You are a friend of man because you are useful to him. In this respect also, God excels in three ways, because greater, more manifold and more lasting usefulness comes to you from Him. A friend may give you his own possessions. But God gives you His own gifts and Himself. "He that spared not even His own Son, but delivered Him up for us all. How has He not also, with Him, given us all things?" (Rom. VIII, 32.) Who among your friends will give his own son or his own soul to you? but God has done it. He gives His own gifts, and Himself, for He gives gifts which are nobler, greater, more permanent in duration and in time, than any man can bestow, and better in relation to the end. God has given many and great gifts to us in the past, while now He gives and continues giving, but in the future He will give His greatest and most manifold gifts.

3. You are a friend of man because perhaps you are

amiable. "A man amiable in society shall be more friendly than a brother." (Prov. XVIII, 24.) But three things make a man amiable, a pleasing countenance, affability in conversation and meekness in action. But God excels in these gifts. Truly is it written that, "favour is deceitful and beauty is vain" (Prov. XXXI, 30), for health lends beauty of complexion and youthfulness to old age. For it is evident that sickness takes away beauty when health is gone and old age replaces the former youthfulness, or death changes the complexion. But most amiable is He Whose "face is full of grace, and shone as the sun. Upon Whom the Angels love to gaze," Whose beauty fades not, but which makes those safe who contemplate it; a beauty which never grows old, but causes rejuvenation; a beauty that never dies, but lives eternally.

Likewise, amiable is he who is more amiable in conversation. "The Lord spoke to Moses as a man speaks to a friend" (Ex. XXXIII, 2.) He is amiable not only to the just, but also to the unjust, inasmuch as He was a friend to Publicans and sinners.

He is likewise amiable because meek in action, "I was as meek as a lamb." (Jer. XI, 19.) (The Love of God X, XI, XII.)

SEPTEMBER 30

Progress in Love of God

1. The state of penitents resembles the glow of a fire, where there is a fire in earthly material. Isaias says (IV, 4), "If the Lord shall wash away the filth of the daughters of Sion, and shall wash away the blood of Jerusalem out of the midst thereof, by the spirit of burning." Truly in this state of penance are found some who are lukewarm, a few inflamed, fewer fervent, and very few ardent (or glowing with love of penance).

2. The state of those advancing on the road of this praiseworthy action of repentance, resembles the ever increasing brightness of a fiery flame, rising upwards more and more, and being enkindled from a charcoal (or spark of love) is nobler in matter and clearer in form. Indeed in this stage of repentance you find not all who are ardent, but some lukewarm, others eager, few fervent, and most rarely ardent repenters. You have a good example in those two disciples of

whom it is written, "Was not our heart burning within us, while He spoke to us on the way, and opened to us the Scriptures." Behold here, and learn from those disciples, that they burned with love from two causes. Behold in these two disciples, motion and action. In their motion consider four things. First, the two were travelling together, in number a united society. Learn not from the masters but from the disciples. Thirdly, they were travelling on a certain day, and not at night. Fourthly, the end of their journey signifies their desire of perfection, "they were going to Emmaus, which means the desire of counsel" (or desire of perfection).

Their action may be described in three ways. 1) They were thinking in their hearts on the Passion of Christ, and therefore "they were sad," and not rejoicing in a worldly manner. 2) They were conversing not about vain things, but "concerning all these good things which had happened"; namely, that which was done in work. 3) The hospitality they showed to the Stranger (namely to the Master). And Jesus approaching these two disciples walked along with them, never rebuked them, but opened and explained to them the sacred scriptures, and thus inspired them with love, causing the flame of love to burn more brightly.

3. Finally, the state of those resting in the peace of contemplation, resembles here the brightly burning flame of light. But nevertheless, you find also among the contemplatives, the zealous, the fervent and very few glowing with Divine love. Of such were those of Jerusalem, sitting there, receiving the Divine fire. Concerning these Gregory says, While they received God in vision they were sweetly inflamed with love." This is a great vision, love without punishment, sweet not burdensome; so that Moses wondered how the bush was on fire and was not burnt. "And the Lord appeared to him in a flame of fire out of the midst of a bush; and Moses saw that the bush was on fire and was not burnt." (Ex. III, 4.) (On the Love of God.)

SUNDAY, OCTOBER 1

Rosary Feast

Our Lady was full of grace which made fruitful the conception of her Son. Hence the Angel said to her, "Fear not, Mary, for thou hast found grace with God. Behold thou shalt conceive in thy womb, and bring forth a son, and thou shalt call His name Jesus. (Luke I, 30.) That indeed, is a work of great admiration and of great dignity, that at once and at the same time she would become the Mother and daughter of God, mother and handmaid, Virgin and mother. Hence, because of this grace she became most dear to God. It is said figuratively of Esther, "she was brought to the chamber of the king, and the king loved her more than all the women, and she had favour and kindness before him above all the women, and he set the royal crown on her head, and made her queen." (Esther II, 17.) Again it is written in Apoc. XII, 1, "A great sign appeared in heaven. A woman clothed with the sun, and the moon under her feet, and on her head a crown of twelve stars."

Wherefore Bernard addresses her thus, "O Lady how familiar thou art with Christ, how close to Him, how immaculate thou didst merit to become! Thou hast found so much favour (grace) with Him that He has remained in Thee, and thou in Him. Thou didst clothe Him. You will be clothed by Him. Thou didst clothe Him with the substance of thy own flesh, but He has clothed thee with the glory of His Majesty."

Although our Lady's greatness in being granted so sublime a favour, cannot be imitated (or fully expressed), still she must be shown every honour, preached and praised, and invoked by us in our every need. For Bernard again says, "In all thy troubles look upon the star of the sea. Call upon and invoke Mary, because it is she who obtains favour and calm for us on life's sea, and is our safest way among life's turbulent waves. She is the anchor by which the ship sails steadily at sea, yea she is the ship in which man is rescued from the waves of temptation. Whosoever neglects to praise her, can scarcely hope to be heard in time of tribulations."

It is necessary therefore, that whosoever desires to obtain favour with God, should approach this mediatrix, approach her with a most devout heart because since she is the Queen of Mercy, possessing everything in the kingdom of God's justice, she cannot refuse your petition. For as Saint Bernard says, "When the sinner asks her for a favour, she shows her heart (her pierced and immaculate heart) to her Divine Son; while the Son shows His pierced side and wounds to the Eternal Father. Wherefore, no refusal can exist, where there are so many signs of charity." Hence it is that the Apostle speaking to the Hebrews (IV, 16) said, "let us go therefore, with confidence to the throne of grace, that we may obtain mercy, and find grace in seasonable aid." For of Mary it has been truly written, "I am the mother of fair love, and of fear, and of knowledge, and of holy hope. In me is all grace of the way. In me is all hope of life and of virtue. Therefore, come over to me, all ye that desire me." (Eccli. XXIV, 24.) (The Hail Mary, 2.)

SUNDAY, OCTOBER 2

The Maternity of the Blessed Virgin

It was most fitting that Christ should be born of a woman.

1. First because in this way the entire human nature was ennobled. Hence Augustine says, "It was suitable that man's liberation should be made manifest in both sexes. Consequently, since it behoved a man, being of the nobler sex, to assume human nature, it was becoming that the liberation of the female sex should be manifest in this, that man was born of a woman. Otherwise, it might seem that the female sex might be despised. Therefore, men, despise not yourselves; for the Son of God became a man. Despise not yourselves, women; for the Son of God was born of a woman."

2. Secondly, because in this manner every diversity of human generation is accomplished. For the first man was made from the slime of the earth, without the cooperation of man or woman. Eve was made of man but not of woman, and other men are made from both man and woman. Hence, this fourth manner remained as it were proper to Christ, that He should be made of a woman without the concurrence of a man.

3. The Blessed Virgin is the mother of God.

For to conceive and to be born is attributed to a person. Since therefore, in the very beginning of conception, human nature was assumed by the Divine Person, it follows that it can be truly said that God was conceived and born of a Virgin. From this very fact moreover, any woman is said to be the mother of her son, when she conceives and begets him. Hence it follows that the Blessed Virgin can be truly called Mother of God. (3a. pars. q. 35, a. 4.)

And Saint Ignatius uses a beautiful example when he says, "In begetting man, a woman is called a mother, although a woman does not give man his rational soul which is from God, but she is called mother, because she gives her substance to the formation of the body. Consequently, a woman is called the mother of the whole man, because that which is assumed from her is united to the rational soul. Likewise, since the humanity of Christ was assumed from the Blessed Virgin, because of its union to the Divinity, the Blessed Virgin is called the mother of the Man, but also the mother of God, although the Divinity was not assumed by her, just as in others the rational soul is not assumed by the mother."

In this manner the dignity of Mary is clearly manifested. For to no other creature, neither to man nor to an Angel was the privilege granted of becoming the mother of God. But this privilege of a special grace was destined for Mary that she should become not only the mother of the Man God, but also the mother of God; and therefore is it written in Apoc. XII, 1, "a woman clothed with the sun," as if completely filled with the Divinity. Hence Saint Matthew says, I, 18, "Now the generation of Christ was in this wise. When as His mother Mary was espoused to Joseph, before they came together, she was found with child, of the Holy Ghost."

3. The mother of God has a certain infinite dignity.

Just as in each created good thing there is something finite which can become something better, so too in every increated good, there is that which is infinite, that can become nothing better. Therefore the goodness of a creature can be considered in two ways. One which is of the essence of it, and so each creature can become something better; or secondly, by comparison to the increated good, and in this wise, dignity of the creature receives a certain infinity from which it is compared to something infinite; just as human nature in as far as it is united to God and the Blessed Virgin, in so far as she is the mother of God, and finally, grace, in so far as it unites us to God. (1 Dist. 44, q. 1.)

SUNDAY, OCTOBER 3

The Feast of the Purity of the Blessed Virgin

"A holy and shamefaced woman is grace upon grace." (Eccli. XXVI, 19.)

1. Such was the Blessed Virgin, who not only had grace common to all but over and above this grace, she also possessed sanctifying grace, so that she was not only holy in her life but likewise in the womb of her mother. Augustine says, "When

we speak of sin, I in no wise wish to impute sin to the mother of God, who was absolutely exempt from all sin, but if all the Saints and holy persons, men and women were united in one place, and asked whether they were without sin, what would their answer be, unless that which Saint John says, "If we say that we have no sin, we deceive ourselves, and the truth is not in us." (1 John I, 8.) Hence of all women, it can be truly said of Mary alone: "My heart doth not reprehend me in all my life." (Job, XXVI, 6.)

In this gift, moreover, we cannot imitate her, because just as we are conceived in sin, so too are we born in sin. But still we should remember this, that God Who preserved immaculate the womb of the Blessed Virgin, required an immaculate home. "Holiness becometh Thy house, O, Lord!" (Psalm XCII, 5.) The house of God is our mind, which should be before all things clean and holy; lest it be said of us, "My house shall be called a house of prayer, but you have made it a den of thieves." (Matth. XXI, 13.)

2. The Blessed Virgin excels even the Angels in regard to her purity; for she was not only pure in herself, but she also secured purity for others, and also because she was most pure in regard to fault; for this Virgin incurred neither original, nor mortal, nor venial sin. Likewise in regard to punishment. For three maledictions fell upon men on account of sin.

The first malediction fell upon woman, that since she conceived in corruption, she bore in difficulty and brought forth in pain. But the Blessed Virgin was immune from this pain and sorrow, for she conceived without corruption, bore in comfort and brought forth in joy the Saviour of the world. "It shall bud forth and blossom, and shall rejoice with joy and praise." (Isaias XXXV, 2.)

The second misfortune fell upon man, that he should earn (or eat) his bread, by the sweat of his brow. From this hardship, the Blessed Virgin was exempt because, as the Apostle says, "virgins who consecrate themselves solely to God, are free from the cares of this world."

The third misfortune befell men and women, that they must return to dust from whence they came. And from this universal law of nature, the Blessed Virgin was exempt, because she was taken up body and soul into heaven. For we believe that after her death, she arose and was taken into heaven. "Arise, O Lord, into Thy resting place—Thou and the ark, which Thou hast sanctified." (Psalm CXXXI, 8.)

Consequently, the Blessed Virgin was immune from every

malediction, and therefore, blessed among women, because she alone bore "the malediction," and carried a benediction, and opened the gates of paradise. Wherefore the name—Mary—which means—"Star of the sea," is proper to her; because just as by means of the star of the sea, navigators are directed to the harbour, so too are Christians directed by Mary to eternal glory. (The Hail Mary.)

The Dedication of a Church

"Holiness becometh Thy house, O Lord." (Ps. XCII, 5.)

1. The Sacrament of the Eucharist ought as a rule to be celebrated in a house, whereby the Church is signified; according to Tim. III, 15, "That thou mayest know how thou oughtest to behave thyself in the house of God, which is the church of the living God." Because outside the church there is no place for the true sacrifice, and because the church was not to be confined within the territories of the Jewish people, but was to be established throughout the whole world. Therefore Christ's Passion was not celebrated within the city of the Jews, but in the open country, so that the whole world might serve as a house for Christ's Passion.

Moreover, the house in which this Sacrament is celebrated denotes the Church and is called a church; and so it is fittingly consecrated, both to represent the holiness which the church acquired from the Passion, as well as to denote the holiness required of them who have to receive this sacrament. By the altar Christ Himself is signified, of Whom the Apostle says (Heb. XIII, 15), "Through Him we offer a sacrifice of praise to God." Hence the consecration of the altar signifies Christ's sanctity. "The Holy One born of thee shall be called the Son of God." (Luke I, 13.)

Hence the church, altar and other things are consecrated, not because they are capable of receiving grace, but because they acquire special spiritual virtue from their consecration, whereby they are rendered fit for the Divine worship; so that man derives devotion therefrom, making him more fitted for Divine functions; unless this be impeded by lack of reverence. Hence it is said, "There is undoubtedly in that place a certain power of God; for He that has his dwelling in the heavens is the visitor, and the protector of that place." (2 Mach. III, 38.) Hence it is that such places are cleansed and exorcised before being consecrated, that the enemy's power might be driven forth. Hence too it is that some say with probability, that by entering a consecrated church one obtains forgiveness of venial sins, just as one does by the devout sprinkling of holy water; quoting the words of Psalm LXXXIV, 3, "Lord, Thou hast blessed Thy land . . . Thou hast forgiven the iniquity of Thy people." And therefore, because of the virtue acquired by a church's consecration, the consecration is never repeated.

2. The faithful Christians are the temple of God, according to the words of Saint Paul, "Be ye holy as the temple of God is holy." They are sanctified by three things which are materially done or found in the church when it is consecrated. First by the washing, secondly by the unction and thirdly by the indwelling of the Holy Spirit.

1. By the washing, for just as the church is washed before being consecrated, so also are the faithful cleansed by the Blood of Christ.

2. By the ointment, for just as the church is anointed (or consecrated with ointment) so are the faithful anointed or consecrated with a spiritual unction, and this unction moreover is the grace of the Holy Spirit. Otherwise they would not be Christians, for Christian means Christ's anointed one.

3. By the dwelling, for wherever God dwells that is a holy place. Holiness becometh Thy house, O, Lord." (Ps. XCII, 5.)

4. A fourth reason might be added why the faithful are sanctified, and that is through the—invocation—or prayers said during the consecration of a church. "Thou, O Lord, art amongst us, and Thy name is called upon by us. Forsake us not." (Jer. XIV, 9.)

Therefore, care must be exercised by us, lest after such sanctification, we, through sin, defile our soul which is the temple of God. (De Humanitate Christi.)

OCTOBER 1

The Effects of Love

1. Love denotes a certain adaptation of the appetitive power to some good. Now nothing is harmed by being adapted to that which is suitable to it; rather, if possible, it is perfected and improved. But if a thing be adapted to that which is not suitable to it, it is hurt and made worse thereby. Hence,

to love a suitable good perfects and improves the lover, but love of a good which is unsuitable to the lover, wounds and renders him worse. Wherefore, man is perfected and improved chiefly by the love of God; but is wounded and rendered worse by the love of sin, according to Osee IX, 10, "They become abominable, as these things which they loved."

2. And let this be understood as applying to love in respect to its formal element, that is, in regard to the appetite. But in respect to the material element in the passion of love, that is, a certain bodily change, it happens that love is hurtful, by reason of this change being excessive just as it happens in the senses, and in every act of a power of the soul that is exercised through the change of some bodily organ.

3. But on the contrary it must be said that—four—proximate effects may be ascribed to love, melting, enjoyment, langour and fervour. Of these things the first, is melting, which is opposed to freezing. For things that are frozen, are closely bound together so as to be hard to pierce. But it belongs to love that the appetite is fitted to receive the good which is loved, inasmuch as the object loved is in the lover. Consequently, the freezing or hardening of the heart is a disposition incompatible with love; while melting—denotes a softening of the heart; whereby the heart shows itself to be ready for the entrance of the beloved. If, then, the beloved is present and possessed pleasure or enjoyment ensues. But if the beloved be absent, two passions arise, sadness at its absence, which is denoted by languor (or ailment); and an intense desire to possess the beloved, which is signified by fervour.

And these are the effects of love considered formally, according to the relation of the appetitive power to its object. But in the passion of love, other effects ensue proportionate to the above in regard to a change in the subject. (1, 2ae. q. 28, a. 5.)

OCTOBER 2

The Angel Guardian

"He has given His angels charge over thee, to keep thee in all thy ways." (Ps. XC, 11.)

1. Each soul has an angel to guard it from the moment of birth.

Man while in this state of life, is, as it were, on a road by which he should tend to the (heavenly) fatherland. In this road man is threatened by many dangers both from within and without, according to Ps. CXLI, 4, "In this way wherein I walked, they have hidden a snare for me." And therefore as guardians are appointed for men who have to pass by an unsafe road, so an angel guardian is assigned to each man as long as he is a traveller. When however, he arrives at the end of life he no longer has a guardian angel; but in the kingdom of God, he will have an angel as a companion in reigning, in hell a demon to punish him.

2. Each soul has an angel appointed to guard it from the moment of birth.

For those benefits which are conferred by God on man as a Christian, begin with his baptism. But those things which are conferred by God on man as a rational being, are bestowed on him at his birth, for then it is that he receives that nature. Such favours demand the guardianship of angels. Hence, from the very moment of birth man has an angel guardian appointed to him, not however before his birth; because the child as long as he is in the maternal womb, is not entirely separated from the mother, but because of a certain intimate tie, is still a part of her, just as the fruit while hanging on the tree is part of the tree. And therefore, it can be said that the angel who guards the mother guards the child while in the womb. But, at its birth when it becomes separate from the mother, an angel guardian is appointed to protect it.

3. Does the Angel guardian ever forsake man?

The guardianship of the angels is an effect of Divine Providence in regard to man. Now it is clear that neither man, nor anything at all, is entirely withdrawn from the providence of God; for in as far as a thing participates being, so far is it subject to the providence that extends over all being. God indeed is said to forsake man, according to the ordering of His providence, but only in as far as He allows man to suffer some defect of punishment or of fault. In like manner it must be said that the Angel guardian never forsakes a man entirely, but sometimes he leaves him in some particular, for instance, by not preventing him from being subject to some trouble, or even from falling into sin, according to the ordering of Divine judgments.

4. Angels do not grieve, either for sins or for the pains inflicted on men. For grief and sorrow are for those things which occur against our will. But nothing happens in this world contrary to the will of the angels and the other blessed,

because their will cleaves entirely to the ordering of Divine justice. Therefore simply speaking, nothing happens in the world against the will of the blessed. Therefore, universally and absolutely speaking, the angels do not will the sin and the pains inflicted on its account; but they do will the fulfillment of the ordering of Divine justice in this matter, in respect of which some are subjected to pains and are allowed to fall into sin. (1a. Q. 113, 4, 7.)

OCTOBER 3

The Sign of True Love

1. *"He that has My commandments, and keepeth them, he it is that loveth Me."* (John XIV, 21.)

That is true love which manifests itself and proves itself in action, for through the manifestation of good deeds, love is shown. For since to love anyone is to wish good to that person and to desire that which he or she desires, it seems that one does not truly love who does not the will of the beloved and fails to do that which he knows the beloved wishes him to do. Therefore, whosoever does not the will of God, does not truly love God, and therefore Christ says, "He that hath My commandments, and keepeth them, he it is, that loveth Me." That is, "he it is that has true love for Me."

But observe that one has the commandments of God, first indeed, in his heart through memory and through constant meditation. But this does not suffice, unless he keeps them in action. Moreover some have (the commandments) in word, in speech and exhortation. "How sweet are Thy words to my palate! more than honey to my mouth." (Ps. CXVIII, 103.) And these people also should keep them in action, because "he who does and teaches, he is the greater in the kingdom of heaven." Hence those who say and do not, are condemned by God. Moreover some have the commandments by hearing, by freely and lovingly listening to them being preached. "He who is of God, heareth the words of God." Neither is this sufficient, unless they observe them, because "not the hearers of the law, but the doers shall be justified." (Rom. II, 13.) Therefore, he who thus has the commandments of God, and keeps them, even then he has an obligation of keeping them unto the end. Hence Augustine says, "he who has (the commandments) in mind, and keeps them in life, has them in speech and keeps them in action, has them in hearing and keeps them in morals, has them by good deeds and perseverance, he it is that loves God."

2. "If you keep My commandments, you shall abide in My love; as I also have kept My Father's commandments, and do abide in His love." (John XV.) To remain in God's love, means to keep His commandments. For the observance of God's commandments is not only an effect of His Divine love by which we love God, but an effect and sign that God loves us. For from the fact that He loves us, He moves us and helps us to fulfill His commandments which cannot be fulfilled unless through God's grace.

And He gives us an example saying, "As I also have kept My Father's commandments." For just as the love with which the Father loves Him, is an example of the love with which He loves us; so He wishes that His obedience be an example for our obedience. For through this obedience Christ showed that He remained in the love of the Father and kept all His commandments even unto death. "He became obedient unto death, even unto the death of the cross" (Phil. II, 8); and abstained from every sin, "Who did no sin, neither was guile found in His mouth." (1 Peter II, 22.) These things must be understood of Christ in as far as He was man. "I always do the things that pleasing to My Father." "Hearken therefore, My children, to your Father. Serve the Lord in truth, and seek to do the things that please Him. And command your children that they do justice and almsdeeds, and that they be mindful of God, and bless Him at all times in truth and with all their power." (Tobias XIV, 10-11.) (John XV.)

OCTOBER 4

The Friendship of God for Man Through Charity

"I will not now call you servants . . . but My friends." (John XV, 15.)

1. Charity is friendship. Not every love has the nature of friendship, but that love which is together with benevolence, when we love someone so as to wish good to him. If, however, we do not wish good to what we love, but wish its good for ourselves (thus we are said to love wine or a horse or

the like), it is love not of friendship, but of a kind of concupiscence. For it would be absurd to speak of having friendship for wine or for a horse.

Yet, neither does well-wishing suffice for the nature of friendship because a certain mutual love is required, since friendship is between friend and friend; and this well-wishing is founded on some kind of communication.

Therefore, since there is a communication between man and God, inasmuch as He communicates His happiness to us, some kind of friendship must be established on this same communication, of which it is written (1 Cor. I, 9), "God is faithful, by Whom you are called unto the friendship of His Son." The love which is based on this communication is charity. Wherefore, it is clear that charity is the friendship of man for God.

2. Through charity we converse with God as with a friend, for nothing is so proper to friendship as to converse with a friend. Moreover, the life of man is twofold. There is his outward life in respect of his sensitive and corporeal nature, and with regard to this life there is no communication or fellowship between us and God or the angels. The other is man's spiritual life in regard to his mind, and with regard to this spiritual life between us and both God and the angels, imperfectly indeed in this present state of life; wherefore it is written (Phil. III, 20), "Our conversation is in heaven. But this conversation will be perfected in heaven, when His servants shall serve Him, and they shall see His face." (Apoc. XXII, 3, 4.)

3. There is no true friendship without return of love. But charity extends even to our enemies, who do not return love. "Love your enemies," writes Saint Matthew, V, 44. This is because if anyone has true friendship for a certain person, for his sake he loves all belonging to that person, be they children or servants or related to him in any way. Indeed, so much do we love our friends that for their sake we love all who belong to them, even if they hurt or hate us; so that, in this way, the friendship of charity extends even to our enemies, whom we love out of charity in relation to God to Whom the friendship of charity is chiefly directed. (2a. 2æ. q. 23, a. 1.)

OCTOBER 5

Clinging to God Through Charity

"He that abideth in charity, abideth in God, and God in him." (1 John IV, 16.)

1. This effect of mutual indwelling (of God in us and we in God) may be understood as referring either to the apprehensive or to the appetitive power. In regard to the apprehensive power, the beloved is said to be in the lover, inasmuch as the beloved abides in the apprehension of the lover, according to Phil. I, 7, "For that I have you in my heart," while the lover is said to be in the beloved, according to apprehension, inasmuch as the lover is not satisfied with a superficial apprehension of the beloved but strives to gain an intimate knowledge of everything pertaining to the beloved, so as to penetrate into his very soul. Thus it is written concerning the Holy Ghost, Who is God's Love, that "He searcheth all things, yea the deep things of God." (1 Cor. II, 10.)

2. As to the appetitive power, the object loved is said to be in the lover, inasmuch as it is in his affections by a kind of satisfaction (or complacency), causing him either to take pleasure in it or in its good when present; or, in the absence of the object loved, by his longing to tend towards it with the love of concupiscence, or towards the good that he wills to the beloved with the love of friendship, not indeed from any extrinsic cause (as when we desire one thing on account of another or wish good to another on account of something), but because the complacency in the beloved is rooted in the lover's heart. For this reason we speak of love as being—intimate—and of "the bowels of charity." On the other hand, the lover is in the beloved by the love of concupiscence and by the love of friendship, but not in the same way. For the love of concupiscence is not satisfied with any external or superficial possession or enjoyment of the beloved; but seeks to possess the beloved perfectly, by penetrating into his heart, as it were.

Whereas, in the love of friendship, the lover is in the beloved, inasmuch as he reckons what is good or evil in his friend as being so to himself; and his friend's will as his own, so that it seems as though he felt the good or suffered the evil in the person of his friend. Hence it is proper to friends to desire the same things and to grieve and rejoice at the same. Consequently, in as far as he considers what affects his friend as affecting himself, the lover seems to be in the beloved as though he were to become one with him. But in so far as he wills and acts for his friend's sake as for his own sake, looking on his friend as identified with himself, the beloved is in the lover.

In yet a third way, mutual indwelling in the love of friendship can be understood in regard to reciprocal love; inasmuch as friends return love for love and both desire and do good things for one another. (1a. 2æ. q. 28, a. 2.)

OCTOBER 6

The Wonderful Privilege of Love

"He that loveth Me, shall be loved by My Father, and I will love him and manifest Myself to him." (John XIV, 21.)

"He who loveth Me, will be loved by My Father." This at first sight seems absurd. For does God love us because we love Him? Far be it! Hence it is written in 1 John IV, 10, "Not as though we had loved God, but because He hath first loved us." It must be remembered therefore, that anyone who loves Christ is not loved because he loves but because he was first loved by the Father. Therefore, we love the Son because the Father loves us. For true love has this quality, that it draws the love of the lover. "Yea I have loved thee with an everlasting love therefore have I drawn thee, taking pity on thee." (Jer. XXXI, 3.) But the love of the Father is not separate from the love of the Son, for it is the same love for both Divine Persons; "for whatsoever the Father does these things also the Son does," therefore, He says, "I also will love him."

But since the Father and the Son love all these things from eternity, therefore God says, "I will love." In the future? We must distinguish, for we must say that love considered as it is in the Divine will, is accordingly eternal; but when considered as it is manifested in the execution of work and effect, it is temporal and therefore in this sense does our Lord say, "I will love him," that is, "I will show him the effect of love"; since "I will manifest Myself to him, and because of this I will love so that I may manifest Myself."

Moreover, let it be remembered that the love of anyone for another is sometimes limited and sometimes unlimited. Limited, as when we wish some one a particular good, unlimited when we wish that person every good. But God loves all things created. He loves them limitedly—even the very devils, because He wishes for every creature a certain good, namely, that they live and understand and exist which are indeed good things. But on the other hand God loves those unlimitedly to whom He wishes every good, namely that they possess God Himself; the possession of Whom is the possession of Truth, for God is Truth. But Truth when it is possessed is then recognized.

Therefore, God Who is the Truth, truly and unlimitedly manifests Himself to those fortunate and blessed souls, and this is what He means when He says, "I will manifest Myself to him" (who loves Me), namely, in the future through glory, which is the ultimate effect of future beatitude. Hence Job XXXVI, 33, says, "God showeth his friend concerning it (beatitude), that it is his possession." And Wisdom VI, 12, advises, "Covet ye therefore, my words, and love them." (John XIV.)

OCTOBER 7

The Divine Manifestation to One Loving God

"If anyone love Me, he will keep My word, and My Father will love him, and we will come to him, and make our abode with him." (John XIV, 23.)

1. There are two things which make man worthy of God's manifestation, charity and obedience. In regard to the first our Lord says, "If anyone love Me." For three things are necessary for a man desiring to see God. First, that he approach God. Secondly, that he lift up his eyes to see God. "Lift up your eyes and see Who has created these things." (Isaias XL, 26.) Thirdly, that he keep himself free from earthly things for the vision of God. For spiritual things cannot be seen by us, unless we free ourselves from worldly things. "Taste and see that the Lord is sweet." (Ps. XXXIII, 9.)

Charity accomplishes these three things mentioned above. For it unites the soul of man to God. "Whosoever abideth in charity, abideth in God." (1 John IV.) Charity directs man's gaze towards God, sets his heart right with God. "Where thy treasure is, there is thy heart also (Matth. VI, 24.) Hence it is written, "where thy love is, there is thine eye." For charity makes us free from worldly things. "But he who loves the world, the perfect charity of God is not in him" (John XII, 15.) On the other hand, whoever loves God perfectly, the love of the world is not in him.

From the possession of charity obedience results, hence our Lord says, "he will keep My word" (or law). Wherefore Gregory remarks that "the proof of love is the manifestation of good works. Never is the love of God a burden, for it accomplishes great things if it is in man, but if love of God is absent, the worker is rejected." When therefore, there exists an earnest will on our part towards God Who is our last end, it moves all the powers of our soul to do those things which lead to Him. But we draw near to God through charity, and therefore charity is that supernatural virtue which enables us to obey His commandments. While through obedience, man becomes worthy to see God. "By Thy commandments (that is, by obeying Thy commandments) I have had understanding. Therefore, have I hated every way of iniquity." (Ps. CXVIII, 103.)

2. Moreover, there are three things by which the Divine manifestation is brought about in man. First, Divine love and in regard to this our Lord says, "the Father will love him." He will love him in the future, in as far as man will experience the effect of God's love, Who has loved us eternally in as much as He willed to do good to us.

Secondly, the Divine Visitation, and in this regard our Lord says, "We will come to him." God truly comes to us in as far as He is in us in a new way, according to which He was not present to us previously, namely, by the effect of His grace, and through this effect of grace God makes us approach Him.

But on the other hand, God comes to us in three ways, and by these same ways we go to Him. He comes to us by performing His effects and we go to Him by receiving the effects of His grace. He comes by enlightening us, and we go to Him through meditation. He comes by helping us and we go to Him by obeying Him, and neither can we obey Him unless we are assisted by Christ.

Thirdly, to behold the manifestation of God, perseverance of both is necessary, namely, perseverance in the love of God and in His Visitation. In regard to this visitation, our Lord says ,"We will make our abode with him." In this statement He points out two things, First, constancy of adhesion to God, when He says "abode." For God comes to some, through faith in Him, but He does not remain, "because they believe for a time, and in time of temptation they fall away." He comes to others by giving them sorrow for sin, still He does not remain with them, because they return to their sins. But in His chosen ones (who love Him) God remains always. He is always with them. He makes His home with them.

Secondly, the familiarity of Christ with man is seen in the words, "with him," namely, with the man who loves and obeys God. He will be with us, inasmuch as He is delighted with us and makes us by His grace to be delighted with Him. (John XIV.)

OCTOBER 8

The Way to Find Jesus

1. "Jesus went aside from the multitude standing in the place." (John V, 13.) Thus declareth sacred Scripture, so that we might know that Christ is not easily found among the multitude and in the whirlwind of worldly cares, but in spiritual solitude. "I will lead her (the spiritual soul) into solitude, into the wilderness, and I will speak to her heart." (Osee II, 14.) For words of wisdom are heard in solitude. The spiritual life of man consists in quietness. "Thus saith the Lord God the Holy One . . . if you return and be quiet, you shall be saved. In silence and in hope shall your strength be." (Isaias XXX, 15.)

"Afterwards Jesus findeth him in the temple, and said to him, Behold thou art now made whole. Sin no more, lest some worst thing happen to thee." (John V, 14.) Two things are here to be noted in this statement, namely, the manner of finding Jesus and the place to find Him. The manner is indeed wonderful, because He is not found unless He is sought earnestly. Hence it is written, "Jesus findeth him," namely, the man who earnestly sought to be cured of his disease. For unless man is aided by Christ, he cannot find Christ. Moreover, the place in which Christ is found is wonderful and holy, namely, in the temple. "The Lord is in His Holy Temple." (Ps. X, 5.) For His mother also found Jesus in the temple.

From this fact, we must realize that the man whom Jesus

finds (or who finds Jesus) is converted not to vanity but to the study of religion, frequenting the church in which he learns to know Christ; because if we wish to arrive at a knowledge of the Founder of our Church we must flee from the multitude of our depraved affections, withdraw from evil associations and take refuge in the temple of our heart which God makes worthy for His visitation and dwelling. (John V.)

2. "Return therefore, ye transgressors, to the heart." (Isaias, XLVI, 8.)

Man should return to the heart. First, as if to the throne of a judge, so that he might repent and become ashamed of his sins. "I meditated at night with my own heart, and I was exercised, and I swept my spirit." (Ps. LXXVI, 7.)

Secondly, man should return to the heart, as if to the fountain of life to guard it. "With all watchfulness keep thy heart, because life issueth out from it." (Prov. IV, 23.)

Thirdly, he should return to the heart, as to the sanctuary of the Divine word so that he might diligently listen to God. "I will lead her (the soul) into solitude, and I will speak to her heart." (Osee. II, 14.)

Fourthly, he should return to the heart, as to the treasury of Divine wisdom so that he might persevere. "Thy words have I hidden in my heart, that I may not sin against Thee." (Ps. CXVIII, 11.)

Fifthly, man should return to the heart, as to the cenacle (or upper room) of peace and restoration, because of the evil ones of whom it is written, "they speak peace with their neighbours, but evils are in their hearts." (Ps. XXVII, 3.)

3. But perhaps, it must be here said, "there has stood One in the midst of you, Whom you know not," that is, the Son of God Whose Divine Wisdom shines in the intellect of all mankind; because whatever light and wisdom there are in men, come to them from a participation of the Word of God. Hence He says, "in the midst," for in the middle of bodily man is the heart, to which a certain wisdom and intellect are attributed. Hence although the intellect has not a corporal organ, still because the heart is the chief organ, it is customary to refer to it as intellect. Hence "to stand in the midst," is said according to this similitude; for "it enlighteneth every man that cometh into the world. Return therefore, to the heart," that is to the intellect, because, "the Light shineth in darkness and the darkness does not comprehend it." (John I.)

OCTOBER 9

The Internal Illumination of the Mind

"I have called you friends, because all things whatsoever I have heard of My Father, I have made known to you." (John XV, 15.)

1. In what does this illumination consist? A true sign of friendship is that a friend reveal the secrets of his heart to his friend. For since it is characteristic of friends to be of one mind and heart, it does not seem that a friend would keep a secret from a friend." Hence it is written, "treat thy cause with thy friend, and discover not the secret to a stranger." (Prov. XXV, 9.)

But how is this true? If our Lord made known all things to His Apostles, does it follow they knew as many things as the Son of God? Saint John Chrysostom says we must remember that, "all things whatsoever I have heard," means "those things which it were fitting for you to hear, I have made known to you; but not however all things absolutely speaking. I have yet many things to say to you which you cannot hear now."

According to Augustine, our Lord used the past tense for the future, because of certainty and truth of the things spoken, so that "all things I have made known to you," may be taken in this sense, "all things which I will do in the fulness of time," concerning which the Apostle says, "Then I shall know even as I am known. In that day I will tell you plainly of the Father," namely, when God introduces us into the Presence of the Father. For all things which the Son knows, the Father knows. Therefore, when the Son reveals the Father to us, He will reveal all things which He knows.

According to Gregory, and this seems a better interpretation, "About Divine things, a twofold knowledge can be had. First, imperfect knowledge, and this is had through faith, which is a foreshadowing of our future happiness and knowledge of heaven." Hence, concerning this knowledge our Lord says: "All things I have made known to you, namely, in faith, according to a certain foreshadowing, as conclusions are, by virtue, in their principles." Hence Gregory says, "All things which He made known to His faithful servants are the joys of interior charity, the banquets of the heavenly mansions, which He impresses daily upon our minds by the inspiration of His love; for while we love the heavenly things which we have heard, we now know the things to be loved, and this very love is knowledge."

2. Moreover, there are three things which dispose us to internal illumination of the mind. First, the withdrawal from all fleeting pleasures. Hence Isaias (XXVIII, 9) says, "To whom shall He teach knowledge? Whom shall He make to understand? except those who are weaned from the milk, those that are drawn away from the breasts"; namely, those who have renounced worldly pleasures and sinful consolations. Hence Saint John, I, 10, commenting on this, says, "the world, (namely, the worldly) knew Him not," and Chrysostom adds to this saying, "The Lord calls the world—the men—who are inordinately attached to the world and wise in the things of the world." On the other hand nothing so disturbs the mind, and causes it to weaken, as improper love of worldly things.

The second thing which disposes us to internal illumination of the mind, is nearness to the very fountain of Light. "Come to Me and be enlightened." (Ps. XXXIII, 6.) Hence Augustine says, "the soul is placed midway between God and creatures, and by turning to God, the soul becomes enlightened, improved and perfected; but in turning to creatures, it becomes darkened, deteriorated and killed."

The third thing which disposes us towards internal illumination of the mind, consists in an interior opening of the mind, which is done by an effort or inclination of man himself. "Open thy mouth wide, and I will fill it." (Ps. LXXX, 11.) That is, open the mouth of thy heart, and the Lord will fill it with the Bread of Life and of knowledge. Hence Augustine says that "just as God by His inborn liberality, fills all creatures with the power of understanding, so through the power of God and through the Wisdom of God all good things come to us through Christ, since by His birth we are favored as to the manner of living, we are consoled as to the condition of living, enlightened in regard to the act of understanding." (De Humanitate Christi, LXII.)

OCTOBER 10

Spiritual Joy

"Rejoice in the Lord always. Again I say, rejoice. Let your modesty be known to all men. The Lord is nigh." (Phil. IV, 4.)

1. It is necessary for each one desiring to advance in perfection, that he possess spiritual joy. "A joyful mind maketh age flourishing. A sorrowful spirit drieth up the bones." (Prov. XVII, 22.) Moreover, the Apostle lays down four conditions for true joy. First, true joy should be straightforward, that is when it exists for the proper good of man, and is not something created but is really God in the soul. "It is good for me to adhere to God." (Ps. LXXII.) Therefore the Apostle says, "rejoice in the Lord." Secondly, spiritual joy should be continual. Wherefore the Apostle says, "Rejoice in the Lord always," and this happens when joy is not interrupted by sin, for then it is truly continual. Sometimes it is impeded by temporary sadness, which means imperfection of joy. For when anyone perfectly rejoices, his joy is not interrupted. Hence it is written, "Rejoice always." Thirdly, spiritual joy should be manifold, for if you rejoice in the Lord, rejoice in His birth. "I bring you good tidings of great joy, for today is born to you a Saviour." (Luke II, 10.) Likewise rejoice in action (or good works) and also in contemplation let joy come unto you. "His conversation has no bitterness." (Wis. VIII.) Hence if you rejoice about the proper good, spiritual joy will flow to you from the good that others do, whether it is present or future good. Hence it is written, "Again I say rejoice." Fourthly, spiritual joy should be moderate, lest vain desires enter in and make it worldly joy. Hence the Apostle says, "let your modesty be known," as if he said, "Let your joy be so moderated that it will not turn into weakness and vanity." "Sweet is he who lives in moderation." (Prov. XII.) Wherefore, Saint Paul says, "let your modesty be known to all men," as if he had said, "let your life be so regulated and moderated interiorly and exteriorly, that no one can reproach you and no one be injured by your conversation."

2. Consequently, when the Apostle says, "the Lord is nigh," he refers to the cause of our joy, for a man rejoices concerning the nearness of a friend. The ever-abiding Presence of God's Majesty is indeed near. "He is not far from

everyone of us." (Acts XVII, 27.) He is likewise near us because of a relationship of nature. "And coming, He preached peace to you that were far off, and peace to them that were nigh. . . . Now therefore, you are no more strangers and foreigners, but you are fellow citizens with the saints, and domestics of God." (Eph. II, 14.) Likewise, God is near us through the indwelling of His grace. "Draw near unto God, and He will draw near unto you." (James II.) God is also close to us by the mercy He manifests in hearing our prayers. "The Lord is nigh to all who call upon Him." (Ps. CXLIV.) He is likewise near us with a reward. "His time is near at hand, and his days shall not be prolonged, for the Lord will have mercy." (Isaias XIV, 1.) (Philip IV.)

OCTOBER 11

The Peace of God

"And the peace of God, which surpasseth all understanding, keep your hearts and minds in Christ Jesus." Philip IV, 7.)

1. Peace, according to Augustine, is a tranquility of order, for disturbance of order is the destruction of peace. This tranquility of order may be considered in three ways, and therefore Saint Paul says, "the peace of God, which surpasseth all understanding, keep your hearts and minds in Christ Jesus." First, peace, as it exists in the beginning of order, namely in God. From God—the very fountain head of all peace, peace flows first and more perfectly to the blessed, in whom there is no disturbance and consequently it flows to holy men and women in this world also. And in as far as a person is the more saintly by so much the more does he or she suffer less from confusion and disturbance of mind. "Much peace have they that love Thy Law, O Lord, and to them there is no stumbling block." (Ps. CXVIII, 165.) But this perfect peace is the possession of the blessed in heaven. Because, moreover, our hearts can not be free from every disturbance, unless God helps us, and since this blessing comes entirely from God, hence Saint Paul calls it, "the peace of God." In this manner, according as peace is considered in its beginning in God, it "surpasseth all understanding," because "it

inhabiteth light inaccessible." (1 Tim. VI, 16.) This peace of God as it exists in heaven, surpasseth all understanding of the Angels and as far as it exists in holy persons on earth, it exceeds all human knowledge, particularly the knowledge of those without the grace of God. "To him that overcometh, I will give to eat of the tree of life, which is in the paradise of God." (Apoc. II, 7.)

Secondly, this peace will "keep your hearts," that is your affections, so that you may not decline from good." With all watchfulness, keep thy heart, for life issueth out from it." (Prov. IV, 23.)

Thirdly, "keep your minds so that in no wise may you deviate from truth." And this you can do by remaining "in Christ Jesus," through Whose charity your affections will be preserved from evil, and through Whose Holy Faith your intellect will remain steadfast in truth. (Phil. IV.)

2. Peace is the greatest good, as is clear from what the Apostle says at the start of nearly all his Epistles. He always prays for grace and peace. "Grace, mercy and peace from God the Father, and from Christ Jesus our Lord." (1 Tim. I, 2.) Grace is indeed the first among the gifts of God, for through it the wicked are justified. Peace, on the contrary, is the last among the gifts of God, because it is perfected in heaven. "God has placed peace in thy borders." (Ps. CXLVII, 14.) For only then will there be perfect peace, when the will rests satisfied in the fulness of every good, pursuing freedom from evil. (Rom. I.)

The good things which the Apostle prays for are twofold, namely, "grace and peace," in which all spiritual good things are included. First of all is grace, which is the beginning of the spiritual life, gace by means of which sin is taken away, is the first step in the spiritual life. On the other hand, the second good is peace, which causes tranquility of mind finally and reconciliation with God. Consequently, while the Apostle prays for the beginning and the end of all spiritual good, (namely, grace and peace), he includes between the two extremes, the desire of every good resulting from grace and peace. "The Lord will give to thee grace and glory." (Ps. LXXXIII, 12.) (Gal. I.)

OCTOBER 12

Preparation for the Contemplative Life Through the Moral Virtues

1. The moral virtues do not essentially, but dispositively, pertain to the contemplative life; because the end of the contemplative life is the consideration of Truth. The moral virtues belong to the contemplative life dispositively. For the act of contemplation, wherein the contemplative life essentially consists, is hindered both by the impetuosity of the passions which withdraws the soul's intention from intelligible to sensible things, and by outward disturbances. Now the moral virtues curb the impetuosity of the passions and quell the disturbance of outward occupations.

Gregory says that "the mind tramples on all cares, and longs to gaze on the face of its Creator." Now, no one can accomplish this without cleanness of heart, which is the result of moral virtue; for it is written (Matth. V, 8), "Blessed are the clean of heart for they shall see God," and (Heb. XII, 14), "Follow peace with all men, and holiness, without which no man shall see God." Moreover holiness, that is, spiritual cleanness of heart is caused by the virtues that are concerned with the passions which hinder the purity of the reason, and peace is caused by justice which is about operations; according to Isaias XXXII, 17, "the work of justice shall be peace"; since he who refrains from wronging others lessens the occasions of quarrels and disturbances. Hence, the moral virtues dispose one to the contemplative life by causing peace and cleanness of heart.

2. Some persons are suitable for the contemplative life. Those who are prone to yield to their passions on account of their impulse to action, are simply more suited for the active life, because of their restless spirit. Hence Gregory says that "there are some so restless that when they are free from labour, labour all the more, because the more leisure they have for thought, the worse interior turmoil they have to bear."

Others on the other hand, have the mind naturally pure and restful, so that they are apt for contemplation and if they were to apply themselves wholly to action, this would be detrimental to them. Wherefore, Gregory says, "that some are slothful of mind and if they chance to have any hard word to do, they give way at the very outset." Yet, as he adds further on, "often love . . . stimulates slothful souls to work, and fear restrains souls that are disturbed in contemplation." Consequently, those who are more adapted to the active life can prepare themselves for the contemplative by the practice of the active life, while those who are more adapted to the contemplative life can take upon themselves the works of the active life, so as to become more apt for contemplation. (2a. 2æ. q. 182, a. 4.)

OCTOBER 13

The Excellence of the Contemplative Life

"Mary hath chosen the best part, which shall not be taken away from her." (Luke X, 42.)

1. The contemplative life is simply more excellent than the active, and this may be proven by eight reasons. The first, because the contemplative life becomes man according to that which is best in him, namely the intellect, and according to its proper objects, namely, intelligibles; whereas the active life is occupied with externals. Hence Rachel, by whom the contemplative life is signified, is understood the vision of the principle; whereas, the active is signified by Lia who was blear-eyed.

The second reason is because the contemplative life can be more continuous although not as regards the highest degree of contemplation, wherefore Mary, by whom the contemplative life is signified, is described as "sitting" all the time at "the Lord's feet."

Thirdly, because the contemplative life is more delightful than the active; wherefore Augustine says that, "Martha was troubled, but Mary feasted, and was delighted."

Fourthly, because in the contemplative life man is more self-sufficient, since he needs fewer things for that purpose; wherefore it was said (Luke X, 41), "Martha, Martha, thou art careful and art troubled about many things."

Fifthly, because the contemplative life is loved more for its own sake, while the active life is directed to something else. Hence, it is said (Ps. XXVI, 4), "One thing I have asked of the Lord, this will I seek after, that I may dwell in the house of the Lord all the days of my life, that I may see the delight of the Lord."

Sixthly, because the contemplative life consists in leisure and rest, according to Ps. XLV, 11, "Bee still and see that I am God."

Seventhly, because the contemplative life is concerned, about divine things, whereas the active life is according to human things. Wherefore, Augustine says, "In the beginning was the Word. To Him Mary was listening. The Word was made flesh. Him Martha was serving."

Eighthly, because the contemplative life is according to that which is most proper to man, namely, his intellect; whereas in the works of the active life the lower powers also, which are common to us and brutes, have their part. Wherefore (Ps. XXXV, 8), after the words, "Men and beasts Thou wilt preserve, O Lord," that which is special to man is added, (verse 10) "In Thy light we shall see light."

Our Lord adds a ninth reason (Luke X, 42), when He says, "Mary hath chosen the best part, which shall not be taken away from her"; which words Augustine explains thus, "Not that thou hast chosen badly, but she has chosen better. Why better? Listen,—because it shall not be taken away from her. But the burden of necessity shall at length be taken from thee; whereas the sweetness of truth is eternal."

Yet, in a restricted sense and in a particular case one should prefer the active life, on account of the needs of the present life. Thus too, Augustine says, "It is better to be wise than to be rich, yet for one who is in need it is better to be rich." (2a. 2ae. q. 182, a. 1.)

OCTOBER 14

Happiness Obtained in a Life With God

1. Since happiness denotes some final perfection, according as various things capable of happiness can attain to various degrees of perfection, so must there be various meanings applied to happiness. For in God there is happiness essentially; since His very Being is His operation, whereby He enjoys no other than Himself. In the Angels the final perfection is in regard to some operation by which they are united to the Uncreated Good; and this operation of theirs is one only and everlasting.

But in men, according to their present state of life, the final perfection is in respect of an operation whereby man is united to God. But this operation neither can be continual, nor consequently, is it the only, because operation is multiplied by being discontinued. And for this reason in the present state of life, perfect happiness cannot be attained by man. But God has promised us perfect happiness when we shall be "as angels . . . in heaven." (Matth. XXVII, 30.) For then in that state of happiness, man's mind will be united to God by one continual, everlasting operation.

But in the present life, in as far as we fall short of the unity and continuity of that operation, so do we fall short of perfect happiness. Still it is a participation of happiness, and so much the greater, as the operation can be more continuous and more one. Consequently, the active life which is busy with many things, has less of happiness than the contemplative life, which is occupied with one thing, namely, the contemplation of truth. And if at any time, man is not actually engaged in this operation, yet since he can always easily turn to it and since he ordains the very cessation by sleeping or occupying himself otherwise, to the aforesaid occupation, the latter seems, as it were, continuous.

2. A life lived for God, or contemplation, brings delight. For contemplation can be delightful by reason of its very operation, because each individual delights in the operation which befits him according to his own nature or habit. Now the contemplation of truth befits a man according to his nature as a rational animal, the result being that "all men desire to know," so that consequently, they delight in the knowledge of truth. And more delightful still does this become to one who has the habit of wisdom and knowledge, the result of which is that he contemplates without difficulty.

Secondly, contemplation may be delightful on the part of its object, in so far as one contemplates that which one loves; even as bodily vision gives pleasure, not only because to see is pleasurable in itself, but because one sees a person whom one loves.

Since then, the contemplative life consists chiefly in the contemplation of God, of which charity is the motive, it follows that there is delight in the contemplative life, not only because of the contemplation itself, but also by reason of the Divine love. In both respects the delight thereof surpasses all human delight, both because spiritual delight is greater than carnal pleasure, and because the love whereby God is loved out of charity surpasses all love. Hence it is written (Ps. XXXIII, 9), "O taste and see that the Lord is sweet." (2a, 2æ, q, 180, a, 7.)

OCTOBER 15

The Merit of the Contemplative Life

The root of merit is charity. But since charity consists in the love of God and our neighbour, the love of God is by itself more meritorious than the love of our neighbour. Wherefore, that which pertains more directly to the love of God is generically more meritorious than that which pertains directly to the love of our neighbour for God's sake. Now the contemplative life pertains directly and immediately to the love of God; for Augustine says that the love of the Divine truth seeks a holy leisure, namely of the contemplative life, for it is that truth above all which the contemplative life seeks. On the other hand the active is more directly concerned with the love of our neighbour, because it is "busy about much serving." (Luke X.) Wherefore the contemplative life is generically of greater merit than the active life. This is moreover asserted by Gregory who says, "The contemplative life surpasses in merit the active life, because the latter labours under the stress of present work, by reason of the necessity of helping our neighbour, while the former with heartfelt relish has a foretaste of the coming rest, that is, the contemplation of God."

Nevertheless, it may happen that one man merits more by the works of the active life than another by the works of the contemplative life. For example, through excess of Divine love a man may now and then suffer separation from the sweetness of Divine contemplation for the time being, that God's will may be done and for His glory's sake. Thus the Apostle said (Rom. IX, 3), "I wished myself to be an anathema for Christ; for my brethren," which words Chrysostom expounds as follows: "His mind was so steeped in the love of Christ that, although he desired above all to be with Christ, he despised even this if thus he pleased Christ."

A sacrifice is rendered to God spiritually when something is offered to Him; and of all man's goods, God especially accepts that of the human soul when it is offered to Him in sacrifice. Now a man ought to offer to God, in the first place, his soul, according to Eccles. XXX, 24, "Have pity on thy own soul, pleasing God." In the second place, man ought to offer to God the souls of others, according to Apoc. XXII, 17, "He that heareth, let him say, Come." And the more closely a man unites his own or another's soul to God, the more acceptable is his sacrifice to God; wherefore it is more acceptable to God that one apply one's own soul and the souls of others to contemplation than to action. Consequently, the statement that "no sacrifice is more acceptable to God than zeal for souls," does not mean that merit of the active life is preferable to the merit of the contemplative life, but that it is more meritorious to offer to God one's own soul and the soul of others than any other external gifts. (2a, 2æ, q, 182, a, 2.)

OCTOBER 16

The Things We Should See in Contemplation

"What thou seest, write in a book." (Apoc. I, 11.)

1. Man ought to see many things in contemplation. He should see his own sins, the punishments of hell, the joys of paradise, the favours of Christ, the needs of his neighbour, and write all these things in the book of his mind. Concerning his sins, man should see how fleeting is sinful pleasure, and how terrible the eternal punishment. Gregory says, "that which affords pleasure is momentary, but that which crucifies and punishes, is eternal." Likewise he should see how vile sin really is. "How exceeding base art thou become, going the same ways over again." (Jer. II, 36.) Likewise, how detrimental sin is to man, because it lessens the goods of nature, deprives him of grace and robs him of future glory. "From the daughter of Sion all her beauty is departed." (Lamentations I, 6.)

Concerning the punishment of hell, man should see its diversity, its painfulness, its everlastingness. First its diversity, "He shall rain snares upon sinners. Fire and brimstone and storms of winds shall be the portion of their cup." (Ps. X, 7.) Secondly, the painfulness, "there shall be weeping and gnashing of teeth." (Matth. VIII, 12.) Thirdly, the everlastingness, "Their fire is not extinguished. Depart from me ye cursed, into everlasting fire." (Isaias LXVI, 24.)

Concerning the joys of paradise, man should see in meditation their purity, their plenitude, their durability. "In his joy the stranger shall not intermeddle." (Prov. XIV, 10.) Secondly, their fulness, "Your joy shall be full." Thirdly, their durability, "I shall see you again, and your joy no one shall take from you." (1 John I, 4.)

Concerning the favours from Christ, man should see a multitude of favours. "What shall I render to the Lord for all the things He has rendered to me?" Secondly, the greatness of the favours, "He that is mighty has done great things for me." (Luke I, 49.) Thirdly, gratitude for the favours received from our Lord. "Freely have you received, freely give." (Matth. X, 8.)

Concerning the needs of our neighbours, man ought to see in contemplation what he would want to have done for himself, if he were in such need, and how great is the weakness of man. "As you would that men should do to you, do you also to them in like manner." (Luke VI, 31.) Likewise, those things which you see in Christ, in the world and in your neighbour, write that in the book of your heart.

2. Observe the statement also, "behold thyself as in a looking-glass," because man ought to behold and examine himself, in the looking-glass of his mind. First, consider the sins committed so that he may repent. "Set thee up a watchtower, make to thee bitterness, and direct thy heart in the right way." (Jer. XXXI, 21.) Secondly, he should consider the punishments which he has deserved, so that he might fear with a holy fear. "Thy visitation cometh." (Mich. VII, 4.) Thirdly, the favours which God has conferred on man, so that he may render thanks to God. Fourthly, the commandments which God has given for man's guidance, so that he may observe them. Fifthly, the rewards which God has promised, so that man may obtain that reward. "Keep a memory of these things. For we have not by following artificial fables, made known to you the power, and presence of our Lord Jesus Christ; but we were eye-witnesses of His greatness." (2 Peter, I, 16.)   (In Isa. XXI.)

OCTOBER 17

The Hidden Manna

"To him that overcometh, I will give the hidden manna." (Apoc. II, 17.)

1. This is a wonderful manna. It can be explained either from its interior sweetness, which is given to holy persons on their journey to heaven, or explained from the part of its eternal sweetness which is granted to the saints in

glory. Both sweetness is so great that everyone who tastes it, exclaims: "What is this?" And both sweetnesses are hidden, because only to a few is a little of this granted to be tasted. The sweetness of contemplation is well signified by manna, because of the sweetness of its flavour. "O taste and see that the Lord is sweet. Blessed is the man that hopeth in Him." (Ps. XXXIII, 9.) That is, he who places his whole hope in God; because to such a one is given the privilege of tasting the sweetness of God; however little it may be the soul is astonished, so that it exclaims rightly, "O Manna, what is it?"

For no one can fully understand its internal sweetness, even though the soul should burn with the desire to understand. Rightly does the Psalmist exclaim, "My soul hath fainted after my salvation," and again, "My soul longeth and fainteth for the courts of the Lord. My heart and my flesh have rejoiced in the living God." (Ps. LXXXIII, 3.) As if the Psalmist had said, "From this I know that Thy tabernacles, that is, the mansions of Thy Father's house, O Lord, are lovable and desirable; because I who am as yet outside of thy courtyard, and not yet within Thy holy temple, anxiously do I desire to wait here, but in desiring I faint, not being able to comprehend what is within. If therefore O Lord, thou dost grant me a foretaste of Thy sweetness in the courtyard, and I cannot comprehend its sweetness, who shall be able to receive and understand all of it in the temple of the living God."

2. Where is it found? "The Lord said to Moses, Behold I will rain bread from heaven for you. Let the people go forth and gather what is sufficient for every day; that I may prove them whether they will walk in my law, or not." (Ex. XVI, 4.) Whosoever desires this sweetness, must ascend from this world to heaven, from the flesh to the spirit, from himself to God; and then he will find the manna. "The mountains shall drop down sweetness." (Joel III, 18.) There are three mountains, namely, the spirit, heaven and God. And upon these three man should collect the manna, by meditating on the individual good things of each mountain, and he should collect daily, because every day he should dedicate himself to prayer and meditation.

Moreover he should collect as much manna as suffices for his needs. For some there are who gather very little fruit, because they pray little and meditate little. Others acquire a great deal of good. Therefore it is written Prov. XXV, 16, "thou hast found honey, eat what is sufficient for thee."

The place where the manna is found, is solitude. "I will bring her (the soul) into solitude and I will speak to her heart." (Osee II, 14.)

Likewise it is found in the early morning. In the morning during prayer and meditation devotion is granted. "In the morning I will stand before Thee, and will see. For to Thee will I pray, O Lord, in the morning thou shalt hear my voice. Hearken to the voice of my prayer, O my King and my God." (Ps. V, 3.) And again Proverbs VII, 17, says, "they that in the morning watch for Me, shall find Me."

Likewise, it is granted to those who abandon sin. Some indeed find God sweet only in prayer, others only in spiritual reading, others in worship. But the perfect find Him sweet and lovable, both in fasting and in discipline, in sickness and in poverty, according to Eccl. XXIV, 11, "in all these I have sought rest," according to the method of the bee, which extracts honey from almost every flower. Hence the Lord says of such persons, "They surrounded me like bees, and they burned like fire among thorns" (Ps. CXVII, 12), because inasmuch as the soul serves God and partakes of God, by so much the more does the soul burn with love for God. (Apoc. II.)

OCTOBER 18

Spiritual Recovery

Spiritual recovery consists in two things, namely, in the gifts of God and in His sweetness (or delights). First, let this scriptural statement be carefully observed, namely, "They shall be inebriated with the plenty of Thy house." (Ps. XXXV, 9.) The house is the church. And this house which is now on earth, will sometimes be transferred to heaven. In both houses there is an abundance of God's gifts. In His house on earth the abundance however is imperfect, whereas in His Father's heavenly mansion, there is the most perfect abundance of all good things, and with this abundance of things spiritual, spiritual men will become perfectly satisfied. "We shall be filled with the good things of Thy house O Lord, for holy is Thy temple, and wonderful in justice." (Ps. LXIV, 5.) And what is more, they shall be inebriated, in so far as their desire of merit will be fulfilled above every measure. For this fulness or abundance, denotes a certain excess. "The eye hath not seen, nor the ear heard, neither has it entered into the heart of man, what things God has prepared for them that love Him." (1 Cor. II, 9), and Canticles V, 1, says, "Eat, O friends, and drink, and be inebriated." Those are inebriated who are not in themselves but outside themselves, they are so filled with spiritual gifts, that their entire mind and intention are centered on God. "Our conversation is in heaven." (Phil. III, 20.)

Secondly, not only will we be refreshed with heavenly gifts, but also with the delights and sweetness of God. "Then shalt thou abound in the delights of the Almighty, and shall lift up thy face to God." (Job XXII, 26.) Therefore, it is written in regard to the second phrase, "Thou shalt make them drink of the torrent of Thy pleasure." (Ps. XXXV, 9.) This is the love of the Holy Spirit, which causes an attack upon the soul like a torrent. "He shall come, as violent storm, whom the Spirit of the Lord driveth on." (Isaias LIX, 19.) And "pleasures," are mentioned, because the Holy Spirit causes delight and sweetness in the soul. "O how good and how sweet is Thy Spirit, O Lord, in us." (Wis. XII, 1.) And the good shall drink of this spiritual drink. "All drank the same spiritual drink." (I Cor. XIX, 1), or drank from "the torrent of Thy delight," namely, of God, because He is called a "torrent." (Prov. XVIII, 4.) A torrent flowing over like a fountain of wisdom, because God's will is so powerful that like a torrent it cannot be resisted.

Thirdly, "for with Thee is the fountain of life, and in Thy light we shall see light." (Ps. XXXV, 10.) The result of recovery or spiritual refreshment is such, that those who are united to the fountain, become inebriated; because they hold their mouth as it were to the fountain of wine, that is, their every desire becomes fulfilled at the fountain of Life and sweetness. And so they become—"inebriated," "for with Thee, O Lord, is the fountain of Life." When this is referred to Christ ,the meaning is therefore, "Thou art the Fountain of Life," for Thy word vivifies all things. "They have forsaken Me, the fountain of living water," (Jer. II, 13), that is, the fountain of all spiritual good, by which all things are vivified. (Ps. XXXV.)

OCTOBER 19

The Sweet Experience from Divine Goodness

"Taste and see, that the Lord is sweet." (Ps. XXXIII, 9.)

The Psalmist exhorts us to experience the effect of Divine fellowship. And concerning this fellowship, the Psalmist does two things. First, he exhorts us to experiment, and secondly, he states the effect of the experiment.

1. He therefore, says, "taste." Experience from a thing is obtained through the senses. In one way, if the thing is present, and in another way if the thing is absent; for when the thing is absent, experience may be secured through vision, smell or hearing; on the other hand, when the thing is present, experience may be obtained through the sense of touch and taste, but through touch, however, from the extrinsic thing present, through taste from the intrinsic thing. God moreover, is not far from us, not outside of us, but He is in us. "Thou O Lord, art amongst us, and Thy name is called upon by us. Forsake us not." (Jer. XIV, 3.) Therefore, the experience of Divine goodness is called "taste." If such be, then you have tasted that the Lord is sweet." (1 Peter II, 3.), and Proverbs XXXI, 18, says, "she hath tasted and seen that her traffic is good."

2. Moreover, there is mentioned a twofold effect resulting from this experience. One effect is certitude of the intellect, another effect is security of the affections. In regard to the certainty of the intellect, the Psalmist says, "And see." For in corporeal things, we first see the thing and afterwards taste it, but in regard to spiritual things, we first taste them and afterwards see; because whoever taste not spiritually, does not recognize spiritual things, and hence the Psalmist says first of all, "Taste."

In regard to security of the affections, it is written, "that the Lord is sweet." Again Proverbs XII, 1, says, "O how good and sweet is Thy Spirit, O Lord, in all things." The Psalmist likewise exclaims, "O how great is the multitude of Thy sweetness, O Lord." (Ps. XXX, 20), and Isaias XXX, 18, declares, "Blessed is the man who hopeth in the Lord. Blessed are all they that wait for Him."

3. When therefore, it is said, "Taste and see, that the Lord is sweet," Psalms XXXIII, and again in Rom. XII, 2, "That you may prove what is the good, and the acceptable, and the perfect will of God;" this is not said so that we might

experiment as if doubting, for this would be to tempt God. For there is a twofold knowledge of God's goodness or will. One is speculative, and as to this it is not lawful to doubt or to prove whether God's will be good or whether God is sweet. The other knowledge of God's will or goodness is effective or experimental, and thereby a man experiences in himself the taste of God's sweetness, and complacency in God's will; as Dionysius says of Hierotheos that "he learns Divine things through experience with them." It is in this way that we are advised to prove God's will, and to taste His sweetness. (2a, 2æ, q. 97, a. 2, Obj. 2.)

OCTOBER 20

The Coming of Divine Consolation

Augustine says, "Who will help me, so that Thou, O Lord, may come into my heart, and fill it; so that I may forget evil, and embrace Thee, my One True Good." There are three things which dispose us to this advent of Divine consolation.

First, a contempt of worldly pleasures. Secondly, devout meditation on the Divine will. Thirdly, a fervent desire of charity. 1. A contempt of worldly pleasures. Hence Saint Paul says (Col. III, 2), "Mind the things which are above, not the things that are upon the earth"; as if he had said, "you cannot mind heavenly and earthly things at the same time." Saint Bernard also declares, "If anyone thinks that this heavenly sweetness can be mixed with worldly pleasures, that this Divine balsam can be mingled with poison, that the gifts of the Holy Spirit will mix with the allurements of this world, that man errs most grievously. Do you think that you can receive the Most Pure Spirit, without renouncing these carnal consolations? Even when you begin to give up these sinful pleasures, sorrow will fill your heart, but if you persevere in renouncing these worldly allurements, your sorrow will be turned into joy. For then your affections will become purified, and your will renewed and sanctified; so that all the things which at first seemed difficult and even impossible to secure, will then be managed with much sweetness and zeal."

2. Devout meditation on the will of God, is necessary to obtain Divine consolation. "I remembered God, and was delighted." (Ps. LXXVI, 4.) Consolation from God will not be

wanting to His chosen ones who think of Him and to whom perfect happiness is not yet granted. But the goodness of God, which has been manifested to man, delights the man thinking frequently of Christ. Hence it is written, "I remembered the works of the Lord, for I will be mindful of Thy wonders from the beginning." (Ps. LXXVI, 12.) That is, mindful of those things which God has granted to the human race from the beginning, namely, the fact that He made Adam to His own image and likeness, that He received Abel's sacrifice, likewise the example of Noah, in whose ark, which was a symbol of the Church, God preserved (Noah and his family) and the animals, during the deluge, likewise the example of Abraham, whose sacrifice symbolized the incarnation and passion of Christ, the Son of God. Yet the Lord Himself came into the world; and these are the things which should delight every saintly soul.

3. A fervent desire of charity is essential, that the Divine Consoler might come into our hearts. Hence Bernard commenting on the words "A fire shall go before Him, and burn His enemies" (Ps. XCVI, 3), says, "It is necessary that the flame or ardor of this holy desire go before His face, into every soul to whom the Lord will come. A flame which burns all the rubbish of every vice, and so prepares in the heart a fitting place for God." It is then that the soul realizes the Presence of God, when it feels itself enkindled with this heavenly fire. This same Holy Spirit of God is in the soul, and desires the beauty of the soul; especially when the soul is inflamed with the love of God and turns wholeheartedly towards God, walking in the way of the spirit, and not pampering the desires of the flesh. To such a soul, who frequently and devoutly devotes itself to prayer and to meditation, the Holy Spirit lovingly hastens. Therefore, whosoever wishes to be a man of such holy desires, that he desires to be dissolved and to be with Christ, let him earnestly desire it, ardently thirst for it, continuously meditate, then will he truly receive God. (The Humanity of Christ.)

OCTOBER 21

Four Ways by Which the Demons Prevent Contemplation

"His truth shall compass thee with a shield. Thou shalt not be afraid with the terror of the night—of the arrow that flieth in the day, of the business that walketh about in the dark, of invasion, or of the noonday devil." (Ps. XC, 5.)

Here four things are mentioned, by means of which demons often attack souls devoted to contemplation. But the infused light of truth protects such souls from these diabolical attacks. First, there is nocturnal fear, secondly, the flying arrow of vain glory, thirdly, undue anxiety about worldly things, fourthly, "invasion of the noonday devil," namely, diabolical deception under the appearance of good.

1. Nocturnal fear is an error or horror, which the devil usually leaves at the place of his expulsion. Gregory says, that the soul when it is at first deceived by the devil, receives joy and finally horror. But the contrary happens when God speaks to the soul. He does not deceive the soul. Hence the Blessed Virgin in being saluted by the Angel, was at first disturbed but afterwards consoled.

2. "The flying arrow," is vain glory, because quickly and sweetly as it were, it enters, but seriously wounds the soul. This spirit of vain glory often attacks and deceives those meditating. Isaias I, 22, says, "thy wine is mingled with water." Wine here signifies the revelation from God (or the voice of God speaking to the soul) which rejoices the heart. Water signifies vain glory, which puffs up the soul and makes it proud or arrogant. Therefore, those people mix water with wine, who rejoice in the revelation made to them, uselessly and deceitfully.

3. "The business walking about in the dark," which prevents contemplation is anxiety or care of worldly things, thoughts of which the devil often causes in the minds of those praying and meditating; so that he might withdraw them from contemplation, and rob them of its strength and consolation.

4. Finally, "the invasion also of the noonday devil," is that diabolical deception under the appearance of good, for example, sometimes when satan sees a devout novice, he suggests to him to watch, to fast, to pray and weep for a long time; so that weakened and disheartened, he might draw the

novice away from the worship of God or make him repent of the good which he has begun.

Therefore, the Lord said to Zacheus who climbed up into a sycamore tree that he might see Christ, "Zacheus, make haste and come down, for this day I must abide in thy house." (Luke XIX, 4.) The sycamore tree signifies indiscreet devotion, in which some novice at times wishes to ascend too high, and to him Jesus says, "Do not ascend too high, but descend quickly, because I wish not only to be with you, but to remain with you a long time." (Apoc. C. 1.)

OCTOBER 22

Divine Familiarity

"The Word was made flesh, and dwelt among us." (John I, 24.)

Here Saint John speaks of the conversation of the incarnate Word. It "dwelt among us," that is, Jesus conversed familiarly among His Apostles as Saint Peter declares. "All the time that the Lord Jesus came in and went out among us." (Acts, I, 21.) Moreover the Evangelist adds this to show the wonderful conformity of the Word towards men, among whom Jesus so conversed that He seemed as if He were one of them. For not only did He wish to be like unto man in nature, but also, with the exception of sin, He wished to be like unto men in constant fellowship and in familiar conversation; so that by sweetness of His conversation He might lead men to higher perfection.

Truly did Jesus Himself say that, "a prophet is not without honor, save in his own country, and in his own home." (Matthew XIII, 57.) And this statement is verified not only in the prophecies to the Jews but also as Origen says, among many of the Gentiles, because by many of their citizens the prophecies were held in contempt and the prophets led to death. For frequent conversation among men and overfamiliarity with them, decreases reverence and breeds contempt. And therefore we are accustomed to respect less those with whom we are very familiar, and we respect more those whom we cannot have as intimates.

But the contrary is true of God. For inasmuch as anyone

becomes more familiar with God, through love and contemplation, by so much the more does one reverence God, and regard Him the more excellent. "With the hearing of the ear, I have heard Thee, but now my eye seeth Thee. Therefore, I reprehend myself, and do penance in dust and ashes." (Job XLII, 5.)

There is a reason for this, because in man there is a certain infirmity and weakness of nature, and when man converses with man for a long time he recognizes these infirmities and weaknesses, and because of these man's respect for man decreases. But since God is absolutely perfect, the more then that a man advances in the knowledge of God, by so much the more does he admire the excellence of God's perfection, and because of this man should reverence God all the more. (John C, IV.)

OCTOBER 23

A Method of Learning Divine Secrets

"Now there was leaning on Jesus' bosom one of His disciples (John), whom Jesus loved. Simon Peter therefore beckoned to him, and said to him, "Who is it of whom He speaketh?" (John XIII, 23.)

1. Peter wishes to know the person to whom our Lord referred when He said, "One of you will betray Me." Since moreover, Peter is always mentioned in the Gospels as being the most courageous and the first to respond because of his fervent love for Christ, why is it that he is silent on this occasion? Why is it that he asks John the question? The reason is, according to Chrysostom, threefold. First, because since he (Peter) was reprimanded by the Master for being unwilling to have his feet washed by Him, he doubts now that any of the Apostles would be so ungrateful as to betray so good a Master. Secondly, Peter was unwilling that the Lord should tell this betrayal publicly so that the other Apostles might hear it. Hence because Peter was a little distance from Christ, and John was closer to Him, he asked John the question. "Who is it of whom, He speaketh?" Thirdly, there is a mystical reason or there is a mystical meaning in this. Through John, the contemplative life is signified and through Peter, the active life is meant; because, through the medium of the contemplative life those leading an active life are instructed in Divine things.

"John therefore, leaning on the breast of Jesus, said to Him, Lord who is it?" (John XIII, 25.)

2. It must be observed, that when Peter beckoned to John to instruct him John was leaning on Jesus' bosom. Moreover, Peter asks John in preference to the other apostles, because he was "leaning on the breast of Jesus." Now John asks the Master. The breast being closer to the mouth than the bosom, John therefore, desiring to hear more secretly and more silently the Divine secret, ascended from the Saviour's lap to His breast.

Mystically, moreover, it can be understood from this incident that inasmuch as man wishes to receive the secrets of Divine wisdom, by so much the more must he strive to approach closer to Jesus. "Come ye to Him, and be enlightened." (Ps. XXXIII, 6), for the secrets of Divine wisdom are chiefly revealed to those who are united to God through love. "He showeth His friend concerning it, that it is his possession." (Job. XXXVI, 33.) "His friend cometh, and shall search him." (Prov. XVIII, 17.) (John XIII.)

OCTOBER 24

The Effects of Contemplation

"The King has brought me into His storerooms." (Canticles I, 3.)

1. "The King has brought me into His storerooms," that is, into His sweetness by giving me His grace. Moreover, grace is called, "storerooms," because from grace flow and are derived special virtues which render perfect the different powers of the soul, and according to the various virtues of the different powers, we differently rejoice and are made happy in the Lord. And being perfected in these special virtues through God's grace, we in a certain manner drink the wine of spiritual joy from the various storehouses (or winecellars) of the Lord. (Cant.)

2. Contemplation decreases sadness.

For the greatest delight consists in the contemplation of truth. Moreover every delight lessens sorrow, and inasmuch as anyone is a more perfect lover of wisdom, by so much the more does contemplation of truth relieve sorrow or grief.

Therefore, men who contemplate Divine things and future happiness rejoice in tribulations, according to Saint James, I, 2, "My brethren, count it all joy, when you shall fall into divers temptations," and even more, men rejoice in the midst of bodily tortures; as the martyr Tiburtius, when he was walking barefoot on the burning coals said, "Methinks, I am walking on roses, in the name of Jesus Christ."

From this incident and from other facts, it is clear that in the powers of the soul there is an overflow from the higher to the lower powers; and accordingly, the pleasure of contemplation, which is in the higher part overflows, so as to mitigate or relieve that pain which is in the senses.

3. Contemplation causes the affections to rest concerning temporal things. "I sleep, and my heart watcheth." (Cant. V, 3.) For contemplative persons are said "to sleep," because they rest from the distractions of the senses; still in regard to their heart they are wide awake since they are more apt to perceive interior inspirations and Divine influences. Just as the blind are not devoted to visible things they remember better, so, too, contemplatives who are not given to external things, perceive all the more, interior inspirations from God.

4. Contemplation increases and strengthens and directs the affections towards God. "Love is as strong as death." (Cant. VIII, 6.) For just as death separates the soul from the body so that it can no longer desire anything, and cannot move around in this life any longer; so the love of Christ truly fills the heart of one who wholly mortifies himself in regard to worldly desires, as if he were insensible to earthly things and dead to the world but living entirely in Christ and for Christ. The true love of Christ never falleth away, never deserts the contemplative and saintly soul. Hence the Apostle says: "Who shall separate us from the love of Christ? Shall tribulation, or famine, or nakedness, or persecution, or the sword? I am persuaded that neither death, nor life, nor any other creature, shall be able to separate us from the love of God, which is in Christ Jesus our Lord." (Rom. VIII, 35.) (Cant.)

OCTOBER 25

How to Recover Divine Sweetness . . .

"In my bed by night, I sought Him Whom my soul loveth." (Canticles III, 1.)

1. Man ought to examine his conscience.

External cares so occupy the soul, that when it desires to return to conscience it finds itself very often wanting in that sweetness (or fervor) which previously it possessed. Moreover, when a man is distracted in mind, and cannot enjoy that sweetness which he formerly experienced, he ought to enter into the secret depths of his heart by seeking Christ. Hence, he should search for Him in his bed, that is, in his conscience. He sometimes seeks and finds not Christ. "In my bed by night, I sought Him, Whom my soul loveth. I sought Him, and found Him not." (Cant. III, 1.) And whenever this happens to man, he ought to rise and seek Him and ask himself if he desired anything or did anything displeasing to Christ, because of which he feels himself now distracted in conscience.

A method of seeking Christ is here noted. "I will rise, and will go about the city. In the streets and the broadways I will seek Him whom my soul loveth." (Cant. III, 2.) Returning to conscience, "I sought Christ, but found Him not." Hence, so that I may find Him, I will continue searching for Him. "I will rise, and will go about the city," that is, through actual contemplation I will re-examine my conscience, search again, "in the streets and the broadways," that is, through every thought, word and action, which I have entertained, said or done and ask myself, if in so doing I did something which displeased Christ. I will seek Him Whom my soul loveth. For if anyone after performing an action cannot return to the sweetness of contemplation, he should remember, that perhaps he has failed in something, because of which he experiences not, the accustomed sweetness. And therefore, he ought to examine the entire city, that is, his conscience.

Moreover, it must be remembered, that conscience is compared to "a bed," in which Christ should rest, and that it is such a narrow bed that only One can rest in it, namely, Christ or Satan. But if we consider conscience and the heart in relation to the various kinds of sin which can be there, it is a "separate city with streets and broadways," that is, with major and minor crimes.

2. To recover Divine sweetness, man ought to recall often the memory of Divine sweetness.

When anyone returns from a state of action to a state of contemplation and finds not Christ, among other things which may inspire him to seek Christ is the memory of the Divine sweetness (or fervor) which he has lost. For since man experiences sometimes in prayer, and actually enjoys Divine sweetness, and later cannot taste such sweetness as before, the memory of that former sweetness should stimulate him to examine his thoughts and affections, and see if by them he has displeased Christ, so that he can find the cause by reason of which he cannot now experience that same Divine sweetness.

3. Man ought to renounce vain and evil thoughts (if he desires to regain Divine favour). Such dangerous thoughts are called "the watchmen of the city." (Cant. III, 3), because they are always ready to arrest and occupy our attention. But we should abandon these evil thoughts, for in such thoughts Christ is not found. Moreover we might say, "they struck me, and wounded me, and took away my veil from me." (Cant. V, 7.) More than this, these evil thoughts strike us when we admit them into our minds, they wound us when we delight in them; but when we consent to them, they rob us of "our veil," by taking away from us the virtues and gifts of God. (Cant. III, and V.)

OCTOBER 26

The Perfection of the Christian Life

"Above all these things have charity, which is the bond of perfection." (Col. III, 14.)

1. A thing is said to be perfect, in as far as it attains its proper end which is the ultimate perfection of the thing. Charity, moreover, is that supernatural virtue which unites us to God, Who is the ultimate end of the human mind; because, "whosoever abideth in charity, abideth in God, and God in him." (1 John IV, 16.) And therefore, as far as charity goes, it is absolutely the perfection of the Christian life.

Man is said to be absolutely perfect in the spiritual life by reason of that in which the spiritual life chiefly consists, but he can also be called relatively perfect, by reason of whatever is united to the spiritual life. Moreover, the spiritual life principally consists in charity, and whosoever has not charity is considered to be nothing spiritually. Hence the Apostle says (1 Cor. XIII), "If I should have prophecy, and should know all mysteries, and all knowledge, and if I should have all faith, so that I could remove mountains, and have not charity I am nothing." Saint John, the Apostle, also declared that the whole spiritual life consists in charity. "We know that we have passed from death to life, because we love the brethren. He that loveth not, abideth in death." (1 John III, 14.) Therefore, in the spiritual life, he is absolutely perfect who has perfect charity.

2. Moreover, one can be relatively or limitedly perfect in whatever way he is united to the spiritual life. This is clear from the words of Saint Paul to the Colossians (III, 14), where he attributes perfection to charity, for after having enumerated many virtues, namely, mercy, kindness, humility, etc., the Apostle adds, "Above all these things have charity, which is the bond of perfection"; because it unites in a certain manner all the other virtues in perfect unity.

But also, in regard to intellectual knowledge some persons are said to be perfect. "That you may be perfect in the same mind, and in the same judgment." (1 Cor. I, 10.) Nevertheless, even though one may have perfect knowledge without charity, such a person is considered to be of no account spiritually.

So also someone can be called perfect in regard to "patience which has a perfect work" (James I, 4), and likewise in regard to any of the other virtues. (Perfection of the Spiritual Life C. 1.)

OCTOBER 27

The Perfection Necessary for Salvation

A rational creature ought to love God with all his strength, for it is written (Deut. VI, 5), "Thou shalt love the Lord thy God, with thy whole heart, and with thy whole soul, and with thy whole strength." But in order that we may love God with the whole heart, mind, soul and strength, nothing must be lacking in us of Divine love, but we must refer everything to God, either actually or habitually. The perfection of this Divine love is given to man in the commandment.

1. The first thing is that man should refer all things to

God as to their proper end, as the Apostle says (1 Cor. X, 31), "Whether you eat, or drink, or whatever else you do, do all for the glory of God." This is truly fulfilled when anyone dedicates his life to the service of God, for thus all things which he does are virtually ordained to God and so man loves God with his whole heart.

2. Secondly, the perfection of Divine love is assigned so that man might subject his intellect to God, believing those truths which are Divinely revealed, as the Apostle says (2 Cor. X, 5), "Bringing into captivity every understanding unto the obedience of Christ," and thus God will be loved with the whole mind.

3. Thirdly, the commandment is given, so that all of man's exterior actions, words and deeds might be established in Divine love, according to the Apostle (1 Cor. XVI, 14), "Let all your things be done in charity"; and thus God will be loved with the whole strength.

4. Fourthly, so that whatever man loves he may love in God and for God, and thus refer all his affections to the love of God. Hence the Apostle used to say (2 Cor. V, 13), "For whether we be transported in mind, it is to God; or whether we be sober, it is for you, for the charity of Christ presseth us"; and thus God may be loved with the whole soul.

This is the way of perfect Divine love which all are bound to observe from a necessity of precept. (The Perfection of the Spiritual Life.)

OCTOBER 28

The Perfection Which Comes Under Counsel

1. The perfection which falls under counsel is that which tends to a likeness of the perfection of the blessed in heaven. It is said in Deut. VI, 5, "thou shalt love the Lord thy God, with thy whole heart, and with thy whole soul, and with all thy strength"; and Saint Luke adds, "with all thy mind," so that the heart might be referred to the intention, the mind to knowledge, the soul to the affections and strength to action. Since "whole," means perfect or to which nothing is lacking; God is loved with the whole heart, soul, mind and strength, if nothing is wanting to us in the perfection of those things; but this manner of perfect Divine love is not proper (or possible) to us in this life but to the blessed in heaven.

For in this heavenly beatitude, the intellect and the will of the rational creature are always centered on God, since beatitude consists in the Divine enjoyment; and moreover happiness does not exist in a habit but in an act. And because the rational creature adheres to God, as to his ultimate end since God is the highest truth then all things are directed by the intention of their ultimate end, and all things which must be done are directed to their final and proper end; hence it is that in the perfection of this heavenly beatitude, the rational creature loves God with his whole heart, for his whole intention is centered on God in all things which he thinks, loves and does. He loves with the whole mind, since his mind is always actually focused on God, beholding Him always, judging all things in Him and according to His truth. The rational creature in heaven loves God with his whole soul, since his entire affection is directed continuously towards God in loving Him, and because all things are loved there for God's sake. The rational creature loves and will love God in heaven, "with his whole strength and force," for the reason that all his exterior action will be the love of God.

2. But although this perfection of the blessed is not possible to us in this life, still we ought to strive to attain it so that we might bring ourselves to a likeness of this perfection, as far as it is possible. And in so doing consists the perfection of this life, to which the counsels of the Gospel invite us to imitate. For it is clear, that the human heart inasmuch as it is more deeply centered on one thing, by so much the more is it drawn away from many things. Therefore, inasmuch as the mind of man is more perfectly consecrated to the love of God, by so much the more is it drawn away from love for earthly things. Hence Augustine says, that "the poison of charity is the hope of possessing and retaining worldly things, but the increase of charity is the lessening of that worldly greed, while perfection destroys all greed and selfish desires."

Therefore, all the counsels which invite us to acquire perfection pertain to this purpose, namely, that the mind of man might be drawn away from affection for worldly things, so that our minds might be more free to tend towards God by contemplating, loving and fulfilling His Truth. (The Perfection of the Spiritual Life; C. IV, and VI.)

OCTOBER 29

Perfection Consists in the Observance of the Commandments Rather Than the Counsels

Perfection is said to consist in a thing in two ways. In one way primarily and essentially; in another way, secondarily and accidentally.

1. Primarily and essentially the perfection of the Christian life consists in charity, principally as to the love of God, secondly, as to the love of our neighbour, both of which are the matter of the chief commandments of the Divine law. Now the love of God and of our neighbour are not commanded according to a measure, so that what is in excess of the measure be a matter of counsel. This is clear from the very form of the commandment, pointing as it does to perfection—for example, in the words, "Thou shalt love the Lord thy God, with thy whole heart"; since the whole is the same as the perfect and since it is said, "Thou shalt love thy neighbour as thyself," for everyone loves himself most.

The reason of this is that the end "of the commandment is charity," according to the Apostle (1 Tim. I, 5) and the end is not subject to a measure but only such things as are directed to the end, thus a physician does not measure the amount of his healing but how much medicine or diet he shall prescribe to effect a cure. Consequently, it is evident that perfection consists essentially in the observance of the commandments; hence Augustine says, "Why then should not this perfection be prescribed to man, although no man has it in this life?"

2. Secondarily and instrumentally, however, perfection consists in the observance of the Counsels, all of which, like the commandments, are directed to charity yet not in the same way. For the commandments, other than the precepts of charity, are directed to the removal of things contrary to charity, with which charity is incompatible, whereas the counsels are directed to the removal of things that hinder the act of charity, and yet are not contrary to charity, such as marriage, the occupation of worldly business and so forth. Hence Augustine says, "Whatever things God has commanded, for instance, 'Thou shalt not commit adultery,' and whatever are not commanded, yet suggested by a special counsel, for example, 'It is good for a man not to touch a woman,' are then done aright when they are referred to the love of God, and

of our neighbour for God's sake, both in this world and in the world to come."

Hence it is that in the Conferences of the Fathers the Abbot Moses says, "Fastings, watchings, meditating on the Scriptures, poverty, and loss of all one's wealth, these are not perfection, but means to perfection, since not in them does the school of perfection find its end, but through them it achieves its end," and he had already said that, "we endeavour to ascend by these steps to the perfection of charity."

Now the perfection of Divine love is a matter of precept for all without exception, so that even the perfection of heaven is not exempted from this precept, but "one escapes transgressing the precept, in whatever measure one attains to the perfection of Divine love," writes Augustine. The lowest degree of Divine love is to love nothing more than God or contrary to God or equally with God, and whoever fails in this degree of perfection nowise fulfills the precept. There is another degree of Divine love which cannot be fulfilled by us in this life, and it is evident that to fail in this is not to be a transgressor of the precept; and in like manner one does not transgress the precept if one does not attain to the intermediate degrees of perfection, provided one attain to the lowest, that is to the love of God.

It is written then (Deut. VI, 5), "Thou shalt love the Lord thy God, with thy whole heart," and (Lev. XIX, 18), "Thou shalt love thy neighbour as thyself," and these are the commandments of which our Lord spoke (Matth. XXII, 40), "On these two commandments dependeth the whole law and the prophets." Hence Augustine says, "the perfection of charity is prescribed to man in this life, because one runs not aright unless one knows whither to run. And how shall we know this if no commandment declares it to us?" (2a. 2ae. q. 184, a. 3.)

OCTOBER 30

The Counsels of the Gospels

"The good counsels of a friend are sweet to the soul." (Prov. XVII, 9.)

Because it is best for man's mind to adhere to God and to Divine things, because it is impossible for man to be intensely and entirely busy about different things at the same time; for this reason, counsels are laid down in the Divine Law, so that man's mind might more freely cling to God, and through which men might be drawn away from the worldly occupations of this life as far as it is possible.

Moreover, human anxiety is occupied usually with three things, namely, it is busy about one's own person, what the person does or whither the person goes, secondly, about persons connected with us, namely, wife and children and thirdly, there is anxiety and worry about external things to be procured which man needs for the necessaries of life. To remove therefore, from man anxiety and worry about external things, the counsel of poverty is laid down in the Divine Law; so that he might renounce the things of this world in which his mind might be centered with a certain and too great solicitude. Jesus said "If thou wilt be perfect, go sell what thou hast, and give to the poor, and thou shalt have treasure in heaven; and come follow Me." (Matth. XIX, 21.) To remove the anxiety connected with a wife and family, there is given to man, the counsel of chastity or continency. "Now concerning virgins, I have no commandment of the Lord, but I give counsel, as having obtained mercy of the Lord, to be faithful." (1 Cor. VII, 25.) To remove the anxiety of man even for himself, there is given the counsel of obedience, by which man places the disposal of his actions into the hands of his superior. "Obey your prelates, and be subject to them. For they watch as being to render an account of your souls." (Heb. XIII, 17.)

Because moreover, the highest perfection consists in this that the mind of man consecrate itself to God, for this consecration and adherence of the mind to God these three things cited above, are especially helpful and suitably pertain to the state of perfection; not as if they are in themselves perfections, but because they are certain dispositions to perfection consisting in this that they lead us to God. They can also be called the effects and signs of perfection. For since the human mind is passionately attracted by a love and desire of a certain thing, it follows that the mind esteems other things of less value. From this fact therefore, that man's mind from love and desire is fervently transported to Divine things, it is clear that it should tend to and rest upon perfection, renouncing all those things which prevent it from adhering to God; not only the care and anxiety about worldly things, but also affection and care of wife and family, and even over-anxiety about oneself.

Because therefore, the above mentioned three counsels are effects and signs disposing to perfection, persons who vow the observance of the above three counsels or promises to God are said to be in a state of perfection. Moreover, the perfection to which the aforesaid three counsels dispose, consists in the surrender of the mind to God, the total surrender. Hence those who make profession of these three vows are called religious, because they have dedicated themselves and thir possessions to God in the manner of a certain sacrifice; dedicated, surrendered and consecrated worldly things by the vow of poverty, their bodies by the vow of chastity and their wills by the vow of obedience. Therefore, religion consists in Divine worship. (111 Contr. c. 130.)

OCTOBER 31

Perseverance

"He that shall persevere to the end, he shall be saved." (Matth. XXIV, 13.)

1. Perseverance is a virtue. For virtue is concerned about the difficult and the good, and so where there is a special kind of difficulty or goodness there is a special virtue. Now a virtuous action may involve goodness or difficulty in two ways. First, from the very species of the act, and secondly, from the length of time, since to persist long in something difficult involves a special difficulty. Hence, to persist long in something good belongs to a special virtue.

Therefore, just as temperance and fortitude are special virtues for the reason that one of these virtues moderates pleasures of touch (which is of itself a difficult thing), while the other moderates fear and daring in regard to the dangers of death (which also is something difficult in itself), so perseverance is a special virtue, since it consists in enduring delays in the above or other virtuous deeds so far as it is necessary.

Perseverance and constancy agree as to the end, since it belongs to both to persist firmly in some good; but they differ as to those things which make it difficult to persist in good. Because the virtue of perseverance properly makes man persist firmly in good against difficulties arising from the very continuance of the act; whereas constancy makes him persist firmly in good against difficulties arising from any other external circumstances. Hence perseverance takes precedence over constancy as a part of fortitude, for the difficulty arising from continuance of a good action is more intrinsic to the act of virtue than that which arises from external obstacles.

2. Man established in grace, needs the help of God's grace to persevere; for perseverance may be considered in three ways. First, when it signifies a habit of the mind by which man firmly stands in virtue, lest he might be removed by distress in sadness from the pursuit of that which is virtuous. Secondly, perseverance is called a certain habit, according to which a man has the desire of persevering in good unto the end of life. And in both of these ways, perseverance is infused into the soul together with the grace of God, just like constancy and the other virtues.

Thirdly, perseverance may be called a certain continuance in good unto the end of life. And to possess this kind of perseverance a man who is established in grace does not need any other habitual grace, but the Divine assistance to direct and protect him against the attacks of temptations. Therefore after anyone is sanctified by grace, it is necessary that he ask the aforesaid gift of perseverance from God; so that he might be protected from evil unto the end of life's journey. For grace is granted to many, to whom it is not granted to persevere in grace. (1a. 2ae. Q. CIX, a. X.)

3. The gift of perseverance does not fall under merit, is not acquired because of merit; but anyone desiring it must seek it from God for himself or for another. For those things which we do not merit, we should implore through prayer; because God hears even sinners begging pardon, which they do not merit, and this is clear from the prayer and pardon and justification of the Publican, "O God be merciful to me a sinner. I say to you, this man went down into his house justified." (Luke XVIII, 13.) (1a. 2ae. q. 114, a. 9, 1um.)

NOVEMBER 1

The Happiness of the Saints

"Come, ye blessed of My Father, possess you the kingdom prepared for you from the foundation of the world." (Matth. XXV, 34.)

The kingdom of heaven is called the glory of paradise. Nor is this wonderful, for kingdom is nothing other than the rule or government of a state. Moreover, wherever there is the best government or rule, nothing is found contrary to the will of the ruler. But the will of God is the salvation of all mankind, "because He wishes all to be saved"; but salvation will be especially in paradise where nothing will be found repugnant to the salvation of man. "The Son of man shall send His Angels, and they shall gather out of His kingdom all scandals." (Matth. XIII, 41.) When therefore, we pray, "Thy kingdom come," we pray that we might share in the kingdom of heaven and in the glory of paradise.

Indeed that heavenly kingdom is most desirable on account of three things.

First, because of the highest justice which abounds there. "Thy people shall be just, and they shall inherit the land forever." (Isaias LX, 21.) Here on earth, the good and bad mingle together, but in God's kingdom there will be no evil and no sinner.

Secondly, the heavenly kingdom is most desirable, because of its most perfect liberty. Here in this world there is no perfect liberty, although all naturally desire it; but there in God's kingdom there will be every liberty which is contrary to every slavery. "The creature shall be delivered from the servitude of corruption, into the liberty of the glory of the children of God." (Rom. VIII, 21.) Not only will men be absolutely free there but they will be kings. "Thou art worthy O Lord—and hast redeemed us to God, in Thy blood, and hast made us to our God a kingdom" (Apoc. V, 10); because all in heaven will be of the same will with God, and God will wish whatever the saints will wish, and the saints, whatever God wills. Hence the will of God will be the will of those in heaven; and therefore all will rule, because the Lord will become the will of all and the crown of all." In that day the Lord of hosts shall be a crown of glory, and a garland of joy to the residue of His people." (Isaias XXVIII, 5.)

Thirdly, the kingdom of heaven is most desirable, because of its wonderful riches. "The eye hath not seen, O God, besides Thee, what things thou hast prepared for them that wait for Thee." (Isaias LXIV, 4), "Who satisfieth thy desire with good things." (Ps. CII, 5.)

Observe also that man will find in God alone everything more excellent and more perfect than everything which he sought after in Him in this world. If you seek delight, you will find the greatest delight there in God. "You will see and your heart will rejoice. Everlasting joy shall be upon your heads." (Isaias LXVI, 14.) If you seek duration of joy, it will be there eternally. "The just shall enter into eternal life." If you seek riches, there in God's kingdom you will find an abundance of riches by reason of which riches exist, and so in regard to all other good things.

Wherefore Augustine says, "Whatever there is, that thou O holy soul can desire, there you will find it entirely in God." (The Lord's Prayer.)

NOVEMBER 2

Purgatory

"Now if any man build upon this foundation, gold, silver, precious stones, wood, hay, stubble; every man's work shall be manifest, for the day of the Lord shall declare it. Other foundation no man can lay, but that which is laid; which is Christ Jesus." (1 Cor. CXI, 12.)

By gold is meant, according to Augustine, meditation on God, through silver, the love of our neighbour, by precious stones, are signified good works. Through wood, hay, stubble, are meant venial sins, which insinuate themselves into those who care for earthly things. For just as these are stored in a house without belonging to the substance of the house and can be burnt while the house is saved, so also venial sins are multiplied in a man while the spiritual edifice remains, and for them man suffers fire or temporal trials in this life or of purgatory after this life, and yet he is saved forever. (1a. 2ae. q. 89, a. 2.)

For venial sins in a man who has charity can be consumed by a certain punishment; and therefore, according to the metaphor, these things are suitably signified which are burnt or consumed by fire. And because inasmuch as any sin is the more serious, by so much the more difficult is it purged or removed. But among venial sins, one sin is found to be more serious than another, therefore, the difference among these is suitably pointed out by the difference between those things which are more easily and more slowly burnt by fire.

Moreover, because all things are included in three things, namely, in the beginning, the middle and the end, according to this, all degrees of venial sin are reduced to three; namely, to wood which remains longer in the fire, stubble which is burnt up at once and hay, which is between these two. According to this, venial sins are removed by fire, quickly or slowly, in so far as man is more or less attached to them.

Moreover, certain venial sins are of greater adherence in the soul than others, according as man's affection for them is more inclined to commit them and more firmly fixed on them. Because therefore those venial sins, which adhere more strongly to the soul are purged more slowly, some souls will be punished longer in purgatory than others; in so far as their affections were the more deeply immersed in venial sins.

But since the severity of the punishment properly corresponds to the seriousness of the fault, and the length of the punishment to the removal of the fault from its subject; therefore, it can happen that one soul remains longer than another in purgatory but is less afflicted, and the contrary is also true. (4, Dist. 21, q. 1, a. 3.)

NOVEMBER 3

The Punishments of Purgatory

1. In purgatory there is a twofold pain or punishment. First, the punishment of the damned, in so far as the holy souls are delayed from enjoying the Divine vision, and secondly, the pain or punishment of sense, in so far as they are punished by corporal fire. And in regard to both punishments, the least punishment of purgatory exceeds the severest punishment of this life. For inasmuch as anything is more desired, by so much the more is its absence the more painfully felt; and because the affections which desire the Highest good after this life are most eager to enjoy God and also because the time of enjoying the Highest Good is now at hand unless something prevents that enjoyment, consequently the holy souls suffer pain especially concerning the delay in enjoying the Divine vision.

Likewise also, since this pain is not an injury but the sense or experience of an injury, the souls in purgatory are all the more sensitive to this pain, for those pains which are in the most sensitive places, in the affections of the soul, cause the greatest grief. And because the entire sensitiveness of the body is from the soul, therefore if any pain or sorrow comes to the soul, the soul especially suffers. But moreover, the soul suffers from the effects of material fire and this must be admitted by all. Therefore it must be that the pains of purgatory, in regard to the pain of the damned and the pain of sense, exceed in severity every punishment or pain of this life.

2. In regard to the location of purgatory, its exact location is not expressly stated in Sacred Scripture, neither can conclusive reasons be set forth as to the determined place of the purgatorial prison. Still it is said that purgatory is probably located close to hell; so that the same fire which punishes the damned in hell, and cleanses the just in purgatory; although the damned in as far as they are inferior in merit, are condemned to lower places. Therefore Gregory says, that just as under the same fire, gold shines and chaff smokes; so under the same fire, the sinner is burned, and the elect purified. (4 Dist. 21, q. 1, a. 1.)

NOVEMBER 4

Praying to the Saints

1. We should pray to the Saints.

This Divine order was established among things, so that all things might ultimately be brought back to God. Hence since the saints in heaven are the nearest to God, the order of Divine law requires that we who are in the body journeying to the Lord, be brought to Him through the intercession of the Saints; which happens in very truth when through them God pours out upon us the effect of His Divine goodness. And because our return to God should correspond to the progress of His goodness in us, just as through the prayers of the saints blessings and favours come to us, so should we return to God, that we might again and again receive God's favours through the medium of His saints. Hence it is that we call upon them to be our intercessors with God, to be our mediators; while we ask them to pray for us.

Although indeed the greater saints are more acceptable to God than the saints of lesser dignity, still it is also useful for us to pray during life to the minor saints, and this because of five reasons.

First, because sometimes a person may have greater devotion to a minor saint than to a greater saint, and the effect of prayer depends especially on devotion.

Secondly, because of the aversion to be removed, for constant correspondence to one thing (and this is true of prayer), begets aversion or dislike for the thing sometimes. For this reason we ask different saints, so that a new fervor of devotion for each saint might be aroused in us.

Thirdly, because to certain saints the work of defending special cases is chiefly assigned.

Fourthly, that proper honor might be shown to all the saints by us.

Fifthly, because the favour which is not obtained through the intercession or prayer of one saint is sometimes obtained through the prayers and intercession of many saints.

2. The saints know when we pray. They are aware of our prayers. The Divine essence is a sufficient medium of knowing all things. God in beholding His own essence sees all things. Still it does not follow that whosoever sees the Essence of God knows all things, but only those who comprehend the Essence of God. Hence, since the souls of the saints do not comprehend the Divine Essence, it follows that they do not know all things which can be known by the Divine Essence. Hence also, the lower Angels are taught certain things by the higher angels; although all the Angels see the Divine Essence. But each blessed sees only those things in the Divine Essence, which the perfection of beatitude requires. The perfection of beatitude requires that a man has whatever he wishes and that he wishes nothing inordinately. Moreover, each one wishes with a right will, so that he knows those things which pertain to him. Hence since no uprightness is lacking in the saints, they will to know those things which pertain to them and therefore they know them in the Word of God. Moreover it pertains to the glory of the saints, that they obtain help for those on earth who need it for salvation. Consequently, "the saints are co-workers with God, and nothing is so Divine," writes Dionysius.

Therefore, it is clear that the saints have a knowledge of those things which are required for this Divine work. And so it is evident that they know in the Word the promises, prayers and devotions of mankind imploring their help and intercession with God. (4 Dist. 45, q. 3, a. 1 and 2.)

NOVEMBER 5

The Saints Pray for Us to God

1. The Saints pray for us.
As Jerome says, the error of Vigilantius consisted in saying that "while we live, we can pray for one another; but that after we are dead, none of our prayers for others can be heard, seeing that not even the martyrs' prayers are granted when they pray for their blood to be avenged." But this is absolutely false, because since prayers offered for others proceed from charity, the greater the charity of the saints in heaven the more they pray for wayfarers; since the latter can be helped by prayers, and the more closely they are united to God the more are their prayers efficacious; for the Divine order is such that the lower beings receive an overflow of the excellence of the higher, even as the air receives the brightness of the sun. Hence, it is said of Christ (Heb. VII, 25), "Going to God by His own power ... to make intercession for us." Wherefore Jerome, writing against Vigilantius says, "If the Apostles and martyrs while yet in the body, and having to be solicitous for themselves, pray for others, how much the more now that they have the crown of victory and triumph."

2. The prayers of the saints to God for us are always heard. The saints are said to pray for us in two ways. In one way by expressed prayer when by their prayers they implore the ears of Divine Mercy in our behalf. In another way, by interpretative prayer, namely, by the merits which they have in God's sight, merits which give not only glory to Him and to them, but are also suffrages and prayers for us; just as the blood of Christ when shed, is said to obtain pardon for us.

Moreover, in both ways, the prayers of the saints, on their part, are efficacious to obtain what they ask. But on our part, there can be a defect so that we do not obtain the fruit or favour of their prayers; and according to this they are said to pray for us in so far as their merits profit us. But when they beseech God for us, by demanding something for us by their prayers, the saints are then always heard; because the saints will only that which God wills, and they seek only that which God wills to happen. Unless we speak of the antecedent will of God, whereby "He wishes all to be saved," which is not always fulfilled. Wherefore it is not wonderful that, even in the saints who pray for us according to this manner of will, sometimes our petitions are not heard. (4 Dist. 45, q. 3, a. 3.)

NOVEMBER 6

The Advantages of Believing in the Resurrection of the Dead

Faith and hope in the resurrection of the dead will win for us a fourfold victory. They will remove from our hearts the sadness we feel for our dead. Secondly, they will take away from us the fear of death. Thirdly, they will make us more anxious and desirous to accomplish good, and fourthly, belief in the resurrection of the dead, which will happen through the power of God will withdraw us from evil.

First, faith and hope in the resurrection of our dead will remove sadness. It is impossible for us not to grieve over the death of an intimate friend, or over the death of a member of our own family; but if we earnestly believe that the dead will rise again, our grief is greatly lessened by this consoling truth. "We will not have you ignorant, brethren, concerning them that are asleep, that you be not sorrowful, even as others who have no hope." (1 Th. IV, 12.)

Secondly, faith in the resurrection of the dead takes away the fear of death, for if man does not hope for another and better life after death then death is certainly greatly to be feared, and consequently man should endure every evil rather than suffer death. But because we believe, and rightly so, that there is another and better life which we will enjoy after death, we should then have no fear of death; nor fear to endure evils and persecutions because of death. "I will put my trust in God, so that through death, He might destroy him who had the empire of death, that is the devil, and might deliver them, who through the fear of death, were all their lifetime subject to servitude." (Hebr. II, 14.)

Thirdly, faith in the resurrection of our dead makes us anxious to do good. For if this earthly life of man is the only life which he lives, there would not be any great inspiration for man to do good; because whatever good he might do would be small, since his action would be determined by time and not by eternity. On the contrary, when we believe, and because we believe that the good which we do here will merit for us an eternal reward on resurrection day, we are by that very fact encouraged to do good and to rejoice at the good accomplished. "If in this life only we have hope in Christ, we are of all men the most miserable." (1 Cor. XV, 19.)

Fourthly, faith and hope in the resurrection of the dead will withdraw us from evil. For just as the hope of a reward inspires us to do good, so the fear of punishment which we believe is reserved for the wicked withdraws us from doing evil. "They who have done good things, shall come forth unto the resurrection of life, but they who have done evil unto the resurrection of judgment." (John V, 29.) (The Creed.)

NOVEMBER 7

The Necessity of a General Judgment

"The word that I have spoken, the same shall judge you on the last day." (John XII, 48.)

Judgment cannot be passed perfectly upon any changeable subject before its consummation, just as judgment cannot be given perfectly regarding the quality of any action before its completion in itself and in its results. Many articles appear to be profitable, which in their effects prove to be hurtful. And in the same way perfect judgment cannot be passed upon any man before the end of his life; since he can be changed in many respects from good to evil or conversely, or from good to better or from evil to worse. Hence the Apostle says (Heb. IX, 27), "It is appointed unto men once to die, and after this the Judgment."

But it must be observed that although man's temporal life in itself ends with death, still it continues dependent in a measure on what comes after it in the future.

1. In one way, as it still lives on in men's memories, in which sometimes, contrary to the truth, good or evil reputations linger on.

2. In another way, in a man's children, who are so to speak something of their parent, according to Eccl. XXX, 4, "His father is dead, and he is as if he were not dead, for he hath left one behind him that is like himself." And yet many good men have wicked sons and conversely.

3. Thirdly, as to the result of his actions, for just as from the deceit of Arius and other false leaders unbelief continues to flourish down to the end of the world; even until then

faith will continue to derive its progress from the preaching of the Apostles.

4. In a fourth way, as to the body, which is sometimes buried with honor and sometimes left unburied and finally falls to dust utterly.

5. In a fifth way, as to things upon which man's heart is set, such as temporal concerns, for example, some of which quickly lapse while others endure longer. Now all these things are submitted to the verdict of Divine judgment; and consequently, a perfect and public Judgment cannot be made of all these things during the course of this present time. Wherefore, there must be a final Judgment at the last day, in which everything concerning every man in every respect shall be perfectly and publicly judged.

Consequently, it must be held that after death man enters into an unchangeable state as to all that concerns the soul; and therefore, there is no need of postponing judgment as to the reward of the soul. But since there are some other things pertaining to a man which go on through the whole course of time, and which are not foreign to the Divine judgment, all these things must be brought to judgment at the end of time. For although in regard to such things a man neither merits nor demerits, still in a measure they accompany his reward or punishment. Consequently, all these things must be weighed in the final judgment. (3 a. q. 59, a. 5.)

NOVEMBER 8

The Discussion of the Cause in the Final Judgment

1. The Lord will be the Judge of men. He will determine the cause of things in the Judgment. He will discuss things with us in the presence of all mankind. First, He will discuss concerning the greatness of His Passion. Hence, He will show all the instruments of His death, namely, the cross, the nails and lance. Likewise, He will show us the wounds He suffered for love of us. "Every eye shall see Him, and they also that pierced Him." (Apoc. I, 7.) Likewise Apoc. XIX, 13, says, "He was clothed with garments sprinkled with blood." Moreover, the sign of the cross will appear before Him. "Then the sign of the Son of Man shall appear in heaven." (Matth. XXIV, 30.) Concerning these things the Lord, our just Judge

will say, "What did you say about these instruments of My death and Passion? What did you do? O sinner! Against you, your conscience speaks. The very heavens accuse you." Christ will accuse you by His wounds, His scars will further declare against you and the nails of His Crucifixion will loudly cry for justice.

2. There will be a discussion concerning omissions of the good which we could have done and should have done, but did not do. "I was hungry and you gave Me not to eat. I was thirsty, and you gave Me not to drink. I was a stranger, and you took Me not in, naked, and you covered Me not, sick, and in prison, and you did not visit Me." (Matth. XXV, 42.)

3. In the Judgment, "Inquisition shall be made into the thoughts of the ungodly." (Wis. I, 9.) Fourthly, inquisition shall be made into their intentions, by "the Discerner of the thoughts and intentions of the heart." (Heb. IV, 12.) Fifthly, concerning sinful words. "Every idle, or sinful word that men shall speak, they shall render an account for it, on the day of judgment." (Matt. XII, 36.) Sixthly, concerning bad actions, "The Lord will examine your works, and search out your thoughts." (Wis. VI, 4.) Seventhly, examination will be made concerning temporal things. "Render an account of thy stewardship." (Luke XVI, 2.) Eighthly, concerning the care of your family. Where is the flock which was given to thee? Ninthly, "The Lord has called against me, the time." (Lamentations I, 15.) And again, "God has given to man, time and place for penance, and he abuseth it unto pride." (Job XXIV, 23.)

4. After the inquisition, there will be an examination of the cause or reason why things were done in life, why sins were committed; and around these must be observed the accusers and the witnesses.

The accusers will be three. The first accuser will be man's own conscience. "Their conscience bearing witness to them, and their thoughts between themselves, accusing, or also defending one another, on the day in which the Lord will judge the secrets of men's hearts." (Rom. II, 15.) Likewise, the devil who is set before man to try him, and who continually observes man and his action, will be man's accuser. "The accuser of our brethren is cast forth, who accused them before our God day and night." (Apoc. XII, 10.) Likewise, the place where man sinned and the persons with whom he sinned, shall accuse him. "The heavens shall reveal his iniquity, and the earth shall rise up against him." (Job XX, 27.) The prophet

Habacuc (II, 11) says, "The stone shall cry out of the wall, and the timber that is between the joints of the building, shall answer." Even more than this, father will accuse his own son, and the son will accuse the father. The son will accuse the bad father, because of the bad example of the father, the son is now being condemned. "For the children that are born of unlawful beds, are witnesses of wickedness against their parents in their trial." (Wis. IV, 6.)

The witnesses will likewise be three. The first Witness will be the Creator Whom we have offended. "Behold my Witness is in heaven, and He that knoweth my conscience is on high." (Job XVI, 20.) And Jeremias XXIX, 23, says, "Because they have committed adultery with the wives of their friends, and have spoken lying words in My Name, which I commanded them not to do, I am the Judge and the Witness, saith the Lord." The second witness will be the good angel, who was given to man to protect him. He will accuse man of much ingratitude for his service. Hence Jeremias (LI, 9) says this of the judgment, "We would have cured Babylon, but she is not healed. Let us forsake her." The third witness will be the stain of sin, which will shine in man's face, "Thy own wickedness shall reprove thee, and thy apostacy shall rebuke thee." (Jer. II, 19.) Likewise Job XVI, 9, says, "My wrinkles bear witness against me, and a false speaker riseth up against my face, contradicting me." Consequently, there will be three witnesses lined up against man according to Deuter. (XVII, 6), "By the mouth of two or three witnesses every word shall stand." (On the Final Judgment.)

NOVEMBER 9

Fear of the Judgment

"Fear the Lord, because the hour of His judgment is at hand." (Apoc. XIV, 7.)

This judgment should be feared by us for four reasons. First, because of the wisdom of the Judge, secondly, because of His power, thirdly, because of His unchangeable justice, and fourthly, because of His just anger.

1. Because of His wisdom, for the Lord knows all things —knows all our thoughts, words and actions, since "all things

are open to His eyes" (Heb. IV, 13), even our most secret thoughts and actions. He hears and knows our words: "For inquisition shall be made into the thoughts of the ungodly, and the hearing of his words shall come to God, to the chastising of his iniquities." (Wisdom I, 9.) And again Jeremias (XVII, 9) says: "The heart of man is perverse, and who can know it? I am the Lord who searches the heart . . . and who gives to everyone according to the labor of his devices." Furthermore at the final judgment the witness for or against us will be infallible, namely our own conscience. Our "conscience bearing witness, and our thoughts between themselves accusing, or defending one another." (Rom. II, 15.)

2. Because of the power of the Judge, for He is all-powerful in Himself: "Behold the Lord God will come in His strength." (Isaias XV, 10.) He is likewise all-powerful over others, because every creature will be gathered around Him and with Him. "The whole world will fight with Him against the unwise, for He will take justice as an invincible shield and will take a true judgment instead of a helmet." (Wisdom V, 20.) For this reason the prophet Job said (X, 7): "No one will be able to snatch them out of His hand." "If I ascend into heaven, thou, O Lord, art there, or if I descend into hell, Thou art present." (Ps. LXXXVIII, 8.)

3. The judgment of God should be feared on account of His inflexible and unchangeable justice. Now is His time for mercy, the day of judgment He will devote to justice solely. Consequently, now is our time, for that day of wrath will be God's day entirely. "When I shall take a time, I will judge justices." (Psalm LXXIV, 3.) "The jealousy and rage of the husband will not spare in that day of revenge. Nor will He yield to any man's prayers, nor will He accept for satisfaction, ever so many gifts." (Proverbs VI, 34.)

4. God's final and unyielding judgment should be feared because of His just anger, for while He will appear to the elect as sweet and pleasant, yet to the condemned He will seem enraged and cruel in so much that they, because of their just condemnation, will say to the mountains: "Fall upon us, and hide us from the wrath of the Lamb of God." (Apoc. VI, 16.) This anger in God on that day will not reveal a disturbance of the mind of God, but an effect of His righteous indignation, namely, an eternal punishment inflicted on unrepentant sinners. Narrow and strict will be the way for sinners in the final judgment. (The Creed.)

NOVEMBER 10

The Power of the Highest Judge

"He will come with great power and majesty." (Matth. XIV, 30.)

Those who refused to listen to Christ when He was humiliated, will behold Him coming in "great power and majesty. For the powers of heaven shall be moved." What is meant by "the powers of heaven"? unless the Angels, Dominations, Powers and Principalities which will appear visibly then at the coming of the Judge; Who will exact from us then a reason for that which He now impartially asks of us. Chrysostom says, "If an earthly King who is about to wage war, commands an undertaking against an enemy, are not the chiefs aroused, and the army called forth, and the entire city stirred up for battle? By so much the more will the heavenly army, those terrible ministers of a more terrible and just Lord advance before their Commander, and by so much the more will they be aroused when the heavenly King rises up to judge the living and the dead."

It must be remembered that the power of Christ judging, will be unconquerable, inexplainable, unbounded. Concerning the unconquerableness of Christ's judgment, Chrysostom says, "Then there will be no power to resist it, no power to escape it, no place to repent, and no time for satisfaction." From the condition then of all things, nothing will remain but lamentation.

Concerning the inexplainableness of the power of the Judgment, Augustine says, commenting on the words of John XVIII, 6, "As soon therefore, as He had said to them I am He; they went backward and fell to the ground. . . . One Voice struck the crowd of betrayers fierce in their hatred. It struck without a spear, struck terrible as an army. The Voice of Christ beat back and struck to the ground Judas and the betrayers; felled them to the ground with the power of its hidden Divinity. What will that Voice do, when Christ will act as Judge? Who then, can resist the Ruler?" As if Augustine had said, "the power of so great a Judge, cannot be explained."

Concerning the unboundedness of the power of Christ as Judge, Daniel (VII, 13) declares, "I beheld therefore, in the vision of the night, and lo, One like the Son of Man came with the clouds of heaven, . . . and His power is an everlasting power," that is a power confined to no limits. , The power of such a Judge is greatly to be feared.

Moreover, just as the power of Christ judging will be unconquerable, so will His wisdom be indescribable and His justice inflexible. Hence Bernard writes, "When the day of Judgment comes, then pure hearts will profit more than cunning words, and a good conscience more than a full purse, since that Judge can neither be deceived by words, nor bribed by money." Moreover to render a just judgment certain things are required, namely, zeal for justice which precedes the judgment, strength of power by which the sentence passed is executed and the light of wisdom, according to which a just sentence is rendered. In Christ as Judge, these qualities will be found in a most excellent manner; for His Justice is unchangeable, His wisdom indescribable, His power unconquerable; which is proven from the testimony of Scripture and the lives of the Saints.

Gregory therefore, concludes by saying, "O how narrow then in the day of Judgment, will be the ways of the wicked! The angry Judge above. A terrifying abyss below. On the right hand, sins accusing, on the left numberless demons dragging souls off to punishment. Within, a burning conscience. Outside, a world on fire. The wretched sinner so harassed by crime, whither shall he go? To hide, will be impossible. To appear for judgment will be unbearable." (On the humanity of Christ.)

NOVEMBER 11

The Time of the Final Judgment

The time of the coming of our Lord as Judge is unknown to all, according to Matth. XXIV, 36, "Of that day and hour no one knoweth, no not even the angels in heaven, but the Father alone." Moreover, God has not given us a knowledge of when judgment day will be because it is a good thing for us to remain always uncertain of the coming of the Judge, and so live from day to day as if today were the day of final judgment. Hence St. Mark XIII, 33, says: "Take ye heed, watch, and pray. For ye know not when the time is." In these words our Lord lays stress upon three things especially; namely, take heed, watch and pray.

1. We should take heed fervently by thinking of the day when the just Judge will come. For that day, that "dies irae," "day of wrath," must be kept before our eyes always. Hence Deuter. (XXXII, 29) says, "O that they would be wise, and would understand, and would provide for their last end." Jerome likewise, declares: "Whether I eat, or drink, or write, or whatever other work I do, that Voice is always ringing in my ears; Arise ye dead, and come to judgment."

2. We should always "watch," by working faithfully, so that we may be found ready for the judgment with good works accomplished. We are said to watch when we have our eyes opened for a vision of the true Light. We watch when we serve God by doing what we believe to be right. We watch when we cast off from ourselves the darkness of the body, and the spirit of negligence or laziness. Consequently, we must watch, because we know not the hour when the Lord will come to judge us either individually, at death, or all together in the final judgment. Hence Augustine commenting on the words, "What I say to one, I say to all, watch" (Mark XIII, 37), observes that, "the day will come to each one, when the Lord's day comes, which day will be such that all will be judged on that day. For this reason, every Christian should watch, lest the arrival of the Lord finds us unprepared. Moreover that day will find us unprepared, if the last day of life finds us unprepared."

3. We ought to pray, by fervently begging Christ's mercy, "so that we may be accounted worthy to escape all those evils which are to come, and to stand before the Son of Man." (Luke XXI, 36.) Here two things are mentioned for which we should pray; namely, we should pray to escape "future evils," and secondly, pray to win eternal happiness. First, "that we may be accounted worthy to escape future evils." Wherefore Saint Matth. XXIV, 20, also says, "Pray that your flight be not in the winter, or on the sabbath"; that is, lest then you wish to flee when it is not allowed nor possible. Moreover, we begin to pray in a real spiritual manner when our faith in God and our love for God, grows not cold; so that the sabbath day of virtue finds us in the service of God.

Secondly, we should pray, "to stand before the Son of Man"; that is, we should then stand secure at the summit of happiness in the Presence of our Judge. "For this is Angelic glory," exclaims Saint Theodore, "to stand before the Son of Man, and to see His Face forever." (The Humanity of Christ.)

NOVEMBER 12

Eternal Death

The wicked, who will suffer eternal death, will proportionately suffer more sorrow and pain than the blessed will possess of joy and glory. The pain of the damned or wicked will be increased. First, because of their separation from God and from all good things. Secondly, because of their remorse of conscience. Thirdly, because of the severity of their pain in hell fire. Fourthly, because of their despair of salvation.

1. The pains of the wicked will be increased because of their eternal separation from God and from all that is good; and this punishment is the punishment of the damned souls which corresponds to hatred. It is a pain far greater than any pain of sense. "The unprofitable servant cast ye out into exterior darkness." (Matth. XXV, 30.) For even in this life, the wicked are possessed of interior darkness, the darkness of sin; but then they will be enveloped by exterior darkness as well.

2. Remorse of conscience will increase the pains of the damned. "I will reprove thee, and stand before thy face, because you forgot God, and cast My words behind thee." (Ps. XLIX, 21.) "Repenting and groaning for anguish of spirit." (Wis. V, 3.) And still this kind of repenting and groaning will be useless; because it will not be on account of the evil the damned committed, but because of the fear and enormity of their pain which they have justly deserved by reason of their unrepented wickedness.

3. The severity and greatness of their pains resulting from the fire of hell, which are the severest pains of all pains; for they will crucify soul and body, as the saints tell us. And just as these self-condemned souls are always dying but never will die, their death is therefore called eternal. For just as one dying may suffer excruciating pains, so do those in hell experience the severest torments. "They are laid in hell like sheep. Death shall feed upon them." (Ps. XLVIII, 15.)

4. Their despair of salvation will increase the pains of the wicked. For if there was given to them any hope of freedom from their pain, their pain would thereby be assuaged, but since every hope is taken away from the damned their pain becomes the severest. "Their worm shall not die, and their fire shall not be quenched." (Isaias LXVI, 24.)

Consequently, the difference between the workers of good and the workers of evil, is perfectly clear; because good works will lead us to life eternal, but evil deeds to everlasting death.

For this reason we should frequently recall these thoughts to mind, because they should inspire us to do good and withdraw us from doing evil. Wherefore, at the end of the Apostles Creed and at the conclusion of nearly all our prayers, mention is significantly made of *"eternal life,"* so that the memory of it might be the more deeply impressed upon our minds; and to this eternal life may we be led by our Lord Jesus Christ, Who is God forever and ever. (On the Creed.)

NOVEMBER 13

The Pains of the Damned

"Fire and brimstone and storms of wind shall be the portion of their cup." (Ps. X, 7.) And Job (XXIV, 19), says, *"Let him pass from the snow waters to excessive heat, and his sin even to hell."*

1. In the final cleansing of the world, separation in the elements will take place so that whatever is pure and noble will remain above for the glory of the blessed, but whatever is impure and dishonorable will be cast into hell for the punishment of the damned. Just as every created thing will contribute to the joy of the blessed, so too all creatures will increase the torment of the damned; according to Wisdom (V, 21), "God will sharpen His severe (and just) wrath for a spear, and the whole world shall fight with Him against the sinner." This also becomes Divine justice; for just as those sinners who through vice fall away from the One Object of Love, namely, God, center their affection in material things which are many and varied, so too, will they be punished in many ways and for many things.

2. "Their worm shall not die." (Isaias LXVI, 24.) The worm (or spirit) placed in the damned ought not to be understood as something material but spiritual, which is for them remorse of conscience. It is therefore called "worm," in as far as it arises from the carcass or rottenness of sin and damages the soul; just as an earthly worm arising from corruption damages or destroys another body by entering it.

3. "Cast him into exterior darkness." (Matth. XXII, 14.) Basil commenting on, "the voice of the Lord divideth the flame of fire," says, that by the power of God the brightness of the

fire will be separated from its burning power, so that the brightness will be granted to the joy of the blessed but the burnt cinders of the fire will contribute to the torments of the damned. For the condition of hell will be such, that all the miseries of the damned will belong to it. Vision morever, considered in itself is delightful, but it can happen that vision may become an affliction, in so far as we see something which is hurtful to us or repugnant to our will. And hence, in hell, the place will be so arranged that nothing will be clearly seen there but only those things which can heap affliction on the heart may be seen underneath a certain darkness. Hence the place is filled with darkness, but because of the Divine plan of arrangement, there is in hell something of light, in so far as it suffices the damned to see those things which can torment the soul.

4. "A fire that is not kindled shall devour the sinner." (Job XX, 26.) Gregory says that, a corporal fire which is of any use, needs corporal support, to keep it burning and nourished. But on the contrary, the fire of hell, since it is corporal, and burns of itself the condemned, it is not kindled by human ingenuity, nor fed by wood; but once created it endures unquenched, and needs nothing for its endurance, and is not wanting in heat." That fire needs not wood or material support to nourish it, for it exists either on its own matter or exists on another matter not through violence, but by nature of an intrinsic principle. Hence, it is not kindled by man but by God Who has established its nature, and this is what Isaias (XXX, 33) means, when he says, "The nourishment thereof is fire and the breath of the Lord as a torrent of brimstone kindling it." (IV Dist. 50.)

NOVEMBER 14

The Knowledge of the Damned

"Then shall the just stand with great constancy, against those that have afflicted them ... and the wicked seeing this, shall be troubled with a terrible fear." (Wis. V, 2.)

1. The damned will be able to use the knowledge which they had in this world. For just as, by reason of the perfect happiness of the saints, nothing will come to them but that

which will be for them a source of joy, so nothing will be in the damned but that which will be for them the material and cause of sadness; and moreover anything which can belong to sadness will not be lacking to the damned, since their sadness is of the worst kind, complete in itself. In the damned therefore, there will be an actual consideration of those things which they formerly knew, as material for sadness; but not as a cause of joy. For they will consider both the evil they have done and the delightful goods which they have lost; and from both considerations they will be tormented. Likewise also, they will be tormented from this, that they will consider the knowledge which they had of future things as imperfect and especially tormented that they lost the highest perfection which they could have now enjoyed.

2. The damned will behold the glory of the blessed. For before judgment day, the damned will see the blessed in glory, not in this manner that they will see the glory of the blessed as it is in itself, but they will only perceive that the blessed are enjoying indescribable glory. Because of this also the damned will be tormented, grieving because of their jealousy at the happiness of the blessed and also because they themselves lost such glory. Hence it is written (Wis. V, 2), "These seeing it, shall be troubled with a terrible fear."

But after judgment day, the damned will be entirely deprived of this vision of the blessed; and this deprivation will not however decrease their pain but will increase it; because they will still possess the memory of the glory of the blessed which they beheld at the judgment or before the judgment, and this will be for the damned a torment; but worse than this, they will be tormented at seeing that they are considered unworthy even to see the glory which the saints have merited to enjoy.

3. The damned will think of God.

God can be thought of in two ways: in one way in Himself, according to that which belongs to Him, namely that He is the Beginning of all Goodness; and in such wise we cannot think of God without happiness resulting, but in this manner God will not be thought of by the damned. In another way God can be considered, and this is in His effects, in so far as He punishes for sin and in this way the thought of God can lead to sadness, and it is in this manner that the damned will think of God; remembering Him only as the Punisher and Enemy of sin in which their evil wills delighted.

NOVEMBER 15

Concerning the Will of the Damned

1. The damned do not repent of the evil which they have done. To repent of a sin happens directly, and indirectly. One repents of a sin directly, in as far as one hates sin; indirectly when one hates sin because of something connected with it, such as punishment or something of this nature. Directly speaking therefore, the damned will not repent of their sins, because the malicious will of sin remains in them; but they will repent however indirectly, in so far as they are afflicted with the punishment which they suffer for sin.

2. All the damned wish to be damned.

Just as in the blessed in heaven there will be the most perfect charity, so in the damned there will be the most complete hatred. Hence, as the saints rejoice in all good things, so the condemned grieve over all good things; and consequently the happiness of the saints, considered by the damned, especially grieves them. Hence (Isaias XXVI, 11) says, "Let the envious people see, and be confounded; and let fire devour thy enemies." Although from the multitude of the damned, the pain of each one is increased, still the hatred and envy of each one increases, because they choose rather to be tormented with many than tormented alone. Since they will be in the greatest misery, and since it happens that envy increases in this life so will the envy of the damned increase as they gaze upon the glory of their neighbors.

3. The damned have a hatred for God.

"Forget not the voices of Thy enemies. The pride of them that hate Thee ascending continually." (Ps. LXXIII, 23.) God is seen, either in Himself, as by the blessed who see Him in His essence, or He is seen by effect as by us and the damned. Therefore, God in Himself, since He is goodness essentially, cannot be displeasing to the will of anyone who sees Him in His essence, and in this way none can have any hatred for Him. But there are certain effects of God, which are repugnant to a depraved will, namely the infliction of punishment and also condemnation of sin by divine law which are repugnant to a will depraved through sin. In this manner God can be held in hatred; not in Himself however, but by reason of His effects. And so the damned seeing God in the effect of His justice which is punishment, regard Him with hatred even as they do the sufferings which they must endure.

4. The damned always blaspheme.

"Men were scorched with great heat, and they blasphemed the Name of God, Who had power over these plagues." (Apoc. XVI, 9.) To the nature of blasphemy belongs a detestation of the divine will. But those who are in hell will retain a perverse will repugnant to the justice of God, in this that, they love those things for which they are punished and wish to use them if they can, and hate the punishments inflicted for sin of this nature. Still they grieve for the sins committed, not because they hate them but because they are punished for them.

So therefore, such a detestation of divine justice is to them the interior blasphemy of the heart. It is credible that after the resurrection vocal blasphemy will be in the damned, just as vocal praise of God is and will be in the saints. Men are prevented here from blasphemy, because of fear of punishments which they hope to evade. But the damned in hell cannot hope to evade punishments, and therefore, in as far as they are without hope, they are inclined to every evil which their perverse will suggests to them. (2a. 2ae. q. 13, a. 4.)

NOVEMBER 16

The Eternal Punishment of the Damned

"These shall go into everlasting punishment, but the just into life everlasting." (Matth. XXV, 46.)

1. Just as merit is deserving of a reward, so crime deserves punishment. But according to Divine justice an eternal reward is due to temporal merit. Therefore, according to Divine justice, eternal punishment is due to a temporal crime. Since punishment has a twofold quantity, namely as regards the amount of punishment and the duration of time, the quantity of the punishment should correspond to the nature of the crime, so that in so far as anyone sins the more grievously, the more severe should his punishment be. Wherefore Apoc. XVIII, 7, says, "As much as she hath glorified herself, and lived in delicacies (that is in sin), so much torment and sorrow give ye to her."

But the duration of the punishment does not correspond to the duration of the crime, for adultery is perpetrated in a moment or punished with slight punishment, even according to human laws. But the duration of punishment is directed towards the evil intention of the sinner. For sometimes a person who sins in a particular city, by that very sin, becomes exiled forever from his fellow citizens, or sometimes incurs the death penalty. Sometimes, on the other hand, his sin is such that he is not considered deserving of perpetual banishment from his native city, and therefore, he can conveniently be a member of society, his punishment being either prolonged or shortened in so far as it is expedient to cure him of crime; so that he might be able to live in his own city or town, live conveniently and peacefully.

And so likewise, according to Divine justice, a person because of serious sins deserves to be entirely separated from the City of God and from everlasting fellowship with God; which may happen through every mortal sin by which man sins against charity, the bond uniting us to that glorious city of God. Therefore, through mortal sin, which is contrary to the charity of God, a person becomes excluded from the society and fellowship of the saints and deserves eternal punishment.

But on the other hand, there are those who commit venial sins, and these do not deserve to be deprived forever from fellowship in the Holy City. In so far as their punishment will be shorter or longer will depend upon whether their purification be greater or small; which results from the fact that venial sins adhere to their souls in a greater or smaller degree. But in this world and in purgatory punishment is imposed according to the plan of Divine justice.

2. Moreover the eternal punishments of the damned are useful—in two ways. First, because even in the damned, Divine justice is observed, which is acceptable to God for the sake of justice. Secondly, the blessed rejoice concerning these punishments, since in them, they see the justice of God and the blessed rejoice that they, through God's grace, have escaped these eternal punishments. All the wicked condemned to eternal punishment will be punished by their own iniquity and will burn for something else, namely, that they have squandered and abused God's many graces and lost the eternal happiness which they now see the saints enjoying. It will torment the damned to know they could have avoided the evils for which they are now being punished eternally, had they co-operated with the help of God.

3. There is no hope in the damned.

Isaias, LXV, 14, says, "My servants shall praise for joyfulness of heart, and you shall cry for sorrow of heart, and shall howl for grief of spirit." Just as it is a condition of happiness, that the will should find rest therein, so it is a condition of punishment that what is inflicted in punishment should go against the will. Now, that which is not known can neither be restful nor repugnant to the will. Wherefore Augustine says that the Angels could not be perfectly happy in their first state before their confirmation, or unhappy before their fall, since they had no knowledge of what would happen to them. For perfect and true happiness requires that one should be certain of being happy forever, else the will would not rest.

In like manner, since the everlastingness of damnation is a necessary condition of the punishment of the damned, it would not be truly penal unless it went against the will; and this would be impossible if they were ignorant of the everlastingness of their damnation. Hence, it belongs to the unhappy state of the damned that they should know that they cannot by any means escape from damnation and obtain happiness. Hence it is written (Job XV, 22), "He believeth not that he can return from darkness to light." (2a. 2ae. q. 18, a. 3.)

NOVEMBER 17

We Must Believe in Life Everlasting

1. Conveniently placed at the end of all our desires is life everlasting. This end or purpose of our desires is fittingly set down at the conclusion of the Apostles Creed, where "Life Everlasting," is mentioned. "I believe . . . in life everlasting. Amen." Our belief in eternal life is opposed to those who say that the soul dies with the death of the body. If this were true, man would be of the same nature or state as the beasts of the fields, and the words of the Psalmist would be proper to both man and beast; namely, "Man when he was in honor did not understand. He hath been compared to senseless beasts, and made like to them." (Ps. XLVIII, 21.) The human soul is like to God by being immortal, but from the part of sensuality the soul of man is likened to the beast. When therefore, anyone believes that the soul dies when the body dies, such a person departs from the likeness of God and is compared to beasts. Against those heretics it is written, "And they knew not the secrets of God, nor hoped for the wages of justice, nor esteemed the honor of holy souls. For God created man incor-

ruptible, and to the image of His own likeness He made him." (Wisdom II, 22.)

2. Now, it is easy to believe this because of the testimony of Christ. For two things are necessary for man to know, namely the glory of God and the pains of hell. For wise men inspired by this glory and terrified by these pains should be retarded from committing sin. But the glory of God and the punishments of hell are very difficult things for man to fully understand. Hence it is said of glory, Wisdom IX, 16, "Hardly do we guess aright at the things that are upon the earth, and with labour do we find the things that are before us. But the things that are in heaven, who shall search out?" But it is not difficult concerning spiritual things, because, "God Who is in heaven will send His Holy Spirit from above upon all, so that the ways of them that are upon the earth may be corrected, and men may learn the things that please Him." (Wis. IX, 17.) And therefore, God came from Heaven and became Man to teach us heavenly things.

It is also difficult to realize the pains of hell. "For no man hath been known to have returned from hell." (Wis. II, 1.) And this has reference to the damned. But this cannot be said now of God; because just as He came down from heaven to teach celestial things, so He arose from hell that He might keep us out of hell. (On the Creed.)

NOVEMBER 18

Seeing God Face to Face

"Now this is eternal life. That they may know Thee, the only true God, and Jesus Christ, Whom Thou hast sent." (John XVII, 3.)

1. Every natural desire is implanted in our hearts by Almighty God for some very definite purpose. Now it is impossible to have a natural desire for no purpose. But that would be the case, if it were not possible for us to arrive at an understanding of the Divine Substance which all minds naturally desire to know. Therefore, we must logically conclude that it is possible that the substance of God, or God in Himself, be seen by the intellect and by separate spiritual substances and by our souls.

Moreover, this immediate or direct Vision of God, this Vision of God face to face, is promised to us by Sacred Scripture. "We see now through a glass in a dark manner; but then face to face." (1 Cor. XIII, 13.) But it is wrong to understand this to be a corporal vision, as we imagine in the very Divinity there is a corporal face. But this cannot be understood in a bodily manner, since God is incorporeal. Nor is it possible that we will see God with our bodily eyes, since bodily vision which resides in us is only concerned about material things. Consequently, we will see God face to face, for we will see Him directly, as a man whom we see face to face.

Moreover, according to this Vision we are especially made like unto God and share in His blessedness. For God Himself understands His substance through His essence and this is perfect happiness. Hence it is said in (1 John III), "When He appears, we will be like unto Him, and we will see Him as He is." And Luke XXII, 29, says: "I dispose to you, as My Father hath disposed to Me, a kingdom, that you may eat and drink at My table, in My kingdom." This statement by our Lord cannot be understood as meaning bodily food and drink, but of that nourishment which is received at the table of Wisdom, and of which Proverbs IX, 5, speaks thus: "Eat My bread, and drink the wine which I have mingled for you." Therefore, those seeing God in that manner in which He sees Himself, eat and drink at the table of God and enjoy this same happiness because God is happiness.

2. "This is eternal life." We say that those things which move themselves to action, are properly speaking said to be alive, and all actions to which the operator moves are called the operations of life, as the action of wishing, understanding, feeling, moving and increasing. Moreover, among the actions of life, the highest and noblest is the act of the intellect, that is the act of understanding, and therefore the act of the intellect is especially life. Since therefore, the intelligence is life, and to know is to live, it follows that to know the Eternal Object of all our desires is to live Eternal Life. But God is the Eternal Object, consequently, to know and to see God is eternal life. Therefore, the Lord says that eternal life consists in seeing God, principally in as far as His entire substance. But love is the moving power to this Vision and a certain completion of it. For from the delight which is in the Divine enjoyment and which love causes, there is also the completeness and beauty of happiness; but the substance of this happiness consists in Vision—in seeing God face to face.

NOVEMBER 19

Eternal Life

1. The first thing in eternal life is that man will be united to God. For God Himself is the reward and the end of all labours. Now in this consists our perfect vision of God, secondly, in a love the most fervent, for in so far as a thing will be known better, the more perfectly it will be loved there; thirdly, there will be a union of the highest praise. Augustine says, "We will see, we will love, and we will praise." "Joy and gladness shall be found therein, thanksgiving and the voice of praise." (Isaias LI, 2.)

2. There is also in eternal life the complete and perfect fulfillment of our every desire, for there each blessed will have more than he or she desired and longed for. The reason for this is because nothing in this life can perfectly fulfill our every desire, for God alone satisfies and exceeds our desires in an infinite manner, and hence, it is that perfect satisfaction is found and will be found in God alone. Augustine exclaims, "Thou hast made us, for Thyself, O Lord; and our hearts are restless until thy rest in Thee."

And because the saints will possess God perfectly in heaven, it is clear that He will fulfill all their desires, and even excel them in glory. And therefore the Lord Himself says, "Enter into the joy of Thy Lord." (Matth. XXV, 21.) Augustine says, "All joy will not enter into those rejoicing there, but all those rejoicing will enter into joy." "I shall be satisfied when Thy glory appear" (Ps. XVI, 15), and again, "Bless the Lord, O my soul . . . Who satisfieth thy desire with good things." (Ps. CII, 3, 5.)

For whatever is delightful, all that delight will be there in abundance. For if delights are sought, there they will be found —the highest and the most perfect delights; because of the delight in "the summum bonum," in the highest good. "Then shalt thou abound in delights in the Almighty, and shall lift up thy face to God" (Job XXII, 26), and again, "At Thy right hand are delights even to the end." (Ps. XV, 11.)

Likewise, if honours are sought, there in eternal life will be found every honour. Men may desire here to be kings and bishops, but there both honours will be found. The king will be there with his loyal subjects, the bishop with his faithful souls. "O Lord, Thou hast made us to our God a kingdom and priests." (Apoc. V, 10.)

Likewise, if knowledge is sought, there in eternal life will be knowledge, the most perfect, because there we will know the nature of things and all truth, and whatever we desire to know we will know, or whatever we wish to have, we will possess it in eternal life. "Now all good things came to me together with her, and innumerable riches through her hands" (Wis. VII, 11), and again, "To the just their desire shall be given." (Prov. X, 24.)

3. There, in life eternal is most perfect security. For in this world there is no such thing as perfect security, because, inasmuch as one has many things and greater dependents, by so much the more does he fear and need all the more. But in life everlasting, there is no sorrow, no labour, no fear. "My people shall sit in the beauty of peace" (Isaias XXXII, 11), and again, "He that shall hear Me, shall rest without terror, and shall enjoy abundance, without fear of evils." (Prov I, 33.)

4. There, in life eternal is a suitable society or association of everything good, which society is delighted chiefly in good. Therefore, the saints will possess all these goods and other ineffable things and each one will love the other's good as his own. And hence, each person will rejoice in the other's happiness as if it were his own, so that inasmuch as the joy and happiness of one in heaven is increased, so is the joy of all increased. "The dwelling, in Thee, is as it were of all rejoicing." (Ps. LXXXVI, 7.) (The Creed.)

NOVEMBER 20

Of Those Who See the Essence of God One Sees It More Perfectly Than Another

"Star differs from star in glory." (I Cor. XV, 41.)

1. Of those who see the Essence of God, one sees Him more perfectly than another. This, indeed, does not take place as if one had a more perfect likeness of God than another, since that vision will not spring from any likeness; but it will take place because one intellect will have a greater power or faculty to see God than another. The faculty of seeing God, however, does not belong to the created intellect naturally, but is given to it by the light of glory which establishes the intellect in a kind of deiformity.

Hence, the intellect which has more of the light of glory will see God the more perfectly and he will have a fuller participation of the light of glory who has more charity; because where there is the greater charity there is the more desire and desire in a certain degree makes the one desiring apt and prepared to receive the object desired. Hence he who possesses the greater charity, will see God the more perfectly and will be the more beatified.

Since the end corresponds proportionally to those things which are for the end, it must needs be that just as some things are differently prepared for the end, so they share differently in the end. Moreover, the vision of the Divine substance is the final end of each intellectual substance. But intellectual substances are not all equally prepared for the end, for some are of greater virtue and some of lesser virtue. But virtue is the way or royal road to happiness. Therefore it must be that in the Divine vision, exists a diversity since some souls see the Divine substance more perfectly and some less perfectly.

Hence it is that our Lord points to this difference of happiness, when He says: "In My Father's house there are many mansions." (John XIV, 2.) By these words of Christ is refuted the error of those who claim that the reward of all is equal. For just as from the mode of vision appears the different degrees of glory in the blessed, from this it would seem that the glory is the same. But the happiness of each one springs from this that he sees the substance of God, which is the same Object that makes all blessed; still all do not receive from the object of their vision equal happiness.

The diversity of seeing by the blessed will not arise on the part of the object seen, for the same object will be presented to all, namely, the Essence of God; nor will it arise from the diverse participation of the Object seen by different similitudes; but it will arise on the part of the diverse faculty of intellect, not indeed, the natural faculty but the glorified faculty. (1a. q. 12, a. VI.)

NOVEMBER 21

The Holy Life of the Blessed Virgin

"My flowers are the fruit of honor and riches." (Eccle. XXIV, 23.)

1. Our lady was full of grace in her every conversation. Hence of her it is figuratively said in Esther II, 15, "She was exceedingly fair, and her incredible beauty made her appear agreeable and amiable in the eyes of all." She is that Rebecca —a lady of exceeding beauty, a most beautiful virgin. Hence it is written of her in Canticles IV, 7, "Thou art all fair, O My love, and there is not a spot in thee." It says, "all fair," because in mind and in heart, she was most beautiful, spotless; so that never was there a woman like unto her.

Wherefore Saint Bernard commenting upon these words of Canticles, "Thou art all fair," says, "She was most beautiful in countenance, most pure of heart, and most holy in soul. If you carefully investigate, you will find there is nothing of beauty, nothing of purity, nothing of candor and of glory, but shines forth from her soul." By this plenitude of life, therefore, she had magnetic power, for just as a magnet attracts iron to itself so the holy Virgin attracted to herself the Word of God from heaven above. Consequently, the Blessed Virgin was the royal dwelling, adorned and shining with the gems of virtue of soul and body, beautified by grace, recognized in heaven by her appearance and beauty of soul, so distinguished among the heavenly citizens that she won to herself the attraction of the King of Kings; and brought to herself the heavenly messenger from the throne of the Most High.

Even though we cannot imitate Mary entirely in possessing the grace of her holy life and conduct, still, we should practice her virtues as much as we are able; so that we might strive to have like her, purity of mind and body, patience and constancy in times of trials, and endurance in the perseverance of good works. For Saint Bernard says, "If you wish to obtain Mary's help in adversities, do not abandon the example of her holy life and conduct." (Angelic Salutation.)

2. The Blessed Virgin practiced and exemplified in her life, the actions characteristic of all the virtues. Other saints are known for certain special virtues, one was humble, another pure, another merciful; as Saint Nicholas whose example of mercy and kindness are so well known; but the Blessed Virgin

shone forth in the example of every virtue; for in her you find the one glorious example of humility; "Behold the handmaid of the Lord"; and as a result, "the Lord regarded the humility of His handmaid"; the example of her virginity, "since I know not man"; and the example of every virtue, as is clear from her holy life and conduct. (The Hail Mary.)

NOVEMBER 22

Happiness

"We shall be filled with the good things of Thy house O God our Saviour." (Ps. LXIV, 6.)

1. The house of God is not only that mansion in which God dwells but it is also Himself, because He is in it; and into this house He will bring us. Moreover, God Himself lives in this house. "We know if our earthly house of this habitation be dissolved, that we have a building of God, a house not made with hands, but eternal in heaven." (2 Cor. V, 1.) This house is a house of glory, for it is God Himself. Moreover, man abideth in this place, namely, in God, in as far as his will and affections are united to God through charity, "for whosoever abideth in charity, abideth in God, and God in him" (1 John IV, 16), and in as far as to the intellect, through the knowledge of truth. "I go to pprepare a place for you." (John XIV, 2.) This place is God Himself in Whom exists the excellence of all perfection. Truly God has prepared a place, as He has given to each one of us the power to enter that abiding place.

2. "We will be filled with the good things of Thy house," because true happiness will be granted to us, that is God Himself. It is impossible for man's happiness to consist in any created good. For happiness is the perfect good which perfectly satisfies the appetite, else it would not be the last end if something yet remained to be desired. Now the object of the will, of man's appetite, is the universal good, just as the object of the intellect is the universal truth. Hence it is clear that nothing can perfectly satisfy man's will unless the universal good. This is not to be in any creature, but in God alone; because every creature has goodness by participation. Wherefore God alone can completely satisfy the will of man, according to the word of Ps. C, 11, 5, "Who satisfieth thy desire with good

things." Therefore God alone constitutes man's happiness, for He alone is the universal fount of goodness itself; the Universal Object of the happiness of all the blessed, since He is the infinite and perfect good.

But this highest good, the more perfectly it is possessed the more is it loved and other things despised, for the more we possess it the more we know it. Hence it is written (Eccles. XXIV, 29), "They that eat Me shall yet hunger." Whereas in the desire for wealth and for any temporal goods the contrary is true, for when we already possess them we despise them and seek others; which is the sense of our Lord's words (John IV, 13), "Whosoever drinketh of this water," by which temporal goods are meant, "shall thirst again." The reason of this is, that we realize more their insufficiency when we possess them, and this very fact shows that they are imperfect and that the Sovereign Good does not consist in them.

3. Divine Beatitude embraces all other beatitudes or happiness. For whatever is desirable in any happiness, whether true or false, preexists wholly and in a more remarkable degree in the divine beatitude. As to contemplative happiness, God possesses a continual and most certain contemplation of Himself and of all things else; and as to that which is active, He has the governance of the whole universe. As to earthly happiness, which consists in delight, riches, power, dignity and fame, He possesses joy in Himself and all things else for His delight; instead of riches He has that complete self-sufficiency which is promised by riches; in place of power, He has All-powerfulness (or Omnipotence), for dignities, He has the government of all things; and in place of fame, He possesses the admiration of all creatures. (1a. q. XXVI, a. IV.)

NOVEMBER 23

Degrees of Happiness

"In My Father's house there are many mansions." (John XIV, 2.)

1. The different mansions mean the different participations of happiness, that is, the different participations in the Divine knowledge and delight. The absolute perfection of happiness consists in God alone, for He alone knows Him-

self and loves Himself, in as far as He is knowable and lovable; for He infinitely knows and loves His infinite truth and goodness. And in regard to this, the very highest good which is the object and cause of beatitude, cannot be greater and less, since there is but One Highest Good, namely, God.

Moreover, the perfection of beatitude can be considered according to certain conditions of time, nature and grace, and so one person can be happier than another; according to the attainment of this Good and the capacity of each man; because inasmuch as a man is more capable of receiving this Goodness, by so much the more does he share in it, and this because he is better disposed and ordained for its enjoyment; to which he is disposed in two ways. For beatitude consists in two things, first in a Divine Vision, and for this man is prepared and disposed through purity of soul. And therefore, inasmuch as anyone has his heart elevated the more above earthly things, by so much the more perfectly will he see God. Secondly, the perfection of beatitude consists in enjoyment, and to this end man is disposed through love. Therefore, he whose heart is the more inflamed with the love of God, the more will he be delighted with the Divine possession.

2. But an answer is sought concerning the labourers in the vineyard (Matth. II), to whom was given a penny each as a reward for their labour. Here this penny or reward means nothing more than the mansion in the Father's house. Hence it would seem there are not many mansions. It must be remembered that the rewards of eternal life are one and many. Many indeed, according to the diverse capacity of those meriting the reward and in this way there are many mansions in our Father's house. On the other hand, the mansion is one in three ways; first because of the union with the Object, secondly, on account of the same measure of eternity for all, and thirdly, because of the love uniting all.

First, because of the unity of the Object. For all the blessed see and enjoy the same Object and therefore one for all; but it will be seen and loved differently by all; as if someone should show a fountain to another so that all might drink from it at will. He who has the largest vessel receives more than one who has a smaller receptacle. Therefore, there is but one fountain in which to share, but the measure of those receiving from it is not the same.

Secondly, because of the same measure of eternity, since all will possess eternal life because the just will go into eternal life or happiness, but they will possess that happiness differently by reason of their capacity.

Thirdly, because of charity, uniting all and causing the happiness of each one of the blessed to be the happiness of all and vice versa. "Rejoice with them that rejoice." (Rom. XII, 15.) (John XIV.)

NOVEMBER 24

The Endlessness of Perfect Happiness

"Mary hath chosen the best part, which shall not be taken away from her." (Luke X, 42.)

Origen held that man can become unhappy after attaining final happiness. This however, is evidently false because of four reasons. First because of the general notion of (perfect) happiness; secondly, because of the specific nature of Happiness; thirdly, because the withdrawal of Happiness would be a punishment; fourthly, because perfect union with God can never be severed or lost. Origen's opinion is therefore evidently false.

1. First because of the general notion of happiness. For since happiness is the perfect and sufficient good, it must needs set man's desire at rest and exclude every evil. Now man naturally desires to hold to the good which he has and to have the certainty of his holding; otherwise he must necessarily be troubled with the fear of losing it, or with the sorrow of knowing he will lose it. Therefore, it is necessary for true Happiness that man have the assured opinion of never losing the good that he possesses. If this opinion be true, it follows that he will never lose Happiness, but if it be false, it is in itself an evil that he should have a false opinion; because the false is an evil of the intellect just as the true is its good. Consequently, man will no longer be truly happy if evil be in him.

2. Secondly, it is again evident if we consider the specific nature of Happiness. For man's perfect Happiness consists in the vision of the Divine Essence. Now it is impossible for anyone seeing the Divine Essence to wish not to see It. Because every good that one possesses and yet wishes to be without is either insufficient, something more satisfying being desired in its place; or else has some inconvenience attached to it, by reason of which it becomes wearisome. But the vision of the Divine Essence fills the soul with all good things, since it unites it to the source of all goodness; hence

it is written (Ps. XVI, 15): "I shall be satisfied when Thy glory shall appear"; and (Wis. VII, 11), "All good things came to me together with her," that is, with the contemplation of wisdom. In like manner, neither has it any inconvenience attached to it, because it is written of the contemplation of wisdom (Wis. VIII, 16): "Her conversation hath no bitterness, nor her company any tediousness." It is thus evident that the blessed or perfectly happy man cannot forsake Happiness of his own accord.

3. Moreover neither can he lose Happiness through God taking it away from Him. Because, since the withdrawal of Happiness is a punishment, it cannot be enforced by God the just Judge except for some fault; and he that sees God cannot fall into a fault since rectitude of the will, of necessity, results from that vision (of the Divine Essence).

4. Nor can it be withdrawn by any other agent. Because the mind that is united to God is raised above all other things and consequently no other agent can sever the mind from that (perfect) union. Therefore, it seems unreasonable that as time goes on man should pass from Happiness to misery, and vice versa; because such like vicissitudes of time can only be for such things as are subject to time and movement. But perfect Happiness is consummate perfection, which excludes every defect from the happy. And therefore whoever has this Happiness has it altogether unchangeably. This is done by the Divine power, which raises man to the participation of Eternity which transcends all change. Hence the endlessness of perfect happiness is evident. (1a. 2æ. q. V, a. IV.)

NOVEMBER 25

The Fourfold Vision of the Lord

"Have I not seen Christ Jesus Our Lord?" (Cor. IX, 1.)

It must be noted that we read of a manifold vision of the Lord. First, a corporal vision which has passed. "Afterwards He was seen upon earth, and conversed with men." (Baruch III, 38.) Secondly, a spiritual vision which is present. "Be still and see that I am God." (Ps. XLV, 11.) Thirdly, an eternal vision which will be in the future; concerning which John says, "Father, I will that where I am, they also whom Thou hast given Me, may be with Me, that they may see My glory." (John XVII, 24.) The fourth vision will be also future and momentary. "Then they will see the Son of Man coming in a cloud with power and majesty." (Luke XXI.) The first vision was of Christ in this world; the second, in the mind; the third will be in heaven; the fourth will be at the judgment.

The first vision of Christ gave to the world an example of how to live and this in three ways. First, He was seen as a poor man and ragged, so that He might curb inordinate greed and desires of wealth. "I am poor and sorrowful." (Ps. LXVIII, 30.) Thus the shepherds saw Him, "as poor and abject," so that He might restrain our unworthy ambition for honours. "We have seen Him despised, and the most abject of men, a man of sorrows and acquainted with infirmities." (Isaias LIII, 3.) He was afflicted and suffered so that He might restrain our sinful desires and lusts of the flesh.

The second vision of Christ, the spiritual one, gives in three ways help to those advancing. First, it gives strength to the repentant by showing them their faults and punishments. This spiritual vision is to the soul what the sun is to the land. Secondly, it affords hope to those struggling in life by holding out to them a reward, just as the Lord did to the laborers in the vineyard. Thirdly, this spiritual vision of our Lord gives joy to contemplatives by offering them a foretaste of heaven, as the shopkeeper does with his choice wine. "Taste and see that the Lord is sweet." (Ps. XXXIII, 9.)

The third vision of our Lord, namely, the eternal vision, gives us a desire of reaching our true home because of three things. First, because of the true joy. "You shall see and your heart will rejoice because of a sweet and delightful light." (Isaias LXVI, 14.) Secondly, on account of the multiplicity or plurality of the joy. "Then you shall see and abound and thy heart shall wonder and be enlarged when the multitude of the sea shall be converted to thee." (Isaias LX), because, "we will see Him as He is and He will be all things to all men." For God will be to the intellect the fulness of light; to the will, an abundance of peace; to the memory, the continuation of eternity. Thirdly, the eternal vision gives us a desire of reaching our true home on account of the eternity of the joy awaiting us on our arrival. "His servants shall serve Him and they shall see His face and reign with Him forever and ever."

The fourth vision of the Lord, namely, our momentary vision of Him will inspire hatred or fear of sin because of three things. First, because of the crimes perpetrated against the coming of the Judge. "Behold, He cometh," said the Lord of hosts, "and who shall stand to see Him?" Secondly, this eternal vision will inspire hatred and fear of sin because of the severe punishment of evil doers. For the thief seeing his fellow there condemned, will tremble the more because of his own crime of theft. Thirdly, the eternal vision of the Lord will cause hatred and fear in the sinner, when he realizes the eternal good things he has lost through his own fault. "The just shall see and shall rejoice and the innocent shall laugh them (the condemned) to scorn." (Job XXII, 19.) (1 Cor. IX.)

NOVEMBER 26

Eternal Joy

"Because thou hast been faithful over a few things, I will place thee over many things. Enter thou into the joy of thy Lord." (Matth. XXV, 21.)

1. These few things are all the things which are found in our present life, for these things are as nothing in comparison to heavenly things. Hence, our Lord wishes to say that because you have been faithful by reason of the good things you have done in this life, "I will place you over many things," that is, I will give to you spiritual treasures which excel all the good things of this present life. He that is faithful in that which is least, is faithful also in that which is greater." (Luke XVI, 10.)

2. The greatness of the reward is the result of our faithfulness. "Enter into the joy of thy Lord." For joy is a reward. "I will see you and your heart will rejoice." (John XVI, 22.)

Some one might also say, "Is not vision or some other good likewise a reward?" I answer that if another thing is called a reward, still joy is a final reward. For joy is nothing other than a rest for the soul in a good possessed. Hence, by reason of the end joy is called a reward.

Wherefore, our Lord says, "Enter into the joy of thy Lord." It must be said that joy is twofold, namely, joy concerning external goods, and joy about internal goods. Whosoever rejoices in external goods, enters not into joy, but joy enters into him. On the other hand, he who rejoices over spiritual goods enters into joy. "The King hath brought me into His storerooms." (Cant. I, 3.)

Or again, the container is greater, in a certain sense, than the thing contained. Since therefore, joy is about something which is less than the human heart then joy enters into your heart. But God is greater than the heart, and therefore, he enters into joy who rejoices in God.

Likewise, "enter into the joy of thy Lord." That is, rejoice in the Lord, for the Lord is Truth.

Or again, "Enter into the joy of thy Lord," that is, rejoice in Him in Whom and concerning Whom the Lord rejoices, namely, concerning the enjoyment of Himself. Therefore, man rejoices in the Lord when he is rejoiced as the Lord. Hence the Lord said to His Apostles: "That you may eat and drink at My table, in My Kingdom, that is, that you may be blessed in that in which I am blessed." (Luke XXII, 30.) (Matth. XXV.)

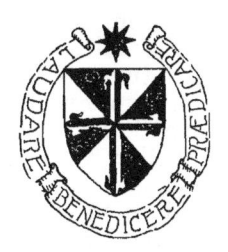

SPIRITUAL TOPICS FOR RETREATS

(Material for Retreats. Priests giving Retreats or Missions will find excellent ideas for conferences in these 17 subjects, translated from various works of the Angelic Doctor.)

1. The Voice of God Calling Us.
2. First Charity Must Be Regained.
3. Second Death.
4. The State of Perfection.
5. The Usefulness of The Vows.
6. The Good Use of Time.
7. Is Poverty Required for the Perfection of Religion?
8. Does Obedience Pertain to the Perfection of Religion?
9. The Necessity of the Three Vows.
10. The Perfection of Religion Consists in the Three Vows.
11. The Vow of Obedience Is the Most Powerful of the Three Vows.
12. The Sin of Religious and of Priests.
13. How a Religious May Sin Easily and Repent Quickly.
14. Concerning the Works of the Active Life.
15. Concerning the Study of the Letters (or Sciences.)
16. Concerning the Works of Religious.
17. Concerning Fidelity.

SPIRITUAL EXERCISES FOR A RETREAT

The Voice of God Calling Us

"I heard behind me a great voice as of a trumpet." (Apoc. I, 10.)

This voice is the summons of the Lord, Who calls and re-calls us fleeing from Him. "Thy ears shall hear the word of One admonishing thee behind thy back." (Isaias XXX, 21.) "Return, return, O Sulamitess" (Cant. VI, 12), that is, O captive soul, "Return, return, return, so that We may behold thee!" (Cant. VI, 12.) Why does the Canticle of Canticles say, "return, return?" So that in childhood, in manhood, in old age and in senility we might return to the Lord. Or because four things cause us to flee from God, namely, the boldness of youth, and these people flee to the East; secondly, the delay of death, and these flee to the West; thirdly, the love of riches, and these people flee to the South, and fourthly, the fear of adversity, these persons flee to the North.

Therefore the Lord cries out to all classes. "Return from the East," because youth, prone to evil, dies quickly. "Return from the West," because the aged have not long to live, and when man turns away from God he cannot live long. "Return from the South," for the vanity and riches of "this world quickly passeth away." (I John II). "Return from the North," the adversity and trials of this world cannot injure you; unless you wish to be injured by them.

The Voice is called great, because a great Friend calls, and calls for great things. Moreover He calls in four ways. The Lord calls us by the preaching of the word of God, secondly, by giving us favours, thirdly, by His inspirations and fourthly, by punishment. And these four are noted in Proverbs (I, 24), "I called, and you refused. I stretched out My hand and there were none that regarded. You have despised all my counsel, and have neglected all my reprehensions."

The "great voice called as a trumpet," and calls to a spiritual banquet where the soul is refreshed. "The Lord of hosts shall make unto all people in this mountain, a feast of fat things, a feast of wine, of fat things full of marrow, of wine purified from the lees." (Isaias XXV, 6.) (Apoc. I.)

The First Charity Which Must Be Regained

"I have something against thee, because thou hast left thy first charity." (Apoc. II, 4.)

1. "Thy first charity," that is the state of thy first charity when you were fervent. You have left that state through lukewarmness caused by excessive laziness. Hence, many persons when they should advance by ascending from good to better, fail by descending from the heights of sanc-

tity to the lowest depths of degradation; like Nabuchodonosor's (Daniel II) dream. "The head of this statue was of fine gold, but the breast and arms of silver, and the belly and thighs of brass. The legs of iron, and the feet part of iron and part of clay."

2. "Be mindful therefore from whence thou are fallen" (Apoc. II, 5), that is, from what state of dignity and by what cause have you fallen; for, led on by the tempest of temptation, thou hast fallen. "We have all fallen as a leaf." (Isa. LXIV.) "From whence," that is from heaven where we had hope and happiness and merit. "Where have we fallen?" that is to the earth, because we think of nothing else but things earthly. "By what cause?" through pride. "How art thou fallen from heaven, O Lucifer, who didst rise in the morning? How art thou fallen to the earth that didst wound the nations? Thy pride is brought down to hell." (Isaias XIV, 12.) Therefore Baruch III, 10, says to the sinner, "How happeneth it, O Israel, that thou are in thy enemies' land? Thou art grown old in a strange country. Thou art defiled with the dead. Thou art counted with them that go down into hell."

3. "Do penance, and do the first works." (Apoc. II, 5.) "Behold thy ways in the valley and do quickly what thou hast to do, and do penance"; (Jer. II), by repenting with the heart, confessing with the lips and by satisfactory good works, which are the three essentials of those returning repentant to God and of those fleeing from Egypt. "The God of the Hebrews called us to go three days journey into the wilderness, and to sacrifice to the Lord our God." (Ex. V, 3.) "The three branches are yet three days, after which Pharoah will remember thy service, and restore thee to thy former place." (Gen. XL, 12.) From which it is clear that by true penance, virtues and graces which were lost by us through sin will be restored. Therefore, Christ said, "do penance," and not merely "receive" penance. For many receive penance but few do penance, or voluntarily take penance upon their own accord. They make good promises but poor returns.

Penance makes us approach the kingdom of God. It also causes the Angels to rejoice. It enables us to regain the friendship of God. Therefore, penance must be performed at once, because there can be no work of merit nor reason for excuse nor wisdom to delight in, without penance being intended and performed.

4. "Or else I will come to thee, and will move thy can-

dlestick out of its place, except thou do penance." (Apoc. II, 5.) "Or else," that is if you do not repent and return to your former state, namely, to your first charity, I will come to you in death or in judgment. "To thee," that on account of thee, punishment must be inflicted on your body and soul. "Quickly," this is said so that the quickness and unexpectedness with which the Lord will come will occasion fear and anxiety. "The day of the Lord shall so come, as a thief in the night. For when they shall speak of peace and security, then shall sudden destruction come upon them. And I will move thy candle." (I Thess. V, 3); that is, I will take away gifts and virtues, by which candles are signified; or I will separate thee from thy church, and I will give another thy place. "I will move thee from thy place," that is, I will remove thee from the place of thy virtue and from the congregation of the faithful. (Apoc. II.)

The Second Death

"He that shall overcome shall not be hurt by the second death." (Apoc. II, 11.

1. The death of the soul is twofold, first, death through sin, secondly, death by punishments; the first because of faults, the second in hell. Likewise, the death of the body is twofold, namely, in loss of life and in eternal damnation.
The first death of the soul is likened to the first death of the body in many ways. For just as the body at first becomes weak, afterwards sick and then death follows, and afterwards it is borne away, later buried, and finally covered by stone or clay; so also the soul is at first weakened by temptation or bad thoughts, after that, the soul becomes sick by harmful pleasures; later it dies through sinful consent of the will, then it is seduced or led away through force of habit; after that the soul becomes buried in sin through custom, and finally it is a prey to hardheartedness.
2. Likewise, just as the death of the body hurts us, so does the death of the soul cause us injury. The death of the body separates the body from the soul and the death of the soul separates the soul from God.
The death of the body separates us from parents, friends and relatives, but the death of the soul separates us from

association with the Angels and Saints. "He hath put my brethren," that is the Angels, "far from me, and my acquaintances," namely the Saints, "have departed from me. My kinsmen have forsaken me, and they that knew me have forgotten me." (Job XIX, 13.) The Angels not only abandon the sinful soul, but they become its enemies, and will stand against the soul in judgment. "All her friends have despised her, (the soul) and are become her enemies." (Lam. I, 2.)

The death of the body deprives us of corporal vision but the death of the soul robs us of spiritual vision and of every spiritual perception. Moreover the death of the soul is most injurious; for it can hurl the soul into eternal fire. The death of the soul is injurious, because of the severity, diversity and everlastingness of the punishments; which three things are pointed out by the Psalmist in these words: "Thou, O God, shall bring them down into the pit of destruction." (Ps. LIV, 24.) The diversity of the punishment is noted in the words, "Thou shalt bring," that is God shall lead the sinners from punishment to punishment. The everlastingness of the punishments is pointed out by the words, "into the pit"; from whence no sinner can depart who once falls into that pit.

The death of the body causes us to lose the riches of this world, but the death of the soul deprives us of heaven's treasures. "Our inheritance is turned to aliens." (Lam. V, 3.)

3. Likewise the death of the soul injures us seriously, unmercifully and incurably. "Thy bruise is incurable. Thy wound is very grievous; for I have wounded thee with the wound of an enemy with cruel chastisement. By reason of the multitude of thy iniquities, thy sins are hardened." (Jer. XXX, 12.)

Still this injury to the soul is curable, as long as the soul is in the body, but after the soul leaves the body the wound or injury is incurable. Whosoever therefore, desires not to be injured by a second death should seek to be cured here of the hurt caused by the first death; and show our wounds to the Good Samaritan Who cures them by pouring on them the wine of compunction and the oil of consolation. "When a man shall know the wound of his own heart and shall stretch forth his hands in this house, then hear Thou, O Lord, in heaven in the place of Thy dwelling, and forgive." (3 Kings VIII, 30.) Hence Augustine says, "Are not O God the bowels of Christian mercy in Thee, Whose body died from wounds when Thy soul departed from it?" (Apoc. II.)

The State of Perfection

1. **The religious life implies a state of perfection.**

That which is applicable to many changes in common is ascribed, antonomastically, to that to which it is applicable by way of excellence. Thus the name of fortitude is claimed by the virtue which preserves the firmness of the mind in regard to most difficult things, and the name of temperance, by that virtue which tempers the greatest pleasures. Now religion is a virtue whereby a man offers something to the service and worship of God. Wherefore, those are called religious antonomastically who give themselves up entirely to the Divine service, as offering a holocaust to God. Hence Gregory says: "Some there are who keep nothing for themselves, but sacrifice to Almighty God their tongue, their senses, their life, and the property they possess."

Now the perfection of man consists in adhering wholly to God and in this sense religion denotes the state of perfection. To offer something to the worship of God is necessary for salvation, but to offer oneself wholly and one's possessions to the worship of God belongs to perfection.

We must remember that it pertains to religion not only to offer sacrifices and other like things that are proper to religion but also proper to all the acts of all the virtues, which in so far as they are referred to God's service and honour become acts of religion. Accordingly, if a man devotes his whole life to the Divine service, his whole life belongs to religion; and thus by reason of the religious life that they lead those who are in the state of perfection are called religious.

Although religion or the religious life is a state of perfection, it is also a more suitable place of repentance. For the religious state was instituted chiefly that we might obtain perfection by means of certain exercises whereby the obstacles to perfect charity are removed. By the removal of the obstacles to perfect charity, much more are the occasion of sin cut off, for sin destroys charity altogether. Wherefore, since it belongs to penance to remove the causes of sin, it follows that the religious state is a most suitable place for penance.

2. **It is not required that a religious be actually perfect.**

For religion denotes a state of perfection with the intention of striving for perfection. Hence it is not necessary that whosoever is in religion be perfect, but that he or she is tending to perfection. For he who enters religion does not make profession to be perfect, but he professes to strive to attain perfection; even as he who enters the schools does not profess to have knowledge, but to study in order to acquire knowledge. Hence a religious is not a violator of his profession if he be not perfect, but only if he despises to tend to perfection. (2a. 2ae. 186. a. 1 and 2.)

The Usefulness of the Vows

"Vow ye, and pray to the Lord your God." (Ps. LXXV. 12.)

One and the same work done in fulfillment of a vow is better and more meritorious than if it were done without a vow, and this because of three reasons.

First, because to vow is an act of worship, which is chief among the moral virtues. Now the more excellent the virtue the better and more meritorious the deed. Wherefore, the act of an inferior virtue is the better and the more meritorious for being commanded by a superior virtue, whose act it becomes through being commanded by it, just as the act of faith or hope is better if it be commanded by charity. Hence, the works of the other moral virtues (for example, fasting, which is an act of abstinence; and being continent which is an act of chastity) are better and more meritorious, if they be done in fulfillment of a vow, since thus they belong to the divine worship being like sacrifices to God.

Wherefore Augustine says, "that not even is virginity honorable as such but only when it is consecrated to God, and cherished by godly continence."

Secondly, because he that vows something and does it subjects himself to God more than he that only does it; for he subjects himself to God not only as to the act but also as to the power, since in future he cannot do anything else. Even as he gives more who gives the tree with its fruit than he who gives the fruit only. For this reason we thank not only those who give, but also those who promise to give.

Thirdly, because a vow fixes the will on the good immovably. But to do anything of a will that is fixed on the good, belongs to the perfection of virtue; just as to sin with an obstinate mind aggravates the sin and is called a sin against the Holy Ghost. (2p. 2p. q. 88. a. 6.)

The Good Use of Time

"God has given man time and place for penance, and he has abused it unto pride." (Job XXIV, 23.)

In one way time is our own, because we can do with it what we wish either for good or for evil; for God has left man to be his own counsellor, and so before man are life and death, good and evil and that which he desires will be given to him. But sometimes God takes away His own time, and then we cannot do what we wish but we receive what we deserve. Therefore Sacred Scripture says: "Whatsoever thy hand can do, do it earnestly, for neither work nor reason, nor wisdom, nor knowledge shall be in hell." (Eccles. IX, 10.)

God has moreover, given to us time as an opportunity; secondly, as a help; thirdly, as a warning; fourthly, as a reminder. As an opportunity, so that we might return to Him. "The Lord waits for us so that He might have mercy on us." (Isaias XXX, 18.) Therefore, let us seek the Lord while we are able to find Him, lest death should suddenly overtake us, and then, we have no time to repent.

Time is given us as a help, because the quality of time aids us to do penance if we wish. Extreme heat, cold, rain afflict us. But if we patiently suffer these inconveniences, we do penance. But if we complain against the Lord now, so will it be in judgment against us. He has called "time out" as it were against us.

Time is likewise given to us for a warning, because just as after the day in which men labour, comes night, in which they may rest, so after this life comes death. Hence those who labor in this life for Christ, rest afterwards with Him. And just as after labor a reward or pay is given at night, so after this life Christ gives to His workers their reward.

Time also serves as a reminder, because every day God admonishes us to fear the darkness of hell, from which no one returns if he enters that infernal darkness. The change of time and of seasons likewise reminds and admonishes us that all things are changeable and that we should not fix our heart entirely on transitory things.

God has given us time, or periods of time, such as childhood, boyhood, manhood and old age, so that we might do penance in time. From early childhood penance should begin, but few there are who wish to do penance in childhood or even in manhood; while in our old age we are scarcely able to repent and so all time is lost in so far as doing penance is concerned. The power or even the desire to do penance is scarcely in us at old age, if we have neglected to repent until then. It is good therefore, to repent while the power to do so is in the will, because the time will come when every power of doing good will be taken away from us.

In these days of unemployment and of universal depression, what use have the unemployed made of their idle hours, or to what advantage have those who were blessed with work turned their free time? Much laziness, loafing and abuse of time have wrecked hundreds of homes and thousands of lives.

It behooves us all then to make good use of our time, and especially of our free time or leisure hours. "Therefore, whilst we have time, let us work good to all men, but espcially to those who are of the household of the faith." (Gal. VI, 10.) (Apoc. II.)

Is Poverty Required for Religious Perfection?

"If thou wish to be perfect, go, sell all what thou hast, and give to the poor, and come, follow Me, and thou shalt have treasures in heaven." (Matth. XIX, 21.)

1. The religious state is an exercise and a school for attaining to the perfection of charity. For this, it is necessary that a man wholly withdraw his affection from worldly things, since Augustine says, speaking to God: "Too little doth he love Thee, which he loveth not for Thee." Wherefore he says that charity increases with the lessening of cupidity, and is perfect charity where cupidity is no more. Now the possession of worldly things draws a man's mind to the love of them; hence Augustine says: "That we are more firmly attached to earthly things when we have them, than when we desire them—for why did that young man go away sad, except because he had great wealth? For it is one thing not to wish to lay hold of what one has not, and another to renounce what one already has; the former are rejected as foreign to us, the latter are cut off as a limb." And Chrysostom says: "that the possession of wealth kindles a greater flame as the desire for riches becomes stronger."

Hence it is that in the attainment of the perfection of charity the first foundation is voluntary poverty, whereby a man lives without property of his own, according to the saying of our Lord: "If thou wilt be perfect, go, sell all thou hast, and give to the poor,—and come, follow Me."

2. And although almsgiving is a work most acceptable to God, still poverty (religious poverty) by which the giving of gifts is excluded, pertains to the perfection of religion, because the renouncement of one's own wealth is compared to almsgiving as the universal to the particular and as the holocaust to the sacrifice. Hence Gregory says: "that those who assist the needy with the things they possess, by their good deeds offer sacrifice, since they offer something to God and keep back something for themselves; whereas those who keep nothing for themselves offer a holocaust which is greater than a sacrifice."

Wherefore Jerome also says, in speaking against Vigilantius: "When you declare that those do better who retain the use of their possessions, and dole out the fruits of their possessions to the poor, it is not I but the Lord Who answers you: 'If thou wilt be perfect, go, sell all that thou hast, and give to the poor. . . .'"

Afterwards Jerome goes on to say: "It is a good thing to give away one's goods by dispensing them to the poor. It is a better thing to give them away once for all with the intention of following the Lord, and free of anxiety, to be poor with Christ." (2a, 2æ, q. 186, a. 3.)

Obedience Belongs to Religious Perfection

Religious perfection consists chiefly in the imitation of Christ, according to Matth. XIX, 21, "If thou wilt be perfect, take up thy cross daily, and follow Me." Now the obedience of Christ is especially commended, according to Phil. II, 8, "He became obedient unto death."

1. The religious state is a school and exercise for tending to perfection. Now those who are being instructed or exercised in order to attain a certain end, must follow the direction of someone under whose control they are instructed, as disciples under a master. Hence religious need to be placed under the instruction and command of someone, as regards things pertaining to the religious life. Now one man is subject to another's command and instruction by obedience, and consequently obedience is required for religious perfection.

As the Philosopher says, "by performing actions we contract certain habits, and when we have acquired the habit we are best able to perform the actions. Accordingly, those who have not attained to perfection, acquire perfection by obeying, while those who have already acquired perfection are most ready to obey; not as though they need to be directed to the acquisition of perfection, but as maintaining themselves by this means in that which belongs to perfection."

2. The necessity of compulsion makes an act involuntary and consequently deprives it of the character of praise or merit; whereas, the necessity which is consequent on obedience is a necessity not of compulsion but of a free will, inasmuch as a man is willing to obey, although perhaps he would not be willing to do the thing commanded considered in itself.

Wherefore, since by the vow of obedience a man lays himself under the necessity of doing for God's sake, certain things that are not pleasing in themselves, for this very reason that which he does is the more acceptable to God, though it be of less account, because man can give nothing greater to God than the subjection of his will to another's for God's sake.

Hence in the Conference of the Fathers (Coll. XVII, 7), it is stated that "the Sarabaitæ are the worst class of monks, because through providing for their own needs without being subject to superiors, they are free to do as they will; and yet day and night they are more busily occupied in work than those who live in monasteries." (2a, 2æ, q. 186, a. 5.)

It Is Required for Religious Perfection That Poverty, Continence and Obedience Should Come Under a Vow

It belongs to religious to be in the state of perfection. Now the state of perfection requires an obligation to whatever belongs to perfection, and this obligation consists in binding oneself to God by means of a vow.

But it is evident that poverty, continence and obedience belong to the perfection of the Christian life. Consequently the religious state requires that one be bound to these three by vow. Hence Gregory says, "When a man vows to God all his possessions, all his life, all his knowledge, it is a holocaust"; and afterwards he says that this refers to those who renounce the present world.

Our Lord declared that it belongs to the perfection of life that a man follow Him, not anyhow but in such a way as not to turn back. Wherefore, He says again, "No man putting his hand to the plough, and looking back is fit for the kingdom of God." (Luke IX, 62.) Now, this unwavering following of Christ is made firm by a vow, wherefore a vow is requisite for religious perfection.

Gregory says that "religious perfection requires that a man give God whatever he has vowed." But a man cannot actually give God his whole life, because that life as a whole is not simultaneous but successive. Hence, a man cannot give his whole life to God otherwise than by the obligation of a vow.

Among other services that we can lawfully give is our liberty, which is dearer to man than anything else. Consequently when a man of his own accord deprives himself by vow of the liberty of abstaining from things pertaining to God's service, this is most acceptable to God. Hence Augustine says, "Repent not of thy vow; rejoice rather that thou canst no longer do lawfully, what thou mightest have done lawfully but to thy own cost. Happy the obligation that compels to better things." (2a, 2ae, q. 186, a. 6.)

Is It Right to Say That Religious Perfection Consists in the Three Vows?

The religious state may be considered in three ways. First, as being a practice of tending to the perfection of charity; secondly, as quieting the human mind from outward solicitude, according to 1 Cor. VII, 32, "I would have you without solicitude"; thirdly, as a holocaust whereby a man offers himself and his possessions entirely to God; and in corresponding manner the religious state is constituted by these three vows.

1. First, as regards the practice of perfection, a man is required to remove from himself whatever may hinder his affections from tending wholly to God, for it is in this that the perfection of charity consists. Such hindrances are of three kinds. First, the attachment to external goods, which is removed by the vow of poverty; secondly, the concupiscence of sensible pleasures, chief among which are venereal pleasures, and these are removed by the vow of continence; thirdly the inordinateness of the human will, and this is removed by the vow of obedience.

2. In like manner the unrest of worldly solicitude is aroused in man in reference especially to three things. First, as regards the distribution of external things, and this solici-

tude is removed from man by the vow of poverty; secondly, as regards the control of wife and children, which is removed by the vow of continence; thirdly, as regards the disposal of one's own actions, which is eliminated by the vow of obedience, whereby a man commits himself to the disposal of another.

3. Again a holocaust is the offering to God of all that one has. Now man has a three-fold good. First, the good of external things which he wholly offers to God by the vow of voluntary poverty; secondly, the good of his own body, and this good he offers to God especially by the vow of continence, whereby he renounces the greatest bodily pleasures. The third is the good of the soul, which man wholly offers to God by the vow of obedience, whereby he offers God his own will by which he makes use of all the powers and habits of the soul.

Therefore, the religious state is fittingly constituted by the three vows. (2a, 2æ, q. 186, a. 7.)

The Vow of Obedience Is the Chief of the Three Religious Vows

Gregory says that, "Obedience is rightly placed before victims, since by victims another's flesh is sacrificed, but by obedience one's own will is sacrificed." Now the religious vows are holocausts. Therefore, the vow of obedience is the chief of all religious vows, and this for three reasons.

First, by the vow of obedience man offers God something greater, namely, his own will; for this is of more account than his own body, which he offers to God by continence, and than external things, which he offers God by the vow of poverty. Wherefore, that which is done out of obedience is more acceptable to God than that which is done of one's own will, according to the saying of Jerome to the monk Rusticus. "My words are intended to teach you not to rely on your own judgment," and a little further on he says,."You may not do what you will; you must eat what you are bidden to eat, you may possess as much as you receive, clothe yourself with what is given to you." Hence, fasting is not acceptable to God if it is done of one's own will, according to Isaias LVIII, 3: "Behold in the day of your fast your own will is found."

Secondly, because the vow of obedience includes the other vows but not vice versa, for a religious, though bound by the vow to observe continence and poverty, yet those also come under obedience, as well as many other things besides the keeping of continence and poverty.

Thirdly, because the vow of obedience extends properly to those acts that are closely connected with the end of religion; and the more closely a thing is connected with the end the better it is.

It follows from this that the vow of obedience is more essential to the religious life. For if a man without taking a vow of obedience were to observe, even by vow, voluntary poverty and continence, he would not therefore belong to the religious state, which is to be preferred to virginity observed even by (private) vow; for Augustine says, "No one, methinks, would prefer virginity to the monastic life." (2a, 2æ, q. 186, a. 8.)

The Sin of Religious and of Priests

Seemingly the sins of those who are in a state of holiness and perfection are the most deplorable, for it is written (Jerm. XXIII, 9), "My heart is broken within Me, . . . for the prophet and the priest are defiled; and in My house I have found their wickedness." Therefore religious and others who are in the state of perfection, other things being equal, sin more grievously.

For a sin committed by a religious may be in three ways more grievous than a like sin committed by a secular.

First, if it be against his religious vow, for example if he be guilty of fornication or theft, because by fornication he acts against the vow of continence, and by theft against the vow of poverty; and not merely against a precept of the Divine Law.

Secondly, if he sin out of contempt, because thereby he would seem to be more ungrateful for the Divine favours which have raised him to the state of perfection. Thus the Apostle says (Heb. X, 29), "that the believer deserveth worse punishments who through contempt tramples under foot the Son of God." Hence the Lord complains (Jer. XI, 15), "What is the meaning that My beloved hath wrought much wickedness in My house?"

Thirdly, the sin of a religious may be greater on account of scandal, because many take note of his manner of life. Wherefore it is written, (Jer. XI, 15), "I have seen the likeness of adulterers, and the way of lying in the Prophets of

Jerusalem; and they strengthened the hands of the wicked, so that no man should return from his evil doings."

2. On the other hand, if a religious, not out of contempt, but because of weakness or ignorance commit a sin, that is not against the vow of his profession,—without giving scandal, (for instance if he commit it in secret) he sins less grievously in the same kind of a sin than a secular, because his sin if slight is absorbed as it were by his many good works and if it be mortal, he more easily recovers from it. First, because he has a right intention towards God, and though it be intercepted for the moment, it is easily restored to its former object. Secondly, he is assisted by his religious brethren to rise again; according to Eccles. IV, 10, "If one fall he shall be supported by the other, but woe to him that is alone, for when he falleth he hath none to lift him up."

The just sin not easily out of contempt, but sometimes they fall into sin through ignorance or weakness from which through God's grace, they easily arise. If, however, they go so far as to sin out of contempt, they become most wicked and incorrigible, according to the words of Jeremias (II, 20), "Thou hast broken My yoke, thou hast burst My bands, and thou hast said: ... I will not serve." (2a, 2ae, q. I, 86, a. 10.)

The Works of the Active Life

1. Religious who are engaged around works of the active life, depart not from the true concept of religion. For the religious state is directed to the perfection of charity, which extends to the love of God and of our neighbour. Now the contemplative life which seeks to devote itself to God alone belongs directly to the love of God; while the active life, which ministers to our neighbour's needs, belongs directly to the love of one's neighbour. And just as out of charity we love our neighbour for God's sake, so the services we render our neighbour redound to God, according to Matth. XXV, 40, "As long as you did it to one of these My least brethren, you did it to Me."

Consequently those services which we render our neighbour, in so far as we refer them to God, are described as sacrifices, according to Hebr. XIII, 16, "Do not forget to do good, and to impart, for by such sacrifices God's favour is obtained." Therefore it belongs to religion to offer sacrifices to God.

2. Religious engaged in the works of the active life, are not deprived entirely of the fruit of the contemplative life.

Now the perfection of the religious consists in the contemplation of divine things, for Dionysius says that, "They are called servants of God by reason of their rendering pure service and subjection to God, and on account of the indivisible and singular life which unites them by holy reflections, that is, contemplations, on invisible things, to the Godlike unity and perfection beloved of God." But service and subjection rendered to God are not precluded by works of the active life, whereby a man serves his neighbour for God's sake. Nor do these works preclude singularity of life; not that they involve man living apart from his fellow men, but in the sense that each man individually devotes himself to things pertaining to the service of God; and since religious occupy themselves with the works of the active life for God's sake, it follows that their action results from their contemplation of divine things. Hence they are not entirely deprived of the fruit of the contemplative life.

3. Such religious are not in the world. A man may be in the world in two ways. In one way by his bodily presence, in another way by the affection of his mind. Hence our Lord said to His disciples, "I have chosen you out of the world," and yet speaking of them to His Father He said, "These are in the world, and I come to Thee." (John XV, 19.) Although then, religious who are occupied with the works of the active life are in the world as to the presence of the body, they are not in the world as regards their affections and bent of mind, because they are occupied with external things, not as seeking anything of the world, but merely for the sake of serving God; for "they . . . use this world, as if they used it not." (I Cor. VII, 31.) Hence James (I, 27) after it is stated that "religion clean and undefiled before God and the Father . . . is . . . to visit the fatherless and widows in their tribulations," added, "and to keep one's mind unspotted from this world," namely to avoid being attached to worldly things. (2a, 2ae, q. 1, 88, a. 2.)

How a Religious Who Sins Slightly May Rise Quickly

We have already said that if a religious, not out of contempt, but from weakness and ignorance, commit a sin not against the vow of his profession, without giving scandal, his sin, if slight, is absorbed by his many good works, and if it be mortal, he quickly recovers from it through prompt cooperation with God's grace; and by the good example and assistance of his fellow religious.

First, because he has a right intention towards God, and though it be intercepted for a moment, it is easily restored to its former object. Hence Origen commenting on Ps. XXXVI, 24, "When he shall fall he shall not be bruised," says "The wicked man, if he sins, repents not, and fails to make amends for his sin. But the just man knows how to make amends and recover himself; even as he who said, 'I know not the man,' shortly afterwards when the Lord had looked on him, knew how to shed most bitter tears, and he who from the roof had seen a woman and desired her, knew how to say: 'I have sinned and done evil before Thee O Lord.' "

Secondly, the religious is assisted by his fellow-religious to rise again, according to Eccles. IV, 10, "If one fall he should be supported by the other, but woe to him that is alone, for when he falleth he hath none to lift him up."

Hence Augustine says, "From the time I began to serve God, just as I scarcely found better men than those who have made progress in monasteries, so have I not found worse than those who in the monastery have fallen." (2a, 2ae, q. 186, a. 10.)

The Study of Letters (or Sciences)

The study of letters (or secular sciences) is becoming to religious in three ways.

1. First as regards that which is proper to the contemplative life, to which the study of letters (or the sciences) help in a twofold manner. In one way by helping directly to contemplate, namely, by enlightening the intellect. For the contemplative life is directed chiefly to the consideration of divine things, to which consideration man is directed by study. Hence it is said in praise of the righteous, "that he shall meditate day and night on the Law of the Lord." (Ps. I, 2), and "The wise man will seek out the wisdom of all the ancients, and will be occupied in the prophets." (Eccles. XXXIX, 1.)

In another way the study of the sciences is a help to the contemplative life indirectly, by removing the obstacles to contemplation, namely the errors which the contemplation of divine things frequently beset those who are ignorant of the scriptures. Thus we read in the Conferences of the Fathers that the Abbot Serapion through simplicity fell into the error of the Anthropomorphites, who thought that God had a human shape. Hence Gregory says: "that some through seeking in contemplation more than they are able to grasp, fall away into perverse doctrines, and by failing to be humble disciples of truth, become the masters of error." Hence it is written (Eccles. II, 3), "I thought in my heart to withdraw my flesh from wine, that I might turn my mind to wisdom and might avoid folly."

2. Secondly, the study of sciences is necessary to religious institutions for preaching and other like works; wherefore the Apostle (Tit. I, 9) says, "Embracing that faithful word which is according to doctrine, that he may be able to exhort in sound doctrine and to convince the gainsayers." Nor does it matter that the Apostles were sent to preach without having studied the sciences, because, as Jerome says in his letter to Paulinus, "Whatever others acquire by exercise and daily meditations in God's law, was taught them by the Holy Ghost."

3. Thirdly, the study of science is becoming to religious as regards to that which is common to all religious orders. For it helps to avoid the lusts of the flesh. Wherefore Jerome said to the monk Rusticus: "Love the science of the scriptures and thou shalt have no love for carnal vice." For it turns the mind away from lustful thoughts, and tames the flesh because of the toil that study entails according to Eccles. XXXI, 1, "Watching for riches (riches of virtue) . . . consumeth the flesh."

It also helps to remove the desire for riches, wherefore it is written (Wis. VIII, 8), "I . . . esteemed riches nothing in comparison with her, namely wisdom, and (1 Mach. XII, 9), "We needed none of these things," namely, assistance from without, "having for our comfort the holy books that are in our hands."

A devout and careful study of the sciences also helps to teach obedience. Hence Augustine says: "What sort of perverseness is this, to wish to read, but not to obey what one reads?"

The philosophers professed the study of letters in the matter of secular learning; whereas it becomes religious to devote themselves chiefly to the study of letters in reference to the doctrine that is "according to Godliness." (Tit. I, 1.) It becomes not religious whose whole life is devoted to the service of God, to seek for other learning, save in so far as it is referred to sacred doctrine; and unless as Augustine says, "it is necessary for confounding heretics." (2a, 2ae. q. 1, 88, a. 5.)

The Works of Religious

1. Are the works of Religious, to be preferred to the works of those who do not occupy themselves with the salvation of souls? It must be remembered that two works can be compared to one another in many ways. In one way according to their genus, just as we say that continency excels virginity in the separate good of continency. In this way the active life is more fruitful than the contemplative, but the contemplative is more meritorious than the active. Zeal for the salvation of souls, is a sacrifice most acceptable to God; if it is properly exercised; so that our first care should be for our own salvation, and afterwards for the salvation of others. "For what shall it profit a man to gain the whole world and suffer the loss of his own soul?" (Matth. XVI, 26.)

2. One action is preferred to another because of the will, good will, of the person performing the action. For that work which is more willingly performed is judged the better, and that person whose work is done from fervent love of God, his or her work is the more meritorious.

3. One work can be compared to another work, not in itself but in relation to another act; just as abstinence is preferred to the eating of food, still to take food with another on account of charity is to be preferred to abstinence.

Thus compared, the works of Religious are incomparably superior to the works of those who do not consecrate themselves to the salvation of souls. For those things which Religious do, are referred to that root or principle by which they have vowed their whole life to God. Hence we must not consider what they do, but the fact that they have consecrated themselves by vow to do each thing for God. And so Religious are compared to those who do some special good work, just as the infinite to the finite. For whosoever gives himself to another to do all things which he commands, gives himself infinitely more than one who gives himself to another to perform a certain work. Hence even if a Religious, according to the demands of his religion, should do some work however small in itself, still it receives great attention and merit, because of its relation to the first obligation, by which that Religious consecrated it and himself entirely to God.

4. Still if all things are equally compared with all things, the works of Religious are by far greater and the more excellent. For although to procure the salvation of others is greater than to work solely for one's own salvation, speaking

generally, still to work for one's own salvation in every way, is to be preferred to working for the salvation of others, while neglecting our own salvation. For if anyone works wholeheartedly and perfectly for his own salvation, by so much the more does such a person perform many special good works, for the salvation of others. (Quodlib. 2, q. 5, a. 1.)

Faithfulness

"Be thou faithful unto death, and I will give thee the crown of life." (Apoc. II, 10.)

1. "Be thou faithful," that is keep the faith. As if our Lord had said, "Be always faithful, that is keep faith or be faithful; just as a faithful wife keeps faith with her husband, as a servant with his master, as a friend with a friend. The faith which a wife should have for her husband, is that she should have no love or affection for another man. Concerning this very thing, Osee II, 20, says, "I will espouse thee to me in faith, and thou shalt know that I am the Lord."

The faith which a servant ought to have for his master, is that he attend to his affairs well, guard them carefully and distribute them justly. Concerning this faith the Lord said, "Who (thinkest thou) is the faithful and wise servant?" (Luke XII, 42.) And Saint Paul speaking to the Corinthians says, "Now it is required among the dispensers, that a man be found faithful." (1 Cor. IV.)

The faith which a friend should place in a friend, is that he defend his friend at all times and forsake him not in time of need. Concerning this, (Eccl. VI, 14) says, "A faithful friend is a strong defense, and he that hath found him hath found a treasure." Nothing can be compared to a faithful friend. No amount of gold or silver is worthy to be compared with the goodness of a faithful friend.

"Unto death," inclusive. As if our Lord had said, "even to avoid death, do not renounce your faith. Even unto death fight for justice." (Eccle. IV, 33.)

2. "And I will give to thee the crown of life;" that is, everlasting life, kingly life, or "the crown of life," that is the honor of living always, which is not the world's crown. "Let us crown ourselves with roses before they be withered." (Wis. II, 8), that is, with worldly honor which quickly perishes.

"Woe to the crown of pride, to the drunkard of Ephraim, and to the fading flower." (Isaias, XXVIII, 1.) The roses or flowers from which the earthly crown is made, are temporal riches, carnal pleasures, worldly honors. "Give a flower to Moab, for in its flower it shall go out, and the cities thereof shall be desolate." (Jer. XLVIII, 9.) Because the flower that fadeth bears no fruit. The world gives this fading crown to its heroes. But Jesus gives the first crown, the crown of everlasting life to His faithful and unconquerable soldiers of the Cross of Christ. (Apoc. II.)

EXPLANATION OF REFERENCES

Throughout these Meditations references have been made at the end of each Meditation to some work of St. Thomas Aquinas, O.P., whence the topic for meditation was adapted. For the most part, references have been made to his immortal masterpiece—*The Summa Theologica*. Hence persons not familiar with the divisions of the *Summa* of the Angelic Doctor, in order to understand the references, will do well to *remember*, that St. Thomas' *Summa* is divided into three parts, and that the second part is sub-divided into what is known as, the first part of the second part, and the second part of the second. Such references then, as (1a. q. 8, a. 7), would mean—the First Part of the *Summa* (Prima Pars in Latin), question 8, article 7.

Also 1a. 2ae. q. 87, a. 3, would refer to the first part of the second part of the *Summa*, question 87, article 3. Thirdly, 2a. 2ae. q. 53, a. 1.—would refer to the second part of the second part of the *Summa*, q. 53, article 1. (In Latin it would read, secunda, secundae, q. 53, a. 1.)

Keeping these general divisions in mind, there will be no difficulty in understanding from what part of the Universal Doctor's *Summa Theologica*, most of the meditations have been taken. Some few references have been made to St. Thomas work "Against the Gentiles" (Contra Gentes).

The *Summa* of this saintly and illustrious Dominican scholar contains some three thousand articles and ten thousand objections, among which will be found a refutation of the errors of all time, a clear, logical, and powerful defense of Christ and His infallible teaching.

The prayers of St. Thomas Aquinas, printed at the end of these Meditations, have been taken from an excellent little volume, entitled "St. Thomas Aquinas Book," by the late Father Thomas M. Schwertner, O.P.; in which volume will be found also Novena Prayers for the Six Sundays in honor of St. Thomas, and can be obtained from the Rosary Press, Somerset, Ohio, through whose courtesy the St. Thomas prayers have been here reprinted.

E.C.McE.

M v. Feuerstein
ST. THOMAS AQUINAS
Non Recipiam Mercedem Nisi Te, Domine

"May I Receive no reward, but Thyself O Lord."—St. Thomas Aquinas.

ADDENDA

PRAYERS OF ST. THOMAS AQUINAS, O.P.

BEFORE HOLY COMMUNION

(The prose prayers of St Thomas have been divided into single lines so that they can be said better, aloud, in unison.)

PRAYER BEFORE HOLY COMMUNION

O Almighty and Eternal God,
Behold I draw near to the Sacrament
of Thy only-begotten Son,
our Lord Jesus Christ!
I come as infirm
to the Physician of life,
as unclean to the fountain of mercy,
as blind to the light of eternal splendor,
as poor and needy,
to the Lord of Heaven and earth.
I implore the abundance of Thy immense bounty
that Thou wouldst deign
to cure my infirmity,
to wash away my uncleanness,
to enlighten my blindness,
to enrich my poverty,
to clothe my nakedness,
that I may receive the Bread of angels,
the King of kings,
the Lord of hosts,
with so great reverence and humility
with such contrition and devotion,
such purity and faith,
with that purpose and intention
as is profitable to the salvation of my soul.
Grant me, I beseech Thee,
not only to receive
the Sacrament of the Body and Blood of the Lord,
but also the essence,
and virtue of the Sacrament!
O most mild God, grant that the Body
of Thy only-begotten Son,
our Lord Jesus Christ,
which He took from the Virgin Mary,
I may so receive
as to deserve
to be incorporated
with His mystical Body,
and to be numbered
among His members!
O Most loving Father,
grant that Thy beloved Son,
Whom now in life
I am about to receive veiled,
I may perpetually contemplate,
revealed face to face!
Who liveth and reigneth with Thee
in the unity of the Holy Ghost,
one God forever and ever.—AMEN.

LAUDA SION

BEFORE HOLY COMMUNION

Sion, lift thy voice and sing:
Praise thy Saviour and thy King:
  Praise with hymns thy Shepherd true:
Strive thy best to praise Him well;
Yet doth He all praise excel;
  None can ever reach His due.

See today before us laid
The living and life-giving Bread
  Theme for praise and joy profound!
The same which at the sacred board,
Was, by our Incarnate Lord,
  Given to His Apostles round.

Let the praise be loud and high;
Sweet and tranquil be the joy
  Felt today in every breast;
On this festival divine,
Which records the origin
  Of the glorious Eucharist.

On this Table of the King,
Our new Paschal offering
   Brings to end the olden rite;
Here for empty shadows fled,
Is Reality instead;
   Here instead of darkness Light

His own act at supper seated,
Christ ordained to be repeated,
   In His memory divine;
Wherefore now with adoration
We the Host of our salvation
   Consecrate from bread and wine.

Hear what Holy Church maintaineth;
That the bread its substance changeth
   Into Flesh, the wine to Blood.
Doth it pass thy comprehending?
Faith, the law of sight transcending,
   Leaps to things not understood.

Here beneath these signs are hidden
Priceless things to sense forbidden;
   Signs not things, are all we see;
Flesh from bread, and Blood from wine;
Yet is Christ in either sign,
   All entire confessed to be.

They, too, who of Him partake,
Sever not, nor rend, nor break,
   But entire their Lord receive.
Whether one or thousands **eat**,
All receive the self-same meat,
   Nor the less for others leave.

Both the wicked and the good
Eat of this celestial Food;
   But with ends how opposite!
Here 'tis life; and there 'tis death;
The same, yet issuing to each
   In a difference infinite.

Not a single doubt retain,
When they break the host in twain,
   But that in each part remains
What was in the whole before;
Since the simple sign alone
Suffers change in state or form,
The Signified remaining One,
   An the Same for evermore.

Lo! upon the altar lies,
Hidden deep from human eyes,
Bread of angels from the skies,
   Made of the food of mortal man;
Children's meat to dogs denied;
In old types foresignified,
In the manna Heaven supplied,
   Isaac, and the Paschal Lamb.

Jesus, Shepherd of the sheep!
Thou Thy flock in safety keep.
Living bread! Thy life supply;
Strengthen us, or else we die;
Fill us with celestial grace;
Thou who feedest us below,
Source of all we have or know,
Grant that with Thy saints above,
Sitting at the feast of love,
   We may see Thee face to face!

VERBUM SUPERNUM

The Word, descending from above,
   Though with the Father still on high,
Went forth upon His work of love,
   And soon to life's last eve drew nigh.

He shortly to a death accursed
   By a disciple shall be given;
But to His twelve disciples first
   He gives Himself, the Bread from heaven.

Himself in either kind He gave:
   He gave His Flesh, He gave His Blood;
Of flesh and blood all men are made;
   And He of man would be the Food.

At birth our brother He became:
   At board Himself as food He gives;
To ransom us He died in shame;
   As our reward in bliss He lives.

O saving victim! opening wide
   The gate of heaven to man below!
Our foes press on from every side;—
   Thine aid supply, Thy strength bestow,

To Thy great Name be endless praise,
Immortal Godhead, one in Three!
Oh, grant us endless length of days,
In our true native land with Thee!

PANGE LINGUA
BEFORE HOLY COMMUNION

Sing, my tongue, the Saviour's glory,
Of His Flesh the mystery sing;
Of the Blood, all price exceeding,
Shed by our Immortal King,
Destined for the world's redemption,
From a noble womb to spring.

Of a pure and spotless Virgin
Born for us on earth below,
He, as Man with man conversing,
Stayed, the seeds of truth to sow;
Then He closed in solemn order
Wondrously His life of woe.

On the night of the Last Supper,
Seated with His chosen band,
He the Paschal victim eating,
First fulfils the Law's command;
Then as Food to all His brethren
Gives Himself with His own hand.

Word made Flesh, the bread of nature
By His word to Flesh He turns;
Wine into His Blood He changes:—
What though sense no change discerns!
Only be the heart in earnest,
Faith her lesson quickly learns

Down in adoration falling,
Lo! the Sacred Host we hail;
Lo! o'er ancient forms departing,
Newer rites of grace prevail;
Faith for all defects supplying,
Where the feeble senses fail

To the Everlasting Father,
And the Son, who reigns on high,
With the Holy Ghost proceeding
Forth from Each eternally,
Be salvation, honor, blessing,
Might and endless majesty.

A SHORT PRAYER WHICH ST. THOMAS SAID DAILY

Grant me, I beseech Thee, O merciful God! ardently to desire, prudently to investigate, truly to acknowledge, and perfectly to fulfil that which is pleasing to Thee, to the praise and glory of Thy Name. Amen.

(On June 29, 1878, Leo XIII granted an indulgence of 300 days to all who, with a contrite heart, recite this prayer)

PRAYERS OF ST THOMAS AQUINAS
After Holy Communion

I give Thee thanks,
O holy Lord, Almighty Father,
Eternal God, who hast deigned
through no merits of mine,
but only through Thy own mercy,
to feed me, a sinner,
Thy unworthy servant,
with the precious Body and Blood,
of Thy Son,
our Lord Jesus Christ.
And I pray
that this Holy Communion
may not be for me
a subject for punishment,
but a salutary pleading for pardon.
May it be to me
the armor of faith
and the shield of good will
May it be
the extirpation of my vices,
and the increase of charity and patience,
of humility and obedience,
and of all the virtues;
a firm defense
against the snares of all enemies,
visible and invisible;
a perfect quieting
of all my affections,
both carnal and spiritual;
a firm adhesion to Thee,
the one and true God,

and the blessed consummation of my end.
And I pray Thee,
to deign to lead me, a sinner,
to that ineffable banquet,
where Thou with Thy Son
and the Holy Spirit,
art the true light,
the full plenitude,
the everlasting joy,
the consummate delight,
the perfect felicity of Thy saints.
Through the same Christ, our Lord. Amen.

ADORO TE

AFTER HOLY COMMUNION

O Godhead hid, devoutly I adore Thee,
Who truly art within the forms before me;
To Thee my heart I bow with bended knee,
As failing quite in contemplating Thee.

Sight, touch, and taste in Thee are all deceived;
The ear alone most safely is believed:
I believe all the Son of God has spoken,
Than Truth's own word there is no truer token.

God only on the Cross lay hid from view;
But here lies hid at once the Manhood too;
And I in both professing my belief,
Make the same prayer as the repentant thief.

Thy wounds as Thomas saw, I do not see;
Yet Thee confess my Lord and God to be;
Make me believe Thee ever more and more;
In Thee my hope, in Thee my love to store.

O Thou, Memorial of our Lord's own dying!
O living Bread, to mortals life supplying!
Make Thou my soul henceforth on Thee to live;
Ever a taste of heavenly sweetness give.

O living Pelican! O Jesus, Lord!
Unclean I am, but cleanse me in Thy Blood,
Of which a single drop for sinners spilt,
Can purge the entire world from all its guilt.

Jesus! Whom for the present veiled I see,
What I so thirst for, oh, vouchsafe to me!
That I may see Thy countenance unfolding,
And may be blessed Thy glory in beholding.
(The following is usually sung after every stanza)
Jesus, Eternal Shepherd; hear our cry;
Increase the faith of all whose souls on Thee rely.

PRAYER OF ST. THOMAS TO OBTAIN THE VIRTUES

Almighty God, Thou who knowest all things,
Thou who art without beginning or end,
Thou who dost bestow,
preserve and reward the virtues,
vouchsafe to confirm me
in the firm foundation of faith,
to protect me
with the indestructible shield of hope
and to adorn me
with the wedding garment of charity.
Grant that in justice
I may be subject to Thee,
that with prudence I may shun
the snares of the evil one,
and with fortitude patiently endure adversity.
Grant that I may freely share
what I have with those that have not,
and that what I myself have not

I may humbly seek from those that have.
Grant that the guilt I have committed,
I may sincerely confess,
and the punishment I endure,
I may bear with equanimity.
Grant that I may not envy my neighbor his goods,
and that I may always thank Thee for Thy gifts.
In rest and motion,
may I be always reserved!
May I preserve my tongue from vain-glorious words,
guard my feet from transgressing,
restrain my eyes from wandering glances,
withdraw my ears from the noise of the world,
incline my head humbly,
lift up my mind to heavenly things,
despise what is transient,
long only after Thee.
Subdue my flesh,
purify my conscience,
honor the saints,
praise Thee worthily,
increase in blessings,
and end my good works by a holy death.
Implant in me, O Lord, the virtues that I may be toward holy things devout,
in earthly duties prudent,
in my behaviour troublesome to no one.
Give me, O Lord, heartfelt repentance, sincere confession,
and the grace to make perfect satisfaction.

A FREQUENT PRAYER OF SAINT THOMAS

Creator beyond human endurance,
Who out of Thy wisdom'd treasures,
didst establish three hierarchies of Angels,
setting them in wonderful order to preside over the empyrean heaven,
and Who hast most marvellously assorted the parts of the universe;
Thou Who art called the fountain-head of life and of wisdom,
and the one over-ruling principle;
be pleased to shed the ray of Thy brightness,
over the gloom of my understanding,
so as to dispel the double-shadow of sin and ignorance in which I was born;
Thou Who makest eloquent the tongue of babes,
instruct my tongue,
and shed the grace of Thy blessing upon my lips.
Bestow on me keenness of wit to understand,
the power of a retentive memory,
method and ease of learning,
subtlety for explaining,
and a gift of ready speech.
Teach me as I begin,
direct me as I advance,
complete my finished task for me,
Thou who art our Lord Jesus Christ.
Lady most holy,
be my helper and my comforter against the attacks and snares of the ancient foe,
and of all my enemies. Amen.

PRAYER TO ST. THOMAS FOR THE PROPER CHOICE OF A STATE OF LIFE

O Blessed Thomas, thou who didst early hear in thy heart the call of the Master to lay aside the trappings of this world to follow Him in poverty and humility; thou who didst run after the Lord in the odor of His ointments, trampling underfoot all the blandishments of the senses; thou who by prayer and meditation didst seek to discover that thou wert going in the right direction, I pray thee, with all the fervour of my heart, to obtain for me the grace to know what is the Divine good pleasure in my regard. Help me to choose aright the state of life for which I have been destined. Do not let me be turned aside by any earthly consideration from following over the way which the good Master has selected for me. Help me to realize my vocation, to make myself daily more worthy of it, to pursue and increase constantly the glory of God, to work out my salvation with fear and trembling and to merit the heavenly reward which God has promised those who do His will. Amen

AFTER HOLY COMMUNION
PRAYER OF ST. THOMAS TO THE BLESSED VIRGIN

Dearest and most blessed Virgin Mary,
Mother of God,
Overflowing with affection,
Daughter of the Sovereign King,
and Queen of the Angels:
Mother of Him Who created all things,
this day and all the days of my life
I commend to the bosom of thy regard
my soul and body,
all my actions, thoughts, wishes, desires, words, and deeds,
my whole life, and my end:
so that through thy prayers
they may all be ordered
according to the will of thy beloved Son.
Amen.

TOPICAL INDEX

A

Adoption, Our Divine	219
Andrew, Saint	7
Angel, Guardian	422
Annunciation, see Blessed Virgin	
Apparition, of Christ	211
Ascension of Christ	252
Ascension, the Usefulness of	253
Ascension, the Cause of Our Salvation	255

B

Baptism	222
Baptist, Saint John	13
Beatitudes	235
Beatitudes, Rewards of	237
Banquet, the Threefold	308
Blessed Virgin Mary—	
Annunciation of	8
Apparition of	102
Assumption of	351
Compassion of	190
Fruit of Her Womb	55
Espousals of	77
Expectation of	32
Help of Christians	9
Holy Life of	494
Immaculate Conception of	19
Intercession of	66
Nativity of	385
Purification of	91
Pure Heart of	291
Rosary of	415
Virginity of	54
Visitation of	298
Blood, the Most Precious	180
Burial of Christ	186
Spiritual	187

C

Carefulness, Need of	122
Charity, Degrees of	409
Excellence of	363
Clinging to God Through	427
First Charity Must Be Regained	504
Increase of	410
Precepts of	390
Perfect	406
Of God in the Passion	155
We Merit Through Charity	243
Christ's Birth, Circumstances of	45, 47
Christ, Born to Suffer and Die	43
Goodness and Usefulness of Christ's Birth	41
Christ's Active Life	72
Abiding in Christ	109
Associations	63
Austere Life	71
Conduct Towards the Law	75
Clinging to Christ	106
Christ, Circumcision of	56
Conversation of	70
Imitation of	98
Christ's Pains of His Passion	151
Passion of Christ	152 to 192
Poverty of Christ	73
Presentation in the Temple	92
Temptation of Christ	148
Yoke of Christ	89
Christ Endured All Sufferings	149
Priesthood of	82
Church, Dedication of a	420
Three Things Mystically Understood in a	196
Cleanliness, Need of Perfect	194
Conversion Must Not Be Put Off	105
Consolation, Divine	435
Contrition	328
Duration of	329
Contemplation	438, 439
Four Ways the Demons Prevent	451
Effects of	454
Things Seen in	443
Contemplative Life	433
The Merit of	442
Counsels of the Gospels	462
Courage, see Fortitude	
Creator	303
Cross, Death of the	393
Darkness and Shadow of the	286, 363

D

Damned, Pains of the	482
Knowledge of the	483
The Will of the	485
Eternal Punishment of the	486
Darkness of the Cross	286
Death	143
Of Christ	133
Eternal	481
Second	506

TOPICAL INDEX

Of Lazarus 178
Devotion 375
  Cause of 376
  Effects of 376
Dew, Heavenly 37
Desert, the Voice of One Crying in . 36

E

Evangelist, St John the 44
Epiphany of Christ 56
  Order of Christ's Manifestations 58
Eucharist, the Sacrament of
    227, 280, 281, 282, 283 to 289

F

Faith, Advantages and Need of 359
  Effects of 361
Faithfulness 522
Father, Our Heavenly . . . 257
  Our Confidence in the . . 259
  The Father, Our Consolation 260
Familiarity, Divine 452
Fasting 144
Fear of the Lord 365
Fortitude 370
Folly 337
Friend, the Divine 177

G

Gate, the Narrow 114
Gift of the Most High . . . 266
Glory, the Possession of . . 260
  Vain 353
  Vain is a Capital Vice . . 354
God, Advantages of Reflecting on 303
  Attraction of Man to . . 228
  The Gift of the Most High 247
  The Gift of the Son of . . 29
  Happiness in a Life with . 495
  Our Father 305
  The Holy Name of . . . 68
  The Governor of All Things 304
  Keeping the Word of . . 79
  Immutability of 301
  The Presence of 300
  Reconciliation to 160
  Offerings Ourselves to . . 93
  The Temple of 87
  Love of 404
  How We Must Worship God 138
  Serving God 136, 139
  Searching for 62
  The Greatest Love and Worship Belong to 277
  The Peace of 440
  Sacrifices Offered to . . . 381

The Saints Pray for Us to . 471
  Seeing God Face to Face . 489
  The Voice of God Calling Us 492
Good, Doing 125
Goodness, Divine . . . 130, 448, 456
Gospels, Counsels of the . 427
Grace of Christ 79
  The Life of 242, 333
  Man's Knowledge of . . 230
  Meriting Eternal Life Through 245

H

Haste, see Precipitation . . 342
Happiness in a Life with God 440
  Degrees of 496
  Endlessness of Perfect . . 498
  Which We Must Avoid Here 324
  Of the Saints . . . 457, 461
Heaven, Conversation in . . 256
Hell, Our Lord's Descent Into 201
Holy Name of God 68
  The Suitableness of the Name Jesus 51
  The Usefulness of the Name of Jesus 52
Holy Ghost, Apparition of . 272
  The Gifts of 232
  The Manifold Blessings of 279
  Preparation for the Reception of 262
  Operations of 265
  Not Given to the Worldly 263
  How We Are Moved to do Good by 268
  The Spirit Descending and Remaining with Us 273
  A Sin Against the . . . 278
Hope, the Lack of 334
  Object of 362
Humility, Christ's 69
  The Need of 382
  Our Lord Commands Us to be Humble 386
  Man Subjects Himself Through 384

I

Immaculate Conception, Feast of 20
Imprudence 339
Immutability of God 278
Incarnation, Advantages of . 38
  A Wonderful Gift of God . 16
  The Need of 11
  The Time of. 19
  A Most Suitable Remedy . 12
  If Man Had Not Sinned Would God Have Become Man? . . 18
  Desire for the 25
  A Work Proper to the Holy Spirit 31
  No Merits Preceded Union of 28
Intemperance 344
Imprudence 339

TOPICAL INDEX 535

J

Jesus, at the Door	90
Judge, Power of the Highest	478
Judgment, General	473
Fear of the	476
Discussion of	474
Final	474
Justice	368

L

Lance and Nails, Feast of	154
Law, Christ's Conduct Towards the	67
Learning Divine Secrets	453
Letters, the Study of the Letters or Sciences	519
Life, Beginning of the New	216
Belief in Everlasting	488
The Contemplative	404
The Excellence of the Contemplative	405
In Christ	110
Eternal	491
The New	209
Three Persons Restored to Life by Our Lord	207
The Works of the Active	481
Love of Christ for Us	175, 262
Of God	306, 403
Advantages of the Law of	402
The Fourfold Good of the Law of	400
Divine ———— -	3
Divine Manifestation to One Loving God	429
The Causes of	413
The Effects of	421
Why Love Our Enemies?	397
Improper Love of Oneself	336
Mutual	394
Of the Highest Good	411
The New Commandment of	395
Perfect	396
Precept of	360, 361, 373
Progress in	414
The Sign of True Love	424
The Wonderful Privilege of	428
Lord, Following the	95
Loretto, Translation of the House of Our Lady of	23
Lust, the Daughters of	345
Ways to Conquer	346

M

Man, the Friendship of God for	425
The First Man's Innocence	244
Manna, the Hidden	444
Magi, Diligence of	59
Marriages, Spiritual	65
Mary, see References to Blessed Virgin Mary—	
Meditation, Usefulness of Meditating on the Mysteries	88
Mercy	399
Merit	242 to 245

N

Nature, Fitting for the Son to Assume Human	26
Manner of Repairing Human	15
Negligence	343
Night, the Departing	22

O

Obedience of Christ	76
Belongs to Religious Perfection	512
Required for Perfection	511, 513
Vow of	515
Obstacles to Contemplation	416

P

Pains of the Damned	475
Passion, Our Lord's	131
Of Christ, see References to Christ—	
Patience	388
Paul, Conversion of	80
Peace of Christ	213
And Victory Through Jesus	112
Penance, the Sacrament of	33, 326
Worthy of	34
The Repentant Soul	46
Perfection of the Christian Life	457
Consists in Observing the Commandments	461
Necessary for Salvation	458
Of Religion Consists in the Three Vows	514
State of	508
Under Counsel	459
Piety, the Gift of	234
Prayer, Advantages of	246, 247
Continual	379
Devotion During	345
In the Garden	127
The Lord's	249
Manner of Praying	378
Perseverance in	464
Prayers of Saint Thomas Aquinas	527 to 532
Unanswered Prayers	250
Pride	317
Wickedness of	348
The Beginning of Every Sin	349
The Way to Avoid It	352

TOPICAL INDEX

Precipitation	342
Prudence	367
Purity	418
Purgatory	46
Punishments of	468

R

Recovery, Spiritual	446
Redeemer, Christ Our True	167
References, Explanation of	525
Reflection	. 279
Reformation, Interior	123
Religion, the Perfection of	518
Religious, the Works of a	517, 521
The Sin of a	516
Remains of Sin	327
Renunciation	115, 203
Resurrection of Christ	203 to 206
Advantages of Belief in	472
Retreats, Topics for	503 to 523
Resurrection, Our Spiritual	210
Reward, Our	120

S

Saints, Praying to	469
Sanctity	141
Sacred Heart of Jesus	290
Sacrifice of Christ	150
Offered to God	381
Scourging of Christ	142
Seed, the Divine	128
Sin, Venial and Mortal	313, 318, 323
Penalties of	223
Divine Favor in Arising from	. 332
Sinners, State of	104
Sonship, Divine	49
Soul, Repentant	39
Indwelling of Divine Persons in the	220
Solicitude	331
Sorrow, Advantages of	389
Sloth	338
Sign of True Love	391
Sufferings of Christ	150
Supper, the Lord's	198
Spirit, Holy, see Holy Ghost references	

T

Temperance	372
Temple of God	94
Temptation of Christ	149
Things, Heavenly	99
Thorns, Crown of	145
Time, the Good Use of	510
Of the Last Judgment	479
Trinity	254, 274

V

Vigilance, the Need of	124, 133
Vine	124
Vineyard, the Lord's	117
Virtue, the Garments of	356
True and Great	357
Cardinal	366
Of Religion	373
Vision of the Lord, Fourfold	491
Vocation of Mankind	309
Vows, Usefulness of the Three	509
Voice of God Calling Us	503

W

Watch, Always	134
Water, the Living	217
Wheat, the Grain of	146
Well, the Delightful	85
Wine, the Good	67
Threefold	69
Wisdom, the Study of the Incarnate	100
Woman, the Samaritan	169
Word of God	83
Disposed to God's Word	86
Keeping His Word	87
Works, Good	119
Worship of God	. 277
Wounds of Christ	190
Wounds of Nature	312

Y

Yoke of Christ	96